LADY GREGORY, FIFTY YEARS AFTER

IRISH LITERARY STUDIES

LADY GREGORY, FIFTY YEARS AFTER

edited by
(Eleanor) Ann Saddlemyer and Colin Smythe
(1932 –

Irish Literary Studies 13

1987
COLIN SMYTHE
Gerrards Cross, Bucks.

BARNES & NOBLE BOOKS
Totowa, New Jersey

First Published in 1987 by Colin Smythe Limited
Gerrards Cross, Buckinghamshire

British Library Cataloguing in Publication Data

Lady Gregory, fifty years after.—(Irish Literary
studies, ISSN 0140–895X; 13)
1.   Gregory, Isabella Augusta, *Lady*
2.   Authors, Irish—20th century—Biography
I.   Saddlemyer, Ann   II.   Smythe, Colin
III.   Series
822'.912   PR4728.G5Z/

ISBN 0–86140–111–5

First published in the U.S.A. in 1987 by
Barnes and Noble Books, Totowa, N.J.07512

Library of Congress Cataloging in Publication Data
Main entry under title:

Lady Gregory, fifty years after.

(Irish literary studies, ISSN 0140–895X; 13)
Includes index.
1. Gregory, Lady, 1852–1932—Addresses, essays,
lectures. 2. Authors, Irish—20th century—
Biography—Addresses, essays, lectures. I. Saddlemyer,
Ann. II. Smythe, Colin. III. Series.
PR4728.G5Z637 1987   822'.912 [B] 84–6012
ISBN 0–389–20360–2

Produced in Great Britain
Photoset by Grove Graphics Ltd, Tring, Herts,
and printed and bound by Billing & Sons Ltd., Worcester

In memory of
Richard Graham Gregory
1909–1981

CONTENTS

INTRODUCTION

'We work to add dignity to Ireland.' It is now over fifty years since the death of Augusta Gregory, who as playwright, folklorist, essayist, poet, translator, editor, theatre administrator and nationalist, contributed so much and so uniquely to the realization of modern Ireland. Surely it is time for reassessment, a freeing of her spirit and achievements from the shadow of her colleagues, a fresh — perhaps a first — look at this remarkable woman.

We begin this volume therefore with images of Lady Gregory, as she saw herself and as others perceived her. Inevitably the portraits are contradictory — the partially comic, partly pathetic Queen Victoria theme resting uneasily with the veteran playwright and producer; the self-styled 'Fighting Temeraire', to quote O'Casey, 'flitting through life like a robin with the eye of a hawk';[1] distant to some, approachable to others; for Yeats a blend of Castiglione and Queen Victoria, to O'Casey a mixture of Jesus Christ and Puck. Inevitably, too, some of the strongest memories have their setting in Coole, where Yeats, like many others, 'found at last what I had been seeking always, a life of order, and of labour, where all outward things were the images of an inward life'.[2] It is fitting, yet deeply ironical, that many of the most graceful phrases concerning her life are quotations from the friend who profited most from her constant care and self-effacement. But collaboration from Lady Gregory meant a willing surrender of self to the greater importance of work and country (terms which she considered almost synonymous). We include therefore, reminders of her partnership with friends other than Yeats, and see her also as wife, mother, lover. It seemed fitting, also, to devote an appendix to the life and work of her beloved son Robert.

Chatelaine of Coole with a 'genius for entertainment, benevolent patron and defender of artists, she was that and more. In the words of one of the memorialists in this volume, 'the hospitality of her mind was as generous as her house'. All rooms, all interests, all actions, led at last to the honour and dignity of Ireland, to the rescue of its folklore, the dissemination of its epics, the glorification of its language and heritage. That those activities were many and varied can be seen from the chronology and checklist that frame this volume. Yet even within the world of the theatre, which she served so faithfully and steadfastly, her name did not long outlast her; although her publishers kept her works in print for at least 20 years after her death, sales were minimal, and few people appeared aware that they were still available. Apart from a few of her plays, most of her works went out of print in the years 1946–52 and were only revived with the inauguration of the Coole Edition in 1970.

Slowly, very slowly, the situation has begun to turn around. Elizabeth Coxhead's *A Literary Portrait* of 1961 and her edition of the *Selected Plays* in 1962, followed by other studies of her work, culminating in the purchase of the Gregory archives by the Berg Collection of the New York Public Library, have done much to introduce a younger generation of scholars to the woman whom Bernard Shaw once hailed as 'the greatest living Irishwoman'. At last in 1985, the full-length biography by Mary Lou Kohfeldt has appeared.

In addition to encouraging a reassessment of her work, this collection of essays is a celebration, therefore, of the tenacity, fervour, and craftsmanship of an extraordinary woman. We lament the loss of three voices in particular, all of whom had agreed to contribute to this volume — Elizabeth Coxhead, Michele Dalmasso, Micheál MacLiammóir; but fortunately their words and memories are recorded elsewhere.[3] Nor have we included records of those friendships and enthusiasms that are fully described by Lady Gregory in her own writings. The Olympians of her youth — her husband's generation — she recalls at length in *Seventy Years*. The long slow struggle to regain Hugh Lane's pictures for Ireland threatened to overshadow her many achievements in her later years: 'No peace for my mind, no rest for my pen, until his desire is accomplished, his last direction carried out.'

Characteristically she concludes this vow with the words, 'We must try to bring the English Government to honesty'.[4] The emphasis is apt in more ways than one, for nationalism informed all her work and even affected the formulation of her spiritual beliefs, while her insistence on honesty of response and action coloured her public conduct and determined the comic techniques of her plays. And these two characteristics, combined with her concern for the word both in its Irish and Anglo-Irish manifestations, serve as the driving forces behind the accomplishments of a lifetime of service. Her last sentiments return to the source: 'I am proud,' she wrote in *Coole*, 'that I . . . have worked for the honour of Ireland.'⁵ Always she remained true to herself.

Except for some of the 'Fragments of Memory', commentaries by Andrew E. Malone (reprinted from *The Dublin Magazine*, 1932) and Bernard Shaw (never before published), all the critical and biographical material in this volume has been specially commissioned. Of the memories, those by Anne Yeats, Brinsley MacNamara and Gabriel Fallon have never before been published, and we have kept to a minimum any duplication with E. H. Mikhail's useful *Lady Gregory: Interviews and Recollections* (1977). We include new letters, elaboration for the first time on her relationships with W. S. Blunt and John Quinn, some of her own poetry, and fresh examinations of her work where can be seen the many variations, in Mary FitzGerald's happy phrase, of Lady Gregory 'at play with language'.

This collection, therefore, reveals a multi-talented woman who made full use of her life to support and guide an important literary movement and to claim due homage for her country.

Ann Saddlemyer
Colin Smythe

May 1986

ACKNOWLEDGEMENTS

The editors and publishers wish to thank the following for their permission to publish extracts of works under their control.

As the surviving heirs of the literary estates of Lady Gregory and Robert Gregory, we are indebted to Mrs R. de Winton and Mrs R. Kennedy for permission to include unpublished letters and other writings by Lady Gregory and Robert Gregory. Lady Gregory's unpublished letters and other writings including the original versions of 'A Woman's Sonnets', and Robert Gregory's letters are copyright © 1987 by Anne de Winton and Catherine Kennedy.

W. S. Blunt's revised version of 'A Woman's Sonnets' and extracts from his letters and diaries, the unpublished parts of which are copyright © 1987 by the Syndics of the Fitzwilliam Museum, Cambridge, are published here with their permission.

Extracts from Gabriel Fallon's History of the Abbey Theatre copyright © 1987 by the Estate of Gabriel Fallon, are published by permission of James Nolan.

Extracts from Me & Nu: Childhood at Coole are copyright © 1970 by Anne de Winton, by whose permission they are printed here.

Extracts from "Memories of Coole" by the Rt. Rev. Arnold Harvey are published by permission of the Very Rev. Brian Harvey and The Irish Times.

Unpublished extracts from manuscripts of Lady Gregory and Douglas Hyde that are in the possession of the John Quinn Papers in Special Collections and the Henry W. and Albert A. Berg Collection, New York Public Library, Astor, Lenox and Tilden Foundations, are published with their permission. Extracts from the Douglas Hyde papers in the possession of the National Library of Ireland are published by permission of the Trustees. The copyright in all the works of Douglas Hyde is vested in Douglas Sealy, Christopher Seally and Lucy Sealy, by whose permission all these extracts appear.

The extract from The Splendid Years by Maire Nic Shiubhlaigh and Edward Kenny is published by permission of Edward Kenny.

Extracts from Sean O'Casey's 'The Lady of Coole' are published by permission of Eileen O'Casey, as are the four unpublished letters, copyright © 1987 by Eileen O'Casey, Breon O'Casey and Shivaun O'Casey. Extracts from *Inishfallen Fare Thee Well* © 1949 by Sean O'Casey, renewed 1977 by Eileen O'Casey, Breon O'Casey and Shivaun O'Casey, are published by permission of Macmillan, London and Basingstoke, and the Macmillan Publishing Company, New York.

Bernard Shaw's 'Note on Lady Gregory's Plays' copyright © 1987 The Trustees of the British Museum, The Governors and Guardians of the National Gallery of Ireland and Royal Academy of Dramatic Art is published by permission of the Society of Authors as agent for the Shaw Estate.

Unpublished material by W. B. Yeats, is copyright © 1987 by Michael B. Yeats and Anne Yeats, and is published with their permission. Extracts from the published works of W. B. Yeats are printed here by permission of Michael B. Yeats and Macmillan, London and Basingstoke, and for North America by permission of Anne Yeats and the Macmillan Publishing Company, New York. W. B. Yeats's *Memoirs* are © 1972 by M. B. Yeats and Anne Yeats. *The Trembling of the Veil* is copyright 1924 by Macmillan Publishing Co., renewed 1952 by Bertha Georgie Yeats. 'Upon a House Shaken by the Land Agitation' is copyright 1912 by Macmillan Publishing Co., renewed 1940 by Bertha Georgie Yeats; 'An Irish Airman Foresees his Death' and 'Shepherd and Goatherd' are copyright 1919 by Macmillan Publishing Co., renewed 1947 by Bertha Georgie Yeats; 'Coole Park, 1929' and 'Coole Park and Ballylee, 1931' are copyright 1933 by Macmillan Publishing Co., renewed 1961 by Bertha Georgie Yeats; 'The Municipal Gallery Revisited' is copyright 1940 by George Yeats and renewed 1968 by Bertha Georgie Yeats, Michael Butler Yeats and Anne Yeats; 'Reprisals' is copyright © 1957 by Macmillan Publishing Co.

We have not been able to find out who controls the rights of some of the copyright material published in this volume. To these individuals we tender our apologies and request that they get in touch with the publishers.

CHRONOLOGY

COLIN SMYTHE

1852 14/15 March (midnight). Birth of Isabella Augusta, seventh daughter of Dudley Persse of Roxborough, Co. Galway; by his second wife, *née* Frances Barry.

1879 Visits Nice and Rome with her mother and invalid brother Richard, who dies 8 September.
Meets Sir William Gregory for the first time since his return from Ceylon.

1880 4 March. By Special Licence, marries the Rt. Hon. Sir William Gregory, Privy Councillor (Ireland), Knight Commander of the Most Noble Order of St. Michael and St. George, of Coole Park, Co. Galway, and 3 St. George's Place, Hyde Park Corner, at St. Matthias' Church, Dublin.
March to May. Honeymoon in France, Greece and Italy.

1881 20 May. [William] Robert Gregory born.
July to August. Sir William and Lady Gregory visit Holland and Germany, Robert remaining at home with his nanny. (He does not accompany his parents on any of their trips abroad.)
October. They set out for Egypt via Europe, returning to England in May 1882.
2 December. Lady Gregory meets Wilfrid Scawen Blunt, and his wife, Lady Anne, for the first time.

1882 23 October. 'Arabi and His Household' is published in *The Times*, and published as a separate pamphlet by Kegan Paul, Trench & Co. later that year.
December. Begins love affair with Wilfrid Scawen Blunt which lasts for eight months.

1885 October. Sir William and Lady Gregory leave for India, returning to England in April 1886.

1887 October to May 1888. The Gregorys visit Rome.

1888 *Over the River*, about St. Stephen's parish in Southwark, is published.

1

1892   26 January. 'A Woman's Sonnets' published anonymously
       in the Kelmscott Press edition of W. S. Blunt's *Love Lyrics
       and Songs of Proteus with the Love Sonnets of Proteus*.
       6 March. Sir William Gregory dies.
       Lady Gregory sells 3 St. George's Place.

1893   Supplement to *Over the River* published anonymously.
       A Phantom's Pilgrimage, or Home Ruin published anony-
       mously by W. Ridgway of Piccadilly.

1894   Rents a flat in Queen Anne's Mansions, London, which she
       maintains until 1901.
       Spring. Meets W. B. Yeats for the first time.
       23 October. *Sir William Gregory, K.C.M.G., An
       Autobiography*, edited by Lady Gregory, is published by
       John Murray (London).
       8 December. Second edition of *Sir William Gregory*
       published.

1895   Robert enters Harrow School.

1896   22 March. Her mother dies.
       May to June. In Venice as the guest of Sir Henry and Lady
       Layard, at their home, Ca Capello.
       August. Meets W. B. Yeats again at Edward Martyn's home,
       Tillyra Castle.
       September. Yeats stays at Coole for a few days.

1897   Yeats spends the first of twenty summers at Coole. Sir
       Horace Plunkett, AE (G. W. Russell), Standish O'Grady
       and Douglas Hyde also visitors for shorter periods during
       his stay.
       Yeats and Lady Gregory formulate the idea of a Celtic
       theatre while visiting the Comte de Basterot at his home
       Duras, in Kinvara, Co. Galway.
       Her *A Short Catechism on the Financial Claims of Ireland*,
       Irish Financial Relations (London) Committee, Leaflet no. 8,
       published anonymously.

1898   7 March. *Mr. Gregory's Letter-Box 1813–35*, edited by Lady
       Gregory, published by Smith Elder & Co. (London).
       May. Visits Aran Islands to collect folklore.
       Christmas. Punch & Judy show in Gaelic given at Coole by
       Douglas Hyde and Miss Norma Borthwick.

1899   12 January. Foundation of Irish Literary Theatre, marked by
       Yeats's letter to the *Daily Express* (Dublin).

8 May. First productions of the Theatre: W. B. Yeats's *The Countess Cathleen* and Edward Martyn's *The Heather Field*. Michaelmas Term. Robert enters New College, Oxford.

1900   Discovers and sets up a stone memorial at Anthony Raftery's grave, and starts an annual *feis* there, on 26 August.

1901   *c.* 24 January. *Ideals in Ireland*, edited by Lady Gregory, published At the Sign of the Unicorn (London), M. F. Mansfield (New York).
Writes *Kathleen ni Houlihan* and *The Pot of Broth* with W. B. Yeats, and her own *Colman and Guaire*.
October. *Casadh an tSugáin* by Hyde with her translation published in *Samhain*.
21 October. *The Twisting of the Rope* produced at the Gaiety Theatre, Dublin.
Writes *The Jackdaw* (revised in 1907) and *Twenty Five* (revised in 1903).

1902   2 April. *Kathleen ni Houlihan* produced by W. G. Fay's Irish National Dramatic Company, with AE's *Deirdre*, at St. Teresa's Hall, Clarendon Street, Dublin.
April. *Cuchulain of Muirthemne* published by John Murray (London), and in 1903 by Charles Scribner's Sons (New York).
August. John Quinn travels with Jack B. Yeats from Dublin to the Raftery *feis*, and meets Lady Gregory for the first time, and stays at Coole.
30 October. *The Pot of Broth* produced by the Irish National Dramatic Company at the Antient Concert Rooms Dublin.
October. *Cathleen-ni-Hoolihan* published in *Samhain*.
30 October. *Where There is Nothing* by W. B. Yeats, Lady Gregory and Douglas Hyde published as a Supplement to *The United Irishman.*
December. *Twenty Five* (first version) published in *The Gael* (New York), its title being changed by the editor to *A Losing Game*.

1903   March. Publication of *Poets and Dreamers* by John Murray (London) and Hodges, Figgis, & Co. (Dublin).
14 March. *Twenty Five* (revised version) produced by the Irish National Theatre Company, with *The Hour Glass*, at the Molesworth Hall, Dublin.

May. *The Poorhouse*, translation of *Teach na mBocht*, written in collaboration with Douglas Hyde, published in *New Ireland Review*, and September in *Samhain*.

November. *The Rising of the Moon* published in *The Gael* (New York).

Robert gets a third class in his exams, but does not bother to get his degree conferred. On leaving Oxford University he starts at the Slade School.

1904   *c.* 31 January. *Gods and Fighting Men* published by John Murray (London), and by Charles Scribner's Sons (New York) later in the year.

4 June. *The Poorhouse* produced at the Passmore Edwards Settlement (London).

26 June. *Where There is Nothing* produced at the Court Theatre (London).

20 August. The Patent for the Abbey Theatre is granted in the name of Lady Gregory for six years.

10 December. *Spreading the News* published in New York by John Quinn, in a limited edition of 50 copies.

December. *The Rising of the Moon* published in *Samhaim*.

27 December. *Spreading the News* produced on the opening night of the Abbey Theatre.

1905   25 March. *Kincora* (first version) produced by the Abbey Theatre.

? April. *Kincora* published by the Abbey Theatre, as Vol. 2 of the first Abbey Theatre Series.

16 May. *Stories of Red Hanrahan* by W. B. Yeats and Lady Gregory published by the Dun Emer Press (Dundrum, Co. Dublin).

20 May. *Kincora* published by John Quinn in New York in a limited edition of 50 copies.

9 December. *The White Cockade* produced at the Abbey Theatre.

29 December. *The Travelling Man* and *The White Cockade* published together by John Quinn in a limited edition of 30 copies.

1906   ? February. *The White Cockade* published by Maunsel & Co. (Dublin) as Vol. 8 of the first Abbey Theatre Series.

19 February. *Hyacinth Halvey* produced at the Abbey Theatre.

16 April. *The Doctor in Spite of Himself*, adapted from Molière by Lady Gregory, produced at the Abbey Theatre.

? June. *Spreading the News, The Rising of the Moon* and *The Poorhouse* published by Maunsel & Co. (Dublin) as Vol. 9 of the first Abbey Theatre Series.

10 September. *A Book of Saints and Wonders* published by the Dun Emer Press (Dundrum), in an edition of 200 copies.

20 October. *The Gaol Gate* produced at the Abbey Theatre.

1 December. *The Gaol Gate* published in *The Gaelic American* (New York).

8 December. First version of *The Canavans* produced at the Abbey Theatre.

31 December. *Hyacinth Halvey* published by John Quinn in New York in a limited edition of 30 copies.

1907 23 February. *The Jackdaw* produced at the Abbey Theatre.

9 March. *The Rising of the Moon*, passed by the company in February 1904, at last produced at the Abbey Theatre.

16 March. *The Interior* by Maurice Maeterlinck, translated by Lady Gregory, produced at the Abbey Theatre.

3 April. *The Poorhouse* produced at the Abbey Theatre.

c. 10 April. In Italy with Robert and W. B. Yeats; they return to London on 22 May to deal with threats of English censorship of *The Playboy of the Western World*.

26 September. Robert marries [Lily] Margaret Graham Parry, with Augustus John his best man.

c. 10 October. Enlarged version of *A Book of Saints and Wonders* published by John Murray (London), and Charles Scribner's Sons (New York).

31 October. *Dervorgilla* and the revised version of *The Canavans* produced at the Abbey Theatre.

21 November. *The Unicorn from the Stars* (a rewriting by Yeats and Lady Gregory of *Where There is Nothing*) produced at the Abbey Theatre.

1908 15 January. *The Unicorn from the Stars* published by The Macmillan Company (New York) in an edition of about 10 copies.

19 March. *Teja* by Hermann Sudermann, translated by Lady Gregory, produced at the Abbey Theatre.

4 April. *The Rogueries of Scapin*, adapted from Molière by Lady Gregory, produced at the Abbey Theatre.

20 April. *The Workhouse Ward* (*The Poorhouse* revised) produced at the Abbey Theatre.

13 May. *The Unicorn from the Stars and Other Plays* by William B. Yeats and Lady Gregory published by The Macmillan Company (New York).

25 September. *Dervorgilla* published in *The Gaelic American* (New York) and in November in *Samhain*.

1909   6 January. Richard Graham Gregory, her first grandchild, born.

21 January. *The Miser*, adapted from Molière by Lady Gregory, produced at the Abbey Theatre.

Late January. Very ill, from what was probably a cerebral haemorrhage.

11 February. *Kincora* (revised version) produced at the Abbey Theatre.

14 May. *The Workhouse Ward* published in *The Gaelic American* (New York).

June. *Seven Short Plays* (containing *Spreading the News, Hyacinth Halvey, The Rising of the Moon, The Jackdaw, The Workhouse Ward, The Travelling Man,* and *The Gaol Gate*) published by Maunsel & Co. (Dublin).

August. Fight with Dublin Castle over G. B. Shaw's *The Shewing-Up of Blanco Posnet*, produced on 25 August at the Abbey Theatre, directed by Lady Gregory.

11 November. *The Image* produced at the Abbey Theatre.

November. *The Kiltartan History Book*, with illustrations by Robert Gregory, published by Maunsel & Co. (Dublin).

1910   24 February. *Mirandolina* by Carlo Goldoni, translated by Lady Gregory, produced at the Abbey Theatre.

2 March. *The Travelling Man* produced at the Abbey Theatre.

May. Individual plays in *Seven Short Plays* published separately.

2 June. *The Image* published by Maunsel & Co. (Dublin), as Vol. 1 of the second Abbey Theatre Series.

29 October. *The Kiltartan Molière* (containing *The Miser, The Doctor in Spite of Himself,* and *The Rogueries of Scapin*) published by Maunsel & Co. (Dublin)

10 November. *The Full Moon* produced at the Abbey Theatre.

1 December. *Coats* produced at the Abbey Theatre.

mid December. *The Kiltartan Wonder Book* with illustrations by Margaret Gregory, published by Maunsel & Co. (Dublin).

1911   12 January. *The Deliverer* produced at the Abbey Theatre.
26 January. *The Full Moon* 'published by the Author at the Abbey Theatre Dublin MCMXI and sold for sixpence'.
13 September. [Augusta] Anne Gregory, Robert and Margaret's second child, born.
20 September. The Abbey Theatre Company arrives in Boston, U.S.A.
29 September. Arrives in Boston on S.S. *Cymric*, having written *McDonough's Wife* (originally entitled *McDaragh's Wife*) on the voyage.
16 December. *McDaragh's Wife* published in *The Outlook* (New York).
29 November. Theodore Roosevelt attends performances of *The Gaol Gate* and *The Playboy of the Western World* in New York.
While accompanying the Abbey players, she also gives lectures: Harvard, Yale, Bryn Mawr, Smith College, Vassar, Fenway Court (Mrs Jack Gardner's home, near Boston), New York, Philadelphia, Washington D.C., Detroit, and Columbus, Ohio, are some of the places on her itinerary.

1912   11 January. *McDonough's Wife* produced at the Abbey Theatre by the second company, directed by Nugent Monck.
18 January. Abbey Theatre company arrested in Philadelphia. Through Quinn's defence, the company is acquitted on 22nd.
January-March. Love affair with John Quinn.
6 March. Accompanies Abbey Theatre company from New York on their return voyage to Ireland.
30 March. *Irish Folk-History Plays*, 1st and 2nd series (1. *Grania, Dervorgilla, Kincora*; 2. *The White Cockade, The Deliverer, The Canavans*) published by G. P. Putnam's Sons in New York, and in September in London.
4 July. *The Bogie Men* produced by the Abbey Theatre company at the Court Theatre, London.
12 November. *The Bogie Men* published in *The Fortnightly Review* (London).
21 November. *Damer's Gold* produced at the Abbey Theatre.

19 December. Leaves Queenstown [Cobh] with Abbey Theatre players on S.S. *Majestic* for second tour of America.

1913   14 March. *New Comedies* (*The Bogie Men, The Full Moon, Coats, Damer's Gold,* and *McDonough's Wife*) published by G. P. Putnam's Sons in New York, and *c.* 1 May in London.
April. With the Abbey Theatre company, she returns to Ireland. Severely injures her hand when a heavy door slams on it on board the ship. Arrives back 1 May.
21 August. Catherine Frances Gregory, her third grandchild, born.
15 November. *Our Irish Theatre* published by G. P. Putnam's Sons in New York, and in late January 1914 in London.

1914   1 June. *The Wrens* produced by the Abbey Theatre company at the Court Theatre, London.

1915   January to April. Third tour of North America.
8 April. *Shanwalla* produced at the Abbey Theatre.
8 May. S. S. *Lusitania* sunk by German U-Boat. Her nephew Sir Hugh Lane drowned.
On her intuitional guess, a search is made of Sir Hugh's office at the National Gallery of Ireland, of which he was Director, and found in his desk is the unwitnessed 'Codicil of Forgiveness' with instructions that the 39 French impressionist pictures be returned from the National Gallery in London to Dublin.
25 September. *The Marriage* by Douglas Hyde, translated by Lady Gregory, produced at the Abbey Theatre.
15 October. Sets sail for fourth lecture tour in N. America, her last visit.
Autumn. Robert enlists with the 4th Connaught Rangers.

1916   15 January. Sets sail from New York for Ireland at the end of her lecture tour.
January. Robert transfers to the Royal Flying Corps.
20 May. *Commedie Irlandesi* de Lady Gregory, translated by Carlo Linati, published by Studio Editoriale Lombard (Milano).
29 September. *The Golden Apple* published by G. P. Putnam's Sons (New York) (although Lady Gregory had inscribed a copy to Richard on August 16), and in October by John Murray (London).

November. Yeats is negotiating the purchase of Thoor Ballylee.

1917   February. *Sir Hugh Lane's French Pictures* published by the Chiswick Press (London).
31 March. The Congested Districts Board withdraws objections to Yeats acquiring Thoor Ballylee and agrees to sell it to him, informing him that he can take possession whenever he wishes, although legal transfer cannot yet be completed.
16 May. The title in Thoor Ballylee transferred to Yeats, for the sum of £35.

1918   23 January. Robert shot down in error over N. Italy, and killed. Buried in Padua.
29 January. Public Meeting at the Mansion House, Dublin to press for the recovery of the Lane Pictures to Ireland. *Hanrahan's Oath* produced at the Abbey Theatre.
February. *Sir Hugh Lane's French Pictures*, the report of the 29 January meeting, published, and 500 copies given to the Lane Pictures Committee, by The Talbot Press (Dublin).
1 June to 1 December. The Talbot Press (Dublin) publishes one of the *Seven Short Plays* on the first of each month.
22 November. *The Kiltartan Poetry Book* published by the Cuala Press (Churchtown, Dundrum, Co. Dublin) in an edition of 400 copies.

1919   17 February. *The Kiltartan Poetry Book* is published by G. P. Putnam's Sons (New York), and in March or April by Putnam (London).
18, 20 March. Plays title role in *Cathleen ni Houlihan* at the Abbey Theatre.
March. Directs Shaw's *John Bull's Other Island* at the Abbey Theatre, produced on 25 March.
21 April. *The Dragon* produced at the Abbey Theatre.

1920   6 January. *The Golden Apple* produced at the Abbey Theatre.
31 March. *The Dragon* published by G. P. Putnam's Sons (New York), and in May by Putnam (London) and The Talbot Press (Dublin).
3 April. *Visions and Beliefs in the West of Ireland*, in 2 vols., published by G. P. Putnam's Sons in New York, and on 4 September in London.

16, 23 October, 13 November, 4, 18 December and 1 January 1921. Contributes series of anonymous reports on the activities of the Black and Tans around Coole, under the title 'A Week in Ireland', 'Another Week in Ireland', etc., in *The Nation*.

1921   January. *Sir Hugh Lane's Life and Achievement* published by John Murray (London) and later by E. P. Dutton (New York).
17 March. *Aristotle's Bellows* produced at the Abbey Theatre.
15 May. Margaret Gregory caught in an ambush at the gates of Ballyturin House, Co. Galway. The other four occupants of the car killed in the gunfire, Margaret the sole survivor.

1922   17 March. *The Image and Other Plays* (*The Image, Hanrahan's Oath, Shanwalla, The Wrens*) published by G. P. Putnam's Sons in New York, and in London, October or November.
17 November. *Three Wonder Plays* (*The Dragon, Aristotle's Bellows* and *The Jester*) published by G. P. Putnam's Sons (New York) and in London, July 1923.
Putnam republish *Seven Short Plays* and many of her plays in acting editions.

1923   c. August. First operation for breast cancer.
26 November. *Bubbles* (libretto based on *Spreading the News*, music by Hubert Bath) produced by the Carl Rosa Company at the Opera House, Belfast, and on 11 June 1924 at the Scala Theatre, London.
31 December. *The Old Woman Remembers* recited by Sara Allgood at the Abbey Theatre.

1924   6 February. *Mirandolina*, translated from Goldoni's work, published by G. P. Putnam's Sons (London and New York).
20 February. *The Old Woman Remembers* published in *The New Republic* (New York) and in *The Irish Statesman* (Dublin) 22 March.
12 March. Arabella Waithman, her favourite sister, dies at her home in Galway, Lady Gregory by her bedside.
15 April. *The Story Brought by Brigit* produced at the Abbey Theatre.
April. Roxborough burned.

1926   4 January. *The Would-Be Gentleman*, adapted by Lady Gregory from Molière, produced at the Abbey Theatre.
April. Enlarged edition of *The Kiltartan History Book* published by T. Fisher Unwin (London).

May. *On the Racecourse* published by G. P. Putnam's Sons (London & New York).
Case for the Return of Sir Hugh Lane's Pictures to Dublin, published by the Talbot Press (Dublin).
31 August. Second operation for breast cancer, under a local anaesthetic.

1927   14 March. *Sancho's Master*, based on Cervantes' *Don Quixote*, produced at the Abbey Theatre.
1 April. Acts as witness to Margaret's signature on deed of sale of Coole, "—all—house—woods—gardens".
9 May. *Dave* produced at the Abbey Theatre.
27 May. *Dave* published in *One Act Plays for Stage and Study* presented by P. Wilde, published by Samuel French Inc. (New York).
20 October. Representatives of Land Commission and Forestry Commissions formally take possession of Estate.
7 November. Signs agreement with Forestry Department concerning the lease of Coole House.

1928   May. *Three Last Plays* (*Sancho's Master*, *Dave*, *The Would-be Gentleman*) published by G. P. Putnam's Sons in London, and in the Autumn in New York.
late April. Agrees with Yeats and Lennox Robinson on the rejection of Sean O'Casey's *The Silver Tassie*.
8 September. Margaret Gregory, Robert's widow, marries Captain Guy Vincent Hugh Gough, heir presumptive to the Viscountcy. The marriage is solemnised by the Rev. Arnold Harvey, later Bishop of Down & Connor, who had been Robert's tutor.

1929   Summer. Writes *Michelin*, *The Meadow Gate*, *The Dispensary*, *The Shoelace* and *The Lighted Window*.

1930   *Spreading the News, Hyacinth Halvey and Other Plays*, with Introduction and Notes by Kazumi Yano, published by Kenkyusha (Tokyo) in the English Classics series.
August. *My First Play* (*Colman and Guaire*) published by Elkin Mathews & Marot (London) in an edition of 530 copies signed and numbered by the author.

1931   *c*. 9 July. *Coole* published by the Cuala Press (Dublin) in an edition of 250 copies.

1932   23 May. Death, about 12.30 a.m.
25 May. Burial, beside her sister Arabella in the New [Protestant] Cemetery in Galway. Apart from her family,

the mourners included W. B. Yeats, Lennox Robinson, F. J. McCormick, Arthur Shields, Canon Arnold Harvey (one of the four clerics conducting the Service), P. J. Little representing Eamon de Valera, and Denis O'Dea on behalf of the Abbey Theatre.

8–9 August. Auction of much of the contents of Coole by A. M. Toole of Loughrea.

1941   Coole House demolished.

1946   16 December. *Lady Gregory's Journals*, edited by Lennox Robinson, published by Putnam & Co. (London) and on 25 March 1947 by The Macmillan Company (New York).

1961   *Lady Gregory, A Literary Portrait*, by Elizabeth Coxhead, published by Macmillan (London) and Harcourt Brace and World (New York). Second edition, enlarged, published by Secker & Warburg (London) in 1966.

1962   *Selected Plays*, Chosen and Introduced by Elizabeth Coxhead, Foreword by Sean O'Casey, published by Putnam & Company (London) and Hill & Wang (New York), republished by Colin Smythe (Gerrards Cross) and Macmillan of Canada (Toronto) in 1975.

1970   4 May. Publication of first three volumes of the Coole Edition (*Visions and Beliefs in the West of Ireland, Cuchulain of Muirthemne, Gods and Fighting Men*) by Colin Smythe (Gerrards Cross) and later that year by Oxford University Press (New York).

1971   1 March. *Collected Plays*, in four vols. (Coole Edition vols. 5–8) published.

1974   8 July. *Seventy Years* published by Colin Smythe (Gerrards Cross) and by the Macmillan Publishing Co. (New York) in 1976.

1978   23 October. *The Journals, Books 1–29*, published by Colin Smythe (Gerrards Cross) and later by Oxford University Press (New York).

FRAGMENTS OF MEMORY

PEN PORTRAITS

She came into the room quickly, with a welcoming smile on her face, and I set her down here as I see her: a middle-aged woman, agreeable to look upon, perhaps for her broad, handsome, intellectual brow enframed in iron-grey hair. The brown, wide-open eyes are often lifted in looks of appeal and inquiry, and a natural wish to sympathise softens her voice till it whines. It modulated, however, very pleasantly as she yielded her attention to Yeats. . . . She laughed, as is her way when she cozens. . . . Well she may say that the future will owe her something, and my thoughts moved back to the first time I saw her some twenty-five years ago. She was then a young woman, very earnest, who divided her hair in the middle and wore it smooth on either side of a broad and handsome brow. Her eyes were always full of questions, and her Protestant high-school air became her greatly and estranged me from her. (George Moore, *Ave*, 1911)

I like to write of Lady Gregory from the evening that Edward drove me over to Coole, the night of the dinner-party. There is in the first part of this book a portrait of her as I saw her that night, a slim young woman of medium height and slight figure; her hair, parted in the middle, was brushed in wide bands about a brow which even at that time was intellectual. The phrase previously used, if my memory does not deceive me, was high and cultured; I think I said that she wore a high-school air, and the phrase expresses the idea she conveyed to me—an air of mixed timidity and restrained anxiety. On the whole it was pleasant to pass from her to Sir William, who was more at his ease, more natural. (George Moore, *Vale*, 1914)

*   *   *

Although she confesses to grandmotherhood, she seems scarcely beyond middle life, and there is youth in her smile which makes

13

one forget the gray hair smoothed away from the forehead. Her eyes, keen and dark, light up with a quizzical expression as she talks. (Boston *Sunday Herald*, 1 October 1911)

*   *   *

Outside was a little black figure welcoming us. This was Lady Gregory, and as I had never seen her before, I noticed her fresh complexion, bright penetrating brown eyes, white hair black-veiled, slight tendency to stoutness, black mourning clothes and a little black silk apron. She was most cordial, even to me, the unknown marital adjunct of a man whom she knew and liked, and we went into the tall white house. . . . Lady Gregory wanted to know about John Quinn, and probably she found out, but I looked at the dark, tall, rich room, lit by fluttering candles. Her beautiful warm voice and easy manner went well with this library. . . . Lady Gregory cares for the seven woods in a very practical way, and she showed me groves of young trees and saplings she had had planted. 'Nearly all my book royalties grow into trees,' she said. I liked the commonsense streak in her. Gradually I was beginning to find that she kept herself in no aesthetic citadel, that the hospitality of her mind was as generous as her house. . . . [The tone of her voice] was warm and kind, and uncomfortably full of concentration on me—not on me as the inoffensive marital adjunct of a visiting friend, but me as a body expected to answer for my real self. . . . I felt—as farmers, stone-cutters, workhouse wards, beggars must have felt—that here was a woman without mockery, a human being in whom there was the safety of kindness, and a keen simplicity of interest that warranted understanding. . . . Lady Gregory reads so beautifully that one can't help listening to her. (Signe Toksvig, 'A Visit to Lady Gregory', *North American Review*, August 1921)

*   *   *

There she was, a sturdy, stout little figure soberly clad in solemn black, made gay with a touch of something white under a long, soft, black silk veil that covered her grey hair, and flowed gracefully behind half-way down her back. A simple brooch shyly glistened under her throat, like a bejewelled lady making her first retreat, feeling a little ashamed of it. Her face was a rugged one, hardy as that of a peasant, curiously lit with an odd dignity, and softened with a careless touch of humour in the bright eyes and the curving wrinkles crowding around the corners of the firm little mouth. She looked like an old, elegant nun of a new order, a blend of the Lord Jesus Christ and of Puck, an order that Ireland had never known before, and wasn't likely to know again for a long time to come. (Sean O'Casey, *Inishfallen Fare Thee Well*, 1949)

THE CHATELAINE OF COOLE

I first saw Coole in the summer of 1899, when I went there from Trinity College to read Greek with Robert Gregory, who was about to enter Oxford University from Harrow. A common interest in classics and cricket laid the foundations of friendship, and of the next ten years not one passed without a visit; if it was in the summer, to assist him in forming a cricket XI from the employees and tenants on his estate; if in winter, for rough shooting or coarse fishing in the lake. . . .

At the turn of the century, the house at Coole was the focus of the literary and artistic ferment of the time, as may be gathered from the names of those people of note whom Lady Gregory delighted to entertain from time to time in various combinations. Among those from Ireland were W. B. Yeats (almost invariably), and his father J. B. Yeats, the portrait painter; George Russell (A.E.), poet, painter, mystic and editor of the *Homestead*; J. M. Synge, Sarah Purser, portrait painter and founder of the Tower of Glass; Dr. Douglas Hyde, founder of the Gaelic League and first President of Ireland; Jack Yeats and his wife; his sisters, Lolly and Lily Yeats of the Cuala Press and Industries; the poet Susan Mitchell; the Hon. W. Gibson, afterwards Lord Ashbourne, setting the fashion of Irish kilts which failed to catch on; the writer Standish O'Grady; William and Frank Fay and other members of the Abbey cast; T. W. Lister and R. I. Best, librarians in turn of the National Library; Sir Horace Plunkett, founder of the I.A.O.S.; and Percy Gethin, the artist from Sligo.

Interest in the movement from outside was shown by visits from the Irish-American John Quinn; Augustus John, making studies for a portrait of Yeats; the Carmichaels, father and daughter, from Scotland, authorities on Scottish folklore; Miss Horniman, who financed the purchase of the old Dublin morgue to become the Abbey Theatre, and York Powell, historian from Oxford.

From time to time Edward Martyn, playwright of *The Heather Field*, would ride over for lunch from Tulira Castle to tell with boyish pride of his latest purchase of a French Impressionist painting—now to be seen in the National Gallery—or recommend the liturgical use of Palestrina and plain-song, and talk of his plan for the endowment of a choir in the Pro-Cathedral, Dublin, for the performance of the latter. . . . The company usually fell into two groups: an older, drawn from the literary and artistic world, and a younger, consisting of Robert Gregory's young friends and relations. Except at meals there was little intermingling of the groups. During the day the former conversed, or wrote, or painted, while the younger engaged in outdoor activities. After dinner the intellectuals sat in the library; we younger folk retired to the drawingroom for music, to be summoned occasionally to hear Lady Gregory read aloud her latest play. . . .

Over every assemblage at Coole Lady Gregory presided with charm and unvarying tact, not uncalled for when clashes arose, as they sometimes did, among the members of the *genus irritabile vatum*. She has been called domineering, but dominating is a fairer word. And I have the impression that but for her moderating influence in its crucial years the movement for the formation of a National Theatre might well have disintegrated through disagreements on policy. With all her cares and preoccupations— she was engaged on her plays and versions of early Irish legends— she was sufficiently at leisure from herself to think of others and help them in the ordering of their lives. To W. B. Yeats she was indispensable.

She prescribed for him a balanced regimen of work and relaxation, and insisted on his taking proper meals. After lunch on most afternoons she would read out to him, generally and at length from Spenser's 'Faery Queen'. . . . From the gunroom below his bedroom he could be heard every morning walking up and down intoning his lines. At lunchtime we would hear how many he had written; they averaged rarely more than one-and-a-half or two. . . .

On Sundays two outside cars would draw up at the hall door for the convenience of those who wished to attend church in Gort. Our party occupied the south gallery while the opposite gallery contained Lord Gough's party from Lough Cutra castle. The world of Coole and the world of the British Embassy in Dresden, where Lord Gough was Minister, were poles apart, but a link was found in an annual cricket match between the two estates. . . .

One summer a series of races took place on the lake between two boats, in which the smaller, which eventually won the series, was

manned by W. B. Yeats and his brother, and the larger by Robert
Gregory, his cousin Richard, and myself. The masts and sails were
home-made and the latter decorated with emblems by the artist
member of each crew. One of the races had an abrupt ending. The
boat in which I was contained a passenger in the shape of a large
retriever, Croft, and finding him an encumbrance Robert Gregory's
cousin and myself decided to get rid of him. We stood up and,
swinging him to and fro, prepared to pitch him into the lake, but
at the last heave the boat capsized, and we were flung headlong,
fully clothed, into the water. Robert Gregory, who from behind the
square sail could not see what was afoot found himself similarly
precipitated. . . .

Croft also figured in an incident vividly stamped on my memory.
Accompanied by him, I arrived one morning at the side of the lake
to find Yeats engaged in a desperate struggle to land a large pike.
He had hooked it while rowing in the lake and, unable to secure
it, had brought the boat to the lakeside, and scrambling ashore was
continuing the struggle from the bank. He was completely
exhausted and it was a question in my mind which of the two, the
poet or the pike, would pull the other into his element. Croft took
in the situation at a glance and, dashing into the water, brought the
fish ashore. It was found to weigh over nine pounds. (Arnold
Harvey, 'Memories of Coole', *The Irish Times* 23-24 November
1959).

*   *   *

Grandma walked a lot. Round the gardens, and usually all
through the Nut wood, but if she was going to the farther away
woods, Parc na Carragh, the Isabella or towards Inchy, she'd go
in the donkey trap. Tommy was a dear kind donkey, but not very
interested in what went on, and he wandered along as slowly as he
could. When we went with Grandma we could make him trot now
and again with the use of a great deal of screaming 'go on outa
that,' and the use of ash sticks, which raised a great deal of dust
from his fur, but which he treated with a certain amount of disdain.
Grandma never used a stick on him. She had a spud, which she
carried everywhere with her, partly as a walking stick, but she
loved to attack thistles and nettles growing near her beloved young
trees, and she used this spud to prod Tommy whenever he stopped
in his tracks; now and again he must have felt it, as Grandma

always got to where she wanted in the wood, and of course once he was headed for home, there was no need for a goad. . . .

Grandma adored the woods, and taught us such a lot about them. Every year she planted a lot of young saplings, and endlessly walked round looking at her young plantations, tearing ivy away from the older ones, and seeing that the wire netting was safely around the smaller ones to keep the rabbits away. The weather had to be very bad indeed to keep her from visiting at least the nearest seedlings. She always wore galoshes over her shoes, cotton gardening gloves over her mittens, and armed with her spud went forth daily to wage war against thistle, ivy, nettles, convolvulus and rabbits. I think one of the few times I saw her really furiously angry was when she found that several of her beautiful young larches had been cut down and taken away.

'If they'd *asked* me,' she said when she got home, 'I'd have given them some timber. I've never denied anyone, as they well know, and I could have taken one here and one there and thinned them out at the same time. But to go and cut ten trees from the same spot is sheer vandalism, and I hope that they will be found and punished.' I had never heard her speak like this of anyone before— not even when the Black and Tans killed Malachi Quinn's young wife—shooting at everything as they drove along the road, for fear of being ambushed, they said.

Grandma certainly did give to anyone who came to the house asking for things. I can remember the streams of people out of Gort who came to ask for flowers for their church, for graves of relatives or to put in their windows when there was to be a holy procession along the streets of Gort. Grandma really liked giving for the procession best, because she said that if the flowers were in the windows of the cottages the people living there would enjoy looking at them. Grandma went down to the garden with each person who came, and walked round the garden with them, making an individual bunch of mixed flowers for each one. Sometimes the flower garden looked as though there was not a single flower left in it, and yet Grandma always managed to find something blooming which, with added coloured leaves and buds, made yet another offering to the Roman Catholic Church. (Anne Gregory, *Me & Nu: Childhood at Coole*, 1970)

*   *   *

Lady Gregory seeing that I was ill brought me from cottage to cottage to gather folk-belief, tales of the fairies, and the like, and wrote down herself what we had gathered, considering that this work, in which one let others talk, and walked about the fields so much, would lie, to use a country phrase, 'Very light upon the mind'. She asked me to return there the next year, and for years to come I was to spend my summers at her house. When I was in good health again, I found myself indolent, partly perhaps because I was affrighted by that impossible novel [*The Speckled Bird*], and asked her to send me to my work every day at eleven, and at some other hour to my letters, rating me with idleness if need be, and I doubt if I should have done much with my life but for her firmness and her care. . . .

On the sea-coast at Duras, a few miles from Coole, an old French Count, Florimond de Basterot, lived for certain months in every year. Lady Gregory and I talked over my project of an Irish Theatre looking out upon the lawn of his house. . . . I told her that I had given up my project because it was impossible to get the few pounds necessary for a start in little halls, and she promised to collect or give the money necessary. That was her first great service to the Irish intellectual movement. She reminded me the other day that when she first asked me what she could do to help our movement I suggested nothing; and, certainly, no more foresaw her genius than I foresaw that of John Synge, nor had she herself foreseen it. . . . It is more fitting, however, that in a book of memoirs I should speak of her personal influence, and especially as no witness is likely to arise better qualified to speak. If that influence were lacking, Ireland would be greatly impoverished, so much has been planned out in the library or among the woods at Coole; for it was there that John Shawe Taylor found the independence from class and family that made him summon the conference between landlord and tenant that brought land purchase, and it was there that Hugh Lane formed those Irish ambitions that led to his scattering many thousands, and gathering much ingratitude; and where, but for that conversation at Florimond de Basterot's, had been the genius of Synge? (W. B. Yeats, *The Trembling of the Veil*, 1922)

* * *

We used to go to Coole from Ballylee, mostly when it was too wet to stay at the Tower. We used to be packed off in the pony and trap up to Lady Gregory's and we had several visits there. I don't remember whether Father and Mother were there at the same time, probably not, but when we arrived at Coole, Lady Gregory would put us to work. She always kept a rake and hoe in the porch, with the tennis racquets, croquet hoops, etc., for Michael and me to amuse ourselves, by raking the very large gravel area outside the house, and that provided endless entertainment, and kept us quiet and out of her hair, no doubt.

I remember the house and the grounds, the stables and in particular the walled garden which I hated. It was dark and the walls were high and there was never anybody there and it was lonely, and I felt the strange atmosphere in there. There was a marvellous peach house down at the bottom of it, and there was always a gardener near the peach house who would give me a peach, but further down again beyond the peach house was the row of graves where they buried the dogs.

She put up with us, though I remember one night—I slept at the back of the house—I had nightmares. There were sheep which must have given me nightmares with their baa-ing in the middle of the night, and Lady Gregory came herself and brought me a glass of milk and ginger-snaps.

I don't remember her anywhere else. Mother said she used to come up to Merrion Square quite a lot when she went to the Abbey. Mother told me that when I was very small she took me to Geary's which was a toy shop at the top of Grafton Street that sold jokes, and I bought a squeaky cushion. I put it on the chair Lady Gregory was going to sit on, and she sat on it and it squeaked; Lady Gregory just stood up, removed the cushion and sat down again. Mother was sorry for me as Lady Gregory did not make a single gesture towards it. This must have been before 1927.

Another time during the Troubles when she came up, there was a lot of shooting in Dublin. Lady Gregory insisted on going to the Abbey, and walking back. One night it was particularly noisy with a great number of shots going round the place, and Mother thought it would be best to take the tram and get home a bit quicker. Lady Gregory refused: she wasn't going to take the tram, she wasn't going to be intimidated by the shots coming round the corners, and Mother told me, 'I felt like saying, "It's all very well for you, but it isn't *my* country!"' I think she found Lady Gregory rather a handful.

The grandchildren were never at Coole when we were there, so I remember we could use the rocking horse in the nursery.

I remember Mother telling me that when they were down at

Thoor Ballylee, word reached Lady Gregory that Mother and Father had had the local protestant curate to dinner one evening, and she summoned Mother and said, 'You know, George, it's usual to have the bishop to dinner, the vicar to lunch and the curate to afternoon tea'. Mother wasn't going to tell her that the curate was the only intelligent one of the three! Lady Gregory observed the forms and I think she thought that Mother, being twenty-seven at the time, should know this. By this time we children saw Lady Gregory as an incredibly ancient figure. She had this—what was to us—very long drawing-room, endless bits of furniture, whatnots, and so on, so I could quite see why one wasn't allowed in, and at the end there was a harp which caught the light. The house itself I remember quite well, and in fact for years after when I went into certain country houses, it was the Coole Park sniff, aged leather, ancient mackintoshes in the back hall, tennis racquets in front.

There was a white owl in the stable, and there were lots of strawberries in the garden, and they had a dog which could get under the nets and eat the strawberries. I remember one tea-party with a lot of Gregorys there one afternoon, and there were tiny little scones; I was seated remotely and I thought quite safely, and these scones were too small for two bites and proved too large for one bite and one of the Gregorys drew attention to this and made some remark. And I can still feel the pains in my cheeks while trying to keep the jam scone inside. (Interview with Anne Yeats, August 1982)

*   *   *

Anyway, he was quite at ease with the Old Lady. They got on grand together. They had many things in common besides the theatre. He loved pictures, and she was brimful of what her nephew, Hugh Lane, had done to diamond-clothe the walls of precious buildings with fair paintings of the men of the day, and with those done by their fathers in the old time before. She loved good books, and Sean felt that he was a little ahead of her there. She saw humour sparkle from things thought to be dead, or dull, and so did he; and they often talked and laughed together over tea in a hotel that overlooked the fair form of Stephen's Green; Sean trying to look at home in the posh place, and succeeding in a way; she eating bun after bun, murmuring that she was very, very hungry; and saying that their talk was lovely; though, best of all, she rejoiced that his plays were forcing queues to stand outside her little theatre, ringing a chime of cheeriness into all their chat. So here was Sean, sober and thoughtful, reading a warm invitation to come and spend a week or two in Coole Park, in Galway; eager to go, but a little nervous at the thought of setting out to visit foreign parts. . . .

There she was waiting for him—a trim, stout, sturdy figure, standing upright and still on the platform, ready to guide him safely down to Gort, grimly patient in the midst of the talkative, quickly-moving crowd. A strange, lone figure she looked in a third-class carriage, stuck tight in a mass of peasants and small farmers, and they with baskets on their laps, or live fowl clutched in their hands. . . .

One evening she came in, aglow with a surprise for Sean—a new petrol lamp into which air was pumped so that, she said, we'll have a light that makes the night even as the day of a sunny summer morning. She stood the lamp on a stand on a high table; and a lovely thing it looked with its silver-like stem and opalescent shade. Lady Gregory's maid, Bridget, hovered round while her ladyship pumped air into the petrol bowl, anxiously watching, and murmuring, Let me handle that, leave it to me now, me lady, to be answered with the angry and impatient retort of Doh away, doh away, woman; it's twite simple, and I tan handle it myself. Turning to Sean, she added, And now you'll soon see a light dat never was on sea or land.

She was right, too, for as soon as she put a light to it, the thing gave out a mighty hiss that was half a scream, a bluish-white flame shot up high as the ceiling, the old lady's face, panic in her eyes, became as opalescent as the lamp-shade, and her wildly-puckered little mouth began to send frantic and harmless puffs of air towards the soaring, hissing flame, the agitated mouth suddenly opening wide, between the puffs, to shout at Bridget, Bring a blanket, bring a blanket, Bridget, before de house does up in fire! Sean whipped up a rug from the settee, and placed it between their faces and the flame for fear it might explode; and behind this safety-curtain the three of them juggled, blew, and smothered the thing till the fire died down; standing round it on guard till it cooled, and Bridget could safely carry the silver [stem] and cracked opalescent bowl out of our sight into the kitchen.

—Oh! murmured her ladyship, sinking down to the softness of the settee, a bunishment for my banity; tinking I could do it alone; tinking I knew too much. Back to de tandles dat bring peace and surety to men of doodwill. . . .

He hadn't been ten minutes at the table before he felt he had often been there, to eat soberly, and talk merrily of books and theatre, and of the being of Ireland; she in simple and most gracious ways showing how things were handled; pointing out that dese things were done, not because of any desire for ceremony, but because dey made one more comfortable, and made things easier to eat. So he was soon at rest. . . . (Sean O'Casey, *Inishfallen, Fare Thee Well*, 1949)

*   *   *

This morning I got a letter telling me of Lady Gregory's illness. I did not recognise her son's writing at first, and my mind wandered, I suppose because I am not well. I thought my mother was ill and that my sister was asking me to come at once: then I remembered that my mother died years ago, and that more than kin was at stake. She has been to me mother, friend, sister and brother. I cannot realise the world without her—she brought to my wavering thoughts steadfast nobility. All day the thought of losing her is like a conflagration in the rafters. Friendship is all the house I have.

Lady Gregory better but writes in pencil that she 'very nearly slipped away'. While she has been bringing herself near death with overwork to do all her household duties as few women have ever done things, keeping all in stately order while giving us enough plays, translated or original, often working much against the will, often with difficulties, our base half-men of letters, or rather half-journalists, that coterie of patriots who have never been bought because no one has ever thought them worth a price, have been whispering everywhere that she takes advantage of her position as Director to put her own plays upon the stage.

Of Lady Gregory one can say what Shakespeare said of another, 'She died every day she lived'. (W. B. Yeats, *Memoirs* [1909])

AT THE ABBEY THEATRE

Lady Gregory, now an established member of the committee, paid Camden Street occasional visits. . . . As the work of new dramatists wishing to avail of the society passed from Fay's hands through a reading committee to her, before we saw it, she always insisted on reading over selected pieces to us in her hotel drawingroom. Her odd lisping voice had a peculiar effect on speeches, especially those of the poetic sort, and, later, the strange lilting lines of J. M. Synge, which suffered much through her pronunciation. I think she rather fancied herself as an actress. Years later, when circumstances delayed my arrival at the Abbey for an appearance as Kathleen Ni Houlihan, she horrified Yeats and the company by calmly announcing that she would play the part herself. Her interpretation was hardly a flattering one, not only because of her extraordinary sing-song delivery of the beautiful lines. Her appearance, at times oddly reminiscent of an elderly Queen Victoria, can hardly have been in keeping with the character Yeats had in mind when he wrote the play. But her arrival in such fashion as an Abbey Theatre actress, received, to her delight and Yeats' dismay, widespread publicity, and she often spoke of the occasion afterwards, referring proudly and a trifle pathetically to her appearance in the play as the realisation of a life-long ambition.

But she was a pleasant if at times rather condescending person, who treated us all rather as children in need of special advice. . . . she joined in launching the Literary Theatre. When this failed, she turned, like Yeats, to the most promising of its successors and came to us in 1902, a small, not very striking woman in middle age, full of a great enthusiasm for our work and a conviction that the Irish National Theatre Society should succeed where the Literary Theatre had failed. In these and later years she frequently had her own way as far as the affairs of the society were concerned, for although she was not altogether overbearing, she was tenacious, which is much the same thing. I have many memories of her during these years; presiding maternally at one of those lavish suppers she loved to hold in the theatre on first nights; or, in different circumstances, drawing up her short rather bulky figure, squaring her shoulders and smiling rather grimly in a thin-lipped manner in face of opposition. Or again in later years, bustling with her strange, short-stepped walk through the Abbey, meeting distinguished visitors in the vestibule before the curtain rose on new plays, smiling her rather fixed social smile, or talking rapidly in her odd flat-toned way. . . .

She was a most hospitable hostess. During these early years, her arrival in Dublin for a new play was usually accompanied by an invitation to the Nassau Hotel, where in her austerely-furnished suite, she would entertain a few of us elegantly with tea and French cakes while she discussed forthcoming productions. Occasionally, too, she would have quantities of confectionery sent down to Camden Street, coming in herself later in the evening and, rather like an understanding aunt, sitting beside the stove while we brewed tea and ate. It was in Camden Street during a rehearsal of her play *Twenty-five* that she instituted what was later to become one of the most popular features of Abbey Theatre first nights—the 'Gort Barm-brack suppers'. The Gort Barm-brack was a huge cartwheel of a fruit-cake, filled with the richest ingredients, made specially by her own bakers at Gort for the casts of any of her new plays. It was a huge affair of several pounds weight and usually took two to carry it. It must have been two feet in circumference, and fully eight inches in depth. Wrapped around with silver paper, bits of candied peel and glacé cherries sticking out all over its shiny surface, it held a place of honour on a table near the stove. I will always connect barm-brack with rehearsals and the smell of grease paint. Abbey openings years later would never have been considered complete if there was not one—and it had to be a genuine Gort one—on the table in the greenroom, with a serrated knife beside it for anyone who wanted a piece. Many times have I gulped the last crumb of a slice down before stepping on to the Abbey stage, and many times has my reluctance to part with any of it, even after my cue had come and gone, made me temporarily inarticulate before the footlights. (Maire nic Shiubhlaigh, *The Splendid Years*, 1955)

*   *   *

A constant source of worry was combining the necessary publicity with our strictly limited means. It meant among other things that we had to make as many friends as we could among those who were interested in our project. Here we were helped by Lady Gregory's genius for entertainment. She was able to bring all sorts of people to the theatre to see the plays and to keep them afterwards to have supper on the stage with us, and this became the regular custom on all first nights. Our guests got to know the actors behind the footlights as well as in front of them, and gave us valuable hints by listening to the impressions made by each new play and by hearing remarks, expressions and criticisms not intended for repetition which had been overheard by those in front. Some proportion, at least, of these remarks were friendly or flattering, and this with the social occasion increased our confidence. A new sympathy grew up between us and our audiences.

Another scheme of Lady Gregory's that we liked even better than the first night suppers was the company's own private party after the dress-rehearsal, when she would arrive at the theatre laden with heavy parcels containing cooked chickens, pies and, among other dainties, the mainstay of these parties, a barm brack. No common barm brack this, from a Dublin shop, but one from her home at Gort, a special brand weighing about 10 lbs. and packed thick with raisins, currants and lemon-peel. A single slice of one of these Gort barm bracks was as good as a meal. For the Gort barm brack was the father and mother of a brack. Porter was in it too. The famous Miss Houligan's Christmas Cake could not hold a candle to it. You had to be very intimate with the company to get invited to the party when there was a Gort barm brack in the centre of the table. (W. G. Fay and Catharine Carswell, *The Fays of the Abbey Theatre*, 1935)

*   *   *

At first I only saw her in the distance, but at a near distance. This was early in 1909, when I first found my way to the Abbey Theatre and began to go there every week thereafter. I knew few people in Dublin then, the notable or literary not at all. But I soon learned that there were famous people to be seen in the stalls of the Abbey every Thursday night, and from my sixpenny seat in the pit I began to pick them out.

. . . Yes, that must be Yeats . . . I was to become accustomed to the theatrical way he used to pause for a perceptible moment on the short staircase that led out from the mysterious regions behind, to fling back his wandering forelock and glance around the auditorium in the dreamiest way imaginable. A neighbour in the pit nearly spoiled my hero worship for good by whispering to me once that the pause, and the poetic gesture, and the dreamy glance around, were all for the purpose of telling us who he was, and to give him time to count the number of heads in the house, before meeting Lady Gregory. . . .

At that very moment, in from the vestibule, in the full sail of her widow's weeds, would come the lady who could be none other than Lady Gregory herself, and the two would find seats together. They would remain in close converse until the rise of the curtain, thus managing the theatre in public view, or else trying to put away some of the trouble that Miss Annie Elizabeth Fredericka Horniman might be giving them just at that moment. . . . In the intervals, they

would turn around to have a word or two with the notable people
who had come to see the first night of the new play. . . .

It was some time in the autumn of the following year that I
actually *met* Lady Gregory. I had conceived the unhappy notion of
writing a play myself, and had applied for membership of the
Abbey company so that I might gain some practical stage
experience. They had put me down for a part in the forthcoming
new play and I had called to the greenroom for my script. She was
there, and it must have been the suggestion of her name, Augusta,
that made me feel I had come into an august presence. She regarded
me with a steely eye, and her screwed-up mouth, as in the bust by
Epstein, made me feel that she was weighing me up unfavourably.

Then suddenly, a faint smile began to break over her wintry face
and she told me that I had come just in time to hear her reading
of a little play to the company. I was greatly flattered by her
invitation and felt that all the ice had thawed as if by magic. Her
first seven short plays had been already produced and published
and now I had heard that she was about to launch a further seven.
This one then must be the first of the new series.

While we listened as she read it, her cold eye was upon each of
the players in turn, as if to catch any sign of wandering attention.
I caught the feeling that she was in merciless domination of the
scene as she read on. Whatever they might be thinking of the play,
they had to take it. For the moment she was the grand lady who
could not be doubted or questioned. All Dubliners, until I had
wandered unaccountably in amongst them, they had always found
the Kiltartan language a torture to learn and something even worse
to remember.

That was one of the first things I came to know at the Abbey,
but the players of that day had to learn it, and did. The talk would
be almost beyond the strength of players of today, and that is the
principal reason why the plays are now so seldom seen. And the
reading of them all had always made her so happy, the birth of
each one being celebrated by the striking appearance in the greenroom of what had come to be known as the 'Gort' cake, which was
a barmbrack of huge size and great richness. A treat for the players,
it came in time to be regarded in an unkindly and suspicious way
as something that had a sort of feudal touch about it, the kind of
thing that grand ladies sometimes supplied for high jinks in the
servants' hall. So great lumps of it would remain untaken and be
relegated to the scene dock for consumption by the stage hands.

I was to see exemplified to the full in the course of the next year or two the tender and sympathetic side of Lady Gregory. She was like a child with a toy over some of her little plays, and she had a little play always going on in her mind or partially on paper about this time.

The Abbey Company had gone on their first American tour, and when she came over to join us in Boston in 1911 she had two that she had typed on the voyage over. Her small typewriter, very much the worse for wear, had not been improved by its use on the sea passage and the two scripts that she had produced were barely legible.

Although it was no part of my duties as an extra player, she asked me to retype them for her. I was delighted to be given the opportunity of a first read of them and, on a rented machine, the job gave me the pleasure of many conversations with her at her hotel. She was trying hard to beat out improvements on their original form, and I rose greatly in my own esteem when she adopted a few of my suggestions.

But her playwriting had to be put aside for some time, for she had been caught up in the publicity for the tour. We had been given the services of a professional publicity man by the management that had brought us out but what he had done for us in the newspapers was poor stuff compared with what she now began to do in her stride.

Very soon we were in every newspaper, not alone in Boston but over the whole of the United States. She had spoken at some public function, and thinking of the battles for the Abbey that had been fought and looking forward to those that were to come, she had likened herself to 'The Fighting Temeraire'. It was a stroke of genius on her part, for now in every morning and evening paper we met such striking headlines as 'The Fighting Temeraire speaks again . . . Another victory for the Fighting Temeraire . . . Exclusive interview with the Fighting Temeraire. . . .' I would never know, not even to this day, why she had appropriated the title of Turner's famous picture as a fantastic description of herself, for she was not yet a battered wreck ready to sink in the sunset, but still as a stately warship proudly sailing in the high noon of her day.*

It may have been a sense of the association of 'The Fighting Temeraire' with Nelson's flagship 'Victory', or the sound and

---

* According to an article in the *Freeman's Journal* (28 March 1912) she received the name from a writer (P.S.W.) in the *Chicago Daily Tribune* of 12 February 1912, in a short poem entitled 'A Line-O'-Type or Two' dedicated to Lady Gregory, likening her to the ship in its opening lines. Eds.

colour that was in the word 'Temeraire' itself, or the feeling for
great pictures that had come to her from her brilliant nephew,
Hugh? It is something she has not told us.

It had worked, however, and for the moment she was standing
in the very forefront of Boston society with such a notable leader
of it at that time as Mrs Jack Gardner of Fenway Court, [who]
had all the Boston assurance and place of one whose people might
have come over, quite definitely, with the Pilgrim Fathers—and
mothers.

She was already being regarded as the mother of the Abbey
Theatre, but that role came easy to her. On 'off' days or nights
from her strenuous publicity campaign she would often speak
to one or another of the company about her dearly-loved son,
Robert, and express a longing to be back with her grandchildren
once more.

It had often struck us of late that as she read one of her little
plays that she had become even as any old woman of Ireland. And
we would think that that sort of simplicity must have befallen her
while gathering material for her books and plays in the cabins and
cottages of Clare-Galway, where she had been industriously plied
with folk lore specially invented for her visits, and all of which she
had innocently accepted.

Perhaps not so innocently, but consciously for her purpose,
which was to lead the Abbey away from the elaborate Yeatsian
dream of an art-theatre into a sort of folk-theatre where simple
people could laugh their fill. And if we look at the Abbey today
it is all too easy to see that it was her will with the matter that has
prevailed, rather than the ambitious but unacceptable and
unprofitable scheme of Yeats and Moore and Martyn.

So when she went back very tired from that American tour to
her home at Coole Park and her countryside of 'Gort and
Kilbeacanty and Drimdarode and Daroda' it was to ponder on how
best she might serve that end, by writing many more comedies
herself, and by encouraging comedy to come from the young
authors who were beginning to contribute plays to the Abbey. . . .

What a vandal act [the destruction of Coole] was, born out of
what a vandal thought, that swept it from the face of the earth.
Many are still stunned when they think of it, but it is something
that does not bear thinking about. . . .

[The demolition contractor donated the Coole door knocker to
the Abbey Theatre.] And if ever used it should make as terrible a
sound as the knocking in *Macbeth*, and strike coldly to the heart,

to tell of a dead of shame which was the destruction of Lady Gregory's house. (Brinsley MacNamara, broadcast interview, 1950s, exact date uncertain).

*   *   *

What an atmosphere that old Abbey Green Room had, with its sloping roof, its comfortable arm chairs and settees, its portrait of Lady Gregory (the George Russell one) dominating the fire-place, with the Sargent drawing of the young Yeats to the right of it; the Cuala Press prints of Yeats poems and of his brother Jack's early drawings, of their father's pencil drawings of Synge and Padraic Colum. Then the script safe covering an entire wall and the Carnegie Library book-case (Lennox Robinson being a Carnegie Librarian saw to it that the Green Room was a library centre). Into that Green Room came distinguished visitors from all over the world. One never knew when Lady Gregory or Yeats would appear as we sat round a gate-legged table drinking tea or playing cards with the stage manager watchfully standing-by five steps down and two yards away waiting to respond to 'when my cue comes call me.'

The year 1921 was not the best of times for the Abbey Theatre. Its finances were at their lowest ebb. Ireland's war of independence was rising to a peak-point; the notorious Black-and-Tans were loose upon the land; the streets of Joyce's Dublin were pocked with daily and nightly ambushes; a British curfew declared that citizens must be within their dwellings by 8.00 p.m. When a 9.00 p.m. curfew closed all other theatres the Abbey had remained defiantly open, but the additional hour was just one hour too much. Most of the Theatre's leading players had gone off to the U.S. on a tour of Lennox Robinson's *The Whiteheaded Boy* leaving behind a handful of part-time players—of whom I was now a junior member—a promising School of Acting, and a seasoned actor from the main company who remained behind to direct the School. A gift of £500 from Lady Ardilaun, added to the takings from the London lectures, gave the Theatre a new lease of life and, as soon as the British lifted their curfew to a more reasonable hour from the Theatre's point of view, Lady Gregory left the Black-and-Tan terror of Coole Park, Galway, for the Black-and-Tan terror of Abbey Street, Dublin, and ordered rehearsals to commence.

These she attended in person, primly sitting—a better looking version of Queen Victoria—in the middle seat of the front row of the stalls. The rehearsal over she would gather us around her in the Green Room and distribute her praise and blame. She wanted a little more of this or a little less of that; as for the other thing, it ought not to be even mentioned amongst us if we wished to retain our places in the Abbey Theatre Company. One afternoon she told us that she was bringing Mr Yeats to the following afternoon's rehearsal. William Butler Yeats, she informed us, was a very great poet; and to make clear this fact she drew our attention to the framed Cuala Press copies of his poems that adorned the Green Room walls. There, for instance, was 'The Pity of Love', there 'The Lover tells of the Rose in his Heart', and there 'The Lake Isle of Innisfree.'

These she read to us in her ageing quavering voice with its intriguing habit of transforming 'th's to 'deh's. We duly looked impressed, and with some of us our looks did reflect our inner feelings. I couldn't help wondering how the author of these poems would react to *The Lord Mayor*, the semi-political farce by Edward McNulty (a bank manager related by marriage to George Bernard Shaw) which we were then rehearsing.

The next afternoon we assembled for rehearsal at the usual time and as we stood in the wings were told that Lady Gregory and the poet were out front. The rehearsal went through with a little more vigour than usual, the effect of an upsurge of nerves, undoubtedly due to the fact that we were acting in the presence of two-thirds of the Abbey Theatre's Directorate (Lennox Robinson, the remaining third, with whom we always felt much more at home, being on holidays in Paris). Our acting ability wasn't helped by the report of a small-part player (who had surveyed the auditorium through a hole in one of the flats) that the poet had spent most of the time with his head bent over the pages of some literary journal. The rehearsal over we trooped up the stairs to the Green Room and tried to compose ourselves while we awaited the arrival of that Director whom most of us knew only by sight. Soon we heard a familiar voice saying, 'Now, Willie, I want you to meet the players.' (Good Heavens, she was calling the man 'Willie'; she was one of the few—if indeed there were any others—who had the right to do so.) Our first impression of Lady Gregory's 'Willie' could be summed up in two words 'dignity' and 'distance'. He had a way of looking at you as if he did not see you. His glance seemed to penetrate and go beyond you as if he were intently examining your aura which had somehow slipped round to the back of your neck. He heard our names as Lady Gregory introduced each one of us as if he were standing on the outer edge of the world we inhabited. She did all the talking; he occasionally inclined his head in acquiescence. He took a step forward and boringly examined the Cuala Press copies of his poems. He looked towards the sloping ceiling of the Green Room as if examining it for the first time. He then looked at Lady Gregory, as if to say, 'I take it this interview is at an end.' With a final word of commendation to the respectfully silent group of players Lady Gregory touched the poet's elbow and they left the Green Room together. When the sound of their footsteps died away on the concrete floor that led through the scene-dock to the stage there was an immediate buzz of conversation in the Green Room. Out of it came, with an unmistakable Dublin accent the voice of a small-part player, a not-so-promising member of the School of Acting: 'So that's the man who talks to fairies. Be God, he looks it!'

Augusta Gregory was, without doubt, one of the most remarkable women of her time. . . . The Lady Gregory I knew—though only for the last twenty years of her life—is most vividly described in that delightful book *Me and Nu* by her granddaughter Mrs Anne de Winton. They used to tell me that there was an earlier Lady Gregory, domineering, tough, unresilient. I have never believed it. She was a woman whose 'Yes' was YES and whose 'No' was NO and such a person must always seem formidable to a fickle vacillating world. In my acting days in the Abbey Theatre she was affectionately known as 'The Old Lady'. When word ran through Green Room and dressing-rooms that 'The Old Lady' was out front you could bet your life that everything on the stage that night would be of a high quality. She either liked you or she disliked you and it was well for you if it was the former. Above that she had her favourites. In my time it was her beloved Sally Allgood and her dear Barry Fitzgerald. . . .

She had little time for the middle class, in particular the middle-class mind. She hated pretence, she loved workers, whatever their station; and was more at home with a Seaghan Barlow, the Abbey's stage-carpenter, or a Sean O'Casey or with any of the people of her Galway countryside than she was with many of her own class.

She was an Irish Protestant, but, according to Lennox Robinson, himself an Irish Protestant, she was 'impatient with Irish Protestantism, because before anything else, she was Irish.' 'And though she worshipped every Sunday in the Protestant church in Gort,' writes Lennox, '. . . her heart was really on the other side of the street in that Catholic chapel, with the country people, her country's people. I do not want to suggest that she ever wanted to become a Catholic; far from it but she loved the people and the people were Catholic.'. . .

I stood a few yards from her on the evening of the 27th December 1925 when the Abbey Theatre celebrated its twenty-first birthday. The programme had consisted of *The Hour Glass* by W. B. Yeats, *The Shadow of the Glen* by J. M. Synge, and her own little comedy *Hyacinth Halvey*, plays representing the three geniuses who had made the Theatre. She was visibly nervous as she went on the stage to make a speech. She said afterwards that the only words she thought good were towards the end of it. Here they are: 'Three is the number of perfection—body, soul and spirit; father, mother, child; the three leaves of the shamrock. In the theatre we have the three A's, interdependent, inseparable—Author, Actor, Audience. We are necessary to one another.' In this co-operation of the three A's she had in her own quaint way set out the great fundamental of theatre. Remove one and the edifice falls apart. And then she finished: 'If these three hold together I hope the Abbey will last into the far future, and that (quoting from Yeats's *The Golden Helmet*) 'the long-remembering harpers have matter for their song.' . . .

I had often wondered about the working relationship between Lady Gregory and Yeats since she obviously wanted a theatre at all costs while he wanted a select and aristocratic form of drama. . . . It was in the mid-twenties when Sean O'Casey's plays, to Lady Gregory's great delight, were regularly packing the Abbey Theatre for the first time in its history. By this time Yeats had deeply interested himself in the Noh drama of Japan. . . . Lady Gregory held her peace. It was enough for her that O'Casey's plays were bringing crowds into her little theatre. However, it was not unconnected with Yeats's new departure that on the Friday of a week in which we were playing *Juno and the Paycock* a notice appeared on the call-board to the effect that the distinguished *maitresse-de-ballet* the Irish-born Ninette de Valois would, between the matinée and evening performances on the following day, give a lecture in the Peacock Theatre on the fundamentals of ballet. To this lecture the players were cordially invited. . . .

It was not easy to persuade the players to attend Miss de Valois' lecture, but being interested in ballet I was determined not to miss it and I managed to lure my dressingroom companion, Barry Fitzgerald, to come along with me. When we got to the Peacock we found Lady Gregory there before us. As soon as she saw us she indicated the vacant seats to the right and left of her own. Whatever we thought of this situation it was a royal command

which we daren't turn aside. As soon as we were comfortably
seated she told us that this lecture idea was one of Mr Yeats's
'foolish notions' but that it provided a grand opportunity for the
players to rest themselves between the two performances of *Juno
and the Paycock*! I could see Barry Fitzgerald looking at me but I
hadn't the courage to meet his twinkling eye. I found the de Valois
lecture both fascinating and useful. . . . Barry Fitzgerald was bored
and since Lady Gregory insisted on being quietly facetious made no
attempt to conceal his boredom.

When the lecture was over we invited Lady Gregory to tea and
she accepted. During the meal there was no reference to the de
Valois lecture. But she insisted on telling us of those far-off days
in the Abbey's history when in a desperate attempt to attract people
to go to it she used to pretend she was a patron by putting on a
hat and marching from the Stalls entrance to the Pit entrance
through which she popped after pausing, as if to pay, at the box
office. She would then wait inside for a few moments and begin to
repeat the procedure this time moving from the Pit to the Stalls
entrance. Looking at us both with tears in her eyes she said: 'What
a joy to think that those bad days will never come again!' Tea over,
the three of us walked back slowly to the Theatre. By this time the
queues for the evening performance of *Juno and the Paycock* were
stretching out in length from both entrances. Suddenly Augusta
made us stop at the corner of Abbey and Marlborough Streets in
order to admire the increasing crush of patrons. 'There are times,
my dear friends' she said, 'when I find I can love my fellow-man
with much more ardour than usual; and this'—she pointed to the
queues—'is one of them.' I began to see how much William Butler
Yeats and Lady Gregory differed on this all-important subject of
audiences. Yeats yearned for the select few; Lady Gregory wanted
them in the mass.

She was particularly sensitive about the facts concerning the
foundation of the theatre. When Andrew E. Malone published his
book *The Irish Drama* in 1929 I asked her what she thought of it.
'Well' she said, 'since he praises the directors of the Abbey, whereas
the other book (she was referring to Dawson Byrne's *The Story of
Ireland's National Theatre* published a little earlier) gives all the
praise to the players, I suppose I'll have to say I like it.' Then, after
a pause; 'But it is one of the dullest books I ever read!' (Gabriel
Fallon, unpublished History of the Abbey Theatre)

*   *   *

LADY GREGORY: 1852–1932

ANDREW E. MALONE

Written within a year of Lady Gregory's death, this contemporary appraisal by Andrew E. Malone (the pseudonym of Laurence P. Byrne, 1888–1939), was published in the January–March 1933 issue of The Dublin Magazine. *Errors in some of the names and dates have been silently corrected.*

When Lady Gregory died there were people who said in the conventional phrase, that her loss was irreparable. But her loss was no more irreparable than was the loss of such great figures of the theatre as Euripides, Shakespeare, Molière, or Ibsen. Like these she had done her splendid work for the theatre and the drama; and like them her life had marked a turning point in theatrical history. She had founded a new national theatre, and created a new kind of drama. It was she who gave to the aspirations and ideals of Yeats and Martyn practical shape, as it was she who is generally believed to have suggested that the location of the proposed Irish Literary Theatre should be Dublin rather than London and it was [due] to her influential support that the project materialised. Her house in London was the meeting-place of artists and wealthy patrons of the arts in her day, and it was to her that W. B. Yeats confided his ardent desire to have 'a little theatre somewhere in the suburbs' where his own, and other, verse plays might be staged. In later life she confessed 'The plays that I have cared for most all through, and for love of which I took up this work, are those verse ones of Mr. Yeats.' Had Lady Gregory not become interested in the production of the plays of Mr Yeats at a critical moment in Irish history, it is not improbable that Ireland would still be without its national theatre and the distinctive drama that it has given to the world during the past thirty years.

From her earliest childhood she had been devoted to the peasantry of her native Galway, and throughout her life she loved them with passionate intensity. If she did not quite succeed in shedding her 'ascendancy' and 'landlord' traditions completely, she certainly did succeed in viewing her neighbours with sympathy and

35

understanding. In her childhood days she had seen her home attacked by the Whiteboys, and the attack driven off with the gunfire of her father and his friends, and she had been reared under the imagined shadow of:

> An army of Papists grim
> With the green flag o'er them.
> Red coats and black police
> Flying before them.

In later years she was to become the friend of revolutionaries, and she found their company interesting and profitable. The folklore of her native county fascinated her, and she learned the Irish language the more readily to assimilate it. So she went among her poorer neighbours with that famous note-book which became at the same time the cause of suspicion and the basis of her fame. It was her interest in folklore that in time brought her into the theatre, and it is now quite certain that the theatre she visualised at the London interview with Mr Yeats, where it was first discussed, would be a folk theatre in every sense of the word. It would be a theatre in which plays of Irish life and character would be staged, and which would be a folk theatre because Ireland is in the main a nation of peasants. London could never have been a satisfactory home for such a theatre: in Ireland it would have a solid rooting in the national life, and there it would in time stimulate the growth of a native drama.

Lady Gregory lived to be the most popular playwright of the Irish theatre, and to be regarded by critics in other lands as one of the leading playwrights of her time. Prophets are not generally regarded highly in their own countries, and artists rarely fare better than prophets. Holding a mirror up to nature, or nature up to a mirror, is an occupation not calculated to secure the enduring affection of compatriots or neighbours, even if it does occasionally earn the applause of foreigners, and it may be all the more detested because of that applause. Ibsen was not at first regarded lovingly by his Norwegian fellow-countrymen; and Synge and O'Casey had their plays howled down by Irish audiences. In time, however, compatriots come to forgive, even if they fail to understand. It is a great mistake to think that preaching to the converted is a waste of energy; it is preaching to the unconverted that is often the real waste. Everyone who has experience of addressing large popular audiences knows that they must be told just those things that they already know very well if their attention is to be held: familiarity breeds not contempt but attention. When audiences are sure that the theme is familiar they are willing to appreciate the virtuosity of the performer; otherwise there is the danger of that howling-down process which reformers and critics know so well. Bernard Shaw understood his audiences, he had been a popular orator before he entered upon his career as a dramatist, so he concealed his sincerity by the cap and bells of Jester to Demos. His audience might not have laughed with him, so he persuaded it to laugh at him. Comedy is the direct road to popularity, as it may also be the road to greatest drama. Audiences want to laugh; theatres are filled mainly by adventurers in search of laughter. The greatest laugh of the greatest number is the measure of success in the contemporary theatre.

Lady Gregory secured the greatest laugh of the greatest number in the Irish Theatre. Her plays were performed more frequently than those of any other playwright of the Irish theatre, and *Spreading the News* or *Hyacinth Halvey* evoke the same hearty spontaneous laughter to-day that they did 20 years ago. She has been flattered by the imitation of many who accepted her buffoonery without any thought for her satire, or without her ability to write sparkling dialogue or her technical dexterity. The theatrical conception of the Irishman is still largely composed of a blend of Lever, Lover and Boucicault, and neither Larry Doyle nor Broadbent can alter that conception by the simple expedient of reversing characteristics hallowed by tradition. The stage Irishman is believed to have been driven from the stage by the righteous anger of Irish audiences; but only the staginess has gone, the clowning remains to delight audiences and enrich directors. *The Colleen Bawn* is still popular enough, and *The Lily of Killarney* is made to pay for the production of grand opera by touring opera companies. Bernard Shaw is no more loved in Ireland than is Synge or O'Casey because their Halls of Mirrors are said to contain only distorting mirrors such as were once the attractions in cheap fairs. Christy Mahon and Larry Doyle, 'Joxer' Daly and 'the Paycock' Boyle could not be true to Irish nature when there were such attractive creatures as Myles na Coppaleen, Danny Mann and *Paddy the Next Best Thing* to testify to the contrary. Irish heads are not so hard as Shaw suggested; and the happy-go-lucky rolling stone, with a laugh for life's little ironies and a tear for life's little joys, is still the Irishman beloved of audiences. If he uses a little more bad language in this twentieth century, as he hitches his trousers, it merely means that manners change and human nature remains. The spirit of Lady Gregory's plays is that of Lever and Lover rather than that of Shaw or Synge.

'Comedy is drama that studies universal interests and depicts their meaning or influence, quite as certainly as does the tragic method, but it enlightens us through our sense of laughter,' says Gilbert Norwood, 'not of tears or horror. Its superficial counterpart is farce—the employment of the ludicrous to engage our attention in what does not touch our own heart or interests.' Comedy is the humour of character: farce is the humour of situation. *John Bull's Other Island* is comedy because its humour springs directly from the impact of the personalities of Doyle and Broadbent in contact with Ireland. *Spreading the News* is farce because its entire structure depends upon the deafness of Mrs Tarpey. If Mrs Tarpey had been able to hear correctly the whole series of ludicrous incidents would have been obviated, and Bartley Fallon would never have been known as the typical Irishman upon whom all the troubles of the world 'are sure to fall'. Fallon and Haffigan are brothers in affliction from the lips out; both are representative of the whining type of Irishman which is more common than national dignity can afford to tolerate. Both are comic characters; but the laugh is at Haffigan's shrewdness and at Fallon's cringing imbecility. Fallon simply must be laughed at; he is the typical figure of farce not of comedy. Lady Gregory's humour in her early plays was the humour of situation, of farce, not that of character and comedy. Her comic figures are 'characters' not characters; they have mouths but it is impossible to believe that they also have brains.

'Comedy and not tragedy was wanted at our Theatre,' Lady Gregory said, 'and I let laughter have its way.' It is easier to laugh at a fool than to laugh with the wise, and Lady Gregory in her beginning chose the easier way. Bartley Fallon, Hyacinth Halvey, Davideen, Cracked Mary, and the other eccentric inhabitants of Cloon, are direct descendants of Handy Andy, born about the same time as Shaw's Larry Doyle, Synge's Christy Mahon, and Meredith's O'Donnell. At a moment when pure comedy was being written about, and even by, Irishmen, Lady Gregory wrote her first little farces, and played down to the low conception that Irish people had of themselves. Compared with Fallon and Hyacinth Halvey Christy Mahon is indeed a hero; but Fallon and Halvey evoked hearty laughter and Mahon only a lusty riot.

Lady Gregory was born in 1852, a member of the prominent family of Persse, at Roxborough in County Galway. The family was of English extraction and its outlook and sympathies were as

British as its political view was Unionist. But in Galway the past still is alive, is still vivid in speech, in stone, and in human misery. Young and eager in intellect as it is bright of speech, with a grave sonority that national education and cheap newspapers have combined to take from the English speech of other places. In early life she was attracted by the folk songs and tales of her neighbours and she commenced that systematic collection which has since been given to the world in a series of justly-famed volumes. This folklore was the devouring passion of her early life, compelling her to learn Irish so that she could converse with the peasantry. When she married, in 1880, Sir William Gregory, who had been a Colonial Governor and was a Trustee of the British National Gallery, she lived much in London; and there she met, as one of her husband's close friends Sir Frederic Burton, the artist, archaeologist and scholar, who had been the friend of Davis and Petrie, had known John Mitchel, and had designed the title-page for *The Spirit of the Nation*. In London, also, she came to know W. B. Yeats, George Moore, and Edward Martyn, all three of whom had affiliations with Connacht, and at least one of whom was a comparatively near neighbour in Galway. Edward Martyn, who lived in the next barony in Galway, brought her into close contact with Douglas Hyde and the Gaelic League, and so completed the chain of circumstances which led to the foundation of the Irish Theatre, the rise of the Irish drama, and the use of Kiltartan dialect on the stage.

In 1897 Lady Gregory had a conversation with W. B. Yeats in which he expressed the desire to have 'a little theatre somewhere in the suburbs,' presumably of London, in which poetic drama could be staged. Lady Gregory fixed that ambition upon Dublin, and it was she who made its realisation possible. The circular letter soliciting support for the Irish Literary Theatre was drafted at her house at Coole, and bears the impress of her personality; and it was largely through her efforts that the Theatre actually came into being a year later. She had developed from the little girl who had been scared by 'Fenian atrocities' to friendship with a Fenian leader, support of the Gaelic League, translation and publication of Irish folklore, to the foundation of a theatre and a drama for Ireland. Her great phase began when she undertook the organisation of a theatre for Ireland in Ireland; and then she entered upon a career which was destined to make her name known throughout the world, and to give her an honoured place among the playwrights of her time.

Before she began to write plays, or even to take any part in theatrical affairs, Lady Gregory had accumulated a vast and profound knowledge of the thoughts, beliefs and customs of the West of Ireland. Always a welcomed visitor to the cottages of the peasantry she availed of every opportunity to gather sayings and folk-tales, and to study the dialect which she later used so beautifully in her books and plays. It is doubtful, however, if she ever got anything more than the peasant speech; the mind eluded her. She was of the 'gentry,' the landlord class, and therefore suspect in the troubled times of the 1880s and 1890s; so she viewed the peasantry from without, from above, and as her outlook was essentially comic she saw them as figures of fun. 'There is nothing in literature quite like her bewildered peasantry,' a friendly critic has noted with satisfaction, and he might with truth have added that there is nothing like them in life. They are the product of a rich humanity, a highly-developed sense of humour, and an unconscious snobbery, garnished with their native dialect and idiom, and are very enjoyable on the stage. How effective is her use of the Kiltartan dialect may be noted in her translations from Goldoni and Molière, to whose comedies she gave probably their most attractive dress in English. Some kinship with Molière Lady Gregory certainly had, but she brought little of the wide experience and shrewd observation of Molière to her original work. The fine subtlety of Molière will be sought in vain in her plays: she loved a broad situation, with characters sketched in bold lines, each embodying some simple human quality. Her characters are extravagantly simple, there is no guile in them; they have little of that shrewd cunning which is the mark of the peasant in Ireland as elsewhere.

Lady Gregory's name is associated with more than forty plays; she had been writing plays for over thirty years, and she was the original patentee of the Abbey Theatre and one of its Directors from its foundation to the time of her death. Her industry and energy were marvellous, resembling the Spanish dramatists the Martinez Sierras in their wide range and comprehensive sweep. All her plays have been published, and all but three have been staged at the Abbey Theatre. Her translations from Hyde, Goldoni, and Molière have also been staged and published, and only her translation of Sudermann's *Teja* has not been published.

The one-act plays are mainly farces, or farcical comedies, with an undercurrent of satire, and possibly *The Workhouse Ward* contains a criticism of Irish politics which has escaped notice in the theatre. *The Rising of the Moon* is a delightful comedy of abnormal political conditions: the choice of the police Sergeant when duty and sentiment conflicted was difficult, and the artistry by which

Lady Gregory used the Ballad Singer to rouse his latent patriotism is masterly. This and *The Gaol Gate* are Lady Gregory's highest achievements in the one-act form. *The Gaol Gate* has all the tragic intensity of *Riders to The Sea*, and the final *caoine* cannot fail to wring the hearts of any audience. *The Travelling Man* gives a glimpse of the mystical strain in Lady Gregory which never managed to secure adequate expression.

Some of the most interesting, and the most successful, of Lady Gregory's plays are to be found among those collectively entitled *Folk-History Plays*. Her preparation for such drama had been long and arduous, resulting in the collection and publication of many volumes of folklore and mythology. These *Folk History Plays* are attempts to translate the subjects of Irish historical tragedy into terms of folk drama, and in the Kiltartan dialect she found a medium excellently suited to her needs. Three of the plays are called tragedies, and three tragi-comedies; and five of the total of six have been staged at the Abbey Theatre. 'I had from the beginning' she said 'a vision of historical plays being sent by us through all the counties of Ireland. For to have a real success and to come into the life of the country, one must touch a real and eternal emotion, and history comes only next to religion in our country.' *Kincora* was the first attempt to make that vision a reality; it had several successors but none of the folk history plays has yet had a chance to intermingle in the life of the country. Only at long intervals are they staged, and the travelling company never came into being. So she is popularly known only as the author of little farces, and this is all the more regrettable because her best comedies are folk history plays, and her best tragedy *Grania* has never been staged in Ireland at all.

Kincora takes an episode in Irish history in which the victor of Clontarf is himself crushed by the treachery of Gormleith. There are all the essentials of tragedy, but high tragedy is not achieved. *Dervorgilla* is, next to *Grania*, the best of the folk tragedies. Its single act is devoted to 'the swift, unflinching, terrible, judgment of the young,' showing the aged Dervorgilla having her gifts spurned because she had betrayed her country. 'Do not be afraid to give back my gifts,' she says, 'do not separate yourself from your companions for my sake. For there is little of my life but is spent and there has come upon me this day all the pain of the world and its anguish, seeing and knowing that a deed once done has no undoing, and the lasting trouble my unfaithfulness has brought upon you and your children for ever.' The same theme is treated by Mr. Yeats in *The Dreaming of the Bones* with great effect. It is *Grania*, however, that is her highest achievement in tragedy; because in its emotional content and poetic fervour it is superior to many historical tragedies that have long enjoyed world fame. Deirdre has had her admirers in plenty, Grania but few, and of these Lady Gregory was the most ardent. 'I think,' she once said, 'I turned to Grania because so many have written about sad, lovely Deirdre, who when overtaken by sorrow made no good battle to the last. Grania had more power of will, and for good or evil twice took the shaping of her life into her own hands.' In this three-act tragedy of love and jealousy only three persons are concerned, but in falling under the spell of Grania and her story Lady Gregory achieved her masterpiece in tragedy. It is often said that the one-act play was her proper medium, and it is true that she failed more often in long than in short plays, but *Grania* is a crushing refutation of the statement.

The Story Brought by Brigit is based upon a West Irish folk tale in which Saint Brigit is credited with personal attendance at the Crucifixion. On the stage the play was fragmentary, and drastic revision might have done for it what was done for *Kincora*.

In political satire Lady Gregory was strong: her best comedy effects were satirical, as her best comedies are *The Canavans, The White Cockade* and *The Image*. *The Canavans* satirises an accommodating coward, and is a good effort at satirising an aspect of Irish character that is too rarely given such merciless treatment. King James of the Running, James II, provides a fitting subject for the satire of *The White Cockade:* to see the cowardly monarch packed into a barrel is worthy of the laughter it secures. In *The Image* the factions wrangle while the artists die, and the material goods of life are either wasted or stolen. *The Image* is excellent comedy that will bear seeing many times.

The strain of mysticism which first manifested itself in *The Travelling Man* comes close to triumph in *The Dragon* and *The Golden Apple*, but perhaps fantasy not mysticism would be a more correct title for them. All the best qualities of Lady Gregory's art are exhibited in *The Golden Apple*; humour, humanity, *naiveté*, and a complete faith in the fairy world such as Barrie seems to lack and Maeterlinck possesses. If it was primarily 'a play for Kiltartan children' it is also a play which will delight the children of the whole world.

When all her plays have been studied only a few stand out prominently: *The Rising of the Moon, The Gaol Gate, Grania, The*

Image, The White Cockade, The Canavans, The Dragon, and *The Golden Apple.* To these must be added her translations from the French and the Italian: Molière's *The Doctor in Spite of Himself, The Rogueries of Scapin, The Miser, The Would-be Gentleman,* and Goldoni's *Mirandolina.* Thirteen plays of surpassing merit and interest! No mean contribution to the contemporary drama from a lady whose first play was not written until she had entered middle age. To have a third part of the total output recognisable as excellent is the tribute that Lady Gregory's art demands from the contemporary theatre. The little farces fade quickly from the memory: it has been said that they nearly emptied the Theatre, but that is so far from the fact that exactly the contrary is true. It was these little farces, indeed, which first brought popularity to the Abbey Theatre, and the money they earned enabled other, and possibly, better plays to be staged there.

Lady Gregory's reputation will not rest upon the little farces, which have served their purpose and their time and may be allowed to fade into peaceful oblivion. The most superficial examination of her plays must quickly draw attention to her most obvious limitation as a dramatist, her almost complete lack of imagination. Where she was able to draw from life she was invariably successful, even her fairy and wonder plays were drawn from the life around her, and she was often masterly. If her dialogue has little of the poetry of Synge it has a rhythm of its own that is as pleasing as it is vital and vivid. It has become the custom in Ireland now to laugh at 'Kiltartanese,' but the laughter has been caused by imitators and not by the originator herself. Her dialogue seemed so easy that it proved a temptation to imitators, and induced many to write plays who had neither art nor artifice. Lady Gregory's dialogue is crisp, idiomatic, rich, real, and pleasant: it keeps close to the peasant speech which she knew all her life and in consequence it has nothing of the poetic quality that marks Synge's more imaginative selectiveness. Dialogue was Lady Gregory's strength, as imagination was her weakness: but talk alone will not make great plays, and the bulk of her work was talk only. She could be as tedious and as dull as the worst in the repertory of the Abbey Theatre, but she also scaled the heights with the best. She had not the qualities which would have kept her for a long time on the heights; her material was too thin for that rarified atmosphere.

An observer, a note-taker among the people, rather than a sharer of their inmost lives, she assumed unconsciously an attitude towards the people that was somewhat snobbish. Neither herself nor the people could forget that she was 'the gentry' and they were 'the people'; and no conscious effort to secure confidential contact can be entirely successful. That is why so much of her dramatic work must be considered as in the Lever tradition. It is a striking tribute to the strength of a few Irish writers of the last century that they succeeded in moulding the popular conception of Irish life and character to their own models. It is the neglected Edgeworth, Carleton, and Le Fanu who might have been the better literary models as they were the better literary artists. Time will, doubtless, produce a new concept of the national life, and when that process is complete Larry Doyle will be recognised as no less Irish than Christy Mahon, while Bartley Fallon, Hyacinth Halvey, Malachi Naughton, Davideen, Cracked Mary, and many another of the same kind will share with Handy Andy the space reserved in a museum of national pathology for variations from the normal. Pathology will keep them safely, and the theatre will know them no more. *Grania, The Canavans, The Image, The White Cockade, The Golden Apple, The Dragon, The Gaol Gate, The Rising of the Moon*, and the adaptations from Molière and Goldoni are sure to give Lady Gregory an enduring place amongst the playwrights of her time, and a leading place amongst Irish dramatists of all time.

It is, however, for her great work in founding and guarding the Irish theatre, and so making possible Ireland's great contribution to contemporary drama that the gratitude of Ireland and the world is due to Lady Gregory. She was the Fairy Godmother, as Miss Horniman was the Foster Mother, who made smooth its way and made difficulties seem insignificant. Small in stature, frail of physique she could find the courage to say 'No' either to an author or to Dublin Castle as occasion demanded. She did her great work, and while her death left Ireland poorer her life had made Ireland immensely richer in those things that will count more heavily in the scale than many things that are more highly valued to-day.

'PERFECTION OF THE LIFE': LADY GREGORY'S AUTOBIOGRAPHICAL WRITINGS

MARY FITZGERALD

In *The Winding Stair and Other Poems*, strategically located in a series of meditations on the great questions of life and death, Yeats considers an ultimate reality, 'The Choice':

> The intellect of man is forced to choose.
> Perfection of the life or of the work,
> And if it take the second must refuse
> A heavenly mansion, raging in the dark.[1]

It is a critical commonplace to note that Yeats chose perfection of the work. But the alternative perfection that was not possible for him seems to have been the ultimate choice of his good friend, Augusta Gregory. Although there can be no doubt that she worked hard at 'the work' and that she made some wonderful books and plays in the process, it is clear from her personal writings that she was not only profoundly and intelligently religious—a seeker of that heavenly mansion Yeats refers to—but also a dedicated student and practitioner of the severe art of self-perfection. Her ability to lose herself in Yeats's work, or in the work of other writers; her endless dedication to the Irish dramatic movement that caused George Bernard Shaw to dub her 'the charwoman of the Abbey'; her many personal kindnesses to those she lived with and worked with—all attest to a remarkable discipline and generosity of spirit. But she was also an eager student of lives well lived and an exemplary teacher to the Gregorys who would succeed her. And she seems to have done this with characteristic deliberateness.

When she visited the United States, she wrote, biographies 'were the first thing I looked for on the bookshelves of any house where I stayed'.[2] Her memoirs and journals also record her broad reading in history and biography. And although she has come to be known for her work in the Irish theatre, she was if anything even more prolific in her biographical and autobiographical writings than in her plays. The narrative impulse that worked to such good

45

effect in the production of her dramas found another outlet both early and late in her literary career that resulted in thousands of pages of diaries, journals, and histories of her own life and of the lives of others. Even her accounts of the lives of Hugh Lane and of Arabi Bey, or her editions of the papers of her husband and his grandfather, or her detailed memoir of Coole Park, her home, serve as deflected autobiographies that illuminate her life as clearly as they do her subjects.

Whereas constructing plays did not at first come naturally to her—she learned how, she said, in order to help the Abbey and eventually grew to like playwriting so much that the desire to experiment with dramatic forms became 'like fire in the blood'[3]—biographical writing seems always to have attracted her, perhaps because it was one genre that was not proscribed during her rather strict upbringing,[4] perhaps because she was fascinated by the variety of human nature, a fascination that served her well in her dramatic writing too. And if reading biographies gave her pleasure, writing about lives as they had actually been lived offered her the sort of challenge she relished every bit as much as the desire to experiment onstage. Both were a kind of straining at limits, the one against dramatic conventions, the other against historical record. As she said in her seventieth year, with many plays and books to her credit, 'I can master a play . . . but a bundle of facts are different. In biography even of oneself, one is not free'.[5]

She yielded to truth and to history. She was fond of quoting the remark attributed to the legendary hero Finn that 'the sweetest music is the music of what happens'. And to judge by her fidelity to her journals, her folklore collecting, and even the nature of her plays, Lady Gregory seems to have thought of herself as a recorder of her times. Her primary method of writing historical books reflected an insistence on accuracy in reporting 'what happens'. To that extent it differed radically from her method of constructing plays, which involved plotting a scenario in some detail, inventing dialogue to suit the imagined situation, and revising the result substantially in manuscript. In writing biography, as her remark about the lack of freedom implies, Lady Gregory did not try to impose a prior order on history; rather, she allowed the facts as she found them to shape the book. This meant more work and harder work for her than the writing of her plays, and her method of going about it developed out of the process of gathering folklore. She first put it to work in editing her husband's autobiography. There, dealing with events that had occurred long before she knew him, she wanted to reconstruct what happened as faithfully as possible, and she had his notes to guide her. Ever after, she would research her way scrupulously through all the available materials on her subject: letters, journal entries, remarks jotted in notebooks, library notes. Next, she would type passages that she had selected onto scrap paper (sometimes the backs of advertising circulars from local merchants and even letters from such Abbey notables as Lennox Robinson). When these typed notes had reached an appropriate length, Lady Gregory would cut them up, arrange them in order, and paste them onto other pieces of scrap paper. From this she would type a rough draft, developing a text by adding introductory material and interlarding whatever connecting or explanatory interpolation she thought necessary. This rough draft would typically undergo several revisions, each one created at the typewriter, with further corrections added in manuscript. Until nearly the end of her life she typed all her own successive drafts on a typewriter given her by her friend, Lady Layard.[6] This self-transcription was something of a necessity, as her handwriting was so difficult to decipher that even professional copyists invariably needed a typed version from which to provide a final text. Her typing, although infinitely clearer than her penmanship, was nonetheless equally distinctive, and scholars who have handled her typescripts or the many hundreds of pages that she typed for W. B. Yeats during their long collaborative enterprise at Coole can readily recognize the familiar typeface and technique that signify Lady Gregory's work.

This cut-paste-and-revise method of composition is the source of her chief strength in her autobiographical writings, imparting as it does an unusually close historical accuracy and flavour that result from using unadulterated primary sources; but it also gives rise to her chief weakness, an occasional tendency to obscure her sources or to confuse them with one another. Possibly because of her habitual inclination to self-effacement, Lady Gregory was far more concerned with what actually occurred or what actually had been written or how it had been said than she was with who might have said it or where she might have found it. In this she was not alone, of course: the absence of documentation is fairly characteristic of much casual historical writing—and some scholarly writing—of the period. But there are times when Lady Gregory leaves her reader rather more unclear than is necessary about the factual basis of the material she uses. Typically, she is most careless in this regard when writing about herself: the problem is especially

evident, for example, in her unfinished memoir, *Seventy Years*,[7]
where the scissoring apart and pasting together of passages from
different letters—and from different correspondents—has resulted
in several chapters in which it is impossible at times to distinguish
quotation from interpolation, or to identify which of several
correspondents she is quoting, or even to determine where one
letter ends and another begins. It is, in fact, the worst instance of
this problem, no doubt because it was written very late in her life,
when she was long removed from the events she describes, and
because in compiling it she was forced to rely frequently upon
letters that were themselves undated and out of order. Although
she submitted the final text of the book to her publishers, she was
well aware of its shortcomings: she had worked to complete the
memoir in considerable haste, hoping to earn enough from it to
save Coole from being sold. But the memoir did not appear in her
lifetime—not in fact until more than forty years after her death,
when Colin Smythe brought the final version of the text into print.
And Coole, of course, was not only sold in 1927 but torn down in
1941.

Despite its shortcomings, her cut-paste-and-revise method
worked well enough to enable Lady Gregory to assemble several
autobiographical or semi-autobiographical books, among them
The Autobiography of Sir William Gregory (1894), an edition of
her husband's memories; *Mr. Gregory's Letter Box 1813–35* (1898),
an edition of letters belonging to her husband's grandfather; *Our
Irish Theatre* (1913)—subtitled *A Chapter of Autobiography*—an
account of the origins of the Abbey Theatre; *Hugh Lane's Life and
Achievement, with Some account of the Dublin Galleries* (1921),
the life of her nephew; *Coole* (1931), an impressionistic evocation
of her home; and the posthumously printed *Seventy Years* (1974),
her memoir.[8] Her diaries and journals, now gradually coming into
print,[9] constitute a large proportion of her autobiographical
writings. Although they have obviously not been subjected to the
kind of editing which Lady Gregory used in compiling and
developing her other historical texts, they show a deliberate
construction and a sustained editorial design; she was evidently
well aware that others would read them. She made typed copies of
them, not only to allow readier access to the material they might
contain for her own use in putting together autobiographical works
or other possible histories, but also with an eye to their eventual
publication, either at her own hands or at the hands of some future
editor.[10]

Her biographical and autobiographical writings show a sustained growth in technique. Her first full-length venture in the genre was her preparation of her husband's long autobiographical manuscript for posthumous publication. In many ways, this was an appropriately symbolic beginning for her. It was her marriage to Sir William Gregory that gave her writing talents their first outlet, and the brief pamphlets that she wrote and published during the years of her marriage confirmed her belief in her ability as a writer. A monograph on the Egyptian nationalist Arabi Bey, whom she met with her husband during their visit to the Middle East in the early years of their marriage, had been produced under Sir William's approving eye; he had encouraged her literary interests. After his death, Lady Gregory found in the editing of his autobiography a useful way both to honour his memory and to preserve his public renown, so that the Gregory name might hold its lustre until their young son Robert should reach his majority. Moreover, she wanted Robert to imitate his father's life of public service and perhaps to follow her own artistic pursuits.

She edited the large Gregory manuscript with an eye to providing an informative and readable account of Sir William's life, and it provided her with a model for her future work in autobiography. She submitted the shortened version to historians she knew and to friends and relatives who had known Sir William, asking for their opinion. She was careful to delete references in the text that might not meet with approval, and she was very conscious of the possibility of causing pain to living descendants of persons mentioned in the text. The marked tendency in her later books to obscure the identities of persons mentioned in connection with events or opinions derives from the work she did to avoid offending others in editing her husband's book. The published result of these labours was greeted with approbation by reviewers, and, fired with her success, Lady Gregory turned her attention to mining another fortunate storehouse of publishable material, which she also found under her own capacious roof at Coole: *Mr. Gregory's Letter-Box*, as its published title aptly describes it.

In editing letters, she faced a new challenge. She had to balance the demands of chronology against those of a more topical organizational structure, and the method she evolved for handling the wealth and diversity of the materials in the letter-box was one she continued to use to the end of her life, a combination of chronology and topicality, which provided an episodic structure for the collection. The book begins with 'Orangeism and

Emancipation' and works its way through historical events in a series of chapters dedicated to individual correspondents. It gives both sides of the correspondence as it proceeds, and the result is an insider's view of the unfolding of political events. The major portion of the book is given to Gregory's correspondence with Lord Talbot, and the volume closes with the passage of Catholic Emancipation and with Lord Talbot's life in London, giving the volume as a whole a sense of resolution.

Because in this book Lady Gregory was handling events located at a greater distance in the past than those in her husband's autobiography, she needed more annotation and more editorial apparatus. She supplied an index, and apparently feeling herself on slightly less secure ground than before, she also supplied a title that artfully suggested only a random sampling from an old letter-box. The internal structure of the volume and the deft handling of individual letters and episodes, however, demonstrate that she had actually done a great deal more. The book, like its predecessor, was well received, and it served to keep the Gregory name in view a while longer. In the meantime, of course, Lady Gregory had begun to make a name for herself, not only as the editor of her in-laws' works but as a folklorist in her own right as well. She met and befriended her fellow folklorist and poet, William Butler Yeats, and thereby embarked on an involvement with his work in Irish drama that lasted the remainder of her life and provided the impetus for her to attempt dramatic writing on her own. In 1902, the year of Robert's majority, she wrote her first play. She would eventually write some three dozen more, and the Gregory name would come to be associated in the world at large primarily with her, rather than with the men whose lives she edited.

Her diaries from the earliest days in the theatre are alternately full and sparse, as she suffered from 'the day's war with every knave and dolt', in Yeats's famous phrase, every bit as much as Yeats himself suffered from it. Most of the material from the diaries she put to good, efficient use in her first personally autobiographical book, *Our Irish Theatre*. In it she describes not only the founding of the Irish Literary Theatre and its famous successor, the Abbey Theatre, but also the first dozen years of the struggle to establish an enduring national theatrical movement and a popular repertory company in Ireland.

The book was published in 1913, after the Abbey had become financially independent of its major benefactor, Annie Elizabeth Frederika Horniman, whose munificence was as much a burden as a blessing—because of the many ways in which she intervened in its management. Lady Gregory chronicles the triumphs and mishaps that shaped the Irish dramatic movement, ending the book positively, with the peaceful commemorative 1911 production of John Millington Synge's *The Playboy of the Western World* and the successful—though tumultuous—first American tours. The technique that she employs in the volume is a more chronologically oriented development of the episodic structure she used in producing *Mr. Gregory's Letter-Box. Our Irish Theatre* is largely a history, and although the chapters are arranged around exciting or important episodes in the unfolding of that history, the overall impression is of a smoothly flowing chronological tale. Although the primary intention of the volume is the telling of the Abbey story, Lady Gregory's own involvement is so inextricably woven into that history that in narrating it she gives the account of this period of her life. And like its predecessors, the book is meant to explain the public life of a Gregory to the next generation in the family: Lady Gregory addresses *Our Irish Theatre* to her grandson Richard, so that he may come in later years to understand the way in which she chose to live her life. *Seventy Years*, the final memoir, bears a similarly introductory address to Richard Gregory.

Seventy Years, which should have been Lady Gregory's autobiographical masterpiece, fell short of that goal for a number of reasons. First among these was the breadth of its scope. In order to do justice to the full span of her long life, she needed to multiply her customary research for a book five-fold to seven-fold. Thousands of letters and thousands of pages of diaries and journals had to be scanned and often typed, and although she set to work at the typewriter with her customary doggedness to transcribe and to write, devoting several hours each day to that and to nothing else, the amount of work involved extended the length of preparation time for the book to years instead of the usual months. Then too, Lady Gregory was suffering declining health, battling cancer and also rheumatism as her age advanced. She was further hampered by her worries about Coole, which she hoped would be kept for her grandson, but which her daughter-in-law wanted sold. The need for money to save Coole was acute, and so Lady Gregory pushed on at the Memoirs, as she called *Seventy Years* in the earliest stages. Yeats listened to her reading of the final draft, and after her death he made a brief attempt to edit it, but as he was in declining health as well, he left the book for later scholars to work on.

The published version which Colin Smythe produced in 1974 is the largely unrevised typescript that Lady Gregory had submitted to her publisher, who declined it in that form largely on the grounds of its length, and then bequeathed it to Yeats. In the interests of historical fidelity, Colin Smythe printed it in the form in which Lady Gregory last saw it, without much encumbering editorial apparatus. While this preserved the flavour of the book as Lady Gregory hoped to publish it in 1930, it also obscured some identities of characters and of sources whom Lady Gregory meant to protect in 1930, as she did with *The Autobiography of Sir William Gregory*. Fortunately, however, the names that she habitually hid under misleading initials are available in earlier drafts of the book, preserved among her papers in the Berg Collection at the New York Public Library. Thus, for example, the actresses refered to as N, Q, B, and C in a series of anecdotes about backstage quarrels at the Abbey turn out to be the Allgood sisters, Molly (Maire O'Neill) and Sara (*Seventy Years*, pp. 416–17). Sally is N and B; Molly is Q and C. Similarly, references to Miss Horniman and to playwright and actor Padraic Colum are hidden behind initials (pp. 421, 429). Two useful pieces of information about Yeats appear: it is George Bernard Shaw whom he describes as a watch contemplating a bullock (p. 437), and it is Maud Gonne who is the 'friend' who married in haste to prove to Paris friends that she was no longer under the sway of her former lover (p. 424). The early drafts also show that Lady Gregory not only excised the names of her contemporaries in an effort to cause no embarrassment or discomfort, but she also toned down the bitterness of her recollections of early childhood, eliminating sketches of her odd and unhappy tutors and of the colder aspects of the Persse home, preferring to convey these more subtly in the final text by a continual substitution of the phrase 'the Mistress,' for example, wherever she had used 'my mother' in earlier versions.

One can argue that these obscured identities do not seriously impede the reader's appreciation of the book, but *Seventy Years* also suffers from her tendency to understate her role in events, a practice that one can only account for in terms of rigorous, and probably religiously motivated, self-denial. Where her diaries and journals indicate that she initiated a particular course of action, in *Seventy Years* she invariably describes that action as the result of some group decision. The only exceptions to this rule appear to be those instances where she had already received public recognition for a particular act. This deliberate modesty was worsened by her reading the final draft to Yeats: she minimized her own role partly to magnify his, partly so as not to seem hungry for praise, but also out of her genuine desire not to take too much credit for anything she did. Her selflessness, laudable in itself, robs *Seventy Years* of some interest: the volume becomes more of a record of her observations than of her doings, and the resulting staleness of parts of the book contributed to her publisher's decision to decline it in that form.

Knowing that a revised memoir could not appear in time to save Coole, and wishing to explain to her grandchildren both the importance of Coole House to the Gregory name and her long battle to preserve Coole Park as their inheritance, she set herself to write one final semi-autobiographical work. Entitled simply *Coole*, and published in 1931, the year before she died, this slim volume, containing three of the five chapters she originally wrote for it, employs the episodic or topical approach to evoke the history of the house and its meaning for her. It is an implicit defence of her fight to preserve her house and lands, as *Our Irish Theatre* was a defence of her fight for the Abbey and *Hugh Lane's Life and Achievement* was a defence of Ireland's right to the Lane bequest of French impressionist paintings that had gone to England. Like all its predecessors, *Coole* is a history of the public life of the Gregorys.

She reserved the history of the private life for her diaries and journals, yet even in these she employed editorial decorum and control. Although the characteristic pattern is a jotting down of the day's events, observations, and reflections, together with excerpts from letters received and replies returned, there is always the consciousness of a possible reader over her shoulder. There is very little private personal information in Lady Gregory's journals: for example, although references to Wilfrid Scawen Blunt and to John Quinn are fairly common, nothing conveys more than a professional or family friendship with either man, and it is only the archives of *their* papers that support the fact of her personal intimacy with them.[11] Nevertheless, her journals are extremely valuable research tools, which is clearly what she intended them to be. She pinned letters and other documents into appropriate pages, recorded conversations that might otherwise have slipped into merely mental recollection, and kept an account of her writing and theatrical activities as well as of the comings and goings of family and houseguests. All chronicled items, however, share in common a certain importance: all document things that matter. There is very little small talk—and what little there is is related to work or to significant events in politics or in local land matters—and there is virtually none of the meditation on daily life that one sometimes expects to see in journals. That was not their function as she saw it: they were documents to be preserved for her own use and for posterity, and she was simply too busy to indulge her thoughts more than occasionally. The hasty scribble in which she wrote most of the entries attests both to the great number of matters she was involved in and to the weariness that involvement brought her at day's end.

Her journals have a slightly self-conscious tone overall, but it does not intrude noticeably in most entries. That she considered her journals relatively candid is clear from the fact that she edited them when typing them out—and she *did* type them out herself in hundreds of pages, with the remark that by doing so she had saved somebody a little work some day in the future.[12] Ultimately, then, Lady Gregory's journals were as much a part of her auto-biographical writing as her more consciously constructed published volumes. Volume One of the *Journals*, edited by Daniel Murphy, is now in print, the second should appear in early 1987, and a volume of diaries is in the process of being edited.[13] They are valuable for what they tell about Lady Gregory's writing—not only in themselves but also in the information they contain about her construction of plays and books of folklore and history; and because many of her literary friends were major figures, the journals are useful sources of facts about their lives and works as well. Yeats is chief among these, of course, but George Bernard Shaw and other Irish writers appear, as do English and even American writers like Mark Twain. The journals provide glimpses of the great and famous in their more relaxed and social moods—at dinner, attending the theatre, in casual conversation. Her daily notes also comment on the unfolding of historical events—they are particularly vivid in recounting the violence in Ireland during the Troubles—and they provide the human perspective on events which helps to round out the more academic recountings of the times. All in all, they reveal Lady Gregory to be a painstaking literary craftsman, a tireless worker, an ardent nationalist, and a generous person.

Although her reputation rests justifiably on the plays which made her both admired and famous, Lady Gregory's work in autobiographical and historical writing ranks perhaps with her work in folklore and translation—writing for which she is generally less well known. It shows her to be a master of several genres and forms, and although these may seem to be disparate elements in her literary career, in reality they are complementary manifestations of a single, unified creative impulse that was firmly grounded in close and loving observation of human nature. Lady Gregory understood people, as her various writings attest. Partly she was curious to find evidence of human perfectability; partly she enjoyed studying the common tradition that links past with present and one national or religious group with all others; partly she delighted in the rich variety of the human comedy. She found the whole human experience enacted anew in each individual life, and she lived her own life as if the results of her efforts might well be worth reading. And so they are.

THE CLOUD OF WITNESSES

MARY LOU KOHFELDT STEVENSON

Augusta Gregory discovered she could write plays when she was in her fifties. She had, in fact, been working most of her life to please an audience, a 'cloud of witnesses' assembled by her to give her life the direction, value, and emotional richness she did not get from her family.

When she was born—at midnight between March 14th and 15th, 1852—she was momentarily laid aside because her mother was disappointed she was not a boy. When her mother was attended to and the baby remembered, she was found under a quilt, blue and gasping, nearly dead. After everyone was sure the baby would live, her mother remarked that she 'would have been sorry for such a loss, because the other children would have been disappointed at not having a new baby to play with'.[1]

When Augusta was older and her nurse told her the story, with apparently neither indignation nor comfort, Augusta took it to heart. Though every female child of her time and class was taught she was to live for others, Augusta believed it more than most. The success of her life lies in the manner in which she chose to serve.

There were no important personal relationships in her early life. Though she later praised Mary Sheridan, her Catholic, Gaelic-speaking nurse, for telling her Irish folk tales, she described the woman herself as 'that proud old nurse'.[2] And in any case, Frances Persse continuing to produce a baby every two years for the next seven years—each and every one a boy[3]—her nurse's attention was much divided.

Augusta and all her sisters and brothers referred to their parents as 'the Master' and 'the Mistress'. Dudley Persse, according to an old countryman, was 'a fierce-looking man to look at. He had two big jaw-bones and wore side whiskers and he had big teeth in his head and they were nearly as long as my thumb. He was a big strong man in his day but he used to be suffering from gout.'[4] Augusta never saw her father walk. By the time she was born when he was fifty, he had eaten and drunk so excessively he was

56

paralysed from the waist down. He rode everywhere in his little
donkey cart or on his huge horse or sat in the middle of the yard
in his wheeled chair supervising the massive activity of his estate.
Frances Persse was described by her future son-in-law as 'a very
pretty woman . . . dressed in white of an evening with pearl
decorations',[5] and by one of the children's tutors as 'a tall lady in
black velvet and diamonds'.[6] Augusta saw her mother as artificial
and frivolous as well as 'very handsome, bright and strong'.[7]

Mother and father together presented a powerful and unpleasant
combination. The centre of her mother's life was evangelical
religion. Its chief lesson was that sin was terrible, but if you were
saved, sin did not matter. Augusta said that her mother had taught
her father so well he believed that 'you might be greedy, untruthful,
uncharitable, dishonest—in moderation—that did not really
matter, you would be "washed in the blood" at last'.[8]

Dudley Persse had thousands of acres and hundreds of people
subject to his power. Several attempts were made to shoot him. (In
Knocknagow, a popular novel of Irish country life, the author
quotes the actual statement of an Irish judge: 'I never met an
instance of a landlord being killed, who did not deserve—I don't
say to be hanged, as I am a judge—but I do say, a case of this kind
never came before me that the landlord did not deserve to be
damned!')[9]

Her father's passions were exploitative and short-sighted. He
began an acrimonious, and eventually successful, lawsuit that
lasted through many years of Augusta's youth to obtain the
adjoining estate of Castleboy from his brother. He set up a sawmill
and began cutting timber. Augusta and all the children hated the
sawmill and the ugly scars left on the landscape. Her half-brother
Dudley, heir to Roxborough, quarrelled with his father and left
home on account of it.

Augusta observed that her father manipulated her mother by
'treating her as a spoiled child, doing as he liked in great things,
giving her a dress or paying her compliments to pacify her'.[10] Her
mother indulged the boys, but neither mother nor father gave them
any sense of direction or responsibility. Her mother was stricter
with the girls, and as she grew older, she became more dissatisfied
with all her children and more quarrelsome.

Augusta found no friends among the older sisters and brothers.
The two half-sisters and Frances Persse's oldest daughter Elizabeth
took after the mother and devoted themselves to the attempt to
convert Catholics, an attempt Augusta saw as faintly ridiculous,

using energy and emotion, arousing dislike and uneasiness, in a cause that could not succeed. The older boys were away. Richard, when home, 'seemed to look with disapproval on the younger brothers and sisters'[11] and chose Augusta as the special butt of his dissatisfaction.

The middle girls, Gertrude and Adelaide, were not interested in her. Arabella, only two years older than she, appears to have been a pleasant companion, but Augusta, who had learned early that boys were more important, was not interested in companions from, as she put it, 'the weaker side'.[12]

Augusta spent most of her time with the four younger brothers. If she had seen herself as their leader, rather than their entertainer and junior nursemaid, she might have made something of them. As it was, they ran wild, played tricks on tenants, spent their time at fairs and races. They hunted foxes, rabbits, birds, and—as they grew older—women. Her brother Frank, just younger than she, boasted 'that he had done everything that could be done out of the way—except to kill a man'.[13]

In later life three of her nine brothers drank themselves to death. One had a successful career in the army. Three, including Frank, became farmers and land agents. One seems to have done nothing in particular, and her sarcastic and unpleasant brother Richard held a small judicial post in Galway until his early death from tuberculosis.

The path laid out for the girls was simple and honorable. They were to marry appropriately and have children. (It was also dangerous. Augusta's sister Gertrude died after three years of marriage on the birth of her third daughter.) The girls were not permitted outdoor pursuits. Little attention was paid to their education. Their mother's programme was simple: 'Religion and courtesy and holding themselves straight, these were to her mind the three things needful.'[14]

The most important attribute for a girl could not be acquired. Augusta's family subscribed fully to the prevalent doctrine that a woman's right to be loved depended on her beauty. Everyone agreed that Augusta was not beautiful (except her future husband who insisted he had seen her as a child and told her mother, 'that is the prettiest of all your daughters').[15] She was small, which was considered a defect, with an attentive, intelligent face, dark eyes, and straight dark hair. She wrote: 'it may be I would have been more tempted by dress and society had I nursed any expectation of being admired. But the Mistress, disappointed in a birthday prayer that I might grow not only in wisdom but in stature, made me aware, and this was true enough, that I was not to think myself the equal of beautiful Adelaide, of tall gay musical Gertrude or agreeable Arabella.'[16] Under orders, she gave up hope of romantic love.

She also received many lessons in its dangers. A first cousin once removed, Standish Hayes O'Grady, whose translation from the ancient Gaelic literature became one of the underpinnings of the Irish Renaissance, came visiting, apparently romantically interested in one of the older sisters. He was sent away, Mrs. Persse declaring she had 'a great dislike to the marriage of cousins'.[17] She also had a serious dislike to otherwise eligible young men with no money.

The troubles of her sister Adelaide, who was acknowledged to be a beauty, taught Augusta again that love and the social structure were in conflict. After three years of attending the balls and parties of the Viceregal season in Dublin, after getting religion and wanting to become a nurse, Adelaide finally became engaged. Her family was horrified. Her choice was John Lane, a divinity student several years her junior and, most objectionable of all, not of a landowning family. The Master and Mistress ordered Adelaide not to see him for three years. After two years they gave up and let her marry— their petty cruelty decreeing that she could not be married in the little church on the estate where she had been christened and attended services. Her marriage in the neighbouring parish symbolized her semi-exclusion from the family.

Adelaide and John Lane were unhappy immediately. He did not gain access to the glorified life of the aristocracy which had been part of Adelaide's attraction for him. He had to see his beautiful wife 'with but the background of a curate's lodging in a smoky English town'.[18] Adelaide hated being a minister's wife, hated 'the change from the easy luxury to the narrow cares of a home that had upon it the critical eyes of churchworkers'.[19] Her first child died; others came in quick succession (among them Hugh Lane who with his love of art added another dimension to the Irish Renaissance). Twenty years later it was Augusta who got back from John Lane's mistress his love letters and turned them over to the lawyer to be burned, who paid Adelaide's debts, and attended to the details of their legal separation.[20]

Augusta's first love was not for individuals but for the land. She described the happiest day of her childhood:

when my mother had come to the schoolroom and told us we might leave our books and get ready for a drive up the mountains to the lovely and romantic woods, past Daire-caol, Daroda and Druimdarod to Chevy Chase. We came across the bogs and purple heather and red col [sic], and I have never forgotten the moment of unspeakable ecstasy at the sight.[21]

Her next love was rebel Ireland, to which, she says, she was drawn by 'the wide beauty of my home, from whose hillsides I could see the mountains of Burren and Iar Connacht, and at sunset the silver western sea'.[22] Yet her family already owned and had owned for generations her beautiful home. Cousins and nephews, later sister and brothers, would own more of the beautiful land around her. She recognized early the flimsiness of their legal, exploitative ownership in contrast to the emotional ownership of the country people for whom the land was part of the fabric of their lives.

Exactly how she found the literature that reinforced and broadened her love is not clear. She was buying nationalist literature from the time she was big enough to push her sixpence across the counter of the dark little stationers' shop in Loughrea.[23] She was buying the songs of the Young Irelanders, an intellectual and literary group, mostly Protestants, who in the early 1840s set out to arouse national feeling by an emotional call for the unity of the Irish people—a great race with a great past and a greater future—against the oppressor.

The literature of Young Ireland, like the literature of most subject peoples, is an attempt to make up for the huge injury of having had, in a national sense, bad parents. It suited Augusta well. She selected this verse from Thomas Davis' *Lament for the Death of Owen Roe O'Neill* as representative of it all:

> We thought you would not die, we were sure you would not go
> And leave us in our utmost need to Cromwell's cruel blow;
> Sheep without a shepherd when the snow shuts out the sky,
> O why did you leave us, Owen? Why did you die?[24]

The last line of the poem, which she does not quote, is: 'But we're slaves, we're orphans. Owen!—why did you die?'[25] It is a child's song, an orphan's lament. The literature of rebel Ireland gave a warmth and a width and a passion to Augusta's obscure but urgent feelings of neglect.

The Master and Mistress did not know of Augusta's quiet rebellion. In their self-sufficient blindness, 'it is not likely that the idea of her having any thoughts of sympathies different from their own had ever entered the mind of any of the elders of the house'.[26] Yet she was reinforced in her love for rebel Ireland by the example of her own great grandfather who in 1777 formed and paid for the Roxborough Volunteers whose purpose, like that of similar volunteer armies all over the country, was to force the English, whose armies were busy in America, to grant Ireland more self-government. (William Persse was a correspondent of George Washington; there was a turkey in a glass case at Roxborough to prove it.)[27] When England did permit Ireland its own parliament, William Persse erected a plaque, the lichen-grown letters of which Augusta traced reverently: 'in memory of Ireland's Emancipation from foreign Jurisdiction',[28] which meant something far more revolutionary in her day than in his.

Her nurse Mary Sheridan, who 'professed to take the aristocratic side',[29] was nevertheless a source of rebel lore. Mary had been a nurse in the home of the famous rebel Hamilton Rowan (who was as prolific as the Persses, Mary having cared for ten baby Rowans before coming to Roxborough to care for eleven baby Persses.) Hamilton Rowan, also like the Persses, was a Protestant landowner. He was forced to flee from Ireland with a price on his head because of his active membership in the United Irishmen, who were preparing for an independent Ireland. Augusta was moved by the story 'of his escape from prison in which he was aided by his heroic wife and of the boatmen from whom he tried to hide his face till they said, "We know you very well, Mr. Rowan, and the reward that's on your head and there is no fear that we will betray you." '[30] Here, instead of a wife teaching her husband to be greedy, a father destroying his son's patrimony, she found a wide and encompassing loyalty. And Hamilton Rowan, after six years in France and America, was pardoned and returned to his wife and family and his large estate in Ireland, a circumstance comforting to young Augusta meditating rebellion on the beautiful estate of her narrow-minded family.

Though she writes that 'A part of the romance of my early days had been the whispered rumours of servants, and the overheard talk of my elders of the threatened rising of the Fenians',[31] her love of rebel Ireland was a purely private exercise that did not connect her with contemporary events involving the Fenians. In 1865 when she was thirteen, the office of *The Irish People*—the official newspaper of this supposedly secret society—was raided and its editors arrested. James Stephens, the founder of the Fenians, escaped, was captured, imprisoned, and escaped again within two weeks. According to a literary historian, 'All witnesses reported that in surprise, excitement, and popular identification with the object of a hue and cry, Stephens' jailbreak was one of the high emotional peaks of Irish history'.[32] In 1867 when she was fifteen, an attempt was made to rescue Fenian prisoners from a police van in Manchester. A policeman was shot in the attempt; three young Irishmen were hanged for his murder. Another attempt was made to free Fenian prisoners from Clerkenwell prison. A huge charge of dynamite placed against the prison wall blew out the side of the tenement house opposite, killed twelve people, maimed 120 others, and would have killed the Fenian prisoners had they been on that side of the jail. Augusta mentions none of these events in accounts of her childhood. But when she was fifteen she underwent a religious conversion that turned her away from Irish nationalism, a conversion perhaps caused by a new awareness of its complexities and dangers.

Though she had been continually exposed to religion—beginning with her christening to which her parents brought their own *famille rose* christening basin because the plain white one at the church was cracked[33]—it is not surprising that it took so long to catch her attention. Religion, as it presented itself to her, was a mixture of the repellent and the attractive.

She saw religion impelling her mother and older sisters to the ridiculous and unpopular task of attempting to convert Catholics. Her sister Elizabeth confessed to her, 'I sometimes think how happy you are not to feel called to this business as I do. It is a heavy task.'[34]

On the other hand, religion was a part of the routine of family life. The Bible was read every day, a chapter of the Old Testament in the morning, the New Testament in the evening. The genealogies were skipped but everything else was read unexpurgated, giving, as Augusta says, 'no offence to our ignorance'. She was grateful all her life for the 'driving force, the training to the ear, the moving of the imagination, the kindling of the spiritual side of nature through much listening to the English of the Bible'.[35] But on Sunday the children had to attend church twice; they could not work or play. They were read to out of instructive books for children. Being told 'This is Sunday Sabbath Day; This is why we must not play', the boys would whisper 'This is Sunday Sabbath night; This is why we'll have a fight'.[36]

The children earned their weekly allowance—the sixpence with which Augusta bought rebel song books—by memorizing an assigned Bible verse. It was not a difficult task. Augusta remembered her father examining a younger brother:

'In the beginning,' said my father.
'In the beginning,' said the child.
'God created the heavens and the earth.'
'Yes.'
'Good boy! A prize!'[37]

For a time the children were examined every evening from a card beginning, 'What sin have I this day committed in thought, word and deed?'[38] But they were so much more anxious to tell on their sisters and brothers than to remember their own 'sins' that the practice was given up. It was, however, a habit of mind, a sense of being surrounded by a crowd of eager tattletales, that contributed to Augusta's permanent sense of performing before a cloud of witnesses.

The church itself was cosy and pleasant, almost an extension of their home. 'The friendly little Killinane Church' was attended by 'neighbours from two or three houses' . . . and there was a customary chatting at the door after service, (though the children were in agreement with an early saying of the elder brother, 'I hate the nasty how d'ye do's').[39] The creaking harmonium was covered by a blanket to keep out the damp, until the sexton took the blanket home to his bed and the harmonium creaked even more. During service the sexton would bring in an armload of twigs and dump them on the fire. The fire crackled cosily. The children sat in their upholstered pews and watched the young grouse playing in the nettles outside. When brother Richard 'whose training at the Bar had given him respect for law and order' told the sexton to mow the nettles, the sexton, who knew who had power in God's house, refused indignantly: 'and what would the Master say if I was to cut them before the young pheasants are reared?'[40]

Their minister, William O'Grady, was a son of Lord Guillamore, a brother of their father's first wife, and their second cousin. He was 'liberal and kindly; proud of showing the figs that ripened on his garden walls and the red-blossomed rhododendrons, rare in that limestone soil, growing indeed in peat, for which rumour said he had dug pits to a depth of eighteen feet.'[41] The church was theirs, but Archdeacon O'Grady was the last incumbent before Disestablishment eliminated church livings as a provision for younger brothers. He was succeeded by Archdeacon Burkett whom the little Persses, with precocious snobbery, could not respect because of his Waterford accent.

Archdeacon Burkett encouraged Frances Persse's natural

inclination to constrict life. He advised her not to let the children
have dancing lessons. He told her not to let them perform
Cinderella—not because there was any harm in it, but 'You can't
tell where it might lead to!'[42] So the children continued making up
elaborate charades. Arabella with 'her gift of mimicry and humour'
was the star; Augusta was producer and director.[43]

However, it was their kindly cousin, preaching before
Disestablishment, who gave out two or three times a year the
Athanasian Creed which begins and ends with the stern warning
'which faith except everyone keep whole and undefiled, without
doubt, he shall perish everlastingly'. The congregation also
regularly sang the hymn: 'There is a dreadful hell, With everlasting pains, Where sinners must with devils dwell in darkness,
fire and chains'. And as this was a Protestant church, there was
no possibility of Purgatory, no repentance or conversion at
leisure.[44]

When she was fifteen, Augusta became seriously alarmed. Was
she saved? She concentrated on the problem so completely she
became ill and was taken to a doctor in Dublin. She had always
been the most delicate of the children, never recovering completely
from a childhood attack of whooping cough. In Dublin, the doctor
lifted her thin arm and declared that he had seen nothing like it
since famine times.[45]

The doctor's recommendations have not been preserved.
Augusta continued to concentrate so hard on her problem that she
solved it:

Then of a sudden one morning in the cottage on Lough Corrib her father
had taken as a fishing lodge, she rose up from her bed at peace with God.
All doubts and all fears had gone, she was one of His children, His angels
were her friends. The ballads, the poems and patriotic songs had become
as ashes; His work, the Bible was her only book. She need no longer strive
to do His will, it was her delight to do it. She was a little ashamed of this
ecstasy, a little shy, unwilling to have it known . . . She was very
happy.[46]

She had been threatened with death and hell; she was saved. Aside
from being saved, the chief advantage of this arrangement, as well
as its chief defect, was that other people did not count. The whole
conduct of her life was a matter between her and God and
His angels. 'George Moore, who in fact knew several of her
brothers and sisters, wrote, 'I imagine her without a mother, or

father, or sisters, or brothers, *sans attaché'*.)[47] She wrote, 'My first real memory of myself is at fifteen'.[48] She had found a way to give herself the sense of value she did not get from her parents, a way to distinguish herself from the crowd of brothers and sisters.

As a matter of course, her salvation involved service to others. She spent her pocket money on food and comforts for the poor—who were in great abundance in the neighbourhood. She taught Sunday school. She visited the sick. She paid a teacher to teach sewing to the young girls on the estate, but the priest ordered them to keep away, and did not change his mind when she promised to have in attendance, not herself, but one of the Catholic Miss Dalys of Castle Daly.[49]

Her charities, though important, were neither intellectually nor emotionally satisfying. She later described Arabella as 'a sister, more gifted as I think by nature than myself, but one who for conscience sake surrounded herself with ministers and preachers without intellectual force or training . . . the main difference between us was that she liked to live with her intellectual inferiors, I with my superiors.'[50] Augusta was not going to sacrifice her intelligence to her religion.

Her education had been so negligent as to leave unimpaired her great natural desire for learning. The girls had been taught by a series of 'amiable, incompetent governesses'.[51] Their texts were a few standard history books. When the governesses asked the Mistress for new books, she would ask if the children could answer all the questions in the old ones, which they never could.

Nevertheless, books found their way into the house. One Christmas a box of books arrived as a gift to be chosen from. Gertrude

saying frankly she did not care for reading but would choose the biggest, took and laid on the drawing-room table the two volumes of Chambers' *Encyclopedia of English Literature*.

That was to the younger sister the breaking of a new day, the discovering of a new world. . . . She knew now what to ask for at Christmas or from a brother in good humour, for the boys had more money in their pockets than the girls, given for the shooting of mischievous pests.[52]

The boys were given a penny for every crow they shot, and being good shots, 'they made a fortune'.[53]

Mostly through her brothers and their friends, Augusta acquired

Scott's poems (novels were not allowed), Burns, Montaigne, Arnold's essays, Clough, Hood, Keats, each new volume of Tennyson as it came out, and 'beyond all most enduring of joys Malory's *Morte D'Arthur*'.[54] (However, she was never completely devoted to Tennyson and once startled Yeats by saying that Tennyson had as his God the British Empire and Queen Victoria as his Virgin Mary.)[55] One Christmas her mother let her choose a six volume edition of Browning, the poet 'most understanding of us, the one who gives the heaven in and around us'.[56] After reading an article in the *Times* that made her think Browning might be an infidel, her mother was sorry she gave it. But for Augusta, her favourite authors became, as had been the leaders of the Irish rebellions, a band of heroes devoted to freeing their readers from limited lives and narrow sympathies.

Gradually the literature of rebel Ireland reoccupied its old place in her affections, not seeming after all to conflict with God and His angels. She wrote in a draft of her autobiography: 'Those three— what shall I call them? passions, incentives, influences—which have dominated my life, love of country, faith in the spiritual life, delight in poetry and literature, had taken possession of me I think before I entered my seventeenth year.'[57]

She was, therefore, well prepared when romantic love presented itself to test her. She had just turned eighteen. She declined a coming-out party, preferring to spend her money on the poor. Her formal entrance into society was overshadowed by the just acquired freedom to read novels and Shakespeare. Her brother Frank, temporarily a medical student in Dublin, whom she called 'a wild son of the house', brought home a friend, a Mr. Henry Hart, whom she called, 'a wild undergraduate of Trinity College . . . extremely handsome with the Grecian profile and an athlete, manly.'[58] She noted that he was also Edward Dowden's favourite pupil in literature. These qualities, physical attractiveness, 'wildness', and a love of literature, were exactly those possessed by the two men with whom Augusta did fall in love (in more protected circumstances): the English poet, landowner and freedom fighter Wilfrid Scawen Blunt and American lawyer and art patron John Quinn. They also belonged to the man she married—though by then Sir William was at a later stage in his life.

Henry Hart gave her a copy of *In Memoriam*, but she was too enthralled by Shakespeare to read it. She was learning the sonnets at her dressing table and reading the plays during long hours lying in the heather on Slieve Echtge. Every day Henry Hart went hunting with her brothers, and 'when we met in the evening, I was full of the day's discoveries'.[58] She wrote in a draft of her autobiography that did not find its way into the final version:

One or two things happened. He had come to sit near me in the drawing room one evening. I think they had been racing at a fair that day, and after a minute or two Frank came and touched him and took him out. Frank told me the next day that H. H. was very penitent and asked to apologize. Though I had not noticed it, he had too much to drink. I felt sorry for him and after a day or two, chancing to meet him in the garden we sat down and talked of the violets which I had in my hand. Next day I was told by my mother that I was to be sent to Castle Taylor, that my father, going through the garden in his chair, had not been pleased to see us talking together. I agreed cheerfully. I was exultant about my books, and happy if I took them with me, filled with the new enthusiasm that had come to me.[60]

Henry Hart wrote to her; the letter was intercepted and opened by 'the Authorities', the Master, the Mistress and Archdeacon Burkett. She learned of the letter years later, and that 'the broken seal had but disclosed a friendly note giving the authorship of a once discussed quotation'.[61] A neighbour insisted that 'I could tell by the sound of that young man's voice when he was talking that he was in love with Augusta'.[62] Augusta was a very good girl and insisted, 'I am sure that no thought of love or flirtation had crossed my mind'.[63]

Augusta was crippled all her life by the constrictions of her powerful family. Her successful rebellion consisted in creating for herself another set of 'Authorities' in whose service she could use her abilities and her passions. She referred often to her 'cloud of witnesses', which phrase comes from Hebrews 12, 1: 'Wherefore seeing we also are compassed about with so great a cloud of witnesses, let us lay aside every weight, and the sin which doth so easily beset us, and let us run with patience the race that is set before us.'

She was ready for a wider world, but she was nineteen, and then twenty and then twenty-one. She visited her sister Gertrude several times in Cornwall during the three years of Gertrude's brief marriage and continual pregnancies. She was twenty-two and then twenty-three. Her bad-tempered brother Richard was dying of tuberculosis and she was sent to Cannes each winter as his nurse. When she was twenty-five she met sixty-one year old Sir William Gregory, the owner of nearby Coole Park, back from being widowed and knighted in Ceylon where he had been governor. Sir William seemed to like her. She went again to Cannes with Richard. When she was twenty-six she was nursing her younger brother Gerald at Roxborough and overheard some of the servants saying they had heard the banshee crying for a death, 'and though I had not thought of such warnings being attributed to our family, or being anything but an idle tale, I felt a sudden dread'. She watched Gerald anxiously all night, and going out on the landing to reprove some servants who were making noise, her father's servant came up the stairs to her and said in a hushed voice, 'The Master is dead'.[64]

Her father's death was devastating:

To those of his children still living under the roof it seemed as if all had been shattered around them. Roxborough was such a hive of life, with its stables full of horses, its kennels full of sporting dogs . . . the sawmill with its carpenters and engineers and turners; the gamekeepers and trappers; the long array of labourers coming each morning to their work; the garden so well tilled, so full, at this September time, of grapes and melons and peaches and apples, inexhaustible fruit[65] . . . Must we leave it all? Where would we go? Were we who had been rich now poor?[66]

Her half-brother Dudley had at last inherited. Her mother left Roxborough for the reduced circumstances of a town house on Merrion Square in Dublin.

Augusta was spared having to choose between being dependent on her mother in Dublin or her half-brother at Roxborough by accompanying Richard to Cannes for the fourth and last time. When she returned to Roxborough, she took over the house-keeping. Everything was going wrong. The weather was bad. Agricultural prices were down. Tenants had joined the Land League and were demanding rent reductions. Her brother Dudley, unaccustomed to responsibility or discouragement, spent his time drinking with cronies from his club days in Dublin. A year and a day after her father's death, her brother Richard died.

At the gathering after the funeral, Augusta grew weak and nearly fainted. Her sister Eliza cried, 'Oh, Augusta, *you* must not break down!'[67] She pulled herself together and a few days after the funeral got Dudley into a carriage and to a doctor in Dublin. Looking back, she wrote, 'It surprises me now I did not fret more than I did, I seemed to be convinced that a pretty full life awaited me, and in this world too.'[68]

Just before she turned twenty-eight, Sir William Gregory asked her to marry him, and she accepted. She was reading George Eliot's *Middlemarch* and thought Dorothea's feelings for the elderly, scholarly Causabon were similar to her own about marriage to Sir William: 'How good of him—nay, it would be almost as if a winged messenger had suddenly stood beside her path and held out his hand toward her!'[69]

Sir William did not disappoint Augusta as Causabon did Dorothea, and for the twelve years of their married life, he became one of the cloud of witnesses, the primary one, for whom she performed. After his death she returned to Ireland and the simple triumvirate of God, country and literature. Serving God she made a private matter, but serving Ireland and literature found a perfect object first in W. B. Yeats, then in the Abbey Theatre, and then—her masterstroke—in the writing of her own plays.

THE MARRIAGE

BRIAN JENKINS

Recalling the married couple, one observer expressed surprise that Sir William was 'considered the more important of the two, whereas he actually was merely a charming old gentleman and a good raconteur.' As for Lady Gregory, who was her husband's junior by more than thirty years, 'Nobody could have believed that she would develop into the genius that, long after middle age, she became.'[1] Yet, if the connection was by no means obvious to all, Augusta Gregory did recognize that her short marriage had played no small part in her long life and was central to her later development as 'The Egeria of the Irish literary renaissance'.[2] Her husband had as a Member of Parliament a decade and a half earlier struggled to convince a Commons overwhelmingly English that it would be both 'wise and politic' to foster the 'literary, artistic and scientific' talent of Ireland. Moreover, alliance with William Gregory brought her an ever-increasing circle of friends and acquaintances formed by writers, artists, poets, statesmen and politicians. Both directly and indirectly it served to broaden her mind and deepen her knowledge. Not surprisingly, she devoted fully one half of her memoirs to these twelve years.

Sir William Gregory was far more than 'a charming old gentleman and a good raconteur'. Here was a man who only in middle age had redeemed the promise of youth, which had been mis-spent. Spoilt by attention at home and by success at school, he had gone up to Oxford expecting to make a great mark but had quietly come down four years later without even a degree. Fortune rescued him from failure when the unexpected opening of a parliamentary borough presented him with the opportunity to enter the Commons early in 1842. However, his consuming passion for the Turf distracted him from the tiresome business of seeking re-election and in 1847 he lost his Dublin seat. That same passion also consumed his income, as did the Famine, and in 1857 he began to sell off parcels of his estate in order to settle his debts. Eventually, he was to be left in possession of only one third of the 15,000 acres he had inherited. But the terrible experience of the Famine and the bitter lessons of the Turf were in a very real sense the making of William Gregory. Having lost or squandered so many of the advantages of his birth, 'and everything but *honour* forfeited', he now rebuilt his life and career and emerged from that labour a man of greater strength, maturity and compassion. Returned to Parliament for County Galway in 1857, he held that seat until his resignation to accept the governorship of Ceylon in 1872. There he distinguished himself as a humane and enlightened despot, one anxious to protect the relics of the island's past cultural splendour while promoting its present material prosperity. And his service was rewarded with a knighthood, conferred by the Prince of Wales during his visit to the colony.

Gregory had sought the Ceylon appointment with all the intensity of a quietly desperate man, for his once promising political career had not been crowned by office. The posts which had been offered to him during the 1860s were too minor to be accepted by a man of his age and experience. Yet a growing and discouraging sense of failure was not lessened by the awareness that the Ballot Act was going to make immeasurably more difficult the task even of winning re-election to the Commons. How was landlord or clerical influence to be exerted now that men cast their ballots in secret? Ambitious for fame, but at the age of fifty-five all too aware that time was an enemy, he grasped the governorship as an opportunity to prove his worth and make his mark and to do so in a region of the world which had long held a particular fascination for him. No less important, the post carried a handsome salary which eased his constant monetary problems and enabled him both to propose to and be accepted by the woman he had long adored. Gregory's first marriage, to Elizabeth Temple Bowdoin, the widow of a soldier and the daughter of Sir William Clay, was finally to free him of financial embarrassment. When she died in 1873 he discovered that his wife had lovingly guaranteed that his long ordeal of more than a quarter of a century of crushing indebtedness would be ended. 'She has left everything in the world to me for life, except her personal ornaments which go to her sister', he explained to his mother. 'The legacies are £2,000 to other people and £9,000 to me—besides the life income.' Indeed, Lizzie Gregory's will provided for an annual income of £1,200 and a life interest in the remaining revenues from a trust fund which with the sale of her house in Eaton Square totalled almost £50,000. He promptly instructed his mother to destroy the will which had been drawn up with an eye to protecting the family home of Coole and what remained of the estate from creditors. 'I am now so extremely

well off that I often doubt whether it is worth while to stay on here
and save money,' he wrote from Ceylon in August 1873.[3] Yet stay
he did because the quest for financial security had always been
subsidiary to that for recognition and achievement.

   Sir William resigned his post in 1876 and returned to Britain
during the summer of the following year. After the initial round of
welcoming dinners he travelled on to Coole for a period of peace
and quiet and to ponder his future. At age sixty-two he remained
intellectually vigorous and physically robust, yet an invitation to
make a belated entry into the world of high finance, with the
prospect of becoming chairman of the Erie Railway, was politely
declined. Nor did the thought of immediately re-entering
Parliament hold any great appeal for him, even though speculation
was rife that he would soon 'occupy again the position he once so
worthily filled,' and, somewhat more incongruously, that he was
'the bhoy for Galway'.[4] He would not be goaded by friends who
strove to provoke him to stand with the suggestion that he was
afraid of the Irish nationalists in the Commons, and failed to
respond to the flattery that he was 'too useful a man to be out of
public affairs' and possessed special knowledge which would surely
carry him to a high position.[5] Five years of government in Ceylon
had extinguished all interest in the 'wretched Irish filled squabbles'
into which he would inevitably be drawn, he explained. Instead, he
busied himself redecorating Coole, which he found 'fusty' after the
brightness and freshness of Ceylon houses, and re-arranging a
library which boasted between three and four thousand volumes.
Whenever the weather permitted, he supervised improvements and
embellishments to the exterior of the residence. He took an interest
in the monastic ruins at nearby Kilmacduagh and agreed to pay for
the restoration of the remarkable round tower. But much of his
time was also given to the congenial task of furnishing and stocking
the tall and pleasant town house he had bought in London.
Fashionably located in St. George's Place, a little enclosure off
Hyde Park, it ensured that by the spring of 1878 his life in the
capital was an enviable one: 'A pretty house, prettily decorated,
with artistic surroundings—a good cook and cellar, pleasant
friends, and ample income and good health.'[6] As for employment,
at least of his talents, Gregory concentrated on the affairs of the
National Gallery. From the day of his appointment by Disraeli in
1867 he had been one of the most energetic of the Trustees and with
his return from Ceylon he threw himself into the Gallery's many
battles. However, by the summer of 1879 this glittering life had lost

some of its sheen. Vile weather, a persistent cough (the first hint of the chronic bronchial problems that were to afflict him for the remainder of his life) and the death of Frances Waldegrave had combined to take all joy out of the 'season' as far as he was concerned. It had been Lady Waldegrave (she had remarried Chichester Fortescue) who as one of the leading political hostesses of the day had done much if not most to secure for Gregory the Ceylon appointment, and he described her simply as 'my very dear and truest friend'.[7] Depressed, he returned to Coole in August seeking solitude and health but his spirits soon improved, for there he renewed his friendship with the young Augusta Persse.

In a household dominated by young men who were local Hotspurs, as befitted their descent from the Percys, there was much physical activity but precious little intellectual inquiry. Quiet rather than boisterous, conscious that she was constantly being compared unfavourably with her sisters, who were tall, and either musically talented or more attractive, Augusta found a refuge and consolation in reading. It was this studiousness which interested Gregory in the earnest young woman. They had met soon after his return from Ceylon and before long he opened his large library to her and amended his will to grant her the choice of any six of the near four thousand volumes at Coole. Gregory had long been determined to remarry, for he had no wish to pass his declining years without a companion and a friend. 'Of course I never can feel as I felt for my late dear wife', he had written only a few months after Lizzie's death. 'Still I could have a warm regard and respect for a woman who suited me and that would be enough.'[8] Precisely when he settled on Augusta Persse as that woman is not clear, perhaps because the disparity in their ages discouraged any immediate thought of a union. Yet their paths continued to cross, and not only in Galway. When Augusta escorted her ailing brother Richard Dudley Persse to the Riviera during the winter of 1878–9 she again encountered Sir William, and although very early in the spring he travelled on to Rome, this season may well mark the planting and nurturing in his mind of the idea of marriage. He went to the Italian capital to meet a fellow Irishman, Robert Tighe— whom he described as his 'archeological Gamaliel'—ostensibly to learn more of the city's ancient and medieval past. However, Tighe was about to leave for home in order to get married. Although further advanced in years than Gregory, he had found a bride who was approximately the same age as Augusta. 'He told me that their tastes were quite in conformity, that she hated parties and was not going to have an evening dress in her trousseaux', Sir William confided to 'Miss Persse'.[9]

Several months were to pass before Augusta responded to this somewhat elliptical approach. In the meantime, the brother she had been nursing died and her eldest half-brother, who had succeeded to the family estate and taken possession of Roxborough on her father's death, fell ill and turned to her for care. 'I was tied as before', she later observed.[10] For an intellectually alert woman of twenty-eight, who was small, plain, one of several children as yet inadequately provided for, a dependent who seemed increasingly to be viewed as a convenient nurse, marriage even with a far older man must have appeared an ever more inviting prospect. Moreover, if Gregory looked his age he was a man of considerable charm, some distinction, much refinement, sufficient means and without being a great wit was a fascinating conversationalist. To be mistress of Coole with its heritage and magnificent library, and to have a London house, was to be assured of a cultural richness of life and to enjoy a security otherwise unattainable. Gregory had twice written to her since Rome, once to offer his condolences on the death of her brother and then in December to invite her to Coole while 'chaperones' were staying there. Also, he had protested to her mother the self-sacrifice the family expected of Augusta. So, when in January 1880, she returned to Gregory his copy of *Roderick Hudson*, Augusta attached a note which was something more than a simple critique of that book.

Despite this encouragement Sir William continued to advance cautiously, sensitive as he was to the danger of exposing himself to ridicule as a foolish old man. Thus he first asked Augusta whether he might 'write freely' on the 'most momentous question affecting man and woman's life', and provided her with a graceful means of closing the discussion by promising to remain her 'true and most sincere friend' even should he discover that he had misinterpreted her note. He did request that she 'refrain from communicating the purport of this letter to any one'.[11] Augusta evidently replied by return for only four days later Gregory, again writing from St. George's Place, proposed to her. 'Will you be my wife?' 'Will you marry me at once?' 'Will you come abroad after the marriage to Italy and perhaps Constantinople and then home here for the Summer?' Of course, he did not ignore the great difference in their ages, reminding her of the obvious fact that he was old enough to be her father and warning that while in good health now even the strongest break down unexpectedly. Moreover, she would still be young when he was a very old man and as her life had as yet not been a bright one she ought to consider the consequences should he become another invalid for her to nurse. However, on the positive side 'there is this that we have great similarities of tastes, we both love art and books and travelling, we know something of the character of each other, though I know far more of you than you of me. We can both live quietly, if we think fit, without yearning for balls and dissipation. It is great happiness no doubt to see this beautiful world in the companionship that is the most congenial one can select.'[12]

Friends were quick to congratulate Gregory, not least for his good sense in 'choosing with your head as well as your heart, which latter sometimes makes mistakes'.[13] 'She has an original mind, well cultivated and with the sense of humour inherited from her mother.'[14] Yet, he continued to be more than a little embarrassed by Augusta's youth. 'I dare say you will think it a foolish thing at my time of life to marry a young lady, only 27 [29]', he wrote defensively to his close friend Sir Henry Layard, who was himself married to a younger woman, 'but she is far more mature in thoughts and habits than her years. She has been admirably brought up, is clever and well informed, fond of art and literature—so I trust we may get on happily—I have found myself of late so lonely especially when in the country and by myself that my spirits and health were giving way and I could no longer live without a companion. It is all very well when you are young, but solitude is bad for the old, and last winter tired me terribly.'[15] Nor was Gregory's sensitivity lessened by his bride's appearance, which caused most people to underestimate her age. Naturally, he attempted to make light of the matter, suggesting that 'the Society for the Suppression of Vice' would seize and prosecute him 'for abducting a girl below the proper age', but was insistent that theirs be a very quiet wedding, one free of feasts, toasts and 'gossip', and he promptly took his youthful bride off on an extended European tour.[16] Nevertheless, there was no escaping the fact that many years separated them or that this disparity made all too likely another long separation. Thus shortly after their marriage he brought home for Augusta some verse which he had found and copied out at the Athenaeum:

> Till death us part
> So speaks the heart
> When each to each repeats the words of doom
> Thro blessings and through curse

For better and for worse
We will be one, till that dread hour come

There was, however, the assurance of eventual reunion:

Death with his healing hand
Shall once more knit the band
Which needs but that one link which none may sever
Till, thro' the only good
Heard, felt and understood
Our life in God shall make us one for ever.

Having chosen a young woman of intellectual tastes for his wife, one whom he admiringly described as 'quite a student' and whose smooth hair and subdued apparel reminded him of a 'Jenny Wren' when he saw her among more fashionable 'birds of plumage', Gregory was somewhat nonplussed by this blue stocking's unexpected and expensive preoccupation with 'chiffons and modistes' during their brief stay in Paris at the beginning of the honeymoon.[17] Yet his disapproval could not survive her disarming explanation that her purchases were motivated solely by a desire to please him. In other respects this initial journey set the pattern for he Gregorys' many subsequent overseas expeditions. They were usually concentrated on places of artistic and aesthetic interest—galleries, museums and churches—though the pair did occasionally attend balls and more frequently receptions and dinners to which they were invited by his friends or the local British Embassy or Legation. From Paris they travelled on to Italy and at Naples embarked for Greece, and then journeyed on to Constantinople. There they were handsomely entertained by the Layards, although they arrived shortly after the unpleasant news that Sir Henry had been recalled as Ambassador to Turkey. Lady Layard judged Augusta to be no more than 21 and considered her 'plain but intelligent looking'.[18] Together they visited mosques and bazaars and were carried by the ambassadorial launch to the entrance to the Black Sea and to Scutari, and walked up to the Crimean War cemetery which was beautifully decorated by Judas trees. After twelve days of sightseeing and exploration the Gregorys set out for home, taking a French mail steamer to Marseilles. They arrived in a cold and wet London on 31 May.

Although they again crossed the Channel the following summer, after their son Robert's birth on 30 May 1881, spending much of July and August in the Low Countries and Germany, Augusta quickly tired of foreign travel. No doubt this was due in part to the monotony of those tours in which the artistic rounds were infrequently interrupted by the social, for she increasingly and not surprisingly enjoyed the company of interesting, distinguished and cultivated people. She had met Henry James at Rome, Heinrich Schliemann, the discoverer of Troy, in Athens. 'Museum again' became a daily and rather weary entry in her diary during the summer of 1881. Diligently, she recorded the names of the pictures she had seen, but more to please her husband than for her own pleasure. Of course, on many occasions she was captivated by what she saw. In Ravenna in 1889 she spent half a day copying one work of an Old Master and found further occupation for her pencil sketching the beautiful tower of the cathedral in Modena. Indeed, she would sally forth at 7:00 a.m. to draw 'her "bozzos" of tombs and buildings of the old towns' of Northern Italy, and a proud Gregory happily informed Layard: 'If you hear of a new painter called Augusta dei Sepoteri extolled in the Italian art newspapers you may guess who it is.'[19] But by this date she had overcome her earlier and natural lack of enthusiasm for travels which separated her from their child.

In the years immediately following her marriage, life in London held by far the greatest attractions for this young woman from remote and unsophisticated County Galway. There was the excitement, glitter and variety of 'the season', and visits to Covent Garden, to the museums and galleries, to the Royal Academy— 'music, beautiful flowers, wonderful dresses'—and even to Christie's to attend auctions. Luncheons, teas, dinners and receptions followed one another with an intoxicating frequency. She found herself in the company of Lords, statesmen, diplomats, and politicians. For, his aversion to Ireland's 'squabbles' notwithstanding, Sir William remained politically active if in an informal way. 'Ours is an unfortunate country', he instructed his young wife, 'but if ruled over by a benevolent despot it would be one of the most easily governed and most prosperous of countries.'[20] He created quite a stir in London with a powerful and pessimistic analysis of the plight and prospects of Irish unionists which was printed and privately circulated in January 1881. He warned that in Galway Charles Stewart Parnell, the Home Rule leader, 'might send his umbrella and walking stick as candidates, and they would be instantly elected, in spite of bishops, priests and landlords, *vice* the present members'. The legislation of the past twelve years, for all its friendly intent, had merely 'undermined the structure of the British connection'. while those measures now

in prospect would 'in no time sweep every vestige of it away.'
Although he maintained amicable personal relations with the
'Grand Old Man' (as Gladstone was referred to), sending gifts of
the famous Coole woodcocks, and discussing their mutual
devotion to the Classics, he had lost faith in him as a political
leader. To Gregory's mind, Gladstone was at best the least of the
evils that threatened the Union—he was a restraining influence on
the more radical members of his own party and an obstacle to
Conservatives who might for reasons of political expediency be
willing to make greater concessions to Parnell and company. Yet
Sir William was one of the small group of prominent Liberals who
in 1884 attended a meeting in Dublin, sponsored by the Irish
Executive, and called in the hope of resuscitating the party in
Ireland. But little came of their deliberations. Instead, like fellow
unionists, he watched with impotent fury as the Home Rulers made
all the running in Ireland and the two major parties competed for
their support in Parliament.

If Gregory's earlier career and present but discreet involvement
in politics ensured that he and his wife rubbed shoulders with those
who wielded power, the fact that he continued to devote much of
his time and energy to his duties as a Trustee of the National
Gallery also guaranteed that Augusta was exposed to artists,
writers and poets. Slowly she overcame her shyness when
introduced to this 'delightful society' and took pride in her
mastering of the art of conversation. Of course, in her husband she
had an excellent instructor. 'Sir William Gregory is a very
agreeable man,' she later recalled that Gladstone had remarked, 'I
think the most agreeable I have ever known.' However, her
progress was also aided by a native wit. On one occasion, when
dining out, she lost her gloves, but apologised to the company 'for
arriving bare-handed as a refugee from Ireland, stripped and
despoiled'. The aplomb with which she handled her duties as
hostess at St. George's Place was soon legendary. There were only
twelve places at the Gregory table but the host was able to boast
to Layard: 'We are having small and pleasant dinners, not for
mashed-potato headed swells but "convivers" who put something
into the part.'[21] The Layards were among the guests at a
celebrated lunch on 20 May, 1881, which had been 'quite a
banquet' and had gone ahead though Augusta was far advanced in
her pregnancy. In the drawing-room afterwards she calmly
informed Enid Layard that her confinement had already begun but
that her doctor had given her permission to sit through lunch.
Layard's startled wife immediately rose and encouraged everyone

to leave promptly, and at 9:00 p.m. a son was born whom the Gregorys named William Robert.

Sir William had not behaved well during the pregnancy, for the prospect of becoming a father was not one he welcomed. At his age, the inconveniences of parenthood, not the least of which was the immediate cancellation of travel plans and the probable disruption of daily life and settled ways, perhaps even the fear of being made the butt of ridicule, seemed more obvious than the joys. 'It is a horrible business and each day adds to my discomfiture', he complained to Layard.[22] Indeed, for much of this difficult period he deserted Augusta, leaving her at Coole or with her mother in Dublin while he remained in London. He fussed about his own health, obliged as he was to remain in Britain for the winter, in ignorance of the fact that she was at one time seriously ill. And even after his son's birth he privately voiced the wish that the child be shut up at least until the age of seven.

The Gregorys had planned to spend the winter of 1880–81 in Egypt but the expedition had necessarily been postponed, much to William's undisguised irritation, as a result of the impending birth. However, he was determined to make the journey and they set out the following autumn, having left their infant with one of Augusta's sisters. The Egyptian interlude proved to be a decisive moment in her life. It was here, she later observed, 'that I first felt the real excitement of politics, for we tumbled into a revolution. We arrived there in November after the "revolt of the Colonels" of whom Arabi Bey was one.' Initially, the couple were united in their admiration for Arabi and sympathy for the National movement. They often found themselves standing together in Arabi's defence against fellow members of the small British community in Cairo. But they had at least one ally—Wilfrid Scawen Blunt. It was in Egypt that Augusta first encountered Blunt and began their lifelong friendship. In her memoirs she loyally defended her husband against Blunt's published charge that Gregory subsequently defected from the ranks of Arabi's defenders in order to keep in well with a London society which regarded the colonel and his associates as dangerous radicals. Certainly, after Arabi's fall and his banishment along with a group of supporters to Ceylon, following British intervention in Egypt, Gregory worked long and diligently on behalf of the exiles. He sought a more generous allowance for them and by 1890 was urging that they be permitted to return home, or at least be transferred to Cyprus. Nevertheless, the Gregorys had eventually found themselves at odds over Egypt.

The contrast between her aging husband who increasingly suffered problems with his teeth and from an unsightly eczema, against whom she may have harboured some resentment for his inconsiderate conduct during her pregnancy and apparent lack of interest in their son, and the handsome, romantic and even exotic Blunt was too sharp for Augusta to have ignored. In her diary for the Egyptian period she reserved for Blunt alone the intimacy of his first name, and her favourite adjective to describe him was 'radiant'. Back in England, they co-operated closely in preparing for Arabi's defence when he was placed on trial in Egypt. She could not have failed to be impressed by his quixotic generosity in agreeing to shoulder legal expenses which threatened to reach the figure of £4,000, even though his wife admitted, 'We have not got the money but we can borrow it and if our income is straitened we have the comfort of knowing it is owing to our having done what is right.' It was to Augusta that Blunt showed a copy of an appeal for assistance which he placed in *The Times* and she gave him 'a splendid quotation for the end of it'.[23] Then in the summer of 1883 Blunt and Augusta found themselves standing together on Egypt against her husband. Together with Randolph Churchill and others they sought to discredit the Khedive, but this was a course Gregory deplored. Throughout, his prime concern had been the protection of British interests. 'Blunt is a fanatic and apparently thinks anarchy will create a pure and simple Arab rule', Sir William concluded. 'R. Churchill's only object is to discredit and embarrass the [British] Government, and Lady G. thinks if the Khedive becomes impossible her dear Arabi may be recalled to govern the country.'[24]

Whether or not Gregory was alarmed by the evident strength of his wife's admiration of Blunt, he never gave any indication of having suspected that the relationship was other than a friendship. His surviving letters to Augusta from this period are affectionate in tone and he continued to employ tender diminutives when he addressed her. Nor did he sever relations with Blunt, at least until 1886 and even then the cause of the break was Blunt's provocative support for Irish nationalism. The mid-1880s found Gregory giving serious consideration to a return to public life. He was twice urged to stand for Parliament, in Devonport in 1884 and for the Epsom and Surrey division the following year, but held back from fear that a wintry campaign might soon bring his head 'to the family vault'. He had also been mentioned as a possible candidate for a number of important colonial appointments and it was for this reason that he now wished to distance himself from the reckless Blunt. 'The less we have to do with the Blunts the better', he wrote to Augusta from Coole in June 1886. 'If there had been a question of my getting a foreign appointment my former connexion with him w[oul]d have told against me and his last proceedings are so outrageous that I trust you will not encourage him to come to No. 3 [St George's Place] except during my absence here.'[25]

Sir William was justifiably proud of his record of generosity in his dealings with tenants. He was fully aware that rents on his lands had not been increased in a generation. Although he continued to provide an example of enlightened landlordship, establishing new rents by agreement with the tenantry rather than have them judicially set, Gregory was embittered by his experiences during the land war. Privately, he regretted that his great-grandfather had not retained one of his English estates instead of selling them both a century earlier and keeping those in his native Galway. Watching the drift of events and pessimistic about the future, Gregory believed that he would do well to sell his lands to his tenants in order to be assured of realizing something from his inheritance. Similarly, he regarded Home Rule as a stalking horse for the complete separation of Ireland from Britain and the eradication of the landlord class. It was an opinion his young wife shared, and they eventually resolved not 'to give up to grasping hands the lands that had been bought and cultivated and worked by his great grandfather'. Augusta's position on the Irish question may have been influenced by her upbringing and no doubt she was impressed by her husband's analysis of it, but the determining consideration appears to have been a powerful maternal resolve to guard her son's birthright. And following Robert's death she was to struggle just as gamely to preserve Coole for her grandson. Thus on Ireland she 'fell out of sympathy with W. Blunt'.

Writing to Augusta on the eve of his departure in 1884 for what proved to be a triumphal return to Ceylon (she did not accompany him on this journey but they retraced his steps together the following year) Gregory observed that she knew 'well enough how deep is my affection for you, how steadfast my trust in your honour and right judgment, how confident my expectation that under your guidance our boy will grow up to be a credit to the name which has not been wanting in men of some mark.'[26] Nor was this a mere formal statement by an old man who had to face the possibility that he might never return from a trip of such length. Augusta was his 'affectionate wife' and he had grown somewhat less sensitive about the difference in their ages. He almost enjoyed the gossip that he still pursued her as ardently as he had before their marriage and lightheartedly remarked to friends that she sent him away on his frequent travels in order to have some respite from his 'importunate affection'.

During Gregory's absences, either as a result of brief visits to London to attend meetings of the National Gallery's trustees, or longer journeys, such as those to Ceylon in 1884 and 1890, Augusta was entirely responsible for the supervision of Coole and the estate. She had to confront alone the tiresome domestic problems created by a long-serving housekeeper who was loyal but given to tantrums. 'I am so glad that you have been toadying the servants', Gregory wrote after one explosion. 'It is the only way to make life go on smooth wheels.' He was convinced that it was better for Augusta to tolerate occasional tantrums than for him to go 'through a course of cheats, drunkards and poisoners' in search of a new housekeeper.[27] But the responsibilities thrust upon her, and her husband's respect for her intelligence—for in his letters he discussed the larger national issues of the day and boasted to friends of her 'remarkable political acuteness'—naturally encouraged Augusta to assert her own personality within the marriage. Indeed, having studied the Layards' relationship, Gregory was struck by the sharp contrast between Enid Layard's docility in the face of her husband's many criticisms and Augusta's increasingly spirited replies to his gentle remonstrations. 'Is it not strange that instead of a deep and durable resentment my heart should yearn to a little "spiriting devil" who has so ill treated me that I should constantly miss her', he avowed.[28]

Augusta's intellectual self confidence, the self-assurance she had acquired after so few years of marriage, were on display during the journey through India in 1886. In Madras they stayed for a few days with a former parliamentary colleague of William, and now a colonial governor, Grant Duff. He discovered that Lady Gregory was widely read, knowledgeable and witty, moving effortlessly from a learned discussion of the sonnet form (a form she had practised as a result of her intimacy with Blunt) to a fund of amusing Irish anecdotes. Also, she supplied her host 'with and admirable formula for the slaughter of a mosquito within one's bed curtains,—a not too rare incident in the nightside of Madras:

'Thou wretched, rash, intruding fool, farewell!'[29]

Far from seeking to keep her in the background as Blunt claimed, Gregory spurred his wife's literary endeavours. He revelled in the favourable reception accorded her first published work, a short essay on *Arabi and His Household* which appeared in 1882, and reported with undisguised pride that in London she was known as 'the bright and clever Lady Gregory'.[29] He was soon urging her to write 'a corrected vindication of Arabi and the National party', for she had 'the power of writing well and piquantly'.[30] In 1883 she wrote an account of their journey 'Through Portugal' which not only revealed her descriptive ability but paraded her literary and artistic knowledge and was lightened by a fillip of humour. Following its publication in the *Fortnightly Review* a proud William was quick to report the *Pall Mall's* praise of this 'lively and clever' piece. But he mixed praise with exhortation, pressing her always to make full use of her talent. Her subsequent and lifeless article in the *Fortnightly*, entitled 'Glimpses of the Soudan' and no more than an abstract of work on the *Heart of Africa* 'written by the enthusiastic naturalist, Dr. Schweinfurth', he applauded as very good of its kind but dismissed its kind as unworthy of her attention. She was too original, Gregory flattered, to convert herself into a mere 'lemon strainer'.[31]

William Gregory was also ever an admiring supporter of his wife's dedicated work among the poor. In Galway, she sought to brighten the cheerless lives of the children in the Gort Workhouse by inviting the young inmates to Coole for the day to play in the woods. At other times she took Robert to the forbidding institution to distribute fruit. In London, she devoted herself to the task of aiding the underprivileged children of the parishes of St. George the Martyr, Holborn, and St. Stephen's, Southwark. Children who had formerly arrived at school half starved were soon assured of a good penny dinner. Each Christmas that Augusta spent in London was marked by her tireless efforts to organize a party for the children of the two parishes, complete with a tree which invariably came from the Blunt estate. She would return home late in the evening, having worked all day, sometimes alone, without dinner or supper. The tall house in St. George's Place was annually crammed with clothes, toys and other paraphernalia which she had collected for distribution at the party and Gregory good-naturedly described his home as an old clothes depository and doll's house. If he tolerated the inconvenience he hailed his wife's activities as 'Godly work'. No doubt he endorsed the opinion of one of the clergymen whose parishes Augusta aided, who wrote to Sir

William: 'One cannot be too thankful for this most hopeful sign of the times—the clear, intelligent manner in which many of the aristocracy are studying the interests of the mass of the people and showing sympathetic regard to them and their well-being. Labouring so long in the very thick of the London poor I can estimate the untold value of such marks of kind feeling in soothing angry mutterings and in weakening the force of social agitation.'[32]

There was one final bond which served to strengthen the Gregorys' mutual attachment—their son. As Robert grew from infancy to childhood so his father took a much greater interest in his development. Although he complained that his son was at times scatter-brained Gregory soon discovered that his was 'really a sharp boy'. He gave considerable attention to Robert's education, and undertook himself to coach him in classics. Sensibly he did not seek to force the child's studies, being 'a little afraid of this progress on a very excitable brain'. And as his son grew so did the father's evident affection and pride. 'He is really an excellent boy,' he boasted to Layard, Robert's godfather, 'full of go, but obedient and strictly truthful.' When, because of his small stature, Robert fell victim to bullying at school, Gregory dutifully instructed him in the art of boxing which he had acquired as an Oxford undergraduate almost half a century earlier. All of which added poignancy to Gregory's sense that time's devouring hand was fastening its grip upon him. Increasingly he was afflicted with bronchial asthma, perhaps emphysema, and sought to will himself to live 'for the sake of my boy and my dear good wife'. However, in March 1892 he succumbed, and Augusta provided an eloquent but brief epitaph for their twelve years together when, in a letter to a mutual friend, she wrote: 'As for myself each day seems more sad & empty—& I dare not look forward to the lonely years before me. I have Robert, but only [during] his holidays, and I shall miss more & more that bright, many sided companionship I appreciated so much.'[33]

LADY GREGORY AND WILFRID SCAWEN BLUNT

ELIZABETH LONGFORD

'The difference between men is not manners, or good breeding even. It is that some seem to have loved princesses and some sluts.'[1] So said Mrs Patrick Campbell, the flamboyant actress, to W. B. Yeats in 1908. Wilfrid Scawen Blunt was emphatically one of those men who loved princesses. Apart from the fact that he briefly loved a genuine princess, Hélène of Orleans, all his many loves had star quality, not least Augusta Gregory.

No secret has ever been better kept than Lady Gregory's. It is probable that only two contemporaries suspected her and Blunt of having once been lovers: the husband of one and wife of the other. Not till Blunt's 'Secret Diaries' were opened in 1952 by the trustees of the Fitzwilliam Museum, Cambridge, England (and hurriedly closed again) did a handful of people glimpse the truth.[2] Not till Blunt's official life based on his 'Secret Diaries' was published in 1979, did the true story become available to anyone interested.[3]

Yet the total connection between Lady Gregory and Blunt was far more significant than their sexual one taken alone, and indeed lasted forty times as long: over forty years during only one of which they were actually lovers.

The Gregorys and Blunts met in Cairo in the winter of 1881, Augusta Persse having been married to Sir William Gregory (his second wife) since March 1880, and Wilfrid Blunt having married Lady Anne King-Noel (Byron's grand-daughter) eleven years before. Wilfrid Blunt was already known to William Gregory. In 1863 they had met at a bullfight in Madrid, Wilfrid attracting attention as a dashing amateur toreador aged twenty-three. 'I wondered you were not afraid', said Gregory. 'I was very much afraid', replied Blunt, 'but I would not give in.'[4]

It may have been the courage then shown by Wilfrid which now convinced Sir William that he was a man alongside whom one could fight. At any rate, the Egyptian nationalists of the early 1880s found themselves supported by two remarkable European couples, the Gregorys and the Blunts.

85

This is not the place to elaborate on the complicated politics of
Egypt in 1881 and 1882. But an introductory summary is necessary.
An Egyptian colonel, Ahmed Arabi Bey — by birth a peasant or
fellah — made a series of bids to reform the army and obtain a
moderate share for his people in their country's government. Egypt
had long been subject to a Turkish Khedive and Caliphate and a
Chamber of Notables, while its finances had been under the 'Dual
Control' of France and Britain since 1876, as a result of the purchase
by foreign 'bondholders' of nearly half the total Suez Canal shares.

Neither Great Power was willing to make any concession,
arguing that Arabi was engineering a military coup under cover of
political ideals. The Gregorys and Blunts thought otherwise. Sir
William had been a humane governor of Ceylon, and Wilfrid was
a lifelong opponent of imperialism. Augusta, as an Irishwoman,
could at least understand the claims of small nations, while Anne's
descent from Byron drove her in the same direction.

In this situation the quartet drew close together in Cairo, two of
them gradually becoming closest of all. Lady Gregory has
described the day-to-day process in more vivid detail than Blunt,
though Blunt's final summary of their resultant relationship is
essential reading. In quoting from Lady Gregory's diaries I have
used photostats of her actual notebooks, not the tidied up versions
in her published autobiography, *Seventy Years*.

We must begin by seeing Augusta Gregory as a young wife of
twenty-eight, married to an elderly retired pro-consul, with a baby
boy of nearly a year old who has been left in England. Augusta was
married in a grey dress and hat, as if her husband had conferred
a vicarious maturity on her also. Slight of stature, with a dignified
oval face not unlike Queen Victoria's, Augusta was in fact a small
volcano hiding its secret fires. Her favourite reading as a girl had
been Malory's *Morte d'Arthur*. This taste for Lancelots and
Guineveres was shared by many other Victorians including
Tennyson, William Morris and — Wilfrid Scawen Blunt.
Underneath Augusta too was a glowing romantic in no sense 'grey'.

From her diary we can trace the steps towards her seduction by
Blunt. The path she followed was well trodden, Blunt having
already seduced one married lady many years younger than her
husband, fallen passionately in love with another, lived with a
third in South America, helped to ruin the marriage of a fourth in
Sussex, and been himself drawn from the arms of a little madrilène
by the famous Anglo-Irish courtesan, Catherine Walters, known as
'Skittles'. His *Love Sonnets of Proteus*, of which Skittles was the

heroine, were to be first published in London that year, 1881. For Wilfrid Blunt was a poet; and not only a poet but a sublimely handsome one: tall, lithe and strong, with wavy chestnut hair and passionate brown eyes.

Nevertheless by autumn 1880, while still in England, he had decided to renounce all this and begin a *vita nova*. 'I have just torn up sixty-four love letters I found in my desk, all written this year', he wrote on 29 September.[5] On 3 November he announced the end of Part I of his life — of romance, poetry, the search for happiness with women. Part II would start in Egypt with two worthy objects: reform of Islam involving support for an Arabian Caliphate, and the foundation of an Arabian stud in Sussex built up from pure Arab horses bought in the East.

The first important date for the purposes of this chapter was 18 November 1881, when Sir William and Lady Gregory arrived at Shepheard's Hotel, Cairo. Then comes the key date 2 December. 'Lunched with the Fitzgeralds, Mr. & Lady Anne Blunt . . .' wrote Lady Gregory in her journal.[6] The Blunts had decided to mediate between the British and Egyptians, to smooth Arabi's path. The Gregorys, as new arrivals in Cairo, were rapidly drawn into their circle. Lady Gregory wrote in her diary:

5th December. Boulak Museum with Mr. Brugsch, Mr. Blunt.

14. Rode to Tombs of the Khalifs Mosque with fine pulpit & copper doors. Mr Blunt.

19. Blunts.

25. Xmas Day. Dined Fitzgeralds Blunts . . .

26.   . . . Blunts in tribulation Sir E. M. [Edward Malet the consul] having written a despatch condemning Mr. Blunt's 'interference'.[7]

Blunt nevertheless retorted with letters to *The Times*, which Lady Gregory helped him to draft. For she was a naturally shrewd critic though at present inexperienced. Years later, when she wrote to Blunt asking him if he still possessed any of her 'Egyptian' letters, he replied significantly: 'You talk of having made your political education in Egypt, and so too did I with you, for before that eventful year, 1882, I had never played a public part of any kind or written so much as a letter to *The Times* with my name to it, and we made our education together over it.'[8]

In his *Secret History of the Occupation of Egypt* (1907) Blunt also credited Sir William with bombarding *The Times* in Egypt's cause: 'Nor is it perhaps too much to say', wrote Blunt, 'that Gregory's letters and mine — especially his — were largely the means of obtaining a respite for Egypt from the dangers that threatened her.'[9]

The next threat to Egypt arrived on 6 January 1882 with a notorious 'Joint Note' from Britain and France. This duly provoked the nationalists, and Arabi was appointed Minister of War. Blunt heard from the British Controller of Finance that British policy would probably end in Egypt's 'annexation'. For a moment the indomitable Augusta was shaken by Blunt's uncompromising attitude. Her husband was probably also cautioning her.

2. [February, 1882] Wilfrid in the morning in full Bedouin costume. He is becoming impracticable, says the Chamber is right in holding out, that if England intervenes there will be a bloody war but that liberty has never been gained without blood. In the middle of this Mr. Villiers Stuart came in & began to talk of mummies & the covering of the Sacred Ark. Wilfrid sat looking unutterably disgusted & I gave him the Arabian Nights & some bonbons to console him. He left in the lowest depths, Wm's moderate counsels & the discovery that his letters to the *Times* had not been published being too much for him.[10]

On 4 February Lord Houghton, Mrs Fitzgerald and the Gregorys were invited by the Blunts to luncheon at Heliopolis outside Cairo where they grew fruit and bred Arabian horses on their recently purchased estate called Sheykh Obeyd. How poor Sir William must have hated this expedition.

. . . 2 or 3 sheiks [wrote Augusta] to luncheon — first sweets nougat etc. Then incense burned & coffee — then a bowl of boiled lamb, one of rice, & coloured water. Wilfrid says this sheikh is not what we would call a robber but ravages the villages near him. Ld. H. [oughton] says 'like a man a friend of mine met out riding in the Far West & asked his occupation to which the answer was "Well, sir I may say I am generally out on the steal".'[11]

A week or so later, at a dinner-party with the Malets, Lord Houghton and the Fitzgeralds, the Gregorys rose together in defence of the nationalists. 'We quarrelled over Arabi: W. & I against the rest.'[12] Between 13 February and 1 April, Augusta moved steadily in a pro-nationalist direction, what with William sending more supportive letters of his own to *The Times*, Wilfrid being attacked and indignantly counter-attacking and Lady Anne interpreting for Augusta when the two ladies visited Arabi Bey's wife and family. Before the end of February, the Blunts had decided to leave Egypt: 'a long visit from Wilfrid in the afternoon. He is going back to England to set private opinion right there. He says Arabi and the others are so exasperated by the false reports of them and their motives in the English papers that they have now a very bitter feeling towards England and may give vent to it by some rash act.'[13]

With the Blunts gone by 28 February, and the Gregorys by 1 April, the 'rash acts' by both sides in Egypt multiplied. At home, on 19 May the Anti-Aggression League was addressed by Blunt in London. The Gregorys were not there. Lady Anne talked about 'cowards and curs',[14] and Wilfrid later said Sir William had 'failed' the cause.[15] But as Augusta was to explain in her *Seventy Years*, her husband was loyal — though dedicated to England's as well as Egypt's best interests.

The tally of disasters rose. A trivial local dispute in Alexandria caused a riot and 60 deaths on 11 June. Blunt sent a long-deferred open letter to Gladstone, claiming the Suez Canal was safe in Egypt's hands. Published in *The Times*, it earned its author torrents of abuse: Blunt was 'impulsive, credulous, and exceedingly vain', 'only another Arabi in a frock coat', 'both Blunt and Arabi ought to be shot'. Instead, on 11 July, Alexandria was shot up. A naval bombardment by the Powers reduced all its forts to rubble, killing or wounding every one of Arabi's gunners. The unprotected city was immediately burnt and looted while Arabi retreated to Cairo. Finally, on 13 September 1882, General Wolseley destroyed 10,000 of the enemy in forty minutes at Tel-el-Kebir, incidentally ruining Arabi's career as a much-needed Egyptian leader and pushing Egypt's independence into the far future.

This was the tragic 'climax' of which Blunt was to write years later in his 'Secret Diaries', describing Lady Gregory's part in it. He began by noting that his women friends were stauncher than the men.

More devoted still was Lady Gregory, and with a stronger personal feeling. She during all this trouble had been my secret and most trustworthy ally, the consequent confidante of my political joys and sorrows.[16]

He remembered her, when they first met in Cairo as

a quiet little woman of perhaps five and twenty years, rather plain than pretty, but still attractive, with much good sense and a fair share of Irish wit; hardly more than two years married to a husband greatly older than herself and kept by him rather in the background.[17]

Blunt then recorded that, since popularity was very dear to Sir William Gregory, when the pinch came over Egypt he drew back.[18]

Not, however, his wife, who with a woman's constancy, remained untouched by the decline of its fortunes, and as far as lay in her power served its interests still. This naturally drew us more closely than ever together, and at the climax of the tragedy by a spontaneous impulse we found comfort in each other's arms. It was a consummation neither of us, I think, foresaw, and was a quite new experience in her quiet life. It harmonised not ill with mine in its new phase of political idealism and did not in any way disturb or displace it. On the contrary to both of us the passionate element in our intercourse at this time proved a source of inspiration and of strength.[19]

Valuable though this passage is, it can now be augmented at certain points from Lady Gregory's own diaries.

18 [May] London. Blunts 10 James St.

This was the Blunts' town apartment. Significant that Augusta went round there on the very day of her arrival home.

19. Crabbet. Arab Horses & Egypt!

Crabbet was Blunt's country home in Sussex, where the Crabbet Arabian Stud was beginning to flourish.

26. To the New Cut. Thought myself a very ridiculous little Creature.[20]

Is this something to do with Augusta's falling into Wilfrid's arms? We shall never know, but certainly the prolonged Egyptian 'climax' had begun with the riot in Alexandria a fortnight before.

On 23 October Lady Gregory had shown her mettle by getting an article into *The Times* entitled 'Arabi and His Household'. (She had visited Mrs Arabi a second time after the Blunts left Egypt). Skilfully bringing out the humble domestic set-up — a bare living-room and tiny table with a crocheted antimacassar, the small photograph of Arabi his wife wore, with others of him on the walls, the simple meal she had cooked for her visitors protesting that had she known visitors were coming she would have killed a buffalo! − recording all this and much more, Augusta's article triumphantly swept England momentarily into the pro-Arabi camp. 'I am so glad you intend to write about Arabi's family', Blunt had encouraged her. 'You write so well, & some thing of that sort would be more likely to touch the public than any argument.'[21] Sure enough even Mr Gladstone the Prime Minister found it 'very touching'.[22]

It was a crucial moment. Wilfrid had sent out to Cairo two lawyers at his own expense to defend Arabi, now a prisoner of the British and in danger of execution in a Khedival court. Augusta meanwhile had had a hand yet again in a letter to *The Times*, this time asking for subscriptions to an Arabi Defence Fund. She recommended and translated several lines of Dante's *Purgatorio*, which admirably expressed Wilfrid's proud reluctance to make the appeal:

> To rescue him who lay in prison sore,
> The pangs of wounded pride I gladly bore.[23]

Wilfrid ultimately raised £300, though contributing ten times as much himself. In the end, wrote the jubilant Augusta, Wilfrid 'by his intervention saved Arabi's life'.

Arabi, his family and fellow 'rebels' were eventually exiled to Ceylon, where both the Gregorys and Blunts visited them. The news on 11 March 1884 of General Gordon's death in the Sudan at the hands of the Mahdi put a full stop to Lady Gregory's political campaign: 'That was the end of my essay in politics', she wrote afterwards. Her later work on behalf of an Irish National Theatre, the Irish language and heroic sagas, she saw as *preparations* for the Irish freedom fight, not as the fight itself. Moreover her campaign partner, Wilfrid Blunt, was now officially banned from Egypt and was travelling during 1883–4 in India. Just before he sailed he and Augusta decided that their sexual intimacy must stop. He wrote in his 'Secret Diary':

It ended by a mutual pact made between us in the summer of 1883 . . . that this part of our friendship should be replaced by one of a saner and less passionate kind. With her it resulted in that beautiful sonnet sequence which, with her consent was printed ten years afterwards in the Kelmscott Edition of my Proteus, with the title 'A Woman's Sonnets'. She wrote them for me as a farewell to our passion and put them in my hand the morning that we parted after our last night spent together in the room over the bow-window at Crabbet.[24]

As Blunt said, the twelve sonnets appeared as part of his own *Love Lyrics and Songs of Proteus*. Thus Wilfrid Blunt in his impersonation of Proteus — the god of many shapes — was to take among others the neat form of Augusta Gregory. 'She was pleased with the success of my Kelmscott book', reported Blunt. ' "With that one exception", she said, "I was a good wife to him [Sir William]." And so I am sure she was', added Blunt.[25]

The sonnets themselves, though workmanlike, hardly convey the intensity of emotion which had driven the author to adopt poetic diction. Nevertheless they are valuable for the insight they give into Augusta's passionate adventure.

Another, much longer poem, also emerged from the Gregory–Blunt association: Wilfrid's *The Wind and the Whirlwind* (1883), which Augusta was to describe as 'the real monument of that time'.[26] Its message was simple but devastating. Britain, having sown the wind in Egypt, would reap the whirlwind through the length and breadth of her Empire.

Two more minor points must be noticed before we move rapidly through the later stages of this long and productive friendship. First, Augusta referred to her lover as 'Wilfrid' in her actual diaries but changed this to 'W.S.B.' in the printed versions; after the sexual relationship ended they both apparently reverted to extreme formality in their correspondence — 'My dear Mr. Blunt', 'My dear Lady Gregory'. This was more puritanical than, say, the Duke of Wellington, who addressed former lovers as 'My dearest'.

Second (and more speculative), Augusta's diaries seem to have taken a turn for the better under the impact of Wilfrid's flamboyant personality. There are many excellent anecdotes (Dizzy being late for dinner at Windsor because there was no Mary Ann to dress him) which break up the formerly pedestrian though conscientious accounts of foreign galleries and their contents.

It was not till Blunt became involved with the Irish nationalists that his relations with Lady Gregory were briefly again emotional — though only on paper. While he was imprisoned in Galway gaol and later in Kilmainham, Dublin, for speaking at a banned meeting against evictions, Lady Gregory broke once more into song. But this time, though she addressed him poetically as 'My love', the tone was lyrical rather than erotic.

> My heart is in a prison cell
> My own true love beside
> Where more of worth and beauty dwell
> Than in the whole world wide.

She wrote altogether four prison poems to him in 1888. She also promised to see Blunt's own prison sonnets, *In Vinculis*, through the press while he was abroad, which she duly did. He bequeathed to her his prison Bible, which Lady Gregory's grandson Major Richard Gregory later gave to the Library of University College Galway.[27]

Curiously enough, Ireland not only cemented the Gregory–Blunt friendship but also provoked their only temporary estrangement. Lady Gregory at first denounced Home Rule for Ireland as 'Home Ruin'. Blunt in turn denounced her as suffering from property-owning blindness. By the twentieth century, however, she was not only advocating political Home Rule but Home Rule in a far wider context.[28]

The early Naughty Nineties — naughty for Blunt but not for Lady Gregory — found him preoccupied with other women, and she with editing her late husband's memoirs. Sir William died in the winter of 1892, and Blunt wrote on 9 May: 'Called on Lady Gregory. She is looking aged and sad in her widow's weeds.'[29] But in two years she had completed the memoirs and Blunt was reflecting: 'They are quite admirable and admirably edited by his widow, who will repay him by this pious act for this single infidelity. She is the cleverest and one of the best of women . . . a great help to him in his literary work as she has often been to me in mine.'[30]

It was her deception of Sir William that had pained Lady Gregory most, judging by some lines in 'A Woman's Sonnets'.

> What have I lost? . . .
>   . . . the days when with untroubled eyes
> Scorning deceit, I could hold up my head.
> I lead a double life — myself despise
> And fear each day to have my secret read.[31]

One remembers how young Anne Gregory recalled her grandmother's strong feelings about deceitfulness: 'she turned away', wrote Anne in *Me & Nu*, 'saying something about disliking deception in any form.'[32]

There was a new burst of emotional intimacy in 1905, again through Ireland. Although Blunt never set foot in Ireland after 1888 he was deeply attracted to the Irish literary renaissance. (He had longed to be an Irish MP but, as an Englishman, could not be sponsored by Parnell.) Lady Gregory brought W. B. Yeats several times to visit him both in London and at his latter-day home in Sussex, Newbuildings Place.[33] Anyone whom Lady Gregory liked Blunt tended to like too, and he wrote on 1 April 1898 with almost unqualified pleasure of Yeats being brought round by Lady Gregory. 'An Irish mystic of an interesting type. . . tall, lean, dark, good-looking.' The only two things in Yeats that Blunt jibbed at were his attempts, during seances, to make Blunt see his 'ghosts' (as Yeats said of 'AE', 'he hated to be put to see other people's ghosts'); and Yeats's 'chaunting' mannerisms as a reciter of poetry.[34] One again remembers Anne Gregory recalling how Yeats wrote a poem for her called 'For Anne Gregory', 'and proceeded to read it, in his "humming" voice.'[35]

But despite Yeats's ghosts and humming, Blunt felt flattered to be invited to contribute a play for his Cuchulain series at Yeats and Lady Gregory's Abbey Theatre.[36] The play, called *Fand of the Fair Cheek*, was in rhyming verse and dramatised the rival loves of Emer and Fand. It was sharply reviewed in 1905 by *Sinn Fein*, and more kindly by the *Freeman's Journal*; but in each case the critical reviewer was using *Fand* as a means of attacking the Abbey's theatrical methods. The goddess Fand, complained the former, was less like a Celtic goddess than an 'English parlour-maid in a fit of heroics' and she sang like 'a shop girl'. The fact that the play was written in alexandrines made it 'a curiosity piece, rather than . . . a drama of passion'. This latter criticism (from the *Freeman*) was not unjust. Yet Yeats thought well of *Fand*, since it was the work of a dramatist who had also been a man of action.

Without a drop of Irish blood, Blunt became almost an honorary Irishman, what with his own imprisonment, a much later visit to Newbuildings by Roger Casement, and a farewell message from Casement's death-cell.

Meanwhile it was again Lady Gregory who had crowned Blunt's career as a poet with a somewhat fantastic but undoubtedly magnificent 'Peacock Dinner'. Known also as the 'Poets' Party', it was in fact a luncheon attended by six young poets at Newbuildings on 18 January 1914 in honour of Wilfrid Scawen Blunt. Present were Yeats, Sturge Moore, Aldington, Ezra Pound, Flint, and Plarr. John Masefield had also accepted, but his wife intervened.[37]

Lady Gregory had first broached the idea with Yeats, her plan being that the poets should invite Blunt to be their guest at dinner in London. Owing to his ill-health, however, the celebration was transferred to Blunt's own home, at lunchtime. (She later attributed the plan directly to Pound, with Yeats as intermediary.) Highlights of the entertainment were a roasted peacock in full plumage, culled from the Newbuildings flock, a presentation statuette, seven individual poems in praise of Blunt inside a marble box and some general verses of welcome written and spoken by Pound. (Pound inadvertently congratulated Blunt on the support he had given to the patriot Mazzini — meaning Arabi!) There was only one thing wanting at the party. 'I should feel it lacked reality without you', wrote Blunt to Lady Gregory beforehand. She was not there.[38]

Blunt always considered Lady Gregory a better poet than Yeats. Indeed, when Yeats's great 'Easter 1916' was published, Blunt decided it must really be by Lady Gregory, being 'far too vigorous for Yeats'.[39] Blunt may not have been a good judge of Yeats but he was not mistaken in attributing to Lady Gregory, as partner in action and feeling, a quite exceptional vigour. His excessive enthusiasm for Lady Gregory as a poet is not unlike that of Yeats himself for Lady Dorothy Wellesley.

Blunt supported Lady Gregory in many ways: with a Crabbet Christmas tree every year for her Holborn slum children, and money and support for an official patent as well as *Fand* for her Abbey Theatre.[40] But perhaps his most interesting contribution to her fame was the two-tiered portrait in his 'Secret Diaries', 1913–14:

29 December 1913. Lady Gregory has gone back to Chelsea where she is staying with her other nephew Hugh Lane. We talked over her early married life with which I was connected and her shyness in those days and how she so long was content with an almost silent part in her own house. Sir William did all the talking then and her marriage though he was quite kind to her was always more or less the continuance of an act of condescension on his part. Neither he nor anyone could have guessed the important part she was to play in the world. Sir William came to understand her value in his later years but it was not till his death that she began to assert herself publicly apart from him. Yet she has been the real inspirer of the Irish Literary movement having created Yeats out of almost nothing and half the young Irishmen who now have names, while the Abbey Theatre has been wholly her work. She is the only woman I have known of real intellectual power equal to men and that without having anything unnaturally masculine about her. She is an admirable writer, something of a poet, a good speaker & lecturer & an entirely practical business woman.[41]

The second extract is dated 28 June 1914. Though there is some repetition, it also deserves to be quoted.

Lady Gregory arrived late last night from London where she has been busy with her play and we sat up talking till past 12. She is looking younger I think than a few years ago, things all being prosperous with her and her name and fame established. I feel I have the right to claim something of her success when I remember the timid unambitious woman she was 32 years ago, and that I had so to say the making of her education. It must have been some time in August 1883 that her husband took her for the first time to settle down at Coole and it took another ten years before she emerged completely from her chrysalis.

. . . I asked Lady Gregory what her idea exactly was about Home Rule, was she for or against it? She said she was for it as the least now of evils but what she cared most about was still the land purchase, so curiously are people swayed by their money interests, yet in a sense she is more nationalist than anybody, and has certainly done a larger national work for Ireland with her theatre.[42]

For her part, she acknowledged in her *Woman's Sonnets* three gifts she had gained from her passionate affair with Blunt. First, charity towards other wrongdoers. Second, 'one moment's glimpse of Paradise'. Third, the joy of once having 'made some happiness for you'.

A lady not yet mentioned must provide the postscript to this chapter. Dorothy Carleton, Blunt's junior by over thirty years, his adopted niece and his mistress from 1906 until his death in 1922, was also a close friend of Lady Gregory. Miss Carleton had indeed made a half-hearted bid for Lady Gregory's son Robert, but it was Yeats not Robert who flirted with her at Coole, and in any case she quickly discovered that she was irrevocably in love with Blunt.[43]

To Dorothy, Lady Gregory's literary efforts on Blunt's behalf were noble and endearing. It was she who had been the real author of an appreciation of W.S.B. in Miles's *Literary Nineteenth Century Who's Who*, though it was signed by the distinguished writer Richard Le Gallienne.[44] Again, it was Lady Gregory who had produced the new preface for Blunt's *My Diaries* when they were published in America (Knopf, 1921). She spoke of his 'mastery of living', as if he were 'one of Plutarch's men'. (Perhaps 'one of Malory's men' would have been even more appropriate.)[45]

So in 1923, the year after Blunt's death, Dorothy, as Blunt's executor, found herself writing to his natural daughter Mary in praise of Lady Gregory:

Newbuildings. May 15th 1923.

I have just had dear Lady Gregory here for two days which was a real godsend. She is such a wonderful woman in so many ways and her sympathy & kindness beyond words — I was able to talk over so many things with her, questions about publishing Mr. Blunt's books in America etc. which is the greatest help just now.[46]

We may be sure that at the back of each lady's mind lay the thought of what the other had been to Blunt. Dorothy had read and transcribed much of the 'Secret Diaries', so she knew Lady Gregory's story, while Dorothy's ambiguous position in the Newbuildings household was widely recognised. It was one of those situations which enabled Lady Gregory to practise once more the charity she had learnt in 1882.

> What have I gained? a little charity?
> I never more may dare to fling a stone
> Or say of any weakness I may see
> That I more strength and wisdom would
>   have known.[47]

Augusta Gregory had written out this sonnet and the other eleven for Blunt in her own hand, though disguised. The last six lines of all (which, among others, he altered for the worse on publication) were too sad to be permanently true of such a positive woman.

> For me, the light is dimmed, the dream has past.
> I seek not gladness, yet may find content.
> Fulfilling each small duty reach at last
> Some port of peace before my youth is spent.
>   But come whatever may, come weal or woe
>   I love thee, bless thee, where soe'er thou go.[48]

Her friendship was nothing less than a blessing to Blunt. But her own splendid life was anything but a record of 'small' duties fulfilled, when at last she reached her 'port of peace'.

A WOMAN'S SONNETS

LADY GREGORY

with a commentary by
JAMES PETHICA

Although Lady Gregory's hand had already been suspected in 'A Woman's Sonnets', a sequence of twelve poems which appeared in the Kelmscott edition of Wilfrid Scawen Blunt's poetry in 1892, it was not until the recent release of Blunt's papers that her clandestine affair with him was confirmed, and a manuscript of the poems became available. Showing how extensively they had been altered by Blunt for publication under his own name, the manuscript preserves the sonnets in the form originally written by Lady Gregory in the summer of 1883 as the affair came to an end. Autobiographically rich, the poems belie the familiar image of Lady Gregory as indomitable, black-clad grande-dame of the Abbey Theatre, by revealing a passionate side to her personality that had gone almost unsuspected. During her years of literary notoriety Lady Gregory's often chilling reserve made for uneasiness amongst many of her contemporaries who sensed a deliberate distancing. Even Yeats, clearly writing with her uppermost in mind for the 24th phase in *A Vision*, specified masks of self-reliance and isolation. But an emotionally-guarded style was apparent even before Lady Gregory came to prominence as a writer. George Moore, who knew her in the late 1880s as a 'very earnest' young woman, considered her *noli me tangere* air to be characteristic:

I should like to fill in a page or two about Lady Gregory's married life, but though we know our neighbours very well in one direction, in another there is nothing that we know less than our neighbours, and Lady Gregory has never been for me a very real person. I imagine her without a mother, or father, or sisters, or brothers, *sans attaché*.[1]

'A Woman's Sonnets', in which she temporarily let slip the strong guard she kept on her personal life, allow a revealing glimpse of Lady Gregory's 'inmost heart' (sonnet xi, line 4).

Considering how secretly the affair was conducted, and a continuing, almost rigid discretion evident in their correspondence

of over forty years, it is surprising that Lady Gregory approved
publication of the sonnets, even under Blunt's name; for the poems,
as Blunt was to write, 'tell all our love's history that needs the
telling'.[2] It is also ironical that they should have passed as the
work of a man considered in his own time dangerously personal
and autobiographical in his lyrics, while his own involvement in
the affair inspired only a political poem, 'The Wind and the
Whirlwind'. Initially, Blunt had asked only for use of 'The Eviction'
in his Kelmscott volume, a poem Lady Gregory had sent him in
1888 after his period of imprisonment for anti-eviction
campaigning in Ireland.[3] Sending her proofs of part of the book
on 5 October 1891 he wrote:

You will find your 'Eviction' in this collection, & I have marked in the
margin 'from words by A.G.' If you wd sooner there was no such note,
I will leave it out.[4]

Her response two days later was enthusiastic, and unhesitant even
that a clue to her authorship of the poem might be given:

I am quite vain of having a share in even one of the poems & don't think
my initials will be recognised by the world at large.[5]

It was perhaps this reply which encouraged Blunt to ask for use of
the sonnets as well. His admiration for them had been reflected
years before when inscribing a copy of his *Love Sonnets* to
'Augusta Gregory, from a fellow poet'.[6] But the sequence, an
outpouring and memory of her love, was clearly more sensitive to
Lady Gregory, and the flat tone of her response suggests an
unwillingness to speak of that emotion again:

I shall be very glad if I can be of use to you in correcting [proofs]. I see
no reason why those twelve sonnets should not be published if you think
them worth it—merely calling them 'Sonnets written by a Woman'.[7]

Receiving this permission, Blunt was swift to modify the poems,
noting in his diary on 20 October:

I have remodelled Lady Gregory's twelve sonnets, which I heard from her
a day or two ago she would like to see printed in the new book, though
of course without her name. They are really most touching, and required
little beyond strengthening here and there a phrase and altering a few
recurrent rhymes. As they stand, they are certain to be recognised at their
worth. I tried their effect last night on Berthe [Wagram] giving her a
fabulous account of their origin, and they made her cry.[8]

Yet Blunt's account of his revision of the sonnets is misleading. Besides suggesting a greater enthusiasm for publication on Lady Gregory's part than is apparent in her letter, his diary entry gives no suggestion of the substantial changes in meaning which collation of the poems shows his 'strengthening' effected. The sonnets in their original form are printed here for the first time, with Blunt's revised versions alongside.

A WOMAN'S SONNETS

LADY GREGORY

I

If the past year were offered me again,
And choice of good and ill before me set
Would I accept the pleasure with the pain
Or dare to wish that we had never met?
Ah! could I bear those happy hours to miss
When love began, unthought of and unspoke—
That summer day when by a sudden kiss
We knew each other's secret and awoke?
Ah no! not even to escape the pain,
Debate and anguish that I underwent
Flying from thee and my own self in vain
With trouble wasted, till my strength all spent
        I knew at last that thou or love or fate
        Had conquered and repentance was too late.

II

Ah, my own dear one do not leave me yet!
Let me a little longer hold thy hand.
It is too soon to ask me to forget
Too soon I should from happiness be banned.
The future holds no hope of good for me,
The past I only wish to shut away
But while thou'rt with me and thy face I see
The sun shines on me, it is always day.
And time and fate bring near our parting hour
Which well I know thy love will not outlast—
But then perchance I may have gained more power
More strength and will to bury my dead past
        Ah! try to love me still a moment's space
        'Tis all I ask thee dear, this little grace.

I

If the past year were offered me again,
With choice of good and ill before me set,
Should I be wiser for the bliss and pain
And dare to choose that we had never met?
Could I find heart those happy hours to miss,
When love began unthought of and unspoke
That first strange day when by a sudden kiss
We knew each other's secret and awoke?
Ah, no! not even to escape the smart
Of that fell agony I underwent,
Flying from thee and my own traitor heart,
Till doubts and dreads and battlings overspent,
    I knew at last that thou or love or fate
    Had conquered and repentance was too late.

II

Nay, dear one, ask me not to leave thee yet.
Let me a little longer hold thy hand.
Too soon it is to bid me to forget
The joys I was so late to understand.
The future holds but a blank face for me,
The past is all confused with tears and grey,
But the sweet present, while thy smiles I see,
Is perfect sunlight, an unclouded day.
Speak not of parting, not at least this hour,
Though well I know Love cannot Time outlast.
Let me grow wiser first and gain more power,
More strength of will to deal with my dead past.
    Love me in silence still, one short hour's space:
    'Tis all I ask of thee, this little grace.

III

Where is the pride for which I once was blamed?
The pride which made me hold my head so high?
Who would believe it, seeing me so tamed
As at thy feet I subject, pleading lie—
Pleading for love which now is all my life—
Begging a word that memory may keep,
Asking a sign to still my inward strife,
Petitioning a touch to smooth my sleep—
Bowing my head to kiss the very ground
On which the feet of him I love have trod,
Controlled and guided by that voice whose sound
Is dearer to me than the voice of God.
    And knowing all the time that some dark day
    Indifferent and cold thou'lt turn away

IV

Should e'er that drear day come in which the world
Shall know the secret which so close I hold,
Should taunts and jeers at my bowed head be hurled,
And all my love and all my shame be told,
I could not, as some women use to do
Fling jests and gold and live the scandal down—
I could not, knowing all the story true
Hold up my head and brave the talk of town—
I have no courage for such tricks and ways,
No wish to flaunt a once dishonoured name—
Have still such memory of early days
And such great dread of that deserved shame
    That when it comes, with one all hopeless cry,
    For pardon from my wronged ones, I must die.

III

Where is the pride for which I once was blamed,
My vanity which held its head so high?
Who would believe them, seeing me thus tamed,
Thus subject, here as at thy feet I lie,
Pleading for love which now is all my life,
Craving a word for memory's rage to keep,
Asking a sign to still my inward strife,
Petitioning a touch to soothe my sleep?
Who would now guess them, as I kiss the ground
On which the feet of him I love have trod,
And bow before his voice whose least sweet sound
Speaks louder to me than the voice of God;
    And knowing all the time that one dark day,
    Spite of my worship, thou wilt turn away?

IV

Should ever the day come when this drear world
Shall read the secret which so close I hold,
Should taunts and jeers at my bowed head be hurled,
And all my love and all my shame be told,
I could not, as some doughtier women do,
Fling jests and gold and live the scandal down,
Nor, knowing all fame's bruitings to be true,
Keep a proud face and brave the talk of town.
I have no courage for such tricks and ways,
No wish to flaunt a once well-honoured name.
I have too dear a thought of earlier days,
Too deep a dread of my deserved shame.
    So, when it comes, with one last suppliant cry
    For pardon from my wronged ones, I must die.

V

Whate'er the cost may be I say farewell
I will not see thee, speak to thee again.
If some on earth must know the pangs of Hell
Mine be the torture, mine be all the pain.
What if my life grow blank and void and dead,
If my last hope of love be dashed away—
Better than risk dishonour on the head
Of her in whose arms as a babe I lay.
I have no right to bring such grief as this
Into the lives that linked are with mine,
No right to vex the dead in new found bliss,
With knowledge of my sin and great decline.
    Their peace I seek, and though my soul be rent
    With the hard conflict, I will not relent.

VI

What have I lost? The faith I had that right
Must surely prove itself than ill more strong.
For all my prayers and efforts had no might
To save me, when the trial came, from wrong.
And lost the days when with untroubled eyes
Scorning deceit, I could hold up my head.
I lead a double life—myself despise
And fear each day to have my secret read.
No longer will the loved and lost I mourn
Come in my sleep to breathe a blessed word.
Tossing I lie, and restless and forlorn,
And their dear memory pierces like a sword.
    In thy dear presence only have I rest.
    To thee alone naught needs to be confessed.

V

Whate'er the cost to me, with this farewell,
I shall not see thee, speak to thee again.
If some on Earth must feel the pangs of Hell,
Mine only be it who have earned my pain.
No matter if my life be blank and dead,
Bankrupt of pleasure: it is better so
Than risk dishonour on a once loved head,
Than link all loved ones with my own sole woe.
I have no claim to bring grief's shade on these,
To mix their pure life's waters with my wine,
To vex the dead, dear dead, in their new peace
With knowledge of my sin and great decline.
     For these I leave thee, and, though life be rent
     With the rude fight, think not I shall relent.

VI

What have I lost? The faith I had that Right
Must surely prove itself than Ill more strong.
For see how little my poor prayers had might
To save me, at the trial's pinch, from wrong.
What have I lost? The truth of my proud eyes
Scorning deceit. Behold me here to-day
Leading a double life, at shifts with lies,
And trembling lest each shadow should betray.
No longer with my lost ones may I mourn,
Who came to me in sleep and breathed soft words.
Sleepless I lie and fearful and forlorn,
With their love's edge still wounding like a sword's.
     In thy dear presence only I find rest.
     To thee alone naught needs to be confessed.

VII

What have I gained? A little charity?
I never more may dare to fling a stone
Or say of any weakness I may see
That I more strength and wisdom would have shown—
And I have learned in love lore to be wise:
And knowledge of the evil and the good
Have had one moment's glimpse of Paradise
And know the flavour of forbidden food.
But this, if it be gold has much alloy,
And I would gladly all the past undo
Were it not for the thought that brings me joy
That I once made some happiness for you—
    That sometimes in a dark and troubled hour
    I had, like Jesse's son, a soothing power.

VIII

Thou needst not on me any pityance lay
If I have sinned the judgement has begun.
The joy I knew lasted but one short day,
The clouds descended with the setting sun.
Thou wert my all dear, and too soon I knew
How small a part I could be in thy life—
That all a woman may endure or do
Counts little to her hero in the strife.
Ah dearest, thou wert not at all to blame
Thou hast so many worlds within thy ken.
I staked my all upon a losing game
Knowing thy nature and the ways of men.
    Knowing that one chill day I must repent
    With open eyes to love and death I went.

VII

What have I gained? A little charity?
I never more may dare to fling a stone
At any weakness, nor make boast that I
A better fence or fortitude had shown;
Some learning? I in love's lore have grown wise,
Plucked apples of the evil and the good,
Made one short trespass into Paradise
And known the full taste of forbidden food.
But love, if it be gold, has much alloy,
And I would gladly buy back ignorance,
But for the thought which still is my heart's joy
That once your life grew happier in my hands,
    That in your darkest and most troubled hour
    I had, like Jesse's son, a soothing power.

VIII

I sue thee not for pity on my case.
If I have sinned, the judgement has begun.
My joy was but one day of all the days,
And clouds have blotted it and hid the sun.
Thou wert so much to me! But soon I knew
How small a part could mine be in thy life,
That all a woman may endure or do
Counts little to her hero in the strife.
I do not blame thee who deserved no blame;
Thou hast so many worlds within thy ken.
I staked my all upon a losing game,
Knowing the nature and the needs of men,
    And knowing too how quickly pride is spent.
    With open eyes to Love and Death I went.

IX

I think the day draws near when I could stay
Within thy presence with no thought of ill—
And having put all earthliness away
Could listen to thy accents and be still,
And feel no sudden throbbing of the heart
No foolish rising of unbidden tears
Seeing thee come and go — and meet or part
Without this waste of gladness and of fears.
Only have patience for a little space.
I am not yet so wise to see unmoved
Another woman put into my place
Or loved as I was for a moment loved
    Be not so cruel as to let me see
    The love-light in thine eyes if not for me!

X

Love, e'er I go, forgive me any wrong
I may to thee unwittingly have wrought.
Although my heart, my life to thee belong
I may have vexed thee by some random thought:
One sin against thee I would fain atone
The crime of having loved thee yet unwooed,
The blame, the guiltiness are mine alone—
The woman tempted thee from right and good.
Forgive me also, e'er thy pity cease
That I denied thee, vexed thee with delay,
Sought my own soul to save, sought my own peace,
And having gained thy love yet said thee nay.
    But now for pardon now for grace I plead,
    Forgive me dearest! I thy pity need—

IX

The day draws nigh, methinks, when I could stay
Calm in thy presence with no dream of ill,
When, having put all earthliness away,
I could be near thee, touching thee, and still
Feel no mad throbbing at my foolish heart,
No sudden rising of unbidden tears,
Could mark thee come and go, to meet or part,
Without the gladness and without the fears.
Have patience with me then for this short space.
I shall be wise, but may not yet unmoved
See a strange woman put into my place
And happy in thy love, as I was loved:
    This were too much. Ah, let me not yet see
    The love-light in thine eyes, and not for me.

X

Love, ere I go, forgive me each least wrong,
Each trouble I unwittingly have wrought.
My heart, my life, my tears to thee belong;
Yet have I erred, maybe, through too fond thought;
One sin, most certainly, I need to atone:
The sin of loving thee while yet unwooed.
Mine only was this wrong, this guilt alone.
The woman tempted thee from ways of good.
Forgive me too, ere thy dear pity cease,
That I denied thee, vexed thee with delay,
Sought my soul's coward shelter, not thy peace,
And having won thee still awhile said nay.
    Forgive me this, that I too soon, too late,
    Too wholly gave a love disconsolate.

XI

Wild words I write, wild words of love and pain
To lay within thy hand before we part,
For now that we may never meet again
I would make bare to thee my inmost heart.
For when I speak you answer with a jest
Or laugh and break the sentence with a kiss
And so my love is never half confessed
Nor have I told thee what has been my bliss.
And when the darkness and the clouds prevail
And I begin to know what I have lost
I would not vex thee with so sad a tale
Or tell how all too dear my love has cost.
    But now the time has come when I must go
    The tumults and the joy I fain would show.

XII

The hour has come to part! and it is best
The severing stroke should fall in one short day
Rather than fitful fever spoil my rest,
Watching each gradual sign of love's decay.
Go forth dear! thou hast much to do on earth;
In life's campaign there waits thee a great part—
Much to be won and conquered of more worth
Than this poor victory of a woman's heart—
For me, the light is dimmed, the dream has past—
I seek not gladness, yet may find content
Fulfilling each small duty, reach at last
Some goal of peace before my youth is spent.
    But come whatever may, come weal or woe
    I love thee, bless thee where so e'er thou go!

XI

Wild words I write, and lettered in deep pain,
To lay in your loved hand as love's farewell.
It is the thought we shall not meet again
Nerves me to write and my whole secret tell.
For when I speak to you, you only jest,
And laughing break the sentence with a kiss,
Till my poor love is never quite confessed,
Nor know you half its tears and tenderness.
When the first darkness and the clouds began
I hid it from you fearing your reproof;
I would not vex your life's high aim and plan
With my poor woman's woe, and held aloof.
    But now that all is ended, pride and shame,
    My tumults and my joys I may proclaim.

XII

'Tis ended truly, truly as was best.
Love is a little thing, for one short day;
You could not make it your life's only quest,
Nor watch the poor corpse long in its decay.
Go forth, dear, thou hast much to do on earth;
In life's campaign there waits thee a great part,
Much to be won and conquered of more worth
Than this poor victory of a woman's heart.
For me the daylight of my years is dim.
I seek not gladness, yet shall find content
In such small duties as are learned of Him
Who bore all sorrows, till my youth is spent.
    Yet come what may to me of weal or woe,
    I love thee, bless thee, dear, where'er thou go.

As her first sustained attempt at poetic self-expression[9]—with according directness and originality as well as the flaws of inexperience—the sonnets are of most importance as a record of Lady Gregory's apprenticeship in love; for as Blunt would write thirty years after the affair, 'her connection with me was her first emancipation'.[10] Discussion of his revisions is hence inevitably concerned with the manner in which they alter the autobiographical content of the sonnets. (It is unlikely Lady Gregory herself recognised the extent of the revisions, having almost certainly kept no copy of her dangerously confessional work).[11]

Written in the knowledge of the affair's imminent end through a 'mutual pact' between the lovers, the poems formed part of the drama of their separation. As Blunt later recalled:

She wrote them as a farewell to our passion and put them in my hand the morning that we parted after a last night spent together . . .[12]

Notorious as an amorist, Blunt was more practised than Lady Gregory in the saying of farewells. His revisions consequently tend to emphasize love as 'Passion' rather than as the intensely personal emotion of the poems in original form. Whereas Lady Gregory's second sonnet pointedly laments the impermanence of a particular man's love—

> ◦ time and fate bring near our parting hour
> Which well I know thy love will not outlast— (ii, 9–10)

—in Blunt's revision this recognition has been replaced by a more experienced voice, detached from emotional turmoil:

> speak not of parting, not at least this hour,
> Though well I know Love cannot Time outlast.

This abstracted 'Love' and 'Time' are theoretical in tone, turning the situation from particular to generic. Other changes similarly diminish the sense of Blunt's involvement and responsibility in the affair. In the eighth sonnet, for instance, Lady Gregory's pointed recognition of the dangers particular to Blunt's character is quietly but significantly deleted;

I staked my all upon a losing game[13]
Knowing thy nature and the ways of men.
    Knowing that one chill day I must repent . . . (viii, 11–13)

becomes in Blunt's version:

I staked my all upon a losing game
Knowing the nature and the needs of men
    And knowing too how quickly pride is spent . . .

Her sacrificial love and acknowledgement of impending penance are reduced to a world-weary submission and jaded acceptance of the 'needs' of men in general.

This movement towards a generic and almost abstract tone reflects Blunt's 'philosophy' of love at the time of retouching the sonnets—that particular love is transient and should be enjoyed merely as a facet of a grander 'Passion'. About this time he would write, 'duty is pleasure, pleasure duty, that is all we know on earth and all we need to know.'[14] Such hedonism leaves its mark on the alterations, with their increased emphasis on sensuality. Whereas the end of the affair signals an emotional loss for Lady Gregory:

What if my life grow blank and void and dead,
If my last hope of love be dashed away—
Better than risk dishonour . . . (v, 5–7)

Blunt by contrast contemplates a loss of enjoyment:

No matter if my life be blank and dead,
Bankrupt of pleasure: it is better so . . .

In the ninth sonnet Lady Gregory is seen steeling herself to resist the power of physical love:

I think the day draws near when . . .
. . . having put all earthliness away [I]
Could listen to thy accents and be still.
And feel no sudden throbbing of the heart . . . (ix, 1, 3–5)

In Blunt's version, by contrast, the sensual element is incongruously intensified:

. . . having put all earthliness away,
I could be near thee, touching thee, and still
Feel no mad throbbing at my foolish heart . . .

Most significantly, perhaps, Blunt's revisions remove the ambivalence of Lady Gregory's tenth sonnet, which asks forgiveness not only for 'delay', but also for a presumably physical denial which continued even after Blunt's heart had been won:

> . . . I denied thee, vexed thee with delay. . .
> And having gained thy love yet said thee nay. (x, 10/12)

In deleting this ambivalent 'yet,' Blunt leaves no doubt that consummation took place in the end:

> . . . I denied thee, vexed thee with delay. . .
> And having won thee still awhile said nay.

Similarly, while the affair is for Lady Gregory a 'moment's glimpse of paradise' which gives merely 'the flavour of forbidden food' (vii, 7–8), Blunt achieves a 'short trespass' *into* Love's Eden which allows a more gratifying 'full taste of forbidden food'.[15]

Lady Gregory's parting sonnet is bitter in its recognition of the differing emotional values of herself and Blunt. While accepting that their love must end, she sees that this is primarily because love is, for him, of secondary importance.

> In life's campaign there waits thee a great part —
> Much to be won and conquered of more worth
> Than this poor victory of a woman's heart — (xii, 6–8)

With parting inevitable, her resentment is suppressed, in recognition that a swift separation will, at least, minimise the shock:

> The hour has come to part! and it is best
> The severing stroke should fall in one short day
> Rather than fitful fever spoil my rest,
> Watching each gradual sign of love's decay. (xii, 1–4)

By contrast, in Blunt's version it is Love that has ended, and not just the affair:

> Tis ended truly, truly as was best.
> Love is a little thing, for one short day;

> You could not make it your life's only quest,
> Nor watch the poor corpse long in its decay.

This diminished love, its Passion waned, is disturbingly externalised in the revision, becoming a 'corpse' which is turned from more in distaste than in sorrow. Lady Gregory's pain of separation and wish to avoid seeing a slow falling-off in the love which has cost her so much, are gone, and in Blunt's hands the focus has been suggestively slanted towards the prospect of a next 'quest'.

The personal intensity which the revisions dilute is a primary strength of the poems, for their 'love's history' is, on Lady Gregory's part, one of self-examination, in which guilt is balanced against the joy of love. Her love, because illicit, has a dual nature embracing 'love and death' (viii, 14) together. The poems articulate both an emotional struggle against involvement with a dangerous lover, and a struggle of conscience against the guilt which unfaithfulness induces. Their occasional bitterness shows they were no formal love-offering; it is pain and veiled resentment which gives them their force.

> Wild words I write, wild words of love and pain
> To lay within thy hand before we part . . . (xi, 1–2)

Losing much of this personal intensity, the poems become in Blunt's hands more of a gesture, an exercise in empty courtliness:

> Wild words I write, and lettered in deep pain,
> To lay in your loved hand as love's farewell . . .

Here, as with many of the revisions, the formality of Blunt's language is uncomfortably at odds with the impulsive action described. For though the poems in original form are occasionally sentimental, their simple language is generally effective in expressing pain and troubled conscience. The revisions tend towards a self-consciously 'poetic' language which is sterile in comparison, and often too deliberately literary in the worst Victorian manner ('lettered in deep pain') to be equal to the emotional drama involved. Lady Gregory's 'pain,/ Debate and anguish' (i, 9–10) becomes a lifeless 'smart/ Of that fell agony', her 'trial' (vi, 4) becomes a 'trial's pinch'. Such revisions are too far removed from the mood of the original poems to seem other than heavy-handed. Other changes consistently tone down the harshness of guilt, shame and resentment evident in the original sonnets, with the most emotive of Lady Gregory's phrases being deleted:

> Indifferent and cold thoul't turn away (iii, 14)
> Mine be the torture, mine be all the pain. (v, 4)
> I lead a double life — myself despise (vi, 7)
> Knowing that one chill day I must repent (viii, 3)
> Be not so cruel . . . (ix, 13)

Muted too is the sense of spiritual struggle which the embracing of illicit love involves. For Lady Gregory the pain of separation will be followed by a vain search for peace, and an abiding sense of dishonour. These she recognises as and accepts as penance:

> and though my soul be rent
> With the hard conflict, I will not relent. (v, 13–14)

In Blunt's revision, by contrast, the impact of inner conflict on 'life', the temporal prospect, is clearly more feared than its effect on the 'soul'.

> and though life be rent
> With the rude fight, think not I shall relent.

Throughout, the whole-hearted emotion of the poems in original form is qualified, ironically confirming their recognition of the lovers' differing emotional values. Lady Gregory's 'thou wert my all dear' (viii, 5) becomes 'Thou wert so much to me!', and where she would expose her 'inmost heart' (xi, 4), Blunt offers to reveal a 'whole secret' — a phrase devoid of all suggestion of confession and exposition. The intensity of guilt and shame in the original poems shows how important the affair was for Lady Gregory, while Blunt's versions suggest a relatively 'manageable' experience. She wishes to 'shut away' or 'bury' her 'dead' (ii, 6/12) past, whereas this past is something the worldly-wise Blunt can 'deal with'.

The atmosphere of Lady Gregory's sonnets is predominantly one of guilt. Aware that 'the judgement has begun' (viii, 2), she accepts that this judgement will continue even after the affair ends, penance being a continuation of guilt, fear of discovery of her 'secret' shame (iv/vi), and a consciousness of separation, by dishonour, from friendship with the untroubled souls of the dead. Her loss of 'a blessed word' (vi, 10) from the dead because of her sin is a primary regret, since it is 'their peace' she seeks. Here, perhaps, is the lasting interest of the sonnets in their original form; their exposition of that self-examining moral sense which Yeats saw as a dominant feature of Lady Gregory's character. Assigning her to the 24th Phase in *A Vision*, he wrote that those in the phase

submit all their actions to the most unflinching examination . . . for they but ask without ceasing, 'Have I done my duty as well as So-and-So?' 'Am I as unflinching as my fathers before me?' and though they can stand utterly alone, indifferent though all the world condemn, it is not that they have found themselves, but that they have been found faithful.[16]

The sonnets tempt speculation as to how specifically Lady Gregory's affair with Wilfrid Blunt fed her tendency to self-examination — certainly her wearing of mourning clothes for forty years of widowhood, and repeated calling of attention to that widowhood, suggest a wish both to atone for and disguise her infidelity.[17] 'Dies Irae', a short story she wrote in 1894, eleven years after the affair ended, is highly suggestive of lingering guilt, since it depicts the expulsion of a woman from her home ten years after an adulterous liaison. For this woman too, guilt has been the main penance for illicit love:

Do you know what the terrible loneliness of these years has been? Cut quite away by the consciousness of my sin from fellowship with all good men, and not only from them, but from all the dead I have lost. Their eyes look at me as I lie awake at night, and reproach me with my guilt. There will be no rest in the grave for me; they will be there.[18]

This sense of lost fellowship with the souls of the dead corresponds strikingly to that of the sixth sonnet:

> No longer will the loved and lost I mourn
> Come in my sleep to breathe a blessed word.
> Tossing I lie, and restless and forlorn . . . (vi, 9–11)

Notably, however, the climax of 'Dies Irae' is not in the wife's expulsion from her home, but in its portrayal of her separation from her son. While her husband and daughter judge her unwaveringly, the son attempts to go with her as she leaves:

as she tried to unfasten the door, her son flung his arms round her, sobbing. 'Mother', he said, 'I will go with you. I cannot give you up; I will never leave you.' She unfolded his arms, and kissed him again and again, but then pushed him gently from her, and in a moment had gone out, alone and silently, into the darkness.[19]

This sudden shift of focus at the end of the story is particularly suggestive, for Lady Gregory's diary at the time of writing 'Dies Irae' repeatedly shows a fear of losing the boyish affection of her son Robert.[20] It seems likely that her guilt and fear of discovery, suppressed since the time of the affair, were being refocused as widowhood made his love all the more precious; certainly her love for Robert was the only passionate emotion Lady Gregory allowed herself to display openly in later life. One loose sheet amongst the disordered drafts of her memoirs has an entry written shortly after his death in 1918 showing that intense love explicitly linked to a fear of rejection:

with all the anguish of Robert's death I have lost my one great fear, of losing his affection — Now there is nothing that could hurt me so much to dread.[21]

An underlying sense of unworthiness seems to have accompanied her love for Robert, giving it all the passion of an emotion which might be denied. Having deliberately ended her affair with Blunt, Lady Gregory perhaps committed herself to a life in which the free flow of emotions would ever after be difficult.

> I lead a double life — myself despise
> And fear each day to have my secret read. (vi, 7–8)

More evidence of lingering guilt is suggested in the folk-history play *Grania*, commenced in 1908. Long recognised as the most autobiographically significant of Lady Gregory's plays, its marriage of young princess to old king parallels the disparity of age in her own to Sir William Gregory. Yet no link has been remarked upon between the elopement of Diarmuid and Grania in the play and Lady Gregory's affair with Blunt, though parallels are clear. In both sonnets and play, the woman regards herself as wooer:

> One sin against thee I would fain atone
> The crime of having loved thee yet unwooed,
> The blame, the guiltiness are mine alone —
> The woman tempted thee from right and good. (x, 5–8)

Grania's acceptance of responsibility is equally pointed:

It is not his fault! It is mine! It is on me the blame is entirely. It is best for me to go out a shamed woman.[22]

Grania's wooing of Diarmuid is more emphatic in early holographs of the play than in the published version, and in one discarded scenario she gives him a chain and 'tries to encourage him'.[23] Diarmuid's physical beauty is repeatedly emphasised in these drafts in a manner reminiscent of Lady Gregory's admiration of Blunt's physical charisma.[24] And most importantly, Grania's guilt, like that of the sonnets, primarily comes from having broken a code of loyalty.

It would be a terrible thing a wedded woman not to be loyal — to call out another man's name in her sleep.[25]

'A Woman's Sonnets' identify the autobiographical element intuited, even before the Blunt manuscripts were available, as the likely cause of Lady Gregory's reluctance to produce *Grania*. Noting her apparent unease regarding the play, Elizabeth Coxhead had speculated:

Did she doubt whether, after all, she could hold an audience's attention through three acts with only three persons . . . Or is it, perhaps, that the play tells one truth too many, and that when she came to think it over, she was disquieted by what she had done?[26]

Her affair with Blunt was Lady Gregory's best-kept secret, and necessarily so, for in Catholic Ireland the slightest hint of this buried past would have severely damaged her reputation. Yet if there is little evidence of the affair in her journals and diaries, a percolation of guilts and fears is often apparent in her plays — directly, as in *Grania*, but also in the frequent motif of choosing between an old and young lover, revulsion from the fallen woman, or Lady Gregory's recurrent focus on reputation. Even the light-hearted *Spreading the News* may have originated from some undercurrent of personal fear:

I kept seeing as in a picture people sitting by the roadside, and a girl passing to the market, gay and fearless. And then I saw her passing by the same place at evening, her head hanging, the heads of others turned from her, because of some sudden story that had risen out of a chance word, and had snatched away her good name.[27]

The guilt and self-examination of the sonnets deepen our under-standing of the fear of or fascination with disloyalty that features in many of Lady Gregory's plays, of their frequent focus on the hidden 'heart-secret', and of that sense of lost fulfilment ('my last hope of love' v, 6) which is a recurrent theme in her comedies and tragedies alike.

Her affair with Blunt invites a reassessment of the apparent artlessness which has been taken as characteristic of Lady Gregory's life and writings. The sonnets alone, though seeming to confirm the Yeatsian view of her as a rigid upholder of codes[28], also suggest an emotional spontaneity rebellious against a morality which denied passion. They show Lady Gregory's acceptance of guilt and consciousness of sin, but also her refusal to regret having loved.

> But come what may, come weal or woe
> I love thee . . . (xii, 13–14)

This rebellious desire for passion and self-fulfilment would re-emerge in the assertiveness of the heroines of her later folk-tragedies, and most directly in the passionate complaint of Grania against moral restraint:

What are any words at all put against the love of a young woman and a young man?[29]

'DEAR JOHN QUINN'

DANIEL J. MURPHY

John Quinn, when Lady Gregory first met him in 1902, was a bright young lawyer employed by a prominent New York firm; he was taking his first trip abroad. Born thirty-two years earlier (24 April 1870) to Irish Catholic parents in Tiffin, Ohio, Quinn was an extremely bright child. Precocious for his early years, he was ready for college by the time he was sixteen.

His father at first wanted John to attend West Point, but as John showed no interest in the Military Academy, he enrolled in Michigan University after his graduation from high school. He stayed at Michigan only one year for, through a family connection, he was brought to the attention of Charles Foster, a former Governor of Ohio, who was then leaving for Washington as Secretary of the Treasury in the Harrison cabinet. Foster took Quinn to Washington with him as his assistant. In Washington, Quinn continued his undergraduate studies at Georgetown University, where he majored in law. The years Quinn spent in Washington were immensely important for him; as an assistant to the Secretary of the Treasury, he met many important political figures in the Capital, and he became interested in finance and law; moreover, the cosmopolitanism of Washington replaced the provincialism of Tiffin, Ohio, and made Quinn a confirmed internationalist.

In 1893, he left Washington to attend Harvard, where he majored in international law. After his graduation from Harvard, in 1895, he came to New York as a special assistant to General B. F. Tracy, who had been Secretary of the Navy in Harrison's Cabinet. As a lawyer Quinn was a perfectionist; he prepared each case with assiduous care and researched the smallest detail bearing on every point. Owing both to his legal ability and his pleasant personality, he advanced rapidly. In 1900 he became a junior partner in the firm of Alexander and Colby, but in 1906 their acceptance of an insurance case, against Quinn's advice, prompted him to leave and found his own law firm. As an independent lawyer he subsequently became counsel to several banking institutions, including the Equitable Trust Company and the National Bank of Commerce, a bank that Quinn served for the rest of his life.

For Quinn, law was an occupation, not a way of life. As J. B. Yeats said of him, he was a lawyer only when working at law, 'for which I give God Almighty my personal thanks.'[1] Quinn was also an omnivorous reader, with an enormous appetite for a wide variety of subjects—he read William James, whose pragmatism was a lasting influence in his life; he read Greek and Latin classics, particularly Plato, Horace, and Catullus; read and re-read Meredith, one of his favourite authors; he was familiar with almost all the major Irish and English authors, particularly those of the Victorian and modern periods. In addition, he read a substantial number of historical and political works, and his letters are peppered with references to them. Everything he read he annotated, writing voluminous notes in the margins of his books. But Quinn not only read books, he also collected first editions, a habit acquired early; while a freshman at Michigan he purchased first editions of Wilde, Pater, Hardy, Meredith, and Swinburne. When he went to Washington as an assistant to the Secretary of the Treasury, he continued his book purchasing. Later, when he began his legal career in New York, he continued collecting the same authors, but he now began purchasing some of their manuscripts.

In New York Quinn met many of the prominent Irish-Americans then in politics, and both his Irish heritage and their friendship stimulated his interest in Ireland and its culture; his interest in Irish literature was intensified during his first trip abroad in 1902.

He travelled to Ireland primarily to meet W. B. Yeats and to help, if he could, the Gaelic language movement. When Quinn reached Ireland, both Yeats and Douglas Hyde were attending a festival in the West, organized by Lady Gregory in honour of the poet Raftery. Jack Yeats, the poet's brother, offered to accompany Quinn there, and they travelled from Dublin west to Athenry, and from there followed the crowd going to attend the Raftery festival in Kileeneen. Quinn was fascinated with the unending stone fences along the winding dirt roads, with the newly thatched white cottages, with the steady stream of donkey carts and bicycles from which people called their cheery 'fine day, fine day,' or called out to the American 'a pleasant journey to you'. Jack Yeats introduced Quinn to his brother, who was standing among the four or five hundred present, and he and Yeats waited for Lady Gregory and Douglas Hyde, who were on the platform judging the traditional singing, the recitation of Irish poems and stories, and the folk dancing.

The *Feis* lasted until after nightfall, and when it had concluded, Lady Gregory invited Quinn, W. B. Yeats, Jack Yeats, Douglas Hyde and his wife to stay at Coole for a few days. 'It was black night when the lights of Coole welcomed us,' Quinn writes, 'Lady Gregory got down from the car first, and, turning to me and extending her hand, said with a pleasant smile, "Welcome to Coole". '[2]

Coole astounded Quinn; it was an aspect of Irish life of which he had never dreamed: an intensely cultivated house filled with the history of its owners; its great library, containing rows of leather-bound books; its sweeping woods; the stately gardens; the stables; all were new and exciting to him. But it was not the physical surroundings that enthralled Quinn, much as he delighted in the library and the beautiful old gardens. It was the intellectual intensity of owner and guests, the creativity of everyone that amazed him.

Douglas Hyde wrote a Gaelic play in one day while Quinn was at Coole: 'When we returned in the evening, Dr. Hyde had finished the play and was out shooting wild duck'.[3] The play was Hyde's *The Lost Saint*, and only a hymn remained to complete it. Hyde wrote the hymn the next day while he was looking for wild duck beside Inchy marsh, and he read the play aloud to Lady Gregory, Yeats, and Quinn that evening, 'translating it back into English as he went along'. Lady Gregory wrote that all present felt 'as if some beautiful white blossom had suddenly fallen at our feet.'[4]

Another morning Quinn, Hyde, and Lady Gregory wandered through one of the beautiful old gardens. Lady Gregory 'named over the names of this, that, and the other flower until Hyde said that if she just wrote down the names there was matter for a sonnet ready for Yeats.' But Yeats needed no help from anyone; he had just completed 'The Seven Woods of Coole', of which he was so pleased, Quinn writes, that he repeated it so often Quinn had most of it by heart.[5]

In the evening Quinn listened while Lady Gregory and Hyde read scenarios for plays, or while Lady Gregory read short plays in English and Hyde short ones in Irish. After Lady Gregory retired, Quinn, Yeats, and Hyde would sit up until one or two in the morning, talking about everything, 'but chiefly', Quinn writes, 'about the theatre of which Yeats's mind was full. These were wonderful nights, long nights filled with good talk, Yeats full of plans for the development of the theatre.'[6] Other evenings Hyde and Lady Gregory read their translations of Irish songs and ballads. One evening while Quinn sat and listened, Lady Gregory and Yeats composed a scenario for a play which Hyde spent three afternoons translating into Irish.

Quinn had the greatest admiration for Lady Gregory. He admired the 'stored up richness' of her mind and the amount of work she accomplished; when he came down to breakfast in the morning, he 'would be amazed to find that she had already done two hours of writing'. She had, however, 'the faculty of laying aside her work and making all her guests enjoy to the full the pleasant side of life and the delights of social intercourse. Her enthusiasm was infectious, and those who came into contact with her . . . became or were made her helpers and associates.'[7]

It was not, however, solely the intellectual life or the cultured surroundings at Coole that altered Quinn's attitude toward Ireland; it was also the life and activity he found in Dublin. There he met J. B. Yeats, the Irish painter and father of W. B. and Jack Yeats; at his home Quinn met John Synge, and through Synge, George Russell. While in Dublin Quinn bought ten paintings by Jack Yeats and commissioned J. B. Yeats to paint several pictures of notable Irish political and literary figures. J. B. Yeats called him 'the nearest approach to an angel in my experience'.[8]

Quinn returned to New York filled with enthusiasm for Ireland. In order to introduce the new creative work being done in Ireland to the United States, he organized the Irish Literary Society of New York 'For the promotion of the study of Irish Literature, the Irish language, Irish history, drama, music and art'.[9] He asked Yeats's permission for the Society to produce some of his plays, and Yeats replied that Quinn might try Cathleen ni Houlihan or Pot of Broth as both were in prose and therefore might be simpler for the actors to perform.[10]

Quinn returned to Ireland in 1903 and 1904, and in the meantime arranged for successful lectures in America by Yeats and Hyde. The lecture tour by Hyde in the fall of 1905 was arranged and orchestrated by Quinn, who worked three hours a day, seven days a week from May 1905 until he saw Hyde and his wife off on the White Star Celtic, on 15 June 1906. Although the Hyde tour was a financial success—Hyde realized $64,000—it disenchanted Quinn with the Gaelic societies in America. As he wrote to Lady Gregory: 'I came in for all sorts of criticism over the Hyde tour, and I haven't darkened the door of an Irish "society" since Hyde left the country.

The rankness of the abuse seems to be in proportion to the amount of time they have devoted to the study of Gaelic . . .'[11]

Two other factors influenced him to devote less time to Sinn Fein and other Irish American societies. The first event was the January 1907 battle over the Abbey production of Synge's *The Playboy of the Western World*. Quinn was infuriated by the wail of opposition which Irish-Americans, without ever having seen a production, exploded against Synge and his play. He wrote to Lady Gregory in dejection over the supremacy of 'prairie land and prairie values' in Ireland: 'In place of gentlemen and of the standards of truth and honor and moderation which they had, have come the priest and all the vile things that characterize Irish life—treachery, mendacity, abuse and lying, lying in the press and lying on the platform and lying in private. These are harsh things to say, but I fear they are the truth. I don't feel harshly toward any class of Irishman, but I feel dispirited and discouraged.'[12]

Significant as was Quinn's disenchantment over *The Playboy* riots, by far the most important factor influencing his future was his increasing involvement in American politics. In 1908, he was elected as one of New York's delegates to the Democratic national convention, where he worked to defeat William Jennings Bryan, whom Quinn called a champion of lost causes and an apostle of defeat. Quinn favoured a new man, such as Governor Johnson of Minnesota, who would present a new face for the Democrats. Bryan, however, was nominated and defeated by William Taft, as Quinn had predicted. He wrote to Lady Gregory of his involvement in politics, and she replied, 'It is strange that politics should have drawn you into their net. They are the most unsatisfactory of all human pursuits . . . and I have seen a good deal of them. . . . One loses independence in them, having to go with your party, and they leave so little mark at the end. . . . There are plenty of politicians and there is but one John Quinn, the sympathetic, large-hearted, intellectual and gracious helper and providence of some who are worth it. So come back here and get strong and well and put new life and courage into us.'[13]

Quinn was again a New York State delegate to the Democratic National Convention in Baltimore June 1912, where he again backed an underdog, Oscar Underwood. During the convention, a lot of ballots were traded, and Quinn was furious with Bryan's desertion to Wilson, which he described as 'the treachery that was paid for with the position of Secretary of State'. Describing politics as mere buying and selling, Quinn would have nothing to do with it after the election of 1912.[14]

Six months before his involvement with the Democratic convention, he became involved with the Abbey tour of America, September 1911–February 1912, primarily over the opposition of the American Irish to the production of Synge's *Playboy of the Western World*. There were protests over the production of *The Playboy* in Boston and in Providence, where two hundred customers and fifty police saw the play. In New Haven the Chief of Police submitted a list of cuts to be made before he would permit the play to be produced. Since he had witnessed a rehearsal of Shaw's *Blanco Posnet*, Lady Gregory gladly complied.[15]

When they arrived in New York, Quinn told Lady Gregory he was afraid of what might happen when the *Playboy* was presented. One of his friends had warned him: 'There is a party of rowdies coming to the theatre to-night to make their demonstration.' In a sense, Lady Gregory welcomed the opportunity to confront the demonstrators: 'it is better to let them show themselves. They have been threatening so long; we shall see who they are.'[16]

The New York engagement was a great financial success, in spite of the riots caused by the audience throwing eggs, potatoes, watches—everything not nailed down was thrown at the actors. Twenty-five people were ejected and two arrested for assault before the play could be heard by the audience.[17]

From New York, the company moved to Philadelphia, where they were told to withdraw *The Playboy* or risk arrest. John Quinn, who had come to Philadelphia to see the plays, accompanied Lady Gregory to the theatre, where they found the company under technical arrest. In the end, Quinn arranged to accept warrants for arrest, post bail bonds, and have the hearing put off. After some legal manoeuvering, and the dramatic re-arrival of Quinn during the questioning of a witness, the case was dismissed.[18]

The fight over the right of the Abbey Theatre to perform *The Playboy* had profound implications for the relationship between Lady Gregory and John Quinn. Ever since they had met in Ireland, they had maintained a steady correspondence, but this was the first time that she had met Quinn on his own ground. After the conclusion of the American tour, she stayed with him for about a week, and during that week friendship ripened into love. As the following letters indicate, the affair was not 'one of close and warm affection'.[19] Rather, it was a passionate affair during which Lady Gregory, for a few brief days, loved Quinn deeply.

[Postmarked March 16, 1912] ALS

My very dear John,[20]

I think you are never out of my mind—though sometimes all seems a dream, a wonderful dream. It seems so long for a letter to go or to come, I want to know how you are, what you are doing.

No more pains or aches I hope. How good you were to me! How happy I was with you. How much I love you!

A. G.

[Postmarked March 22, 1912] ALS

My John, my dear John, my own John, not other peoples John, I love you, I care for you, I know, I want you, I believe in you, I see you always. Everything I ever said to you I say over again. Dont think I am fretting, I am proud, I am glad, you are nearer to me than anything, everything else a little far off. Where is the use of writing? You know all this do you not?

A. G.

March 31 [1912] ALS

Dear John—We are still in March, the month I began under your roof! What a long month it always is; & always will be.

Tuesday 2 [April, 1912] ALS

Hadnt posted this—& yesterday your dear letter came! It made me sad & glad—it brought you so near to me, & made me know you are so far away! Oh my darling, am I now lonely after you? do I not awake looking for you—& long to be alone sometimes that I may think only of you. Why do I love you so much? It ought to be from all that piled up goodness of the years. Yet it is not that—it is some call that came in a moment—something impetuous & masterful about you that satisfies me—that gives me perfect rest. I think back to this day month—the Saturday, we did our shopping by telephone—you encompassed me with thought & care. . . . 'Wonderful' yes! quite as wonderful, more wonderful to me than to you. Your dear letter goes into the fire tonight. I must keep it till then. I think I love you better every day. Dear John, yours

A. G.

One month after this letter, Lady Gregory refers to the affair for the last time:

Coole Park
Gort, Co. Galway

Monday May 6 [1912]

Dear John,

Just two months today since I said good bye to America and you! Oh, I have worked so hard in that time yet I seem to have done very little. And these last days I have been going through what is unusual with me a fit of depression. I have felt more profound loneliness than I had felt for many a year. I know that is just paying for past happiness, that rapture of friendship that so possessed and satisfied me. Yet if I must pay the price I wont bemoan it.

Yours affectionately
Augusta Gregory

Although Lady Gregory stayed with Quinn during the Armory Show of February and March 1913 and presumably resumed their relationship, no direct evidence exists that they did so.[21] Indeed the longstanding relationship Quinn had with Dorothy Coates does not seem to have been disrupted by this interlude, although a few years later Miss Coates was replaced in Quinn's affections by Jeanne Robert Foster. What is certain, however, is that Lady Gregory and Quinn remained friends and frequent correspondents until Quinn's death in 1924. Of his death, Lady Gregory wrote:

30 July. A great blow yesterday. A cable from New York 'John Quinn died this morning. . . .' America will seem very distant now without that warm ready sympathy and interest. . . . So my day and night have been sad and I am heavy hearted.[22]

THE PATTERN OF THREE THREADS: THE HYDE–GREGORY FRIENDSHIP

GARETH W. DUNLEAVY

Douglas Hyde and Augusta Gregory—one dedicated to reviving the Irish language, the other to establishing an Irish theatre, both committed to recovering what remained of the Irish folk tradition—were remarkably similar in background and personality. Both were born into the Protestant religion and the Ascendancy class; on the Big House estates where they lived, each had been tutored in cabin culture; both became literary nationalists. Hyde's tutors, all from Frenchpark, Co. Roscommon, were Johnny Lavin, Seamus Hart, and Mrs Connolly; Lady Gregory's tutor at Roxborough, near Loughrea, Co. Galway, was Mary Sheridan. Before they met each had learned to cross and recross the line between Big House and cabin in the west of Ireland. Shortly after they were introduced, at Edward Martyn's Tillyra in 1897, they joined to press a search that each earlier had undertaken alone, for what could be told of the life and recalled of the poems of Blind Raftery. Both withstood abuse for being traitors to their class—the gentle, church-going Hyde once actually was accused of having stated publicly that he wished one day to 'wade through Protestant blood'; Augusta Gregory was charged on the one hand with disloyalty and a desire for popularity, and on the other she was dismissed as quite mad when she took up the study of Irish.[1]

But it was Hyde who had 'brought another enriching influence into my life', Lady Gregory wrote in her autobiography,[2] and his Gaelic League gave her, she said, a basis for focusing her own Irish interests at the gatehouse of Coole where, under her patronage, language classes were formed for the young men and women of Gort, and a branch of the League was organized. For their efforts on behalf of Irish culture, both received American recognition and financial support, through their mutual and intimate friend John Quinn. From his first visit to Ireland in 1902 to his death in 1924, Quinn was unfailing in his vigorous support of that circle of literary nationalists that included Hyde, Lady Gregory, and W. B. Yeats. His organization of Hyde's 1905–1906 fundraising tour of

131

the United States and the 1911 American visit of Lady Gregory's Abbey Theatre produced the financial support both critically needed and conferred the additional prestige on the League and the Abbey that was essential to their survival in Ireland.

Finally, the efforts of both were eclipsed by history, as Ireland moved towards the Easter Rebellion: Hyde was forced to resign from the presidency of the Gaelic League in 1915; Lady Gregory gradually altered her role in the Abbey by the end of the company's third American tour in 1914, choosing a less influential position. Both shared the same view of what was realistic and possible in Irish politics in the post-1916 period. Both experienced the tragic loss of a child: Hyde's daughter Nuala succumbed to tuberculosis in 1916; Augusta Gregory's son, Robert, died in action over the Italian front in 1918. Both mourned together their loss, in 1924, of their friend John Quinn. And after they died, both were erased from Ireland's visual memory, for the houses that had nurtured them, in which their friendship flourished—Ratra in Frenchpark, Co. Roscommon, Lady Gregory's Coole Park near Gort, Co. Galway—both fell to the bulldozer that has claimed so much of the Ireland they knew. Yet each built monuments to the other: in published public interviews, Lady Gregory paid tribute to Hyde and to the stimulus his cause had brought to her life. In her autobiography she wrote that, for her, Hyde was 'first among the builders of the New Ireland', and that his Gaelic League had led to 'an upsetting of the table of values [and] to an extraordinary excitement'.[3] The Gaelic League badge sent to her by Hyde's close friend, Father Eugene O'Growney, she wore with pride, and her loyalty to the language revival from the start was unflagging: 'I went to Galway with W.B.Y. to support the Gaelic movement, very glad we went, for none of the "classes" were there to support it unless priests can be so called.'[4] For his part Hyde repaid her loyalty to the cause of the language and the retrieval of folklore with a stream of letters and cards, well over 250, dating from shortly after their first meeting in 1897 and extending to 1930, two years before her death in 1932. This correspondence, for the most part now to be found in the Lady Gregory papers in the Berg Collection of the New York Public Library, but also in the manuscript collection of the National Library of Ireland and in several private collections, comprises the major record of their long and fruitful relationship.[5]

Hyde's first note to Lady Gregory, dated 19 August 1897, expressed regret at not being able to accept her invitation to Coole

Park, for he had always heard that 'Gort abounded in shanachies and in correct Gaelic', and he was 'very sorry to miss this opportunity of proving it'.[6] Augusta Gregory, who had been seeking Raftery materials for some years before meeting Hyde, welcomed a partner: 'Now don't you think I deserve credit as a detective?' she wrote on 23 October, to report tracking down a shopkeeper who owned a manuscript of interest to Hyde. She regretted not knowing Irish on a recent visit to Spiddal—'quite an Irish-speaking place'—where she had enlisted the aid of two Irish-speaking schoolmasters to collect stories for Hyde. To one of the masters who hoped to assemble and publish his own collection of Irish songs, she sent a copy of Hyde's *Love Songs of Connacht* as a model. She reported to Hyde that she had offered a shilling each for stories written down in Irish or English by the schoolchildren. 'The Celtic Theatre is progressing nicely'; she was sending him a prospectus: 'We want as much *intellect* on the list as possible'.[7] Hyde's letter and accompanying gift of 23 October crossed hers in the mail. The gift, he wrote, is 'a little book of Irish stories printed in Roman characters, with the translation of five of them . . . very simple, and at the same time in good classical Galway Irish, so that if you are really thinking of learning to read the language you will probably find this as easy a stepping stone to it as you could have.'[8] The 'little book' was Hyde's *An Sgeuluidhe Gaodhalach* (1895), his first step in encouraging his new disciple to learn to read Irish. In a twelve-page letter of 26 October he thanked Lady Gregory for locating the man who had a manuscript of Raftery's poems and for telling him about Spiddal's storytellers, reminding her that his *Sgeuluidhe Gaodhalach* would 'make a good textbook if you were going to really learn to read Irish'. Of the 'folk beliefs', as he termed them, that she and Yeats had gathered, he wrote: 'it will be of immense interest and enormous value.' He promised to find more subscribers for the Celtic Theatre.[9] Hyde's private log of the letters he wrote shows that in the years 1897–1900, Augusta Gregory was by far the most frequent recipient of his letters.[10] In November and December 1897, he complained of the 'bad shape' of the poems in the Raftery manuscript and expressed as always his wish that the Celtic Theatre was going well. After a visit to Coole in late December, during which he entertained her and her guests with a Punch and Judy show in Irish, he wrote on New Year's Day 1898 that he had left 'many things behind' and was 'much ashamed of' himself. In a sixteen-page letter of 6 January, he thanked Lady Gregory for a brace of cock she had sent to him at Ratra: 'Your kindness pursues me even when out of sight and reach.' Intrigued by her push to collect Irish stories from the Galway school children with the help of their teachers, he suggested that in the future she insist on all stories being written in Irish. He would then read and make summaries of them, he declared, adding 'perhaps you will be able to read them yourself some day'.[11] By the end of January Hyde had written, 'it is awfully good of you to think of establishing a branch of the League at Coole.'[12]

In February Hyde was busy rounding up pictures and books about 1798, including a picture of Emmet and his last speech, which he sent to Lady Gregory's London address, according to his correspondence. Does she know Lord Castletown? 'Do you think he would take the chair at our Oireachtas in May?'[13] Every letter encourages Lady Gregory's efforts to learn Irish: 'I am glad you are not dropping your Gaelic.' In May he reported that 'everything related to the League has done well and we are all pleased.'[14] Increasing numbers of words and phrases in Irish appear in his letters to her until, in an eight-page letter of January 1899, he wrote a long anecdote, completely in Irish, about a peasant woman who lies in fear on her deathbed lest her soul be taken in charge by an English speaking priest.[15]

Through the winter of 1898–1899, Hyde's letters to Augusta Gregory covered his admiration for Robert Gregory's prowess when they shot the bogs together at Coole, and the latest attack on the language, this time by the Intermediate Education Commission that Hyde feared would 'wipe out the language altogether' or 'so lower the marks that nobody would take it up.' On 20 February he wrote to Lady Gregory that 'the intermediate battle has been fought, and I think won.' All the news about successful rallies and new branches of the Gaelic League formed in the West found its way to her in Hyde's letters.[16] In April Hyde wrote of his vexation at the Gaelic League's newspaper that seemed to oppose the idea of anything Irish in English—for example, the Literary Theatre. Fearful at the possibility of alienating his ally at Coole because of sniping at her theatre in *An Claidheamh Soluis*, Hyde wrote on 7 May, 1899, an uncharacteristically stern note in Irish to its first editor, his long-time friend, Eoin MacNeill: 'I beseech you please to say nothing in *Claidheamh* against the Literary Theatre. Many of our friends, especially Lady Gregory, are on the Executive Committee, so don't go against them. . . . They are not enemies to us. They are a halfway house. They wanted, and they did their best, to do *Oisin* and *Padraig* in Irish, at the same time, in the theatre.' Neither they, wrote Hyde, nor George Sigerson's group, another 'halfway house,' should be condemned.[17]

'What an extraordinary energetic scholar you are to find Raftery's grave and to lay hold of those manuscripts,' wrote Hyde in November 1899. In January, 1900, in a friendly exchange, Augusta Gregory sent to Ratra new Raftery manuscripts for Hyde to copy, and for the table at Coole Hyde sent golden plovers shot on the bogs of Ratra. In May Lady Gregory received a postcard from Hyde, with its triumphant message entirely in Irish: 'This is the best Oireachtas we've ever had. My own place is stronger than it has ever been among the people.'[18] Pleased with and proud of her growing ability to read Irish, demonstrated by her translation of his own poems that he had sent her, Hyde wrote in June, 'I had no idea that you had translated anything like so many, or that you would have been able to translate them anything like so well.'[19] He had decided that he wanted her to write the preface to the book of Raftery's poems. Would she do this? And would she give Yeats his Gaelic League button, enclosed with the letter? 'Please give it to him from me. I hope he'll wear it! It will be a talisman against the *banditti* of the League.'[20] In December 1900 Augusta Gregory became the custodian of more of Hyde's work: 'Irish songs I made, some of them twenty years ago, and printed in various places.' Would she keep them for him, because he might rewrite and republish them some day?[21]

As the Gaelic League approached the peak of its power under Hyde's presidency, he occasionally divulged to Augusta Gregory what he could not voice publicly. His constant strategy had been to depict the League as nonpolitical, nonsectarian—a nonpartisan crusade to save the Irish language. But in a letter of January 1901 he wrote: 'The fact is we cannot turn our back on the Davis ideal of every person in Ireland being an Irishman, no matter what their blood and politics. . . . It is especially true though, that the Gaelic League and the *Leader* aim at stimulating the old peasant Popish aboriginal population and we care very little about the others, though I would not let this be seen as Moran has done.'[22] Responding to this letter, Lady Gregory quoted Yeats's remark about Moran in a recent letter she had received from him: he holds, she declared, 'the point of view of a man who only cares for the mob'. More important to her seemed to be the success of the local language classes in Gort and Galway and the behind-the-scenes bickering over the production of *Diarmuid and Grania*.[23]

By 1901 Augusta Gregory truly had found her work in Ireland

and could 'claim comradeship with other workers as she saw the threads of new interests . . . woven into the pattern' of her life.[24] And by 1901 Douglas Hyde was an integral partner in the weaving of the pattern of three threads—language, the theatre, and folklore. His support for her next project, however, was at first somewhat grudging. In October 1900 she mentioned to him her idea of putting together the Irish legends of Cuchulain in a sort of *Morte d'Arthur*, 'choosing only the most beautiful and the most striking' of these ancient tales.[25] By December 1900 she could record: 'Douglas Hyde came for shooting. . . . He rather snubs my idea of the Cuchulain book. I think his feeling is that only a scholar should do it, and he is bewildered by my simple translation.' No colloquial style was admissible in epic translation, Hyde told her, at which point she speculated to herself that that advice might account for the heavy and formal style of Hyde's own translations of portions of epics. 'However, he gave his consent, which is all I wanted', she concluded.[26] For Hyde, she was 'plucky to tackle the great cycle' as she did. 'It is more difficult than it seems at first sight', he warned.[27] Despite his reservations, he moved rapidly to assist her in securing the sources she needed. He checked the status of Windisch's proposed edition of the Táin with Kuno Meyer and informed her that it was a long way from completion. He told her of the existence of a translation of the Táin in the Royal Irish Academy. In May 1901 she thanked Hyde for his help and asked for the loan of parts of *Irische Texte*, which he possessed, and any of his own manuscripts which he thought might be helpful to her. 'I suppose there is no translation, and that they would be beyond my own powers', she conjectured. Could the parts of interest to her be typed out in modern Irish? 'If the Tain [sic] manuscript in Dublin is any good, I think I will be able to carry out my purpose of bringing out a clear, consecutive, readable story of the Red Branch period with scarcely any divergence from the originals and scarcely any putting in, though a good deal of leaving out.' It is obvious from their letters that, above all, she wanted to produce 'a book with sap and pleasure in it', to use Hyde's phrase to her. Her only regret, she declared, was 'that I can't do it in Irish, which would be better still'.[28]

Hyde saw the advantages of having his disciple's work published in Irish. In the summer of 1901, harried though he was with the looming climax to the struggle to introduce Irish as a subject for the Intermediate Examination, the problems of producing *The Tinker and the Fairy*, and the election of delegates to the congress of the

Gaelic League (he wanted Augusta Gregory to be one of them), he tried to discover how he might help. In a letter to W. B. Yeats of 1 August 1901, he offered to put into Irish 'any portion which she thinks fit, which would make a little booklet. . . . Let me try my hand upon it, with a reasonable amount of latitude, and if she likes I can get it printed as a Gaelic League book. Let her send it to me anyhow and she'll soon see the result, whether it goes well or ill into Irish.'[29] (Why Hyde did not put the offer directly to Lady Gregory is not clear.)

Cuchulain of Muirthemne appeared in April 1902, with a reminder from Lady Gregory in her dedication to the people of Kiltartan that she, 'the woman of the house', had been impelled to tell what the Trinity dons had ignored—the history of the heroes of Ireland. In her autobiography she wrote, 'I had done what I wanted, something for the dignity of Ireland.'[30] She recognized, of course, that Hyde's constant encouragement and assistance, through the loan of his own books and manuscripts and through the queries he directed to his academic friends at home and abroad, had contributed substantially to the completion of her book. No response to *Cuchulain of Muirthemne* pleased her more, however, than the one she received from Eoin MacNeill, a highly regarded Celtic scholar whose own work on *Duanaire Finn* had been in progress since 1897 (it did not appear until 1908): 'It is the truest representation of the Irish heroic age . . . that I have ever seen in English', wrote MacNeill[31]—who as editor of *An Claidheamh Soluis* had had to be warned by Hyde two years earlier against attacking members of the 'halfway house', the dramatic movement, simply because they wrote in English. So well did he regard Lady Gregory's work, in fact, that he later offered to assist her in the preparation of her own treatment of the Finn legends, *Gods and Fighting Men* (1904), on which she had started work soon after receiving proofs of *Cuchulain of Muirthemne*.

During this period Hyde's letters to Augusta Gregory reflect their mutual concern with the structure of his play *Casadh an tSugáin* (*The Twisting of the Rope*), which was performed on 21 October 1901 in Dublin, the first play in Irish to be produced in any theatre. With an English translation by Lady Gregory, it was printed in *Samhain* I (October, 1901) and, again with her translation, in her *Poets and Dreamers* (1903). In a letter to Hyde she wrote, 'I return the play, I have gone through it and noted the changes on to my translated copy. It is certainly an improvement, taking the audience into your confidence about the plan against

poor Moran. . . . It is a delightful play, I am always fascinated by
it, and so sorry for the poor bard in the end. . . . The Sugan must
be printed sometime, but I am "in dread" of anyone getting at it for
acting before our theatre.'[32] Throughout the winter and spring of
1902 Hyde's letters are taken up with his misgivings about the *The
Tinker and the Fairy* as well as with a mysterious plot in the Gaelic
League, presumably against his presidency. In May 1902 he fretted
about the *The Tinker and the Fairy*: 'I don't like the play but did
it to please [George] Moore.' His letter makes clear his wish that
Lady Gregory rather than Belinda Butler had done the
translation.[33] Of the conspiracy to dislodge him from the
leadership of the League, he could write in May that it was no
longer a worry: 'we have strangled it in advance.' He confided,
however, that he would stay away from the annual language
procession in Dublin, using a bad back as an excuse, and that
furthermore, he did not want to be hauled through the streets of
Dublin in a coach: 'I have a great fear of making people jealous.'[34]
Not until September did he find time to make some changes in the
proof sheets of *Gods and Fighting Men* which she had sent to him.
'What a worker you are!' exclaimed Hyde in November 1903,
encouraging her work on her new book.[35] Angry at an Irish-
American who was about to produce a twelve-volume 'Irish
Library' from which Yeats, Lady Gregory, and AE, among others,
were to be left out, in favour of the 'Honourable this' and the
'Honourable that', Hyde pledged to her that he would order all the
branches of the Gaelic League to protest against the publication of
the series in Ireland.

As Hyde approached the zenith of his popularity and prestige as
president of the Gaelic League, he kept Augusta Gregory informed
of his every success, disappointment, and frustration. In July, 1905,
only three months away from the time set for his departure for the
American fund-raising tour arranged for him by John Quinn, he
wrote to her of the 'muddle' caused him by the imminent sale of
Ratra, his Roscommon residence, to the Congested Districts Board
and the Board's wish to sell the estate to Hyde. Moreover, as he
told her, he was at the same time under consideration for
appointment to a teaching post at the University at Cork—and his
eighty-six-year-old father was dying. In panic at this convergence
of events and responsibilities, he had at first cabled Quinn to cancel
the tour—and then, perhaps on Augusta Gregory's advice, and
with assurance from Quinn that Hyde would not incur personal
financial loss, he reconsidered and carried through triumphantly.

From New York he wrote a warm letter immediately after disembarking, describing his reception and Quinn's kindness, which he termed 'beyond anything'. 'I don't know how my tour will turn out, but my success in New York seems commensurate with the send-off that I got from Ireland.'[36] Exhausted by the whirl of speeches, receptions, and press interviews, he made time to write again from New York on 2 January 1906. He was, he said, giving 'thundering speeches to big audiences in theatres'. Knowing that Lady Gregory had long looked forward to an American tour with the Abbey company, he wrote that he thought such a tour would go well with the Irish [Americans], but he was doubtful about the Americans, fearing that they 'never experiment but only go to see proved successes'. Nevertheless, he affirmed that he would see what he could do about the theatre, then closed with a line that he was to repeat in much of his correspondence from the United States, as his tour continued: 'I only wish I were with you at Coole for a day's rest! . . . I'll tell you my experiences later on.'[37]

'Immense meetings everywhere but not much money', Hyde wrote from St Paul, Minnesota, in February, in the midst of his fifty-city tour which had as its only purpose, for Hyde, to raise money for the Gaelic League. Never had he forgotten to mention Yeats and the dramatic movement in each speech, he assured her, having learned that Yeats was planning to come to the United States with the Abbey company. Yet manuscripts of 'The Speech' that Hyde delivered over fifty times in American cities, including the copy revised for his San Francisco appearance in March 1906, with his own handwritten insertions, reveal no mention of the Abbey or of Yeats's and Lady Gregory's work in founding the dramatic movement.[38] Did Hyde's memory deceive him on this matter? Or were tact, discretion, and the practical need to avoid offending members of the Gaelic League in America, who shared the Irish League's suspicion of an 'Irish' theatre that produced (except for Hyde's one-act plays) only plays written in English, responsible for his reluctance to publicize the Abbey? The question of Hyde's timidity in promoting the Abbey's interests in the United States arose again in the midst of the company's 1911 tour, when for the first time it placed a strain on his relationship with Augusta Gregory.

Even before 1911, however, but later in 1906, when Hyde returned from his American tour, his correspondence with Lady Gregory tapered off as he was caught up increasingly in the quarrels, intrigues, and disputes of the Gaelic League. In April 1908 he wrote

wrote that he was bothered with Gaelic League 'alarms and excursions' and 'lots of spite'. Furthermore, 'as I always foresaw', he declared, Father Dinneen was 'at the bottom of it all; his ingenuity in breeding strife is diabolical'.[39] In October of the same year Hyde sent Lady Gregory a copy of the Honours Examination for Irish in the Royal University, proudly pointing out that one of the questions was on the new Irish drama and that nearly all eighteen candidates had written on it.[40] In her answering letter, Lady Gregory thanked him for the news about the examination question, and responded to a news cutting he had enclosed, regarding the dearth of drama written in Irish, with 'now that you have given up this side of your work . . . I think the plays in English, by Irish writers, will have to be used, for a while anyhow, and I am sorry, for as you know, Yeats and I hoped for a Gaelic Dramatic Movement.'[41] Something of their old relationship was evident in a long letter written on 14 July, in which Hyde shared his greatest triumph with his old friend, describing the scene as the University Senate, by a narrow majority, decided that Irish should form an essential part of the university curriculum—indeed, should be a requirement for matriculation. 'It is the greatest blow ever struck for the recovery of our nationality, and it is bound to profoundly affect the country.'[42]

A few years later, all changed, as the Abbey began its tumultuous tour of America with Synge's *The Playboy of the Western World*. As described vividly by Lady Gregory in *Our Irish Theatre* (1913), the United Irish Societies of New York voted to 'drive the vile thing from the stage'. Their resolution was published in the *Gaelic American*, with the result that the performance was disrupted violently, and stinkpots, rosaries, and potatoes were hurled at the stage. An interview conducted backstage at the Maxine Elliott Theatre during a performance of *The Playboy*, published in *The New York Times* of 3 December 1911, testifies to her calmness under fire—and to the trust she had in Hyde and his influence. Singling him out for praise, she explained that his Gaelic League had been founded to revive the language, but had had farther reaching effects: 'although we don't use the Irish language in our plays, still the excitement caused by its revival, the discovery that there was a great deal of legend and culture and song-making still among the people', sent writers 'back to the life of the country itself', instead of leaving them to seek 'an inspiration outside.'[43] Within hours of this interview, before it was published, knowing nothing about it, Hyde had sent a cable to New York disclaiming any connection between the Abbey company and the Gaelic League. Hyde's action, according to John Quinn's biographer, made Quinn 'furious and disgusted': as he saw the situation, Hyde had caved in at threats by the Clan-na-Gael in New York, transmitted to Dublin, to 'sabotage the League's appeal for American funds'.[44] Lady Gregory discreetly omits mention of this incident in *Our Irish Theatre*, but the impact of Hyde's action on Quinn and the company is revealed in a remarkably restrained letter which she wrote to Hyde on 7 December 1911 from the Maxine Elliott Theater: 'Oh Craoibhin, what are these wounds with which we are wounded in the house of our friends? I had been away for a day, and I came back and found John Quinn using strong language and the players sitting sadly and saying, "Have you heard of *Doctor Hyde*?" I have never seen them so troubled. There is not much in the telegram, but at a time of the most abominable attacks it will be used as if it was sent to strengthen our enemies. . . . I would not have it answered. But I do want you to write to me or to John Quinn privately and say what the accusation against us was, and who made it. I need not say that we have never in any way claimed to be connected with the Gaelic League, we are proud of being sheltered by no League at all, of being the only Irish independent body.'[45] Perhaps more gently than he deserved, she told Hyde how in her lectures and interviews she had constantly praised his work, 'which has changed literature from the artificial bird's-eye view of the 19th century to the folk-drama of today', and with her letter she enclosed a copy of the *Times* interview, 'as it contains this statement'. She closed by reminding Hyde that they had been attacked in Washington, D. C. by Jesuits who called them 'hellish', and that priests in New York 'have taken up the cry. . . . We are fighting your battle if you did but know it, and the battle of all who want to live and breathe.'[46] In a lame response Hyde wrote, 'I am sorry you minded my wire.' It was sent, he explained, 'in answer to two insistent cables in two consecutive days, demanding repudiation of connection with the Players, cabled by our own delegates. . . . I might have said much more, but you yourself will acknowledge I could not have said less.'[47] 'The Cable' became a topic of repeated attention in letters that followed. As late as May 1912, Hyde wrote to Lady Gregory: 'As you know, there is nobody in Ireland whose interests I would consult more than your own, if I could without harm to the Gaelic League.'[48]

Hyde's resignation from the Gaelic League's presidency came at the Ardfheis at Dundalk in August 1915, when he recognized that the separatist tide was running strongly against him and that his nonpolitical course was no longer possible. It is curious, but perhaps indicative of the still cool relationship between them, that he did not inform his comrade of nearly twenty years of his departure from the League until December: 'I am no longer President of the Gaelic League. I kept them together for 22 years, but the war was too much for me! I shall tell you about it when I see you.'[49] In a letter of October 1916 he thanked Augusta Gregory for her note on the death of his daughter Nuala, described her death and funeral, and concluded, 'What a dreadful year this has been both public and private. Ireland seems in a hopeless muddle. So does everything, the Gaelic League included.'[50]

Scattered letters from Hyde to Augusta Gregory and various entries in her autobiography and journals show that the friendship survived until her death in 1932. Hyde supported her in her unsuccessful campaign to bring the pictures of her nephew, Hugh Lane, back to Ireland; she, with John Quinn's help, lobbied Yeats on the necessity for a Senate seat for Hyde in the new Irish state. He, she said, should be put on as a representative of literature, 'the intellectual side', as the author of A Literary History of Ireland and Love Songs of Connacht, and as a scholar and teacher whose name was honoured in France and America. 'Yeats was I think convinced', she reported.[51]

Writing to John Quinn, Hyde once had called Augusta Gregory 'a wonderful, wonderful woman, with the pluck of a Joan of Arc'.[52] For her, despite her disappointment in him in 1911, he was the man who had 'given the imagination of Ireland a new homing place'.[53]

LADY GREGORY AND THE GAELIC LEAGUE

MAUREEN MURPHY

Lady Gregory frequently admitted she was not very good about dates and other practical matters of memory because she trained her mind to collect folklore. Indeed she even misdated the founding of the Irish Literary Theatre by a year. It is understandable, perhaps, that she took the founding of the Theatre out of that crowded year 1897 and put it in 1898. 1897 was the date of Yeats's first long summer visit to Coole, the year she began to collect folklore and the year she realized her ambition to learn Irish. For the next few years, from 1897-1901, the span of the Irish Literary Theatre, her work with the Gaelic League was a paradigm of her work with the Theatre: she organized, she nurtured the talent of others, and she contributed her own creative work to the movement. Although the Abbey Theatre later claimed her first loyalty, a loyalty that for some periods was incompatible with the League, her enthusiasm for the Irish language and her belief that the Gaelic League was the transforming force in the Ireland of her time, continued till the end of her life.

In her Introduction to *The Kiltartan Poetry Book*, Lady Gregory describes her longing to learn Irish while growing up at Roxborough, her family's estate in East Galway.

Once in childhood I had been eager to learn Irish; I thought to get leave to take lessons from an old Scripture reader who spent a part of his time in the parish of Killinane teaching such scholars as he could find to read their own language in the hope that they might turn to the only book then being printed in Irish, The Bible. But my asking, timid with the fear of mockery, was unheeded. Yet I missed but by a little an opportunity that might have made me a real Irish scholar and not as I am imperfect, stumbling. For a kinsman learned in the language, the translator of the wonderful *Silva Gadelica* had been sometimes a guest in the house, and would still have been welcome there but that my mother, who had a great dislike to the marriage of cousins had fancied he was taking a liking to one of my elder sisters; and with that suspicion, the 'winged nymph, Opportunity' had passed from my reach.[1]

143

After her marriage to Sir William Gregory in 1880, she tried again to learn Irish. She bought a grammar and tried—with the help of a gardener at Coole—to teac⹂ ι herself Irish. 'But it was difficult and my teacher was languid, suspecting it may be some hidden mockery, for those were the days before Irish became the fashion.'[2]

The 'fashion' wasn't long in coming. Speaking in New York in 1891, Douglas Hyde urged the importance of the Irish language to Irish identity. Hyde repeated his argument in his inaugural lecture as the President of the National Literary Society on 25 November 1829: 'When we speak of "The Necessity for De-Anglicising the Irish Nation" we mean it, not as a protest against imitating what is best in the English people, for that would be absurd, but rather to show the folly of neglecting what is Irish, and hastening to adopt, pell-mell, and indiscriminately, everything that is English, simply because it is English'.[3]

A call for action followed. Eoin MacNeill, editor of *The Gaelic Journal*, in his article titled 'A Plea and a Plan for the Extension of the Movement to Preserve and Spread the Gaelic Language in Ireland', proposed a language movement organized along the lines of another successful Irish mass movement, the Land League. Mac Neill circulated a notice calling for people interested in forming the **Conradh na Gaeilge** or the Gaelic League to meet on 31 July 1893. Those who attended pledged their support to the League's purpose of preserving and encouraging Irish as a spoken language. Douglas Hyde was elected the League's first president. The League differed in its organization and objectives from previous Irish language societies which were scholarly, largely antiquarian organizations. This was a movement to encourage Irish as the vernacular for the Irish people.

Social historians have generally failed to notice the kind of social revolution that resulted from the Gaelic League.[4] While Sean O'Casey characterized the League as a respectable, middle-class, Catholic organization in *Drums Under the Window*, a common interest in Irish language and culture crossed class and religious lines and brought together a very heterogeneous group, people who would not otherwise have had the opportunity for such a diverse experience in the Dublin of their day. It was, as well, Ireland's first adult educational movement.

For Lady Gregory, the Gaelic League made an immense difference, for when she tried to learn Irish for a third time during the summer of 1897, she was successful. She says it was Robert

Gregory's announcement that 'he would give anything to learn Irish' that encouraged her to take it up again.[5] In the end partridge shooting lured Robert from his lessons, but Lady Gregory went on with the work. She gives two main reasons for her success: Father O'Growney's *Simple Lessons in Irish* and her friendship with Douglas Hyde. Father O'Growney, Professor of Irish at Maynooth and a Gaelic League Vice-President, wrote a series of three booklets called *Simple Lessons in Irish* which sold 32,000 copies by the time Lady Gregory began to study them in 1897.[6] Lady Gregory's Irish exercises in copybooks labelled Agústa Gregóre and dated 1897 are among her papers in The New York Public Library's Berg Collection. They indicate that she too worked her way carefully through *Simple Lessons*.

Lady Gregory met Hyde in October 1897, while she was visiting her friend Edward Martyn at Tillyra, Martyn's home in County Galway. As her work in the Irish Theatre helped to seal her friendship with W. B. Yeats, her work for the Irish language was central to the growth of her friendship with Douglas Hyde. Yeats's work involved creating a new poetic and dramatic literary consciousness; Hyde's work disclosed the great wealth of Irish literary and artistic tradition and his excitement was contagious.

Douglas Hyde, An Craoibhín, had founded the Gaelic League, and through it country people were gathered together in the Irish speaking places to give the songs and poems, old and new, kept in their memory. This discovery, this disclosure of folk learning, the folk poetry, the ancient tradition, was the small beginning of a weighty change. It was an upsetting of the tables of values, an astonishing excitement. The imagination of Ireland had found a new homing place.[7]

From the start Lady Gregory saw the goals of the Gaelic League as the same as those she identified for the Irish Theatre. Both were non-political nationalist movements; both were concerned with bringing dignity to Ireland.

Lady Gregory began her service to the Gaelic League by using her talent as an organizer to do what the League needed most: to establish and support League branches around the country. In January 1898 she proposed to Hyde that she establish a branch of the League at Coole. In spite of the demands of preparing *Mr. Gregory's Letter-Box* (1898), she found time to study Irish with Norma Borthwick of the London Branch of the Gaelic League in March and April of 1898.[8] In May she made her pilgrimage to the

Aran Islands staying with the MacDonaghs on Inishmaan, the house that welcomed Eoin MacNeill and John Synge. Synge was making his first visit to the Islands at the same time. Lady Gregory reported seeing him on Inishmore, but they did not meet till his visit to Coole in late June 1898.[9] That July Lady Gregory tried to teach W. B. Yeats some Irish during his summer visit to Coole.[10] In December she brought Miss Borthwick to Coole to teach Irish at the gatehouse.[11]

The first meeting of the Kiltartan Branch of the Gaelic League took place at Kiltartan School on 9 January 1899 with Lady Gregory's friend Father Fahey, Gort's Irish-speaking parish priest, in the chair. Hyde spoke in Irish which Lady Gregory confessed she didn't understand and in English. His remark, 'Let English go their road and let us go ours, and God forbid their road should ever be ours' struck her as being too political.[12] Though she first opposed it, by 1899 Lady Gregory favoured Home Rule for Ireland; however, her motto was that she was 'not working for Home Rule, but preparing for it'.[13] That the League was a non-political nationalist force was particularly appealing to her. While Hyde also firmly believed that the League should be a non-political force and indeed resigned from the League in 1915 when it became politicized, his remark illustrates the Sinn Fein philosophy that was to translate inevitably into political action.

Lady Gregory's enthusiasm for local League activities continued through the year with classes at the gatehouse. Her example was such that her Irish-speaking workmen pledged to speak only Irish among themselves.[14] Vere Gregory, a relative of Sir William, who visited Coole in the summer of 1899, recalled Lady Gregory's earnestness about the Irish language:

She spoke to me very seriously on the subject, and I can recollect being highly amused when she assured me that before long, no one who could not speak Irish would be eligible for any public appointment. In my superior wisdom, I thought it strange, and rather pathetic, that so intelligent a woman could be led to believe such nonsense. Not only have her prophetic words come true, but she had the satisfaction of living to see them verified.[15]

In the same passage, Vere Gregory remarked that Lady Gregory was disheartened because her Irish-speaking tenants didn't understand her Irish. That is not the Myles na gCopaleen scenario that it sounds. Unlike English which has twenty-six letters and forty-four phonemes or basic sound units, Irish has only eighteen letters with which to represent at least sixty sounds. Most European languages have one sound per consonant; Irish has nearly two complete sets of sounds per consonant. For example, 'd' has the sound of the 'd' in 'den' with vowels *e* and *i* but a sound more like the 'th' in 'that' with vowels *a*, *o*, and *u*. If this were not difficult enough, when Lady Gregory was learning Irish there was no standard orthography.

She persisted with her Irish, making 'slow progress' in the summer of 1899 and taking up lessons with a W. Ussher in the fall.[16] While she struggled with spoken Irish, she began to develop real skill as a translator from Irish to English. She amazed Hyde with a translation of Anthony Raftery's poem in praise of Mary Hynes, 'An Posadh Glégeal' for Yeats's article 'Dust Hath Closed Helen's Eye' which appeared in *The Dome* in October 1899. A diary entry for December reveals her method. She was helped by a young farmer named Mulkere to whom she brought her translations for correction. The translations she did in 1899 and 1900, the literal rendering of Irish into English, inspired her to experiment with that language for her *Cuchulain of Muirthemne*.

When Lady Gregory returned to London in the spring of 1900 she translated Hyde's poems from the Irish, translations Yeats read one evening to Mark Twain and to Mrs. Clemens.[17] The spoken language continued to frustrate her. After the Galway *feis* in the summer of 1900, she wrote that she 'understood a little more than last year but still not much'.[18]

In December 1900, Lady Gregory brought Master Conolly, the Irish-speaking teacher from Aran, to teach at the gatehouse; she studied with him until the end of January 1901, when he went to Tillyra, Edward Martyn's home, but she made little progress in understanding the spoken language. Given her difficulty understanding Irish, it is likely that her *modus vivendi* when collecting folklore from Irish speakers was to use an interpreter as she used the Irish-speaking priest from Moycullen when she collected at the Oughterard Workhouse in 1902.

In was Conolly who helped her with her Cuchulain experiment. She gave him an English version of the Death of Cuchulain to translate into Irish; then she translated it literally into English. Hyde was sceptical, but Lady Gregory carried on with her experiment and in the end it was her Kiltartan dialect in *Cuchulain of Muirthemne* that gave Anglo-Irish literature its distinctive idiom. Describing the influence of her Kiltartan dialect on Synge, Lady Gregory said:

Later when my 'Cuchulain of Muirthemne' came out, he said to Mr. Yeats that he had been amazed to find in it the dialect he had been trying to master. I say this with a little pride, for I was the first to use the Irish idiom, as it is spoken, to any large extent and with a belief in it. Dr. Hyde has used it with fine effect in his 'Love Songs of Connacht,' but gave it up afterward on being remonstrated with by a Dublin editor.[20]

In addition to her Irish language and Gaelic League activities on the local level, Lady Gregory represented the Kiltartan Branch at the Gaelic League *Oireachtas* in 1901 and 1902 and she contributed two articles to the League paper *An Claidheamh Soluis* (The Sword of Light): 'Raftery, the Poet of the Poor' (14 October 1899) and 'A Nation's Words' signed Cilltartan (6 July 1901). She was also probably responsible for some of the unsigned reports of the activities of the Kiltartan and the Gort branches of the Gaelic League that appeared regularly in *An Claidheamh Soluis*.[21]

Hyde confided to Lady Gregory about League problems in his letters and on at least one occasion her diary suggests she acted as a sort of peacemaker, probably during a period of tension between the League and the Irish Literary Theatre. 'Then Miss Borthwick and Miss O'Reilly came in and I had a Gaelic League talk with them and found them amiable.'[22]

Hyde and Lady Gregory were both conscious of the kind of support a person of her class could give the League. In an early letter he asked her to sound out Lord Castletown about opening the *Oireachtas*. On the other hand, Lady Gregory's putting Irish interest ahead of class interest earned some disapproval from her Ascendancy family and neighbours. In 1897 she refused to join George Gough of Lough Cutra, private secretary to Viscount Wolseley and father of Guy Gough who would be Margaret Gregory's second husband, in lighting a bonfire to celebrate Queen Victoria's Jubilee because she felt the Queen had neglected Ireland. After she took up Irish, she supported the position of a young farmer named Bartley Hynes who was given a summons in Kinvara in August 1901 because his name which appeared in Irish on his cart was considered illegible. The case was followed with great interest in *An Claidheamh Soluis* which printed the notice from the *Tuam Herald* reporting that both Lady Gregory and Edward Martyn had ordered their carts to be marked in Irish and driven into Kinvara.[23] Some simply thought she was crazy. When O'Casey wrote to her years later that she too had to overcome her background, she replied, 'I was called "mad" when I gave my

personal help to the Gaelic League'.[24] This is not to suggest Lady
Gregory was unconcerned about her reputation as a nationalist
among her own class. She was very concerned because her son
whom she adored was an Imperialist and he was her first loyalty.
Rather she tried to bring what was best to each world.

Lady Gregory not only provided the support of her presence and
her personal resources to the Gaelic League, but she was also able
to bring the Gaelic League to the attention of a wider audience.
When she wrote to Hyde of her plan for an article about the non-
political forces at work in Ireland, he encouraged her and sent
Gaelic League reports. Her article 'Ireland—Real and Ideal'
described George Russell's Irish Agricultural Organization Society
and the Gaelic League.

Lady Gregory's article, much influenced by Hyde and by Gaelic
League policy, is partly concerned with the question of teaching
Irish in the schools. Her description of Irish-speaking children
spancelled by an education through a language they didn't speak at
home has something of the anger of Padraic Pearse's 1912 essay on
Irish education, 'The Murder Machine'. Her essay was an early aid
to the League's campaign to have the Irish language recognized as
a legitimate subject for study in Irish schools.

The last section of her essay spoke of the soul of Ireland and
offered Hyde's translations from the Irish to show Ireland's
imagination. The section also contains one of the first expressions
of the *leitmotif* of her life and work — the dignity of Ireland.
'Poetry and pathos may be granted to us, but when we claim
dignity, those who see only the sham fights of Westminster shake
their heads. But here, in real Ireland, dignity can live side by side
with the strongest political feeling.'[25]

A measure of the effectiveness of 'Ireland, Real and Ideal' was
another essay in *The Nineteenth Century* in August 1899 by
Professor John Pentland Mahaffy, Provost of Trinity College, who
led the opposition to Irish in the National University. In his essay
'The Recent Fuss about the Irish Language' he described Lady
Gregory as:

a western landlady, who promotes Irish among her tenantry and
dependants, and who told me with pride that they were beginning to
appreciate it as no mere spoken idiom, but as a speech that can be printed
and studied in books, so that she hopes for a large development of interest
in the subject throughout her district in the West. She is a woman of large
heart who has lived in the world, and in the midst of her enthusiasm has

retained that strong sense of humour which will protect her from the absurdities into which the advocates of her project continually stray.[26]

In the end Mahaffy's forces were defeated and the Gaelic League had its greatest triumph — some would say its high point — in the decision to make a knowledge of Irish compulsory for entrance to the National University when it was founded in 1908.

Another effort to show the work of non-political nationalist forces in Ireland was Lady Gregory's *Ideals in Ireland*, a collection of essays she edited in 1901. All but Standish O'Grady's 'The Great Enchantment' were concerned at some level with the Irish language and/or the Gaelic League. Lady Gregory did not contribute an essay herself, but her hand is clear in her selection, in her Introduction, and in her translation of Hyde's two essays from Irish and some of Raftery for Yeats's 'The Literary Movement in Ireland'.

Concerned about its reception, Lady Gregory wrote in December 1900, 'The *Ideals* not out yet. I get a little nervous about them, but I think I was right in publishing, to show how strong the national spirit can be, without those who feel it being of necessity followers of William O'Brien or Tim Healy.'[27]

Lady Gregory may have been concerned about Hyde's essay 'The Return of the Fenians,' an essay published in Irish as well as in its English translation. Hyde described a crow hovering over Ireland like an ominous black cloud, a symbol of the Anglicisation of Ireland. He promised that the Gaelic League would destroy the crow with the arrow of the Irish language. The essay does not necessarily show us a militant Hyde: his imagery is almost certainly taken from traditional Gaelic figures of a reclaimed and restored Irish nation.

Lady Gregory needn't have worried; the book was well received. From the point of view of the League, the book was a particular success. Praising it in a review of *An Claidheamh Soluis*, Cú Uladh (P. J. MacGinley) said, 'If you want to understand the spirit that is the Gaelic League, read this book'.[28]

Lady Gregory gave the Gaelic League the royalties for *Ideals in Ireland*; the same year she suggested to Yeats that the proceeds from the Spring 1901 issue of *Beltaine*, the occasional journal of the Irish Literary Theatre, be turned over to the Gaelic League. Yeats not only agreed, but he decided that *Beltaine* should be 'A Gaelic propaganda paper this time'.[29] *Beltaine* was, in fact, succeeded by *Samhain* but its profits for the October 1901 issue were donated to the League.

Two League-related projects demonstrate not only Lady Gregory's genius at organization but also her ability to nurture the talents of others; both influenced the development of literature in the Irish language as well as in the Anglo-Irish literary tradition. She worked to honour the memory of nineteenth century Connacht poet Anthony Raftery and in doing so contributed to the work of Hyde and Yeats. She also encouraged the development of drama in the Irish language.

When Hyde first met Lady Gregory he was in Galway looking for the house where Raftery died. Lady Gregory eagerly joined in the search not only for Raftery locations but also for manuscripts. By September 1899 she was collecting stories about Raftery and, as she had turned over her folklore to Yeats for *The Celtic Twilight*, she turned over her Raftery lore to Hyde.

In an article in *An Claidheamh Soluis*, Tomás O'Concannon, the Gaelic League organizer in the Clare/Galway area, described a conversation at Coole where Lady Gregory said it was a pity that there was no stone to mark Raftery's grave; all present agreed to help.[30] Lady Gregory's article 'Raftery, the Poet of the Poor', written at Hyde's suggestion for *An Claidheamh Soluis* (14 October 1899), was an appeal for subscriptions for Raftery's stone, but she also included some of her Raftery stories and a verse of Raftery's that Hyde printed in *The Religious Songs of Connacht*.

As it happened, Lady Gregory paid for most of the cost of the stone — a high stone with the single word 'Raftery' — that was unveiled and blessed at a Gaelic League *feis* in Killeenan, County Galway, on 26 August 1900. The report of the event in the *Tuam News* (31 August 1900) under the headline 'A Red-Letter Day in Killeenan' describes the platform party of Gaelic Leaguers, local clergy and officials, Lady Gregory, Martyn, Hyde and Yeats. In her diary, Lady Gregory recorded with satisfaction:

They were pleased with the stone, and some objected to the name 'Raftery' alone, without 'Anthony' and I had to explain that Homer also had been known by one name alone. 'He is worthy of this,' one old man said, 'he was such a conversable man.' Redington there, had never heard of Raftery a month ago, and Fr. Considine had been for two years in the parish and had never heard of him.[31]

During that summer Hyde also proposed a joint Raftery project to be published by the Gaelic League, an edition of Raftery's poems with a short biography by Lady Gregory. Lady Gregory went ahead with her Raftery article which appeared as 'The Poet Raftery' in *Argosy* (1901). When their joint project failed to materialize because of the Gaelic League's policy of not publishing translations, Hyde's Raftery collection went to the *Weekly Freeman*. Hyde published the collection in book form in 1903 drawing heavily on Lady Gregory's Raftery article. His gratitude to Lady Gregory for her help to him and for her work to preserve Raftery's songs was expressed in his poem dedicating *Abhráin atá Leagtha ar an Reachtúire* to her. Comparing her to Guaire Aidhne, a sixth century Connacht king and patron of poets, he said:

> A bhaintighearna uasal, a 'Ghuaire' na mbárd
> Tá a bhfad shiar, 'san gCúil sin na ndlúth-choillteadh n-árd
> Ó shabháil tusa clú mo Reachtúire ó 'n mbás
> Ofrálaim go h-umhal duit an duais seo ó m'láimh

> [Noble Lady, Guaire of the bards
> Who lives back in Coole in the tall, dense woods
> Since you have saved the name of my Raftery from death,
> I humbly offer you this prize from my hand.]

Hyde was not the only beneficiary of Lady Gregory's Raftery lore. She supplied Yeats with Raftery stories and translations for three essays, 'Dust Hath Closed Helen's Eye', 'The Literary Movement in Ireland', and 'Literature and the Living Voice'. Later, he returned to Raftery for his poems 'The Tower' and 'Coole Park and Ballylee, 1931'. Lady Gregory's comparison of Raftery to Homer perhaps provided the paradox of the blind poet celebrating a woman's beauty.

Raftery was to figure in another collaborative Irish language project as well, a project that began with Hyde's Christmas visit to Coole in 1898, the winter of Lady Gregory's first year of dedicated Gaelic League activity. Hyde and Miss Borthwick gave a Punch and Judy Show in Irish for the local children at St. Colman's Hall in Gort. That it was an unqualified success certainly inspired Lady Gregory to urge Hyde to write an Irish play for a Dublin audience, for she dated the beginning of a drama in Irish with that event.

I hold that the beginning of modern Irish drama was in the winter of 1898, at a school feast at Coole, when Douglas Hyde and Miss Norma Borthwick acted in Irish in a Punch and Judy Show, and the delighted children went back to tell their parents what a grand curse An Craoibhin had put on the baby and the policeman.[32]

The *Freeman's Journal* for 20 November 1898, describing the Aonach Tír Chonaill (Donegal Fair), mentions an anonymous play (probably by Father O'Growney) called 'Conall Gulban'. While most of the play was in English, there was one scene in Irish.[33]

When Hyde went to Coole after the Gaelic League *feis* at Killeenan in 1900, Lady Gregory and Yeats set him to writing a play in Irish possibly for production by the Gaelic League. 'We thought at our first start it would make the whole movement more living and bring it closer to the people if the Gaelic League would put on some plays written in Irish.'[34] While Hyde, Yeats and Lady Gregory agree that Yeats provided a scenario based on his Red Hanrahan story 'The Twisting of the Rope' from *The Secret Rose* (1897), Hyde was familiar with the basic device of the twisting of a straw rope to get rid of an unwanted suitor. He described it in the note to his version of 'An Súisín Bán' (The White Coverlet) that appeared in *Love Songs of Connacht* (1893). Hyde did not use the words of the song in his play; however, another of the songs 'Tadhg agus Máire' (Teig and Mary) may have inspired the dialogues of praise poetry spoken by Una and Hanrahan in the play.

Hyde's play was produced at the Gaiety Theatre in Dublin on 21 October 1901, during the Irish Literary Theatre's third season. Hyde himself played the part of Hanrahan with Irish speakers from the Keating Branch of the Gaelic League in other roles. Lady Gregory reported on its success in *Our Irish Theatre*, 'it was a delight even to those who knew no Irish — it was played with so much gaiety, ease and charm'.[35]

Although Lady Gregory always called *Casadh an tSúgáin* the first Irish play presented on a Dublin stage, there were two which preceded it: P. T. MacGinley's *Eilis agus an Bhean Déirce* (Eilish and the Beggarwoman) produced by the Daughters of Erin and directed by the Fay brothers in August 1901, and Father Dinneen's *An Tobar Draoidheachta* (The Magic Well) produced by the Ormonde Drama Society at the Gaelic League's Autumn *feis* in 1901.[36] In his memoir, *The Fays of the Abbey Theatre*, William Fay says it was his experience directing *An Tobar Draoidheachta* which brought him into contact with the Irish Literary Theatre:

Mr Moore had intended to produce this little play himself, but he found his experience in dealing with professional actors in London of little use in coaching the Gaelic-speaking amateurs supplied by the League. Indeed it was, if anything, a hindrance, and so he finally sent for me to know if I would take over the job, which I was very glad to do.[37]

First or not, *Casadh an tSúgáin* was enormously popular. Hyde followed it with *An Pósadh* (The Marriage) which had its first performance at the Galway *feis* in 1902 with Hyde in the role of Raftery. Lady Gregory not only supplied the story of Raftery at the poor wedding at Cappatagle, a story she told first in 'Raftery, Poet of the Poor', but she also supplied the ending for the play.[38]

Another Gregory-Hyde collaboration *An Teach Bocht* (The Poorhouse, 1903), was the basis for Lady Gregory's comedy *The Workhouse Ward*. The idea had been hers. 'I intended to write the full dialogue myself, but Mr. Yeats thought a new Gaelic play more useful for the movement, and rather sadly I laid that part of the work on Dr. Hyde.'[39] The Gregory-Hyde *The Poorhouse* wasn't entirely successful when it was produced in English (13 April 1907), so Lady Gregory rewrote it as *The Workhouse Ward* for the following season (20 April 1908).

In addition to her active collaboration with Hyde, she translated his plays from the Irish: *An Tincéar agus an tSídheóg* (The Tinker and the Fairy), *An Naomh ar Iarraidh* (The Lost Saint), *Pléusgadh na Bulgóide* (The Bursting of the Bubble), *An Cleamhnas* (The Matchmaking), *Rígh Séumas* (King James), and *Maistín an Bhéarla* (The Mastiff of the English Language).[40]

Lady Gregory did not write plays in the Irish language herself, but her knowledge of Irish clearly contributed to her work as a playwright. To cite just three examples: the young man's lines near the end of *The Rising of the Moon*, 'Sergeant, I am thinking it was with the people you were, and not with the law you were, when you were a young man', surely come from her translation of An Craoibhín's 'It is with the people I was/It is not with the law I was'; the folk attitude towards the Stuarts expressed in the Irish song 'Preabaim mo chroí le mo Stuart Glégeal' (My heart leaps with my bright Stuart) inspired *The White Cockade*, and Raftery's 'Seanchuis [nó Caisimirt] na Sgeiche' [The History of the Dispute with the Bush] provided the device of the talk with the bush in *Hanrahan's Oath*.[41]

Raftery had been a discovery for her and her Raftery essay in *Poets and Dreamers* a special pleasure:

There was more of my own writing in *Poets and Dreamers* than in anything I had yet published. I felt it more my own. The chapter especially on Raftery had been an excitement. As I heard of him in many thatched houses his image grew. It was almost like Browning's excitement. 'Ah did you once see Shelley plain?' — when some memory of him was given by some labourer or withered hag.[42]

It may be that Raftery provided a dramatic mask for Lady Gregory which permitted her to be more of a nationalist than class or conscience permitted. The Raftery selection she translated for *The Kiltartan Poetry Book* and the vision of Irish history offered by the Raftery poems in *The Kiltartan History Book* reflect her understanding of the way folk history maintained a belief in and commitment to the restoration of a Gaelic Irish nation.

She borrowed that promise of restoration, that motif of the strong defeated by the weak, from Raftery for dialogue in *The Rising of the Moon* and *The White Cockade*. Early in *The Rising of the Moon* the Sergeant defends his duty to maintain the present order: 'Well, we have to do our duty in the force. Haven't we the whole country depending on us to keep law and order? It's those that are down would be up and those that are up would be down, if it wasn't for us.'[43] Later after the young rebel has engaged the Sergeant's deeper loyalty, he is let escape. He takes leave of the Sergeant saying, 'Well, good-night, comrade, and thank you. You did me a good turn tonight, and I'm obliged to you. Maybe I'll be able to do as much for you when the small rise up and the big fall down. . . . When we all change places at the Rising (*waves his hand and disappears*) of the Moon.'[44]

She uses something of the same dialogue in the exchange between Patrick Sarsfield and a Williamite in *The White Cockade*:

First Williamite: Your Majesty would not get very far — we have other
      men.
Sarsfield: Who knows? There are ups and downs.
      A King is not a common man — the moon has risen . . . [45]

After very close communication — visits, frequent letters—Lady Gregory and Hyde became increasingly occupied with the demands of their other commitments. Their correspondence fell off in 1905 and was irregular after that until the 1911 Abbey tour to America when Hyde, pressured by Clan na Gael threats to cut off American financial support to the Gaelic League, cabled from Dublin that there was absolutely no connection between the Abbey and the League. Strictly speaking, he was absolutely correct, but Lady Gregory saw it as an act of gratuitous disloyalty. Among her papers are two letters from Hyde, written six months apart, trying to explain his position to her, but it appears she never completely forgave him.[46]

Loyalty was never an easy issue for her. She was required to mediate between her love for her son and her deep commitment to Ireland, between her loyalty to Yeats and the Irish Literary Theatre and to Hyde and the Gaelic League, and later between her devotion to Yeats and her friendship for O'Casey.

On his side, Hyde, in his later years, minimized Lady Gregory's part in his life and work. While mention of the help of his friend Lady Gregory remained in the text of the second edition of his Raftery book *Abhráin agus Dánta an Reachtabhraigh* (1933), the dedication poem to 'a bhaintighearna uasail' was omitted. What is perhaps more indicative of their lost friendship was Hyde's account of meeting John Quinn for the first time 'in August 1900' at the Killeenan *feis* to unveil Raftery's gravestone.

Saoilim go raibh sé ar aoidheacht leis an mBaintighearna Greagóir. Badh í sinn an bhean-uasal a chuir fá deara an tumba breagh do thogáil do Raifteri, agus saoilim go dtug sí Mac Uí Cuinn leí abhaile go Teach na Cúlach, a háit chómhnuidhe.[46]

[I think he was staying with Lady Gregory. It was she who ordered the fine tomb raised to Raftery and I think she took Quinn with her home to Coole, the place she lived.]

The passage suggests Hyde was not one of the house guests at Coole during Quinn's visit. In fact he was, but not in 1900, for Quinn did not make his first visit to Coole until 1902 when he went to the Killeenan *feis* with Jack Yeats on 31 August.[47] Quinn went on to Coole and so too did Hyde. Indeed, Hyde was at Coole during every one of Quinn's visits. 'One of the chief charms of my repeated visits to Coole lay in the stores of good talk and anecdotes by Yeats and Hyde, who were there at the time of each of my visits.'[48]

While *The Playboy of the Western World* was responsible for the final break between the Gaelic League and the Abbey Theatre, there was always a tension between the League and the Theatre movement over the idea of a national literature in English. Much of this tension is reflected in the pages of *An Claidheamh Soluis* for the spring and summer of 1899. Building a popular language movement, and organizing support for the language against the attack from Trinity's Mahaffy and Atkinson, the pages of *An Claidheamh Soluis* repeated the argument that the Irish language was essential to Irish nationalism. When the Irish Literary Theatre made its Dublin debut on 8 May 1899, the question of Irish literature in English was raised in the 6 May 1899 'Notes'. In her straightforward way, Lady Gregory wrote to Hyde and MacNeill to protest and to call for cooperation between the two movements:

I am a little anxious about the attacks that continue to be made by correspondents in the *Claidheamh Soluis*. I know so well what delight there always is across the channel when any new split or quarrel appears in Ireland and yet this can't be said to be a quarrel, for it is on one side only. I know with what constant and warm admiration Mr. Martyn and Mr. Yeats and others of our own writers speak of the work of the Gaelic League, but these letters would give the impression that they kept aside from it. We all want each other's help in Ireland, and it will be a very great pity if such men are forced out of sympathy with the Gaelic Movement.[49]

In spite of soothing private letters from Hyde, the attacks on he Irish Literary Theatre continued. The 20 May 1899 'Notes' had five items critical of the Theatre; Yeats and Moore, called 'a libeller of life in Ireland', were attacked personally. In the same issue Pearse wrote a letter dismissing Yeats as '. . . a mere English poet of the third or fourth rank' but touching on the real issue, 'If we once admit the Irish literature in English idea, then the language movement is a mistake. Mr. Yeats's precious "Irish" Literary Theatre may, if it develops, give the Gaelic League more trouble than the Atkinson-Mahaffy combination.'[50]

Personal criticism stopped but in its report of Yeats's Trinity lecture on a national literature in English, *An Claidheamh Soluis* (10 June 1899), called the Irish Literary Theatre a 'hinderance' to the language revival. The playwright T. C. Murray wrote to defend Yeats and the Irish Literary Theatre; MacNeill responded with two thoughtful editorials 'What is Irish National Literature?' in the 1 July and 8 July issues once again arguing that language was the basis of national identity. D. P. Moran's conciliatory 'The Gaelic and Other Movement' (8 July 1899) pointed out that the goals of both the Gaelic League and the Irish Literary Theatre were compatible, but it was Yeats himself who demonstrated this compatibility in his speech to the Kiltartan Branch of the Gaelic League which concluded:

Every nation has its own duty in the world, its own message to deliver, and that message was to a considerable extent bound up with the language. The nations make a part of one harmony, just as the colours in the rainbow make a part of one harmony of beautiful colour. It is our duty to keep the message, the colour which God has committed to us, clear and pure and shining.[51]

A 'Note' in the 5 August 1899 issue of *An Claidheamh Soluis* responded gracefully:

Mr. Yeats has done a real service to the movement by his speech at Gort. We make war on ideas not on individuals. No one could expect that writers who had written and spoken English only all their lives should give up such writing. But we could never admit that such work was Irish literature. To do so would be to give up the case of the League. Mr. Yeats's generous statement gives the *coup de grace* to the troublesome heresy; no smaller man will now maintain it, and the League will not have to expend force in combating it. We thank Mr. Yeats for having helped to clear the air, and we thank him also for his generous words of encouragement. A genuine poet sees ever into the heart of things and feels the truth.[52]

In February 1900, before the Irish Literary Theatre's second season, there was some renewed scepticism in *An Claidheamh Soluis* but a 3 March 1900 editorial 'Glimmerings of Dawn' celebrated the Irish Literary Theatre's promise of a play in Irish for the 1901 season. 'The announcement, too, that the first steps towards building up a Literary Theatre in the National Language have been taken will send a thrill of hope through every worker in the cause. Truly we are approaching the dawn.' The Irish Literary Theatre made good their promise with their 1901 production of *Casadh an tSugáin*.

While Lady Gregory defended the Irish Literary Theatre to Gaelic Leaguers, her own articles in *An Claidheamh Soluis* in 1901 suggest that she too was sympathetic to the principle that language was essential to nationality. Her article 'A Nation's Words' starts with the premise that the presence or absence of a word in a language is a revelation of national character. She offers examples of Irish words like *deoraidhe*, the word for 'mourner' which is also used for exile, and the article concludes with an offer of a book prize for the best list of Irish words that reflect Irish national character. Lady Gregory's article may have been influenced by the work of Miss Borthwick whose winning *Oireachtas* essay in 1897 on the topic 'The Influence of Language on Nationality' said that every language had special meaning for the people using its words and phrases, and that these meanings do not translate easily into other languages.[53]

Lady Gregory further demonstrated her belief in language as the informing principle of nationality when she translated Alphonse Daudet's story 'The Last Class' from the French for *An Claidheamh Soluis*. Set in Alsace-Lorraine, it describes a French schoolmaster's

last lesson on the day it is decreed that German will henceforth be
the language of instruction in the district. It concludes:

Then M. Hamel began to speak to us of the French language, saying that
it was the most beautiful language of the world — the clearest, the most
solid; that we must keep it up among ourselves and never forget it,
because, when a people falls into bondage, as long as it keeps its own
language it keeps the key of its prison.[54]

Certainly then, the relationship between the Irish language and
national character and a national literature was the spirit behind
Lady Gregory's interest in a dramatic movement in the Irish
language. She wrote in *Our Irish Theatre*, 'in the beginning we
dreamed of a national drama arising in Gaelic'.[55] Yeats addressed
himself to that dream in the February 1900 issue of *Beltaine* when
he wrote, 'We are anxious to get plays in Irish and can [sic] we do
so will very possibly push our work into the western counties
where it would be an important help to that movement for the
revival of the Irish language on which the life of the nation may
depend'.[56]

First there was talk of an Irish language dramatic company.
Yeats wrote Lady Gregory from Sligo in May 1901, 'I brought a
man to Moore to propose a Gaelic dramatic touring company.
Moore is excited about the scheme, and will try to get money for
it.'[57] Nothing came of the scheme, but the idea was raised again in
1904.[58] It was a response to the Gaelic Leaguers calling for more
plays in Irish as well as to Synge's scheme to form an Irish language
company with Blasket Islanders. Lady Gregory thought seriously
about her part in such a project. She wrote to W. B. Yeats, 'If I
come round to the Gaelic scheme I should be inclined to work it
up in Galway writing plays for them instead of for productions in
English. I might be more useful to the country. But I won't do it
till I feel the want is a real one and not an artificial one.'[59]

In spite of Synge's enthusiasm for staging plays in the Irish
language with the Blasket Islanders, he was regarded by Gaelic
Leaguers — even before *The Playboy of the Western World* — as
the author of plays unpopular with nationalists. When the Abbey
produced *The Playboy* in January 1907, it was not just the play
itself that was offensive but the Abbey's handling of the riot —
calling in the police against Irishmen and taking them to a 'foreign
court' — further outraged nationalists. Pearse did not excuse
Leaguers who rioted. In his article 'The Passing of Anglo-Irish

Drama' in February 1907 he warned that they reinforced Synge's representation of the Irish as a lawless and violent people and urged, instead, a boycott of the Abbey by Gaelic Leaguers.

Lady Gregory, who didn't like the play herself, defended the *Playboy* out of loyalty to the Abbey and to the principle of artistic freedom, but of the three directors, she suffered in the most personal way for her support of the play. She had been admired for the work she'd done for the language by the League; indeed, the reviewer of an exhibition of Jack Yeats's pictures organized by Lady Gregory praised her saying 'Níl Gaedheal i nEireann is fearr 'ná an bhaintighearna' (There isn't a better Gael in Ireland than the Lady).[60] That she would defend such a play hurt and angered her friends in the language movement. She suffered most in her own part of the world where the Gort District Council boycotted her, forbidding the school children to attend her holiday celebrations at Coole. While they were eventually reconciled, the ban was in effect for at least a year for she wrote on St. Stephen's Day in 1907, 'The workhouse children had not been allowed to come for their usual day at Coole because I had refused to take off Synge's Playboy of the Western World during the riot in Dublin'.[61]

While her primary commitment was to the Abbey, Lady Gregory continued to be loyal to the Gaelic League — even after the *Playboy* row. Writing to Yeats in September 1916, she said, 'I can not but be glad all this trouble turns you back to Ireland. I have something of the same feeling; my thoughts turning to the Gaelic League if the theatre should slip away.'[62] Paradoxically, it was the Gaelic Leaguer Eoin MacNeill who saved the Abbey from slipping away. In February 1923, as Minister for Education in the first Free State government, MacNeill received Lady Gregory and Yeats, listened to their concern about the Abbey's financial stability, and proposed a subsidy for the Abbey on the basis of its education work, its teaching of acting and dramatic writing.

That year Lady Gregory saw the plays produced by an Irish language drama group at the Abbey; she regretted that Hyde was not present to see them and that Synge did not live to see *The Shadow of the Glen* in Irish. In February 1924 she was pleased to see a call for an Irish translation of *The White Cockade* from the Dublin drama critic who reviewed the Irish plays at the Abbey. *The white Cockade* was not translated, but she lived to see *The Rising of the Moon* translated into Irish by Sean MacGiollarnath in 1929 for the Taibhdhearc, Galway's Irish language theatre. The Abbey has since produced Irish translations of *The Rising of the Moon* (1952) and *The Gaol Gate* (1966).

Lady Gregory kept up her interest in translation from the Irish until the end of her life. She translated Pearse's 'Mise Eire' in 1922. She noted in her journal in February 1923, that she had read An tAthair Pádraig de Brún's (Father Brown's) translation of Shelley's 'Ode to the West Wind' but preferred her Shelley in English. His translation of the Gospels into Irish, however, was a particular comfort to her in her last years. She mentioned it three times in her journals and in a letter to T. J. Kiernan, her adviser in tax matters, she said, 'My first morning reading is now Father Brown's translation of the Gospel — he has sewn the story together very skilfully — but it is more difficult Irish than *An t-Oileánach* — which I am at the end of — it is a delight.'[63] Through Kiernan she met Robin Flower whose translations from the Irish she admired. In her diary for 11 May 1929, she praised the new translations from the Irish.

Scholars and poets have taken up the Irish translations. Robin Flower with his Scholarship, his form; Stephens with his elfish and lovely genius. My delving is no longer needed, the experts have taken it in hand.[64]

As she looked back on her lifetime, she took particular pride in her own work for the language and for the movement she felt brought most dignity to Ireland. In January 1922 her old friend Wilfrid Scawen Blunt praised her work saying, 'I have always felt that you have done more for Ireland than anyone else. You showed its poetry and beauty, you destroyed that association of vulgarity and ridicule with its people.' She replied, 'It is to the Gaelic League that praise belongs.'[65] The next year she wrote that she agreed with what Michael Collins had written about that Gaelic league. 'Irish history will recognise in the birth of the Gaelic League in 1893 the most important event in the nineteenth century, but in the whole history of our nation it did more than any other movement to restore the national pride, honour and self-respect.'[66] Recalling her own work for the language, she said with uncharacteristic self-satisfaction, 'I sometimes think with a little pride that when Michael Collins and Eamonn De Valera were in their short jackets going to school or marching from it, I was spending time and money and energy bringing back the Irish among my own people.'[67]

An old countryman said of Lady Gregory to Yeats, 'She has been like a serving maid among us'.[68] Her work for the Gaelic League, for the language, as well as for all things Irish was characterised by loyalty, enthusiasm and energy. She served two literary traditions: the Irish as well as the Anglo-Irish; she founded an Irish theatre with Yeats, and she faithfully recorded the oral tradition of the Ireland of her time in what she called 'The Book of the People'.

LADY GREGORY AND SEAN O'CASEY: AN UNLIKELY FRIENDSHIP REVISITED

RONALD AYLING

On the face of it, it was an unlikely as well as an unusual friendship. Though relatively short-lived — lasting in effect from the spring of 1923 until the quarrel between O'Casey and the Abbey Theatre directorate broke out in April 1928 — their acquaintance very quickly developed into a friendship with an unusual degree of mutual warmth, sympathetic understanding and high professional regard.[1]

In his survey of O'Casey scholarship in the MLA publication, *Recent Research on Anglo-Irish Writers*, David Krause fairly sums up what I tried to achieve in an essay on O'Casey and the Abbey Theatre printed in *Sean O'Casey: Centenary Essays* in 1980:

Ronald Ayling's article tends to minimize the influence the Abbey Theatre directors had on O'Casey's early career. He feels that in a practical sense O'Casey received more help and encouragement from Lennox Robinson than is realized, that Lady Gregory's exaggerated influence was more emotional than literary, and that in the final accounting 'O'Casey soon outgrew the playwriting possibilities of the Abbey directorate.'[2]

Subsequently, he goes on to say, of Mary FitzGerald's splendid essay in the same collection of centenary articles:

Mary FitzGerald uses the unpublished sections of Lady Gregory's journal in the Berg Collection to reveal some new insights into the literary friendship of O'Casey and Lady Gregory. . . . This paper strongly modifies Ayling's view of Lady Gregory's influence on O'Casey.[3]

Dr FitzGerald's article, 'Sean O'Casey and Lady Gregory: the Record of a Friendship',[4] is indeed a fine and well-balanced re-assessment of both their private and public relations. It is undoubtedly the best study of the subject that has been written to date, though Elizabeth Coxhead's chapter entitled 'Sean O'Casey', in her pioneering biography *Lady Gregory: A Literary Portrait*,[5] continues to be a necessary introduction.

The present note, far from challenging FitzGerald's estimate, is meant to complement it in essentials, while adding a few details to the overall picture (including four hitherto unpublished letters from O'Casey to Lady Gregory) and qualifying a few minor particulars. I do not think that her writings really modify my view of the friendship between (in Krause's words) 'two seemingly contrary yet specially compatible people'. In my centenary essay I acknowledged that Lady Gregory was O'Casey's best friend on the Board and that there was something special about their friendship, but I was concerned to argue that 'too much reverential attention' has been paid to Lady Gregory's part in O'Casey's success as a playwright and to her critical acumen in telling him that his 'strong point was characterisation'. A. C. Edwards, in an article on 'The Lady Gregory Letters to Sean O'Casey', repeats the common belief that 'Lady Gregory . . . was the first to give encouragement to an unknown product of the Dublin slums whose ink was made from the lead of indelible pencils'.[6] The story about the pencils is correct but the first encouragement was given by Lennox Robinson. There is no evidence that Lady Gregory ever read the first two plays submitted by O'Casey to the Abbey; she did not see *The Shadow of a Gunman* till after it had been accepted for production there; *Nannie's Night Out* was accepted and revised by O'Casey in response to suggestions made by Robinson before she read the typescript; and, indeed, by this time in her long association with the Abbey she appears to be less and less concerned with everyday matters and to be the last of the theatre's directors to read newly submitted scripts, even from recognised Abbey playwrights as O'Casey was by then.

Robert G. Lowery, in starting a new annual publication devoted to O'Casey criticism, went so far as to say:

Was Lady Gregory the founder of O'Casey studies? Perhaps so. Her famous statement about the strength of O'Casey's work was such an acute observation that it has yet to be successfully challenged or refuted. No one will ever mistake Lady Gregory for an academic scholar, but there is no denying that her insight was in the best tradition of literary criticism or that it has been the basis for much of what has been called O'Casey scholarship for nearly sixty years.[7]

Two things should be said by way of response: firstly, that overemphasis on characterisation to the detriment of all else has plagued O'Casey criticism for far too long and, secondly, that what intrigued Lady Gregory in O'Casey's apprentice works (to judge by her written comments at this time) was as much the drama of ideas, the conflict of beliefs in what were clearly ideologically-orientated dramas, as anything else. Of the one and only apprentice play of his that she read and assessed before any of his plays were produced — *The Crimson in the Tricolour* — she wrote:

It is the expression of ideas that makes it interesting . . . and no doubt the point of interest for Dublin audiences . . . I feel that there is no personal interest worth developing, but that with as much as possible of those barren parts cut, we might find a possible play of ideas in it.

That extract comes from her original written summary;[8] her subsequent oral remarks, praising his characterisation, obviously went home to him, initially at least, and it can certainly be argued that this element is predominant in the trilogy of major plays first staged by the Abbey, especially in *The Shadow of a Gunman* and *Juno and the Paycock*. Yet even in those works one can see that the recurrent petty squabbles and often absurd disputes reflect, however farcically, the most serious ideological issues at the heart of the national struggle. Indeed, as early as *The Plough and the Stars* there is a determined attempt to control exuberant individual characters at times in response to larger thematic concerns; while characterisation remains important in this drama, the overall emphasis eventually falls upon the tragedy of the group rather than of the individual. Later plays developed this trend, though O'Casey's delight in idiosyncratic individuals and their outlandish behaviour and speech remained constant throughout his life.

St. John Ervine best summed up the greatest help that Lady Gregory gave Sean O'Casey when he wrote, in *The Theatre in My Time*, that without the assistance of W. B. Yeats and her in their creation and maintenance of the Abbey Theatre, writers like J. M. Synge, T. C. Murray, Lennox Robinson and O'Casey 'would have found no place for their plays and little inducement to write'.[9] In a letter, written on 2 April 1928 (ironically, but a few days before *The Silver Tassie* was rejected), Lady Gregory told O'Casey:

But one of the comforting things I sometimes take to rest on is this of your great success, so good for us all — and for Ireland. And there comes in with this a little grain of pride in the little finger-touch of help I was once able to give you in your early playwriting days.

While one agrees that it was little more than a 'finger-touch' (though considerably more than that when combined with Lennox

Robinson's advice and encouragement), the active support and perpetual interest that she showed in his life as well as his work once he had become an Abbey playwright was of a great deal more value to him, it seems to me. They shared a great many more interests and values than is commonly acknowledged though a number of his later non-dramatic writings were eventually to pay tribute to these affinities while the character of Dame Hatherleigh in *Oak Leaves and Lavender*, though clearly a composite figure with some very un-Gregorian idiosyncrasies, undoubtedly owes something to her indomitable characteristics.[10]

Sean O'Casey, in his many retrospective writings about Lady Gregory,[11] seems to have been more aware of the incongruities in the relationship than she ever appeared to acknowledge. Once O'Casey had become an Abbey playwright, with the brief appearance of his *The Shadow of a Gunman* at the very end of the 1922–23 Abbey season (four performances from 9 to 12 April 1923), Lady Gregory seems to have had no doubt whatsoever about his importance. She took every occasion to encourage and to draw out the fledgeling playwright, still an irregularly employed manual labourer when first she knew him; their discussions ranged over a wide field of topics, including domestic arrangements, his diet (he lived alone and cooked his own meals) and dental care as well as literary and cultural issues. There is little doubt that she put herself out to get to know him and to introduce him to like-minded people whom he would not ordinarily have met. Indeed, she took every opportunity to talk with him personally, drawing him for instance into introspective conversations (probably much to his relief) even at a supposedly literary 'at home' at W. B. Yeats's residence, and, perhaps because there was something very motherly about her and he still grieved over the loss of his own mother, he opened his heart to her in a way that he had seldom if ever done before, and which he was not to do again until, a few years later, he fell in love with the young woman who was to become his wife for the remaining thirty-seven years of his life.

Lady Gregory's journals for the three full years from April 1923 until March 1926 record a number of fascinating discussions with O'Casey and also scraps of gossip that, all told, are fuller and more accurate sources of information than any other about his early life and his opinions as well as about those three years in question, an extremely important period in his literary career and in that of the

Abbey Theatre itself. This was, after all, the time when his playwriting talent first flowered publicly; yet he was, from the very beginning, suspicious of the almost instantaneous popularity of his first two major plays on the Abbey's boards, and tended to trust only the judgements of those people (like Lennox Robinson and Lady Gregory) who had seen merit in the plays of his pre-production apprenticeship. It was also that taxing time in the Abbey's history when the then twenty-year-old theatre faced almost imminent bankruptcy and closure, from which fate — according to Yeats himself — the institution was rescued only by the box office success of O'Casey's writings. Subsequently, it became the recipient of a government grant that was to become an annual subsidy; however, but for O'Casey's advent there would probably have been no Abbey Theatre to be the first theatre in the English-speaking world to receive official support as a national cultural institution.

It is apparent from a host of antagonistic reactions to Lady Gregory's personality that have been recorded over the years that she did not often unbend herself except within a small circle of family and friends. Yet, though there would appear to be huge disparities between the poorly-dressed playwright with a Dublin accent thick enough to be cut with a knife and the imperious-looking Victorian aristocrat always formidably dressed in mourning, a deep sense of empathy and an intuitive understanding bound them together from very early in their acquaintanceship. They always had far more in common than anyone would easily imagine.

On many occasions in her journals Lady Gregory shows her love of and sympathy for the ordinary people, particularly those of her own country world in Clare and Galway. The greatest boast written to herself there is her pride in the loyalty and love of her fellow Connaught men and women. One of the neighbouring landed gentry told her, on his eviction from his property by the Republicans during the Troubles: 'There is no danger for you. You have always been on the side of the people.' Her love of children and working people were other traits that she shared with the tenement playwright. 'I do like meeting workers', she confided to the pages of her journal in an entry for 24 November 1928; and sometime in November 1927 (her letter omits the day) she tells O'Casey with pride that, having seen seven well-acted performances of *Juno and the Paycock* within a week in company with well-filled houses, 'the Abbey is a "Peoples Theatre" '. She meant it, too; the boastfulness in the description may be compared to the attitude of W. B. Yeats who, as early as 1919, in a letter to Lady Gregory conceded that their little theatre had indeed become a People's Theatre but that he strongly resented this development, desiring as he did a more exclusive hieratic audience. Another element that instinctively drew her close to O'Casey was the strong rebel sympathies that they both shared, for all his many criticisms of the official nationalistic movement. Looking back on her life in her late years, she wrote that she had been ' "a rebel" with the Nationalists all through — more than they know or my dearest realised'.

In his person as in his writings O'Casey seems to have embodied some such experience for her; in seeking to get close to him she also recognised that she got closer to the vision and (it must be admitted) the prejudices of a man of the people, who, for all the unusual degree of self-education and dedicated commitment to literature, truly represented the ordinary man in the street. In O'Casey's Dublin plays, the Abbey stage reflected for the first time such experience and helped enlarge the theatre's playgoing public that had been something of a coterie audience for many years. Though fewer working class people attended than either Jim Larkin or Sean O'Casey would have liked (Larkin in the 1920s and 1930s often encouraged his fellow trade unionists to visit the Abbey whenever they could afford to do so), O'Casey's popularity did definitely extend the class orientation of the audience; his work also appealed to Dubliners of all classes who, sated by the Abbey's peasant-based repertoire, found fresh invigoration as well as the shock of an unexpected recognition in his Dublin character types, with their inimitable idiom and inexhaustible fund of humorous stories and repartee.

One can understand, moreover, why Lady Gregory would respond so favourably when she recorded that the worker-playwright's 'desire and hope' in 1924 (as throughout his life), was 'to lead the workers into a better life, in interest in reading, in drama especially', particularly when this aspiration was linked with O'Casey's belief in the Abbey's necessary part in this mission. 'All the thought in Ireland for years past has come through the Abbey', he told her in April of 1923, 'you have no idea what an education it has been to the country.'

The voluminous nature of Sean O'Casey's writings to and (after her death) about Lady Gregory is in itself eloquent testimony to the strength and longevity of his feelings and to that spark of deep understanding that undoubtedly passed between them. It was an affinity — personal as well as professional — that he had seldom if ever experienced in the four decades of his life that preceded their acquaintance, and one which he was not to experience again for another decade — not until he met the American drama critic George Jean Nathan in New York in 1934. Eventually, his relationship with Nathan, wholly professional at first, was to bloom into a full, firm and warm (though mostly epistolary) friendship, based primarily on their mutual regard for each other's writings; the playwright's subsequent correspondence with the critic, which lasted until Nathan's death in the late 1950s, becomes one of the glories of his non-dramatic writings. Up to 1930, however, his correspondence with Lady Gregory is the major literary as well as human highlight of his non-theatrical work. Sean wrote at least forty-four letters to her, of which forty are to be found in the first volume of his collected correspondence superbly edited by David Krause; in the same volume are to be found twenty-three letters to him (there were undoubtedly many more that have been lost or untraced) from one whom he was pleased to acknowledge (in the words of Bernard Shaw) as the indispensable 'charwoman of the Abbey'.[12]

The range of interests traversed in Sean O'Casey's letters to Lady Gregory and the depth of emotional commitment manifested in them are indicative of the very high value he placed upon their friendship. Two examples must suffice: the criticism of Upton Sinclair's play (literary as well as political) and the salute to the Abbey movement in his letter dated October 1924 (pp. 118–119 in the first volume of his *Letters*) and the personal tribute to Lady Gregory in his epistle of 28 March 1928 (pp. 232–233), in which — significantly — he invokes the kindred spirit of his mother, are both especially fine pieces of writing. That is not all, by a long chalk: the extent as well as the nature of his later reflections upon her, written during the period that intervened between her death in 1932 and his own thirty-two years later, speak strongly of the long-lasting remorse that he experienced for having made no real attempt to grasp the hand of friendship that she re-extended to him once the public squabble over the Abbey's rejection of *The Silver Tassie* was over. The most important of these retrospective pieces are undoubtedly those to be found in the last three volumes of his autobiography and, to a lesser extent, in two articles reprinted in the posthumous volume entitled *Blasts and Benedictions;* the autobiographical recollections — and especially the two chapters devoted to her memory in *Inishfallen, Fare Thee Well* — realise in poignant fashion some of the most tender and touching moments in an extraordinarily long and diverse prose narrative.[13]

Mary FitzGerald acknowledges the power of O'Casey's portrayal of 'Blessed Bridget O'Coole', as it appears in *Inishfallen, Fare Thee Well* (Elizabeth Coxhead had earlier likened it to a Rembrandt portrait in words):

His is the loveliest portrait of her written by a contemporary, and the one closest in spirit to the Lady Gregory of the diaries and journals, full of laughter and enthusiasm for life, skilled and dedicated at her work, and endlessly giving of her time and energy.[14]

Like a number of Irish commentators, however, she dislikes several other features:

But O'Casey cannot resist noting her imperfections, partly, one feels, to flesh out the portrait and give it more credibility, but also apparently to blunt the edge of her critical taste and take the polish off her expertise. The 'lisp' he assigns her is really nothing more than the hard-edged 'd' of the Connacht-flavoured English she grew up with. It can still be heard today in the region. But it has the effect of diminishing her stature as well as of livening her speech. It seems to distance her from him, even when they are closest.[15]

This aspect is indeed a matter of taste, and Dr FitzGerald's response is not by any means a singular one; Roger McHugh writes likewise of the dramatist's autobiographical comments:

They do not lack criticism of her; and of her reading — he once caught her reading *Peg O' My Heart* and was exasperated by her enthusiasm for a stupid play full of sentimentality about the workers — or of her odd manner of speech, which he mimics somewhat tediously; but he clearly admired her faculty for putting him at his ease, her practical services to the local people and her undoubted knowledge of and intimacy with them.[16]

Elizabeth Coxhead has ably defended O'Casey's use of the story about Lady Gregory's reading of *Peg O' My Heart*, showing that he had no offensive purpose in mind. The same is true for the lisp that he has her speak (he called it 'her charming lisp' in *Sunset and Evening Star*, the final volume of his autobiography); its use may be overdone in his narrative (as the amount of phonetically rendered Cockney speech is overdone to some extent in both *The*

Plough and The Stars and *The Silver Tassie* and the West Country idiom in *Oak Leaves and Lavender*) but it is not really meant to ridicule her manner of speech.

It is not generally known that there are several unique features about O'Casey's portrait of Lady Gregory in *Inishfallen, Fare Thee Well*, the fourth volume of his autobiographical sequence. Firstly, it was written quite independently of this book (seven years beforehand, in fact); he was completing the second volume, *Pictures in the Hallway*, while it was being composed in January and February of 1942. Secondly, the entire episode — which was later to be the basis of two chapters in *Inishfallen* — was written as a first person narrative, which is true for none of the later autobiographical writings after an initial trial experiment using a first person narrator for early incidents in the chapters that were originally envisaged for the first volume, *I Knock at the Door*. Thirdly, this long essay, originally published as a first person narrative under the title, 'The Lady of Coole' (though his first title was 'I Come to Coole'), was later adapted to fit the third person narrative of the rest of the autobiography, and (revised and expanded) became the individual chapters entitled 'Blessed Brigid O'Coole' and 'Where Wild Swans Nest'.

No other autobiographical incidents have as complicated a genesis; and such an origin has a strong influence on the spirit and tone of the writing as well as upon its style and form. 'The Lady of Coole' is more mellow in mood than the two chapters it eventually became. There is none of the disagreeable side to the relationship in it; this only enters into the narrative when he incorporates it into the telling of his own life story, when accounts of back-stage intrigues at the Abbey, the riots over *The Plough and the Stars* and the internal quarrel with the directors over *The Silver Tassie* surface disconcertingly into his description of his relationship with Lady Gregory. In 'The Lady of Coole' the focus is on her and his own relationship with her; other figures, however important in the Abbey, remain subordinate or off-stage. The opening to the essay shows this clearly, when compared with the beginning of the comparable story, 'Blessed Brigid O'Coole'. Before the memorable first impression of her that is common to both accounts, the stage is set (by the passage I have italicised in the following quotation, which was omitted from the revised version) and incidental figures are kept anonymous so that the emphasis remains throughout on Lady Gregory; the 'long thin man' is identified as Lennox Robinson in the autobiographical chapter, but it is surely more effective to keep him nameless:

I had seen Lady Gregory sometime before, when I had been called to come and see her about an Abbey Theatre's first production of a play of mine. I had set out, clattering proudly through the paved Dublin streets; had passed through the richer entrance of the theatre for the first time; up the narrow staircase, and into the Secretary's Office. A long thin man had risen darkly before me in the dim light, waving a thin hand towards the far end of the narrow room, murmuring, this is Lady Gregory.
Slowly she rose from an office chair, and came forward, her eyes gleaming, hand outstretched, a deep smile on her firm, rugged, and rather brownish face. Dressed in black she was, a simple brooch under her throat, a touch of something white under a long black silk veil that covered her grey hair, flowing gracefully behind, half way down her back — an elegant nun of a new order, a blend of the Lord Jesus Christ and of Puck, an order that Ireland had never known before, and wasn't likely to know again for a long time to come.[17]

'The Lady of Coole' was written at the very time that the Irish Forestry Commission had announced the imminent destruction of the manor house at Coole, and this no doubt contributed to the enhanced mellowness of the portraiture. It is a valedictory salute to the lady of the house, embodying much that was later to appear in *Inishfallen, Fare Thee Well*, but also giving more anecdotal material than could be allowed into the later narrative. The following comic episode is an example; its subsequent omission is regrettable:

— Ah, dere you are, Lady Gregory said, coming up to me and pausing a moment, watching the sun go down over the lands of the Kings of Burren. She went on to the long glass-walled vineries, and came back with a bunch of purple grapes for me. They had an imperial look, but were sour to the tongue, and set my teeth on edge, though I managed to keep my face calm before her peering eyes, and murmur out that they were lovely.
— Oh! what a job we had detting dem back to dood condition again! she said.

An expert had tended the vines long ago, but he was expensive and a common gardener, friend to Lady Gregory, had firmly volunteered to take the vines in charge. He was a man who had gone to a far country in one boat, coming back again in the next, nearly. He constantly chanted into her half willing ear that he could tend them as well as the other fellow, ay, betther than anyone.

— Sam, Sam, deyre berry tender tings, and delicate to mind.

— Isnt that what I'm afther tellin' you all th' time me lady? Isnt it meself that knows more'n I'm able to tell about th' figaries of growth in th' growin' o' grapes? Th' one thing youve got to guard against, with their twistin' here an' their twistin' there, is not to lose your temper.

— Oh, its more than dat, Sam; it's more than a little loss of demper.

— Sure, dont I know that, me lady? That's only th' beginnin'; but a mighty fine beginnin'. You just keep your eyes off the grape threes, me lady, an' I'll go bail I'll bring you a crop of grapes, the like of which was never seen in this counthry since th' year o' one!

— I dont like de word crop given to grapes, said Lady Gregory; it doesnt seem a suitable name for the elegant purple fruit.

— Sure, it couldnt be more unsuitable, me lady; but suitable or unsuitable, it's a good name, an' has its meanin'. An' it's afther sayin' all this I am, th' way you'd hand th' grape threes over to a widely-minded man, who, in a foreign counthry, went knee-deep an shoulder-high through plants an' bushes growin' conthrairy to th' methods of man, only showin' blossoms an' flingin' out fruit be th' dint of sthrivin' afther their knowledge an' their nursin'.

Hiding her doubts deep in her heart, she handed over the grape trees to Sam, and went away on a long, long journey. She came back, still doubtful, but confirming her faith in Sam by imagining grapes hanging thick in her vineries, more richly purple than ever, and puffing out their silken skins with the winey juice inside them.

— Well, how are de vineries? she asked of John, her coachman, driving her along the Gort road to Coole.

— What way would they be but thrivin', me lady? Be all accounts, theyre growin' as they never grew before.

— Well, how are de vineries? she asked of Brigid, and she stepping over the threshold of Coole.

— An' how would they be, me lady, but doin' grand? Be all accounts theyre growin' as they never grew before.

— I dont like dat phrase of dem growing as dey nebber grew before, said Lady Gregory, with a sparkle of anger in her eyes; it sounds too dood to be true. I'll run down to see dem, before I do anoder ting!

Off she went at a run to where they were; and there they were — a sight to see and a sight to remember: They had shot up like magic beanstalks; long, gaunt, angular stems, they had pushed everything aside in their hurry upwards, and had now lifted the glass roof a foot or more above the walls. Bare of fruit they were, and almost bare of leaf, desolate they looked and woebegone.

When the expert came again, he shook his head sadly.

— It will be long, me lady, before we can get them to start life all over again.

— Dat derrible man, Sam; oh! dat derrible man! And all of dem telling me dey were growing as dey nebber grew before.

— Looks as if they were right, said the expert.[18]

At the time O'Casey wrote 'The Lady of Coole' he was living in the midst of the German aerial bombardments of the Second World War that followed hard upon the Battle of Britain in the skies over the south of England. The immediacy of this experience lies behind the poignant recollection of an incident that had occurred to him in Coole eighteen years earlier, where the mistress of the house called to mind her airman son killed in the First World War:

Passing through a room with the blue mountains of the Barony of Loughrea nodding in at the great bow windows, I was shown some of Coole's treasures; and paused in front of a picture of a broadshouldered young man, with an open and courageous face.
— My dear son, she murmured softly; my dear, dear son; lost leading his air squadron over the Italian battlefield. For months and months I had dreaded it, for I knew de German planes were ahead of ours.
I glanced aside, sympathetically at her, and saw that holy tears were trickling down the deep furrows of her tawny cheeks.
— Dear lady, dear friend, I said, softly, pressing her arm, the fall of a young man is a common thing now, and may be still a common thing in years to come; a common thing for young and hopeful life to be cut down before it has had time to blossom and shed its seed. It is for us who have been left standing to turn our thought into a way of deliverance from the cruel and wasteful banishment of our younger·life, with all its lovely visions barely outlined, becoming when they go, a tinted breath of memory.
She forced her head higher, murmuring, we must be brave, and fence our sorrow away so that no shadow may come upon those singing and dancing around us. Come, let us go for a walk in de woods.

The episode is recalled in almost the same words in *Inishfallen, Fare Thee Well*, but the changes, slight though they are, do make a difference; a simpler and more effective experience is in fact realised in this earlier version. One would like to see 'The Lady of Coole' reprinted; it is, arguably, the finest prose portrait of Lady Gregory in existence.

The earliest of the four letters by O'Casey to Lady Gregory that have surfaced since David Krause published the first volume of his edition of *The Letters of Sean O'Casey* is undated, but it was almost certainly written in the autumn of 1924. Lady Gregory had several conversations with him in November of that year about contemporary and older Irish political ballads that she was collecting for the book that was eventually to be published two years later under the title of *The Kiltartan History Book*. Her journal for 24 November records a conversation between them on this subject, during which he offered to send her a copy of his Great War anti-recruiting ballad, 'The Grand Oul' Dame Britannia'. About this time, then, he hurriedly scribbled the following note in longhand on a sheet of plain paper (with the only hint of its date the cryptic preface of 'Monday') as an enclosure to a book I have been unable to trace:

Dear Lady Gregory —

I am enclosing a little book containing a number of Ballads, which may be useful to you. I have marked those that deal with contemporary events — one of them — 'The Flag on the G.P.O.' is by J. J. Walsh.
'The Red Flag' was not written by Jim Connolly as stated, but by Jim Connell. 'The White Cockade' was the air originally chosen, but the song is always sung to the air of 'Maryland'. 'The Call of Erin' was written by Jim Connolly, the Labour Leader.

Sincerely Yours
Sean O'Casey

P.S. I will keep a look-out for others.[19]

The second letter,[20] also written before the writer's quarrel with the Abbey Theatre, is similarly handwritten but bears the date of 'Jan. 6, 1928' and the address is the London home in which he wrote *The Silver Tassie*: that is, 19 Woronzow Road, St. John's Wood, N.W.8.

Dear Lady Gregory —
Here I am in a new home, simple, & just big enough to live in & take a little exercise. Busy trying to choose curtain colourings, & pick out the fair places on the walls for our few little pictures. I have now three pretty little reproductions of V. Van Gogh, one by Corot, two reproductions by Manet; Botticelli's 'Spring', Giorgione's 'Sleeping Venus'; & I am looking for a Daumier reproduction too.
We have a very pretty little garden at the back — about the size of Coole's Tennis Square — where a few flowers bloom, grass grows with some trees hedging the walls. A gardener comes twice a week to keep things trim, & does quite a lot of work for four shillings given every Sunday morning, & a pint of four arf ale every Saturday evening.

I have heard that W. B. Yeats's health isn't too good now, & I am very sorry for this. In a land overflowing with politicians a poet gone will not be missed making a double loss: the loss itself, & the powerlessness to feel the loss. Israel doth not know, my people doth not consider, always looking for the blazing fire, the rush of a big wind, the crashing earthquake, & deaf to the still small voice of colour & line & form in paint & poetry. When will they come to know that the artist is God in a burning bush? I wonder would you give to W. B. Yeats my most earnest wish that he will be quickly alright again.

I have finished the rough grouping of the dialogue of my new four act play, & expect to have the work finally ready by the end of March. The name I have given to the play is 'The Silver Tassie', & it deals with those who go out to the Great War & those who remain behind. The second act is in France & the whole of the dialogue, I think, will be chanted to a plainsong air or Gregorian chant that I will select later on. I am working now on the final draft of the first act.

I hope the Abbey is doing well, & that good audiences are filling the Houses.

And yourself — I hope you are well, & next time I go to Ireland, I must spend a day or two in Coole, & feel the wind that plays in Clare-Galway.

Very affectionately yours,
Sean

A third letter[21] is also handwritten on notepaper bearing the same printed address; dated 'Jan. 8th 1929', its tone only too clearly reveals the barely suppressed irritation and querulousness that was still a residue from the bitter public controversy that had raged over *The Silver Tassie* but a bare eight months previously. The letter is written in response to the receipt of a book that was presumably sent as a Christmas gift but was no doubt intended to be seen as a peace offering; at the very time it was written the playwright was engaged in a heated and protracted public argument with George Russell (A.E.) over art and art criticism:

Dear Lady Gregory —
I have been ill for the last few weeks with severe catharrh [sic] of the stomach, & am still very unwell, so that I will not ask you to forgive me for neglecting to say that I received the book you were thoughtful and kind enough to send to me. [Augustus] John is back from America, & I am sending on his copy to him today.

I don't think 'Days of Fear' is quite so beautiful a book as you seem to think, or as great a contribution to life as AE says it is — AE's making a lot of quaint mistakes lately — but it is the best thing Gallacher has yet written. I read it all some years ago when it appeared from week to week in 'The Republic'.

I was very glad to hear how fine F. J. McCormick was in King Lear. He has done some wonderful work, & the task of Lear must have been a terrible one compressed into a few rehearsals.

I hope next week to be able to go to the wonderful collection of Dutch painting[s] now in Burlington House here. Pity these should be shown in this den of titled incompetents, but that doesn't matter very much.

The baby is going from strength to strength. The doctor who brought him into the world, & who is an authority on babies, says he threatens to reproduce the gigantic stature of the Ancient Gaels. But, most important of all, he has a gleaming eye, a vivid mind & laughs a lot.

I sincerely hope you are well.

Affectionately Yours,
Sean

The fourth letter is almost certainly the last one that O'Casey wrote her; though it has remained unpublished till now, her reply (dated 30 October 1931) was printed by A. C. Edwards in his collection of 'The Lady Gregory Letters to Sean O'Casey' in *Modern Drama* for May 1965.[22] O'Casey's letter, handwritten on printed stationery ('Hillcrest, Chalfont St. Giles, Bucks.'), is dated 25 October 1931. Much more newsy and, indeed, conciliatory in tone, could it be that O'Casey (consciously or instinctively) was aware that Lady Gregory had but a few more months to live? Whether this was so or not, the letter is closer in spirit to those written before his break with her beloved Abbey Theatre. Perhaps getting away from the London house where *The Silver Tassie* had been written and in which he may have been constantly reminded that it was there too that he had also received the Abbey's letter of rejection (in an envelope addressed to him by her) may also have helped. The letter[23] reads as follows:

Dear Lady Gregory —

Above is now our new & permanent address. Stopping down here in a little cottage for a few weeks in the summer (such as it was) we liked the district very much, & decided, if possible, to settle down here for the next few years, if not for the rest of our natural lives. We hunted around continually, never waxing weary, for a suitable home, &, at last, Eileen ferreted out a compact, well built roomy one floor house, hidden away in a lovely garden, filled with beautiful shrubs, garlanded with lovely trees — I know more about trees now than I knew when I was down in Coole — with fruit and vegetable gardens, & backed by a very pretty cherry orchard. The house is on the crest of a hilly part of the Chilterns, near the village of Chalfont St. Giles, & only a few steps from Milton's Cottages; we are within easy walking distance of Beaconsfield, Stoke Poges, The

Chalfonts, Coleshill, Latimer, Amersham, Seer Green & the Households, all beautiful places which are only a few paces away from places as beautiful as themselves. Hillcrest is about 21 miles from London, & an hourly Bus brings us there, whenever we may wish to go, in less than an hour & twenty minutes. We have been here now for three weeks, & so far, I like the place sincerely. I seem to have forgotten to wish for the speed & the noise & the stir of the City. When we — or Eileen, rather — discovered the place, it was occupied, & we had to wait from June till October before we could take possession. I believe the delay was worth bearing, for the place & the surroundings are so pretty & uncommon that a place having similar attractions would be hard to find.

Barry Fitzgerald wrote recently — I got the letter yesterday — & told me you were troubled with rheumatism, & I am sorry to hear this, & hope you feel better now. I suppose the poor summer we had this year had something to do with it.

The Abbey Co must be very excited looking forward to their performances in America. I hope they may have a good time, artistically and financially. By the way, why didn't they or you list one of the big plays by Yeats or by Lady Gregory? The Shadowy Waters; The Image; Countess Kathleen; Aristotle's Bellows? Do you venture to put The New Gossoon, Professor Tim, Ever the Twain in front of these?

England is just now deciding what way she must vote, & Tuesday & Wednesday will see an overwhelming defeat of what is called a mad, red Bolshevist Party. Mr. Baldwin has said that 'we must now end this dangerous, unpatriotic, devilish power once & for all!' And many candidates have on their posters the slogan of 'Now or never'. So Mr. Baldwin pulls down the curtain. He thinks that M. M. Henderson, Lansbury, & Madam Bondfield are the Labour Movement. Imagine a man thinking he can end a power so imperishable that the Gates of Heaven can never prevail against it. Well, well. Remember me kindly to all at Coole. Brian's splendid, & growing up into a fine & vigorous boy.

                    Yours as Ever
                    Sean

'FRIENDSHIP IS THE ONLY HOUSE I HAVE':
LADY GREGORY AND W. B. YEATS

JOHN KELLY

In his autobiographical fragment, 'The Sunset of Fantasy', AE proposes that friendships are made according to a 'law of spiritual gravitation', and argues that his friends were 'drawn to me or I to them by some affinity of mood or identity of character'.[1] Given the extraordinary importance of the friendship between William Butler Yeats and Lady Gregory, not only to their own careers but also to the Irish literary and dramatic revival, we might be forgiven for speculating that they too were brought together by some such occult spiritual destiny. We should, however, resist such speculations as being at once too mysterious and too simplistic. This was a friendship that grew out of more worldly and more complex needs than are dreamt of in AE's philosophy, and one that was further complicated by strains and adjustments throughout its thirty-five year duration. The purpose of this study is to trace the elements of this relationship, its psychological, social, political, and artistic dimensions, and to examine its progress through time.

Timing was, as we shall see, of the utmost importance in getting the friendship started, for it had to attend upon a mutual recognition of shared interests that had not been possible until the late 1890s. Certainly it had not occurred at their first meeting in the summer of 1894 when Lady Gregory recorded briefly in her diary that she had met 'W. B. Yates', looking 'every inch a poet, though I think his prose "Celtic Twilight" is the best thing he has done'.[2] There is a suggestion here, common to those meeting Yeats for the first time, and not only the first, of pose. She, however, was unlikely to be over-impressed by a young poet no matter how decked out in poetical trappings for she had experience of the breed, having seen Browning plain and, as his mistress, Wilfrid Scawen Blunt perhaps even starker. Nor, evidently, was the poetry itself greatly to her taste; at this stage she would have found its heterodoxy and mysticism suspicious, its nationalistic tone dangerous, and its affinities with the decadent movement distasteful. *The Celtic Twilight*, with its simple stories and sketches of Irish country life, suited her much better and she would eventually come to imitate something of its manner and themes in her own more restrained collections of Irish folklore and beliefs. The first meeting was, then, worthy of record but not of great excitement; the pull of the 'spiritual gravitation' too weak to bring about another meeting until two years had elapsed.

Friendship, in the Yeatsian schema, is a relationship in which head and heart are in a measurable equilibrium: love a relationship in which the head is constantly at the mercy of the heart's overmastering irrationality. As in his poem 'Friends', friendship can be weighed in the mind, but love only experienced as it kicks the emotional scales over reason's measuring bar. In this sense his friendship with Lady Gregory is more susceptible to analysis and interpretation than his passion for Maud Gonne, but analysis and interpretation are by no means straightforward. We may begin by identifying the psychological, social, artistic and political imperatives that attracted them to each other, but we must not forget that these imperatives were intricate and sometimes paradoxical. The sex and age difference suggest that psychologically the friendship owes something to a mother-son relationship, and Susan Yeats's maternal shortcomings rendered her eldest child particularly susceptible to such an involvement. The social differences point to a hostess-protegé relationship, in which the worldly-wise lady of the big house takes up a gauche, unhappy but talented young man, and helps to bring him out and shape his career. Certainly Lady Gregory played this role, especially in the early days, and it was one that Yeats found congenial. Then there is the patron-artist relationship, in which Coole becomes a modern Penshurst or Urbino, where Lady Gregory presided over a gathering of geniuses:

> They came like swallows and like swallows went,
> And yet a woman's powerful character
> Could keep a swallow to its first intent . . .[3]

The benefits of such a rural salon to Yeats were incalculable, and are gratefully celebrated in his poetry. The arrangement also appealed to his sense of tradition since it allowed him to adopt the position of an Ancient Irish *fili* at the board of his lord, a position that not only suited his notion of decorum but also touched a more instinctive response: 'I think I was meant not for a master but for a servant . . . and so it is that all images of services are dear to me'.[4]

The relationships sketched here suggest a one-way process, an unreciprocated giving by Lady Gregory of maternal affection, of social assurance, of artistic purpose and freedom. But the friendship was also animated by alternating and compensatory movements. If Lady Gregory conferred a quasi-maternal affection, Yeats returned a quasi-filial regard and admiration which fulfilled one of her deep psychological needs. If she as hostess could introduce him to influential and useful members of the British and Irish establishments, he could bring her into artistic and literary circles that would otherwise have been closed to her. And if she as patron provided a salon and financial support for his art, he, after some initial reservations, encouraged and promoted her own ventures into literature and drama. Their literary and cultural interests were moreover complementary and mutually useful: she could help him to folklore and provide him with appropriate dialect when necessary, while he gave her advice on dramaturgy and helped her to shape her plays and other writings. The friendship was, then, held together by several double strands of shared and self interests: it was consequently flexible, highly tensile and resilient.

If the friendship flourished in London it was rooted in Ireland, and this dimension — which may be described in its larger terms as political — was a further source of strength. Both made Ireland crucial to their art, Yeats because he thought he would find there the passion and imagination that had disappeared elsewhere in Europe, she for more involved personal and economic reasons. Both were distanced from the Irish people by birth and religion, and yet both were seeking to establish an Irish identity at a period of intense national self-consciousness. It was the excitement of this enterprise that first brought them close, and the late 1890s became a time of shared and heady optimism. After the turn of the century sober realities intruded in a series of public controversies over Abbey Theatre policies and the Lane Pictures, but the hostility they faced from a new generation and a new class of Irish critics, writers and actors confirmed rather than lessened their sense of interdependence and mutual interests.

In her recent biography of Lady Gregory, Mary Lou Kohfeldt asserts that there was 'an emptiness at the heart of their union; they were using each other'.[5] Like much in her book this is too reductive and simplistic. That mutual attraction may also involve the recognition of mutual advantage by no means invalidates a friendship; nor need it lead to 'emptiness at the heart'. What, in any case, are we to understand by 'the heart' in this context? What was the central motive power which sustained the relationship through so many years? Dr. Kohfeldt does not tell us, any more than she defines what she means by 'using'. To pluck the heart out of the mystery of this friendship involves, as a preliminary, a close scrutiny of the psychological make-up of the two protagonists and an examination of the experiences which had shaped and modified their views up until their successful meeting in the summer of 1897.

*

In seeking a key to Lady Gregory's behaviour, we should do well to begin by meditating upon the paradoxes through which those who knew her tried to describe her nature. Yeats picked out a central paradox as he stood before her portrait in the Municipal Gallery:

> But where is the brush that could show anything
> Of all that pride and that humility?[6]

Pride and humility are usually placed at far ends of the emotional spectrum: in Lady Gregory, however, they appear to have been curiously intermixed. Yeats was attracted by both these aspects of her character. The humility, a product of what I describe later as her Esther Summerson complex, put her entirely at his service, as house-keeper, personal assistant, typist, and provisioner of food and money. Nor were its benefits merely physical; her constant attention and deference boosted him psychologically in days of public discouragement and self-doubt. In its more wholesome manifestations this humility became a studied *noblesse oblige*, characterized by a politic but not inauthentic series of charitable acts and sacrifices. But there is a less pleasant aspect, for its roots lay in the neglect she had suffered as a child, a deprivation which had found its compensation in the hero-worship of her unruly brothers. Being a girl, she learned that she could win affection from them by an outward and calculated subservience to their wishes and a subtle but persistent flattering of their male egos. In later life she could never exorcise this desperation of the deprived child, eager for approval and sensitive to unjust neglect, and it tips the 'Martha' element in her nature into a frequent and sometimes distasteful quest for praise and esteem, which leads her to interpolate her books of memoirs and reminiscences with reports of all the compliments, great and small, that were paid to her. Yeats was later to celebrate her 'pride established in humility',[7] but 'established' claims too much stability for what was always a more complex and uneasy mixture.

Lady Gregory's pride was perhaps even more attractive to Yeats than her humility. In a world of shifting standards and social mobility she stood for traditional values. He stressed her 'half-feudal' background and was particularly impressed by her code, an inherited and aristocratic value system, which gave her the strength to act decisively in difficult or ambiguous situations. It was a code that he, perpetually vacillating and reasoning with himself, treating each moral or social problem as unique and perplexing, longed to adopt. Given the restlessness of his temperament, his adoption of it could only be intermittent, and their greatest fallings-out occurred when she felt that he had transgressed against it through weakness or self-interest.

Pride and humility were one set of paradoxes. Yeats's observation that there was 'in her life much artifice, in her nature much pride' points to another, as does Thomas Kiernan's variation on the same theme: 'a woman of great goodness, simplicity and guile'.[8] Artifice and guile seem at odds with simplicity and pride, and yet these contradictions are central to any understanding of her situation and behaviour. She was vulnerable on many counts: as a woman in a man's world; as a plain but intelligent girl neglected by a family and society that preferred beauty and conventional thought; as a landlord in an epoch of agrarian unrest and political uncertainty. Guile and artifice were necessary to survival, or at any rate to those things she wished to survive, and we do her an injustice if we fail to take account of this and insist upon viewing her (as she wished to view herself) as merely the simple widow of Coole, just as much as if we see all her actions dictated (as Dr. Kohfeldt would have us believe) by machiavellian design.

Such paradoxes were grounded in her personality, but during the 1890s her county neighbours noted what they took to be a paradox in her public life. The woman who in 1893 had been so vigorously opposed to Home Rule that she went to the trouble of publishing an anonymous pamphlet proclaiming its dangers, was, only five years later, proudly announcing that her mission was to prepare for it. A tentative shift in allegiances had begun before her association with Yeats, but he helped accelerate and direct it. Their search for Irish indentities is an essential factor in their relationship, which is not fully comprehensible without some understanding of the motives which led her to an increasing sympathy with nationalism.

*

The friendship that had not prospered in 1894 looked more promising when they met at Edward Martyn's house two years later and Yeats's unexpectedly long visit to Coole the following summer cemented it. By 1897 Lady Gregory had more need of Yeats and he had more need of her. The mid-nineties had been unsettling for both of them, a time of emotional uncertainties, new perceptions of the world, and important changes in life-style. These changes began to alter Yeats's life soon after his first meeting with her, when he left the shelter of his father's house to set up for himself, at first as a lodger of Arthur Symons, and later in his own rooms. For her the process of change had begun earlier, when in 1892 shortly before her fortieth birthday, she became a widow. The death of Sir William Gregory left her with an eleven-year-old son to educate and a mortgage to pay off. It signalled, if not a farewell to London and cosmopolitan life, at least a drastic reduction in their pleasures. It meant finding new roots and, given her limited financial resources, it seemed that these roots must be put down in Ireland. Her girlhood had been spent in the family seat of Roxborough, and her husband's estate at Coole, although now a precious trust for her son, had engaged far less of her time and emotional allegiance. At first there appeared to be no problem about returning to Roxborough and running it as she had run it before her marriage. Unhappily, the master of the estate, her brother William (who had inherited when his brother Dudley died barely a week after Sir William) was drinking heavily and suspected that her attempt to reinstate herself as chateleine was in reality a bid to usurp his position. He peremptorily ordered her to leave the house and never darken its doorstep again, an incident that she records in the language of high Victorian melodrama: 'on the last night of the saddest year of my life, in bitter cold, Robert & I left my old home & took refuge at the Croft . . . there is a terrible difference in my life'.[9] As it happened, drink did for William quicker than had been anticipated — he died less than two months later — but the psychological shock was profound: her husband's death had narrowed the London scene, her brother's drunken frenzy had brought home to her just how homeless she was: clearly it was Coole or nothing.

She was, in any case, from too long a line of Irish landlords ever to have neglected Coole. All her instincts and traditions dictated that she should protect it for Robert and to this task she began to devote her considerable talents and propensity for self-sacrifice. She neglected her own meals to save money for the mortgage, sacrifices carefully recorded in her diary. But she knew that in the 1890s there was more to holding onto an estate than merely forgoing an extra course or succulent delicacy. Although the terminal crisis of her class was not to occur until the 1920s, it was already evident to those who would see that Ascendancy power had been deeply undermined, and that the lull in the Land War was no more than a temporary respite. Her absence abroad during the worst of the land agitation had not disguised the situation from her. She had seen soldiers garrisoned at Roxborough to protect her brother from assassination, and in 1887 had been caused financial embarrassment when the Coole tenants won a 25% reduction in rents. If anything, living in England had made her more conscious that, dangerous though the unrest in Ireland might be, the challenge from without was far more ominous. Gladstone's espousal of Home Rule was a dereliction never to be forgotten or forgiven, as the spiteful accumulation of gossip and innuendo about him in her autobiography illustrates. Even the death of Parnell and the welcome defeat of the first Home Rule Bill could not mask the knowledge that a large section of the British people now preferred dealing with the nationalists to propping up a small landed class that was doing too little too late. The British connection was no longer to be relied upon, and if many of her rustic neighbours could ignore that fact she, an habituee of smart London dinner tables, had it thrust upon her. At one such dinner James Lowell had cheerfully informed her that 'we landlords must make up our minds to the spread of democracy in the nineteenth century and be the Jonah thrown to the whales'.[10] She must have winced at his choice of the uncompromising 'and', rather than a concessionary 'or': it seemed that, come what may, she, Robert and Coole were to be sacrificed upon the unsanctified altar of British political expediency. She wrote *A Phantom's Pilgrimage, or Home Ruin* as a dire warning of the consequences of this policy, but even the return to power of the Conservative and Unionist Party could hardly lighten the gloom. In the November of 1894, the year in which she first met Yeats, Lord Morris, one of her shrewdest Irish friends in London, was still taking 'a pessimistic view of Ireland, thinks we have not touched bottom, that the new land bill will pass, & property be sliced away by degrees'.[11]

It was an unhappy prospect and one that she intended to circumvent if possible. She could not afford to live in London, but she took a *pied-à-terre* there, partly to pursue her own now intermittent absentee social life, but also to keep up links with the British establishment should 'Home Ruin' indeed triumph. This was prudent; so, too, was her other policy, now being pursued at a national level by the Conservative Government, of trying to kill Home Rule with kindness. Her emotions and sense of duty dictated that she should preserve Coole for Robert; financially she had little choice but to live there, especially as the old links with Roxborough broke: the deaths of her mother, and of her sister Ada, seemed not merely the loss of close relatives, but to signify a break with a past that could not come again in Ireland.[12] Relations with her mother and her family had never been easy, and her experiences of social life in London made her more acutely aware of the growing differences between her and her class. After the death of his drunken father, the installation at Roxborough of her nephew, William Arthur, and his unendurable mother-in-law, Rose, shocked her into a recognition of how far she and things had changed: 'after the good, the high minded, society I had enjoyed in London, they seemed so empty, narrow trivial & common — Rose's swagger so vulgar & so blatant'.[13] By December 1894 she had reluctantly reconciled herself to her destiny: 'Poor Coole looking dreary — but I feel it my right place, & must try to stay on & do my best by it'.[14]

Thus the mid-nineties found her poised between London and Ireland, but committed more to the latter by financial necessity and dynastic duty. Her drunken brother had surprised himself on his inheritance of Roxborough by the discovery that he enjoyed 'the power & authority' of mastership. She, too, was to find compensations in her role as *grande dame* of Coole, although in her case a display of power was neither possible nor desirable. For she was wiser than her brothers; if London had taught her that the Ascendancy position in Ireland was more tenuous than it may have appeared in the midst of a privileged and easy-paced life west of the Shannon, her work on Sir William's memoirs, and the preparation for *Mr Gregory's Letter-Box*, deepened her critique of political structures in Ireland, as did her reading of Froude, 'which has opened my eyes to the failings of the landlords, & I may say of *all* classes in Ireland in the past, & makes me very anxious to do my duty & to bring Robert up to do his'.[15] Nor were her lessons all drawn from history; the behaviour of her kinsmen at Roxborough and Castle Taylor towards their tenants was involving them in immediate trouble and storing up future antagonism. Her neighbour, Edward Martyn, although a Catholic, despised the country people he lived among and was disliked by them in his turn. Lowell's warning that the Irish landords were to be thrown to the whales was beginning to seem ominously prophetic, and by April 1895 she herself acknowledged that time was running out:

I feel that this Land Bill is the last of "Dobson's Three Warnings" & am thankful that we land-owners have been given even a little time to prepare & to work while it is day. It is necessary that as democracy gains powers, our power should go, & God knows many of our ancestors & forerunners have eaten — or planted sour grapes & we must not repine if our teeth are set on edge. I would like to leave a good memory & not a 'monument of champagne bottles' & with all that, I hope to save the *home*, house & woods at least for Robert.[16]

As an abstract force, Democracy seemed menacing and irresistible; translated into the denizens of Gort and its environs, it might prove more negotiable. To say that she set out to win their affection would be too crude, for charity and good works were a Victorian duty she had already willingly embraced at Roxborough and in Southwark. Nevertheless, she saw that charity had a political as well as an ethical dimension, and she began to cast round for suitable benefactions. The Workhouse had long been a target for small charities, and now Robert was marched off there in his school holidays to dole out sugar-sticks to the old gaffers. But she soon found that her religion told against her playing a fuller role; when she tried to organize work schemes — an idea she had picked up in charitable activities in London — she was quickly made aware of the ' "local & religious jealousies" that so often bring the best intentions to nought in Ireland'.[17] Her attempts to help the nuns in the Gort convent by arranging sales of their needlework in London promised to be more effective, but she could not warm to the task; the rag trade, in no matter how worthy and ecumenical a cause, was too much like vulgar huckstering: it was not dignified. And dignity was important to her. If in seeking the protection of an Irish identity she was obliged as she later told Yeats, to accept the 'baptism of the gutter' it must be on the understanding that the gutter was thereby to be cleansed and sweetened.

*

There were complex social and psychological forces at work behind her decisions and behaviour. Although the relationships between landlords and tenants in Ireland were, as modern historical scholarship has shown, more intricate than earlier partisan accounts would lead us to believe, certain basic facts remained. A relatively small and predominantly settler class had achieved political power, but was outnumbered by the natives and, uncertain of their ultimate (or even more immediate) attitudes and allegiances, depended upon a cultivated sense of superiority or caste to protect and bolster its own identity. Augusta Gregory had been brought up amid prejudices close to those that Yeats had known in the Sligo of his childhood, where as he reports, everyone he knew well 'despised nationalists and Catholics'.[18] He had attempted to deracinate (or rather reroot) himself through his friendship with John O'Leary and by associating himself with the popular literary traditions of Young Ireland. For Lady Gregory the transition was more difficult and went against even more powerfully structured reflexes. The way forward for her, as for Yeats, was to work, if not for an alliance, at least for an accord between the landlords and the 'people', meaning by the 'people' the peasants and small tenant farmers. Like Yeats, and many of the representatives and writers of her background, she was suspicious of the Catholic middle classes.[19] They presented the most dangerous political threat and they could still arouse the old bigotted sneers, as when she described John Dillon, a leading nationalist politician and also a university-educated and cultivated man, at a London reception as 'looking gloomy & not at home in his clean shirt'.[20] Men not at home in clean shirts were not likely to raise the dignity of Ireland; but they were apt to bring in undignified proposals for Home Rule or the redistribution of land. Worse still, they were likely to pervert a basically honest and reasonable tenantry by inciting it to lawlessness and undignified disrespect for its social superiors. Chiding Wilfrid Scawen Blunt for his support of Irish nationalism in the 'eighties, she had promised to send him ' "United Ireland" some day, Parnell's paper, to show you how vulgar and virulent it is — so unlike the Irish people, the poor who are so courteous and full of tact even in their discontent'.[21] She thought her point proved when her brother Gerald, who had required a posse of soldiers to protect him only a little while before, received a silver salver as a wedding gift from his tenants, but was begged not to make the presentation public for fear of Land League reprisals against them.[22]

If the Ascendancy could no longer impose its will by force, it could perhaps mitigate the worst that men in uncomfortably clean shirts could do by assuming a social and moral authority that would help to draw out the innate courtesy and tact of the people. She noticed that Edward Martyn was disliked by his tenants largely because he 'neglects gracious things'.[23] Dignity, a stately combination of self-possession and graciousness, was such an authority; it was a caste possession that could be conferred on an emerging nation which had attracted a bad overseas press on this score. She had been disgusted with the frequent denunciations of the Irish people by absentee landlords in London, and by the way in which such accounts enforced the stereotype of a lazy, dishonest and dirty nation among the English. By promoting an Ascendancy 'code' among the people at large one would be raising their own self-consciousness and confidence, enhancing them in the eyes of foreigners, and helping to raise a barrier against the excesses of an unbridled and levelling democracy. One would also, naturally, be dignifying one's own adoption of an Irish identity. 'Dignity' consequently became her watchword, and its promotion the goal of her Irish plans. But how was she to raise Irish dignity? Although growing more nationalist in outlook, she could never bring herself to enter politics, or join the Irish party. Its leaders lacked dignity, and in any case prudence warned her that she should keep all her political options open. Before she met Yeats, Lady Gregory was desperately in search of an Irish role. Literature was an enticing possibility, but her own creative writing seemed to lack direction and she was running out of editorial tasks. By hitching her literary wagon to Yeats's rapidly ascending star, she found a path for her Irish ambitions, an outlet for her own creative impulses, and enough work to appease a conscience in which Duty was a constant imperative.

For if Dignity, the product of her pride, was one of her watchwords, Duty, the product of her humility, was the other. While she was casting round for a dignified occupation she busied herself with sacrifices both on behalf of Robert and Coole, and for the poor. A policy of service and enlightened paternalism was a shrewd strategy at this juncture in the history of her class, but it would be unfair to suggest that the only motive of her benefactions was expediency. As a girl she had developed a strong sense of social duty, which had been underpinned by her religious fervour. It was also intensified by her position in her family. As a plain and unwanted daughter, she had compensated for her neglect and sense of inferiority by seeking to be of service to others, and this unremitting self-effacement had induced what we might describe as her 'Esther Summerson complex'. Like the self-abnegating heroine of *Bleak House* she found a palliative for her own self-doubts and social inconsequence in helping others. 'Dame Durdon' and 'Mother Hubbard' are among the names given to Esther; Lady Gregory variously recalls descriptions of herself as 'Martha the serving maiden', the 'charwoman of the Abbey', and even the Virgin Mary.[24] Just as Esther Summerson calls attention to the apparently unexpected compliments she has attracted, so Lady Gregory's diaries and autobiographical works are scrupulous in recording the many unsolicited tributes to her altruism, intelligence, generosity, and even modesty. As resident benefactress at an Irish Bleak House, she could satisfy many of her needs; she was securing a home for Robert; she was doing good as a Christian ought, and she was winning the thanks and compliments of the grateful poor which, as she already perceived, might be an insurance against times of future unrest.

Both Esther Summerson and she confronted a similar dilemma when faced with the disaffected poor. We recall Esther and her friend Ada's visit to the destitute and sullen brickmakers with the ineffectual do-gooder Mrs. Pardiggle. While Mrs. Pardiggle rattles on to no purpose, the two girls are made 'painfully sensible that between us and these people there was an iron barrier, which could not be removed by our friend. By whom, or how, it could be removed we did not know. . .'.[25] At this point the baby of one of the brickmakers dies and Esther's spontaneous overflow of sympathy helps to build at least a temporary bridge between the two classes. The young Augusta Gregory, also perplexed by the sullen poor, asked similar questions: 'How is love to take the place of bitterness, and sympathy to bind class with class instead of hatred keeping them asunder?'[26] Private charities and personal sympathy were an answer for her as for Esther, but her poor were rural, not industrial, and she could look back to golden girlhood days when all had been harmonious in the quasi-feudal community of Roxborough. *Bleak House* is among other things an elegy for a moribund aristocracy. Lord Dedlock lives, like Lady Gregory, according to a superb code of conduct, but in his case it is a code that has become a shell, at once suppressing his true feelings, and blinding him to the changes taking place in the large world. She was more alert to the value of such a code in a non-industrialised Ireland, and trusted that, mobilised in tandem with a strong sense of Duty, it could restore something of the community of the prelapsarian days before the Land League, 'the time when we lived in peace and charity with all men and loved our people as they loved us'.[27] She was too shrewd to hope for a total restoration of what was in any case a myth, and knew that 'the country will never be quite the same again, for good or ill . . .'[28] Much hangs on that qualifying 'quite': something might be achieved, or saved, and the people given true leaders rather than middle class rabble-rousers. The town of Cloon in her plays, named after a local townland, and her quaint folklore, are attempts to recreate that cosy world of her childhood and to offer its values to contemporary Ireland.

Esther discovers herself to be the daughter of an important lady; Augusta Gregory never forgot she was one, and this is a crucial difference between them. Her social position led to her stress upon Dignity and her adherence to an unquestioned code of behaviour that at once fascinated Yeats and disturbed him. Accommodating this code to a changing social situation was no easy task and her early stories are attempts to explore her relationship to the people behind the discreet anonymity of a pseudonym. 'A Philanthropist', a reavealing study in projected autobiography published in 1891, registers the essential difference between her and Esther Summerson. A well-to-do Anglicized Irishwoman becomes so involved in helping the poor on a western estate (run down, like Tom-all-Alone's, through being in chancery) that she agrees to marry the local doctor in order to remain in the district and carry on with her good works. No sooner has she made this impetuous decision than she begins to have second thoughts. Such a marriage would involve loss of caste, and she perceives that she will no longer be 'the lady who stooped from a high level but a mere doctor's wife . . . living in that small staring house at the entrance of the town'.[29] This is of course precisely the choice that Esther is happy to make in marrying Woodcourt who, like Dr. Quinn in 'A Philanthropist', is a dispensary doctor. But there were limits to Lady Gregory's identification with the people and she could not finally consign her heroine to such a misalliance; at the end of the story, the attempt to break class boundaries accidentally causes the death of the doctor, and the heroine leaves Ireland for position and comfort in England.

In 'A Gentleman' a story published in 1894, Lady Gregory again took as her theme the relationship of the landlords to the people.

The daughter of a Putney plutocrat, newly arrived in Ireland, is irritated by the easy-going casualness of her gardener, but gradually learns to respect his wisdom and delicacy of feeling. After his death she discovers he was a descendant of the 'King of the Burren' and contrasts his dignified tombstone with her father's vulgar memorial in London. The story begins with an apparently stage-Irish figure but as it proceeds discloses his fine sensibility. It presents a view of the people as simple, kindly, pious and, if apparently somewhat feckless, unwaveringly loyal to the landlords. It thus endorses a picture of Irish society much approved by thinking Unionists, and given political expression by her friend Lord Randoph Churchill's proposals for 'Tory Democracy', in which landlord and honest countryman form a natural alliance against the vulgarity (and power) of plutocracy. Her paternalistic representation of the Irish countryman was never essentially to change. In her comedies especially, the characters behave and talk like overgrown children: wayward sometimes, mistaken often, but finally guileless and biddable.

*

By the time of Yeats's first extended visit to Coole in 1897, then, Lady Gregory was looking for an Irish role, he for an Irish base and hostess. In many respects they were arriving at the same destination from different directions. She was seeking to shake off the prejudices of her class, to find a sense of community and rootedness in Ireland that had eluded her in London, and thereby to help ensure the survival of Coole into the future. He had attempted to become *declassé* in the 'eighties and to find popularity and influence as a nationalist poet. As the 'nineties unfolded he began to perceive that not only had he failed, but that his efforts had in any case been misdirected. While he had not given up hope of inspiration and perhaps an audience among the rural poor he had grown disillusioned with the state of the country as a whole. 'Ireland is greatly demoralised in all things', he wrote to a correspondent in September 1894, explaining that

My experience of Ireland during the last three years has changed my views very greatly, & now I feel that the work of an Irish man of letters must be not so much to awaken or quicken or preserve the national ideal among the mass of the people but to convert the educated classes to it on the one hand to the best of his ability, & on the other — & this is the more important — to fight for moderation, dignity, and the rights of the intellect among his fellow nationalists.[30]

To convert the educated classes was a more difficult task than he imagined. They tended to be Ascendancy in outlook, and he had already by 1894 alienated many of them through his nationalism and his attacks on the academic tradition of Trinity College. He was to have some success at Lissadell in introducing the Gore-Booths to Irish literature and folklore, and Edward Martyn's house was open to him, but otherwise his impact among the patrician classes was slight. Yet his desire for such influence grew as the decade went on, for what this letter registers is a discontent, later to become more anguished, with the development of modern Irish society, and in particular with the rise of a middle class rooted neither in the land nor in a tradition he could regard as cultivated. He began to believe that a Unity of Culture might still be brought about through an alliance between the 'educated' classes and the country people, for he argued that both had access to a common heritage, the learned through their scholarship and the peasantry through their folklore. This, once understood, would give Irish literature, perhaps uniquely in the modern world, the opportunity of becoming 'universal', since it could thus

prolong its first inspiration without renouncing the complexity of ideas and emotions which is the inheritance of cultivated men, for it will have learned from the discoveries of modern learning that the common people, wherever civilization has not driven its plough too deep, keep a watch over the roots of all religion and all romance.[31]

As we have seen, an accord between the educated classes and the peasantry also had great political and cultural attractions for Lady Gregory, and it was soon evident to him that she was exactly the sort of patron he needed: a sympathetic member of the Ascendancy who nevertheless had ready access to the people and their lore, and who, like him, put a high premium upon 'moderation, dignity and the rights of the intellect'.

If the development of Yeats's thought prepared him to appreciate Lady Gregory's gifts when he met her again, the emotional entanglements of his private life made her no less valuable to him. Her aristocratic code provided him with a firm path of conduct upon the shifting and uncertain way of what he called the *hodos chameliontos*, and her appetite for duty made her assiduous in attending to his well-being at a time when his being was far from well. His experiences on the '98 Committee, a radical organization formed to orchestrate the centennial celebrations of the 1798 Rebellion, had exacerbated the unhappiness in both his public and his private life. He had undertaken the work largely to be nearer Maud Gonne but proximity without promise merely intensified his frustrated desire. The behaviour of the patriotic committees also left much to be desired, for there was incessant wrangling, bad faith, and even dishonesty, confirming his growing distaste for the middle-classes and the rough and tumble of populist politics. His letters of the spring of 1897 reiterate his wish 'to reduce my life to perfect order', and this finally led him to Sligo where his uncle, George Pollexfen, 'reduces my habits into order as a mangle does clothes'.[32] The desire for peace is insistent, but it is noticeable that in the context of his available retreats securing it seemed to involve a reduction, a flattening out, the oppression of a necessary but indiscriminate wringer. After some weeks in Sligo he wrote to say that he would visit 'Tillyra for a month & then go to Lady Gregory of Coomb [sic], Galway, & then return back here'.[33] But he did not return for long to his uncle's mangle — the few days at Coole lengthened into months, for this was a haven where order was neither reductive nor oppressive, which offered a sanctuary from the growing hostility of the world, and companionship that would so bolster him in spirit and body that he could not only 'labour in ecstasy', but return to the world with refreshed confidence and determination.

If Yeats found that the two sides of Lady Gregory's nature satisfied his needs for a rôle-model and a sympathetic and painstaking friend, she could detect in him attributes and weaknesses that made him a perfect recipient for her particular gifts and resources. Her upbringing and temperament, 'all that pride and humility', attracted her to two kinds of men: the 'strong men of the world', her unruly brothers, Blunt, Quinn, Roosevelt, and de Valera, whom she could admire; and the sensitive but vulnerable men whom she could mother. Yeats filled both roles. In desperate need of care in 1897 and 1898, he yet had the artist's strength and was achieving recognized mastery in a field that she was also eager to enter. His arrival in her life could not have come at a more opportune moment, for, with Robert away at school for long periods, her maternal instincts were seeking a fresh outlet, especially since an earlier protégé, Paul Harvey, the orphaned son of a friend, had recently relinquished the role of surrogate son. As his confidante, she had taken care that he ate regularly, saved him from an imprudent marriage, and engineered him into one that suited both of them (since it took an otherwise unprovided niece off her hands). Once married, however, his centre of interest had naturally and disconcertingly shifted. She was made to feel neglected in the bridal home which, as she tartly remarks in her Diary, she had helped furnish. Into the emotional gap left by young Harvey's defection, stepped Yeats, an even more suitable and deserving recipient of her friendship, since in 1897 his personal affairs were as miserable as they were ever to be. He had sent Olivia Shakespear 'weeping away' but was no closer to Maud Gonne, and, weakened by a poor diet and nervous anxiety, he hovered close to a breakdown. Coole provided him with a healthy regimen of good country food and fresh air, as well as a sympathetic listener to whom he could pour out his literary plans and amatory woes. He was always grateful for the sympathy of women; he had nearly asked Eva Gore-Booth to marry him because she pitied him, and Olivia Shakespear had furthered their liaison by sympathising as he unpacked his troubles to her. Lady Gregory had been trained to be a good listener all her life, and she posed no amatory threat. Although her affair with John Quinn was to show that her sexual interests were far from dead, there is no evidence that they obtruded where Yeats was concerned. She was safe, kind, and understanding. Her age, experience, and social standing enabled her to advise him both on his relationship with Maud Gonne and on the more practical affairs of his life.

She had a large and sequestered house which offered refuge when the world became troublesome, and servants enough to ensure that he did not become too troublesome. It had not always been thus. An earlier confidante, Katharine Tynan, had complained during one of his visits that he was 'an extremely bothering visitor. He thinks all the rest of the world created to minister to him, and there is no rebuffing of him possible. I did nothing while he was here, nor should I if he was here a twelvemonth'.[34] His sisters concurred with this view, but at last he had found a hostess who not only thought that the rest of the world was created to minister to him, but who had it in her power at Coole to create such a world. The cossetting of Yeats never failed to astonish visitors and even amazed regular inhabitants like her granddaughters. The daughter-in-law was more acerbic, observing that Lady Gregory's sedum plants seemed to be in flower for much of the year and that while they were, Yeats would be at Coole.[35] It is easy, perhaps irresistible, to be merry over the way that Yeats was treated and about his undisguised relish for such treatment, and the last words on this must be George Moore's delicious accounts.[36] But even Moore never underestimated the immense physical and psychological value that such tending conferred upon him. Yeats may have been, like his uncle George, something of a hypochondriac, but he was unusually vulnerable to nervous indispositions of a debilitating kind. By inviting him to Coole, Lady Gregory gave him the psychological confidence and material support to enable him to write, and no account of their friendship can begin anywhere but with this fact: without her constant help many of his greatest poems would have remained no more than mouthfuls of air.

*

It is nonetheless evident that the relationship found its sources at a far deeper level than that of merely hostess and protégé. Yeats's subconscious understood this, and in February 1909, shocked by the discovery that she was in danger of death, his wandering mind imagined that it was his mother who was ill:

Then I remembered that my mother died years ago and that more than kin was at stake. She has been to me mother, friend, sister and brother.[37]

This familial omnigatherum might be supposed to out-Freud the most dedicated Freudian, but it is significant that his first impulse was to identify Lady Gregory with his mother. How far the deprivation of maternal affection influenced the development of Yeats's character is a moot point, but that such deprivation occurred is beyond doubt. Shortly after his birth his father abandoned the promise of a comfortable professional life for the indigent Bohemianism of art, and Susan Yeats, as William Murphy has shown, felt acutely this decline in status and the worry that it brought.[38] Left alone with her children for long periods in dismal circumstances, her frustrations found vent in scolding her eldest child. At best Susan Yeats struck her nearest and dearest as 'not at all good at housekeeping and childminding. She was prim and austere, suffered all in silence. She asked no sympathy and gave none . . .' and her husband once told his daughter 'that her affection was a matter that one *inferred*. No one ever saw it or heard it speak'.[39] What did speak and repeatedly, was an irritation with her son that perhaps grew out of deep-seated dislike. She subjected her husband to 'dreadful complaints of everybody and everything', but especially of Willie. 'It was always Willie' J. B. Yeats recalled, and reported elsewhere that 'Willie used to get the blame for everything . . .'[40] Susan Yeats's first 'stroke' occurred in the winter of 1887–8 (although the symptoms suggest that her illness was, as in the case of many of the Pollexfens, more psychological than physical) but her relationships with her household had evidently been clouded for many years before this. After her breakdown she becomes a shadowy figure, apparently keeping much to her room. She hardly rates a mention in Yeats's correspondence — on her unexpected death in 1900 he wrote to Lady Gregory that 'it is long since my mother has been able to recognize any of us, except with difficulty', and went on to confess that his sorrow at her passing was vicarious: 'I think that my sister Lily & myself feel it most through our father'.[41] Only a few months after Susan Yeats's death, Olivia Shakespear's mother died and Yeats wrote to her for the first time since the end of their affair: 'I know that you cared for nobody else as for your mother, & when a mother is near ones heart at all her loss must be the greatest of all losses'.[42] The conditional mood in which this is phrased, like the carefully qualified 'at all', is as poignant, given his most recent loss, as it is revealing.

Ireland was, partly for this reason, always a motherland, not a fatherland, for Yeats. The attachment she did not feel for him was directed by his mother towards Sligo, where she had spent a happy and comfortable girlhood, and some of whose legends she knew. Sligo, apart from its other homely associations, became a territory invested by a withheld maternal affection, its folklore associated with Susan Yeats, and her memory related to the 'racial' memory.[43] He was later to use gender as a metaphor for national characteristics, describing Ireland as a feminine nation with a masculine imagination, and England as a masculine nation with a feminine imagination. Lady Gregory fitted well into this typology. A woman and identified, like his mother, with a western landscape and soon even with the folklore of that landscape, she had nevertheless a masculine imagination: 'how unlike a woman's work', he was to say of *Kincora*, 'so powerful and so on'.[44]

Even before he met Lady Gregory Yeats had made numerous attempts to fill the emotional vacuum caused by his mother's lack of warmth. In Dublin he had engaged the affections of the maturer ladies. Ellen O'Leary confessed him her 'favourite among our young men' and he was 'a special favourite' of Mrs. Sigerson.[45] Although his relationship with Katharine Tynan began to worry his susceptibilities it was never one of sexual interest: she, older

than he by six years, acted in the role, if not of mother, at least of
older and masterful sister. It is significant that he picked out for
particular praise her poems 'The Heart of a Mother' and 'The Dead
Mother', both of which have themes of maternal affection. In fact,
the sexual passion that Yeats did raise, inadvertently, in his early
years in London, was in the apparently capacious breast of a
mature woman with whom he took tea while working at the British
Museum, and who surprised and alarmed him one afternoon by
proposing that he should marry her.[46] The vulnerability and
boyishness that made him appealing to these ladies were not lost
on Lady Gregory, but she was in a better position to understand
the causes of that vulnerability. She, too, had been neglected by her
mother (she even claims that she was left lying forgotten at her
birth until noticed by a nurse),[47] and grew up a conscious
disappointment to her parents both on account of her sex and her
lack of beauty.

Her psychological support did not involve merely the capacity to
listen endlessly to tales of love gone wrong. She had been taught
to defer to men at Roxborough, but there are ways of conducting
dialogues even deferentially, and this friendship was a dialogue.
On an early visit he delighted her by telling her that she was an
anvil upon which he beat out his ideas,[48] and if her diaries show
rather too much of the Esther Summerson in her submissive
reaction to his views, there is no doubt that her advice was freely
given. Above all she took him seriously. She believed in dignity;
he was a man to whom dignity mattered so much that he was
prepared to construct a series of *personae* to achieve it. He had felt
its want for too long, amid the bantering of an irreverent family
and an ego-puncturing poverty.

> The ignominy of boyhood; the distress
> Of boyhood changing into man;
> The unfinished man in his pain
> Brought face to face with his own clumsiness[49]

Ever since seeing Irving play Hamlet he had been working at a role
to protect the vulnerability of his character and recast it into the
created effect of personality. Lady Gregory had been onto the pose
at once, 'every inch the poet', but she was not a woman who
thought that poses were a bad thing *per se*; she had played a role
as ugly duckling at Roxborough, taught herself to be a
conversationalist in the cut and thrust of London dinner parties,
and was in the process of finding an Irish identity that would

protect herself and her son. Moreover between their first and
second meetings Yeats had come to realise that, in seeking the
security of a mask, he needed the confidence of the sort of code that
she had inherited. Looking back on these days as he drafted 'Coole
Park' in 1929 he described himself as a 'weather cock, shuttle cock,
comeleon (sic)' and recalled his desperate need for direction and
understanding:

> Here a straw on every wind that blows
> Here I beaten by every wind that blows
> The characteer of my own mind unknown —
> But hiding under youth's embittered pose
> That ignorance[50]

The growth of their friendship in 1897 took place during a
particularly sensitive time of self-appraisal. She met him at Tulira
in June, 'white, haggard, voiceless, fresh from the Jubilee riots
which he had been in the thick of',[51] and admonished him in terms
that were to be repeated throughout their relationship. The Jubilee
was to prompt her into making her first overt gesture towards
nationalism when she refused to light celebratory bonfires and
'George Gough was sadly grieved by my disloyalty & wrote an
impassioned letter — a sort of wail over a lost soul'.[52] The soul
was not entirely lost: she excused herself on the grounds that
Victoria had never done anything for Ireland, and in any case not
lighting a bonfire was a far cry from aiding and abetting a riot,
which is what Yeats had come close to doing. Lady Gregory
disapproved of these Dublin disturbances in wholly characteristic
terms — 'not a very dignified proceeding' — and Yeats himself
conceded to her that he could not approve of them 'not because of
respect for the Queen . . . but because he thinks the impulse should
come from the <mob> people themselves, & not thrust upon them
from above'.[53] This got to the heart of the matter: the relationship
between impulses from below and leadership from above seemed
to her precisely what the future of Ireland devolved upon, and
Lady Gregory, a landowner and tax-payer — unlike Maud Gonne
— had very decided views on the subject. These came to the fore
in what was perhaps the most crucial exchange between them in
these first years of the friendship. In February 1898 he revealed that
Maud Gonne was planning to incite hungry tenants in Kerry to kill
their landlords and seize food:

I was aghast, & spoke very strongly, telling him first that the famine itself
was problematic, that if it exists there are other ways of meeting it, that

we who are above the people in means & education, ought were it a real famine, to be ready to share all we have with them, but that even supposing starvation was before them it wd be for us to teach them to die with courage than to live by robbery.[54]

She explained that such acts would blunt the people's moral sensibility, and this was an argument that went straight to the heart of Yeats's essential conservatism:

He was very much struck & said he had only thought of the matter as it wd effect her [i.e. Maud Gonne] − not as it would affect the people . . . but that now he saw how wrong such a line would be & he would try to dissuade her from it.[55]

His father had disapproved of Maud Gonne's 'Red Indian feathers' and easy endorsement of violence, but this was the first time he had heard a reasoned critique of her behaviour, and it was all the more potent in that it came at a time when his experiences on the '98 Centenary Committee were disillusioning him about the idealism of Irish nationalism. From now on, although he would not acknowledge the fact until 1903, Yeats began to withdraw from the more popular and radical manifestations of nationalism, and for this, at least in part, Lady Gregory was responsible.

It was not merely a question of politics. Lady Gregory's code covered matters of personal and social conduct too, and this was an area in which Yeats had always been unsure of himself. The pages of *Autobiographies* and *Memoirs* abound in examples of the ways in which his social timidity led to insincerity and awkwardness. Lady Gregory had been brought up to a style of behaviour that he at once envied and yet had difficulty in appropriating. This difficulty emerged soon after his first extended visit to Coole. Lady Gregory's maternal bounty had followed him to London in the form of frequent hampers of game, bottled fruit, and port (which he fell into the detestable habit of mixing with hot water). Such was the profusion of her gifts that he found himself in a moral quandary:

I have a kind of feeling that I ought not to let you do all these little kind things for me, things that I should do for myself. Yet it is a great pleasure to have these little kindnesses shown to one, altogether apart from the things themselves. I wish I saw clearly in the matter. I have reasoned myself out of the instinct & rules by which one mostly governs one's self & have only that uncertain staff reason to trust to & so am in continual doubt about simple things.[56]

The doubt continued. In June 1900 he confessed to her that 'Apart from opinions, which I judge too sternly, I scarcely judge people at all & am altogether too lax in my attitude towards conduct'.[57] Already one laxness of conduct had angered her, although she had said nothing of it: he had spent the money from an article she had written and given to him for his daily needs on an extravagant trip to Belfast to see Maud Gonne. His 'lax . . . attitude towards conduct' was often to exasperate Lady Gregory's admired 'sterner conscience', and in the new century was to lead to 'the one serious quarrel' he ever had with her.

For the present it was her fund of sympathy rather than her strength of conduct that he had most need of, for his always troubled relationship with Maud Gonne was going through a particularly agonizing period. In December 1898 he evidently learned of her affair with Millevoye for the first time and her revelations, and the intense coversations they provoked, threw him into an emotional turmoil. 'Much more has happened than I can tell you here', he wrote to Lady Gregory, 'for one shrinks from writing many things, but it will be a great relief to talk to you about much that I cannot write . . . I am always, my most true friend, your friend . . . '.[58] He was to recall this period as 'a time of great personal strain and sorrow . . . I was tortured by sexual desire and disappointed love . . . I was never before or since so miserable as in those years that followed my first visit to Coole.'[59] Lady Gregory's sympathy and constant support were crucial and gratefully acknowledged; in late 1898 he was to write: 'I do not know what I could have done these last two or three years but for your kindness, your most watchful & patient goodness. You have been to me a well of peace and happiness.'[60] At each emotional crux in his life she was to come to his aid with similar understanding and sound advice: at the time of his desolation over Maud Gonne's marriage in 1903; during the even more harrassing period of her separation in 1905; when he was wooing a reluctant Iseult Gonne; and in the turbulent weeks leading up to his marriage in the autumn of 1917.

This combination of sympathy and conscience was to remain Lady Gregory's major contribution to the friendship. But what the relationship had in addition from 1897 to 1904 was an excitement, a sense of self-discovery that did not, and perhaps by its nature could not, come again. The delight was mutual. For Lady Gregory her new friend was at once someone to mother, to console, and to show off. Here was a gifted man of nationalist persuasion who was also a social asset, who could show London hostesses that Ireland was not so easily to be patronized. Her Diary records the pleasure of bringing him out, almost as she might a debutante daughter, only with the aim of introducing him to powerful editors, politicians, men of letters and hostesses he would otherwise have missed. Reviewing the season in 1897, she recalled giving 'some nice little dinners here too — Yeats always — partly for his sake & partly for my own, to make all go off well for he is always brilliant & charming', and confessed herself 'quite proud of my young countryman'.[61] Among those she presented him to were Knowles, the editor of *The Nineteenth Century*, Edward Clodd the folklorist, Wilfrid Scawen Blunt, William Lecky the historian, and Reginald Smith the publisher, although an arranged meeting with Henry James fell through. In his turn, Yeats introduced her to a more daring literary London, to Lionel Johnson (after solemnly promising her that he would not get drunk at dinner), Althea Gyles, the Rhyses, Barry O'Brien and numerous others. Nor was it only in London that he was of value: his visits to Coole helped to cheer up what had hitherto often been a lonely and dismal house. During that first prolonged stay she found him 'most brilliant — pouring out his ideas in rapid succession — hair splitting — fanciful — full of wit & poetry, deep & subtle thought', altogether 'a most brilliant charming & lovable companion — never out of humour, simple, gentle — interested in all that went on — liking to do his work in the library in the midst of all the coming & going.'[62]

The excitement of these days was generated by national as well as personal satisfactions. They shared a sense of euphoria as the possibilities for Irish cultural nationalism seemed to expand almost daily, and as their Irish identities appeared to grow surer. A new component in Lady Gregory's search for an identity was a careful attempt to de-Anglicize herself. What had begun as an unobtrusive disengagement, the negative fact of not lighting loyalist bonfires, gradually grew more emphatic. Yeats's influence had much to do with this, but his influence had something to work on, and increasingly this was a feeling of anger that England really had, as Lowell had foreseen, ditched her Irish allies. Yeats reminded her in March 1897 'that England has always betrayed its garrison — the Protestant industrial colony — the [Protestant] Church — the landlords . . .'[63] The animus that had once found expression in malicious gossip about Gladstone, now broadened into an attack on England as a whole. In the days of more certain Unionist hegemony, the Ascendancy had preserved its sense of social and

racial identity by insisting upon its differences from a stereotype of
the 'mere Irish'; as that hegemony weakened the more farsighted
sought a rapprochment with the people and tried to authenticate
their Irishness by defining it against a stereotype of Englishness.
'The people', Lady Gregory noted, 'have grown to hate England
through their love for Ireland — Our class is now through dislike
of England growing to care for their own country.'[64] Disparaging
remarks about Anglo-Saxon attitudes become frequent in her
Diary, and her one non-English forebear, a Huguenot great-great
grandmother gains an extraordinary prominence in her genealogy.
The very over-insistence of this sort of racial special pleading
betrays the vulnerability of the position she was trying to defend,
and Sir Richard Burton, weary of her perpetual harping on her
Irishness, told her quite bluntly that she had no Irish blood at all.
She records that she was 'able to prove that I had' but does not
explain how; with her genealogy it cannot have been easy.[65] The
parish priest in Gort inadvertently underlined Burton's point when
he remarked, upon hearing that Robert was learning Irish, that he
hoped to see him become more Irish than the Irish. This was no
doubt kindly meant but it reveals how little the people of her
locality looked upon her or her family as 'genuinely' Irish. There
was too, the lingering suspicion that her Protestantism was of the
militant kind. Roxborough had been notorious for its proselytizing
and, for all she might say in her memoirs, it is difficult to believe
that as a fervent adolescent she had not partaken in the work. Be
that as it may, such suspicions die hard in Ireland. Yeats,
accompanying her on folklore expeditions dressed as always in
black, was thought to be a Protestant missionary, and later a
relative of the Fay brothers maintained that they 'had lost their
faith' at the Abbey Theatre 'owing to Lady Gregory who had taken
to "prosletism"'.[66] She threatened George Moore with a libel
action on this point but his accusations were far from being the
only ones, and indicate the abiding strains on her Irish stance.

Such accusations merely intensified her desire to establish an
Irish identity the more securely and throughout her books and
prefaces she constantly, and sometimes tediously, reminds herself
and her readers that she is Irish and that all she writes is for the greater
glory of Ireland. Her new-found enthusiasm was sustained by two
public events. The controversy over the Financial Relations, which
argued that England had been persistently over-taxing Ireland,
seemed to offer the Anglo-Irish a last opportunity to re-assume
leadership of the nation through Lord Castletown or Horace

Plunkett. Indeed, for a time Lady Gregory and Yeats saw Plunkett as the possible successor to Parnell, a potential national leader of firm but moderate views and drawn from the Ascendancy, who might at once unite the country and keep it from the demagogues of the Irish Party. Over-taxation united all classes since it hit everyone's pocket either directly or indirectly, and for a time, although only a short time, Irish politicians of every persuasion found common ground. The Boer War, which coincided with the high-point of Gaelic League propaganda, also made it easy to despise England. Events in South Africa demonstrated that the world's mightiest Empire was fighting on dubious moral grounds with a badly-led army and generating, because of this, a vulgar jingoism among the people at large. Proof positive of the decline in national moral fibre was provided when, returning through London during victory celebrations, 'a young woman rushed at Yeats & tickled his face with a feather';[67] English degeneracy could, it seemed, sink no lower. Meanwhile the Gaelic League was painting Ireland as the home of simple honour and elevated thought, in hazard from the filth of England. Lady Gregory and Yeats, as well as AE and others, took up the League's views and convinced themselves that their anti-English outlook had a moral as well as a cultural validity. When George Moore revealed that he was writing an article on 'The Decadence of England' she commented that it was 'a subject we all agree on'.[68] Her old friend Blunt noticed and applauded the change, telling her that he had 'always considered the true test of Irish nationality was hatred of England'.[69]

The view of Ireland as the home of almost unlimited idealism found full expression in a book of essays, *Ideals in Ireland*, edited by Lady Gregory, but was not long to survive the founding of the Irish Literary Theatre. That volume contains an essay by D. P. Moran, a representative of the new men in Irish public life who neither knew nor respected the Ascendancy code. In the late 'nineties both Yeats and Lady Gregory thought that they could subsume such men into a unified literary movement which, gaining strength from its diversity of interests, would nevertheless be held together by shared ideals. The new century was to show that they were mistaken. Moran was to be a thorn in the side of the Abbey Theatre and the unremitting attacks of his paper, and of those like him, were to dispel the cultural euphoria of these years.

*

For the time being this euphoria sustained itself upon the excitement of their shared discoveries in folklore. Folklore had always attracted her; as a young woman she had begun her *Emigrant's Notebook* in an effort to record an Ireland that was disappearing, and a letter on Irish superstitions published in the *Spectator* in 1895 shows that her interest in such matters persisted and predated her friendship with Yeats.[70] This was the great age of folklore and it was soon evident to her that this might be a way of making her literary mark and of enhancing the cultural importance of Ireland. In London she had 'talked of folklore & superstitions' with such celebrated authorities as Edward Clodd and Alfred Nutt, and discovered that gathering such material was an occupation valued on both sides of the Irish Sea. Sir Alfred Lyall was 'much struck' with what she had collected and the editor of the *National Review* proved himself 'interested about folk lore & the Celtic movement'.[71]

Her brief meeting with Yeats at Tulira in the summer of 1896 inspired her to systematize her researches, and the collection continued vigorously during his long stay at Coole in the following year. She maintains that her motive was to improve his health by bringing him out into the fresh air, but she must also have calculated that she was uniquely placed to render him this service, for she had access to the people in a way denied to him even in Sligo. She was, too, in her Esther Summerson guise, prepared to do the collecting herself and to type it up in a legible form, 'very good training,' as she wrily commented, 'if I ever want to be a private secretary!'[72] But more than harmless drudgery was involved: while it seems probable that she would have begun her collection even without Yeats's impetus, that impetus was important in revealing to her that such studies might be of more than merely antiquarian interest; they might, in fact, be a further aid in overcoming the social and religious barriers that divided her from the people. Her efforts on behalf of the Gort workhouse had been checked by religious differences; now, under Yeats's guidance, she 'found startling belief & came to the conclusion that Ireland is Pagan, not Xtian'.[73] Yeats recollected that she once told him that she had longed 'to turn Catholic, that I might be nearer the people, but you have taught me that paganism brings me nearer still'.[74] Yet the paganism she discovered was of a more domesticated kind than that which excited Yeats, and her interest in folklore differed from his in that he was striving to find the vestiges of a lost faith and an imaginative energy that would help him to create a unity

of culture for Ireland, whereas she was seeking to reassure herself
that the people were spiritual and idealistic rather than political and
threatening. Thus her folklore, although collected and prepared for
publication under Yeats's aegis, differs from his. He is trying to fit
the stories he hears into some larger system; she is content to deal
in quaint tales where idiom and expression support a paternalistic
view of a people curious and curiously naive. This is especially the
case in what we might describe as her contemporary folklore, that
concerning the Boer War and the Great War where she parades
ignorance as winsome, rather as an over-fond parent might repeat
the whimsical utterances of a precocious child who is trying
ingenuously to make sense of a world it cannot yet fully
comprehend. In her most extensive collection of folklore. *Visions
and Beliefs in the West of Ireland*, it is Yeats who characteristically
offers interpretation and theory: her part is merely to record the
tales.

Her compilation of folklore might be seen as an extension of her
editorial work: instead of preparing papers in the possession of one
family, she was now arranging the oral possessions of a people. But
her activity was not quite so passive as this suggests. In all his
comments on folklore, Yeats had stressed that it must be 'literary',
not 'scientific', meaning that it must be rendered in the idiom of the
people. It was this idiomatic flavour which made Douglas Hyde's
collections and translations so exciting to him but, no matter how
much he might purify it, he himself could never capture the dialect
of the tribe. For the stories in *The Secret Rose* he had leant heavily
on Paterian elaboration, suitable enough for the exquisite dis-
criminations in taste that occupied Pater, but at odds with the
rumbustious life and loves of a figure like Red Hanrahan. He was
to tell Katharine Tynan early in the new century that no one could
'write well in dialect unless he has been brought up talking it . . .
or has made a most exhaustive & scientific study of it like Synge
& Lady Gregory'.[75] Her *Emigrant's Notebook* and her short stories
demonstrate that Lady Gregory had experimented with Irish idiom
before she met Yeats, but his encouragment made this a more
conscious endeavour, and one which was to be of benefit to him.
It was a key element in their collaborative playwriting, and she also
revised the Red Hanrahan stories, transposing his literary English
into country speech. 'They are but half mine now', wrote Yeats,
'and often her beautiful idiom is the better half'.[76]

If collecting folklore, the patient accumulation of material on
behalf of Yeats, Ireland, and the people, appealed to her humility,

her work on the epics was a product of the other side of her nature, in that it satisfied her pride and desire for heroism. Once again, however, the basic task was editorial and scholarly rather than creative, the compilation and selection of material from a welter of texts, and the careful stitching together of a coherent narrative. It was a more ambitious project than the folklore, arising as it did out of her wish to do for Ireland what Malory had done for England, and Lady Charlotte Guest, the mother of her great friend Enid Layard, for Wales. Yet, although Malory had long been among her favourite books, her abnegating nature needed an excuse to undertake such a task and this was provided when Robert Atkinson, a Trinity professor, denounced Gaelic literature as silly and indecent. Having piously elicited Yeats's and Hyde's permission, Lady Gregory set out to prove otherwise. Once more her purpose was to raise the dignity of Ireland, this time by establishing Gaelic mythology as an important and proud national possession and, in so doing, hold up a heroic mirror to her countrymen in which they might recognize and learn to imitate the old virtues amid the venialities of the modern world. The idiom in which she chose to do this was the crucial factor. Hers is not the first rendering of the mythological cycles in English since both Standish Hayes and Standish James O'Grady had produced such translations, and the latter's *History of Ireland* had exerted a seminal influence on Yeats and AE. Yet the style of both the O'Gradys is heavily influenced by their classical training, and too prone to unwieldy latinisms and extended similes. Lady Gregory's text avoids these, substituting instead a style soon to become known as 'Kiltartanese'. It is a style of studied simplicity and carefully placed idioms, too carefully placed for extended readings, when the repetitions and colloquialisms recur with a regularity that becomes mannered. Rather more than stylistic texture is at issue here, as a comparison with Synge will indicate. Both studied country idioms, both made notes on what they heard, but Synge is able to invest his language with a vividness and salt lacking in Lady Gregory. His superior knowledge of Gaelic has something to do with this, but so, more importantly, does the dynamic of his imagination. The patrician, and perhaps the woman, in Lady Gregory wished to see the peasantry, when not led astray by rabble-rousers. as gentle, courteous souls, and her language endorses this conception. The eloquence of Synge's characters is an altogether more energetic and volatile thing: it resides not in courtesy but in emotional hunger and deprivation, even cruelty.

The richness of imagination and language in his plays is an extravagant compensation for what life has denied. Synge and Yeats have intensity and even ecstasy, but her attempts to attain such moments of emotional or spiritual pressure are unconvincing both in the epics and in her plays. It is significant that, notwithstanding Yeats's disapproval, she bowdlerized her bardic material. She could rationalize this censorship by arguing that the books were to be read by children, or that it denied Atkinson and Mahaffy further ammunition for their attacks on Gaelic literature, but there is surely a deeper reason: the extravagance of the Gaelic imagination pointed to a power that she could neither appropriate nor tame, for it introduced a view of the world that would be for ever beyond her.

Yeats's hyperbolic reception of *Cuchulain of Muirthemne*, 'the best book to have come out of Ireland in my time', is well known.[77] To explain this hyperbole as simply the rent now due on Coole hospitality would be to misunderstand the nature of the relationship. Yeats could and frequently did exaggerate the literary achievements of his friends, not because they were friends (he was also capable of penetrating criticism, as Lady Gregory had reason to know) but because his friendships were grounded in shared attitudes towards life and the kind of literature that expressed those attitudes. *Cuchulain of Muirthemne* was published at a time when his views on Irish literature and society were undergoing a painful reappraisal. He had chosen to be an Irish poet because he thought Ireland would provide an audience and an energy of imagination not to be found elsewhere. Although his experiences in the theatre were now beginning to shake that confidence, Lady Gregory's books helped to shore up his hopes by drawing attention to the Irish qualities he most wished to exalt, and by arguing that they were still an essential component of a continuing racial memory. 'The fruit of all these stories', he wrote in his introduction, 'is the quick intelligence, the abundant imagination, the courtly manners of the Irish country people.'[78] As his treatment in Dublin, that 'unmannerly town', grew increasingly bitter, and it became clear to him that urban Ireland was turning its back on these traditional virtues, a compensatory belief that they survived among the country people (a belief that Lady Gregory insisted upon) became ever more necessary and congenial. Yet his reception of her two epic books show how quickly his faith even in this was waning. In *Cuchulain of Muirthemne* he had identified the courtly behaviour of the bardic heroes with the surviving courtesy of the modern peasant; by the time he comes to write of *Gods and Fighting Men*, however, he finds that this ancient courtesy 'has gone perhaps out of the world', and he closes not in an assertion but in the conditional:

If we would create a great community — and what other game is so worth the labour? — we must recreate the old foundations of life . . . as they must always exist when the finest minds and Ned the beggar and Sean the fool think about the same thing, although they may not think the same thought about it.[79]

*

By the beginning of the new century the friendship had already settled down into a productive alliance, but in one respect it disappointed Lady Gregory. While pleased to have a young literary lion as her friend, and delighted to aid him materially and in his collection of folklore, she still felt her own desire for authorship thwarted. No amount of editorial success could make up for this, and she was afraid of turning out to be 'one of those dull people who edit books'.[80] She was constantly looking for openings for her creative gifts and trawling for the encouragement that would give her the confidence to use them. It was inevitable that she should find her opportunity in drama. Looking back, Yeats, who always had a propensity for viewing both the public and private world in apocalyptic terms, professed himself amazed at her sudden transformation into a playwright, for he had not suspected a literary gift.[81] This was impercipient; from childhood she had been an avid reader, and her brief affair with Blunt had brought out the poet in her. We have seen how she used the short story to explore her own relationship to Ireland, and the editing of her husband's memoirs and his father's letters, though undertaken, she insisted, as acts of family piety, earned her a heady measure of literary acclaim. Her friend Lecky had shrewdly prophesied that 'I shall go on writing, says that it is "like drink" '.[82] By the mid-nineties she was fast using up her editorial material and was thrown back on her own resources. Like a number of middle-aged women of her class in Ireland, she thought in the first place of short stories which would draw upon her knowledge of County Galway and its families, and even become projections of her own position and perplexities. Her models at this time were Jane Barlow and Emily Lawless, but both demonstrated the difficulties facing Ascendancy ladies who wished to go native in their writings. In Barlow's *Irish Idylls*, the problem is one of narrative stance. She creates the small village of Lisconnel, as Lady Gregory had invented the small community of Cloon in 'A Philanthropist', and is eager to give a sympathetic portrait of the simple lives of the people there. Yet as so often in nineteenth century Anglo-Irish fiction, the narrator feels obliged to explain the eccentricities of Irish manners and speech too directly and obtrusively. Although she identifies herself as an inhabitant of Lisconnel, her register of language and sophistication of perception reveal her as a knowledgeable outsider speaking to unknowledgeable outsiders. The instability of narrative tone is felt in the sudden switch between Irish country dialect and classical allusions, French *mots justes*, and passages of studiedly fine writing. Lady Gregory had a keener ear for peasant speech and more consistency, but the underlying uncertainty of the authorial stance, the tendency to explain and justify, and therefore to patronize, was harder to overcome. Emily Lawless, very similar to Lady Gregory in upbringing and outlook, was also a potential, but finally impossible model, dividing her characters as she does too starkly between a sentimentalised and a brutalised peasantry. Lady Gregory had no desire to show the Irish as brutal. Violet Martin, the Ross of 'Somerville and Ross', was also a good friend, and some of the characters and humour in 'A Gentleman' (for example, the landlord's wayward nephew and O'Loughlin's scrapes) are reminiscent of *The Irish R.M.*. But Yeats did not like Miss Martin (the antipathy was mutual) and Lady Gregory, under his guidance, found her humour too robust, too far from the Celtic Twilight and too near the stage Irishman; her comedy was to be a gentler thing.

In 1900 Lady Gregory 'dreamed that I had been writing some article & that W. B. Y. said "It's not your business to write — your business is to make an atmosphere".'[83] But it was no longer a question simply of articles. The dramatic movement was providing new possibilities that she was eager to explore. She wrote her first play on her way back from Italy in this year, a simple rhyming account of a local Gort saint which was not published until much later.[84] Meanwhile Yeats was collaborating on *Diarmuid and Grania* with George Moore but finding an appropriate register of language as difficult to achieve as ever, and *Hail and Farewell* gives a wonderful account of the bizarre lengths to which he and Moore felt obliged to go in search of an answerable style.[85] Watching his plays on the stage had brought home to him the necessity of establishing an authentic folk voice, a task that was not only laborious in itself but constantly in hazard from Moore's preciosity. Lady Gregory saw her opportunity. She had, as always, been helping Yeats with the typing of his drafts, and now she began helping 'with words as well'. Within a few days she was 'going through "Grania" altering Moore's words'[86] and her career as a dramatist was almost underway.

In fact, the Irish dramatic movement provided new scope for her talents at every level. Initially her social position, authority and organizational skills were most in demand. Yeats's long-nursed ambition to set up Irish travelling companies had come to nothing, and in 1897 he was thinking of taking a theatre in a London suburb. Lady Gregory, well aware of the seriousness with which he regarded his playwrighting, managed to convince him in their famous conversation at Count Basterot's that he could fulfil his dramatic ambitions and still keep within Ireland's (and her) orbit. Her contacts and social prestige were important in transforming these dreams into realities: she lobbied parliamentary friends to pass legislation which extended theatrical licensing in Dublin, and used her influence in finding rich subscribers for the Irish Literary Theatre. She went on to play an important managerial role at the Abbey, backing Yeats up in quarrels with critics, playwrights, and actors, and yet also applying her tact to good effect in disputes which his lack of diplomacy, and sometimes lack of common sense, had aggravated. Coole, far from the prying eyes of Dublin, could be used for directors' meetings, sometimes almost conspiratorial in nature, as well as a base from which to plan the season's productions or discuss future policy. Even if she had never written a single play, Lady Gregory would still have been crucial to the history of the Abbey Theatre.

But write she did. As we have seen, her beginnings were characteristic; making herself useful by revising Yeats's text, half editor, half amanuensis, she gradually worked her way into the position of collaborator, and finally creator in her own right. The more we learn of these collaborations, the larger her contribution appears and while a definitive account of their work together must await a more detailed analysis, an undertaking now in the very capable hands of James Pethica, it is possible to say something of the qualities that each brought to the task. Although very different, these qualities were for a time complementary, and they centred particularly on problems of language and structure. Yeats had a dramatic imagination; conflict, intensity, and passion were always central to his poetic endeavour, but he lacked a language that could render the demotic expression of Irish life, what he described as 'country emotion'. Lady Gregory had that language, and had already delighted him by translating his folklore into it. Her imagination was not, however, primarily dramatic but narrative; her plays grow out of words and situations rather than action and conflict.

The pattern of the collaboration was set with the composition of *Cathleen ni Houlihan*: Yeats had the dream, but Lady Gregory translated it into idiomatic speech. The process was repeated with *Where There is Nothing*; Yeats had the idea, Lady Gregory helped him with the language, and finally recast it for him as *The Unicorn From The Stars*. Neither is a great play, and *Where There is Nothing* is the more uneven of the two, but it has an energy and intensity that *The Unicorn from the Stars* lacks. Paul Routledge's vision is extravagant, didactic, and bombastic, but retains the power to disturb; domesticated in the later play it becomes wordy and ultimately diminished. Under Yeats's influence, Lady Gregory felt it necessary to try for vision from time to time, but lacked the imaginative energy and conviction to sustain such aspirations. *The Image* is an example of her inability to distinguish between daydream and vision, and so belies the promise of the Preface and disappoints in theme and action. At her best she knew this. Grania, the heroine who is closer to autobiographical representation than any of her other characters (significantly, she never allowed *Grania* to be produced, although it is one of her best plays), expresses the fundamentally sceptical and pragmatic nature of her creator. When Diarmuid unfolds his vision of Tir na nOg, she replies 'I have not had the full of my life yet, for it is scared and hiding I have spent the best years that are past . . . I would wish to bring you back now to some busy peopled place.'[87] This is precisely the opposite in sentiment to Deirdre's romantic lament for the pastoral idyll of Alba which so many of the poets of the Irish Revival found inspiring, but it no less precisely corresponds to the matter-of-factness that is a main ingredient of Lady Gregory's make-up. She was not given to seeing fairies at Coole, although Yeats, and even more AE, apparently discovered myriads there, and Tir na nOg for her as for Grania would have been 'very strange . . . and very lonesome'.[88] Thus, while ventures into 'spirituality' were always a temptation to her as she searched for the dignity of significance, she is far more successful when she abjures symbolism and returns to homely retellings of the Christian stories, as in *The Story Brought by Brigit*, which keep within her orthodoxy of thought and register of language.

Her most satisfactory plays, and her most successful collaborations, are the short 'folk' plays. These suited her talent, and the limitations of that talent, and in the first years of their work were what Yeats wanted. At this time he still believed that the intellect of Ireland was 'romantic and spiritual rather than scientific and analytical', and hoped that 'the war of immortal upon mortal life [which] has been the moving thought of much Irish poetry' might inspire many new Irish plays.[89] The most important of these plays would be poetic dramas, but he also saw that to create a truly national theatre he must appeal to a wider audience through a series of folk plays which would sound similar themes in a minor key. For this he needed Lady Gregory, and she contributed largely to *The Pot of Broth* and to *The Hour-Glass*. Such a simple mode of writing could not content Yeats for long, nor does it show him at his best, and his imagination soon turned to the Red Branch mythological cycle for his subjects. Lady Gregory went on to write her own folk plays, at first predominantly comedies, a little later histories, then dramas involving the relationship of the natural to the supernatural life, and finally lively, sprawling pantomimes undertaken in two cases for her grandchildren.

Drama solved one of the problems that faced Ascendancy fiction writers, that of point of view, for in avoiding narrative it enabled her to adopt an apparently more objective stance. In fact, her plays continue to endorse the view of the people she had first presented in the *Emigrant's Notebook* and her short stories, the sympathetic patrician's view which finds them talkative, amusing, essentially kind-hearted, and endlessly gullible. This gullibility is the spring of many of her plots and she is prone to push it to such absurd lengths that many of her characters are little more than variants of the stage-Irishman: they lack the vulgarity associated with the stereotype, but they certainly surrender little in stupidity. In the shorter, fast-moving comedies, such as *Spreading the News* or *Hyacinth Harvey*, the speed of incident permits a suspension of disbelief at such improbable silliness, but in other plays (for example *The Full Moon, Coats, The Bogie Men* and *The Canavans*) her prolixity so slows the action that egregious error grows wilfully tiresome as a simple mistake is relentlessly milked for its comic possibilities.

Many of her discussions with Yeats about playwriting centre

upon problems of construction. In this respect the collaboration was a case of the blind leading the blind, for neither she nor Yeats had much practical experience of the theatre in the beginning, and neither had conspicuous ability in construction at any time. Both are at their best in one-act pieces, although for different reasons. Yeats is always seeking the point of maximum intensity (in extolling Shakespearean tragedy he always, as in 'Lapis Lazuli', cites such moments) but his imagination is so fertile that he finds it difficult to shape his material. She pointed to the problem in a letter of November 1902, warning him that 'you are like Puppy after a chicken when you see a new idea cross the path, tho' it may but end in a mouth full of feathers after all'.[90] Gradually he learned to subordinate everything to the climactic moment, and the concentration this involved reduced his structural problems, especially after he discovered the Noh form. In focussing on moments of high drama he was playing to his strengths, for the creation of 'character' in its understood sense had always presented difficulties, and if he could not gain a command of Irish idiom, he was likewise incapable of differentiating character through individual speech mannerisms. Lady Gregory had almost the opposite problem. She could register idiomatic patterns of speech but lacked the excitement of new ideas or the ability to sustain moments of intensity. Her difficulty was knowing when to stop the flow of language, or to develop ideas or incidents that would give that flow its appropriate dramatic occasion. Aristotle argued that action was the first requisite of drama; in one of her more revealing observations she describes drama as a matter merely of speech. Plays with long or would-be intricate plots, such as *The Canavans* and *The White Cockade*, sag under the sheer weight of words that slow the action and confuse the themes. Such failures involve more than artistic competence; a limiting paternalism is also at work. Delighted with the scampish scrapes that her characters get into, and the quaint way they express themselves, she indulges herself and them. At first the Abbey's need for short curtain-raisers imposed a necessary and benign discipline upon her; when she grew more ambitious her difficulties grew more acute. Only towards the end of her career did she manage to make a virtue of her lack of constructive skill by writing a number of baggy pantomimic plays based on folk stories and aimed at a juvenile audience.

Her early folk plays are a product of the Esther Summerson part of her nature; she wished to be of service both to the Abbey in providing plays and comic relief, and to the people by portraying them in a sympathetic, even cosy, light. It is significant that although she supported the production of *The Playboy of the Western World* in the teeth of controversy, she did not personally care for the play. Her tragedies are, however, an expression of the other side of her temperament. *Kincora*, *Grania*, and *Dervorgilla* celebrate powerful women who alter history through their sexuality. Like Lady Gregory, they are attracted to 'strong' men or, lacking these, impose their own strength on the menfolk they have. Although structurally weak (*Kincora* required extensive rewritings to get it even into its present shape) these plays try to dramatize emotions and attitudes not found elsewhere in her creative work, although the Witch in *The Golden Apple* and the Princess in *The Dragon* are late if sketchy treatments of strong women. Her later plays are also concerned with the development of heroic qualities, especially self-sufficiency, and have a distinctly didactic element. In *The Jester*, a group of over-refined young princes are re-united with long-lost cousins who have gone native, and the play proposes that each side should learn from the other, the rude but tough cousins gaining manners and dignity from the princes, the princes getting in return 'wisdom of woods, and the way to outrun the wild deer, / Till we'll harden our minds with courage, and be masters of hardship and fear'.[91] It is a parable which makes actual the long wished-for union between the Ascendancy and the people, although it is significant that the cousins, too, turn out to have royal blood. In fact, lurking behind a number of Lady Gregory's plays is the desire for a strong man, an aristocratic hero, who will unite a people confused by false bourgeois aspirations and lead them to dignity and national self-consciousness. This is the theme of *The White Cockade* and *The Deliverer*. Even more pervasive is an attack on middle-class values and their political consequences, represented by the time-servers in *The White Cockade*, the anti-Parnellites in *The Deliverer*, the West Britons in *The Canavans*, the Unionists in *The Wrens*, the villainous Doctor in *The Golden Apple* and the counter-hopping tailor's son in *The Dragon*. All are men who would be uncomfortable in clean shirts, all disrupt the vision of a dignified Ireland, organized from the top into an orderly, benevolent and harmonious society.

Although equipped with a strongly dramatic imagination, Yeats was not a born dramatist. Nor was Lady Gregory: they made themselves competent at their craft. They did this partly by mutual help at the writing stage, but they had also a theatre where they could test their experiments in performance. They could monitor, and even produce each other's work over a period of time, suggesting alterations and amendments. Their correspondence, Yeats's in particular, is full of advice as to how their plays may be made more theatrically effective. Technically, the collaboration was thus a continuing process, involving not only the writing of new plays, but also the revision of old ones. Aesthetically, its value is harder to judge. She always made a point of deferring to his artistic judgments and in *Our Irish Theatre* states unequivocally that the production of poetic drama is the Abbey Theatre's *raison d'etre*.[92] Yet, a few years later she apparently told Maurice Browne that the Abbey had started with the 'liability' of confusing 'theatric with literary values', and on the same American tour confessed that had she 'not become interested in the Gaelic movement . . . I should doubtless have turned my attention to the music halls of England'.[93] Yeats would have regarded this as an artistic fate a good deal worse than death, but it would have suited her talents. Her friendship with Yeats, however, kept her more constantly at aesthetic attention and prompted her to experiment. In some of the middle plays this produces a sense of strain and a too obvious and reductive striving for significance, but its final effect was to result in a canon more varied and more ambitious than she would otherwise have attempted.

*

By 1904 the first flush of the friendship was over. The sense of discovery inevitably passed and gave way to a relationship of more settled rhythms. This was not merely a case of emotional familiarity; it involved the growth of administrative responsibility in the theatre and, no less importantly, a disillusionment with the possibilities of Irish literature. The late nineties had been a period of expanding hopes which the new century punctured. They had founded an Irish Theatre to express a Romantic idealism: in the event it stirred up tensions and contradictions that had larger national and cultural implications, and its development was more contentious than they could have foreseen. As these contentions grew more bitter they found it necessary to close ranks behind an authority that was at once artistic, social, and economic. A hint of things to come was given in 1902 when they combined to squash the production of James Cousins's play *Sold*, the first of many unilateral artistic decisions that were to bring them into conflict with audiences, writers and actors. A more damaging dispute broke out in 1904 when the actors Dudley Digges and Maire Quinn, together with Maud Gonne and Douglas Hyde, resigned from the company over the production of Synge's *In the Shadow of the Glen*. By 1905 both Yeats and Lady Gregory had concluded that the loosely democratic structure of the National Theatre Company would be a perpetual stumbling block to their ambitions for the Abbey, and used Coole to plan a coup that would give them and Synge directorial (and in effect dictatorial) control of the Company. This led to a further secession by actors and playwrights, as did the row over *The Playboy of the Western World* in 1907. In the following year the directors found it necessary to part company with the Fays. They also resisted Dublin Castle's attempts to censor them by going ahead with a production of Shaw's *The Shewing Up of Blanco Posnet*. Miss Horniman let it be known that she wished to discontinue her subsidy and caused much extra difficulty over this when in 1910, owing to a misunderstanding, the theatre remained open on the day of the King's death. The withdrawal of Miss Horniman's money made fund-raising an urgent necessity but they were able to secure the Theatre by giving lectures and mobilising wealthy or influential friends. Such friends had already been of value in supporting the Company on its visits to London, and Lady Gregory helped to win it a larger international reputation by organizing and leading several arduous American tours, during which she courageously stood up to violent attacks from Irish-American opponents of Synge and even arrest in Philadelphia.

This account gives the bare bones of the difficulties and crises that were a regular part of running the Abbey Theatre but says nothing of the day-to-day worries about props, scenery, inefficiencies, back-stage intrigues, and jealousies among the actors. Even so, it reveals how much at a merely practical level the Abbey owed to this friendship. Without Yeats and Lady Gregory the Irish dramatic movement would not have started, and had it lost them at any time between 1899 and 1918 it would not have lasted more than a few weeks. Nor is it likely that either of them would have been able to carry on alone, the strain would have been too great. More than this, their gifts and talents were complementary: Yeats's creative drive and impetuosity kept things moving, her diplomacy, eye for detail, and practicality ensured that things got done without ruffling more feathers than strictly necessary.

That many feathers nevertheless were ruffled is an indication of how sensitive and complex the artistic and political situation in

Ireland was becoming. They had hoped to find 'a tolerant welcome'[94] in Ireland for the dramatic movement but quickly discovered themselves under attack from several different quarters. Lady Gregory did all she could in a vain attempt to appease such hostility. She sacrificed *The Poorhouse* to Douglas Hyde for translation into Irish in an attempt to win over the Gaelic League which was deeply suspicious of a 'national' theatre using English as its medium. She assiduously tried to cultivate D. P. Moran who, notwithstanding his contribution to *Ideals in Ireland*, had taken to criticising the Theatre in *The Leader* for its supposed paganism, Protestantism (he was not over-scrupulous in differentiating between the two), and lack of national feeling. The production of Synge's plays brought a rupture with Arthur Griffith and with his weekly paper *United Irishman*, hitherto a friend and supporter. Even Lady Gregory's applied tact could not prevail against combined opposition like this, and the trust in 'a tolerant wlecome' soon seemed a distant and ironic dream. As early as May 1902 she advised Yeats not to send his books to the Dublin papers for review since they 'have evidently an idea they shd be sort of truffle dogs where you are concerned, to scent out heresy however concealed'.[95]

This growing impatience was reciprocal. While Dublin was becoming more critical of Yeats, and to a lesser degree of Lady Gregory, he himself was changing in outlook towards Irish affairs. He had come to the realization that his 'mission in Ireland is to serve taste rather than any definite propaganda',[96] an ambition which was so precisely Lady Gregory's own that she must have smiled at his sudden discovery of an idea which she had done so much to inculcate. In preparing for a lecture on Robert Emmet he was astonished to find 'how far I have thought myself out of the whole stream of Irish feeling on such subjects. I am just as strenuous a Nationalist as ever, but I have got to express these things differently.'[97] The *Playboy* riots, the death of Synge and the quarrel with the Dublin Corporation over the Lane pictures demonstrated the arduousness of serving taste, but strengthened their alliance and their determination to impose dignity on their countrymen even in the latters' own despite. As Yeats's discouragement with popular opinion grew, he found a relationship between his developing literary views and the aristocratic, social authority which impressed him at Coole. Literary style became associated for him with good breeding. The people could only be 'conquered by an ideal of life upheld by authority' he announced, and took to defining style as 'but high breeding in words and in argument'. 'Protestant social prejudice' which he had deplored in the previous decade, he now praised for keeping 'our ablest men from levelling passions'.[98]

Yeats's always volatile nature was under particular strain at this time. Physically, this took its toll in a number of nervous complaints which gave Lady Gregory cause for concern. Intellectually, it was a period of reappraisal and his experience of Coole played an essential part in this rethinking. His larger aim in the 'nineties had been to create a Unity of Culture in Ireland that would make possible what he described as 'Unity of Being'. His experiences in running the Theatre taught him how far more difficult it was to create a cross-class cultural unity than he had imagined, and by 1909 he came to realize that he had been on the wrong track. He had been seeking Unity intellectually and critically,

whereas Unity of Being . . . is found emotionally, instinctively, by the rejection of all experience not of the right quality, and by the limitation of its quantity. Of this I knew nothing . . . Nor did I understand as yet how little that Unity, however wisely sought, is possible without a Unity of Culture in a class of people that is no longer possible at all.[99]

If it was no longer possible generally, Coole offered a microcosm of what it might be, and he saw the house increasingly as an outpost of true cultural values in a rampantly philistine world. His reading of Nietzsche and Castiglione helped him in different ways to amplify and focus these ideas. Nietzsche's philosophy could explain and sanction his sense of separateness, and invested his stance of cultivated hero outfacing the mob with a mask of nobility. The influence of Castiglione, although less rousing, was pervasive, for *The Courtier* celebrated the duties as well as the rights of position and birth. Castiglione's Urbino seemed close enough to Lady Gregory's Coole for both to be illuminated by the comparison, and when he thought Lady Gregory in danger of death, words from *The Courtier* so moved him that he 'felt all his sorrow as though one saw the worth of life fade for ever.'[100] Nietzsche sets up a code of the individual; Castiglione a code of manners. They sharpened the terms of a debate Yeats had already begun with himself on the relationship of tradition to the individual talent. Increasingly, he had come to regard tradition as encompassing not only a literary style but also a style of conduct and behaviour, and the unruly and rancorous attitudes of his

Dublin critics intensified this view. Yet a man whose poetry is located in the dramatisation of self-division and for whom the concept of antinomy was to be crucial, found it difficult to submit himself to some pre-existent code, no matter how satisfying this might be from a larger cultural viewpoint.

*

This 'quarrel with himself' inspired a series of poems about Coole which articulate Yeats's continuing debate with himself about his friendship with Lady Gregory and the values that she and her code embodied. They also explore his growing realization that his cultural aims are out of joint with the times, that Coole represents a social order and way of life that are obsolescent. His meditations upon these themes helped to change him from a poet of the 'Celtic Twilight' into a modernist, a transition that went far beyond questions of style.

The earliest Coole poem, dated September 1900 and beginning 'I walked among the Seven Woods of Coole', was written to preface his play *The Shadowy Waters*.[101] The play, like much of his poetry in the 'nineties, centres upon a desire to escape the primary, everyday world for an antithetical, paradisical state of being. This quest had been the theme of many of the poems in *The Wind Among the Reeds*, poems which tremble uncertainly on the brink of an always unachieved revelation. The wind in the reeds, the everlasting voices uttering themselves through nature, recall an Edenic state but also remind the poet that the Fall has put it out of reach. This first Coole poem, however, makes a new and fruitful proposal: as he walks among the Seven Woods Yeats speculates that Eden may be there, the natural and supernatural mirror images of each other. 'Is Eden far away', he asks the immortal shadows which are the source of inspiration,

> or do you hide
> From human thought, as hares and mice and coneys
> That run before the reaping-hook and lie
> In the last ridge of the barley? Do our woods
> And winds and ponds cover more quiet woods,
> More shining winds, more star-glimmering ponds?[102]

This is still Yeats of the 'nineties, seeking what he was later to describe as the holy city of the imagination, but it is a Yeats who, while posing the same questions, does so in a calmer, a more assured tone. Coole has given him a focus; its numinous woods and legends provide the topography of an earthly paradise that can reconcile the natural and supernatural, the primary and antithetical. The place was always to be a domain of spirits for him, but after the 'nineties less one of elemental creatures than of human shades — a sanctified spot still, but a spot now sanctified by mortal memories.

In 1900, Yeats was later to remark, everyone got down off their stilts.[103] The descent for Yeats involved the recognition that the symbolist movement and the Irish Literary Revival had not been the harbingers of a new dispensation, 'the revolt of the soul against the intellect', that he had prophesied. A changing perception of the world compelled him to those changes in style noticed by contemporary and later critics. Coole became more important than ever in providing him with both psychic and physical distance from an increasingly hostile world, and in its continuing cultivation of those unfashionable virtues he thought most necessary to a healthy culture. It is significant that two poems about Coole, 'In the Seven Woods' and 'When I from that reed-throated whisperer' stand like book-ends at either side of the period of transition as key expressions of his new departure in thought and articulation. Both, like the Coole poems written between, extol those qualities he had come to associate with Lady Gregory and set them up in an increasingly desperate defiance against what he saw as the rancorousness, deceit and vulgarity of the modern world. Each poem in the series registers a shift in attitude towards a bleaker and more pessimistic view of the state of society and of the historical situation.

'In the Seven Woods', like 'I walked among the seven woods of Coole', celebrates the demesne rather than the house and, as in the earlier poem, the woods are still numinous — 'Quiet wanders there and the Great Archer hangs his quiver above Pairc-na-lee' — but it is now less an earthly paradise than a refuge. Of course, Yeats's poetry had praised refuges before, most famously in 'The Lake Isle of Innisfree', but Coole is not as in earlier locations a place of escape from the world, but a place of rest and recuperation in which the poet can take stock of his situation. The poem places him in the woods of Coole where he has 'put away/The unavailing outcries and the old bitterness/That empty the heart',[104] but things 'put away' are not destroyed. They remain out of sight, but as the poem reminds us not out of mind, and the temporary nature of the respite is accentuated by the temporal adverb in 'I have forgot *awhile*/Tara uprooted'. The image of Tara, the ancient seat of Irish kingship, uprooted was suggested by a recent desecration of the site[105] but gains a wider and more powerful association by its juxtaposition with images of artificiality and rootlessness as the modern world hangs 'its paper flowers from post to post'. Just as traditional organic societies are destroyed to be replaced by the transient sensationalism of contemporary life so is heroic majesty reduced to the new commonness of Edward VII and his recent coronation. Arboreous Coole, however, with its lime-tree (not paper) flowers is a place of roots in more than one sense. Its peace is of natural not artificial things, a point deftly enforced by the assonance and soothing labials of the first three lines contrasted with the discordant 'c's and 't's of the next four, as the harmonious sounds of the rural world, its hums and faint thunder, give way to the recollected 'crying about the streets' of urban restlessness and triviality. This restlessness and triviality were to weigh more heavily upon Yeats over the coming years, but in 1902, he was still close enough to his mood of the 'nineties to rest contented that Quiet and the enigmatic Great Archer might still bring round the revelatory or apocalyptic moment. The tenses of the verbs in the poem endorse this optimism, moving from the past perfect 'I have', through the present 'I am', to the promise of a projected future 'but awaits His hour'. What the Great Archer purposes with his arrows is left as cloudy as the quiver itself, but has both a national and artistic reference. Describing his experiences among the nationalists in September 1899 he told Lady Gregory 'our "patriots" intreague [*sic*] against each other & lose all fine perceptions of any truth in crude angers. Yet doubtless the gods are but biding their time somewhere'.[106] In the poem this allusion to a hoped-for but vague promise gains precision by its association with 'the Great Archer', Apollo, the 'far-darter', much on Yeats's mind since his recent reading of Nietzsche:

I have always felt that the soul has two movements primarily: one to transcend forms, and the other to create forms. Nietzsche . . . calls these the Dionysiac and the Apollonic, respectively. I think I have to some extent got weary of that wild God Dionysus, and I am hoping that the Far-Darter will come in his place.[107]

The poem looks forward then to a new movement in Yeats's thought and poetry. Dionysian transcendence, with its longing for a new dispensation, the mood of the first Coole poem, seemed no longer appropriate to a world where 'new commonness' was crying down the old traditions, and he turned to Apollonian control. Elsewhere he described the Dionysiac spirit as 'sad and desirous', but the Apollonic as 'joyful and self-sufficient', the qualities exhibited by Quiet 'laughing and eating her wild heart' amid the Coole woods. The image of 'Quiet', a personified abstraction, hearkens back to a 'nineties manner that he was in the process of abandoning. Henceforward he will associate the desired Apollonian qualities directly with Lady Gregory and with Coole, and so make the indefinite definite, the abstract concrete.

In giving Coole a greater physical presence in the poetry, Yeats had also to face up to its historical situation. The economics of faeryland had been of as little concern to him as the gastric consequences of a diet of honey and beans on Innisfree, but Coole could not so readily elude its political and social contexts. 'Man cannot know truth but he can embody it', Yeats was to write, and he found that this was also true of women and houses. But embodiment, incarnation, entails falling into time, and subjection to the changes that time can bring. Lady Gregory had been conscious from the early 'nineties that time was running out for her and her class, and that Dobson's three choices loomed. After the turn of the century the clock seemed to speed up, or at least strike more menacingly, and in the summer of 1909 she found herself in dispute with her tenants over rent reductions, an event which deeply engaged Yeats's emotions and which spurred him to another Coole poem, now known as 'Upon a House Shaken by the Land Agitation'.[108] It is an undisguisedly Tory poem, grounded in the belief that social and economic inequalities are necessary to nurse exceptional virtues. The economic threat to Lady Gregory affected him so intensely because it was also a threat to him and to a way of life that had been of inestimable value to him. The penury of his pre-Coole days had, he felt, led him to write with too conscious a purpose so that he detected 'a lack of life's own values behind my thought'.[109] He expanded this personal experience into a general conviction 'that where all must make their living they will live not for life's sake but the work's, and all be the poorer'. Coole and its wealth allowed those associated with it to escape from this impoverishing treadmill:

This house has enriched my soul out of measure, because here life moves without restraint through spacious forms. Here there has been no compelled labour, no poverty-thwarted impulse.[110]

It is this enrichment that the poem seeks to celebrate and the original title, 'To a Certain Country House in Time of Change', made it clear that his homage was directed towards a specific house. In re-titling the poem Yeats moved the specificity from the house to the historical moment; the new title suggests that Coole is to be seen as representative of a whole class, a whole way of life, and at the same time makes the historical process more definite. This new awareness of historical challenge gives the poem an urgency not found in 'In the Seven Woods'; what had seemed in the earlier poem a secure refuge against the levelling hostility of the world is now itself under attack from that world. Thus the later poem is an appeal against the march of time and social reform — an unfashionable cause, as Yeats knows, and so he is at some pains to make his pleading persuasive. He is careful to frame his argument not as a plain statement of fact, but as a series of apparently open questions which nevertheless invite the answer he wants, both through the terms in which they are posed and through the climactic drive of rhythm and phrasing, which, as in 'No Second Troy', sweep the reader on with no opportunity to demur. Moreover, he assiduously avoids naming names, or alluding to specific classes or situations that might provoke dissent. The argument is conducted in terms of architecture — the relationship of grand house and mean roof-trees — so aesthetizing and blurring the sharp issues of economic and social rights and wrongs. Some adroit revisions further help to blur these issues. The poem originally began 'How should the world be better if this house . . . became too ruinous . . ?' This posits a straight evaluative question susceptible to economic and even moral answers that Yeats had no wish to hear. By altering 'better' to 'luckier', and by again drawing attention to the element of chance later in the poem ('How should their luck run high enough'), he makes the question no longer one of applied economics but of a benign Fate which mysteriously but marvellously confers gifts and graces otherwise denied to mankind. The world is luckier in that it has houses like Coole, but it is not merely luck that creates them: chance and choice must operate together through the agency of time. If chance is luck, choice involves marriage and careful breeding, 'the best knit to the best', and a self-conscious and self-sustaining sense of tradition 'Where wings have memory of wings'. The Nietzschean image of the eagle which Yeats uses to symbolize this sense of superiority becomes current in the poetry of this time but here is used in a particularly absolute way. In 'To a Wealthy Man . . .' and 'To a Shade' he was to suggest that art might eventually develop finer sensibilities among the plebeians by providing 'the right twigs for an eagle's nest', but in this poem the gulf between the eagles and the rest seems unbridgeable: no amount of time will give the lesser breeds the luck to climb to the highest gifts.

Precisely what these patrician gifts are is left vague until the end of the poem, which begins by gesturing towards indefinite plenitudes of rich imprecisions, 'laughing eagle thoughts', and 'all that comes of the best knit to the best'. Part of Yeats's problem is that he could never put an exact valuation on these gifts. The value of Coole to him had been calculable; it had given him psychological and physical space to work in, but these advantages were of less obvious application to the larger world. 'Upon a House' is, like many of the Coole poems, an essentially private poem taking on a public role and finding the two modes difficult to reconcile. At the end we discover that most important among the glories of Coole are 'the gifts that govern men' and 'a written speech': authority and authorship, two attributes that Yeats now thought interdependent in the creation of a fine culture since 'No art can conquer the people alone — the people are conquered by an ideal of life upheld by authority'.[111] Specifically he was thinking of Sir William Gregory's governership of Ceylon and Lady Gregory's comedies, her 'written speech . . . of high laughter', but when he tries to expand his theme to include earlier generations, 'Time out of mind', and perhaps the Ascendancy class as a whole, he has more difficulty in finding anything more exemplary than visions of general good and imprecise Nietzschean virtues.

If previous generations were a problem, so were future ones. Time is a central figure in the poem (as it will be in subsequent Coole poems), but it is an ambiguous one. The force of the poem relies heavily on the excitement of a climactic thrust towards completion, towards

> gradual Time's last gift, a written speech
> Wrought of high laughter, loveliness and ease . . . [112]

There is an ambiguity about 'last' that leaves the poem unresolved for all the assurance of its closing rhetoric and rhythm. Literature is not the latest but the 'last' gift that Coole may expect; it is the 'last' in being the greatest but also in being the final, the ultimate. If this is the case, what can 'gradual Time' produce next, except anticlimax? It seems that Coole has even now come to the end of its cycle. The poem registers a contradiction in Yeats's thinking that was forced into articulation for the first time at this period. He had gone to Ireland for his themes because he thought he could find there passion and cultural cohesion. Failing to find these qualities among the people he turned to the 'cultivated classes', but discovered that they, even when not Anglophile and suspicious of him, were in decline. Coole under Lady Gregory comes, therefore, to constitute an epiphanic moment whose glory is intensified and defined by its own imminent demise. 'Upon a House' ostensibly celebrates the necessity of crucial gifts while indirectly acknowledging that the time for such gifts is running out.

Lady Gregory's illness in 1909 helped to focus these conflicting feelings, for it made her death, and the end of Coole as he had known it, a sharp reality. Nearly all the poems that he wrote for her from that time forward were premature elegies, anticipating her end and the end of all that she had come to represent for him. This is certainly true of 'These Are The Clouds', written nearly a year after 'Upon a House', and in a more pessimistic mood. History is triumphing, and the poem has a strange conditional and future-perfect feel to it, as Yeats looks forward to what time must soon bring

> The weak lay hand on what the strong has done,
> Till that be tumbled that was lifted high
> And discord follow upon unison,
> And all things at one common level lie.[113]

'Upon a House' celebrated the 'high' gifts of Coole; this one mourns that what 'was lifted high' ('builded' in the draft, making the Coole association even closer) is to be levelled down to the merely 'common', the adjective, of course, implying both 'shared' and 'vulgar'. In this poem it seems that even the mean rooftrees will hardly be the sturdier for Coole's fall.

The second half of the poem snatches a moral and creative victory from the defeat that history and its agents, the weak, have inflicted. For Lady Gregory to have succeeded in anything in such conditions is seen as a signal achievement and

> so much the more thereby
> Have you made greatness your companion,
> Although it be for children that you sigh . . .[114]

The last line is ambiguous. If we did not know from biographical sources that Lady Gregory was well past the menopause by the time it was written, we might be forgiven for supposing that she was a barren woman longing to bear a child. What Yeats means, of course, is that she sighs *on behalf* of her child and grandchildren because they must live in a world where 'all things at one common level lie', and perhaps themselves participate in that commonness. Once again, Yeats is reluctant to entertain the thought that the Coole tradition might be carried on, even by Robert or his children. He has an almost proprietorial interest in 'gradual Time's last gift', it is a thing between him and Lady Gregory (and, in 'Coole Park', a handful of others) but it is not to outlast his generation.

The ambiguity of Yeats's attitude towards the Coole heirs and the possible future of the house is even more apparent in 'The New Faces', a poem that he wrote on the way home from a visit to Coole in December 1912, but which, on Lady Gregory's orders, he suppressed for a decade. Like 'Fallen Majesty' and 'A Friend's Illness', the poem is a premature elegy which contemplates a world without Lady Gregory, but, unlike them, it also treats the theme of inheritance — a question of vital interest to Lady Gregory, whose actions since 1892 had been primarily motivated by a desire to keep Coole intact for Robert, and which Yeats had made a central concern of 'Upon a House'. He begins by telling her that if she dies first he will never revisit the gardens or the house where 'we wrought that shall break the teeth of Time', and in the second half of the poem envisages Coole after both he and Lady Gregory are dead:

> Let the new faces play what tricks they will
> In the old rooms; night can outbalance day,
> Our shadows rove the garden gravel still,
> The living seem more shadowy than they.[115]

The poem was not published in *Responsibilities,* as one might have expected, but in *Seven Poems and a Fragment* in 1922. There are two possible explanations for this ten-year delay. Yeats might have thought it artistically inferior, or he might have considered that it offended against tact. The artistic explanation will not do; the poem is an accomplished one, and once it had been finished (within a few days of his beginning it) was not further revised. Professor Jeffares has more plausibly argued that the poem was not published because Yeats did not wish to remind Lady Gregory of her illness and increasing age,[116] but letters which have come to light since he wrote his article show that Yeats had had no hesitation in sending the poem to her on completion, and that it was she who asked him to hold it back.[117] If the poem was suppressed as a matter of tact it was tact not towards Lady Gregory but towards her descendants. She saw at once that the poem slights her son and grandchildren. The new faces at their tricks can only be Robert and his heirs, and the references to them are all but contemptuous: the superficiality of 'faces', the triviality of tricks, contrast with the adventurous energy of the shadows as they rove the gardens. Evidently 'gradual Time's last gift' will not pass to a later generation; on the contrary, the poem raises questions about Yeats's attitude to Robert, an attitude which seems to have been a good deal more ambivalent than the later elegies would suggest. While he admired some of his pictures, he had serious reservations about his will and determination. He passed on to Lady Gregory Hugh Lane's opinion that Robert would not work unless he needed money,[118] and reflections on the future led him to candid and sombre conclusions:

I thought of this house, slowly perfecting itself and the life within it in ever-increasing intensity of labour, and then of its probably sinking away through courteous incompetence or rather sheer weakness of will for ability has not failed in young Gregory.[119]

Robert Gregory's death left the question hanging, and the nature of the death gave Yeats the opportunity to resolve his doubts by gathering him into the artifice of epiphany. The unachieved past was redeemed by a present impulse of delight and a hyperbolic because unachievable future.

*

That Yeats should criticise Robert for lack of will is not without irony, for it was a reproach he frequently made against himself. He had always looked for passion in his own writing and admired it in that of others. In the 'nineties passion had presented itself in awesome but vague energies; now under the influence of Nietzsche and the 'Great Archer', he began to seek an Apollonian precision. One of the distinctions of Coole for him was that there 'passion and precision' were one; powerful feeling was controlled and directed by an inherited code of behaviour. It is to this code, which he associated partly with Nietzsche and partly with Castiglione, that he appeals in many of the poems written between 1900 and 1914, and it was all the more attractive to him because he felt in his own nature an excess of passion but an insufficiency of precision and balance. When writing to Lady Gregory during the dispute with her

tenants that inspired 'Upon A House', he explained that he was being
so vehement because 'I am always afraid of the sensitiveness,
created by imaginative culture, making one over yielding that I
perhaps push things the other way'.[120] He continued to ruffle in a
manly pose for all his timid heart, and this often led him into over-
reaction, especially in theatre disputes. Lady Gregory was able to
mitigate the worst consequences of his misjudgements through a
tact which, although sometimes applied too obviously, was
grounded in a consciousness of her social and moral distinction.
Synge shared with her this enviable assurance; Yeats had never
known either 'to lose the self possession of their intellects', for both
were able to 'isolate themselves, Synge instinctively and Lady
Gregory consciously from all contagious opinion of poorer minds'.
He contrasted his own position:

I do neither one nor the other, being too talkative, too full of belief in
whatever thought lays hold on me to reject people from my company, and
so I only keep from these invasions of the soul, which in old days used to
come upon me also, by a series of angry outbreaks which are pure
folly.[121]

He was obliged to analyse this vacillating state in some depth in the
summer of 1910 when Edmund Gosse wrote an intemperate letter
to Lady Gregory whom he accused of meddling in his attempts to
secure a Civil List Pension for Yeats. Yeats's reluctance to write a
letter of remonstration caused high feeling at Coole, and led to 'the
one serious quarrel I have ever had with Lady Gregory, because the
first that has arisen from unreconcilable attitudes towards life'.[122]
It was an extraordinary episode, one which forced him to examine
the grounds of his conduct and to question his relationship to Lady
Gregory and her code. In a series of painfully convoluted letters to
Robert Gregory and notes to himself, he explained that he was
unable to act spontaneously as they did because he had replaced
natural impulse with analytic reason in order to avoid any
judgement that is not authentic, until at last analysis has destroyed
all natural instinct about behaviour. His arguments, uneasily
oscillating between self-accusation and self-justification, postulate
a form of negative capability, but one based upon reason rather
than imagination. As the days of inner turmoil pass, he begins to
construct an *apologia* grounded in a distinction between defined
social relations and artistic freedom:

As I look back on the whole thing, I come to see that Lady Gregory and
Robert expected me to act at once, on a code. All my life I have, like every

artist, been proud of belonging to a nobler world, of having chosen the slow, dangerous, laborious path of moral judgment. And yet the moment the code appears before me in the personality of two friends, I am shaken, I doubt myself.[123]

Although he concedes that he has on this occasion failed to follow either path ('I neither dealt with the matter like an artist, nor as a man of the world. I allowed myself to accept the code . . . without obeying it'), he grows more confident that it was his artistic duty to repudiate the code:

far from the moral nature having anything to do with the code, it begins with the rejection of it, and attains power by listening to minute, almost secret, ungeneralized thought. But of all forms of courage this is the most difficult, for this ungeneralized thought has never any support but in itself.[124]

In a few days he had come a long way: beginning with excruciating self-accusation, he ended by congratulating himself on a superior kind of courage, and glorified his action (or, rather, non-action) as a signal battle in the war between good and bad art: 'All good art is experience; all popular bad art generalization'.[125] It is difficult to remember by now that the whole dilemma has revolved around the writing of a letter to one friend asking him to apologize for abrupt words to another.

His final position has not only forced him to define his own situation, but also to reveal his candid view of Lady Gregory's writings. His claim that 'every artist' is proud of living outside the conventional code puts Lady Gregory's status in some question, since she too is an artist. He tries to get round this by arguing that she is, in effect, an inferior artist:

Being a writer of comedy, her life as an artist has not shaken in her, as tragic art would have done, the conventional standards. Besides, she has never been a part of the artist's world, she has belonged to a political world, or to one that is merely social.[126]

Although predominantly a writer of comedy, she had by 1909 the tragedies *Grania*, *Kincora*, and *Dervorgilla* to her credit, as Yeats knew well, and his remarks can only indicate that, for all his support of her career as a playwright, he had significant reservations about its absolute value.

In these years Yeats had come to the conclusion that in order to 'oppose the new ill-breeding of Ireland, which may in a few years destroy all that has given Ireland a distinguished name in the world' he could 'only set up a secondary or interior personality created out of a tradition of myself'.[127] He was finding that the definition of that 'tradition' was a more difficult task than he had realised. It was not perhaps until 'Meditations in Time of Civil War' that Yeats worked out the full consequences of this quarrel with himself. In that poem he sets up individual 'emblems of adversity' to strengthen the mind, whereas the artifacts of mere inheritance, taken for granted, weaken the will and 'take our greatness with our violence'.[128]

*

The attractions of the code and the impossibility of accepting it are a social aspect of those series of oppositions which are central to Yeats's character, and that he could not so easily argue himself out of the sense of guilt that the Gosse episode left with him is felt in the poem originally entitled 'Notoriety'. This, the final poem of *Responsibilities*, closes a sequence that began with 'In the Seven Woods' and, although it celebrates the human qualities of Coole, does so in a far more sombre mood. The movement of the poem turns upon three verbs: 'surmise', 'find', and 'forgive'. What are surmised, and only surmised, are companions in a hostile world of dull asses; the earlier, confident belief that such kindred spirits were to be found in Irish society at large has dwindled to a mere conjecture. But at Coole his tentativeness gives way to certainty: here are to be found not only companions, but companions who provide vital qualities, 'A sterner conscience and a friendlier home'. The 'sterner conscience' is that which Lady Gregory had exhibited while he was backsliding during the dispute with Gosse; although Yeats knows he cannot wholly appropriate it, he understands how important her code is to him in offering a set of principles which serve as touchstones in confronting the easy slanders and facile compromises that modern life presents. The involved syntax and movement of the poem register just how difficult it is to live up to that code and to show magnanimity in the face of public obloquy and George Moore's insidious satire.[129] The poem is a sonnet composed of only one sentence, a sentence complicated with parentheses and dependent clauses which so qualify the final expression of forgiveness that it is all but nullified.

Yet Coole is, as ever, more than a training camp for moral uplift: it also fulfils fundamental emotional and domestic needs not found elsewhere. He was worried that his description of it as 'a friendlier home' might offend his father and his sisters; that he retained the phrase in spite of this risk reveals how much Coole had become part of his inner emotional life.[130] The house here, as in 'In the Seven Woods', is a place of refuge, not of escape, but the tone of the two poems is very different. It is no longer the birds, bees, gardens and trees of Coole that afford the poet peace and perspective, but human qualities, the sense of values shared among equals, of belonging to a small, sequestered, but vital group, standing against the world.

The promise of the 'Great Archer' has failed to materialise, defeated by the unforeseen turns of the world, 'those undreamt accidents', that have made the poet notorious. Any affirmation in the poem is provisional; the levelling force of contemporary history is felt even more strongly here than in the earlier poems. 'Ancient ceremony' has perished 'this long while', and if vestiges remain at Coole, they do so under an 'ancient roof'; the house has become a last outpost in a transacting age.

Lady Gregory's response to the Gosse affair was severe but short-lived; she thought Yeats had failed her, and let him know it, but bore no lasting grudge. She forgave this as his other lapses, but she did not forget; some years later in New York she and John Quinn, who had quarrelled with Yeats, and whose apartment and bed she was sharing, spent a happy morning adumbrating Yeats's shortcomings and this was one of the items on an extensive list. We should not make too much of this; no doubt she and Quinn wound each other up, and she was shrewd enough to know that there was no surer way of flattering her lover than by discrediting the man against whom he had a grudge.[131] The episode was perhaps a necessary catharsis, a purging of irritations that had inevitably built up over so many years of close relationship.

*

Lady Gregory conducted her affair with Quinn with great circumspection; Yeats's sexual activities were less careful and the tranquillity of Coole was shattered one summer when one of his girl-friends thought that she was pregnant. This proved to be a false alarm, but Lady Gregory suggested that he should get married, not merely to avoid such unseemly panics, but because with increased taxes, a smaller income, and the onset of war, she was less able to take care of him at Coole than hitherto. She was privy to his last proposal to Maud Gonne in the summer of 1916, and he kept her fully informed of his growing affection for Iseult. She also received a constant flow of letters from Normandy during the summer of 1917 narrating his second attempt to win Iseult's hand. He was again refused, and wrote to her from London of his new plans to marry George Hyde-Lees in terms that show the intimacy and candour that existed between them:

I want to get rid now of all ambiguity & to make my relationship definite & final. I go to Mrs Tuckers on Monday, & now that Iseult knows that I will not allow anything to break our friendship . . . she seems to me content, though a little indignant, as Maud is also, with what they think my prosaic marriage plans . . . All this will seem strangely cold & calculating. But I have only come to it − in my way − after sleepless nights & prayer. About 3 mornings ago I awoke calm & decided − had a last interview with Iseult & wrote the deciding letter. . . I certainly feel very tired & have a great longing for order. . .[132]

But order − the state he had been looking for on his first visit to Coole − was a little longer in coming for, no matter how 'prosaic', his plans were not to go smoothly, and it was at this stage that Lady Gregory played a crucial role in bringing about the marriage. Had it not been for her, the wedding might never have taken place.

Mrs. Tucker, George's mother, was suspicious of Yeats's motives, as well she might have been, and tried to prevent the marriage. Characteristically, and with Mrs. Tucker's knowledge, Yeats set out at once for Coole to consult with Lady Gregory and gain her blessing on his union. Even before he arrived Lady Gregory had received a businesslike letter from Mrs. Tucker, asking her to help break off the engagement, since 'it was only a mutual interest in astrology that they shared, which is, so Mr Yeats tells me "a very flirtatious business".' She explained that the whole affair was one of 'most annoying misconceptions' and felt 'that only you can convince him of the entire undesirability of this engagement'.[133] Lady Gregory, of course, had no intention of convincing him of any such thing, and within an hour of his arrival at Coole he was writing to George that 'Lady Gregory thinks that we should get married as soon as possible & that I should bring you here before the weather grows very cold', and that she was 'very pleased at the thought of our marriage, & thinks it the best thing that could have befallen me.'[134] Lady Gregory thereupon sat down and wrote an evidently full and satisfactory letter to Mrs. Tucker who, in thanking her on 9 October, went on to say that as 'long as Georgie has no idea of what I told you I think all will be well now. I am much re-assured by your opinion of Mr. Yeats' feelings'.[135] To make sure that George should have no inkling of what had befallen, Lady Gregory wrote her a friendly note to which George replied that she was glad that 'you above all others' should be happy at the thought of his marriage'.[136]

Lady Gregory also took the precaution of writing in the same vein to Yeats, and just as well that she did for she had apparently delivered herself of a few home truths during their discussion about the marriage and now, having named the day, he was going through an agonized emotional crisis of 'wild misery'. Her letter, however, gave him

great pleasure for you had hurt me very much by something you said about being married in the clothes I bought to court Iseult in. . . . I know I have not been selfish or had any vulgar motive. When you write you need not speak of this letter. I send it to you that I may keep nothing back. I believe that in spite of all I shall make her happy and that in seeking to do so I shall make myself happy. She has great nobility of feeling. I have always believed that the chief happiness & favour of my life has been the nobility of three or four women friends.[137]

Lady Gregory was, of course, *prima inter pares* among these friends and her latest service to him was to produce excellent results. Despite the prosaically unpromising beginning, Yeats's marriage was a success. He was seeking those qualities that he had found at Coole and within a few weeks of the wedding was identifying his bride with his old friend. 'My wife is a perfect wife, kind, wise & unselfish', he wrote to her, 'I think you were such another young girl once.'[138]

*

Barely three months after Yeats's marriage Robert Gregory was killed in Italy. A moving passage in *Seventy Years* gives an account of how Lady Gregory received the telegram and of her numbed journey to Galway to break the news to her daughter-in-law.[139] The fact that there were still grandchildren and, most importantly, a grandson helped to mitigate the dynastic consequences of the death, but she must have understood at once that the chances of a Gregory remaining at Coole into the middle part of the century were now drastically diminished. It seemed that the great ambition of her life since her widowing had come to nothing.

Yeats was not so affected. In some ways the death of Gregory fitted with his historical and personal perception of Coole: that it had reached the apogee of its cultural destiny by the beginning of the century and that inheritance could only mean dilution. He had registered his ambiguous attitude towards Gregory's character in a diary entry already cited[140] and although the absoluteness of death put his reservations into a different perspective the ambiguity could never be quite exorcised, not even in the great elegy.

That he should write an elegy was never in question; he learned of the death in a letter from Lady Gregory of 2 February which had the postscript, 'If you feel like it some time — write something down that we may keep — you understood him better than many.'[141] He would no doubt have written something in any case, but this was a command that he could not refuse, and, besides, she kept him up to the mark. A few days later she added Margaret's appeal to her own: 'If you would send even a paragraph — just some thing of what I know you are feeling — to the Observer — or failing that the Nation — she would feel it a comfort'.[142] Lest 'what I know you are feeling' should furnish insufficient copy, she also sent him 'typed notes . . . not to use but to waken your memory to different sides of him.'[143] As it turned out, these 'typed notes' were to be of great value; not only did they provide him with facts, but also, in wakening his memory 'to different sides' of Gregory's character, helped him to resolve some of the nagging questions about the nature of his achievement.

These questions and hesitations obtrude into his *Observer* article, and into letters he wrote to John Quinn and Iseult Gonne in the immediate aftermath of the death. He told both that he felt the loss more for Lady Gregory's sake than for Robert's, and tried to describe to them Robert's attributes:

I think he had genius. Certainly no contemporary landscape moved me as much as two or three of his, except perhaps a certain landscape by Innes, from whom he had learned a good deal. His paintings had majesty and austerity, and at the same time sweetness. He was the most accomplished man I have ever known; he could do more things than any other.[144]

This does not quite take away as much as it gives, but it sounds like a man trying to convince himself. Yeats *thinks* Gregory has genius, and tries to justify this supposition by citing a few paintings, limited both as to genre ('contemporary landscape') and quantity ('two or three'); moreover, it appears that even these may perhaps be derivative of, and slightly inferior to, their model, the landscape of Innes. Writing to Iseult Gonne the following day, Yeats now credited Gregory with 'a strange pure genius, full of vast austere rhythms. I always felt that he had a luckless star and have expected the end'.[145] The descriptions (or are they qualifications?) of Gregory's genius, 'strange', 'pure', 'full of vast austere rhythms', hardly bring it into closer focus. The *Observer* article is more definite, but only by taking Lady Gregory's hint about 'the different sides':

I have known no man accomplished in so many ways as Major Robert Gregory . . . His very accomplishment hid from many his genius. He had so many sides . . . that some among his friends were not sure what his work would be. To me he will always remain a great painter in the immaturity of his youth . . . Though he often seemed led away from his work by some other gift, his attitude to life and art never lost intensity — he was never the amateur.[146]

Rupert Brooke was twenty-eight when he was killed, Wilfrid Owen twenty-five; Robert Gregory was in his thirty-eighth year, an age by which most great painters have gone well beyond the 'immaturity of . . . youth', and staked their claim to genius with more than two or three pictures. This Yeats knew, and the recurrent qualifications, 'hid from many', 'not sure what his work would be', 'immaturity of his youth', 'often seemed led away from his work', indicate his lack of ease. Nor could the list of Gregory's other accomplishments have been very convincing to anyone who had known him. The Oxford Greats Examiners would have been amused to hear the young man upon whom they had conferred a third-class degree described as a 'classical scholar', and there is little evidence that his knowledge of art history or modern literature was in any way exceptional. Lady Gregory was all too aware of this. Her urgency in importuning Yeats to write an elegy arose from the very fact that without a poem so little would remain. In her letters she spoke of 'the cruel shortening of a life that was still so full of possibility . . .' and lamented that he 'had not built or planted or brought treasure, all he has left are those few beautiful pictures — & a good name'.[147]

The *Observer* paragraphs had been an immediate response, written at pressing request, and from the first he intended 'later on some fuller & more meaning thing'.[148] In addressing himself to a poem that would be fuller and more meaning, he had to review his attitude towards Gregory and to assess more exactly the achievements and meaning of his life. Given the relatively limited evidence of those achievements, and his ambivalence towards them, this was never going to be easy. One resource for avoiding a too intimate and problematic approach was to use a traditional form to distance and dignify the occasion. Thus when he first attempted 'to write something in verse about Robert' he found himself 'trying a poem in a manner like one that Spenser wrote for Sir Philip Sidney'.[149] The pastoral elegy had many advantages: it linked Gregory with the epitome of the all-round Renaissance man and suggested to Yeats how the various accomplishments that Gregory could be supposed to have mastered might be rendered poetically. Furthermore, the eclogue, traditionally a vehicle for discussion of philosophical and other matters, enabled him to air his new theories on the progress of the soul. Finally, it allowed him to escape a too awkward discussion of Gregory's art and life by structuring the poem around a 'goatherd and a shepherd . . . talking in some vague place . . . in some remote period of the world'.[150]

If the manner of the poem was an imitation of Spenser, the content, apart from the final lines based on *A Vision*, was Lady Gregory's. Indeed, her presence in the poem is hardly less prominent than Gregory's, and recalls Yeats's comment to Quinn, that he felt the death more for her sake than her son's. Moreover, as a few comparisons will show, her letters to him during February provided the prose original for his verse:

Thank you for what you say of my darling . . . the mechanics of my life do not much change — I had to see work done in the woods yesterday — for Richard instead of for Robert . . . I think more of those few pictures he has left — & of the extraordinary patience & courtesy he kept through all those difficult negotiations with the tenants . . . Now neither Convention nor War seems to interest me — just like the old cricket matches when my interest failed when he had been bowled out . . . I want to do all business as diligently as before — Hughs pictures — the Abbey — work here — & not to be a trouble to anyone — but a spring seems to have broken.[151]

Yeats renders this in lines 35 to 42:

> She goes about her house erect and calm
> Between the pantry and the linen-chest,
> Or else at meadow or at grazing overlooks
> Her labouring men, as though her darling lived,
> But for her grandson now; there is no change
> But such as I have seen upon her face

> Watching our shepherd sports at harvest-time
> When her son's turn was over.[152]

Lady Gregory told him

I am glad you are writing something more about Robert — especially a poem, it seems as if the intensity and crystallization of thought in verse would go best with ones memory of him — In spite of wife & children & his love for them & for me & for Coole, I keep thinking of the 'birds flight from tree to tree' — Margaret was saying how he never thought of money — or worried about it — & . . . she noticed how very few personal possessions he had . . . He had not built or planted — or brought treasure, all he has left are those few beautiful pictures — & a good name.[153]

and this became

> he alone had gathered up no gear,
> Set carpenters to work on no wide table,
> On no long bench nor lofty milking-shed
> As others will, when first they take possession,
> But left the house as in his father's time
> As though he knew himself, as it were, a cuckoo,
> No settled man. And now that he is gone
> There's nothing of him left but half a score
> Of sorrowful, austere, sweet, lofty pipe tunes.[154]

Yeats's verse is statelier than Lady Gregory's prose, but that stateliness is bought at the cost of emotional involvement; as Frank Kermode succinctly puts it 'We study at a distance what cannot engage us'. The eclogue is a difficult form for a modern poet, but it can be made to work as Hardy and MacNeice, among others, have proved. The stiffness in Yeats's poem comes partly from his inability to command a convincing country speech — an old problem that passing references to griddle cakes, milking-sheds, and rinsing-pools cannot solve — and partly from his uncertainty about what he wants to say. If the poem reads like a translation, it is not merely because of its Virgilian associations but because he is translating the raw material of Lady Gregory's grief into a pastoral mode that chills and distances it. He cannot feel as she does and yet has no clear sense of how he is to order the mixed feelings that he does have. The clue to future thinking is found here, 'As though he knew himself, as it were, a cuckoo,/No settled man', but it is lost in a pastoral staging at once too contrived and too obtrusive. Paradoxically, in its uncertainty this poem is perhaps a more authentic account of Yeats's real feeling about the historical Gregory than the other elegies, for he presents him as a talented young man who

> Now that he is gone
> There's nothing of him left but half a score
> Of sorrowful, austere, sweet, lofty pipe tunes.[155]

This was, of course, precisely what anguished Lady Gregory, who could have found little consolation or celebration in the lines. What consolation the poem offers, comes from the Goatherd's visionary speculations on the progress of Gregory's soul in an unChristian after-life, speculations from which the orthodox Lady Gregory and his down-to-earth widow could have gained but scant comfort.

Yeats probably showed Lady Gregory the poem for the first time when he went to stay at Coole with his bride in early April, and her reactions to it are unknown. It is hardly the poem she had expected, for she had looked for 'the intensity and crystallization of thought' that 'would go best into ones memory of him'. 'Shepherd and Goatherd' lacks both intensity and 'crystallization', and, almost certainly at her urging, he began another elegy during his visit. In this new poem Yeats developed lines of thought he had touched upon in his *Observer* comments and in the eclogue, and turned to poetic advantage the doubts he entertained about Gregory. In particular, he wanted to present Gregory's divided aims and plurality of interests as an illustration of a perfect identification of the man of action with the man of contemplation. Since this is a theme which much occupied Yeats, his imagination is more fully engaged in this poem than in 'Shepherd and Goatherd' and the 'true', under-achieving, biographical Gregory is transformed into a Paterian hero who has lived his life to its full intensity. Much of the success of the poem depends, as in many others where Yeats is attempting to mythologize his friends, upon its convincing the reader that this transformation is more than mere grandiloquence, more, that is, than a superior kind of poetic special pleading. Critics worried by possible objections on this score tend to point to Milton, and argue that the facts of Gregory's life are of no more interest to this poem than are those of that other lamented Anglo-Irishman, Edward King, to 'Lycidas'. Milton's relationship to King was, however, very different from that of Yeats to Gregory and, more importantly, to Lady Gregory. The poems about Robert were no mere exercises in the elegiac mode, but a written memorial in which a proud and grieving mother took a sometimes all too active interest:

I have done nothing but . . . discuss with Lady Gregory the new stanza that is to commend Roberts courage in the hunting field. It has been a little

thorny but we have settled a compromise. I have got from her a list of
musical place-names where he has hunted & hope for a new representation
of the place. I have firmly resisted all suggested eloquence about aero
planes "& the blue Italian sky." It is pathetic for Lady Gregory constantly
says it is his monument — "all that remains." I see that she feels that his
pictures are as it were his thought but not himself.[156]

Yeats had, therefore, a more difficult task before him in writing this
poem than had faced either Milton or Spenser: he was closer to
Gregory than Milton had been to King, so that the historical
presence cannot be so easily subsumed into the mythical; and,
unlike Spenser's subject, Sidney, the historical presence had far less
of the mythical in his achievements. Not only had Yeats to write
a public celebration of a man about whom he had mixed feelings,
but he had to do it in a way that, without compromising his own
integrity, would satisfy a close friend and mother who was herself
afraid that her son had failed to gain the worldly triumph that she
thought was potentially his.

Once more Yeats turned to a traditional form, this time to
Cowley's Ode on William Harvey. The ode proved a more
congenial vehicle than pastoral blank verse, and in this poem
tradition confers decorum without imposing conventionality; it
distances the poet sufficiently from his raw material and yet enables
him to sound the personal note all the more powerfully by allowing
it to break through that very decorum. Following the practice of
many of his mythologizing poems, Yeats begins with the here and
now and establishes a rooted, domestic location in which to ground
his later affirmations. In this case it is the turf fire and the ancient
tower of Thoor Ballylee, Yeats's first house, and his first experience
of settled married life with his new wife. Gregory himself does not
enter the poem until Yeats has welcomed Johnson, Synge and
George Pollexfen, three apparently random ghosts from his past
but each illustrating in isolation gifts that Gregory is supposed to
have combined. With Gregory's first appearance, almost half way
through the poem, Yeats indicates at once the double nature of his
role — as personal friend and yet also as a symbol of Renaissance
man:

> my dear friend's dear son,
> Our Sidney and our perfect man[157]

One notices, as in 'Shepherd and Goatherd', how far Gregory's
significance for Yeats is associated with his mother — that he was
before all else 'my dear friend's dear son'. This gives the plural

possessive pronouns, 'our', of the next line a measure of maternal as well as poetic license by allowing the hyperbolic comparison with Sidney to assume the tact of a mother's friend's overstatement. The following stanza establishes Gregory as a local man, a man to whom the flora and fauna of the Tower's landscape were actual experiences, and onto the immediacy of this physical presence Yeats begins to graft Gregory's mythical claims. He opens with the equestrian prowess he shared with George Pollexfen, and the names of the places where his exploits took place, insistently provided by Lady Gregory, help once more to underscore a physical, geographical and biographical presence. His ability as a horseman is attested in the naming of names; his ability as a painter was always in more doubt, and when Yeats turns to this aspect of his achievement he is more circumspect. The certainty of fact gives way to the tact of interpretation:

> We dreamed that a great painter had been born
> To cold Clare rock and Galway rock and thorn,
> To that stern colour and that delicate line
> That are our secret discipline
> Wherein the gazing heart doubles her might.[158]

'We *dreamed* that a great painter had been born' insists upon little more than a perhaps phantasmagoric hope, especially since the poem later indicates that dreams may come through the gates of horn as well as ivory ('What made us dream that he could comb grey hair?'), but the following lines absorb Gregory through the generosity of the plural pronouns into a tradition of visionary artists — stretching back to Blake and Palmer — among whom Yeats himself wished to be numbered. Without making any explicit claims for Gregory's talent as a painter Yeats has managed to confer importance upon him by association.

Thus far the poem has proceeded with tact and with a detailed texture that gives credence to the claims being advanced. Now Yeats moves into an assertive mode, proclaiming Gregory as

> Soldier, scholar, horseman, he,
> And yet he had the intensity
> To have published all to be a world's delight.[159]

We have had a stanza upon his horsemanship; his soldiering, scholarship and intensity we must, however, take on trust. It is significant that Yeats does not include 'painter' in the list of Gregory's proven abilities, so that his Paterian intensities are rather one-sided, more straightforwardly athletic than Pater would have thought strictly satisfying. Although Johnson and Synge have been invoked as examples of the choice that Gregory was to have made, there is little in the poem to convince us that he had Johnson's scholarly gifts, and even less to allow us to suppose that he partook of Synge's creative genius. For this reason, one must modify Frank Kermode's brilliantly suggestive argument that the poem dramatizes the dilemma facing the Romantic artist of becoming a man of action or a man of contemplation. The theme seems more akin to the idea that those whom the gods love die young, a notion close to that Lady Gregory advanced when she described her son to Yeats as a bird which flies from tree to tree in the knowledge of its early death.[160] Unease with the poem arises from the fact that although, as Harold Bloom puts it, Gregory is more an Edward King than a Sidney, Yeats insists on trying to pass him off as a Sidney. This results in an unconvincing hyperbole: the overused 'all', in the unmediated assertions 'all he did done perfectly', 'all life's epitome', and 'yet he had the intensity/To have published all to be a world's delight' (which prompts the question why by the age of thirty-seven he had 'published' so little). The nagging doubt which this rhetoric tries to override also manifests itself in the curious image of the penultimate stanza

> Some burn damp faggots, others may consume
> The entire combustible world in one small room
> As though dried straw . . .[161]

Both Lady Gregory and Yeats had to agree that the compensation for Gregory's under-achievement lay in the promise provided by his intensity, intensity always being a privileged word in the Yeatsean lexicon. Intensity is, of course, a primary Paterian virtue, but Pater commends his readers to burn with a hard, gem-like flame, a persevering and all-but unquenchable energy, far different from the momentary flash of 'dried straw', which can generate little heat and but brief illumination. Yeats must have been aware of the limiting nature of his metaphor, and indeed, used it later during an unsettled time to disparage his own lack of consistency.[162]

'In Memory of Major Robert Gregory' is a more unstable poem than is often recognized, and a close reading shows how difficult it was for Yeats to suppress the doubts and ambiguities he felt about its subject. The fact that Lady Gregory was in constant attendance during the composition did nothing to mitigate the problems that faced him, and yet it would be wrong to see the desperate attempts at hyperbole as merely Yeats's deference to her maternal insistences. Gregory's death, notwithstanding his children, solved the problem of inheritance for Yeats. Nothing became Robert so much as his untimely but military end; through it he could be drawn into the myth of Coole from which Yeats had previously excluded him on account of his lack of will. That lack of will, the plurality of interests that it generated, was now turned to poetic account, and Gregory emerges as a somewhat athletic Paterian hero who acts in accordance with a preordained fate. For once in a Coole poem Time becomes an accessory rather than an enemy: in the poems about Lady Gregory, her memory is envisaged as defeating Time; in the poems about Robert, Time wins. They invoke an unachieved Future: promise can be exuberantly celebrated for there is no longer the fear that promise will not be realized. Death, discourteous to the physical Gregory, enabled Yeats to be courteous to his memory.

Frank Kermode argues that 'An Irish Airman Foresees His Death' was probably written before 'In Memory of Major Robert Gregory'. In the absence of any conclusive evidence I should say that it was written concommitantly, or slightly afterwards. It seems to me to be Yeats's attempt to write the stanza that Lady Gregory had called for in the longer poem, 'about aero planes "& the blue Italian sky" ', but in writing it he went beyond her 'suggested eloquence' and further in his attempts to establish Gregory as a Paterian hero. Gregory's achievement in the arts and his promise as a painter are now dismissed:

> The years to come seemed waste of breath,
> A waste of breath the years behind[163]

and he is taken out of any historical context

> Nor law, nor duty bade me fight,
> Nor public men, nor cheering crowds[164]

In fact, Gregory had been an Imperialist in his youth and was so interested in the conduct of the War that, before he enlisted, Yeats used particularly to send him all the London gossip about it. Nor did he initially join the Royal Flying Corps, but was commissioned in the Connaught Rangers, a regiment of the line. Thus he could hardly have been impelled by 'a lonely impulse of delight', at least in the first instance of his enlistment. Later Gregory, like many young officers faced with the incomprehension of civilians at home, found among his men and fellow officers, in the comradeship of the field, the authentic grounds of action.[165] But, unlike a number of the officers on the Western Front — one thinks inevitably of Sassoon or Owen — he did not become disillusioned with the conduct of the War; on the contrary, military discipline suited him, it offered another code, and one that imposed order and purpose upon a life which so far (outside the sportsfield) had not been conspicuous for its will and discipline. Years before, the young Irish artist, Henry Lamb, had wondered at finding such an athletic and soldierlike young man studying art, and it seems that active service and the discovery of aerial warfare had provided him at last with his true vocation; had he lived he might well have remained in the service at the end of hostilities and ended up as a high-ranking R.A.F. officer.

Yeats's poem suppresses these contexts and contingencies in order to present its subject as the Paterian man seeking self-defining intensity. The rhythms and phrasing have been justly praised for creating the sense of balance essential to the poem's theme, but the nature of the choice, carefully disengaged by the poet from the insistencies of life in favour of a self-absorption in mere action and death, offers a less vibrant and less satisfying destiny than that advocated by Pater.

The final Gregory poem, 'Reprisals', was written some years after the death but, because of Lady Gregory's objections, not published until long after Yeats's own demise. It is a polemical poem, in which Yeats uses a favourite device of calling up a ghost to comment upon the course of history. In this case Gregory's sacrifice is invoked to condemn the action of the Black and Tans. While he lies among the cheated dead, those on whose behalf he fought and died are committing atrocities upon the Kiltartan people. Lady Gregory objected to the poem because she thought it dishonest. Yeats was living at this time in the safety of Oxford and had little first-hand experience of what was going on in Ireland. Moreover, the 'cheated dead' theme had already become a journalistic commonplace and she had no wish to have Robert involved in a posthumous polemic carried on in terms of clichés. She also found Yeats's moral outrage over the barbaric killing of Mrs. Quinn bogus

> Where may new-married women sit
> And suckle children now? Armed men
> May murder them in passing by
> Nor law nor parliament take heed.[166]

since the matter had indeed been taken up by Parliament where the Chief Secretary had spoken sympathetically and promised a legal enquiry. Yeats defended himself by arguing that he had written the poem on the chance that it might be seen by some men of importance and so influence British policy in Ireland. In fact, Lady Gregory was already engaged in changing British public opinion far more effectively through a series of less polemical but more powerfully factual articles in the *Nation*. Her criticism of the poem is just; Yeats was animated in writing it by justifiable anger at the barbarous behaviour of the Black and Tans, but the rhetoric is too facile, too much of the newspapers, too little mediated through immediate experience. It is moreover at variance with his earlier poems on Gregory. The theme of 'An Irish Airman' was that he had chosen his death on personal grounds, to gain the private statisfactions offered by 'a lonely impulse of delight', and, if this was the case, Yeats can hardly argue now that he has been 'cheated'. That he insists on doing so shows how far Gregory is being manipulated in the later poem for Yeats's merely polemical purposes.

After the death of Robert, Yeats's attitude to Coole could resolve itself into valediction without the complication of succession. The house would end with Lady Gregory, and a vital literary episode come to a close, not merely the Irish Literary Revival but the Romantic movement itself. This prospect was artistically and emotionally congenial to him: he always sought to view the world in terms of dramatic starts or sudden arrests and the actual break up of Coole, already anticipated in his earlier poems, enabled him to mythologize its achievements more securely. The later Coole poems unequivocally celebrate what is gone.

*

Marriage and the death of Robert made significant changes in the private lives of both Yeats and Lady Gregory, but historical changes were no less profound. Coole is a microcosm of Anglo-Ireland in its war experience, for the Great War took a heavy toll of young men, who would otherwise have inherited, and it is not too much to say that it was the slaughter on the Western Front that dealt the final blow to the Ascendancy.

Any post-war inheritance would, of course, have been a chancier thing because of the outbreak of the Troubles. Unlike Yeats, who spent most of this period in the safety of Oxford or lecturing in America, Lady Gregory lived through the violence and uncertainty day by day, and on occasion had good cause to be contemptuous of his inability to grasp the true nature of the situation. Her anonymous reports on the Black and Tan outrages in the London *Nation* alerted the British public to the shameful crimes being committed in its name and helped to turn opinion against the war. The outbreak of the Civil War deeply distressed her as Yeats, both on account of the destruction and death it brought, but also, characteristically, because it brought the dignity of Ireland low in the sight of others:

We agreed in the comfort of being out of England where we should have to hang our heads whatever causes may have contributed. I read him Una's letter saying how contemptuous the Germans are of us and "what we want to know is, what do you think of Ireland?" When there is lunacy in a family, I said, one doesn't write to ask members of it what they think of its state.[167]

As the War petered out, however, she became increasingly Republican in her stance. This was partly because she divined in de Valera one of the 'strong men' to whom she had always felt attracted. Her diary entries about him take on a cloying almost adolescent tone, and she was careful to leave out baskets of apples for him should he happen to pass by Coole. Her policy of sympathizing with the Republicans was also a politically shrewd move given her position, a lonely widow in a sequestered house of the kind and traditions that were being put to the torch all over Ireland. She had no reason to fear the Free Staters, who were the government in power and committed to upholding law and order; any trouble would have come from the die-hards and it was no harm to let them know that they had her sympathy. The nose for political realities that had kept her out of trouble in the 'nineties had lost nothing of its acuteness. Thus it was that while Roxborough burned and, as she noted, King's County [Meath] was cleared of Ascendancy families, she lived on in Coole almost unscathed.

Almost but not quite. There were occasional prowlers round the house, and after one attempt at forcible entry Yeats even came over from Ballylee to stay with her as her protector. But by far the most serious incident occurred while Lady Gregory was in England. Her daughter-in-law Margaret, leaving a tennis match with two off-duty British army officers and the wife of one of them, was ambushed by the IRA. She alone survived, not it seems because she was a Gregory but because she was a woman (the officer's wife had refused to leave her husband's side when offered the chance of safety). One can only speculate on what would have happened to Major Robert Gregory had he survived the war and joined that ill-fated outing.

Apart from her mild and judicious flirtation with the Republicans, Lady Gregory kept out of politics. Her work for Ireland found its occasion in the long and dreary campaign to have Hugh Lane's French Impressionist paintings returned to Dublin. Lane, her nephew, had originally intended them for a new Dublin gallery but after receiving rebuffs and insults from the Dublin Corporation and various Irish newspapers, had left them instead to the Tate Gallery in London. A later codicil to his will bequeathed the paintings once again to Dublin, but this was unsigned, and before the matter could be put beyond legal doubt he was drowned in the sinking of the *Lusitania*. The trustees of the National and Tate Galleries in London insisted that the pictures were legally theirs, and produced evidence to indicate that Lane had given categorical promises to them. Lady Gregory, however, claimed that Ireland had a moral if not legal right to the collection, and produced evidence that her nephew had given no less categorical undertakings to Dublin. It was an agitation perfectly, too perfectly indeed, suited to her temperament and needs. In the first place it enabled her to be doing something to raise the dignity of Ireland, something which while not overtly political could at once guarantee her nationalist credentials and perhaps sublimate the resentment she felt towards England for Robert's death. Moreover, the endless procession in all weathers from office to office, from person to person, the rebuffs and dusty answers, all pandered to her Esther Summerson complex: once more she took upon herself the role of unworthy handmaiden performing her duty against all the odds. Yet the campaign also appealed to the other side of her nature, to her guile and artifice. She quickly and ruthlessly ousted D. S. MacColl as Lane's biographer when it became clear that he would not toe the party line, and when she took up the book in order that it should be written 'from the Irish point of view' she quietly suppressed unwelcome facts, as she had suppressed inconvenient details in her *Times* article on the Egyptian nationalist, Arabi, forty years before. But it was not only her servitude and guile that were involved in this King Charles' Head of a campaign. There was also her pride; she thought she could take on and beat the British establishment

over the pictures as she had so often taken on and beaten the
Dublin establishment over the Abbey Theatre. She refused
therefore to give an inch, although the legal questions involved
were always ambiguous. MacColl had outlined an obvious and
wholly satisfactory compromise at some length in a friendly letter
of 1917:

I wish, as fervently as you can, that the public discussion also had been
avoided, for it seems to me that a satisfactory compromise could have been
privately arranged. You say that you feel bound to try to carry out what
you are convinced were Lane's last wishes. But the Board also is bound to
stand for its legal rights, backed as they are by a very strong moral claim
to the pictures. It is clear that you & the Irish friends were not aware how
deeply Lane had committed himself to us: on the other hand you have
evidence that he encouraged Irish hopes at the last, & the codicil points to
that impulse being uppermost in his mind when he wrote it; though
whether he thought it binding, unattested, no one can say. For these
reasons, & others I feel that Ireland has a claim & that is why I press upon
the Trustees the desirability of making concessions. But your side has
rejected the olive-branch with contumely, & you are going to call up the
bitter political passions of people who care nothing for pictures in the
attempt to get your full formal pound of flesh. It is a heavy responsibility
especially at the present time. Why should we not join hands rather in
arranging a reasonable settlement? When we get away from the discussion
of 'rights' & of fluctuating 'intentions' & all the rest of it, & consider the
good of our two peoples, the truth of the matter is that pictures exhaust
their virtue in any one place after a certain period, especially in a
comparatively small place like Dublin, & to have for a time a fresh set of
pictures in their stead would help to stimulate much more the few students
who are likely to look at them. Moreover, even from the Irish point of
view, more Irishmen would see the group of pictures in London than
would ever do so in Dublin. Therefore I am convinced that a scheme of
alternate exhibition is the right solution, & I would use any influence I have
to bring it about. And if you want Hugh Lane's benefaction to exert its own
utmost influence you will agree to it.[168]

But she would not yield to arbitration now, and later, when she
would have, British attitudes had hardened. A great deal—far to
much—of her own and Yeats's time was then spent on fruitless
efforts, for both were long dead when a settlement was reached in
1959. Although Yeats found the agitation increasingly tedious he
never wavered in its support, writing a small treatise on the issues
for the *Observer* and generally 'nobbling the press'[169] and as many
British peers, politicians, and public servants as he could lay his
hands on.

This apart, the friendship in the last period settled down to one of relaxed familiarity. He visited her almost daily when at Ballylee and stayed with her frequently when the Tower was uninhabitable. During her trips to Dublin on Abbey, Lane Pictures or, later, medical matters she was always cordially invited to stay at the Yeatses. Mrs. Yeats did not always find this as much fun as her husband. At home after an operation in 1931, her recuperation was rudely interrupted when Yeats brought Lady Gregory up for medical treatment 'and since then — thats 11 days ago — life has been a perpetual fro and to and to and fro . . . Christ how she repeats herself now . . . she'll tell you the same saga quite literally three times in less than an hour, and repeat it again the next day, and the day after that too . . .'.[169a]

Lady Gregory's health continued to deteriorate and Yeats remained with her almost permanently during her last year. This terminal vigil he owed to the long friendship but, as a busy married man with children, it was also something of a chore, and initially he had hoped that a typist might stand in for him. This she would not hear of, and he dutifully stayed on, knowing that he was waiting for an inevitable end. There could not be the urgent sorrow of 1909 when the sudden and unforeseen possibility of her death had overwhelmed him. When death at last came, he was not present but hurried back from Dublin to Galway, where he recorded the occasion and his feelings in a prose account that he chose never to publish.[170] There was, indeed, no need, for he had already said his public farewells to her and to Coole in his two topographical elegies, 'Coole Park' and 'Coole Park and Ballylee'.

*

Both poems belong to that paradoxical genre that Yeats had made his own in writing of Coole, the pre- rather than post-mortem elegy. 'Coole Park', as the drafts show, began as a personal, even confessional, tribute to Lady Gregory, dwelling upon all that she had done to save him from his youthful timidities and uncertainties. In its final form the poem attempts to go beyond individual gratitude by widening the scope of her influence to include Hyde, Synge, Lane and Shawe-Taylor, and so confer upon it greater historical significance. It thus confronts the same problems as those presented by the elegies on Robert Gregory in that Yeats wishes to invest his friend with a mythological status, while insisting upon a detailed historical reality as the basis for this transformation. Lady Gregory is at once in nature and time, and yet transcends, or defies, both. Through her influence Coole has witnessed 'great works constructed there in nature's spite' and, like nature, time, too, has been frustrated:

> They came like swallows and like swallows went,
> And yet a woman's powerful character
> Could keep a swallow to its first intent;
> And half a dozen in formation there,
> That seemed to whirl upon a compass-point,
> Found certainty upon the dreaming air,
> The intellectual sweetness of those lines
> That cut through time or cross it withershins.[171]

Critics have rightly noted that this stanza reverses the movement of the first part of 'The Second Coming'; whereas that poem announces the disintegration of modern civilization, 'Things fall apart, the centre cannot hold', this maintains that at least at Coole there was, although temporarily, a concentration, not a loosening. There the best learned not to lack conviction in spite of all their timid hearts but to find 'certainty upon the dreaming air'; nor did impetuous men sink to 'passionate intensity' but found 'intellectual sweetness'.

The poem not only sets up Yeats's positive values against the negatives of 'The Second Coming', but enumerates and glorifies those Coolean attributes that he had celebrated individually in other poems on the house. Here there is pride, but it is pride established in humility; here there is passion, but it is passion that finds an almost mathematical precision 'upon a compass-point'; here contradictory or incomplete temperaments found harmony and wholeness. Hyde's noble blade contrasts with Yeats's timid heart, Synge's slow meditativeness with Lane's and Shawe-Taylor's impetuosity; yet all these contradictions were brought into a unity by Lady Gregory's powerful character.

These are rich and powerful claims, and part of the power and poignancy of the poem comes from the understanding that the qualities it invokes are irrecoverably lost. For this is both an elegy and a lament. Although Lady Gregory has not quite died, her death is an explicit fact in the future perfect tenses of the final stanza, and three of the five Coole visitors named in the poem are long gone. Although the poem suggests that scholars and poets of after times will benefit from the achievement of Coole, they have merely an observer status and, as in 'On a House', any suggestion of genuine continuity is hardly entertained. Those drawn to Coole in its great days 'found' — the verb is repeated — that which stimulated them to greater work than they would otherwise have attained, but now the woods, the sycamores and the lime-trees, are 'lost in night', the western cloud alone luminous, caught in the dying rays of a sinking tradition. By the final stanza even these planted trees have been superseded by saplings rooting where they can among the ruins, the walls which begot the dance-like glory of Coole are reduced to broken stone, and the 'scene well set' is a shapeless mound. There are to be no fresh woods or pastures new for Coole or for what it represented. Even the central image of the swallows underlines the temporary, summer nature of its great days. The poem conceives of Lady Gregory's stewardship there as an epiphanic moment amid the welter of history: a concentrated but brief period of roughly fifteen year's duration which focused disparate talents and intentions into a unity of being, of 'Thoughts long knitted into a single thought'.

In his youth, Yeats had dreamed of Unity of Being on a national scale but by the time he paid his first visit to Coole it already seemed a fading goal. This poem salvages something of his dream and claims for Coole a limited but actual unity created through Lady Gregory's agency in the very teeth of nature and an historical phase inimicable to such an endeavour. It was something that Yeats desperately wanted to believe in, and the poem shows in its contradictions the strain of this desperation. We are told, for example, that part of Lady Gregory's greatness was that she could keep her visitors to their 'first intent', and yet the second stanza confesses that Hyde abandoned his first intent, poetry, in favour of prose. The fact of the matter is that Hyde had made all the major decisions of his life before he even knew Lady Gregory. A passing acquaintance with Hugh Lane's biography also reveals that so far from keeping to his 'first intent', his shilly-shallying between Dublin and London caused years of trouble and controversy. The relationship between Lady Gregory and Synge was also more problematic than might be gathered here, and the publication of his letters reveals how little she was privy to his first intent, or to his subsequent development. Both Lady Gregory and Yeats habitually overstated the contribution of John Shawe-Taylor, her kinsman, to the development of modern Ireland: in fact, he played a minor part in the movement to redistribute land that had begun long before him and which would have progressed as it did without him.

The strain in the poem is further felt in the discrepancies of tone between the precise naming of names — Hyde, Synge, Lane,

Shawe-Taylor, together with the careful biographical descriptions of their characteristics — and the rich imprecision of the language used to describe their achievements: 'Great works constructed there', 'Thoughts long knitted into a single thought', 'A dance-like glory'. These splendid phrases assert more than they, or history, can deliver. For this poem is in the end what it threatened to become during certain stages of its composition, a personal poem recording Yeats's great and specific debts to Coole and Lady Gregory. None of the other figures invoked in the poem owed her so much, and in none of their lives did she play the central role that the poem claims. Yet in writing the poem, and especially in writing it specifically for a commemorative book on the house, Yeats wanted to make more than merely personal gestures. He wished at once to celebrate a friend, but also to insist that together they had made their impression upon history. In his youth Yeats hoped to recreate Unity of Being in some undefined public future; as a sadder but wiser aged man he was obliged to abandon these public ambitions, and locate them in a domestic past glorified by memory. Yeats died disappointed in his larger cultural aims, but characteristically his disappointment issued in defiance rather than defeat. In some of the later poems this can lead to theatricality, even melodrama, but in this poem his claims and exaggerations are poignant rather than hectoring, for, in so far as they relate to his relationship with Lady Gregory, they are founded upon real achievement and personal debts.

'Coole Park and Ballylee 1931' was written two years later, two years in which he had watched Lady Gregory's health decline towards an inevitable end: the woman of 'powerful character' is now 'somebody that toils from chair to chair'. The poem is more ambitious than its predecessor and focuses on the public, traditional role of Coole, rather than upon the epiphanic glory of Lady Gregory's influence. Yet, once again, the underlying theme is time, time's defeats, and the relationship of tradition to history. The opening image of the stream flowing into the lake associates Yeats's Tower geographically with Lady Gregory's demesne at Coole, but at another level offers a traditional platonic image of the soul's progress, while, at another, the racing waters of Yeats's impetuous intellect contrast with the serenity of Lady Gregory's lake, suggesting their different but complementary qualities of mind (as early as 1898 he had described her as a 'well of peace'[172]). Meditations upon the mysterious progress of the soul lead inevitably to a contemplation of the physical present of bodily decay and the close of a tradition. Nor does this poem proffer the consolation of even the tentative inheritance represented by the future scholar and poet of the earlier poem. Lady Gregory is unequivocally 'a last inheritor'; the high horse is riderless; the accumulated tradition now a 'great glory spent'.

The fourth and fifth stanzas describe what that great glory constituted in terms even more expansive than those of 'Upon a House'. Here the 'best knit to the best' are given a complete social and intellectual distinction:

> Where *none* has reigned that lacked a name and fame
> Or out of folly into folly came.[173]

The line of cultured and dynastic excellence that signalized Coole is similarly conveyed as absolute:

> Marriages, alliances and families,
> And *every* bride's ambition satisfied.[174]

The language is close to that of 'A Prayer for my Daughter' but the optative mood has given way to the past perfect and muted optimism has been replaced by pessimism. The tradition is dead; modern man shifts about at the mercy of mere fashion or, more dangerously for one of Yeats's temperament, 'mere fantasy'. The melodrama that such fantasy could induce is already present in the poem

> in a copse of beeches there I stood
> For Nature's pulled her tragic buskin on
> And all the rant's a mirror of my mood . . . [175]

The ranting soul becomes a more habitual Yeatsean property from this out, especially after the death of Lady Gregory, and expresses itself in the extravagant disgust and frenzy that animate many of his last poems. Here it is a passing mood for it is contained and subsumed by Coole and the tradition Coole represents. As in 'Upon a House', the closing lines emphasize that the final fruit of this tradition is great — that is to say Romantic — art but, as in the early poem, Yeats describes the achievement of this art in terms that are assertive, rich, and yet imprecise:

> We were the last romantic — chose for theme
> Traditional sanctity and loveliness;
> Whatever's written in what poets name
> The book of the people; whatever most can bless
> The mind of man or elevate a rhyme . . . [176]

This series of question-begging phrases insists upon being taken on its own terms, although it is not easy to say with any accuracy what these terms are. The stanza is a final attempt to authenticate and celebrate the alliance between the 'cultivated classes' and the people that Lady Gregory had first looked for in her *Emigrant's Notebook* and Yeats since his decision to be an Irish poet. In *Autobiographies* he tells how, deprived by the post-Darwinians of the faith of his childhood, he made a 'new religion'

almost an infallible Church of poetic tradition, of a fardel of stories, and of personages, and of emotions, inseparable from their first expression, passed on from generation to generation by poets and painters with some help from philosophers and theologians. I wished for a world where I could discover this tradition perpetually, and not in pictures and in poems only, but in tiles round the chimney-piece and in the hangings that kept out the draught.[177]

Coole had provided the perpetual discovery of this tradition, and 'Coole Park' closes with a general benediction on that 'new religion', the almost 'infallible Church of poetic tradition' through which he hoped to sanctify, 'bless' and 'elevate'.

*

A few months after Lady Gregory's death Yeats moved to Riversdale, his last home; he was to survive her for less than seven years. They are years that see yet more changes in his poetry and outlook, changes at least partly attributable to her absence. In a celebrated poem he had proclaimed that 'Things fall apart, the centre cannot hold'.[178] As 'Coole Park' tells us, she had acted as the centripetal force for Yeats, not merely in her capacity as hostess, but in her attitude to life, in what she embodied. Lacking that centre, lacking Coole as an image and actual location of tradition and continuity, his view of the world falls if not apart, at least into extremes. Without the Castiglionean graces that Lady Gregory embodied and bestowed, the Nietzschean aspect of his temperament gained dominance. A coarsening is involved. The cultural plenitude that he associated with breeding and which he celebrates in the Coole poems, shrinks to the mechanics of mere eugenics, while *sprezzatura* becomes frenzy and hysterical rage. 'Three Songs to the One Burden'[179] illustrates the change. The first section endorses easy violence and enforced eugenics; in the second, Henry Middleton and his house Elsinore replace the dismantled Coole as the image of what the Anglo-Irish tradition has now become. What at Coole was individual, courageous, and traditional is now eccentric, defensive, and introverted, the Seven Woods shrunk to a storm-bitten green. This is an extreme example, but the last poems and plays sound in different keys the fall of Anglo-Ireland, and the supersession of a tradition that he thought might have made Unity of Culture possible. The symbol of the great house gone is the theme of *Purgatory*, 'The Curse of Cromwell' and 'The Black Tower'. The recognition that the tradition is lost leads to desperation as well as defiance, and in some poems the 'rant' that briefly attracted him in 'Coole Park and Ballylee' is allowed too free a rein and loose frenzy postures as emotional energy. Lady Gregory's presence might have saved him from his more melodramatic poses, even from his flirtation with O'Duffy and the Blueshirts and the malevolent over-excited simplicities of *On the Boiler*. In these last years her influence defines itself the more clearly by its very absence.

*

To sum up a friendship of such length, complexity and richness must be to simplify, yet certain salient facts stand out. In the first place, while the relationship had a profound influence on both their lives, it changed his more than hers. Had she not met him her life would have been immeasurably less rich but its basic contours would have remained constant. She would have still guarded Coole for Robert, still tried to find a rapport with the people, still attempted to make something of a literary name. She would probably have produced articles on folklore for *The Nineteenth Century* and the *Spectator*, busied herself with the Gaelic League, and written short stories which, while less sentimental than Jane Barlow's, lacked the panache of Somerville and Ross. Yeats's friendship did not alter the direction of her life but gave it focus. His encouragement of her writing, although slow at first, became a constant and necessary reassurance, and not infrequently tipped into overpraise.

Her influence on him did alter the direction of his life and it is far harder to envisage what would have become of him had they not met. There would have been more hack journalism to make ends meet and so less time for poetry. He would have attempted to have his plays staged, but the brief histories of the Masquers and the Theatre of Ireland suggest that productions would have been fitful and unsatisfactory. Although Lady Gregory overstates her part in the Abbey Theatre, her presence was crucial to Yeats for administrative as well as artistic reasons. Her applied tact prevented the Irish dramatic movement from disintegrating at several points of crisis. And without the constant resources of his own theatre Yeats would not only have been a different playwright, he would also have been a very different poet.

The practical assistance that she rendered Yeats went beyond the provision of money, board, and administrative and secretarial help. Coole not only offered him space and time to write, it also surrounded him with the tangible symbols of a tradition and quality of life that seemed a microcosm of the cultural unity he wished to establish at a national level. Yeats was an idealist, but he was an idealist who needed to test his ideas on his pulse. Coole came to represent the pulse of Ireland, or at least the Ireland he cared about. In the troubles of its unfolding contemporary history he saw played out the problems and contradictions of his own cultural and political attitudes. His experience of Coole helped him to define those attitudes more confidently, and at the same time taught him how unlikely they were to be implemented in the twentieth-century world. Without Coole as both a refuge and an example, this discovery might have led to isolation and despair, feelings not at all conducive to his poetic sensibilty. Coole saved him from this desolation, and from the extremism it might have provoked, by providing him with a haven in which he could recuperate his imaginative energies and distance himself from the exhausting and potentially corroding squabbles of public life.

But the core of the relationship's value lay in the more intimate emotional and psychological nourishment it provided. 'I have lost one', he wrote to Mario Rossi shortly after her death, 'who has been to me for nearly forty years my strength and my conscience.'[180] Her friendship was crucial in giving him stability. As we have seen, she took the place of the mother he had imperfectly known, and yet her 'sterner conscience' and her code of behaviour also offered qualities that his amiable but weak-willed father had conspicuously lacked. He felt he 'had to escape this family drifting, innocent, & helpless, & the need for that drew me to dominating men like Henley & Morris . . .'[181] Morris and Henley, however, had their limitations. Morris, irritable by nature and involved in a Socialist propaganda Yeats found uncongenial, could not long serve as a satisfactory surrogate father, while

Henley, whose interests included the thickness of steaks and collecting slang names for sexual organs, was a little too robust for so sensitive a poet. Lady Gregory with her masculine code but feminine sensibility fortified Yeats's will, but also offered sympathy and understanding. It was a combination that probably saved him from more than one nervous breakdown, and the severe collapse of Arthur Symons, the most intimate of his male friends, made him reflect upon his good fortune: 'He had the subtle understanding of a woman & his thought flowed though life with my own, for many years, almost as if he had been one of the two or three women friends who are everything to me. And now he has been eaten like a fish by that kingfisher & his bones flung out of doors'.[182] The 'kingfisher' was Rhoda, Symons' wife, whom Yeats thought had driven his subtle friend over the edge of sanity. He was more fortunate, for Lady Gregory restored and strengthened his mental balance. As he wrote to Dorothy Wellesley in May 1936:

I long for quiet; long ago I used to find it at Coole. It was part of the genius of that house. Lady Gregory never rebelled like other Irish women I have known who consumed themselves & their friends; in spite of Scripture she put the new wine into the old bottles.[183]

A LANGUAGE FOR HEALING

ROBERT WELCH

. . . here, on the edge of the world, dreams are real things, and every heart is watching for the opening of one or another grave.[1]

When Bridget Ruane came to Lady Gregory to tell her that she could bring back people from the dead with some of the herbs that, Bridget claimed, revived Jesus, she said that she got this knowledge from her brother. He had it out of a book that he found one day on the road before him, put there maybe by God himself, maybe by the little people. And when Lady Gregory asked what language the book was written in, Bridget Ruane retorted: 'What language would it be but Irish?'[2] Incidentally, the herbs that were claimed to have revived Jesus were the *garbhlus* (dandelion) and the *slánlus* (plantain).

I cite this story, not just for its picturesque quaintness, but because it takes us to the heart of Lady Gregory's preoccupation with the Irish language, and not only hers, but that of a whole generation of writers and thinkers in the 1890s and the early years of this century: Hyde, Moore, Yeats, Father Peter O'Leary, and, of course, Patrick Pearse. Their idea was that the Irish language was attached to a community fully alive, and being so attached, it had the innate power of delivering, to those people still fortunate enough to speak it, a sense of belonging, of familiarity, of being at home in a world where things disclosed themselves in a radiant clarity and freshness. Furthermore, and this is where the Bridget Ruane story has its point, the language comprised and uttered (outered) not just the community of all those that spoke it and shared a common background, but one in which the individual was attached to a whole system of understanding and significance, where the dandelion or the plantain could be read as having a place in the crucifixion and the resurrection themselves, where the fields around the cottages were seen as being charged with all kinds of potential energy. A neighbour of Lady Gregory told her that the *slánughadh* (ribgrass) is good for lumps, but warned that if the wind changed when picking it there was a danger of losing one's mind.

The world that opened up to Lady Gregory here was, obviously, a vital one, alive with significances, all of which emanated from a language which was on the point of extinction, and which, it must be said, the class from which she came had conspired to eradicate.

It would be possible to erect a theory which would seek to 'explain' the passionate interest Lady Gregory and members of her class had in Gaelic and in Gaelic culture as a form of exorcism of a collective Anglo-Irish guilt, an attempt at reparation to a peasantry, who were, really, in no need of sympathy or understanding, and who were, anyway, on the point of taking over. But this will not do, not because it is historically inaccurate, though like all clumsy political rationalizations it has some truth in it, but because it does not sufficiently explain the depth, quality and intensity of the work done on Gaelic and on Gaelic culture in the 1890s and later, first by Hyde, then by Yeats, then Lady Gregory, then strangest of all, George Moore, in the stories he wrote for translation into Irish, which later became *The Untilled Field*.

In *Hail and Farewell* Moore tells us how, in the 1890s, he grew more and more disgusted with English life; how walking the streets he thought he could see the exploitation and insensitivity which the English were displaying towards the Boers on every face, like a mask of tiredness and exhaustion. The English language itself, he had grown to feel, had lost all vivacity: the verbs were loose and tired.[3] All of English culture was a shambles, a ruin of dead Imperial magnificence. And because she had lost all the real energy of dominion, all that was left for her was to tyrannize, mindlessly. This coarsened everything in England, and so Moore, for reasons both naive and profound, joined the Irish literary revival.

Taking the cue from Moore, the turn back to Ireland and its culture may be better understood if we take it out of the context of Anglo-Irish guilt for a moment and place it against a European background. And the figure that looms into sight here is the disturbing one of Søren Kierkegaard, whose preoccupation was the meaninglessness and futility of modern collectivised industrialised life. In *The Present Age* of 1846 he diagnosed the inner condition of Western man under democratised capitalism as one of continual unremitting anxiety, unease, *dis*ease, where no one really speaks to anyone else: all is negotiation; people draw together only in committees; there is no full response to life, and therefore language itself is only a murmuring of the living dead, a soothing exercise in jargon. Our love, even our lust, is diluted into a matter of social convenience. Recalling Kierkegaard's trenchant exposure of the deadness, the *tension* of modern democratic civilisation, we can better understand the kind of crisis Moore went through before he left London for Ireland. Maybe, too, we can be less cynical about his account of hearing a voice on the Hospital Road in Chelsea, telling him to go back; and about the trouble Lady Gregory took to learn Irish in order to make some contact with the disappearing vitality of the world inhabited by Bridget Ruane. Here, in Gaelic-speaking County Galway was a world which was, still, outside the modern one of industrialization, monotony, and Kierkegaardian tension; and the Irish language was the means by which this world declared itself to itself, by which it truly spoke, and when it did so it connected with a whole system of significance and meaning which stretched back thousands of years.

The key texts here are Hyde's *Love Songs of Connacht* of 1893 and Yeats's review of it in the *Bookman* in the same year. Yeats wrote that these love songs, which Hyde had translated into the English of the Irish country people, disclosed something of an Edenic quality. Emotion in them seemed to find the right image, effortlessly. The lives of the people who wrote these songs, their being, stood out, authentically. Language for them, Yeats concluded, on the basis of Hyde's prose translations, was not a matter of tense negotiation, but a total speech opening out of the unconscious depth of their living past, diametrically opposed to that of the men on Kierkegaard's committees:

The soul then had but to stretch out its arms to fill them with beauty, but now all manner of heterogeneous ugliness has beset us. A peasant had then but to stand in his own door and think of his sweetheart and of his sorrow, and take from the scene about him and from the common events of his life types and symbols, and behold, if chance was a little kind, he had made a poem to humble generations of the proud.[4]

Yeats, though he made a number of attempts, never learnt Irish. Lady Gregory had been eager to learn it from childhood, but the 'disclosure' of the Gaelic world that Hyde's book embodied for her awoke an 'astonishing excitement'.[5] She began to collect bits and pieces of folklore around Coole, but the figure who offered her entrance into the networks of intermeshed significance that she saw the Irish language as retaining was the blind nineteenth century poet, Raftery, a figure who was to have an enormous symbolic force for the Irish writers of the 1890s.

Tragically isolated by poverty and blindness, and yet deeply in touch with the inner life of his people, it is understandable that the

writers of the revival, themselves deeply antagonistic to many of
the tendencies of their own time, trying to maintain an inner
connection with a deeper life, should be drawn to such a tragic
embodiment of a culture totally antithetical to the modern world.

It was from an old woman that Lady Gregory first heard the
famous song in which Raftery sang the praises of a beautiful girl
from Ballylee, Mary Hynes, and this song she translated, with the
help of one of the small farmers near her, for Yeats's essay on Mary
Hynes, 'Dust Hath Closed Helen's Eye'. Here are two verses from
the translation:

> I would not grudge you a song every Sunday evening,
> Punch on the table or wine if you would drink it,
> But, O King of Glory, dry the roads before me
> Till I find the way to Ballylee.
>
> There is sweet air on the side of the hill,
> When you are looking down on Ballylee;
> When you are walking in the valley picking nuts and blackberries,
> There is music of the birds in it and music of the Sidhe.[6]

The original verses would have read very like the following, taken
from Hyde's collection of Raftery's songs, *Abhráin atá Leagtha ar
an Reachtúire* (1903):

> Níor mhór liom ceol duit gach aon oídhche Domhnaigh,
>   Puinnse ar bord agus dá n'ólfa fíon,
> A's a Righ na Glóire go dtrimigh an bóthar,
>   Go bhfagh me an t'eolas go Bail'-uí-Liagh.
>
> Is aoibhinn aerach ar taobh an tsléibhe
>   Ag breathnughadh síos ar Bhail'-ui-Liagh,
> Ag siubhal sna gleanntaibh 'baint cnó agus sméara
>   'S geall ceileabhar éan ann le ceoltaibh sidhe.[7]

There are a few minor differences between the Hyde text and Lady
Gregory's translation, but she may have worked from a slightly
different version of the song. What is striking about the translation
is the directness of the statement, the naturalness of the speech, the
way it brings before the mind's eye a complete world:

> . . . she said, 'Raftery my mind is easy,
> You may come today to Ballylee'.
>
> When I heard her offer I did not linger,
> When her talk went to my heart my heart rose.

> We had only to go across the three fields,
> We had daylight with us to Ballylee.

It was this world of the 'three fields', Gaelic, closely-knit, in which language speaks a community, and in speaking gives it identity, recall, definition,which Lady Gregory wished to disclose in her work on Irish. I use the word 'disclose', because it is a word she herself often uses in speaking of what Hyde's work meant to her in the 1890s. Her use of English in the translation is an attempt at an adequate representation of the fullness of Raftery's song in its community: she wants it to be human, alert, and vivid, so that the details of the encounter with Mary Hynes will stand out in unaffected clarity. This is why she makes use of the English speech of the Irish country people and why she translates as literally as she can:

> Going to Mass by the will of God,
> The day came wet and the wind rose.

She wants her English to be an opening back into that lost community, her book to be a 'book of the people'.[8]

The essay she wrote on Raftery, and which later became the first piece in *Poets and Dreamers*, gave her, she tells us, immense pleasure.[9] Appropriately, it begins with the speech of two old women in Gort Workhouse, recalling stories of Raftery. Her own prose moves out of the speech of the old woman from Kilchreest almost as soon as the essay opens:

Raftery hadn't a stim of sight; and he travelled the whole nation; and he was the best poet that ever was, and the best fiddler. It was always at my father's house opposite the big tree, that he used to stop when he was in Kilchreest.[10]

It is this kind of memory, of the poet coming and creating a community of people drawn together to hear their language, voiced and shaped in words that were (in the phrase of one of the people she talked to) 'so strong and stiff', that attracted Lady Gregory. A neighbour told her:

He used to stop with my uncle that was a hedge schoolmaster in those times in Ballylee, and that he was very fond of drink; and when he was drunk, he'd take his clothes off, and run naked through the country. But at evening he'd open the school; and the neighbours that would be working all day would gather into him, and he'd teach them through the night; and there Raftery would be in the middle of them.

'In the middle of them': it is easy to imagine how Lady Gregory would be drawn by that last phrase, with its sense of communal life, and a language fully attentive to all the profound nuances of history and circumstance. He was the embodiment, for her, of the consciousness of the countryside, his work a drawing together of memory and the actuality of life around him. He wrote poems for and about people, and at one time, she tells us, he had a long conversation with a bush under which he sheltered on a rainy night. The bush, in the poem, speaks out of the legendary past and then goes into an account of Ireland's trials and tribulations, until it prophesies that, according to the Revelation of St John, 'in the twenty ninth year the Irish shall score' (clearly a wise-after-the-event reference to emancipation). At the end of the poem Raftery says that this was how he and the bush, together, gave an account of Ireland: 'É féin 's an Sgeachán i bpáirt le chéile'. Again here, as with Bridget Ruane, the herb healer, the landscape is a code that may be read and deciphered, but everything depends on the language. Once that is lost, all the old codes, all the gathered history that Raftery imagined as compacted in the bush, are gone.

Yeats and Lady Gregory were both preoccupied by centrality; both searched for a writing that would speak out of its own time and place for the people of that time and place. In 1886 Yeats had praised Ferguson for what he called *his* centrality, but Ferguson was given this praise because he chose to work in Irish mythology. Here, in Raftery, was the type of poet Yeats had early wished to become, who would speak out, disclose, the collective experience of the life around him, vivifying that life, and thereby making language more and more human, unlike the dead words of negotiation and committees. In 'Cill Aodáin', Raftery's famous poem about his birth place in County Mayo, he writes of himself standing in the middle of his own people, having made the journey back:

> Fágaim le h-umhachta go n-éirigheann mo chroidhe-se
>   Mar éirigheas an ghaoth, nó mar sgapas an ceo
> Nuair smuainighim ar Chearra a's ar Ghaillin taobh
>   thíos de
>   Ar sgeathach a'mhíle no ar phlainéad Mhuigh-Eo . . .
> 'S da mbeinn-se mo sheasamh i gceartlár mo dhaoine
>   D'imtheochadh an aois díom agus bheinn arís óg.[11]

Lady Gregory's version of these lines is simple and straightforward, trying to turn the English back into an attentiveness to the
movement and clarity of the Irish and the world which it defines:

I leave it in my will that my heart rises as the wind rises, or as the fog
scatters, when I think upon Carra and the two towns below it, on the two-
mile bush, and on the plains of Mayo . . . . And if I were standing in the
middle of my people, age would go from me, and I would be young
again.[12]

Once having thought of it, once having found her way to these
songs of Raftery, it would have been simple enough to translate
them into unaffected English. And yet those phrases above do
disclose a pre-famine world, do open it up to us, even now. It must
have taken considerable courage deliberately to turn her language
away from any respectabilizing tendency towards the immediacy
and simplicity of her originals. In doing this she was not just
seeking contact with a Gaelic world, the vestiges of which still lay
around her estate; she was also turning aside from the anonymity
and lifelessness of modern English, trying to translate that language
itself into Irish, rather than just transacting the more predictable
enterprise of translating specific Gaelic poems into reasonable,
acceptable English. Her English is *un*reasonable, *un*acceptable,
which is why it strikes.
    She was, if you like, trying to repair a broken circuit. Like
Bridget Ruane, she would be a healer, but a cultural one. Is there
not a sense in which she became a healer to Yeats, drawing him into
a fuller relationship with the landscape around Coole, the hidden
history of which she was trying to disclose, and with the people for
whom he had always wanted to speak? In the fullest sense of the
word she took him (and Synge and Hyde and AE) into her care.
Through her Coole became a place where what she called the 'two
great landslips' of nineteenth century Ireland, 'the breaking of the
social life of the people by the Famine, and the breaking of their
intellectual life by the shoving out of the language' were
acknowledged and an attempt made to repair some, at least, of the
damage.[13]
    She got Hyde writing plays in Gaelic to bring the Gaelic League
'closer to the people', and one of these, *An Pósadh*, was based on
a story she had heard about Raftery. A marriage took place
between a poor servant boy and girl at Cappaghtagle which

was only a marriage and not a wedding, till Raftery chanced to come in;

and he made it one. There wasn't a bit but bread and herrings in the house; but he made a great song about the grand feast they had, and he put every sort of thing into the song — all the beef that was in Ireland; and went to the Claddagh, and didn't leave a fish in the sea. And there was no one at all at it; but he brought all the bacach and poor men in Ireland, and gave them a pound each. He went to bed after, without them giving him a drop to drink; but he didn't mind that when they hadn't got it to give.[14]

From this she wrote out a scenario, and, according to Hyde's own account at the first performance of the play in Galway, brought it to him and said 'Cur Gaedilge air!'. From her account in *Our Irish Theatre* it is fairly clear that she was responsible for the outline and much of the dialogue, and that Hyde 'put the Irish on it'. She did consult him though, about the changes she made in the original story. For *Poets and Dreamers* she translated Hyde's Irish (possibly with the assistance of Hyde again) back into English. The single manuscript of the Irish version would appear to be lost. She does say it was in considerable demand.

An Pósadh, first performed at the Galway *feis* in 1902, with Hyde playing the part of Raftery, draws together all that has been said so far about Lady Gregory's conception of Irish culture; the significance of Raftery for her in gaining entrance to it; and the way she thought that English might be made to open back into some kind of vital relationship with that culture.

In her introduction to her translations of Hyde's plays in *Poets and Dreamers* she speaks of the old dialogues between Patrick and Oisin and between Raftery and death. 'The creation of acting plays', she says, 'is the natural outcome of this tradition.' It might also be added that if you are trying to revivify aspects of a cultural life which have been forgotten or which have slipped, if you are trying to make those aspects stand out clearly ('*in a steillebheathaidh*', as the Irish phrase would have it), then drama is your medium. It is social, in that it involves a community; and its language is received directly, not abstracted by the technology of print. In the performance of that tiny play in Galway (the city where, Lady Gregory tells us, Raftery had his first talk with death) the poet who, for her, was the embodiment of Gaelic culture, was played by Hyde, the man who, if anyone could, would reconnect the broken circuit of Irish language and life.

The opening of the play follows the story fairly closely: Mary and Martin are just married; they sit down to their meagre meal of bread and a couple of eggs when an old blind fiddler puts his head in through the door. They invite him to share what they have but he eats it all. Then the story of their poverty comes out, and Martin tells the old man that he is going to have to take to the road to earn his keep, and that Mary will have to go into service. The old man starts to play the fiddle, which draws the attention of a couple of young boys passing the road. He tells them to let it be known that it is Raftery 'that is calling to them', and that the people of the neighbourhood should come, bringing presents for the newly married woman. The house fills with people bearing their gifts — meal, bacon, butter, and so on: even an old miser is made to hand over a valuable fleece. Raftery also gets money from each visitor, all of which he gives to the couple at the end before he departs silently. Then a young man comes in:

YOUNG MAN: What is going on here at all? All the cars in the country gathered at the door, and Seagan na stucaire going swearing down the road.
OLD FARMER: Oh, this is the great wedding was made by Raftery — Where is Raftery? — Where is he gone? —
MARTIN (*going to the door*): He's not here. I don't see him on the road. (*Turns to young farmer.*) Did you meet a blind fiddler going out the door — the poet Raftery?
YOUNG MAN: The poet Raftery? I did not; but I stood by his grave at Killeenan three days ago.
MARY: His grave? Oh Martin, it was a dead man was in it!
MARTIN: Whoever it was, it was a man sent by God was in it.[15]

Lady Gregory records the impact the Gaelic words 'Is fear marbh do bhí ann' made on her at that performance in Galway.

The two main changes to the original story as Lady Gregory heard it are clear: first, the people of the neighbourhood do actually come in, whereas in the story Raftery's imaginative powers alone are a compensation and he and the young couple go to their beds hungry; secondly, in the play, Raftery returns from the dead. The young couple are strangely isolated at the beginning, cut off from the people around, and they are soon going to have to leave each other. The dead man comes in, in rags, with his music and his language, and in minutes the house is filled with laughter, noise and giving. Raftery has come to repair a broken circuit in the community, and he does it through the language. The play derives its force from the sense it gives of old lines of connection, between life and language, young and old, living and dead, being restored through the activity of speech. Raftery, in Lady Gregory's English, is a dramatic embodiment of all that she would make her own art achieve.

Raftery, then, was for Lady Gregory (and to some extent for Yeats) an entry point into the Gaelic world which she wished to re-activate. She did an immense amount of work on him which Hyde saluted in the generous dedication to her of his collection of Raftery's poems, 'an Baintighearna Gregori ón gCúil' (Lady Gregory from Coole). He said that she saved Raftery's fame from death: 'Ó shábháil tusa clú mo Reachtúire ó'n mbás'.

From Raftery her work in translation opened out to other poems and songs in the mouths of the country people, and she made the stark telling versions of 'Dónal Óg' and 'A Blessing on Patrick Sarsfield' that are in the *Kiltartan Poetry Book*. But the next major project that she undertook was the daunting one of providing in the English of the country people a readable account of the entire Cuchulain saga.

And so I came by the road nearest to me to the old legends, the old heroic poems. It was a man of a hundred years old who told me the story of Cuchulain's fight with his own son . . .[16]

So she writes in the *Kiltartan Poetry Book*. She wanted to restore to those old tales an immediacy which she felt they would have had in a Gaelic-speaking culture, and which she could reclaim, to some extent, by using 'the English spoken by the Irish people, which keeps so much of the idioms of the Irish original'.[17] She consulted Yeats, she tells us, who hesitated at first, but eventually agreed that the project was a good idea. 'I am provided with work for the rest of my life', she wrote in 1900.

Douglas Hyde, it seems, took longer to come around:

He rather snubs my idea of the Cuchulain book. I think his feeling is that only a scholar should do it, and he is bewildered at my simple translation. I had got Conolly to put the Death of Cuchulain, of which I had only the English version, into Irish, and had translated it back literally into English. 'Of course an epic should not be translated in colloquial style', he says, which accounts for his translations of bits of epics being heavy and formal, quite different from his folk-tales and peasant poem translations. However, he gave his consent, which is all I wanted, though I don't yet know if the task will be beyond my strength and time.[18]

In *Seventy Years* she gives us an account of how she laboured at this extraordinarily demanding work, assembling all the nineteenth century translations of the Cuchulain tales, trying to find her way into some comprehension of the Old Irish originals, themselves often poorly or partially edited. She would sometimes work all day in the Reading Room of the British Museum, eat at an Austrian restaurant nearby, then go back and work until nine or ten o'clock at night.

It must be said that even at this stage her knowledge of spoken Irish was still fairly elementary. In a diary entry for the summer of 1900 she gives an account of a *feis* at Galway, where she says she understood a little more Irish than the previous year, 'but still not much'. She was more confident with the language when it was written down but in no way had she anything like a reading knowledge of Old Irish. With the 'Death of Cuchulain', for example, she got Sean Conolly, a teacher from Aran, to make a modern Irish version of the partial translation by Whitley Stokes that had appeared in *Revue Celtique* for 1877, and which Eleanor Hull had included in *The Cuchullin Saga* (1898). This she then turned into English, with, one presumes, the assistance of Conolly. With other texts she had access to recent or relatively recent editions with modern facing translations and she would have had enough Irish to form some notion of the way the language worked in the original.

With Raftery she had direct experience of oral tradition; there were people still living who could remember him. Furthermore the landscape in which he lived and travelled and of which he had sung was one that had been familiar to her all her life. The world of Old Irish saga, however, was much more foreign and remote: old men did have stories of Cuchulain but the texts which she was working from were difficult and obscure, not just to her, but to the scholars themselves. The translations too were stilted or inflated, or both.

Very simply, she wanted to bring the stories back to the people themselves. She wanted her book to be a link between the old Gaelic world and the Ireland of the new century. Her language, based on the Kiltartan dialect, she saw as a means of recreating an Irish community which would comprise the living and the dead figures of Irish legend. Again, she was thinking of her medium not just as a means of conveying the content of the old stories but as a mode of disclosing their living reality. Her aim was not the creation of literature, as such, but rather the restoration of continuity, the re-establishment, in the deepest sense, of community. In her dedication to the people of Kiltartan she writes:

I have told the whole story in plain and simple words, in the same way my old nurse Mary Sheridan used to be telling stories from the Irish long ago, and I a child at Roxborough.[19]

Then she goes on to attack the arid learning of Trinity College, which is a dead place because the scholars there (she is thinking of Atkinson, who claimed that Irish literature was uniformly 'low') have no living link with the old world, which means they have no speech. Her own language here flashes with assurance and vehement mockery:

And indeed if there was more respect for Irish things among the learned men that live in the College in Dublin, where so many of these old writings are stored, this work would not have been left to a woman of the house, that has to be minding the place, and listening to complaints, and dividing her share of food.

They, she implies, are not dividing their share of what they have been given and what they have inherited. Instead they store the books, and make no attempt to bring them back to where they belong and where they come from. They do not try to accomplish what she later said Synge had done:

He tells what he owes to that collaboration with the people . . . The return to the people, the reunion after separation, the taking and giving, is it not the perfect circle, the way of nature, the eternal wedding-ring?[20]

Synge himself wrote to Lady Gregory that her *Cuchulain* was part of his 'daily bread', but not because of the content: 'Many of the stories, of course, I have known for a long time, but they seem to gain a new life in the beautiful language you have told them in'.[21] This was exactly her objective.

How successful are her versions of the Cuchulain sagas? Modern scholars would find them often disappointing in detail, for example in the story called 'The Championship of Ulster'. Cuchulain, alone amongst the heroes of Ulster, meets the challenge of a huge churl who comes to Emhain Macha. The churl dares anyone to cut off his head as long as he can do the same to whomever takes up the challenge on the next day. No one is prepared to keep the second part of the bargain, save Cuchulain. The day after Cuchulain takes off the stranger's head he comes and tells Cuchulain to stretch out his neck on the block so he can behead him. The story continues (first in the Irish of Henderson's edition of 1899, from which Lady Gregory worked):

'Is confere dombere form', ol Cuchulaind, 'déna mo marbad gilrath. Nimba coipere em tucius fort arér', or sé 'Toingtea ém', or Cuchulaind, 'dia m-bé ug mu conferi pidam sitigithir coir uasatt'. 'Ní fédaim t'airrlech' (ol an) baclach, métt an cipp hocus gairdi do pratad & gairdi do taoiph'.

Rosíni Cuchulaind orsuidiu ann m-braduid gu n-dechsad fertraig ferocloic idir gach dá assnoi do & rosinit a prathoid go ndechaid tar an ccepp don oile taiph. [22]

This is Henderson's very ponderous translation of the above:

'You keep me in torment', quoth Cuchulainn. Despatch me quickly; last night, by my troth, I tormented you not. Verily I swear if you torment me, I shall make myself as long as a crane above you'. 'I cannot slay you', quoth the baclach, 'what with the size of the block, the shortness of your neck and of your side' [sic!]. [Henderson meant the side of the body].

Then Cuchulainn stretched out his neck so that a warrior's fullgrown foot would have fitted between any two of his ribs; his neck he distended till he reached the other side of the block.

The nightmarish clarity of the Old Irish, its acute circumstantial terror (inadequately conveyed in Henderson's version: his use of *sic* is a sign of discomfort and embarrassment) is the kind of thing that readily appeals to us, now. Where Henderson is embarrassed, Lady Gregory in her version cuts drastically:

'You are keeping me in torment', said Cuchulain; 'put an end to me quickly. For last night', he said, 'by my oath, I made no delay with you'. Then he stretched out his neck. . . . [23]

It would be very easy to argue that Lady Gregory was a bowdlerizer who wanted to dignify the old texts and did so in an unsympathetic and very Victorian way. But this would be to ignore what Yeats (who was himself concerned about her excisions), Synge and Hyde most admired: her energetic narrative thrust, and the lively speech which seemed to make the heroes stand out afresh. The passage continues:

But when the axe came down, it was with its blunt side, and it was the floor it struck, so that Cuchulain was not touched at all. And all the chief men of Ulster were standing looking on, and they saw on the moment that it was no strange clown was in it, but Curoi, son of Daire, that had come to try the heroes through his enchantments.

'Rise up, Cuchulain', he said. 'Of all the heroes of Ulster, whatever may be their daring, there is not one to compare with you in courage and in bravery and in truth. The Championship of the heroes of Ireland is yours from this out, and the Champion's Portion with it, and to your wife the first place among all the women of Ulster. And whoever tries to put himself before you after this', he said, 'I swear by the oath my people swear by, his own life will be in danger'.

With that he left them.

The virtue of a prose like this can easily be underestimated. It is written for the ear rather than for the eye, and carries its circumstantiality in the naturalness of its phrasing. The placing of the word 'danger' towards the end is dramatic and clear, and shows the kind of alertness to the possibility of rhythmic emphasis that was (and still is) a feature of Irish country speech. The word, 'danger' incidentally, is based on a thoroughly dull phrase in Henderson's translation, 'sore scathe', which is, in fact, conjecture, there being a lacuna in the Irish text at this point.

She can also attend to matters of detail in her version and call up the telling word to answer to the Irish. There is an earlier scene in 'The Championship' where Cuchulain, Laegaire Buadach and Conall Cearnach are tested at Cruachan by Maeve to see who should be given the precedence over the warriors of Ulster. The three are put into a room to sleep by themselves and three great beasts in the shape of cats come out of the cave under the fairy mound of Cruachan. Terrified, Conall and Laegaire leap up into the rafters, but Cuchulain faces the one assigned to him:

when one of the monsters came to attack him, he gave a blow of his sword at his head; but the sword slipped off as if from a stone.[24]

In the Irish this reads:

in tan dosíned in beist a brágit cosin n-esair, dounsi Cuchulainn béim din claidiub na cend doscirred di mar bad do charraic.[25]

And this Henderson translates as:

when it stretched its neck out for eating, Cuchulainn gave a blow with his sword on the beast's head, but (the blade) glided off as 'twere from a stone.

Clearly Lady Gregory has her eye on the Irish text when she substitutes 'slipped' for 'glided' as a translation for 'doscirred'. The

Irish verb (modern Irish 'scior') has a sense of abrupt suddenness, an impact of surprise, which 'glided' does not convey.

While correcting the proofs of *Cuchulain of Murthemne* she was already at work on her second compilation of saga and legend, *Gods and Fighting Men*, tales of the Irish mythological figures and Ossianic lore and legend. In setting down versions of the tales of Finn she seems to have been more at home than she had been with the formidable remoteness and strangeness of the Ulster cycle, probably because the Finn tales were always closer to folk tradition (she was able to supplement the tales in books with a good deal taken from oral narration); because she had the assistance of Eoin MacNeill, who was working on his authoritative *Duanaire Finn* for the Irish Texts Society at the time; and because she had now worked hard enough to develop self-confidence. Her methods and achievement here do not differ substantially from those of her *Cuchulain*.

Yeats, Hyde, Moore and Lady Gregory, all in their different ways, exhibited a dissatisfaction with the English language of their own time. The reasons for this are many and complex, but one common element in their attitude can be summarized simply: they had come to feel that English had petrified into a language of journalists and Imperialists; that it was a dead machinery of social negotiation and control rather than a fully living tongue, which should open out to, disclose, indeed even *create* reality. 'Art', Yeats was later to declare in mature triumph, 'is but a vision of reality',[26] by which he did not mean that it sought to record the day-to-day but rather that art should work into the fullest possible apprehension of things, to say them as they vibrate in their being. Language is the gracious holding and unfolding of that apprehension, and is, properly, the 'abounding glittering jet' that springs out of 'life's own self-delight'.[27] For both Yeats and Lady Gregory, this is what speech should attain, the kind of hesitant but delighted fullness Heidegger works towards in his discussion of 'saying' in 'A Dialogue on Language'.[28]

For Lady Gregory and Hyde and Synge Irish was a language more fully integrated with the life of Being itself: it spoke out of, it 'said', a great network of codes, sympathies, experiences, depths; it belonged. The landscape, the flowers, the plants to be found growing in the ditches, and all the significances of those things, their history and associations, their energies that could be used for healing, all these found a voicing in the Irish language. The problem was that, because of the forces of modernization and the aftermath of colonial suppression, this great network of interconnection was on the point of disappearance. It was a tragic enterprise, but the only thing to do was to try and re-awaken the sense of value inhering in that network or code, and the Gaelic League was one great effort in that direction. Another was the English writing of Yeats, Lady Gregory and Synge.

Lady Gregory saw the Gaelic League and the literary movement as being very closely related. She saw herself, in her work on Raftery, Cuchulain and Finn, as attempting to open up the lines of communication between the Irish language and the literary movement. But she also wanted to bring back *to the people* their sense of themselves in a speech, which, while English, had about it some of the realising, emphatic, and natural qualities of Irish. She had a vision (again, we should recall Yeats's Blakean use of this word, as having to do with seeing the essential rather than the commonplace) of a community restored, where people would live in a world which was not dead and *codified*, but alive and energetic; speaking a language which could, whenever necessary, call upon the network of collaboration that obtains between people when they are truly themselves, unfettered by isolation, sadness, apathy or committees. This is why the Raftery play, that collaboration between herself and Hyde, is so moving: it discloses on stage the possibility of 'union after separation', the phrase she used to describe the art of Synge. Raftery comes back from the dead, and in her translation, he speaks an English that recalls the old language, but which is marked, even deformed, by the loss of it. She would write a language to heal; she would be a Bridget Ruane to Anglo-Irish literature.

NOTE ON LADY GREGORY'S PLAYS

BERNARD SHAW

[Bernard Shaw, in a speech on behalf of the Abbey Theatre delivered in London on 3 February 1910, had some especially commendatory things to say about Lady Gregory's dramatic writings. When report of this encomium came to the attention of Lady Gregory's literary agent, Curtis Brown, he urged her to appeal to Shaw for a written text that might be utilized for exploitation of her American editions. On 27 September 1910 Shaw, holidaying in Parknasilla, complied with the request by drafting a shorthand 'screed' (British Library Add. Mss. 50703, fols. 193–6, captioned 'Note on Lady Gregory's Plays for Curtis Brown') that purported to be a verbatim report of the earlier extemporaneous remarks. A typewritten transliteration of the draft (BL Add. Mss. 50703, fols. 197–9) was made by Shaw's secretary in London and duly forwarded to Dublin. Inexplicably, the publishing firm G. P. Putnam's Sons appears to have quoted only one brief extract, in an advertisement for the American edition of Lady Gregory's *Irish Folk-History Plays*. Thus the text of Shaw's tribute to Lady Gregory is now published *in extenso* for the first time.   Dan H. Laurence]

Mr Bernard Shaw, speaking at a meeting in London in 1910, alluded to Lady Gregory's plays in the following terms:
'I know of no more conclusive refutation of the theory of irresistible vocation in fine art than the case of Lady Gregory. No dramatist, living or dead, has shewn the peculiar, specific gift of the born playwright—the gift of Molière, for instance—more unmistakeably than Lady Gregory. If ever there was a person doomed from the cradle to write for the stage, to break through every social obstacle to get to the stage, to refuse to do anything but write for the stage, nay, to invent and create a theatre if no theatre existed, that person is the author of Hyacinth Halvey, of The Workhouse Ward, and of The Rising of the Moon. There are

274

authors who have achieved considerable reputation and success as writers for the theatre, who have not had a tenth of her natural faculty for the work. Yet it never, as far as I know, occurred to her spontaneously to write a play at all. She had, on occasion, turned her hand to writing with invariably entertaining results; but it always was 'on occasion': she does not seem to have volunteered anything. I see no reason to suppose that she would ever have written a line if nobody had ever asked her to. Her activities as the wife of an active member of the governing class were to all appearances quite enough for her.

'Fortunately for the world the public duty of nursing the Irish National Theatre thrust itself on her before it was too late. In those early days of the struggle of that institution for existence, everybody had to do what they could. I must not say that the actors had to shift the scenes, and the actresses to darn the wardrobe, the authors to write the playbills and paint the scenes, and the managers to sweep out the box office and so forth; but I feel quite sure that whenever anything was wanted, whether it was a scrubbing brush or an Irish play, Lady Gregory was appealed to as general housekeeper to supply it. The scrubbing brush she bought, and may even have wielded; but as the oilshops did not keep Irish plays, and Mr Yeats and the other great writers on the staff could not keep up with the demand, she had to produce them herself; and thus was discovered one of the most remarkable theatre talents of our time. There never was a clearer proof of the fact that it is not your hopelessly stage-struck, or book struck, or paint struck, or music struck monomaniac that makes our great artists, but rather the practical geniuses who will do anything in the air, and who respond to a public need and not to their individual ambition or vanity.

'Lady Gregory's success needs no confirmation from me. They never fail to do the one thing which we all demand from a play, which is, not as stupid people say, to amuse us—though Lady Gregory's plays are extremely amusing—but to take us out of ourselves and out of London and out of the stuffy theatre whilst we are listening to them. The early ones, from Spreading the News to The Workhouse Ward, have fun and bustle enough—what people call action—to make excellent Variety Theatre turns in the hands of capable Irish comedians. The later ones: The Image and the sequel to Hyacinth Halvey, are subtler and finer: they present to us a group of Irish people to whom absolutely nothing at all happens; and yet their imaginations work so furiously that at the fall of the curtain they have gone through a whole tragedy of what they would themselves call "heartscalding" experience. In this double command of the world of fancy, and the world of the vividest, funniest fact, Lady Gregory's genius strongly resembles that of Molière; and I am not surprised to learn that she has translated several of his plays for use by the Irish National Theatre.'

FOUR FRENCH COMEDIES:
LADY GREGORY'S TRANSLATIONS OF MOLIÈRE

MARY FITZGERALD

Although no less an authority than George Bernard Shaw has noted Lady Gregory's similarity to the seventeenth-century French playwright Jean-Baptiste Poquelin, better known as Molière, the fact that she became a translator of four of his plays resulted from an accident of history.[1] When the Abbey Theatre received its patent in 1904, one clause in the legal contract was designed to placate the owners of other Dublin theatres by guaranteeing that the new repertory company would not encroach on the traditional offerings of its potential rivals: the patent restricted the Abbey to performances of contemporary Irish dramas and continental masterpieces.[2] So in exactly the same way that she became a playwright, stepping in with something of her own when 'comedies were needed' in the early days of the Irish dramatic movement, she later became a translator of continental pieces. When the need for greater breadth of offerings became apparent, Lady Gregory stepped in again. As she described the event herself in *Our Irish Theatre* in 1913,

We wanted to put on some of Molière's plays. They seemed akin to our own. But when one translation after another was tried, it did not seem to carry, to 'go across the footlights.' So I tried putting one into our own Kiltartan dialect, *The Doctor in Spite of Himself*, and it went very well. I went on, therefore, and translated *Scapin* and *The Miser*.[3]

And, she might have added in 1924, *The Would-Be Gentleman*.

It happened very much the way she describes: Lady Gregory seems to have fallen into translating French masterpieces, rather than to have chosen the task. The Kiltartan Molière that resulted from her willingness to take on yet another burden at the Abbey Theatre blends her folklore interests with her dramatic abilities. Looking at her versions of *Le Médicin malgré lui*, *Les Fourbéries de Scapin*, *L'Avare*, and *Le Bourgeois Gentilhomme* can tell us something about her literary and linguistic abilities, her dramatic technique, and her ability to subordinate herself to the mind of another writer—something she did very well for a select few of her contemporaries as well as for Molière.

Lady Gregory may never have planned to be a translator, but she certainly had prepared for it: in a sense, her offer to translate Molière for the Abbey was simply putting to use a skill she had taken great pains to develop. She had, of course, been translating Irish into English as part of her own study of the language, and also in pursuing her interest in folklore and in writing for the early Irish Literary Theatre, the experimental project that became the Abbey Theatre. She was, moreover, fluent in French and knowledgeable about French literature. Her facility with French seems to have been part of her general facility with languages—she knew Irish, French, Italian and German reasonably well. As a child she had learned the rudiments of the French language from her tutors, as did her brothers and sisters, and she had polished this book-learned French in her young adulthood during her tours of duty as family companion to her invalid brother on the continent. She developed an ease in translating from conversational French into conversational English, as her idiomatic handling of Molière's plays attests. That she chose to translate them not into standard but rather dialectal English was partly the result of her major interest in the folklore of her native region and the language in which she heard it expressed, partly a recognition of the folklore quality she recognized in the plays, and partly a concession to the prevailing trend at the Abbey. As she and Yeats put it in a document that survives under the heading *Paragraphs from Samhain, 1909*:

the folk drama, for which our Theatre has given the opportunity, has a great number of writers, and especially of late there have arisen young men of great promise whose future is probably bound up in the future of our Theatre. The creation of a folk drama, was, however, but a part of the original scheme, and now that it has been accomplished we can enlarge our activities, bringing within our range more and more of the life of Ireland, and finding adequate expression for the acknowledged masterpieces of the world. A theatre, as we conceive it, should contain in its repertory plays from the principal dramatic schools. We have begun with . . . Molière . . . [because his] affinities with folk drama have made [his plays] easy to our players.[4]

There is also the hidden suggestion that the perceived affinities between classical French masterpieces and contemporary Irish plays indicated that the Abbey repertoire might well be seen by future generations to be every bit as 'classical' as its French predecessor.

Lady Gregory referred to her translations as *adaptations* of Molière, and her use of that word was more conservative—at least for the first three plays that were translated in the period from 1905 to 1909—than it needed to be, which gave rise to the sort of misunderstanding about her versions that can be seen in the following comment from an American newspaper during the Abbey tour of 1911:

It is perhaps not fair to refer to 'The Kiltartan Molière'—little known in this country—as a translation. Lady Gregory wrote it for the Abbey Theatre at a time when there were few new plays, translating not so much the words of 'Les Rogueries [*sic*] de Scapin' and the other plays it contains, as their spirit into the speech of the Irish villages.[5]

In fact, her translations of *The Doctor in Spite of Himself*, *The Rogueries of Scapin*, and *The Miser* are virtually verbatim reproductions of the originals, if one makes slight allowances for the occasional word-inversions and other dialectal phrasings that the Kiltartan idiom demands. Thus, for example, in *The Doctor in Spite of Himself*, the line 'toutes mes études n'ont été jusqu'en sixième' becomes 'All I could do never rose me from the bottom of the school,' and 'De grace, Monsieur, ne dissimulez point avec nous' becomes 'Don't be humbugging us now if you please'. Her translation is invariably faithful to the original, as well as comfortably smooth in English, and it is always informed by a sure comic sense and lightness both of spirit and of diction. Sometimes, too, in comparing the French and Kiltartan versions line by line, one is surprised by how closely an Irish expression renders the French. Thus, for example, in *Scapin*, 'm'assassiner' is given as 'to destroy me', and in *The Miser*, 'ne m'assassinez point' becomes 'Don't make an end of me altogether'. Also in *The Miser*, 'ce que je viens de dire' is given the appropriately idiomatic rendering, 'the thing I am after saying'. Sometimes too, Lady Gregory manages even to surpass the original, while remaining true to its literal meaning, as when, in *Scapin*, she gives Silvester's bullying cry, 'Je lui donnerais tout à l'heure de l'épée dans le ventre' as 'I'll spit him on my sword'. One member of the Abbey audience, who evidently knew Molière's French well enough to recognise how well she had done her job, asked her after the first performance of *Scapin* what the original of her line 'blobby tears' was.[6] It was 'ces larmes désagréables qui défigurent un visage'. It was also one of the largest liberties she ever took with a Molière line.

Lady Gregory not only kept rather rigorously to the literal sense of lines, but she also preserved nearly the whole structure of each play. Although she took some liberties in this regard with her 1924 translation of *Le Bourgeois Gentilhomme*, making changes that were necessitated by the limitations of the Abbey stage and the company, for the three plays that appeared as *The Kiltartan Molière* (*The Would-Be Gentleman* was published in *Three Last Plays* [1928]), she adheres closely to the form of the originals. She makes very few cuts—a line here or there in most cases—and these are almost invariably the sort of cuts made in a rehearsal, a pruning of lines which clog the pace of the action, such as an elimination of repetition or a shortening of a monologue. The only exception to this rule is her cutting of the double-entendre flirtation at the end of Act II, Scene II of *Le Médecin*, where Sganarelle tells the beautiful Jacqueline that he wishes he were 'le petit poupon fortuné qui tétât le lait de vos bonnes graces' with its accompanying low-comic stage business. Although this one instance of censorship might seem to be ascribable to Victorian sensibilities in the translator, it was probably a rather more hard-headed understanding of the dangers of affronting the volatile sensibilities of the Abbey audience that caused Lady Gregory to eliminate the scene, which is brief and does nothing to advance the action— though it may well get a laugh from those members of a modern audience whose consciousness has not yet been raised by the woman's movement. Apart from this one instance, however, Lady Gregory makes no substantive cuts in her first three translations from Molière. (*The Would-Be Gentleman*, as we will see, presented special problems and was cut rather more extensively.)

She gives the plays as they were originally written. There is no rearrangement of plot or structure; scenes follow one another exactly as they do in the originals. Although Lady Gregory does not follow the French practice of announcing a new scene in her text whenever a character enters or exits the stage, she presents all the scenes in sequence, running them together into larger units. She does not alter characters: everyone who appears in Molière appears in Lady Gregory, though occasionally she anglicises the French name, as 'Martine' to 'Martha' in *The Doctor in Spite of Himself*. Furthermore, she adds no lines to *The Doctor* or *The Miser*, and adds only three brief lines to *Scapin* in places where some slight clarification was wanted. In short, the Kiltartan Molière is very near to Molière himself.

The Abbey first considered performing the works of Molière in late August 1905. Yeats and Lady Gregory, apparently with Miss Horniman's eager concurrence, decided to ask John Millington Synge—who was at the time the third of the trio of Abbey directors—whether he would approve the undertaking of such a project. Yeats wrote Synge on 15 August 1905, saying that he and Lady Gregory wanted to do Molière and asking Synge whether he would agree in principle to such a plan, with the specific Molière play to be presented to be decided upon later. He added, however, that he and Lady Gregory had been thinking of *The Doctor in Spite of Himself* for the coming Beltaine 1906 season, and that Miss Horniman had found 'a fine eighteenth century translation' of the play.[7] Synge agreed, and as we know from Lady Gregory's account in *Our Irish Theatre*, Miss Horniman's fine eighteenth-century translation was only the first of several to prove unsuitable on the Abbey rehearsal stage, and Lady Gregory then made her offer to translate *The Doctor* herself.

She was very busy when she volunteered for the assignment. The years during which she translated the plays that appear in *The Kiltartan Molière* were tumultuous years at the Abbey and a time of peak creativity for her. When she began her translation, the Abbey company was in the midst of a bitter reorganization battle that eventually saw the secession of a number of the finer actors and writers, among them Padraic Colum, and the consequent formation of the rival Theatre of Ireland. The battle lasted all the time that Lady Gregory worked on her translation—though it obviously had nothing to do with it—and in fact the Theatre of Ireland held its first meeting two nights after the first Abbey production of the Molière play. The protracted fight was a constant strain on Lady Gregory's time and concentration, but the chronic headache caused by this bit of 'theatre business' was not her only distraction. In addition to helping with the work of other playwrights, she was rehearsing her own new play, *The White Cockade*, and writing the whole of her sequel to *Spreading the News*, *Hyacinth Halvey*. The main character in that short comedy, Hyacinth, may owe his name to the influence of Molière—a Hyacinth appears in *Les Fourbéries de Scapin*, which Lady Gregory may well have looked into while thinking about *Le Médecin malgré lui*. Despite all her obligations at the Abbey and at home in Coole, she worked steadily at the translation from early autumn and on through the new year, sending the completed typescript to Dublin, where Synge received it on 15 February 1906.[8]

He pronounced it 'admirable' and predicted it would go well, and in this he was right, as the production, which starred the Fays, Sara and Molly Allgood [Maire O'Neill], and Arthur Sinclair among other early Abbey luminaries,[9] earned good reviews from the Dublin critics, who noted that the audience had enjoyed it.[10] Lady Gregory's Kiltartan dialect was still new enough to be spared the abuse that eventually came to be heaped upon it: nobody yet thought that it obscured the full flavour of Molière, and those who did not know much of Molière presumably found the play so similar in tone and in technique to Lady Gregory's *Spreading the News*, with which the Abbey Theatre had opened two years previously, that the dialect seemed perfect for the content. The plot, in which young lovers are united as a result of an angry wife's design to get revenge on her husband by telling strangers that he is a doctor so as to entangle him in some comic difficulties, is sufficiently harmonious with Lady Gregory's own short comedies that one might not at first be aware that it is the work of another playwright in another culture in another century. How well Molière and Lady Gregory match each other may be seen in one brief excerpted exchange, the protagonist's conversation with one of the young lovers at the beginning of Act III. Molière gives it as follows:

SGANARELLE: Diable emporte si j'entends rien en médicine! Vous êtes honnête homme, et je veux bien me confier à vous, comme vous vous confiez à moi.
LEANDRE: Quoi? vous n'êtes pas effectivement . . .
SGANARELLE: Non, vous dis-je: ils m'ont fait médecin malgré mes dents. Je ne m'étais jamais mêlé d'être si savant que cela; et toutes mes études n'ont été que jusqu'en sixième. Je ne sais point sur quoi cette imagination leur est venue; mais quand j'ai vu qu'à tout force ils voulaient que je fusse médecin, je me suis résolu de l'être aux dépens de qui il appartiendra. Cependant vous ne sauriez croire comment l'erreur s'est répandue, et de quelle façon chacun est endiablé à me croire habile homme. On me vient chercher de tous les côtes; et si les choses vont toujours de même, je suis d'avis de m'en tenir, toute ma vie, à la médecine. Je trouve que c'est le métier la meilleur de tous. . . . Enfin le bon de cette profession est qu'il y a parmi les morts une honnêteté, une discrétion la plus grande du monde; et jamais on n'en voit se plaindre du médecin qui l'a tué.
LEANDRE: Il est vrai que les morts sont fort honnêtes gens sur cette matière. [Act III, Scene i]

Lady Gregory's rendition is both close to the literal meaning of the original and equally comic in tone and in effect:

SGANARELLE: Devil mend me if I know anything all about it [medicine]! You are a gentleman, and I will tell you no lie, as you told me no lie.
LEANDRE: You are not really a doctor!
SGANARELLE: I am not. I tell you they made me a doctor in spite of myself. I never had tried for such great learning as that. All I could do never rose me from the bottom of the school. What it was first put the notion in their heads I don't know, but so soon as I found they had their minds on making me a doctor by force, I made up my own mind I would be one at the expense of whoever would meet with me. You would hardly believe now the way the mistake has spread itself, everyone believing me to be a very skilful man. They are coming to consult me from all parts, and if things go on the way they are doing, it is as well for me to stick to doctoring to the end of my life. It seems to me it is in our profession, the dead always keep a civil tongue, they are very decent indeed, you will never hear them make a complaint against the doctor that killed them.
LEANDRE: That is true. The dead keep a very honourable silence upon that point.[11]

Lady Gregory's version of Molière sounds sufficiently like her own works that the Kiltartan phrasing seems almost natural to his characters.

The success of *The Doctor in Spite of Himself* prompted Lady Gregory to try her hand at another Molière play. The one she chose next was *Les Fourbéries de Scapin*, perhaps under the influence of *The Playboy of the Western World*, which had just had its tumultuous first performances in January 1907. Perhaps she wanted to show Synge, and Ireland, what a classic and continental Christy Mahon might look like. In any event, on 4 March 1907, she wrote to Synge that although she was struggling with the after-effects of influenza, she was 'translating "Scapin" as hard as I can for Easter Monday, we must have some new work'.[12] However, either because she missed that 2 April deadline, or for some other reason, the play was not performed until April of the following year. In the meantime, while translating it, she had seen the first production of her own *The Rising of the Moon*, and her collaboration with Douglas Hyde, *The Poorhouse* (afterwards revised as her apparently allegorical comedy, *The Workhouse Ward*).[13] She had also written and produced *Dervorgilla*, rewritten Yeats's *Where There Is Nothing* in its entirety as *The Unicorn from the Stars*,[14] and translated Hermann Sudermann's

Teja for production only two weeks prior to *Scapin* itself. It was rather a full year.

The play premièred on 4 April 1908 and was even more enthusiastically received than *The Doctor in Spite of Himself* had been. It had a markedly different cast from its predecessor, as both Fays had left the Abbey and as neither Allgood sister played in it. The female leads were Eileen O'Doherty and Maire Ni Gharbhaigh; the male roles were played by Sydney Morgan, Fred O'Donovan, J. M. Kerrigan, and Arthur Sinclair. *Scapin* proved a livelier play in translation than *The Doctor*: Lady Gregory's strategic cuts and clarifications speeded up the action of the original, and Synge directed the play in what must have been an energetic fashion, if the reviewer for the *Freeman's Journal* is to be believed:

Lady Gregory's translation of *Les Fourbéries de Scapin* is most admirable in every respect, and this is saying a great deal, when one remembers how completely the dash and go, the life and soul of these comedies depend upon the vivacious dialogue with its keen wit, its sprightly sarcasms, its epigrams, and words and phrases for which English equivalents are not by any means readily to hand.[15]

Perhaps buoyed by the success of her first attempt at translating Molière, Lady Gregory seems to have approached *Scapin* with confidence: her purpose in this 'adaptation' seems to have been not only to translate the play, but to improve upon it as well—without straying too far from the literal sense of the lines. The translation is particularly close to the original, but Lady Gregory makes some careful cuts and sharpens the pace of the dialogue thereby. Long-winded speeches are condensed by excising lines that state the obvious—as when the heroine Zerbinette appears onstage going for a walk *announcing* that she intends to take a little air; or by eliminating lines that repeat something that has just been said. But her most usual cut in translating the play is to reduce as much as possible the occasional static moments when the action appears to pause while various characters indulge in philosophical reflections on love and life. Thus, Lady Gregory cuts those lines in Act III, Scene i, in which Zerbinette explains herself, her actions and her views of love. This saves Silvestre from having to stand speechless for five minutes or so, waiting for his cues. (As the Abbey actors prided themselves on the elimination of all unnecessary gesture, so long a silence would be awkward to fill with action.) Lady Gregory also adds three brief lines to the original: one a minor piece of stage business, a direction to look in another pocket—'No, the other one'—while Geronte is rummaging for the ransom money he needs; another, 'He's a liar' as the lead-in to a brief speech that makes that point; and 'He will not get off free. I'm the one that will punish him', which also clarifies the speech of Scapin's in which it occurs at the end of Act III, Scene i. Speaking of the dangers of being found out, he says in the original:

Ces sortes de perils ne m'ont jamais arrêté, et je hais ces coeurs pusillanimes qui, pour trop prévoir les suites des choses, n'osent rien entreprendre. . . . Il ne sera pas dit qu'impuniment on m'ait mis en état de me trahir moi-même, et de découvrir des secrets qu'il était bon qu'on ne sut pas.

Lady Gregory gives this as:

It is not fear of that sort would ever stop me. I hate those sort of timorous persons that will never go into anything fearing some harm might come of it . . . It must never be said that I let myself be slandered, accused of betraying my master's secret, and that the slanderer got off free. He will not get off free. I'm the one that will punish him.[16]

The minor additions make the point more clearly. Even so, Lady Gregory's cuts and clarifications are few, and Scapin appears in Kiltartan very much as he first appeared in French.

When *Scapin* proved popular, it was inevitable that the directors would try once more, and so a third Molière play was scheduled for the following season. Lady Gregory took on *L'Avare*, which was produced on 21 January 1909. She translated it while working on her *Kiltartan History Book*, and perhaps because of that, it shows the greatest concentration of Kiltartan idioms of any of the three Molière plays that she attempted in these years. Despite having as fine a cast as any of the plays so far—Sara and Molly Allgood as Frosine and Marianne, and Arthur Sinclair as the Miser himself, with strong Abbey regulars in supporting roles—it earned Lady Gregory the first bad reviews she received for her translations, chiefly on the basis of the perceived discrepancy between the French names and action and the Kiltartan dialect. It has in common with its predecessors a closeness to the literal meaning of Molière's lines, and it improves upon some of the original by substituting nouns for pronouns or for unclear referents in various lines, as when the lover Cléante says in French that he will depart with 'this amiable person,' and in Kiltartan, that he will

take Marian. In this play too, Lady Gregory shortens long speeches
when they take off on philosophical tangents, and so increases the
pace of the dialogue. But the opening speech of Valère is a little
more cloying than the original, and in other places throughout the
play the dialect seems to devolve into mannerism. Valère enters, in
Act I, uttering the first lines of the play:

What ails you and what is vexing you, Elise, and you having given me
your word you would never break with me? Is it right for you to be fretting
at the time I am so well content? Is it that you are sorry now for the good
words you said to me? Are you drawing back from the promise I maybe
hurried you into, with the strength of my asking and my love?[17]

This considerably embroiders the simpler original of Molière:

Hé quoi! charmante Élise, vous devenez mélancolique, apres les
obligéantes assurances que vous avez eu la bonté de me donner de votre
foi! Je vous vois soupirer, hélas! au milieu de ma joie! Est-ce du regret,
dites-moi, de m'avoir fait heureux? et vous repentez-vous de cet
engagement où mes feux ont pu vous contraindre?

The first impression that such an opening made on the critics lasted
through the play and beyond, so that the *Irish Times* and the *Irish
Independent*, while acknowledging that the audience had liked the
play, both pointed out how hard it was to believe that the French
characters portrayed in *The Miser* could possibly speak in the
accents of Kiltartan. The *Independent* went so far as to say, 'It was
not Molière.'[18]

Whether because of the reviews, or because she was tired of
Molière herself, believing either that she had exhausted the plays of
his that she wished to translate or that she was losing her
effectiveness as his translator, Lady Gregory gathered her three
plays into a single volume, *The Kiltartan Molière*, as if to write an
end to her French translations. She may also have been
disheartened by the death of Synge on 24 March 1909. Certainly
she was much taken up with theatre business again: the Abbey
patent was due to expire, and the directors of the theatre had to
find new sources of funding for the period beginning in 1910.
Moreover a new crop of playwrights, soon to be known as the
'Cork Realists'—Lennox Robinson, R. J. Ray, and T. C. Murray—
were producing new plays for the theatre, making her extra
translations less necessary and freeing her to return to her own
creative work. *The Kiltartan Molière* was published in 1910,

and although the three plays it contained were revived and toured by the company, Lady Gregory did not attempt another French translation for sixteen years.

She had enough to do as it was. Those years saw her write seventeen plays, translate Carlo Goldoni's *La Locandiera* from the Italian (her *Mirandolina*), collect two volumes of folklore and *The Kiltartan Poetry Book* and *The Kiltartan Wonder Book*—not to mention several volumes of her plays; and to write *Our Irish Theatre* and the biography of her nephew Hugh Lane. Much of her energy in these years was taken up, too, with the fight to regain the Lane bequest of thirty-nine French impressionist paintings for Dublin, and with her directorial duties at the Abbey. She was also, like all of Ireland, absorbed in the ongoing conflict of the Troubles and the Civil War. The Abbey did not escape unscathed: Lennox Robinson wrote her at Coole on 8 July 1924 that some stray shots from the street had penetrated the windows above the Abbey stage and that some troops had barricaded themselves in the upper windows with books for a time.[19] Her son Robert had been killed in World War I, and her daughter-in-law narrowly missed execution in an ambush near Coole—everyone else in the carriage was killed but she was spared apparently because of Lady Gregory's known nationalist leanings. Her own life was threatened—and her bravery in response to that threat was commemorated by Yeats in 'Beautiful Lofty Things'. The comedies of Molière were apparently far from her mind.

But when the Civil War had ended, and the Abbey Theatre was experiencing the exhilarating renewal that the plays of Sean O'Casey brought it, another small historical accident returned her to work on Molière. In 1924, the year that her own work appeared in Japanese translation,[20] Lady Gregory was approached by Abbey actor Barry Fitzgerald, who had seen a production of *Le Bourgeois Gentilhomme* at the Comédie Française while visiting Paris. He asked her to put it into English, and so at the age of seventy-two she began to do just that, dedicating the final result to him.[21]

She began work on the play, using a 1723 edition, on 28 October 1924, noting in her journal for the day: 'read it through, and think it will go very well translated and abridged.'[22] The problem, of course, was that *Le Bourgeois Gentilhomme* is both a comedy and a ballet, and the Abbey company was prepared for only half of the designation. Because of that fact, the play posed more problems of translation than the three Molière works she had done earlier, and the result is more an adaptation than its predecessors. Despite the potential problems, Lady Gregory set diligently to work in late October. Aided by the wet winter weather, which kept her indoors and at her writing table, she finished the translation in just two months, noting in her journal of 29 December: 'I have sent off the *Bourgeois*. A relief.'[23] Some of the difficulty it presented—and her solutions to the problem—can be seen in her journal note for 23 November, written when she was roughly half-way through her play:

I talked to [Abbey orchestra director John] Larchet and to Sally [Allgood] about the *Bourgeois*. I proposed making a feature of the songs, having French airs to them, and at the last, as we can't have the apotheosis of old Jordain [sic], as Coquelin did, bursting into triumphant music, the Marseillaise. . . . Larchet likes the idea and will help us, and I lay awake in the night thinking of it—making Jourdain say 'Then if I'm not a Turk I'm still a good French citizen—Give us a good marching tune!' And I think of putting Sally and all the players who can sing on the stage as musicians in the first act, just wearing some of our heroic cloaks over their dress, and little paper half masks from Christmas crackers, that they may sing. I began putting words to 'O Richard O mon roi'! 'Alas my king and lord: Now all abandon thee: In the wide world no song is heard: Save mine to hold your memory'. . . .[24]

More staging details follow. As this note indicates, Lady Gregory takes greater liberties with *The Would-Be Gentleman* than with her previous translations of Molière. She cuts scenes, shifts lines from one character to another where needed, eliminates the ballet and incorporates her own versions of the songs, and in general tailors the play to the Abbey company. Still, she preserves the sense and spirit of the original, and where she does not cut lines, the text is invariably faithful to the original. Her translation, moreover, is less militantly Kiltartan than in previous years, and her sensitivity to nuance in the French original is as good as ever. She renders 'Taisez-vous', for example, as 'Can't you hold your tongue', conveying the comparative politeness of the formal *vous* by phrasing the French *command* as an English *request*. 'Tais-toi', apparently, would have been translated simply as 'Hold your tongue'.

Her twenty-odd years' experience as a playwright and critic of others' plays can be seen to be at work in the alterations she makes in the French original to make it work on the Abbey stage. She blends Act I and Act II together, in order to avoid Molière's first-act ending, which involves dancing. She transfers lines between the Music Master and the Dancing Master, imparting a better logic to their arrangement in the process. As she had done since the beginning of her translating, she cuts repetitive lines and any exchanges of dialogue that do not directly advance the action of the plot. She incorporates the singing more fully into the action, taking her cue from the original, in which Count Dorante praises the singing of the waiters: Lady Gregory has the Count ask for a song. And she handles, very deftly, the difficulty of presenting the banquet ballet. When the Count, in the original, brings up the subject of dinner, a servant says 'Tout est prêt, Monsieur', after which the stage directions indicate the six cooks who have prepared the dinner dance together, and carry in a table covered with various edibles. As this is clearly out of keeping with traditional Abbey Theatre procedure, and just as clearly beyond the capabilities of the company, Lady Gregory simply presents *hors d'oeuvres* onstage, and has Mr. Jordain mention that the dinner 'will be set out in the next room. These are just some little nick-nacks to begin on till it is ready.' She also eliminates the Count's peroration on the glories of the food that has been prepared for the banquet. Similarly, at the end of the play, she omits the dance finale and substitutes a marching song; though the lines and the choice of song are not quite what she planned in her notes of November 1924, they are also not far removed from it. She cuts the closing lines back to Mme. Jourdain's last speech and to the last speech of Count Dorante: when it is clear that the young lovers have successfully hoodwinked Mr. Jourdain and are about to be joined in marriage, Dorante turns to address the only remaining fear that bothers Mme. Jourdain:

Et afin, Madame Jourdain, que vous puissiez avoir l'esprit tout à fait content, et que vous perdiez aujourd'hui toute la jalousie que vous pourriez avoir conçue de monsieur votre mari, c'est que nous servirons de même notaire pour nous marier, Madame [Dorimène] et moi.

To which Mme. Jourdain replies, 'Je consens aussi à cela'.
    In Lady Gregory's ending, the Count says

And Mrs Jordain, to make your mind quite easy, and that you may give up any jealous thoughts or suspicions of your husband let me tell you that this lady and myself will be joined in marriage at the same time.

To which Mrs. Jordain replies, 'I consent to that too!' and Mr.

Jordain says, 'Come on, now. Let the music strike up', after which the onstage characters *'march around the room before going out, to the air of Malbrook s'en va-t-en guerre!.'*[25] The *Marseillaise* has given way to a lighter air, and Mr. Jordain has a quieter and less boastful last line, but the idea is still the one that Lady Gregory worked out with Sara Allgood and John Larchet. Even in her last translation, and close to the end of her life, Lady Gregory is faithful to the literal sense of the play as Molière wrote it, exept for those instances where the needs of the company make changes inevitable—and even in her changes, she looks for a hint in the original on which to base her alterations.

Like its three predecessors, *The Would-be Gentleman* demonstrates Lady Gregory's skill as a translator and as a dramatist. We are used to thinking of her as talented, reserving higher praise for others who wrote with her, like Yeats and Synge. But her talents were largely shaped by her own hard work and determination, and her dramatic and linguistic gifts were endlessly honed and polished by self-discipline. Despite her hard work, and despite her image, she had an enormous sense of fun and good humour. What her four French plays, the Kiltartan Molière, show us is not only self-sacrificing dedication to a theatrical ideal, not only another aspect of a multi-faceted talent, but rather a fine— even brilliant—mind profitably at play with language.

IN RETROSPECT: LADY GREGORY'S PLAYS FIFTY YEARS LATER

LORNA D. YOUNG

More than half a century has passed since Lady Gregory completed her last play, *Dave* (1927)[1], and during that time accelerated social and artistic changes have altered our perspectives on many aspects of both life and art. Nonetheless, within the total work of a dramatist successful in his or her own day there may well reside those universal qualities that eventually survive even the most radical upheavals. Whether this will happen in Lady Gregory's case only the future will reveal, but it does seem appropriate to look once more at the most significant of her dramatic accomplishments and try to pinpoint what is of contemporary and possibly continuing value and relevance in her plays.

It will be recalled that at the beginning of Lady Gregory's career as a dramatist in the early years of this century, she was wholly concerned with assisting her colleagues in the construction and dialogue of plays designed to enhance the rising Irish dramatic movement. She soon realised, though, that she could in fact write complete plays of her own. Strangely enough, the original stimulus did not come from a particular interest in drama, or an innate urge to express herself through writing plays—though this came later with the unexpected acclaim of her work. The new Irish dramatic movement's necessity became the mother of her invention, and eminent success as a playwright was to evolve from her tentative, self-effacing offerings to Yeats's theatre.

Lady Gregory's dramatic career is in fact rooted in paradox—a fine literary foundation for her, as it turns out. The intellectual daughter of an Irish country landowner, and brilliantly married, she moved comfortably among the aristocracy, statesmen, artists, poets, the notables of her day. But prior to all this she had since childhood immersed herself in the smaller world of the country people of Galway, and she came to use their speech as the language of all of her dramatic work, and the stuff of their lives and dreams for much of the content. Yeats was right when he observed that

291

Lady Gregory saw the glory of the world reflected in a peasant mirror.[2]

The Gregory canon includes comedy, tragedy, folk-history plays and plays of the supernatural, but there is often considerable overlapping, and there are tangible links of various kinds among the different categories and the individual plays. It is difficult, though, to try following a curve of her dramatic development, for the line, if it could be called a line, does not curve merely. It circles, mounts up and outward, and is always on the move, offering a different vista at almost every turn. She never stopped making experiments, and, importantly, she moved fairly steadily from the purely outer of the early comedies to the more subtle inner, or psychological, in works such as *Dervorgilla* (1907) and *Grania* (1911). Progression from the more lighthearted to the intensely serious is normal for Lady Gregory in following the course of a genre: it is the observable trend pursued from *Spreading the News* (1904) through to *The Image* (1909) in comedy, from *The Canavans* (1906) to *The Deliverer* (1911) in the historical plays, and from *The Full Moon* (1910) to *The Story Brought by Brigit* (1924) in the 'supernatural' group.

An important concept connecting Lady Gregory's naturalistic plays with her religious dramas and wonder plays is her view of man in relation to the supernatural, whether ancient Celtic or Christian. Commencing with man in his natural element in plays such as *The Jackdaw* (1902, revised 1907) and *The Workhouse Ward* (1908), she moves to a rather different plane in her treatment of certain simple or 'cracked' characters whose contact with another world lends them special wisdom. A striking example of this is Cracked Mary in *The Full Moon*, a daft character related to some of Yeats's creations of the same type; but Lady Gregory's have special orientation and significance in line with her own view of the natural and supernatural. She was also much impressed with George Russell's vision of man as a fallen god,[3] and this could be either a pagan or a Christian concept—the latter if one can conceive of man before the Fall as a god-like creature. In any event she moved towards an emphasis on the essential divinity and uniqueness of each person, however humble, and his direct link with the divine. Both these aspects are present in her last play, *Dave*. Her use of disguise is significant, and occurs regularly throughout her plays, the ultimate disguise being the clay of our mortal bodies, which in the end will be put off like the garment of the ragged green man in *The Jester* (1918), revealing a god beneath.

Perhaps more obvious but of great interest also is her view of the life of the imagination and spirit, beginning with the overblown private dreams of the simple folk in *The Image* and moving on to the more socially oriented ambitions of the leader or reformer who would free a captive people or bring back the Golden Age—dealt with seriously, even bitingly, in *The Deliverer* and whimsically in *Aristotle's Bellows* (1921). The leader, the reformer and the idealist were very close to Lady Gregory's heart, but she also had abounding sympathy with the dreams and longings of the people she knew so intimately, and used them to symbolize both the fruitfulness and the vanity of human aspirations.

A study of the comedies reveals her rapid development in play design and in characterization and psychological insight. She moved onward from the reassuring base of a technical coup— *Spreading the News*—ever expanding as a humorist, an interpreter of the folk mind, a writer of fantasy, and a commentator on the life of the imagination and the spirit. In no one work, of course, does she achieve all of these things, though *The Image* is the most comprehensive of the comedies in this respect. Perhaps the most notable features of the whole body of the comedies are the variety of approach and techniques, and the richness and diversity of characterization.

Lady Gregory excelled in the compact medium of the one-act play. Only two of her comedies, *The Image* and *Damer's Gold* (1912), are longer. In the one-act form she could fully demonstrate her theme, or elaborate on an incident pointing to a significance beyond its surface value. She became successful in writing short plays that possess the qualities by which fine drama is judged: inner and outer harmony co-ordinating design and meaning, and the two modes of irony which give strength and depth to either comedy or tragedy—the surface irony provided by properly managed audience omniscience, and the intrinsic irony of the spirit of the play, which may be opposed to or different from what it appears to be. An interesting example of this latter quality is *Spreading the News*, which with its rumour theme is more properly the material of tragedy, but is here inverted and restated in comic terms.

Spreading the News is her best known and most popular comedy, and a good deal has been written about it over the years. This early play exemplifies some of her most successful techniques. One of these is a pattern she adapted from Molière, where the beleaguered Bartley Fallon, hearing that his friend Jack Smith has been 'murdered', is reduced to the state of an automaton:

JAMES RYAN: . . . You don't know that he was followed, and that he was laid dead with the stab of a hayfork?
BARTLEY: The stab of a hayfork!
SHAWN EARLY: You don't know, I suppose, that the body was found in the Five Acre Meadow?
BARTLEY: The Five Acre Meadow!
TIM CASEY: It is likely you don't know that the police are after the man that did it?
BARTLEY: The man that did it!
MRS TULLY: You don't know, maybe, that he was made away with for the sake of Kitty Keary, his wife?
BARTLEY: Kitty Keary, his wife![4]

The effect in performance is hilarious, and the device works admirably because Bartley, a character drawn from life, is a melancholy romantic egotist who is as involved in his own fabric as a silkworm in its cocoon, and quite unable to cope with an involved social tangle. The 'polyphonic' pattern here will be recognized again and again throughout Lady Gregory's plays. In this particular instance she devises a pentagonal arrangement of dialogue[5] which accords well with the rapid tempo and densely social nature of the play.

The dramatist's strong controlling hand could go unnoticed in a performance of *Spreading the News*, but a study of the text reveals a tight judicious rein from beginning to end. The dialogue is brisk and follows the swift movement of both the action and the course of the rumour, though both these aspects seem to be flying 'this way and that way'. Intensity is built up from one situation to the next with great skill. The important exposition section is brief, to the point, and highly amusing: the characters converge, disperse and reassemble in a hectic mêlée that issues in a sort of false climax, for the final outcome is consummated outside the borders of the play; the dénouement begins after the curtain falls. *Spreading the News* itself seems to begin and end nowhere, and structurally is· almost totally exposition and development. The play is blown up like a huge bubble which comes to bursting point at the close. A small miracle is achieved in this comedy, with the action always rising and never actually culminating; and yet all is articulated with logical, even mathematical, precision. In its course the play presents character delineation, a study of social psychology, and indeed even a philosophical reading of an ever-present aspect of human life—the spreading of rumour and consequent character defamation—transposed from the minor to the major mode.

The genial comedy *Damer's Gold* is equally original, but untouched in technique by the influence of Molière, though Lady Gregory may have been stimulated to write a play about a miser as a result of translating and adapting his *l'Avare* as *The Miser* (1909) for the Irish stage. And like Molière she chose the comic vein for this more nearly tragic subject. *Damer's Gold* is one of the few of her plays that portray a family rather than a community or social group. Damer is in a sense the patriarch of his tribe, though not on friendly terms with his next of kin—brother Staffy, sister Delia and nephew Simon. Simon is important as a symbol of Damer's own youth, and serves as a nexus between Damer's past and present. The relatives are, as might be expected, after the miser's gold. The plot spins and twists and finally resolves itself around a changed Damer. Simon has won all Damer's gold in a card game with his uncle, and Damer is astonished and delighted to realize he has such an astute and doughty young kinsman. 'The dead spit and image of myself he is'—and he tells Simon that 'The Royalty of England and of Spain cannot touch upon yourself. I am prouder of you than if you wrote the wars of Homer.' The miser makes an about-face: he wants no more of heaping and hoarding of coins, but wishes now to see and enjoy the busy world, like his nephew, 'for it's long I'll be lying when my eyes are closed and seeing nothing at all!'[6]

The three main characters, Damer, Delia and Simon, are evenly matched protagonists: Damer and Simon have power, and Delia has a kind of glory with her glittering pictorial imagination. The three of them take turns as focal points, and all win something in the end. There is a kind of enchanted dust hanging over this play that blinds the beholder to all sorts of unbelievable things; almost everything that happens strains credulity, yet it all holds together with a kind of reasonable unreasonableness that blurs the individual oddities and makes us forget almost entirely that every one of the characters in the play is amoral. But, in a manner utterly different from the way in which *The Rising of the Moon* (1907) detaches itself with such ease from the burden of ethical bonds, this play floats almost imperceptibly into a stratosphere of its own, and so delicately that not even the touchy audience of the day would dream of decrying *Damer's Gold* as a slur on the morals of the Irish peasantry. Perhaps this is because the total ethos is so obviously detached, and the play moves so debonairly from start to finish, that *Damer's Gold* conveys the impression of being in this world, but in some delightfully whimsical way not quite of it.

A gift for languages eased Lady Gregory's way into translating and adapting plays by a variety of dramatists from different eras and nationalities. She was fluently conversant with Irish and French, and made excellent translations from the Irish of several plays of her compatriots, Douglas Hyde and Father Peter O'Leary, and from the French of Molière, her master in comic techniques. She was sufficiently skilled in German and Italian to translate a play each from Sudermann, Goldoni and d'Annunzio.[7] All this brought in additional richness to the already varied fare being presented to the Dublin theatre-goers.

She began her translations in 1901 with Hyde's rollicking little comedy *The Twisting of the Rope*, which is based on an Irish folk tale. Within the next two years she translated Hyde's *The Lost Saint*, *King James*, *The Nativity* and *The Marriage*, all published in her volume *Poets and Dreamers* in 1903. *The Lost Saint* and *The Nativity* are tender little miracle plays, and their influence can be felt in Lady Gregory's own dramas in this genre.

The year 1906 saw the first production of *The Doctor in Spite of Himself* (1906) rendered into the Kiltartan dialect from Molière's *Le Medecin malgré lui*—a startling innovation had an immediate success. In 1907 her version of Hyde's *The Poorhouse* was presented, and the next year the first performance of *The Rogueries of Scapin* (1908) from Molière's *Les Fourbèries de Scapin*, and *Teja* (1908) from Sudermann's play of the same name were given. In 1910 she published the two Molière translations along with an additional one, *The Miser*, from *L'Avare*, under the title *The Kiltartan Molière*. That year also saw the first production of *Mirandolina* (1910) from Goldoni's *La Lacondiera*.

Much later, in 1926, she translated and adapted Molière's *Le Bourgeois Gentilhomme* as *The Would-be Gentleman* at the request of actor Barry Fitzgerald, to whom the play is dedicated and who played the title role with great success. This was her last venture of this kind—a happy conclusion to a notable body of translations, and fittingly a comedy well suited to her particular genius.

Emerging clearly from a collective view of the comedies is the impression of a multitude of loquacious people busily expressing themselves, much of the time, through 'the talk that is all', each character curving off into something individual and curious, like the 'live' foliage and animals of Gothic architecture. The tragedies, on the other hand, though indeed concerned with character, deal more generally with the human spirit under various forms of pressure and anguish. In the end one remembers not so much the uniqueness of a tragic protagonist as the weight and strength of the human soul itself shining through the character: the old woman in *The Gaol Gate* (1906), Grania or Dervorgilla in their plays. These latter two tragic characters are, of course, much less their historical selves than studies of what Lady Gregory terms the strong ones of the earth, in the toils of betrayal, bitter disillusionment, or harrowing remorse. It is noteworthy, too, that most of her major tragic characters are women.

Lady Gregory designated and published *Dervorgilla* as a Folk History play, but it is more fruitfully considered as tragedy, and is in fact included under tragedies in the Coole edition of her plays. It has satisfying richness and depth as a study of the historical twelfth century lady of that name through whose love affairs— according to tradition—the English were first brought into Ireland. The play concerns itself simultaneously with Dervorgilla's guilt consciousness and the social and political outcome of her apparent betrayal of Ireland. The whole forty-year scope of the Dervorgilla story is encompassed in one act, in part through episodes of recall evoked in conversations with her two old servants and through the songs of a wandering bard; and in part through a group of young people surrounding the now elderly Dervorgilla. The interplay among these principals projects the revelation of the Lady's true identity, the collapse of her present respected status, and her courageous submission to final and complete rejection by the new generation—and symbolically, for all time. In this latter respect *Dervorgilla* is a companion piece to Yeats's powerful play *The Dreaming of the Bones*, with its ominous and haunting refrain: 'Never, never shall . . . Dervorgilla be forgiven.'

The historical Dervorgilla has since been vindicated, and Frank O'Connor in *The Backward Look* refers to her as a much maligned lady of great piety 'whose marriage to two unmitigated ruffians [whose rivalry for Dervorgilla brought the English into Ireland] she had nothing whatever to say to'. O'Connor considers Dervorgilla's last speech in Lady Gregory's play 'as noble as anything in Irish literature'.[8]

Dervorgilla has a clear kinship with classical tragedy, with the bard acting unconsciously as a seer, and with its chorus of young people who, although an integral part of the plot, also represent and reflect the new generation. The constant play of irony, the sense of impending doom, and the prevailing tension, all contribute to the classical tragic tone. But above all Lady Gregory delineates with unflinching fairness the tragic Dervorgilla, who bears a crushing weight of responsibility but who seems at the end to be almost transfigured in her chastened acceptance of the burden of personal and 'national' guilt.

A glance over the titles of plays written and produced in the first twenty years of the dramatic movement reveals the extent to which Irish myth, legend and history had aroused and inspired the dramatists and poets of the time. Scarcely anyone writing plays in those days had not tried a hand at revivifying and glorifying Ireland's past as part of the upsurge of nationalism, and perhaps never have art and patriotism been so closely and intensely interwoven in a modern nation. Lady Gregory was no exception, though in fact her historical dramas reflected, on the whole, more 'psyche' than history.

Her folk history plays are experimental sorties into Irish mythology and history, and portray in a quite unusual way some of the heroes and events of the past, but using the language and to a certain extent the thought processes of her Kiltartan contemporaries. There is a signal originality in the conception and creation of these dramas.

She had embarked on an ambitious programme. The time span encompassing these plays is very long, all the way from the prehistoric in *Grania* up through the eleventh century in *Kincora* (1905, revised 1909), *Dervorgilla* of the twelfth century, *The Canavans* of the Elizabethan period, *The White Cockade* (1905)—seventeenth century—and *The Deliverer*, which in portraying the young Biblical Moses as a parallel figure to Charles Stewart Parnell simultaneously echoes Old Testament times and the late nineteenth century. The chief unifying factor among the history plays is locale, for they are all set in Ireland—in the case of *The Deliverer* Egypt is an alternate for Ireland and symbolizes it. The shade of Kathleen ni Houlihan looms up behind all these plays except *Grania*, which is left within the ambience of the primitive epic.

Her first history play, *Kincora*, is a serious if not wholly successful attempt to transcribe actual historical events and characters into dramatic terms, for the most part in the light of documentary evidence. The characters here move stiffly, though they are large heroic figures, quite different from her far more human 'pretending' Giant of *The Golden Apple* (1915). What she has produced in *Kincora* is a closely reasoned assemblage of historical data arranged for stage presentation; the approach is academic. Lady Gregory really did not achieve much here to advance the cause of historical drama. Even in the case of *Grania* and *Dervorgilla*, which are profound and deeply moving, the plays are much less historical than psychological or tragic dramas. For in these two plays in particular she has used legendary or historical situations and persons for the purpose of working out a specific concept which has taken possession of her and which demands expression: in other words the history actually becomes a means to an end other than itself.

In the so-called comic histories, however—*The White Cockade*, *The Canavans* and *The Deliverer*—Lady Gregory abandons the heavy heroic approach applied to *Kincora*, and substitutes, much more successfully, the free play of her own imagination, expressing herself with a deft light touch shaded with varying levels of irony from the gently sardonic to the bitterly grim. Famous historical figures are portrayed, among them Patrick Sarsfield and James II in *The White Cockade* and the youthful Moses, alias Parnell, in *The Deliverer*. She sets these historical characters down amidst the Irish peasantry, and whirls them along to the cheerful accompaniment of Kiltartan wit and whim.

The unique quality of the history plays, certainly in terms of production, lies in the fact that the small core of aristocratic persons in the casts is surrounded by voluble and picturesque groups of vivid Kiltartan people who ultimately supply the impetus and energy that carry the plays triumphantly on their course. Though these plays embody and project considerably more 'folk' than history, they do not really suffer too much from this imbalance, and they do exemplify yet another aspect of Lady Gregory's inventive genius.

Four of Lady Gregory's plays are especially concerned with religious themes: these range from the miracle-type drama *The Travelling Man* (1909)[9] to *Dave*, her own version of the morality play. Between these two are the almost unclassifiable *Shanwalla* (1915) and her Passion play, *The Story Brought by Brigit*. *The Travelling Man* was written in collaboration with Yeats, though the play appears under her name and bears her unmistakable stamp. It contains both the fruit of their experiments and ideas, and the seed of her future work in areas of the supernatural. The play is a dramatization of one of the many early Christian folk tales centering around the concept of Christ appearing to humble people in the guise of a stranger; his identity will be revealed as the climax of an event that begins as a quite natural affair and then moves, either slowly or suddenly, into the realm of the supernatural. *The*

Travelling Man, in its simplicity of language, balanced design and essential purity, has a kinship with the legends of Tolstoy.

Based on the solid foundation of Douglas Hyde's religious dramas and her own experiments in *The Travelling Man* and *The Deliverer*, *The Story Brought by Brigit* emerges as an ingenious mingling of Biblical history and Irish legend, of New Testament persons (including Christ) and St Brigit, 'Mary of the Gael'. Elizabethan English is used: the words of Jesus and St John are taken verbatim from the King James Version of the Gospels. The restrained Kiltartan dialect which surrounds the Biblical language has, happily, a natural affinity with Elizabethan English. A particularly strong feature of this play is that Lady Gregory manages the suspense throughout so skilfully that one can almost believe, time after time, that something will surely intervene to save the Galilean from death; and this is handled in the best classical tradition.

One of the rather typical 'Gregorian' touches in *Brigit* is the kind of apologia she offers for Judas. She shows him as an avaricious man who betrayed, certainly, but who seemed to believe that Jesus would extricate himself from harm as he had done in the past. The age-old question of the ultimate guilt and evil of Judas is delicately but pointedly treated in a few words. One's reactions at the end are not unmixed, and one can almost pity this shortsighted, weak and acquisitive man who has sinned more greatly than he seemed at the time aware of. In the play, St Brigit bids him 'Go ask His forgiveness even now. He never refused any.' The anguished Judas replies: 'What is your chattering to me? He looked at me a while ago as he passed the road. It is I myself that betrayed the Son of God!'[10]

Lady Gregory's one morality play, *Dave*, is a long one-act drama dealing with the effect of a mystical dream on a downtrodden youth of the early nineteenth century, worked out somewhat allegorically, but with the traditionally stark figures of Man, Good and Evil recast as colourful, passionate West of Ireland folk. It is for this play that she used a poem of George Russell's as the core of meaning:

> The gods have taken alien shapes upon them—
> Wild peasants driving swine
> In a strange country. Through the swarthy faces
> The starry faces shine.
> Under grey tattered skies they strain and reel there;
> But cannot all disguise

The majesty of fallen gods,
The fire beneath their eyes.[11]

Lady Gregory carries this concept a step further and links it with the eternal destiny of man. After an apotheosis of rage at his constant victimization by a fellow-servant, who finally knocks him senseless, Dave has a dream which he later relates as his vision of 'a beautiful green place . . . with the sound and feeling of home' and a brother who holds out a hand to him. His master's young wife, the benevolent Kate, has been watching over the lad as he sleeps, and softly croons an ancient hymn which describes heaven as a garden. Dave wakes, and tells her about his dream. Kate believes that 'it is certain the Man above never sent you here without some little flame of His own nature being within you. . . . Mind you never let that flame be quenched in you.'[12] Dave is now moving from 'Man unredeemed' to a type of 'Adam redeemed': he is about to begin a new life of labour and sacrifice on behalf of his needy 'brothers', which will lead him back to the heavenly country of his vision.

Dave is a tumultuous play, full of action, conflict and cross purposes, portraying the evil in man through the wicked servant Timothy and the good through Kate and the renewed Dave. Kate's simply piety, expressed in her song, creates 'a ladder to the stars' on which the spirits communing with the sleeping boy can descend and ascend. She sings of heaven, while heaven is the stuff of Dave's dream. When the play ends we do not see Dave, but we know that the starry or transfigured face is shining through the swarthy one.

Lady Gregory's most charming experimental dramas are her wonder plays for children, where she blends human characters and scenes with some of the paraphernalia of myth and fairy tale. The genre was of her own contrivance and is without precedent in Irish theatre. With her comedy *Damer's Gold* she was already bordering on the magical world of the wonder plays; reality had begun to slip its moorings and she was on her way to enchanted seas.

Her second wonder play, *The Dragon* (1919), is in marked contrast to the first one, *The Golden Apple*. Where the latter drama is a re-blending of familiar folk tales and myths, *The Dragon* is much more original, though the dragon fable on which the story turns is familiar enough. Where *The Golden Apple* is episodic and the characters are basically stock types, *The Dragon* has almost unbroken continuity of action within one stage set, and there is some fascinating characterization. *The Dragon* is less a wonder play and more a character comedy than *The Golden Apple*. All but two of the characters change as a result of the incidents in the play—even the dragon changes—and some of them, notably the King and Queen and the Astrologer, are quite distinctive and delightfully idiosyncratic. The King is, by his malleable nature, almost bound to be a different man 'in the end of all', but the Queen and the Astrologer are fine rigid comic types, rather Molièresque, and most effective in their total inflexibility.

Aristotle's Bellows forsakes the enchanted and exotic settings of the earlier wonder plays and localizes familiarly in the Galway dwelling of the surly Conan, who is dissatisfied with the way God made the world. He discovers a magic means of changing all this through an old pair of bellows believed by the folk to have been owned by Aristotle. But Conan finds, after all his changes are made and he has not been able to restore his world to something like the golden age of Greece, that things are in fact worse than they were before. In her notes to the play Lady Gregory writes that if there is a moral to the story it is given in the words of Conan's mother: 'It's best make changes little by little, the same as you'd put clothes upon a growing child.'[13] The Mother is the one who, with the bellows, reverses the spells and restores all the enchanted characters to their original state. It is his sister who expends the final blast of the bellows on Conan, to bring him around at last to a reasonable frame of mind. As the play ends he remarks contentedly: 'Well, what good neighbours we all are, and what a comfortable family altogether. . . . The world is a very good world, the best nearly I ever knew.'[14] Ironically Conan, who wanted to change others, is the only one who is permanently affected by the magic of the bellows.

The theme of change runs all through the wonder plays and is handled differently in each one. In the case of *Aristotle's Bellows*, which is really a folk fantasy, change is effected by the mechanical (though magic) device of the bellows. The people here are not really characters—they are types as fixed as the Queen and the Astrologer in *The Dragon*. The play, of course, is for fun, and is really the most original of these later dramas. One might say that the 'hero' of the play is the *leitmotif*: the idea expressed by the mother that true change cannot be created magically or suddenly, but must evolve in accordance with the laws of human development.

The final play of the group, *The Jester*, was written as a school Christmas entertainment, and its connection with the rest of her work lies in the character of the Jester, who instigates change, and who first appears in ragged green clothes. The villain here is the Ogre, who has enslaved five little Wrenboys; they are persuaded by the Jester to exchange identities with five little Princes, and try living a totally different kind of life. Finally, after a succession of misadventures, the Jester unmasks the wicked Ogre, restores the Ogre's little captives to their rightful place as the long-lost cousins of the Princes, and reveals himself as the ancient shape-changer, the god Manannan, Son of the Sea: 'I am Manannan, that men are apt to call a Jester . . . and a Disturber . . . upsetting the order of the world, and making confusion in . . . its ways.'[15] He then initiates the process of putting things to rights: the Ogre is suitably chastised, and the Jester-god goes on his eternal way.

A happy feature of this children's play is its symmetry. There are two sets of five little boys, and initially each boy is only half a person. Not until the Princes are physically strong and courageous like the Wrenboys, and the Wrenboys are schooled in gracious living and in the arts, will all ten boys be complete individuals.

The Jester is the significant character here, appearing first as a ragged green man, whose medium is laughter and comedy, and whose method is the 'ordering' of the disorder and disparateness of which comedy in the classic sense is composed. Ragged strangers in Lady Gregory's plays always prove to be personages of high significance: one recalls the dusty tramp of *The Travelling Man* who is Christ in disguise, the ballad singer in *The Rising of the Moon* who is an escaped rebel leader, the travelling woman in *Kincora*, the young bard in *Dervorgilla*, the 'beggar' in *Grania*. The Jester here wears green, a fairy colour—also the colour of nature. He deliberately creates disorder so that he may cause the eyes of the characters to be opened; they themselves must then complete the task of restoration.

Lady Gregory's approach to her art, from first to last, was romantic rather than classical, though her method and motivation required the strict discipline of the traditionalist. It seemed quite natural for her to contain romantic themes within classical strictures and still venture as far and probe as deeply as she wished to do. Perhaps it is because she began to write plays in middle life, and did most of her work as old age approached and set in, that she avoided the harsh realism of the Cork group of dramatists, or of O'Casey and those who followed him: she was not interested in social reform through drama. Her natural inclination was toward humorous satire, fantasy, the supernatural. What predominates, particularly in the comedies, the comic histories and the wonder plays, is buoyant good humour, a joy in human quirks, and an abundance of rich comic dialogue keeping pace with and counterpointed deftly into plot design and movement. In whatever genre or blended genres she was working, the integrity, vitality and inventiveness of the plays, and in almost all cases their immediate adaptability to the stage, assured her of front rank status among contemporary Irish playwrights.

It was Lady Gregory's avowed intention in writing plays to interpret Ireland first to the Irish, then to the outside world, and in so doing make her contribution to the glory of her country. In her lifetime she achieved this goal, surprising herself, her colleagues and theatre-goers at home and abroad with a steady flow of plays of exceptional charm and originality. This study has concentrated on some of the outstanding aspects of her accomplishments as a playwright in her own day; but to what extent may her best work be considered significant for our time, and perhaps also for the future? One may approach this problem from two directions, viewing the plays as stage productions viable or otherwise today, or as literary dramas which can be enjoyed in the reading and which have something important to say to playwrights and devotees of the drama now or in the future.

Lady Gregory wrote for her own time, always with her country and its problems and needs in the forefront of her mind. Since then the Irish political and social situation has changed, and plays like *The Rising of the Moon* and *Dervorgilla* have lost a good deal of their nationalistic impact on an Irish audience. They now seem to have just about retreated to the category of nostalgic drama—the light in which any audience of today would be likely to view them, unless accepting them simply as comic[16] or tragic plays. The most outstanding of the pure comedies, on the other hand, have all the qualities of good drama in this genre, and share with the plays of Molière and Congreve and Wilde the ability to transcend their contemporary settings and language, and to charm audiences of today—Irish or otherwise—who delight in comic characterization, witty dialogue and ingenious situations. Among these would rank *Spreading the News*, *Hyacinth Halvey* (1906), *The Workhouse Ward*, and perhaps also *The Jackdaw*, *Aristotle's Bellows* and the comic history *The White Cockade*.

The tragedies do not fare so well today, despite depth of tragic penetration and impressive psychological insight—with the possible exception of *Dervorgilla* when considered primarily as the story of a tormented woman, rather than as a villain of Irish history. And *The Gaol Gate*, with its heroic Mother, would seem not to hold too much promise for an audience now, even with the gripping pathos of the unfolding situation and the transcendent quality of the final speech.

As to the supernatural and wonder plays, there might be special circumstances under which *The Travelling Man* and *Brigit* could be successfully given today, or *Aristotle's Bellows* and *The Dragon*. But it has to be borne in mind that almost all of her best works are brief, and the occasions for producing three one-acters in an evening, or a curtain-raiser before a full length play, are less frequent now, even for amateur dramatic societies; and it is unlikely at present that the clock would be turned back to accommodate what today seems a rather quaint custom.

The founders of the Irish dramatic movement regarded themselves as the sponsors of a literary theatre, which presupposes that the best of their works would in fact have lasting literary value in addition to their immediate function as effective and important stage plays. And of course some of their dramas have found a secure niche in literature in the English language. Lady Gregory's assured place would seem to be here.

Her plays are, for one thing, eminently readable; they spring to life from the printed pages, enthralling the reader with their dramatic virtuosity. They are a continuing delight in their profusion of memorable lines that bubble with comic vagaries of language. In an age of cynicism her plays lift the spirit with their tolerance and sheer enjoyment of humanity. And they reach into deeper territory through her keen exploration of motive and the fascinating and perplexing relationships that are forever spinning between and among human beings. Her characterization and management of interrelationships are noteworthy of themselves, but extend beyond this to her view of man in a larger context than the social one: his polarity with a divine force.[17] Surely these are among the qualities that ensure a place in the future for the outstanding works of a dramatist of the past.

Lady Gregory's plays have continued to grow in critical attention and acclaim, as evidenced by the accumulating volumes written about her, and by the inclusion, in her complete works, of plays and prose that had remained in manuscript until recently; so that from a literary standpoint her reputation has steadily increased. This in itself may prove to be a prophetic signal of an exciting renaissance of her plays as she designed them—for the stage—perhaps beginning with the year 2004, the centenary of the founding of the Abbey Theatre.to which she had contributed so richly in her time.

THE GLORY OF THE WORLD AND THE PEASANT MIRROR

ANN SADDLEMYER

In 1926, six years before Lady Gregory's death, W. B. Yeats published *A Vision, Estrangement,* and his *Autobiographies* with the updated *Trembling of the Veil.* So close to Yeats during the initiating and writing of the events recorded in his autobiography, Lady Gregory described in her journal the pleasure of reading *Estrangement*:

> Many nice words about me, bringing back the memory of those years of close companionship. I miss it. When I am too long without a friend at hand to talk with I feel, not lonely, but insincere—never speaking my whole mind.[1]

But what were her thoughts concerning Phase 24 of *A Vision,* where she and Queen Victoria are sandwiched between Synge (Phase 23, 'The Receptive Man') and AE (Phase 25, 'The Conditional Man'), on the way to the darkness of the moon? Here 'at the end of ambition' dwell those where all is sacrificed to a code of personal conduct formed from social and historical tradition; where moral strength and great humility reside uneasily beside great 'impersonal pride'; where there is no philosophic capacity or intellectual curiosity, though philosophy and science are accepted; and where intolerance for those who break or resist the code is balanced by tolerance for all the world's evil beyond the code. Artists of Phase 24, 'born to moral arrogance', create an art 'where individuals only exist to express some historical code, or some historical tradition of action and of feeling, things written in what Raftery called the Book of the People'; they despise the Bohemian 'till he turns gypsy, tinker, convict, or the like and so finds historical sanction'. Most dismissive of all is Yeats's assertion that those bound to Phase 24

submit all their actions to the most unflinching examination, and yet are without psychology, or self-knowledge, or self-created standard of any kind . . . and though they can stand utterly alone, indifferent though all the world condemn, it is not that they have found themselves, but that they have been found faithful.[2]

There is much in this blunt portrait that captures Lady Gregory's true likeness: home-maker and guardian of the Seven Woods for son, then grandson, so that the Coole demesne would remain in the careful hands of tradition; supporter of the Gaelic League and organizer of co-operatives; fighter of worthy, unpopular causes such as Arabi Bey's Egyptian nationalist stand against the excesses of Turkish rule and anti-Conscription for the Irish in 1918; pro-Republican in 1922; public objector to the hunger strike of 1923; insister on the right to call the tune in the theatre she worked so selflessly and long to create and support; tireless campaigner against 'the overgovernment' for the return of Hugh Lane's pictures to Ireland; indomitable challenger of all who refused to honour the restoration to Ireland of its ancient dignity.[3] Well might Yeats see in her 'a nature wearied out by over-much judgment' and thus the creator of a world 'where no one is ever judged, a high celebration of indulgence'.[4] 'Lady Gregory, in her life much artifice, in her nature much pride, was born to see the glory of the world in a peasant mirror.'[5]

Her own diaries and journals confirm this sense of duty and tradition. In reply to a request for her 'Maxim of Life', she wrote on 20 January 1925 'my old thought': 'it is my desire to live by law and love. Law the serenity of order; love the joy of self-sacrifice.'[6] For many years she carried about with her an extract from Plato's *Republic*, 'A man . . . if in this life . . . having adorned his soul not with any foreign ornament but with her own proper jewels, Temperance, Justice, Courage, Nobility, and Truth, he awaits thus prepared his journey to Hades'.[7] And her *Folk History Plays*, about 'strong people of the world', she dedicated to Theodore Roosevelt, 'one of the world's strong men'. Even the physical resemblance to Queen Victoria has frequently been remarked upon.

Yet despite their many years of unbroken friendship and the external correspondences, Yeats's bold image seems less than complete, the character sketch somehow deficient. For when we examine her published essays and statements and her private letters and memoirs, again and again it can be observed that her thoughts turn towards that most 'self-created standard' of all—that of the image-maker, the dreamer, the visionary, the fabulist. Even in

those little comedies Yeats commended elsewhere for their
'merriment and beauty'[8], sympathy lies not with the world of
'roast and boiled and all the comforts of the day'[9], but with the
outsider, the dreamer whose dream cannot possibly be achieved in
this world, whose desire is beyond any mortal code or tradition.
'The more ecstatic the vision the more impossible its realisation
until that time when, after the shadows of the earth, the seer shall
"awake and be satisfied" ', she wrote in her notes to *The Image*. It
is not reason, 'that binds men to the wheel', which captures her
interest and affection, but 'the call of some of those unruly ones
who give in to no limitations, and dance to the sound of music that
is outside this world'.[10] 'For who knows what windows may have
been opened to those who are under the moon's spell?'[11] To
explain her imaginative entry into the mind of the dreamer and
idealist as merely 'a high celebration of indulgence' and 'moral
arrogance' is to miss the inner life and message of the plays and
their maker.

When we look more closely still, we find that even the 'historical
code, or some historical tradition of action and of feeling', the Book
of the People itself, is celebrated not for 'historical sanction'—a
phrase more applicable to Yeats's own search for complemen-
taries—but for the soul of place, out of which one finds the expression of the individual soul. She confided in an interview:

Another of my objects—the one nearest to my heart—is the making of the
soil of Ireland sacred by getting legends known. By translating a legend,
or some piece of folklore, we may give to the hills and the fields a new
meaning, a new colour, a new inspiration for those who make their homes
among them—thus, as I say, bringing back the soul of Ireland to herself.[12]

'Love of country, *tirgradh*, is I think the real passion; and bound
up with it are love of home, of family, love of God', she wrote of
the ballads of the west of Ireland.[13] In that folklore (rather than
through the 'Book History' taught by the much-scorned professors
of Trinity College[14]) she recognized the real history of the soul of
a people, clothed in fantasy, dream and myth, the property of the
story-teller, the artist, and the poet. A comment very similar to one
found in Synge's notebooks[15] occurs in her introduction to *The
Kiltartan Poetry Book* (1918):

Religion . . . has left Heaven itself far off, mysterious, intangible, without
earthly similes or foreshadowings. I think it is perhaps because of this that
the country poets of to-day and yesterday have put their dream, their

vision of the delectable Mountain, of the Land of Promise, into exaggerated praise of places dear to them.

Seventeen years earlier while holidaying in Italy, she had expressed the same belief in source in a letter to Standish O'Grady, editor of the *All Ireland Review*:

Do you not agree with me that while we in Ireland have plenty of Nationalism, we want more of the parochialism, which is the key note of so much of the great art of Italy? The Italian cities for the most part recognised, and were proud of their own artists, and tried to keep them busy at home, and the artists liked to put their best work into their own birth place. . . . And whatever subject the artist took in hand he put, without any loss of reference, the stamp of his own countryside upon it. . . . Perhaps some day a painter who has grown up and dreamed of heavenly things in Connaught will be content to wrap his Madonna in the shawl he knows rather than in the Italian veil he does not know, and to let his Holy Children have their playground among the grey rocks of Burren or the brown bogs of Slieve Echtge.[16]

On 16 March 1903, in reply to a question sent forth from the Chicago *Daily News* on 'What Ireland Needs', she elaborated this idea further, relating it to her own private dream of a cycle of history plays touring the country schools:

. . . in my mind our greatest need is a wise parochialism. I would like to see the people of my own Galway thinking not less of the personality of Ireland as a whole, but certainly thinking more than they do of the personality of their own county. I should like to see, in the national schools reading books in Irish and English, which would teach historical events and the legends and the poems associated with Slieve Echtge and Cruachmaa and Burren and Aughrim, and the other places the children can see from their doors. I feel certain that a wise education should begin by cherishing what is already in the minds of the children, and not by bringing to them barren knowledge of far-off places and events.

As she was to write in her diaries after listening to Yeats expound his system, 'But the Divine is in us, around us, that at least is certain.'[17]

Inevitably those legends and poems, that love of place and response to land-soul, led her to the study of the Irish language and involvement with the Gaelic League. Here again, her own adopted townland became central, 'for Gort is on the borderland that speaks English, though it has not quite forgotten Irish'.[18] As we know, she began with the living memories of the last bard of Ireland, Raftery, seeking out his unmarked grave and translating his poetry. But it is a short step from dreams of the past and of place to dreams of what might-have-been, and even more important, of the unseen presence. 'Here, on the edge of the world, dreams are real things, and every heart is watching for the opening of one or another grave', she wrote to *The Speaker* in 1903.[19] They can be found even in those street ballads which celebrate loss and defeat rather than victory:

The song-writer, the poet, would find a better mission were he to tell of the meaning of failure, of the gain that may lie in the wake of a lost battle. If he himself possessed the faith that is the evidence of things unseen, he would strive to give spiritual vision to trembling and discouraged men.[20]

Lady Gregory did indeed have a philosophy, found not, however, in the history of tradition and codes, but within herself and her own desire to celebrate that evidence of things unseen. Towards the end of her life she wrote in her copybook, 'One day last week I thought how we had been always told to try and get to Heaven: but should we not rather have been told to strive to live there, to bring it about as now.'[21] This is the claim of the idealist, the personal dream, that cannot depend on the sharing of others, no matter how much co-operation and collaboration is necessary to the institutional life of the body. ' "Sinn Fein"—we ourselves—is well enough for the day's bread, but is not "Mise Fein"—I myself— the last word in art?'[22] It is one's own heart-secret. It is to follow the path of the candlestick maker rather than that of the baker, that 'useful and necessary tradesman', who 'accepts the established order of things' and 'sets his life by the hands of the clock and has all the peaceful virtues of the good citizen', or of the butcher, 'a more picturesque figure', whose voice rings heartily in its loud platitudes, and whose 'belief in himself and in the stroke of his knife, being sincere, gives him an air of sincerity', but whose trade is in 'dead meat, and the stirrings of life disturb his calculations'.

But the candlestick maker is not so well served, nor does he find such ready apprentices. The idealist, the seer, he cannot go with the crowd. He may still say, as an old maker of candlesticks said long ago, 'Mine heritage is unto me as a speckled bird: all the birds of the forest are against it.' Yet he holds up the light and hands it on from generation to generation, taking it from under the bushel that it may search the dark corners of the house. 'I know I am restless and make others so!' The drowsy many hear his cry and close their ears and eyes; they have eaten and drunk, and they want to sleep undisturbed by the hammering of metal or the flash of sudden flame.[23]

Inherent in her praise of these candlestick makers, the image-makers and dreamers, the strong and lonely people of the world, is the acknowledgement that they will surely fail in this world at this time. Their dreams and actions are doomed to misunderstanding (they may even misunderstand their own visions, as does Paul Ruttledge of *Where There is Nothing/The Unicorn from the Stars*[24]); or if heard, they will be met with derision, scorn, perhaps imprisonment, even death. No matter, the fight must go on, the dreamer persevere: 'We must just fight on', she wrote to one helper over the struggle to regain Hugh Lane's pictures, '—& I know we must win in the end. "Great is truth & it must prevail"—but it [is] sometimes hard to keep patience!' And elsewhere, 'I am writing to any I think may help—but of course as usual, dont mean to be dismayed by another set back.'[25]

'We are one with our time; we are in the movement; nothing is impossible.'[26] Colleagues and helpers, though their dreams—and their actions—may differ, provide the encouragement necessary to persevere. After one setback over the Lane pictures, she wrote, 'Rather heartbreaking. But the help of real friends, you among them, warms one's heart & keeps courage up!'[27] Of the 1923 hunger strikers she reported to another correspondent,

The authorities seem to think that all but a few, perhaps ½ a dozen—will give in—& that this residue must be allowed to die. They will certainly be the men with most courage, the ones one has the most sympathy for.[28]

A handful of worthy companions; the strengthening of 'the muscles of the mind' by battle[29]; sustenance from the unseen world that exists around, about and within us; even the certainty of danger and defeat; the delight of exploring the hitherto unknown that is constantly within reach; most of all, striving to achieve the conditions of Heaven here and now—these are the planks on which she based her life and work. They bear strong resemblances to the 'psychology and self-created standard' of her life-long friend and closest colleague. But whereas Yeats confided in her totally, and broadcast much also to the world, her heart-secrets remained private, like many of the most significant events of her own life held close, confided partially to some, entirely to none.

Her plays, however, do give her away, even without benefit of the letters, journals, and notebooks published since her death. Sometimes she admits it herself in her notes: 'I have myself a leaning towards sentimentality', she wrote of her early play

Twenty-Five, then tried to exorcise the 'weakness' in *The Jackdaw* and *On the Racecourse*.[30] And although she self-effacingly referred to her plays as providing 'a base of realism' for her colleagues' 'apex of beauty'[31], she willingly admits that though rooted in Kiltartan soil and local tales, even her little comedies move readily into the world of what-if and where-ever, delighting in 'our incorrigible genius for myth-making, the faculty that makes our traditional history a perpetual joy, because it is, like the Sidhe, an eternal Shape-changer'.[32] In an article describing the first *Playboy*-ridden American tour she commented revealingly of her own dramaturgy:

> The same fable written by a realist would have been intolerable, and Synge could have been one if he liked. I myself consciously lift my comedies out of common life by some extravagance of idea or of language, that the imagination may play more freely and the bubble catch some radiance from fancy's prism before it breaks. Yet before that breaking one must have given the illusion of reality as the old juggler gave it at O'Ceallach's house, sending hare after hound up a silk thread.[33]

'Sending hare after hound up a silk thread' aptly describes her method with the townsfolk of Cloon, who though rooted in place and language delight in weaving tales out of minute casual details until all reality is transformed into some new and glorious shape ready to take off into yet further astonishing adventure. Frequently the transformation is merely that of turning reality inside out (or upside down) so that we might see more clearly, as in *The Unicorn from the Stars, The Jester, The Bogie Men, The Wrens, The Full Moon, Damer's Gold, Aristotle's Bellows, The Dragon*. At other times the contrasts of opposites touch a darker vein of conflicting loyalties, as in *The Rising of the Moon, The White Cockade, The Canavans, Dervorgilla, Kincora, Grania, The Shoelace, The Workhouse Ward, Hyacinth Halvey, The Deliverer, The Travelling Man*. Sometimes this contrast is also with 'olden times', as in *Unicorn, Coats, The Full Moon, Aristotle's Bellows* and *The Jester*. But always, the shadow of another world hovers nearby, no matter how much she 'lets laughter have its way'.[34]

The Otherworld and its visions come to light most clearly when Lady Gregory herself lets her mind go 'miching', breaking through 'the English hedges into the unbounded wonder-world', as she describes the process in her notes to *The Jester*. Here on the other side of the full moon are visions of which the realists with their 'clogged sight' are unaware. 'Take care but it was no dream!' warns

Malachi Naughton of *The Image*. 'Let you go out looking yourself
so in the night time. And if you do go, it is likely you will see
nothing but the flaggy rocks and the clefts, for it's not all are born
to see things of the kind.'[35] All are image-makers in this play, and
all learn the pain of loss, scorn and derision when their heart-
secrets are revealed. 'Oh yes, oh yes, I'll be wary this time and I'll
be wise,' retorts Peggy Mahon, the old midwife, as she retreats to
her own poor cabin, 'I'll be as wise as the man that didn't tell his
dream!'

But the dream itself remains intact: 'And sure when we had to
believe it, we must believe it'. Darby Costello's simple explanation
reverberates throughout the plays. We hear it as early as her two
folk-history plays, *Kincora* and *The White Cockade*, where despite
treachery, deceit, and belittlement Brian holds firmly to his vision
of peace throughout Ireland and Sarsfield remains loyal to a king
who is no king. Through it all, both leave their names 'set in clean
letters in the book of the people'. It surfaces in *The Rising of the
Moon*, where a raggedy beggar awakens an earlier loyalty in the
Policeman's breast, turning him into a 'fool' prepared to sacrifice
reward and perhaps even uniform to help a political prisoner
escape. (She stressed to the players that the Policeman did not
change his mind, but acted out of 'a deeper instinct, his Irish heart
and memory of youth that had been moved unconsciously to
himself'[36].) It resounds in Dervorgilla's final speech, in her
realization that 'a deed once done has no undoing'. It is linked with
laughter in *The Golden Apple*, whose wicked Witch recognizing
defeat, breaks her three rods of mastery, for 'I that have been on
the flood tide, I will not wait for the ebb, or live a woman without
courage for ever!'[37] And it rises to a crescendo of triumph in *The
Jester*, whose laughing magician 'never could know the meaning of
that word "impossible" '.[38]

Frequently, even as we celebrate the courage and purity of the
dreamer's vision, we are forced to realize that he dances, as do
Cracked Mary and Davideen in *The Full Moon*, 'to the sound of
music that is outside this world'. McDonough can work magic with
his pipes to call forth mourners for his wife's funeral, but has not
Orpheus's power to bring his wife back from the dead; Grania can
persuade Diarmuid to rescue her from Finn, but she cannot woo his
loyalty and heart's ease; Conan's wonderful bellows can turn things
inside out, but he cannot make the world a better place. Awareness
of impossibility turns to bitterness in *The Deliverer*, where the
Moses/Parnell figure is welcomed, then as quickly suspected,

despised, rejected and finally killed by those for whom he has given up all to lead. 'That young man to have read history he would not have come to our help', laughs old Malachi bitterly to himself.[39] Betrayal needs no friends with enemies like these.

On the whole, however, the image-maker and his inevitable loss are treated with warm sympathy ranging from the poignancy of loss to rueful laughter, from the ironic acknowledgement of what might have been to a celebration of the dream recognized. Nowhere are all of these qualities more skilfully interwoven than in what were to be three of her last plays: *The Story Brought by Brigit* (1924), *Dave*, and *Sancho's Master* (1927).

From the time she began *The Travelling Man* with Yeats in 1902, a simple re-telling of the legend of The King of the World and a beggar woman who, once she tastes the delights of life's 'earthly side' cannot recognize her saviour in the gentle ragged tramp who appears at her door, Lady Gregory had been tempted by the thought of presenting the Christ figure in Irish folk dress. Writing of an exhibition of Jack Yeats's paintings in November 1901, she had praised his *Simon of Cyrene bearing the Cross*:

The pathetic figure of the Man of Sorrows is surrounded by a rushing, living crowd, mocking, scornful, indifferent, the crowd that is always found to scoff at any representative of a lost cause, of 'captive good attending captain ill' in every age, in every country.

I would like to see the other Stations of the Cross painted in the same manner, and reproduced to take the place of the glaring, conventional lithographs of our country churches and chapels. And it seems fitting and natural that an Irish artist should be the best interpreter of the terrible and tragic journey of Him who was on that day thought to be an earthly failure, and whose cause has lived and conquered through two thousand years.[40]

In 1911 she redirected her thoughts towards that other Biblical leader, Moses, but political bitterness marred the folk image. Finally, eleven years later, 'the great subject took hold of me', she writes in her notes, 'and so filled my mind that I was forced to get it into words'. A programme note justified her method further:

Our tradition, and that of Gaelic Scotland, speak of St. Brigit as 'the foster-mother of Christ,' and I have been told by poor women of Slieve Echtge that she succoured both Blessed Mother and Child when they were brought here by a Heavenly Messenger for safety in Herod's time, and that she 'kept an account of every drop of blood He lost through His lifetime.' So it is not going very far from that tradition to suppose she may have been present at the end of His life as at the beginning, and have told the story in her own way, as she had seen it in the body or in vision.[41]

Lady Gregory's version of Christ's last days and betrayal is consistent with those characteristics informing her life and work. Here Brigit serves as the beggar messenger, having travelled from afar in search of the end of her vision, 'a Young Man having wounds on him'; and, like the holy beggars before her, she observes and relates, but does not act or judge. Instead, Joel, an eager young boy from the mountains intent on making Jesus an earthly saviour, vividly recounts his hopes and disappointment over this leader who rejects one kingdom in favour of a further vision. It is he, not Peter, who is shown as betraying Jesus, when he cheers for Barabbas, and it is he who brings us the news of the trials in the immediacy of his Kiltartan dialect. And it is Joel's human anguish that echoes the agony of the cross as he realizes what he has lost:

My bitter curse on you, where you deceived me a while ago, making me call out against the best man the world ever saw! You have a great wrong done me! If he was not a rebel itself, his name will surely be written in the book of the people! His friendship would be better to me than all the world's gold.

Judas in comparison remains a poor, benighted figure, who betrays his master because he himself is rejected and whose departure is noted with as much pity as scorn:

JUDAS. I am going to that death and that punishment whatever it may be. And all I bring with me is the knowledge that he is the Christ that was promised to Israel, and it is little profit it will be to me, and it is hard I earned it! (*He snatches up the rope and rushes off.*) . . .
ST. BRIGIT. He might find kindness yet for one good deed he did, laying a wide flagstone in a desolate boggy place, where it is a great comfort to them that pass the way.

Other homely details domesticate the story further. A chorus of women keen Mary's loss, lilting in the manner of the Irish street ballad singer. An opportunistic tinker acts as mock-chorus, first to Joel by accepting a wily scribe's bribes to stir up a drunken crowd against the Nazarene, later to the grieving women when he accepts a Soldier's pay to nail Jesus to the cross. Final judgment is voiced by the boy Joel in words that recall all of Ireland's (and the world's) dreams and betrayals:

That's the way of it! All the generations looking for him and praying for him. We wanted him, and we got him, and what we did with him was to kill him. And that is the way it will be ever and always, so long as leaves grow upon the trees!

Less than a year after the completion of *The Story Brought by Brigit* Lady Gregory 'travelled a little further on the road that leads from things seen to things unseen'.[42] On 18 October 1924 she entered in her Journal, 'Perhaps I may do another play after all. I wish I could get that idea I am trying to live in "instead of striving to get to Heaven striving to bring Heaven about us on earth" into dramatic shape.'[43] Three months later she wrote again, 'W. Whitman finds hope for all even "the old man who has lived without purpose and feels it with bitterness worse than gall". I am trying to get some form into that idea for a play, the belief in good awakening good.'[44] Finally, after reading a poem by George Russell (AE) in *The Irish Statesman* which celebrated the Gods in alien shapes ('Through the swarthy faces/The starry faces shine')[45], she began her morality play *Dave*.

In this one-act play, the last new work she was to see produced, she again weaves the familiar threads of domestic comfort, petty pride (this time genealogical rather than material), envy, crossed tempers, and fancy—in short, the normal range of human frailties—that can be seen in all her peasant plays. But here all is simplified, stripped of the strange and wonderful, the weaknesses and strengths of character carved out boldly without their creator's usual softening of the edges. The plot too has a directness and simplicity in keeping with the majesty of theme—the awakening of a soul. As with *The Story Brought by Brigit*, this idea had haunted her for many years, perhaps originating in *The Unicorn from the Stars*, her rewriting of Yeats's *Where There is Nothing*, then treated comically in *The Full Moon*, harshly in *Grania*, folklorically in *Damer's Gold*. Finally the theme surfaced in 1917 as a wonder play in *The Dragon* which, she noted,

was begun seriously enough, for I see among my scraps of manuscripts that the earliest outline of it is entitled 'The Awakening of a Soul,' the soul of the little Princess who had not gone 'far out in the world.' And that idea was never quite lost, for even when it had all turned to comedy I see as an alternative name 'A Change of Heart.'[46]

But *The Dragon*, although a successful comedy, was too lost in the world of childhood, too taken up with wonders and bold

adventures, too trivialized with the minutiae of playmaking, to
bear the weight of serious message. Nor could a play designed for
children sufficiently isolate the childlike simplicity found in Dave's
sudden awakening to a greater vision. So instead of the immediacy
of her earlier plays, here she found it necessary to set the play back
in time a hundred years to the famine, distancing the audience from
the peasant environment, investing her old farmer with an 'ancient
dignity'[47] and emphasizing the serving man's brutality to Dave
and hypocrisy to his master. Against this frieze-like background,
she creates the transformation of the 'by-child reared in the
workhouse' from a sullen, surly animal into a courageous visionary
'that has found his treasure and must go share it with his kin'. No
magical potions or devices, no ragged messengers from abroad are
employed, merely a blow on the head and Dave's mistress's belief
in his goodness:

KATE. It is certain the Man Above never sent you here without some little
    flame of His own nature being within you.
DAVE. That is a great thought if it is true.
KATE. It is true, surely. Mind you never let that flame be quenched in you.

With these words in his ears and the vision of a heavenly garden
in his mind, Dave leaves, shouldering only his spade, to comfort
the suffering and the hungry.

'I will never be content or satisfied till I will come again to that
dream.' It is but a short step from Dave's confident vow to that
arch-dreamer Don Quixote, a subject which had fascinated Lady
Gregory throughout her life. As early as 1898 she used the
inseparable pair, Quixote and his equally fantastic follower,
Sancho Panza, as symbol of England's vision of Ireland, 'part
boastful quarrelsome adventurer, one part vulgar frollicking
buffoon'.[48] When she wrote her first folk-history play, *Kincora*,
she balanced the kingly figures of Brian, Malachi and Maelmora
with three quirky, quarrelsome servants in her first dramatic
representation of the two inseparable qualities that inform
Cervantes' great story. 'This play gives me the greatest joy', Yeats
wrote in his journal, 'colour, speech, all has music, and the scenes
with the servants make one feel curiously intimate and friendly
with those great people who otherwise would be far off—mere
figures of speech.'[49] Then in *The Golden Apple*, the most
successful of her wonder plays for children, she attempted to
disguise her theme in Rury, King of Ireland's Son, and his steward

Simon Maor, 'the Prince seeking a fabulous cure outside the bounds of nature, and his servant groaning and grunting after him, encumbered by reason and bodily fear'.[50] Yet still Quixote would not rest. And so, within the last year of her playwriting career, *Sancho's Master* was born.

Despite Shaw's assertion that 'Don Quixote cannot be put on stage',[51] *Sancho's Master* captures the essential qualities of the cherished dreamer and the shrewd peasant visionary. Here in one play we have the 'base of realism' in Sancho's homely sayings and sensible judgments rising, in Quixote's visionary idealism, to 'the apex of beauty'. Although proclaiming true Manchan chivalry, 'I will fight for the weak against the strong; for the poor against the rich, for the oppressed against the oppressor. I will make the surpassing beauty of the lady I love to be acknowledged through the whole of the living world!', her Quixote carries with him much that is reminiscent of the barony of Kiltartan. 'That is no sense to sit idle, while all the oppressors of the world make slaves of their fellow men at their ease', he objects to the well-meaning friends who try to dissuade him. 'I am going out for the doing away with tyranny; to face danger wherever it may come!' 'To loose the chains of captives—to raise the fallen and cast down. This is my business.' Here is no grand folly brought on by the reading of romances, but a deep sense of the world's wrong which tales of knight errantry confirm and support. Dulcinea may or may not be beautiful, as Quixote himself admits (she does not appear); what is important is that he believe. 'The business is that without seeing, you believe and confess, affirm and maintain it!' And what he believes is that the world's wrongs can indeed be righted, that his calling is 'to defeat violence—to succour and help the miserable'. But he is careful to define his role within earthly bounds:

The religious, with all peace and quietness implore Heaven for the good of the world. But soldiers and knights, of whom I would be one, defend it with the strength of arms, the edge of the sword. And so are God's ministers on earth, and the arm by which He executes justice.

*   *   *

The only difference is, that they were saints, and fought after a heavenly manner; and I am a sinner and must fight after an earthly manner. They conquered heaven by force of arms, and I cannot tell what I may conquer by force of suffering.

'It's likely he is another sort of knight from those now in fashion,' comments Sancho Panza somewhat ruefully, as he contemplates his and his master's bruises. But even though, as Sancho objects with dignity, 'jests that hurt are no jests', it is not bruises that finally defeat this romantic idealist, but ingratitude and ridicule. Broken not by scorn but by discourtesy, Quixote returns at last to his own country estate, having made a discovery greater than knight errantry:

Freedom is best. It is one of the best gifts heaven has bestowed upon men. The treasures that the earth encloses or the sea covers are not to be compared with it. Life may and ought to be risked for liberty as well as for honour. I have had a fine lodging; I have had banquets here. But the obligation of returning favours received are ties that obstruct the free agency of the mind. I will go back to my own poor place.

It is a particularly Irish lesson.

So much for the 'madness of the master'; what of the 'foolishness of the man'? The play's title again is distinctly Gregorian, for despite his gullibility and greed, cowardice and crustiness, Sancho Panza has an innate dignity that raises him above the horseplay and buffoonery and makes him a fitting companion for his visionary master:

It was allotted to me to follow him. We are of the same townland. I have eaten his bread, I love him, he returns my kindness. He has promised me an island. And so it is impossible anything should part us, but the sexton's spade and shovel.

Loyalty and companionship are virtues fitting to reside beside the compassion and justice that are the lot of the visionary. They are perhaps in the end the only compensation for the expected, but always surprising, failure.

For the world is not yet free of the dreamer seeking to realise the perfect in a community not ready for its Millenium, and where he may meet with anger or the ridicule that scorches or have the name thrown at him that Festus flung at St. Paul.[52]

'I don't think I'll tempt my luck again', Lady Gregory wrote in her journal as she embarked on *Sancho's Master*, 'but I do feel this subject ought to make a big play'.[53] In choosing Cervantes' great legend for her last public statement in the theatre, combining the wisdom, laughter and earthiness of Kiltartan with the lonely splendour of the dreamer, she once again confirmed her own private philosophy and lifework. 'It is the visionary who is the really practical worker, for he works with the faith that moves mountains, while the so-called practical man is still assuring the world of the impossibility of even cutting a tunnel through that mountain.'[54]

LADY GREGORY'S CONTRIBUTIONS TO PERIODICALS: A CHECKLIST

COLIN SMYTHE

Although the following list contains over 180 primary entries, it is still of an interim nature, for I am doubtful that a complete listing will ever be possible: not only did Lady Gregory write anonymously and pseudonymously, but her work appeared under other people's names, W. B. Yeats and Wilfrid Scawen Blunt, to name two.

Although Lady Gregory's hand was quietly in much that was published by Yeats in periodicals, I am restricting entries to those works in which she had a major share: *Cathleen ni Houlihan*, *The Pot of Broth*, *Where There is Nothing*, *The Hour Glass*, the tales in the Dun Emer *Stories of Red Hanrahan*, and those articles by Yeats in which he made use of her folklore material.[1]

I am especially indebted to Mary FitzGerald, Daniel J. Murphy, Maureen Murphy and James Pethica for all their help and the time they have spent searching for elusive items. However, some articles[2] have resisted all attempts at discovery: the only clue may be a reference in a letter, or in one of her own or the Abbey Theatre press-cutting books,[3] where incorrect or no information given makes further research necessary. Where an entry in the checklist is marked by an asterisk, this indicates that I have not seen it except in one of the press-cutting books, and the student would be wise to check these.

Lady Gregory was a most determined collector of newspaper cuttings, but there may still be a large body of material in North American papers and journals, published at the time of her tours there, apart from those items still undiscovered in British and Irish periodicals. I would be grateful for news of any additions to this list, so that they can be incorporated into the bibliography of Lady Gregory's writings that will appear in the final volume of the Coole Edition.

In general, the style below follows that of Allan Wade's *A Bibliography of the Writings of W. B. Yeats*,[4] with the page numbers added. With a few important exceptions, I have omitted all interviews and reports of lectures. I hope to provide a list of these at some future date. The following checklist includes only those articles published in her life time.

THE CHECKLIST

Note: C. E. followed by a number, used throughout this list, refers to the Coole Edition of Lady Gregory's Works (1970-), details of which are to be found on p. 402. This system has been used throughout the notes to all the contributions to this volume in order to eliminate repetition.

1882

ARABI AND HIS HOUSEHOLD

(Letter)
The Times, October 23, p. 4a-c.
Printed as a separate booklet the same year.

THE TRIAL OF ARABI PASHA. BY WILFRID SCAWEN BLUNT

(Letter)
The Times, November 27, p. 8c.
Lady Gregory translated the lines from Dante at the end of the letter. See p. 91 of this volume.

1883

[PARAGRAPH ON ARABI]

(Anonymously)
The Times, February 28, p. 8b.

THROUGH PORTUGAL

Fortnightly Review, October 1, pp. 571-80.
Reprinted in *Living Age* (Boston), November 10, pp. 359-65.

1884

GLIMPSES OF THE SOUDAN

Fortnightly Review, March 1, pp. 377-84.
Reprinted in *Living Age* (Boston), April 5, pp. 41-46.

1890

IRENE

(Poem)
The Argosy, October, p. 352.

1891

A PHILANTHROPIST

(Signed Angus Grey)
The Argosy, June, pp. 468-83.
Reprinted in *Living Age* (Boston), August 1, pp. 270-79

1892

ARABI PASHA. BY W. H. GREGORY

(Letter)
The Spectator, February 13, p. 235.
A reference in one of Lady Gregory's letters indicates she wrote this.

1894

A GENTLEMAN

(Signed Angus Grey)
The Argosy, July, pp. 72-81.

1895

IRISH SUPERSTITIONS

(Letter)
The Spectator, April 20, p. 533.

EOTHEN AND THE ATHENAEUM CLUB

Blackwood's Magazine, December, pp. 797-804.
Also printed in *Living Age* (Boston), December 2, pp. 748-55.

1896

DIES IRAE

The Sketch, March 25, p. 376.

GORT INDUSTRIES

Erin, November.
Reprinted as a broadsheet. So far no trace has been found of this periodical, although the broadsheet is quite explicit as to its origin, describing it as 'an Illustrated Journal of Art and Industry'.

1897

IRISH VISIONS

(Anonymously)
The Spectator, July 10, pp. 46-47.

THE TRIBES OF DANU. BY W. B. YEATS

The New Review, November, pp. 549-65.
The first of the series of essays with material contributed by Lady Gregory. However, Frayne & Johnson in *Uncollected Prose* vol. 2, 1975, attribute rather more to her than would appear to be the case. A 'friend' footnoted on p. 64 as probably being Lady Gregory is more likely to have been her friend Miss Charlotte Elizabeth MacManus, the novelist, who lived at Killeaden, Co. Mayo, not far from Coole. Charlotte and Letitia were names used in the MacManus family, while as far as I can ascertain, neither of Lady Gregory's grandmothers was named 'Miss Letty' (p. 67).

Although the whole series was to have been taken by *The New Review*, before the end of 1897 it changed format and editorial policy, and the editor retired, so the later essays appeared elsewhere.

1898

THE PRISONERS OF THE GODS. BY W. B. YEATS

Nineteenth Century, January, pp. 91-104.
The second of Yeats's series of articles, that were based largely on material given him by Lady Gregory, which subsequently appeared in her *Visions and Beliefs in the West of Ireland*, 1920, C.E.1.

TREE PLANTING

The Irish Homestead, February 12 and 19, pp. 141-42, 164.
Reprinted in *The Kilkenny Moderator*, February 23, p. [4d], 26 p. [5e] and in *Irish Forestry*, vol. 33, no. 2, 1976, pp. 94-98.

THE BROKEN GATES OF DEATH. BY W. B. YEATS

Fortnightly Review, April, pp. 524-36.
The third of Yeats's articles containing material provided by Lady Gregory.

SOME FOLK STORIES OF USHEEN

Daily Express (Dublin), September 17, p. 3.

IRELAND REAL AND IDEAL

Nineteenth Century, November, pp. 769-82.

CHILDREN'S FOLK TALES
Kilkenny Moderator, Christmas Number, December, p. 25.

1899

THE WEST AWAKE!
(Anonymous, but probably by Lady Gregory)
Fainne an Lae, January 21, p. 19.

IRELAND IN BOND STREET
(Signed G)
Daily Express (Dublin), February 25, p. 5.

AN ITALIAN LITERARY DRAMA [ON D'ANNUNZIO'S *DREAM OF A SPRING MORNING*]
Daily Express (Dublin), April 8, p. 3.

OUR COTTAGE HOMES
The Irish Homestead, May 27, pp. 368-69.

PUBLIC MEETING AT KILTARTAN
(Anonymous, but most probably by Lady Gregory)
An Claidheamh Soluis, July 29, pp. 314-15.

LECTURE AT GORT
(Anonymously)
An Claidheamh Soluis, August 12, p. 342–43.

MEETING IN KINVARA, CO. GALWAY
(Anonymous, but probably by Lady Gregory)
An Claidheamh Soluis, August 12, p. 349.

THE LANGUAGE MOVEMENT IN IRELAND
The Speaker, August 12, pp. 151-152.
Reprinted in part in *An Claidheamh Soluis*, August 19, p. 365.

IRELAND BEWITCHED. BY W. B. YEATS
The Contemporary Review, September, pp. 388-404.
The fourth of Yeats's articles based on Lady Gregory's material.

RAFTERY, THE POET OF THE POOR
An Claidheamh Soluis, October 14, pp. 488-49.

'DUST HATH CLOSED HELEN'S EYE'
(Translation of poem in Yeats's article)
The Dome, October, pp. 162-63.

IRISH LITERARY THEATRE
(Letter dated October 27)
Irish Weekly Independent, October 28; reprinted in *Irish Daily Independent* October 30, p. 6e, and *The Irish People*, November 18.

POLITICAL PROPHECY
(Letter)
The Spectator, November 11, p. 693.

[LETTER ABOUT RAFTERY'S GRAVE]
An Claidheamh Soluis, December 2, p. 605.

1900

'MAIVE,' AND CERTAIN IRISH BELIEFS. BY W. B. YEATS
Beltaine, February, pp. 14–17.
Material provided by Lady Gregory appears on pp. 14–15.

LAST YEAR
Beltaine, February, pp. 25-28.
Reprinted in *Our Irish Theatre*, C.E.4, pp. 190-93.

THE FELONS OF OUR LAND
Cornhill Magazine, May, pp. 622-34.

AN IRISH POET [LORD BOWEN]
(Letter)
All Ireland Review, March 10, p. 2.

IRISH FOLKLORE STORIES
I   MOUNTAIN THEOLOGY
    The Westminster Budget, August 24, pp. 15-16.
II HERB HEALING
    The Westminster Budget, August 31, p. 15; September 7, p. 13.
The above two articles reprinted in *Poets and Dreamers*, 1903, pp. 104-20, and C.E.11, pp. 84-93.

III CURES BY CHARMS

The Westminster Budget, September 14, pp. 13–14.
Reprinted in *Poets and Dreamers*, C.E.11, pp. 273–76.

IRISH WITCH DOCTORS. BY W. B. YEATS

Fortnightly Review, September, pp. 440–56.
The fifth of Yeats's articles, using material provided by Lady Gregory.

RAFTERY'S GRAVE

An Claidheamh Soluis, September 8, p. 406.

AN IRISH POEM [A SORROWFUL LAMENT FOR IRELAND]

The Leader, October 20, pp. 123–24.
Reprinted with a shortened introduction in *Poets and Dreamers*, 1903,
pp. 98–103, and both versions appear in C.E.11, with notes on
variations in the text, pp. 80–83, 271–72.

SIR FREDERIC BURTON

The Leader, December 8, pp. 231–32.

[ON *IDEALS IN IRELAND*]

(Letter)
All Ireland Review, December 15, p. 5.

RIVAL POETS

With an illustration by Jack B. Yeats.
The Irish Homestead's Celtic Christmas, December 8, pp. 14–16.

1901

THE POET RAFTERY

The Argosy, January, pp. 44–58.
A revised version was printed in *Poets and Dreamers*, 1903, pp. 1–46,
and both versions appear in C.E.11, pp. 15–42, 229–46.

A NATION'S WORDS

(Signed Cilltartan)
An Claideamh Soluis agus Fainne an Lae, July 6, p. 262.

THE LAST CLASS

Translated from the French of Alphonse Daudet.
An Claidheamh Soluis agus Fainne an Lae, July 27, p. 1 of supplement.
Reprinted, with slight changes, under the title 'The Last Lesson', with
an illustration by Jack B. Yeats, in *The Gael* (New York), August
1902, pp. 261–64.

ON THE EDGE OF THE WORLD

The Speaker, August 17, p. 547.
Reprinted in *Poets and Dreamers*, 1903, pp. 193-195, and in C.E.11, pp. 134-35.

THE LEGEND OF DIARMUID AND GRANIA

(Signed A. G.)
Samhain, October, pp. 16-19.

THE TWISTING OF THE ROPE

Translation of Douglas Hyde's *Casadh an tSugáin*.
Samhain, October, pp. 30-38.
Reprinted in *Poets and Dreamers*, 1903, pp. 200-15, and C.E.11, pp. 139-48.
Also reprinted in *Poet Lore* (Boston), March 1905, pp. 1–22, and *Current Literature*, April 1906.

AT 9, MERRION ROW

The Leader, November 2, pp. 158-59.
On an Exhibition of paintings by Jack B. Yeats.

AN GRUAGACH UASAL

The Irish Homestead's Celtic Christmas, December 7, p. 19.
Gives the original Irish text with Lady Gregory's translation.
Reprinted in *Folklore and W. B. Yeats* by Birgit Bramsbäck (Uppsala) 1984, pp. 141-42.

1902

MISTRAL, THE CRAOIBHIN OF PROVENCE

The Leader, January 4, pp. 310-11.

AWAY. BY W. B. YEATS

Fortnightly Review, April, pp. 726-40.
The sixth and last of Yeats's folklore articles using Lady Gregory's material that she had given him. Her contributions to this article subsequently appeared in the chapter of this name in her *Visions and Beliefs in the West of Ireland*, 1920, and C.E.1.

AN ANCIENT CONVERSATION

All Ireland Review, April 12, 19, 26, pp. 87, 103, 123.
Prefaced by a note by W. B. Yeats in the issues of April 5, 12, pp. 75, 87.

LEGENDS OF THE RATHS

> *Galway Archaeological Journal*, Vol. II, pp. 116-17.

[A LETTER TO STANDISH O'GRADY]

> *All Ireland Review*, June 21, pp. 244-45.
> Partially reprinted in *The Freeman's Journal*, titled 'An Irish Catholic', June 24, p. 5, and *The Tablet*, July 5, pp. 36-37 under the heading *Irish Religious Art*.

'O KING IN HEAVEN'

> Translated from 'Aithrighe an Reachtuire' ('Raftery's Repentance') *A Broadsheet*, September.
> Revised and reprinted in *Poets and Dreamers*, 1903, pp. 28-29, and both versions printed in C.E.11, pp. 31, 247.

LAND CONFERENCE

> (Letter)
> *The Irish Daily Independent and Nation*, September 25, p. 5b.

WEST IRELAND FOLK BALLADS

> *The Monthly Review*, October, pp. 123-35.
> Revised and reprinted in *Poets and Dreamers*, 1903, pp. 47-65, under the title *West Irish Ballads*, and both versions printed in C.E.11, pp. 43-55, 251-62.

CATHLEEN-NI-HOOLIHAN. BY W. B. YEATS

> *Samhain*, October, p. 24-31.
> Published separately by the Caradoc Press, 1902, in *Plays for an Irish Theatre*, vol. II, 1904 (every play in this volume being a collaboration between Yeats and Lady Gregory), and in many other editions.

THE LOST SAINT

> Translation of Hyde's *An Naomh ar Iarraid* (which appears on pp. 14-18).
> *Samhain*, October, pp. 19-23.
> Reprinted in *Poets and Dreamers*, 1903, pp. 236-43, and C.E.11, pp. 160-64.

A LOSING GAME

> *The Gael* (New York), December, pp. 384-88.
> Reprinted in *Lost Plays of the Irish Renaissance* (eds. R. Hogan & J. Kilroy) 1970, pp. 51-63, and *Collected Plays I*, C.E.5, pp. 279-89.
> Submitted with the title *Twenty Five*. which was changed by the editor as he felt that the majority of his readers would not be familiar with that card game. The revised version, first produced at the

Molesworth Hall on 14 March 1903, was published in C.E.5, pp. 1-11.

THE NATIVITY
Translation of Hyde's *Dráma Breithe Chríosta* (which also appears on the page).
Weekly Freeman, Christmas Number, December 13, p. 11.
Reprinted in *Poets and Dreamers*, 1903, pp. 244-54, and C.E.11, pp. 165-70.

A STORY OF THE COUNTRY OF THE DEAD
As told to Lady Gregory.
The Irish Homestead's Celtic Christmas, December 6, pp. 15-16.

THE WHIRLIGIG OF TIME AND THE IRISH LANGUAGE
The Leader, December 6, p. 235.

1903

IRISH JACOBITE SONGS
The Speaker, January 24, pp. 413-15.
Reprinted as 'Jacobite Ballads' in *Poets and Dreamers*, 1903, pp. 66-75, and C.E.11, pp. 56-61.

'IT'S MY GRIEF I AM NOT A LITTLE WHITE DUCK'
Translation from Hyde's poem.
A Broadsheet, February.
Reprinted under the title 'An Craoibhin complains because he is a poet', in *The Kiltartan Poetry Book*, 1918, pp. 17-18; 1919, pp. 54-55, and C.E.9, p. 38.

*WHAT IRELAND NEEDS. 'WISE PAROCHIALISM IS GREATEST NEED OF IRELAND'
Daily News (Chicago), March 16.

THE HILL OF HEART'S DESIRE
Translated from Raftery's *Cnocín Saibhir*.
The Green Sheaf, no. 1, p. 3.
Reprinted with slight revisions in *Poets and Dreamers*, 1903, pp. 30-31, and C.E.11, p. 32. It also appeared in *The Kiltartan Poetry Book* under the title 'His Praise of the Little Hill and the Plains of Mayo', 1918, pp. 8-9; 1919, pp. 37-38, and C.E.9, p. 29.

CAEL AND CREDHE
Translation from the Irish.
The Green Sheaf, no. 5, pp. 3-5.
Reprinted in *The Gael* (New York), May 1904, p. 164 and with slight

revisions in *Gods and Fighting Men*, 1904, pp. 207–10, and C.E.3, pp. 172–74.

HANRAHAN

Extract from *Casadh an tSugáin*, with an illustration by Jack B. Yeats. *A Broadsheet*, August.
Reprinted in *Poets and Dreamers*, 1903, pp. 231–14, and C.E.11, p. 147.

THE BURSTING OF THE BUBBLE

(Signed G.G.)
Translation of Irish passages in Hyde's *Pleusgadh na Bulgoide*.
New Ireland Review, May, pp. 164–85.
Later in 1903 published as a separate booklet. Hyde lost the original text of the play, and had to rewrite it from Lady Gregory's translation (See *Our Irish Theatre*, 1913, p. 84, and C.E.4, p. 55).
Reprinted in *Poets and Dreamers*, C.E.11, pp. 178–93.

THE POORHOUSE

Translation of Hyde's and Lady Gregory's *Teach na mBocht*, which appears on pp. 13–18.
Samhain, October, pp. 19–24.
Published with *Spreading the News* and *The Rising of the Moon* as vol. 9 of the first Abbey Theatre Series, 1906, pp. 47–59, and in *Collected Plays IV*, C.E.8, pp. 293–301.

A POT OF BROTH. BY W. B. YEATS

The Gael (New York), September, pp. 310–13.
Published in *Plays for an Irish Theatre* vol. II, 1904, and separately in 1905.

THE HOUR GLASS. A MORALITY. BY W. B. YEATS

The North American Review, September, pp. 445–53.
Printed in a *very* limited edition in pamphlet form for copyright purposes, 1903. Reprinted in *Plays for an Irish Theatre*, vol. II, 1904.

'A GOLDEN CRADLE UNDER YOU'

Translation from the Irish
A Broadsheet, October.

ANCIENT IRELAND

Review of P. W. Joyce's *A Social History of Ancient Ireland*.
The Academy and Literature, October 31, pp. 463–64.

THE RISING OF THE MOON

The Gael (New York), November, pp. 376-78.
Reprinted in *Samhain*, December 1904, pp. 45-52. Reprinted in *Seven*

Short Plays, 1909, pp. 79-96, and *Collected Plays I*, C.E.5, pp. 57-67, and many anthologies.

THE WINTER OF AGE

Translated from Hyde's Irish.
The Irish Homestead's Celtic Christmas, December 5, p. 7.
Reprinted in *Poets and Dreamers*, C.E.11, pp. 266-67.

RED HANRAHAN. BY W. B. YEATS

The Independent Review, December, pp. 478-85.
Reprinted in *Stories of Red Hanrahan*, 1905, pp. 1-15.
Although the title page has 1904, it was not published until May 1905. The difference between publication date and title page may have caused Yeats to misremember which of the early Dun Emer volumes was published in a different year, and account for his giving, in his later volumes of poetry, the year of publication of *In the Seven Woods* as 1904, when the date on the title page — 1903 — was correct: it was published in August.

[KING JAMES]

Translation of Douglas Hyde's *Righ Seumas*, which appears on the same page.
The Weekly Freeman, Christmas Number, December 12, p. 4.
Reprinted in *Poets and Dreamers*, C.E.11, pp. 171–77.

1904

IRELAND IN LETTERS. LADY GREGORY TELLS OF AN INTELLECTUAL REVOLUTION

The Book Monthly, April, pp. 468-473.
It would appear that Lady Gregory checked the text of this interview before publication.

THE MARRIAGE

Poet Lore (Boston) March/April, pp. 135-140. Translation of Hyde's *An Posadh*.
Reprinted in *The Golden Book Magazine* (New York), September 1927, pp. 327-32.
Originally published in *Poets and Dreamers*, 1903, pp. 216-35, and later in C.E.11, pp. 149-59.

LADY GREGORY WRITES [CORRECTING A MISTAKE IN A REVIEW OF *GODS AND FIGHTING MEN*]

The Athenaeum, April 2, p. 433.
The review had appeared in the March 26 issue, p. 394.

THE GOBAN SAOR

Galway Archaeological Journal, Vol. LV, pp. 73-77.

[EXTRACT FROM A LETTER TO THE HON. JUSTIN McCARTHY]

The Gael (New York). September, p. 308.

ACCEPTANCE OF MISS HORNIMAN'S OFFER OF THEATRE

(One of 22 signatories, signed Agusta [*sic*] Gregory)
Samhain, December, p. 54.

'A STONE OF THE BUILDING'

(Letter)
The Freeman's Journal, December 13, p. 5.

1905

A MODERN ART GALLERY FOR DUBLIN

(Letter signed by Jane Barlow, S. H. Butcher, Augusta Gregory,
Douglas Hyde, Martin Ross, E. O. E. Somerville [*sic*], Emily
Lawless, George Russell (A.E.), and W. B. Yeats)
The Times, January 5, p. 6c; *The Irish Times*, January 5, p. 8 as *A
Modern Art Gallery for Dublin*.
A shorter version was published as a broadsheet with reproductions
of signatures.

WHY WE WANT THE PICTURES

An Claideamh Soluis agus Fainne an Lae, January 7, p. 8.

GALLERY OF MODERN ART IN IRELAND

(Letter)
The Times, February 16, p. 8a.
It followed a letter about the Gallery by the Prince of Wales and was
addressed to 'Americans living at home or in England'.

LIVING LEGENDS OF THE FIANNA

The Monthly Review, February, pp. 74-92.

RED HANRAHAN'S VISIONS. BY W. B. YEATS

McClure's Magazine (New York), March, pp. 469-71.
Reprinted in *Stories of Red Hanrahan*, 1904 (1905) pp. 40-46, with the
title 'Hanrahan's Visions'.

MODERN ART GALLERY FOR IRELAND

(Letter signed Angus T. Gregory)
Daily Star (Montreal), April 4, p. 5.

LIVING LEGENDS OF THE SAINTS

Monthly Review, November, pp. 63-84.

SPREADING THE NEWS

Samhain, November, pp. 15-28.
Originally published by John Quinn in the U.S.A. on December 10 1904.
Reprinted in vol. 9 of the first Abbey Theatre Series, with *The Rising of the Moon* and *The Poorhouse*, 1906, pp. 3-29; in *Seven Short Plays*, 1909, pp. 1-30; *The Golden Book Magazine* (New York), September 1925, pp. 355-62; *Collected Plays I*, C.E.5, pp. 15-29, and in many anthologies, and theatre editions.

AN FEAR SIUBHAIL

Translation by 'Torna' (pseud. of Tadhg Ua Donnchadha) of *The Travelling Man*.
Samhain, November, pp. 29-35.

1906

THE TRAVELLING MAN

The Shanachie, Spring, pp. 55-63.
Reprinted in *Seven Short Plays*, 1909, pp. 163-79; *The Outlook* (New York), 4 November 1911 as *The Traveling* [sic] *Man*; *The Golden Book Magazine* (New York), October 1931, pp. 274-79; *Collected Plays III*, C.E.7, pp. 19-28, and in many anthologies and theatre editions.
There is a note by Lady Gregory in the Berg Collection of the New York Public Library stating that this is the first printing of the play, but it was preceded by the edition of *The White Cockade* and *The Travelling Man* published in New York by John Quinn in one volume on 29 December 1905 for copyright protection purposes. However, the version Quinn published was revised for the *Shanachie* printing. The Rider's Song by Yeats is very different.

THE HAUNTED ISLANDS

Monthly Review, May, pp. 68-88.

A NOTE ON SPREADING THE NEWS

(Signed A. G.)
The Arrow, October 20, p. 3.
Reprinted in *Collected Plays I*, C.E.5, pp. 254-55.

HYACINTH HALVEY

Samhain, November, pp. 15-35.
Originally published in a limited edition by John Quinn for copyright
purposes, and slightly shortened before publication here.
Reprinted in *Seven Short Plays*, 1909, pp. 31-78; *Collected Plays I*,
C.E.5, pp. 31-56, and in many anthologies and theatre editions.

[A NOTE ON] THE CANAVANS

(Signed A. G.)
The Arrow, November 24, pp. 3-4.

THE GAOL GATE

The Gaelic American , December 1, p. 2.
Reprinted in *Seven Short Plays*, 1909, pp. 181-94; *Collected Plays II*,
C.E.6, pp. 3-10, and in many anthologies and theatre editions.

CAPTAIN HEADLEY'S SONG

Supplement to *The Arrow*, 8 December.
Printed under a reproduction of an engraving of Queen Elizabeth I,
on a single sheet of paper.
Reprinted in *Irish Folk-History Plays, Second Series*, 1912, pp. 22–23,
and in *Collected Plays II*, C.E.6, p. 189.

1907

[NOTES ON] THE WHITE COCKADE AND THE JACKDAW

(Signed A. G.)
Programme supplement to *The Arrow*, February 23, p. 3.

AN EXPLANATION

The Arrow, June 1, pp. 2-4.
Reprinted in *Our Irish Theatre*, C.E.4, pp. 194-95.

NAPOLEON AT ST. HELENA

(Letter)
The Times, August 13, p. 9d.
Reprinted in *Mr Gregory's Letter-Box 1813-35*, C.E.20, p. 215. It
introduced a letter from Major Poppleton about Napoleon on St
Helena.

HOE DIE NIEUWS VERSPREI'T

Bilingual adaptation of *Spreading the News* in Afrikaans and varieties
of English.
Die Volkstem (South Africa), November 6, 13, 16, p. 4 of each issue.

1908

MODERN ART IN IRELAND
(Letter)
The Spectator, January 25, p. 147.
Reprinted in *Tuam Herald*, 8 February, p. 2d.

[NOTE ON *THE WORKHOUSE WARD*]
(Signed A. G.)
Abbey Theatre *Programme* for the play's first production, Easter Monday, April 20. *The* in the title was omitted when printed in the *programme*.

THE FORESTER'S YEARBOOK
(poem)
The Leader, May 9, p. 180.
A slightly different version appears in Colin Smythe, *Guide to Coole Park, Home of Lady Gregory* (Gerrards Cross), 1973, pp. 26, 29; 2nd ed. revised and enlarged, 1983, p. 45.

[NOTE ON *DERVORGILLA*]
(Unsigned)
Abbey Theatre *Programme*, May 29.
Reprinted as part of the note to the play in *Irish Folk-History Plays, First Series* 1912, pp. 205–6; and in *Collected Plays II*, C.E.6, pp. 289–90.

SOME THOUGHTS AT GALWAY EXHIBITION
Manchester Guardian, September 25, p. 14a.

DERVORGILLA
The Gaelic American, September 26, p. 3 [Set in six columns of very small type].
Reprinted in *Samhain*, November, pp. 13–27; *Irish Folk History Plays, First Series*, 1912, pp. 154–86; and *Collected Plays II*, C.E.6, pp. 93–111.

[NOTE TO *THE WHITE COCKADE*]
(Unsigned)
Abbey Theatre *Programme*, November 26.

OLD IRISH FAIRY TALES [I. THE TALE OF THE THREE SONS, II. THE WISDOM OF SOLOMON]
Pall Mall Gazette, July–December, Christmas Double Number, pp. 756–58.

Reprinted under the titles *The Three Sons* and *King Solomon* in *The Kiltartan Wonder Book*, 1910, pp. 66–78; and in *The Kiltartan Books*, C.E.9, pp. 180–85.

MR. RUTHERFORD MAYNE'S PLAY AT THE GAIETY
(Letter signed Angus T. Gregory)
The Freeman's Journal, November 2, p. 9f.

1909

AN ADVICE

Translation from Hyde's Irish.
A Broadside, April.
Reprinted in *Poets and Dreamers*, C.E.11, p. 265.

THE WORKHOUSE WARD

The Gaelic American, May 15, p. 3.
Reprinted in *Seven Short Plays*, 1909, pp. 143-61; *The Golden Book Magazine* (New York), June 1929, pp. 100–03; *Collected Plays I*, C.E.5, pp. 97-105, and in many anthologies and theatre editions.

THE JACKDAW

The Gaelic American, June 12, 19, p. 3 in each issue.
Published virtually simultaneously in Ireland in *Seven Short Plays*, pp. 97-142; *Collected Plays I*, C.E.5, pp. 69-93, and in many anthologies and theatre editions.

A WARNING

Translation from Hyde's Irish.
A Broadside, July.
Reprinted in *Poets and Dreamers*, C.E.11, p. 266.

MR. SHAW'S PLAY . . . ABBEY THEATRE'S REPLY
Statement by W. B. Yeats and Lady Gregory dated August 1921.
Evening Telegraph (Dublin), August 21, p. 5c. Printed with cuts on same date in *Evening Mail* (Dublin), p. 5g. Reprinted in *The Times*, August 23, p. 4e. For reprints together with statement issued on 22 August, see next entry.

MR. SHAW'S PLAY. PIECE NOT TO BE WITHDRAWN
Statement signed by W. B. Yeats and Lady Gregory, dated 22 August.
The Irish Times (with the previous statement), August 23, p. 7.
Reprinted by itself elsewhere in the Irish and British press, including *The Daily Express* (Dublin), August 23, p. 5f; *Evening Telegraph*

(Dublin), August 23, p. 3e; *The Times*, August 24, p. 8c; *The Arrow*, August 25, pp. 1-2; later reprinted in *Modern Drama* (Lawrence, Kansas), May 1966, pp. 2-3; *Uncollected Prose by W. B. Yeats* vol. 2, 1975, pp. 378-80. *Our Irish Theatre*, C.E.4, pp. 216-18, contains the second half of the first statement and all the second.

MR. SHAW'S PLAY IN DUBLIN. THE OFFICIAL CORRESPONDENCE
Letter to Sir James Dougherty
The Irish Times, August 24, p. 7e.
Printed the same day in *The Times*, p. 8c, with the August 22nd statement, and by itself in *The Daily Express* (Dublin), p. 5d; and *Evening Telegraph* (Dublin), p. 3d.

MORE ABOUT "BLANCO POSNET." THE PLOT THICKENS. STATEMENT BY LADY GREGORY
Evening Telegraph (Dublin), August 24, p. 3c.
Also printed in that day's *Evening Mail* (Dublin), p. 5c.
Reprinted in *The Irish Times*, August 25, p. 7f.

AN INTERESTING STATEMENT . . . ON THE TRIUMPH OF THE ABBEY
Signed by W. B. Yeats and Lady Gregory.
Evening Telegraph (Dublin), August 26, p. 3c. Evening Mail (Dublin), August 26, p. 5d.
Reprinted elsewhere, including *The Times*, August 27, p. 8d; *The Irish Times*, August 27, p. 9a; *The Daily Express* (Dublin), August 27, p. 8e. Later reprinted in *Modern Drama* (Lawrence, Kansas), May 1966, pp. 3-4.

1910

NOTE ON "THE IMAGE"
(Signed A. G.)
Royal Court Theatre *Programme*, June 1-2.
Reprinted, with slight changes, as part of the note to the play published by Maunsel in 1910, pp. 99-101, in subsequent collections, and in *Collected Plays II*, C.E. 6, p. 296.

THE IRISH NATIONAL THEATRE
(Letter signed by Lady Gregory and W. B. Yeats).
The Times, June 16, p. 12f.
This appeared elsewhere in the London and Dublin press, including *The Irish Independent* under the title *The Future of the Abbey Theatre*; *The Standard* under the title *Repertory Theatres*, on June 16; and *The Nation*, June 18, p. 425.
Reprinted in *Modern Drama*, May 1966, pp. 4-6.

1911

DUBHAIRT SÉ DABHAIRT SÉ
Translation by An Seabhach ('The Hawk', pseud. of Padraig Ó Siochfhradha) of *Spreading the News*.
An Claidheamh Soluis agus Fainne an Lae, July 29, pp. 8-11.

THE COMING OF THE IRISH PLAYERS
Collier's National Weekly (New York), October 21, pp. 15, 24.
Reprinted in *Our Irish Theatre*, C.E.4, pp. 144-50.

*A REPERTORY THEATRE
Herald Tribune (New York), November 26.

McDARAGH'S WIFE
The Outlook (New York), December 16, pp. 920-25.
Reprinted under the title *McDonough's Wife* in *New Comedies*, 1913, pp. 133–54, and *Collected Plays*, C.E.6, pp. 113–25.

1912

THE IRISH THEATRE AND THE PEOPLE
The Yale Review, January, pp. 188-91.
Reprinted in *Our Irish Theatre*, C.E.4, pp. 140-43.

KILTARTAN FAIRY TALES [THE TAILOR. THE MISFORTUNE. THE MIRACLE. THE MAN THAT WENT BEYOND GOD]
The Delineator (New York), February, pp. 95-96.
'The Tailor' and 'The Misfortune' were reprinted in *The Kiltartan Books*, C.E.9, pp. 202-3, 198-99.

THE STORY OF THE IRISH PLAYERS: OUR TRIALS AND TRIUMPHS
Sunday Record Herald (Chicago), February 4, part 7 (Drama-Music-Art Section), p. 1.

MAKING READY FOR HOME RULE
World Today (Chicago), March, pp. 1891-92.

*WHY THE IRISH LOVE IRELAND
Brooklyn Citizen (Brooklyn, N.Y.), March 17.
Reprinted as a broadsheet.

HOW TO FOUND A NATIONAL THEATRE
Literary Digest (New York), March 30, p. 643.

THREE KILTARTAN FOLK TALES [AUTHOR'S INTRODUCTION
'THE MEANING OF FOLKLORE'. THE STARS. THE OLD MAN.
THE WOMAN IN THE STARS]
The Outlook (New York), April 27, p. 978-85.

[ON THE ABBEY THEATRE]
(Letter correcting a report in a previous issue)
The Times, October 9, p. 11d, early edition only.

THE BOGIE MEN
Fortnightly Review, December 1, pp. 1165-74.
Reprinted in *Forum and Century* (New York), January 1913, pp.
28–40; *New Comedies*, 1913, pp. 1–23 and *Collected Plays I*, C.E.5,
pp. 107–18.

1913

SYNGE
The English Review, March, pp. 556-66.
Reprinted with changes in *Our Irish Theatre*, 1913, pp. 119-39, and
in C.E.4, where both versions have been collated, pp. 73-83.

*LADY GREGORY'S STRENUOUS EFFORT TO FOUND NATIONAL
THEATRES AND QUELL MOBS DISSATISFIED WITH PLAYS
The Sun (New York), March 9.
Early versions of passages later to appear in *Our Irish Theatre*, 1913,
pp. 112-18, 175-76, 180, 199, 200-1, 201-2, 202-4, 205-6, 210, 216-18,
and C.E.4, pp. 67-70, 99-100, 102, 110, 111, 111-12, 113.

CONVERSATION IN IRELAND
The Independent (New York), April 17, pp. 857-60.

LADY GREGORY'S MESSAGE
The Freeman's Journal, May 10, p. 9e.
A shortened version appeared in *The Irish Times* the same day.

THE AMERICAN MONEY
(Letter)
Irish Independent, September 8, p. 7a; and printed under the heading
'Americans & the Art Gallery' in *The Irish Times*, September 8, p. 7.

1914

PAT AND FRITZ
(Poem)
The Nation, September 19, p. 866.

1915

SIR HUGH LANE'S BEQUESTS. LADY GREGORY AND THE ART GIFTS TO DUBLIN
(Letter)
The Times, October 5, p. 5d.

1916

SIR HUGH LANE'S PICTURES
(Letter)
The Times, December 6, p. 12d-f.
Reprinted in *Sir Hugh Lane: His Life and Legacy*, C.E.10, pp. 224-25.

THE HUGH LANE PICTURES
(Letter)
The Observer, December 24, p. 12b.
Reprinted in *Sir Hugh Lane: His Life and Legacy*, C.E.10, pp. 224-25.

1917

SIR HUGH LANE'S PICTURES. MR. W. B. YEATS'S REPLY
(The postscript to this letter contains quotations from Lady Gregory)
The Observer, January 21, p. 12b-d.
Reprinted in *Sir Hugh Lane: His Life and Legacy*, C.E.10, p. 237. The entire letter is printed on pp. 228-38.

HANRAHAN'S OATH
The Little Review, November, pp. 6-16, 33-38.
Reprinted in *The Image and Other Plays*, 1922, pp. 100-33, and *Collected Plays I*, C.E.5, pp. 159-76.

1918

IRISH WRITERS PROTEST [AGAINST CONSCRIPTION]
(Letter composed by Lady Gregory and signed by her, W. B. Yeats, James Stephens, George Russell ('AE'), Douglas Hyde (An Craoibhin).)
The Evening Telegraph (Dublin), May 22, p. 1, *The Nation*, May 25, p. 199, under the heading 'Irish Writers and Conscription' and other papers.

1920

A WEEK IN IRELAND
(Anonymously)
The Nation, October 16, pp. 63-64.

ANOTHER WEEK IN IRELAND
(Anonymously)
The Nation, October 23, pp. 123-24.

'MURDER BY THE THROAT.' — *MR LLOYD GEORGE.*
(Anonymously)
The Nation, November 13, pp. 215-16.

A THIRD WEEK IN IRELAND
(Anonymously)
The Nation, December 4, p. 333.

A FOURTH WEEK IN IRELAND
(Anonymously)
The Nation, December 18, pp. 413-14.

1921

A FIFTH WEEK IN IRELAND
(Anonymously)
The Nation, January 1, pp. 472-73.

IRISH SETTLEMENT
(Letter)
The Times, March 23, p. 6d.
Reprinted in the *Irish Independent*, March 24, p. 4 under the heading
'Dail Eireann and Peace — What Lady Gregory Heard'.

NOTES ON WILFRID SCAWEN BLUNT
The Nation (New York), December 7, pp. 660-61.

1922

SIR HUGH LANE'S PICTURES
(Letter)
The Irish Times, November 30, p.8a.
Reprinted in *Sir Hugh Lane: His Life and Legacy*, C.E.10, pp. 240-42.

1923

WAR IN IRISH FOLKLORE
Manchester Guardian Commercial, May 10, pp. 40-42.

THE IRISH REMEMBER
The New Republic (New York), May 16, pp. 320-21.

THE HUNGER STRIKERS
(Letter signed by Lady Gregory, Lennox Robinson and James Stephens)
The Irish Times, November 13, p. 8; and *Irish Independent*, November 13, p. 6.

1924

THE OLD WOMAN REMEMBERS
The New Republic (New York), February 20, p. 339.
Extracts (5th candle to the end) reprinted in *The Literary Digest* (New York), March 1, p. 38; and *in toto* in *The Irish Statesman*, March 22, pp. 40-41; *A Little Anthology of Modern Irish Verse* (ed. L. Robinson), 1928, pp. 1-5; Ann Saddlemyer, *In Defence of Lady Gregory, Playwright*, 1966, pp. 103-106; and *Collected Plays II*, C. E. 6, pp. 355-61.

CONNAUGHT AND THE POETS
Connacht Tribune Tourist Supplement, March [? 17 — no day given], pp. 1a-b, 7e-f.

SIR HUGH LANE'S BEQUEST
(Letter)
Irish Independent, March 13, p. 6.

[NOTE ON *THE STORY BROUGHT BY BRIGIT*]
Abbey Theatre *Programme*, April 15-19 (Holy Week).
Reprinted in *Collected Plays III*, C.E.7, p. 398.

SIR HUGH LANE'S DESIRE
The Irish Statesman, May 31, p. 359.

THE LANE PICTURES
The Irish Statesman, June 21, p. 460.

1926

HOW GREAT PLAYS ARE BORN: THE COMING OF MR. O'CASEY
Daily News, March 27, p. 6.

SIR HUGH LANE'S PICTURES
(Letter)
Manchester Guardian, July 14, p. 18.

THE HUGH LANE PICTURES. DUBLIN'S CHANCE
(Letter, signed by W. B. Yeats and Lady Gregory)
The Times, July 29, p. 8a-b.

THE LANE PICTURES
(Letter)
The Nation and Athenaeum, August 14, p. 552.

1927

ON THE RACECOURSE
The Golden Book Magazine (New York), September, pp. 364-68.
Published separately the same year. Reprinted in *Collected Plays I*,
C.E.5, pp. 193-204.

[REVIEW OF FRANK GALLAGHER'S] *DAYS OF FEAR*
The Nation and Athenaeum, December 15, pp. 422, 424.

1929

FRANK GALLAGHER'S *DAYS OF FEAR*
The New Republic (New York), March 20, Spring Book Section,
pp. 141-43.

1930

CLAY PEOPLE LONG FAMOUS
Arts and Decoration (New York), April 30, pp. 106, 117, 133.

APPENDIX

ROBERT GREGORY: ARTIST AND
STAGE DESIGNER

RICHARD ALLEN CAVE

Robert Gregory's access to adulthood must have brought him a formidable burden of responsibilities: the private loneliness experienced by an only child intensified by an expectation that his would be a glittering career that extended far beyond the confines of the family circle. After the first decade of his life (Robert was born on 20 May 1881) he had lacked a father's guidance and friendship, for Sir William had died in 1892. His mother adored him but was sensitive of the dangers of possessiveness; her brother Frank Persse was a trusted adviser during Robert's minority. Privately Lady Gregory kept most of Robert's letters to her from his first story composed at the age of five to those sent from the Italian Front in the Great War;[1] in the fullness of grief at his death in action on 23 January 1918, her one consolation was that her enduring fear over the years could never now be realised: she could not lose his love.

Watching her grandson growing up at Coole gave her one especial delight: that of noticing how Richard inherited 'some of his father's little courteous ways'.[2] Courtesy was a virtue the family cherished: Sir William's successful Governorship of Ceylon depended much on it; Lady Gregory's unstinting hospitality at Coole is legendary; and noticeably she makes strength in magnanimity even in the face of his undoing the proof of Brian Boru's heroic stature in her first tragedy *Kincora*, where it earns King Brian what he most greatly prizes — a name in the book of the people. The same was true of Robert Gregory: recording in *Seventy Years* the tributes and messages of condolence sent her on the occasion of his death, his mother saw it as a fitting decorum to set down the responses of the Kiltartan villagers who had been his cricketing, shooting and hunting companions beside the words of artists, statesmen and relatives. The memory of a Gort workman — 'He would give me a whole hand'[3] — is a moving testimony of Gregory's worth.[4]

But being a fine flower of courtesy does not amount to a career

347

(it is of the essence of that Renaissance-like *sprezzatura* Yeats admired in Robert that it does not strive for its achievements nor seek to advertise its distinction) and the shaping of careers that would add dignity to the cause for Ireland's independence was Lady Gregory's paramount ambition by 1902 when Robert came of age. There was the example of his cousin, Hugh Lane (six years his senior), who, though he was fond of quipping 'I have nothing but my taste', had lived in penury for five years or more acquiring it and perfecting his knowledge of art history, had established himself as a dealer in paintings in Pall Mall Place in 1898 and after four years was well on the way to amassing a considerable fortune and a resplendent private collection. The autumn of 1902 was to find Lane organising an Exhibition of Old Masters in Dublin, the first of a series of enterprises designed to awaken Irish perceptions to the heritage of fine art possessed within the country's great houses and to educate a taste for contemporary movements in painting on the continent that might lead to the establishing of a Gallery of Modern Art in the city. September 1902 marked a move to prominence in the Nationalist cause of another cousin, John Shawe-Taylor (1866–1911) who, in calling for a Land Conference 'succeeded' (in William O'Brien's words) 'where the genius of Gladstone failed'.[5] Both young men were of Persse stock and Lady Gregory recognised in them a quality she too shared, as did Robert: an energy that can take hold of people's minds and an audacity in the pursuit of what they felt instinctively to be right. All four in fact possessed in good measure what John Butler Yeats felt was the dominant note in Hugh Lane's personality: 'a strange combination of extreme sensitiveness with absolute intrepidity'.[6]

By 1902 Lady Gregory's own literary career had taken wing; the editing of *Ideals in Ireland* (1901) and now the publication of *Cuchulain of Muirthemne* had opened to her a wider-ranging public than had read *Sir William Gregory* (1894), *Mr. Gregory's Letter-Box* (1898) or her account of Arabi Pasha's household (1882). Hardly a year was to pass between this and her death that did not see a publication from her or the staging of a play as she immersed herself in the cause of the Irish Literary Theatre. To her delight, Robert was for some years to participate in several of these adventures, matching his taste and skill to her invention as playwright and director.

When he came of age, Robert Gregory was in his third year of reading Classics at New College, Oxford. It must be admitted he was no scholar in the accepted academic sense, he took four years over Greats and like his father before him, went down in 1903, without taking a degree. A developing trait of self-absorbtion would have proved a stumbling-block had he decided to try for Parliament, which is how Sir William's public career began. His was not a mind that could apply itself rigorously as Hugh Lane's had done to the mastery of a single field of intellectual or artistic endeavour; his joy in the variety of life's possibilities was too rich for that. It was rather the *scope* for sympathy of the mind that Yeats in his most famous elegy defines as scholarly: the range of competence at its command and the ease with which new skills and insights could, as with his mother, be acquired at will. Yeats was to have direct experience of that mind at work in the rapidity with which Gregory mastered the art of stage design to meet the poet's most exacting demands; in his companionship at Coole; and more particularly while travelling in Italy in the spring of 1907 with Robert and his mother.

Even as a student these qualities were apparent. To read Gregory's letters alongside his mother's autobiography for his Oxford years is to appreciate that his was a full life, and in its way studious, if not rigorously academic. The style of the letters is direct, transparently honest even in admitting to moments of personal failure; the interest is confined entirely to the factual, no phrase is coloured by emotion or gestures towards the analytical; the tone is wholly impersonal — a manly record of events. Only occasionally does Gregory rise to a joke:

I breakfasted with the subwarden Mr. Rashdall the other day, it was rather an amusing performance: only 2 out of the 6 guests turned up & it was too late to go out into the byways etc; the other man who was at Harrow with me opened the conversation promisingly by asking the subwarden, an old Harrovian and proud of the fact, whether he had ever visited Harrow.[7]

The early promise that got Robert a scholarship from Elstree to Harrow in 1895, taking 'a brilliant examination', 'clearly first — some of the Greek was too much for him, but his Latin excellent, the Latin verses capital', was not maintained, though prose and verse composition remained in his own view his 'strong points'.[8] Lady Gregory records in *Seventy Years* her anxiety at the time of the Harrow scholarship examination: 'His masters speak so well of him I sometimes think he must get one, and then I remember his little careless ways and the excitement he will be in about coming home and hope dies'.[9] Whether out of carelessness or excitement (he had just spent five weeks of the Easter vacation 1900 in Italy with Lady Gregory seeing the Alps, hearing his first *Lohengrin* at La Scala, and being shown the Vatican in the company of the Comte de Basterot), Robert failed his divinity examinations, the 'Little Go', at the first attempt and was unexpectedly sent down. Later informing his mother how easily he passed at the second shot, he adds: 'I feel my time rather wasted now, as I could have got through with much less knowledge apparently'.[10]

A revealing entry in *Seventy Years* reads:

December 1900. Robert came . . . Is working for Mods. at Greek sculpture and Greek plays . . . and really interested in his work, but very much enjoys the shooting.[11]

That 'but' endorses one's impression of Robert's priorities at this time and it is typical of Lady Gregory that she observes, accepts and does not judge. Of the college Collections in March 1903 (a trial run for the university examinations), Robert observed:

So far I have only had 2 papers looked over for which I got B— for (Gk. History) and — — for Moral Philosophy, which is just middling. I ought to improve a good deal on these marks by the time Greats comes off.[12]

Despite the help of a coach in his final term ('Jenkinson by name, a very nice young man, who has only just gone down') Gregory's hope proved over-sanguine; philosophy particularly proved intractable, seeming 'as misty to me as before I started'.[13] Later Gregory's interest in Greek tragedy apparently revived: writing to Synge about the autumn and winter programme for the Abbey in 1906, Yeats commented 'Robert Gregory is inclined to translate the Antigone for Miss Allgood'.[14] Was it Robert's insight that alerted Lady Gregory to the potential tragic stature in Sara Allgood? Her three finest tragedies were composed between the summer of 1906 and the winter of 1908/9 in *The Gaol Gate*, *Dervorgilla* and the revised *Kincora*; in each the ill-fated heroine was played by Sara Allgood.

Though references to his achievements in boxing, shooting, rowing and cricket abound in Gregory's letters from Oxford, the overall impression is not that of the well-known Oxford stereotype, the sporting hearty; the tone is not boorish but one of cool understatement. He may, as on 21 May 1902, observe, 'I have been getting a lot of cricket up here lately', but he continues, 'too much in fact as it often wastes the whole day, so I am not going to play in all the matches in future'. But one can gauge his serious commitment to the game from the explicit instructions he sends his mother about handling the local ground at Coole during the particularly wet May of 1903, should weather conditions in Gort be as adverse as in Oxford. Amusingly, both now and later in his life, it was usually Lady Gregory who waxed passionate about Robert's prowess in retailing his news to others, often breaking into her private musing as recorded in her journals, or into a letter to Synge about Abbey policy, to record his latest batting score. (By contrast, after his Harrovian days she kept silent about his academic performance.) Gregory was not only to captain the Kiltartan side but to play for the Phoenix Cricket Club (Dublin), and the Gentlemen of Ireland. As a boxer he fought as a lightweight for Oxford against Cambridge and, while living in Paris, was a candidate in the Amateur Championship of France.[15]

Though Gregory's education was chiefly in England, he watched developments in the intellectual renaissance in Ireland with interest, recounting in his letters the reactions of his college peers to his mother's and Yeats's publications. Of *Cuchlain of Muirthemne*, he reported on 21 May 1902: 'Everybody I have heard from about the book have [sic] liked it very much. Jennings our literary critic likes the idiom very much'; Schuster, a particular friend with whom he planned a walking tour in the Pyrenees after Greats, is described in a letter of 23 February 1903 as 'reading the wandering tribe and the workhouse stories and is delighted with them; I think it [*Poets and Dreamers*] ought to be a great success'. Robert's own criticisms are reserved for 'my booksellers', because they 'refuse to send for Standish O'Grady's publications as he has not a London agent, so I am fighting them, but the chief villain hides and I can only get at his minions which is no good';[16] and significantly for detailed comment on the production of the books themselves as aesthetic objects: 'The new "Wind Among the Reeds" [the fourth edition bound in vellum] has come from Elkin Mathews. It is very fine I think, though the gold leaf has not been put on very carefully in some places';[17] and of *Poets and Dreamers*: 'The book arrived yesterday & I think makes up very well; the binding too is very nice, but I hope it will hold together, as my copy does not seem very secure'.[18]

To extend concern for his Land policies from Ireland to England, John Shawe-Taylor asked Gregory to try to get the Oxford Union to debate the issue; on 6 November 1902 Robert informed his mother: 'I asked all the people who [m] I know but they were either not interested in it, or cannot spend any time in working up the subject; or are against land purchase'. However, Gregory's suggestion appears to have excited sufficient cordial feeling amongst the Irish undergraduates to found an Irish Club. Robert announced its creation in a letter of 28 November 1902, but added the tart rider:

. . . it chose for itself the name of 'St. Patrick's Club'; which is not very interesting; I tried to get them [to] defer naming it until some more suggestions were offered — the only others being at the time the Shamrock, the Hibernian and the Oxford University Irish; I thought the last the best of a bad lot. There is to be a debate on Compulsory Land Purchase, but no voting "for fear the club should become political". I have to open a debate on the same subject on Monday at the New College Debating Club.

On 7 December he reported that 'The Land sale debates went off all right; Compulsory Purchase was defeated at the New College XX Club by fourteen votes to seven. At the Irish Club it would have been carried almost unanimously but there was no voting'.

The history of the Irish Club during Robert's remaining terms at New College seems to have been marked more by postponements of intentions than by actual achievements. Early in March 1903, he wrote to Lady Gregory asking her to apologise to Yeats for the last minute cancelling of a dinner at which the poet was to have been a guest, hoping it had not 'upset his plans'.[19] Early the following term on 7 May, Robert wrote an urgent plea to his mother:

I have to read a paper on Irish Journalism, I hear, next Tuesday to the Irish Club. I have not much time to think about it, so any suggestions you could write would be very welcome.

The Club ask me to write to Yeats to know whether he could come down on 23 June to the dinner, which will apparently come off really this time.[20]

A week later he wrote a yet more urgent plea for some additional funds to help clear his bills, admitting he would need 'about £100 more than I expected'. Perhaps to palliate this blow somewhat with a show of respect for his mother's intellect, he continues:

I was to have read my paper on Irish journalism last night, however owing to some other club meeting that night only about 10 men turned up so I am to read it 3 weeks hence and I shall probably improve it in the meantime. The chief points were as you suggested the disinterested work

of young men; and the difference between journalism in Ireland & England
is that in England readers prefer the bad, & get what they want, but in
Ireland it is as yet only a portion of the population which desire the bad,
and they determine the quality [not?] only of what is supplied to
themselves, but to all the rest, who take what they are given without
asserting their choice; and that as journalism is bound to be for the most
part a commercial undertaking, the best chance of improvement is rather
in the improvement of the taste of the readers, than in attacks upon the
papers themselves. As I have to make the paper last 20 minutes it is not
easy to fill up the rest of the time.[21]

The concluding sentence amounts to an appeal for still more useful
copy.

D. J. Gordon and Ian Fletcher, writing a brief appraisal of
Gregory in *Images of a Poet*, comment that 'His Mother hoped
very early that her son might prove to be a distinguished
painter'.[22] There is no actual evidence of this in her autobiographical writings nor any suggestion in the correspondence
that Robert was at any time under pressure to pursue such a career.
Certainly Lady Gregory records her pleasure at Robert's sketching
when he accompanied her on holiday excursions and she seems to
accept his proficiency as a matter of course; but chance had happily
shaped her own life too frequently for her to have wanted to set
him on a determined path. The letters from Oxford include
caricatures of Oxford personalities, references to a picture of Emer
worked under the inspiration of Lady Gregory's *Cuchulain*,
sketches of views from the window of his digs, a bookplate
designed for a relative and visits when in London to art exhibitions.
Art occupied as strong a place in his affections as sport. It was not
until the Easter vacation 1903 that painting was fixed on as the next
phase of Robert's education and then the choice appears to have
been decidedly his. On 20 April, Lady Gregory wrote asking
Synge's guidance:

My son has set his mind on working at art, & as a beginning to spend a
couple of years learning drawing & painting — in either London or Paris.
Paris I should think is best. Do you happen to know how one shd. set to
work? Does a student go to art schools — or to studios? What are the
studios open to pupils? Are there regular terms — or does one go at any
time of the year? Any information wd. be welcome — not that there is a
very great hurry as he has another term at Oxford, but I want to begin
getting a little information.[23]

A major influence on his decision must have been the recent

success of the scheme for set and costumes for *The Hour Glass*
which Sturge Moore in consultation with Yeats had devised from
sketches supplied by Robert.[24] These show a remarkable sense of
line and feeling for texture, atmosphere and spatial relationships,
carried off with evident freedom and *brio*. A striking feature too
is the energy of the contrast between the magisterial figure of the
Wise Man—his stance and gesture echoing the austere lines and
angles of the beams that define his study—and the gang of carefree
students; that energy sensitively complements the source of the
play's dramatic vitality in the conflict between the Wise Man's
inflexible, precise logic and the richness and mystery of the world
he seeks to confine within the dictates of reason. Gregory's sketch
evokes a medieval world of learning and asceticism without a
clutter of historical details such as would have been deemed an
essential feature of a period setting by most British stage designers
in 1903. Yeats was delighted (the finished decor was 'profoundly
impressive' to Joseph Holloway)[25] for it confirmed in practice
many of his slowly evolving theories for reforming contemporary
stage presentation.

In the event Synge's advice was not required: the following
autumn Gregory started classes at the Slade School of Art in
Bloomsbury, London. What caused the change of plan is not clear,
but several possibilities suggest themselves: the need to have Robert
within easy access to help with further theatrical ventures; the more
informed advice that Hugh Lane could offer; the influence of
Ricketts and Shannon, themselves former students at the Slade,
who by now were becoming close friends of both Yeats and Lady
Gregory. Perhaps there was a wish to improve his drawing and
composition in order to take proper advantage of a visit to an
atelier in Paris. At the Slade Robert found himself under the
supervision of George Moore's sometime friend, Henry Tonks, an
exciting but formidable teacher as Augustus John had learnt at
some cost:

He was a sharp critic. . . not given to mincing his words. His natural
benevolence was disguised under an austere and forbidding mask. . .
pretentiousness or "cleverness" more than anything moved him to wrath.
Tonks had a passion for teaching drawing and the Slade was his
mistress.[26]

As Yeats was to be away in America during the winter months
1903–4 on a lecture tour, Robert moved into his rooms in 18

Woburn Buildings. These comprised 'two rooms and a little kitchen in a small house in Woburn Place, a narrow street with tiny shops more like a village street than a London one. The rooms were "ninetyish", dark brown (or blue?) walls, dark bookcases crammed with books; for artificial light there were only candles.'[27] This was not ideal studio accommodation for an artist but the situation was most convenient for the Slade. Robert initially attended classes in Drawing and Composition (taking a certificate in drawing in 1905) and in Art and Craft Design; in his final year he entered for Painting and Fine Art and a course on the History of Art. There is no doubt that art was the right choice of a career: the letters of the Slade years strike an immediate contrast with those from Oxford; there is a relaxed freedom of tone and the sense of a personality joyfully discovering itself through work that demands patience and application. The cool detachment has gone and is replaced by a willingness to inform and give details.[28]

> 18 Woburn Buildings
> Oct 7 [1903]

My dear Mama — I have not yet got much idea about the Slade, or the life, or the teaching to tell you. I have only been looked at once during the last two days and then I was only told — 'be careful about your proportions', without any definite correction — however I daresay I shall find out what they want by degrees.

The first day — (I forget if I told you) I was (3 times) told — 'that's all wrong start it again'. However I think I am improving a bit already, and seeing the proportions better. At first I thought I was the worst there, but I now find with relief that some of the others are a degree worse. . . .

Jack and Mrs. Jack were coming to dine here tomorrow, but they have just found that they were engaged.

I got a note from Cockerell, & am going round to see him in the luncheon interval tomorrow. Wilfred Blunt sent me a wire this morning about the shooting, so I wired accepting.

I haven't made any friends at the Slade yet, but Cockerell says he can introduce me to one or two. I enjoyed the rehearsals in Dublin very much — I think both plays ought to be splendid when staged.[29]

Yeats took me to Dowden's whom I liked very much, but his taste in pictures would make me have misgivings as to his literary taste.

When are you to be over; I expect to enjoy myself here very much then, as even without having anyone to talk to except Mrs. Old — I have really got on very well; and I am feeling quite fit.

> Your loving son,
>   Robert Gregory.

Robert was clearly looking forward to making a closer friend of Jack Yeats, the poet's brother, who was beginning to establish a reputation for himself in London with two exhibitions of 'Sketches of Life in the West of Ireland' at the Walker Art Gallery and Baillie's. Sir Sydney Cockerell (1867–1962) is an interesting contact, established presumably by W. B. Yeats (they had been friends of long standing) though he was known to Lady Gregory as an intimate of Wilfred Scawen Blunt's circle. Cockerell, after acting as William Morris's secretary at the Kelmscott Press, was at this date in partnership with Emery Walker, an expert on typography, who had advised Elizabeth Yeats over the establishing and management of the Dun Emer Press. Given Robert's interest in the quality of book production and his initial enrolment in Craft Design at the Slade, one wonders whether he considered developing a specialist knowledge in the field after the example of Ricketts and the Vale Press (1896–1904) or whether Yeats encouraged the pursuit and the friendship with Cockerell in the hope that Gregory might help his sister (Robert was to design several devices and a frontispiece from 1904 for use by the Dun Emer Press). Dowden's rooms in Trinity College, where he was Professor of English Literature, were a popular haunt for Dublin's *literati* but his well-known scepticism about the prospects of a literary renaissance in Ireland may account for Robert's critical stance. Mrs. Old, formerly Arthur Symons's bedmaker in the Temple, had been Yeats's servant-housekeeper since his move to Woburn Buildings in 1896.

After a term at the Slade Gregory decided to confine his attention exclusively to drawing where, even in Tonks's opinion, he was making marked progress.

18 Woburn Buildings
Friday.
[22 January 1904]

My dear Mama—

I'm afraid I've been a long time in writing — but so far I have had a very uneventful life. I have come on a good deal with my drawing and Tonks was quite complimentary to me yesterday — said I had made an immense advance since he had seen my work last and gave me a good deal of general advice — told me not to overwork myself which I did not expect to hear from him. I have given up the designing classes and now go only to the modelling to which I can go as many nights as I like. I dined with Masefield on Sunday night when we cooked our own dinner Mrs. Masefield being away. I have just started boxing at Macpherson's in Sloane St., and am going to combine dancing lessons as they can be given at the same time and at the same place. We have also started all manner of games at the Slade which are good exercise. I have had rather an annoying cold all the week — it has never got very bad but is always a nuisance. I go to the Clays tomorrow night. I don't feel very keen on the prospect.[30]

I am very glad to hear the plays were so good. Are the company coming over this year? . . .

Did you and Uncle Frank come to any further decision about the Studio - I have not inspected any here. . . .

I may go up to Oxford tomorrow fortnight for a day's hunting — Schuster[31] refuses to live with his brother during his engagement and has taken rooms in Long Wall.

. . . There is a show of Blake's work at Carfax[32] but I have not been able to see it yet.

Your loving son
Robert Gregory

The shift from mention of Masefield to boxing is an apt pattern of association for it was an interest the poet shared; he often at this date accompanied Jack Yeats, another enthusiast, to matches in London. In Robert's experience the Clays, old family friends, were kindly but somewhat oppressive in being inclined to suspicion and dogmatic criticism of the new movements in art and literature that were exciting him. The latest performances of the Irish National Theatre Society had been on 14 January with Seumas MacManus's *The Townland of Tamney* and Yeats's *The Shadowy Waters*.

The question of where to site a studio at Coole was to cause Lady Gregory anxiety for some months to come,[33] while Robert himself was facing the prospect of finding new accommodation pending Yeats's return from the United States — a problem soon to be solved by his growing friendship with an older Slade student, William Wilfred Cave. Cave, from Bramborough in Cheshire, had entered in 1901 and during this particular session (1903-4) was to take First Prize in both Figure Painting and Head Painting, and Certificates in Painting and Figure Composition, which doubtless explains the deferential tone of Robert's references to him.

Late January saw the publication of Lady Gregory's *Gods and Fighting Men*.

18 Woburn Buildings
Friday
[29 January 1904]

My Dear Mama—

Many thanks for your letters cake toffee turkey and book — the last arrived today and looks very well — I must keep a look out for reviews. The turkey I had for dinner on Wednesday for a couple of guests — it was excellent and I have been lunching and breakfasting off it ever since. The toffee was very useful — but my cold is as good as gone now. I had tried a Turkish bath last week but I got a fresh chill coming out so it did not get a chance.

I went to the Clays on Saturday, it was quite a nice dinner; I liked the Clays very much; Felix seemed very interested in everything. The niece who is supposed to have such genius sat next me at dinner — she was quite nice, and a great admirer of Cuchulain; they all seemed excited at hearing the new book was to be out soon. My drawing has been getting on all right. Tonks came round to me when I was drawing a cast and said 'it's too niggly, still it shows improvement' and today he talked to me quite a lot and drew a head on my paper which took him quite a long time — and told me that in some ways my drawing wasn't bad, so I feel I am in his good books.

Cave is coming round to tea on Monday here and I am going to see his studio. He is the most graceful draughtsman in the Slade at present, but some of his drawings rather want vigour . . .

I go to Oxford next Friday to have a day with the Heythrop. I went to a couple of theatres, in the pit, Joseph Entangled by Jones and Letty by Pinero. The first quite artificial — it began as if the plot would be clever like some French farce but ended feebly while the characters are quite superficial.[34] Letty was the first play of Pinero's I had seen, and I was inclined to think it rather good at first — but afterwards I saw that all the reality of the play turns upon Letty's character and that one cannot grasp clearly from the play.[35] I forget if you saw it. Urquhart looked in on Sunday — he has left the Slade and gone to the Westminster school — and is I think beginning to appreciate the Slade much more now — for one thing the Slade people work infinitely harder than do his fellow students. . . .

Boxing and dancing have been getting on all right and the exercise is very good for me. . . .

Weather here is awful rain or fog or both almost every day. When will you come to town?

Your loving son,
Robert Gregory.

As February advanced the need to find new accommodation

became pressing. Yeats delayed his sailing from New York by a week 'because I have been so busy that I have not been to see anybody socially here':[36] he left on 9 March with the expectation of being in London by the 18th. Illness slowed down Gregory's search.

18 Woburn Buildings
Monday
[8 February 1904]

My dear Mama,

This has been rather a broken week of work I'm afraid. I either hurt myself wrestling at the Slade or got a chill on Wednesday & was rather bad all that night and Thursday — however I decided to go up to Oxford and take my chance of getting cured by a day's hunting. Friday was beautifully fine and a good meet of the Heythrop and there was a 2 hours run over good country; but I was not up to it and stopped after the first half. However the day out and the exercise did me a lot of good and I am quite fit again now. . . .

I dined with the Clays on Wednesday and was not very well then, and I think it was the rich dinner and the riding on top of the bus that settled me.

I went to tea with Miss Monsell[37] today — not a very interesting tea-party, but Cockerell came in at the end — & we had a talk. He is off to Egypt in a week.[38] I have been reading Gods & Fighting Men. I had read the 'Gods' in the proofs but not the Finn Stories. I think they excite me even more than the Cuchulain stories do; there is I think more extraordinary beauty in them. I hear Mr. Blunt's review in the Speaker is out but have not seen it.

Cave came round here the other day and gave me some good criticisms. He is very candid — and warned me before he looked at my drawings that if he did not think them any good he would say so — or else say nothing. However he says they are quite promising though they have no beauty or anything of that sort.

I think that the studio on top of the laundry would do very well. Cave is very anxious I should paint a big picture for the competition this summer which would mean at least two months work — but I am very doubtful. I went round to Cliffords Inn — two possible sets of rooms — £42 a year each but I think I can get them for less — they need a good deal to be done to them — painting papering carpets etc. I am going again to settle definitely.

Tonks abused me today and told me my drawing was not up to the mark — 'looked like a tracing on glass' — he was quite right — but I did better afterwards.

The Sketch Club subjects this month are 'The Judgement of Solomon' —
A visit — and an open landscape.

There is greater excitement here over the war than over the Boer war;
Japanese flags flying, etc.[39]

I finished this letter today Wednesday.

Your loving son,
Robert Gregory

Throughout February Lady Gregory was at Coole, restocking
her 'Seven Woods' and collecting properties for the staging of
Synge's *Riders to the Sea*.

18 Woburn Buildings
Tuesday
[1 February 1904]

My dear Mama: Thanks very much for the turkey which is magnificent;
it is in process of being cooked now, but in a neighbouring house as it was
found to be too big for the oven in the stove. I have had a good weeks
work and got on a good deal I think; I have not settled anything definitely
about rooms, but I have just got your letter saying Yeats will be back soon
(I don't think he can be back as early as the 6th) — so will hurry things
along. I am trying to get up a tea party for next Tuesday with Miss Monsell
as nucleus. An Oxford man has just come to the Slade who was up at the
same time as me at Christ Church; he is a very nice man I think — and
very well read, which is quite surprising for a Slade man.

Mrs. Old has put in for the post of bedmaker at my new rooms. I should
think I had better take her unless it would interfere with her duties to
Yeats.

It will be grand your coming on the first. It has made a lot of difference
getting to know most of the men at the Slade for even though I don't see
them much outside the school I don't feel cut off from everybody as I did.

The difficulties of planting seem very great. It will be very nice though
to have a birch wood, as we have not had one before.

I have been very well lately and doing a good deal of boxing at the Slade
— but wrestling is the favourite amusement there. I went to see the 'Duke
of Killicrankie' by Marshall at the Criterion on Saturday — it was quite
amusing, the plot is impossible, but the acting and some of the dialogue
very good — it is called a Farcical Romance which describes it very
well.[40]

I have just been to see some rooms at Grays Inn. I went this morning
& heard particulars and wired to you then, and went again & went over
them, & have almost settled to take them; I hope wisely. There is a
bedroom, two sitting rooms — one would do as a studio — a bathroom WC,

kitchen, coal hole — all for 50 pounds — with £15 to the present owner, as he has put in electric light, fireplaces, skylights, wall papers, linoleum on all the floors which was very necessary as the floors were too far gone to stain. Two windows look over the gardens & the others over Grays Inn Road. There would be room for another if I got a friend to come in with me but anyhow they are hardly more expensive than the Cliffords Inn rooms, and they are just ready to move into. The only question is the length of time I must take them for. If I can sublet them, there should be no difficulty in doing so, but I have not seen the agreement they wish to draw up. . . .

I wish you were here to decide, but I must do it myself tomorrow, as several people are also debating about taking the rooms.

Your loving son,
Robert Gregory

When Lady Gregory came to London in March, she gave a dinner party for Ricketts, Shannon, Yeats and Hugh Lane, who during the evening urged Shannon, according to an entry in the latter's diary, 'to accept a commission for a sketch of Lady Gregory, which I promised to do though I wonder if I shall'.[41] The respectful acquaintance of the Gregorys with Ricketts and Shannon now blossomed into friendship. On 16 May over dinner with Yeats, Lady Gregory tried to persuade Shannon 'to sell her the Harmsworth Venus to hold in trust for the Dublin Museum'. True to character she frankly informed him 'she had actually enquired at her bankers to see if she [?could] stand it'. Shannon's canvas was proving something of an embarrassment to him: in addition to Lord Harmsworth who commissioned it and Lady Gregory who wished it to grace Hugh Lane's prospective gallery, the collector, Sir Edmund Davis, was also to put in a bid. Was it perhaps to tip the balance in her favour that Lady Gregory that same evening broached a further project? Shannon's diary notes 'Lady Gregory with great kindness commissioned me to paint a portrait of her son'.[42]

Robert sat for a drawing in the afternoon of 22 June but, though Shannon had a prominent place in Lane's exhibition of Irish Artists at the Guildhall and social contacts between the artist and the Gregorys were not infrequent during the following winter[43], progress on the portrait was not reported until early in 1905. On 23 January Robert attended his first sitting when, as Shannon records, he 'made a sketch of head . . . on an old piece of canvas preparatory to doing portrait'.[44] Ricketts began to delight in Robert's wit and personality: 'Young Gregory had lunch with us, he told us amusing gossip about the Dublin Picture Gallery scheme, how everything there turns into politics; the whole scheme is amazing and ridiculous. . . . the whole nation seems to be given over to academic agitation in a world of Gilbertian seriousness'.[45] Clearly Ricketts and Shannon saw a very relaxed side of Robert.

At this date Gregory and Wilfred Cave decided to share a house together at 28 Delamore Terrace, Royal Oak, overlooking the canal at Little Venice. While the rooms were being set in order Robert lived with the Clays in Kensington.

19 Hyde Park Gate, S.W.
Sunday. [p.mk 29 January 1905]

My dear Mama. I am not yet in rooms but hope to be next week; they are in a rather disreputable state. But I think papering and staining will make them all right for the present. Cave is taking the better rooms on the first floor which are high and have big windows and balcony. I am taking the second floor and am having the walls distempered. We have been busy shopping getting sheets blankets towels etc. at the sales. They have not cost us much but I don't know if they are any good — we are getting some nice old wooden kitchen chairs which came from Buckinghamshire at 6/6 each

which I should not think was too dear as they are a beautiful colour & well made. There is also in the same shop a very nice old settee of ash & oak about six or seven feet long which I half think of getting at £3-10. There is nice inlaid wood at the back. Work has been broken a good deal by all this room and general hunting — but I have had some whole days at the Slade and we are drawing twice a week in the evening. Tonks told me I was getting on well with my drawing. I find it impossible to do any work here but I must get the tree scene done and will try & send it this week. I thought your ash and willow wings very good especially the ash. I am very comfortable here and like the Clays very much. The only subject on which we quarrel is the French Impressionists & Degas in particular. Sir Arthur went to see them & 'they made him sick'. I have had one sitting from Shannon — he did a sketch in oils of my head and drew a sketch of composition which seemed to be something like this but it wasn't worked

out. I was there the whole day but did more talking than work. Ricketts made himself very agreeable. He is doing a very fine picture of Daphnis and Chloe — I think — two figures with a river background. He says Mrs. Goldman is the most impossible sitter — that he had to give up a full face portrait which would have been better as it needed more drawing which he could not do. . . Did you see a book on the legends of Britain or some such name — I saw a review of it in the St. James Gazette — and it gave extracts which read like your Cuchulain turned into journalese.

. . . I was sent six woodcock today — I don't know whether you forwarded them or not as they were unpacked down stairs.

Your loving son
Robert Gregory

The 'tree scene' here refers to a design for the wood of Clontarf where Lady Gregory set the prologue of her tragedy *Kincora* to be staged on 25 March. The delay over designing this setting and the speed with which it had to be executed no doubt in part contributed towards Robert's decision to effect a design more stylised than representational; when first seen in Dublin it was the occasion of considerable critical acclaim. The designing of scenery in general and tree scenes in particular was causing many a headache for the directorate of the Theatre Society after the opening of the Abbey on 27 December 1904. It is possible that Lady Gregory merely forwarded suggestions of what she would like Robert to do both to inspire and prompt him to action. However, from the previous November Yeats had been anxious over his brother Jack's agreement to provide scenery for Synge's new play *The Well of the Saints* to be staged 4 February 1905; it was to comprise 'some tree wings, a cottage and two big chairs'.[46] Not convinced that Jack knew what was required or that he would produce anything acceptable in time, Yeats consoled Synge by assuring him that he would ask Robert to oversee such designs as his brother produced: 'He is enthusiastic about decorative scenery and Ricketts has told him that some great painter or other advised a favourite pupil to make scenery'.[47] The ash and willow wings Robert refers to here would be apt for Synge's play but are likely to be of Lady Gregory's devising for her own comedy, *Spreading the News*, which had shared the bill with *On Baile's Strand* at the Abbey's inauguration the previous December. In the event Jack Yeats failed to produce the necessary work and the settings for Synge's play were a rushed and composite affair designed by Pamela Colman Smith and Edith Craig.

As early as 1904 Yeats was thinking of *stylised* design for outdoor settings (such as he had already achieved with the indoor settings for *The Hour Glass* and *On Baile's Strand*) but taking its inspiration now from Japanese art; shortly Gregory's work for *Kincora* was to please him not so much because it was beautiful in an orthodox way but for its 'high grave dignity and that *strangeness* which Ben Jonson thought to be a part of all excellent beauty'.[48] Lady Gregory's prologue excited Yeats because it showed the penetration of the human by the spirit world (Aoibel of the Sidhe woos Brian in a dream-vision), a subject he was to explore himself in his Noh-inspired dance plays; Robert's achievement was in finding a suitable visual decorum of the familiar transfigured into strangeness to complement the stage-action. This achievement is the more remarkable for the hassle which accompanied its completion — a week or more after his last letter, Robert was writing to apologise for still not sending any designs.

28 Delamere Terrace
Royal Oak.
[mid-February]⁴⁹

My dear Mama. I'm very sorry indeed for not having written or sent the designs; I have been in a great fuss moving into these rooms, and I have been trying to get the design done in the middle of it — but I found I could not get what I wanted at all. I send a sort of thing very feeble though. I have torn up several others. The designs in the sketch book I left behind at Coole, and I thought I had told you when writing but I must have forgotten. I don't know at all where they were — probably in the library. What other designs do you want if there is time for me to do them — I could give my time to them now? Shall I come over at any time or is that not worth while?⁵⁰ I moved in here last Wednesday — but in an awful state of confusion. The house is rather a ruin but it is being got right and I think we will be very comfortable in time if all goes well. Our woman is a dirty old creature and a nuisance in many ways and I think we will have to get rid of her. She does not even cook decently. Cave has made his rooms very nice and mine I think will be when I have got curtains etc. I saw James Silvester and Hoare yesterday and we went to John Bulls Other Island together which I thought very good indeed.

[?James] says he is going to Oxford today and will make inquiries about my things. Gilbert Murray is being elected a fellow and tutor of New College — splendid for the College but it may take up too much of his time.

Slade work is very disturbed during the last few days — but I am getting into it again.

I went to Jack's show — some good things in it I think — and with Jack to see boxing one evening. He seems fairly cheerful tho' he has not sold a picture yet — nor has Miss Monsell and another [?lady] who are also having shows at B[aillie]'s Gallery.⁵¹ I think I may settle permanently here if a woman can be got to do satifactorily for us. But the room is not very big for painting tho' the light is good. Our kitchen is nice and big and we have our meals in it as a rule. I have papered the walls green — rather too green to be nice for painting but I shall probably paint a good deal in Cave's room which he has papered with a beautiful brown paper.

The canal is really very fine and it is nice having no houses close in front of us. I went down to Kennedy's place in the country last Sunday for the night and the country air was very nice. I have been rather ill for a few days with a chill inside — but only a slight attack and I am very well now. Hoare is going to Italy and wants me to join him there at Easter but I don't think I shall go so far — I shall quite possibly come home.⁵² I got a note yesterday from Hugh to come and help him and Dermot O'Brien to choose pictures from the French Impressionists but it arrived too late being forwarded from Hyde Pk. Gate.⁵³ I dine with the Clays on Saturday.

They were very nice and kind, and I was very comfortable there. We were rather inclined to argue too much though — as they were very anxious to convert me from liking Degas, Bernard Shaw, Tolstoy etc. etc. and devoted most of our meals together to it.

This is a rough sketch of the view from the window. . . .

Your loving son
Robert Gregory

Lady Gregory appears to have grown somewhat anxious and persistent over the matter of designs for *Kincora* (advertised for 25 March) to judge by the sudden increase in letters from Robert during February 1905. It was an ambitious venture, her first full-length historical play and a tragedy, for which the varying scenic demands were more exacting than for any of the works staged to date by the National Theatre Society — indeed a third scene beside

the woodland landscape and Brian's tent at the Battle of Clontarf
was required: the hall of the hero's fortress at Kincora.

28 Delamere Terrace.
[p.mk.18 February 1905]

My dear Mama. The design I sent was meant for a repeat pattern for a
curtain — I can draw it out more carefully if necessary — if Fay can paint
it once he can go on repeating it or let someone else do it.

I don't quite understand what other scenes are wanted — is the tent scene
the only one? You see I never read the revised play — and am rather vague
about what is wanted.

The Prince's gift and [?R's letter] are splendid. I have not seen Hugh.

Jack and Mrs. Jack had tea here, I saw Masefield yesterday who has been
writing a lot of plays. He hopes to be sent over to review Kincora. He and
Jack were going to see boxing tonight — but I have to go to the Clays.

We have just got a new woman who looks as if she would be good and
clean.

Your loving son
Robert Gregory

Shannon's progress on portraits was slow, as his diary entries
reveal; inspiration flowed spasmodically once a basic pose had
been decided on. On 13 April he notes 'In morning roughed out
Gregory's portrait on a new canvas in turps under Sienna black
blue and white as forcible as possible in thin turps';[54] he worked at
it again on 18th and 21st in preparation for a sitting from Gregory
on 28th: 'I did the head and altered the shirt. He stayed to lunch
and I did a few touches afterwards. He went after tea.'[55] Once
again Ricketts appears to have found Robert's conversation
engaging: 'Young Gregory to lunch, he gave us amusing accounts
of Dublin and politics. Ireland I fear is really only half civilised, a
sort of provincial Poland. I am inclined to think the Irishman a
solemn sort of beast, provincial in temper, suspicious and quite
lacking in humour.'[56] The most recent scandal concerned a Corot
landscape, purchased with several paintings from Lane's Staats
Forbes exhibition and given to his gallery by the Prince and
Princess of Wales, then on a state visit to Ireland; several
intellectuals were trying to prove the painting a forgery to discredit
Lane's reputation.

28 Delamere Terrace.
[p.mk.5 May 1905]

My dear Mama; I am settled here again all right, tho' I have not got working very regularly yet. Cave came back the night before me so we timed it very nicely.

I have been sitting to Shannon and go again today, and I think that the portrait will be a good one — but it is not carried very far yet. Nothing exciting is happening at the Slade — the work is rather feeble on the whole.

I haven't heard whether the Royalty has been taken yet.[57] People seemed interested about the plays here — and a lady who had been in France had read about Kincora in the Paris New York Herald.

Rothenstein (Albert)[58] had been offered the staging of the plays at the Repertoire Theatre — (Gt. Queen St) and as he does not want to do it he offered them to me but I did not feel at all inclined to do them.

Cave has done some good work since I was away but nothing is carried very far. I have been to the Academy, which is a worse show than ever. There is a fine Furse — his last picture — and that is all.[59]

I am going to start painting at the Slade next week — I don't expect to do very much but I think it will help my drawing doing it occasionally.

I have got some wood blocks and have started experimenting but it seems very difficult to work them properly.

. . . Tonks has a show at Carfax next week — it will be very interesting seeing his work.

Your loving son
Robert Gregory

The Great Queen Street Theatre was leased from 1902 to 1907 to Hans Anderson's German Theatre Company, though between their seasons of repertory the theatre was often sub-leased to visiting companies (the Abbey was to give *The Playboy of the Western World* there in June 1907). The Mermaid Repertory Theatre which was in quest of a designer had been founded by Philip Carr with the express purpose of reviving neglected Early English Classic plays; Jonson's *The Silent Woman* and W. S. Gilbert's *The Palace of Truth* were performed during the weeks beginning 8 May and 23 May respectively. Though Gregory refused the invitation, its offer suggests that his work currently for the Irish National Theatre Society was making a name for him as a designer of potential in *avant-garde* theatre circles.

28 Delamere Ter.
Royal Oak.
[p.mk.16 May 1905]

My dear Mama. I have not heard at all whether the Clays are coming over or not. Won't you come over anyhow — especially as you do not care for staying at Coole. I have got working pretty well. I am just beginning a Judgement of Paris for the Sketch Club which I expect to spend some time over. I cut my first woodcut the other day — it was a failure — it was meant to be a mermaid with a cross — the idea being suggested by the story of the saint who was turned into a mermaid. I forget her name. I enclose a rough sketch — I thought it might do as a sort of colophon for Saints. Oakley has done a very good woodcut of a man's head — it seems to suit his line very well.

I went to stay with the Kennedys at Cookham last weekend — it was beautiful weather and was very pleasant altogether.

The Miss Yeats sent to me stories of Red Hanrahan. I am ordering a couple more from them.

. . . Cave is working well now I think. He is coming some time in the Summer — but he is afraid to come for long as he is not sure that he will be able to work at Coole. He is thinking of going to Paris for a short time in Autumn — if he does I dare say I will as Kennedy and [?] are also going. They are going to work there for some time I think. Tonks has a show on this week in Carfax; it is very interesting; and one can learn a lot from it. . . .

Your loving son
Robert Gregory

Work on Yeats's *Stories of Red Hanrahan* had been completed at the Dun Emer Press by Lady Day of 1904 but it was not published till May the following year. The volume included a design by Gregory showing the four aces from a pack of cards spread over the four provinces of Ireland depicted by a landscape of towers and castles separated from each other by a fast flowing river. The undoubted success of this illustration blending a complex symbolism with a vigorous and clear design may have momentarily turned Gregory's interest again in the direction of the craft of book production. *A Book of Saints and Wonders*, published by the Dun Emer Press in 1906, did not contain the mermaid colophon forwarded with the letter, which is fussy in execution and aesthetically unappealing for the disturbed rhythms created by the opposition of a starkly angular cross with the sinuous form of a mermaid and the waves in which she sports; instead he executed a device in red of a bell, waterfall and fish, again remarkable for its assured line and its emblematic lucidity. There is no record of whether Cave spent a short while at Coole in the summer of 1905 or whether the projected Paris venture occurred.

Tuesday
[30 January 1906]

My dear Mama. I have got settled here and am going to the Slade regularly! Tonks has been to me a good many times and told me he liked my composition very much. He was round at Shannon's on Friday and talked very nicely about my work. I went to John's school last night and drew. John was there and did a fine drawing. I am rather inclined to go there 2 days in the week.

I went to Lady Inger on Sunday.[60] The first acts dragged rather — nobody knew what it was about. The women were very bad, and the audience was very stupid. I thought the last part very fine, like an Elizabethan play, but the audience howled with laughter over the finest passages. There was some slight excuse as the translation was comic at times but they might have got over that. I hope your toothache is gone by now. Cave is bad with influenza which began with toothache & swollen face. Shannon says the portrait is practically finished. He wants to be asked to send to the R.H.A. as it saves trouble, perhaps you could find out if that is possible. The John drawings are here, but one very badly smudged I am sending back to J to see if he can remedy it.

Your loving son
Robert Gregory

Gregory was to come increasingly under the influence of Augustus John as his work at the Slade drew to a close. After a brilliant career at the Slade, John had spent a short period as art instructor at University College, Liverpool but, returning to London, he had joined with William Orpen in 1904 to open the Chelsea Art School in Rossetti Studios, Flood Street. By this date his interest in the venture was beginning to wane though the school was to survive for a further eighteen months. John's gifts as a draughtsman were much admired; Will Rothenstein considered his drawings even in his student days 'so remarkable that they put mine and Shannon's too into the shade'.[61] Robert and his mother purchased a number of John's sketches: fourteen are itemised in the sale catalogue of the contents of Coole as situated on the staircase and landing. John attracted a number of disciples through his school, notably Henry Lamb and James Dickson Innes (1887–1914) who entered the Slade during Robert's final year, winning in 1906–7 a scholarship and in 1908–9 the Prize for Figure Composition. Gregory consorts ill with this band who affected a bohemian gypsy existence and mode of dress, but perhaps it was their freedom from position, responsibility and a mother's sense of

national duty that was their attraction. From John and Innes he was
to learn much and he tried (not always successfully) to integrate his
friends into his mother's circle at Coole. When in 1907 Shannon
proved too busy during Yeats's time in London to undertake a
portrait sketch to act as frontispiece to Bullen's forthcoming
Collected Edition of the poet's work, Robert recommended John;
and Lady Gregory sufficiently supported her son's advice to send
an advance of £18 of the fee to enable a financially embarrassed
John to get to Coole for the summer. Yeats was only lukewarm
about the results while Lady Gregory was downright disapproving;
and, to placate John and ease a difficult situation, Gregory advised
Yeats to consult Will Rothenstein for an opinion about the
suitability of the design for his purpose — a cunning move, given
Rothenstein's distinction as a connoisseur of contemporary art and
his admiration for John's work in particular. Yeats informed Bullen
he found it 'a wonderful etching but fanciful as a portrait'; adding
'But remember that all fine artistic work is received with an outcry,
with hatred even. Suspect all work that is not.'[62] Whatever
Bullen's reaction Lady Gregory was adamant in her dislike and the
etching never graced a volume of Yeats's work until a year after her
death.

> Queen Anne's Mansions,
> St. James's Park. S.W.
> [p.mk.12 February 1906]

My dear Mama. I have not very much news from here. Shannon could not
get a frame in time for the picture to be sent to the R.H.A. — he was not
as a matter of fact very keen on sending it, I think — nor was I for there
is some very queer drawing about it which I should much like him to get
right before it is shown — I think it is moderately like. I hear Mr. Goldman
is delighted with his wife's portrait. He had not seen it until it was hung
at the International, and now spends all his spare time there looking at it.
I am glad Hyacinth's rehearsals are going so well.[63] I have not been to any
plays for Cave has been down with flu for the last fortnight, the swelling
of the face being only one of the symptoms, & I have stayed in in the
evenings looking after him. I read the first vol of 'Marius' to him while he
was in bed. I have also read Wilde's Dorian Gray, of which I had heard
a great deal and was very disappointed in it, and his 'Intentions' which I
thought very fine. I have been drawing well I think, doing more finished
drawings than I have done before — going on with the same drawing two
or three days. I have started on the Sketch Club subject — the death of
the first born — which will be good if I can carry it out, but I'm afraid the
effect I'm trying for is rather beyond me — a family mourning over its

firstborn, while as a background in the night outside the Israelites are all streaming away along the streets with donkeys carrying loads etc.

I went to hear Will Rothenstein lecture on art at the Junior Art Workers' guild, and made a short speech myself which I was afraid was platitude, but I was glad to find that most people thought it unintelligible. They were a very dreary lot of people. . . . I hope that your toothache was settled finally before you left Dublin.

Your loving son
Robert Gregory

After 22 May 1905, when Shannon recorded in his diary that he had 'worked on portrait of Gregory doing shirt at first badly then outlined thickly and darkened wall behind',[64] he had abandoned it until 23 November, when he repainted the canvas with 'fresh oily "emphatic painting" '; on 8 December, he 'repainted from life Gregory's head [and] played racquets for him' and on 30 January 1906 Robert sat 'for finishing touches'.[65] Still not content and doubtless sensing Gregory's apprehension about its success, Shannon rehandled much of the portrait from life on 13 March in preparation for an official viewing five days later: 'Lady Gregory came to tea with Gregory and Yeats[.] She liked the picture of her son I believe though she seemed less satisfied with it as a likeness[.] Its really much more like than it was'.[66] It was not eventually offered for hanging at the Royal Hibernian Academy.

Robert's hopes for his composition on the Death of the First Born proved over-sanguine as the prize entry was by Innes whose version 'was a glorious show of desert and pyramids, while the firstborn themselves, a muddled little group of three figures, were relegated to a shadow in the middle distance'.[67] The judgement occasioned some amusement as Innes despised his efforts at figure composition, the prime object of the exercise, preferring to concentrate all his energies on the depiction of landscape. As Gregory turned increasingly towards a manner of landscape-painting that had kinship with Innes' mode so he too considerably reduced the human content in his work: landscape was not a setting for a figure subject but figures, usually diminutive, often in consciously held poses, offset the grandeur, the distances, the strange lines and masses of natural forms. The mannerism in the handling of figures strengthens by contrast a sense of the *permanence* of landscape, giving it, as Yeats felt, the quality of vision. Given what was to be his own subsequent attitude and practice, Gregory's strictures on Shannon's 'decorative' handling of the living figure during his last months at the Slade show how decisive an influence John and Innes were to be on his development between 1906 and the time of his first one-man show in 1912.

28 Delamere Terrace,
Royal Oak.
[p.mk.9 March 1906]

My dear Mama. I'm very sorry to hear you are not well yet. I hope Galway is doing you good; when did you think of coming over? — at present my idea was to go back to Coole about the 23rd, but if you have any plans I could easily alter it.

Kennedy is very anxious for me to go abroad, but I feel that next year I should get a lot more value from the pictures. I have started painting at the Slade, but have only had one day at it at present. I am improving my composition and I think it will be interesting anyhow, but I don't know whether it will be successful; I am trying rather an experiment in composition.

I saw Yeats yesterday and read his Baile's strand additions — I think them very fine indeed; finer than anything he has done. I am trying to think about staging but find it hard to get my mind off the painting. John is sending you his Gipsy dictionary[68] — he is very depressed and rather ill just now — I hear a lot about him as he is doing drawings of a girl I know. The portrait has not had anything done to it — noone has seen it I believe, and Shannon does not say anything about doing more to it, so I don't know what he intends. I forget if I told you of the show at Agnews;[69] Ricketts has a good thing there[70] so has Shannon; but he also has a very indifferent one — he is not a forceful draughtsman, but can draw very well when he is interested sufficiently; but he does not really feel any joy in the living figure, I think, except in as much as it is decorative material.[71] I wonder if the studio will be ready before I come back; I suppose not. Cave goes away on Saturday as he has not yet recovered from his flu; he should have gone before — he has not been able to do much work. I hope to see you soon either in London or at Coole.

Your loving son
Robert Gregory.

After the production of *On Baile's Strand* that opened the Abbey in December 1904, Yeats revised the text for performances in Oxford, Cambridge and London and then 'entirely rewrote it up to the entrance of the Young Man and changed it a good deal from that on to the end, and this new version was played . . . in April 1906'.[72] Once again, against pressure of time, Gregory was to achieve a noble setting for the piece and on this occasion he took control of the lighting, experimenting to achieve moments of pictorial climax to complement the action, particularly with what Yeats through his revision had made the point at which the complex of tragic ironies begins to come to prominence with the arrival of the wildly resolute stranger who poses such a challenge to Cuchulain's allegiance to Conchubar. Dublin admired but failed to appreciate fully what an original talent the Abbey possessed in Gregory; admittedly it is the mark of a successful designer not to intrude his own work on an audience's attention at the expense of the play his settings serve to enhance, but Gregory was achieving effects of outstanding originality which there was little to equal on the rest of the British stage. Being in no way tutored as a designer for the commercial theatre, he had no lessons to unlearn in reaching for freshness of expression in his art; trained as a draughtsman in the classical tradition, he recognised the virtue of clear lines and uncluttered masses and the power of the artist to create visual tension and highlights to complement the dramatist's changing moods and moments of emotional intensity. Perhaps the very boldness and assurance of his approach, the sense of his mastery of his medium, invited audiences to take his contributions to the Abbey for granted. Certainly the most informative accounts of his work to have survived come from members of the theatrical profession who could best recognise the scope of his innovations.

In retrospect the symbolism of Shannon's portrait of Robert Gregory, whatever its merits as a painting, appears singularly unapt:[73] the patrician bearing, the assurance implicit in the carriage of the head, the ease and mastery of self that the painting suggests is the essence of the sitter's personality consorts ill with the impression conveyed by Gregory's actual work as a painter as revealed in his two exhibitions. There the mood is private, introspective, modernist rather than traditional in feeling and expression, whether one takes as one's perspective the history of European or of Irish art. Shannon's Robert Gregory is an ideal of the self as painter but an idealisation that does not, like Yeats's 'In Memory of Major Robert Gregory', attempt to encompass, even when it cannot explain, the complex antithetical drives that went to the making of his unique personality. In Shannon's statement there is little hint of soldier, scholar or horseman and no suggestion whatever of an inner, deep-rooted unease detected by the painter, Henry Lamb.

Augustus John acted as Gregory's best man when in 1907 he

married Lily Margaret Graham Parry of Rhydoldog, Rhayader, a younger contemporary at the Slade. The marriage was on 26 September, a month after their engagement. In choosing the following year to study at Jacques-Emile Blanche's atelier in Paris, *La Palette*, they joined Henry Lamb who had followed John to Paris after the demise of his Chelsea School. Photographs of this date showing Gregory clad, sportsman-like, in Norfolk suit and thick-ribbed stockings contrast markedly with contemporary descriptions of Lamb and in particular Innes, who in John's eyes 'cut an arresting figure' in Quaker hat, coloured scarf and long black overcoat.[74] It was the incongruities in Gregory's lifestyle and position that Lamb felt best accounted for both his uncertainty of performance and of direction in these years; indeed Lamb questioned whether he had a secure talent.[75] It was perhaps a similar vein of self-doubt that spurred Gregory on to apply himself rigorously to landscape painting after 1909, largely at the expense of his work in stage design — a burst of effort that culminated in two London exhibitions at the Baillie Gallery in 1912 and at the Chenil in 1914.

The currently preferred style at the Slade, where the influence of Tonks, Steer, Sickert and the New English Art Club was considerable, was Impressionist in inspiration; Ricketts and Shannon when working in oils were cultivating a Renaissance manner either Spanish or Italianate; the sympathies of Jacques-Emile Blanche, Gregory's mentor in Paris, were rooted in Impressionism, though with a flamboyant, bravura edge — to none of them did Gregory owe a profound allegiance. It is difficult now to gauge exactly which of the trio — Gregory, Innes or John — initiated a technique for painting landscape in flat colour which they each began to explore and perfect *circa* 1907–8. Though Post-Impressionism was not to have much impact on English art-circles before Fry's famous exhibition of 1910, all three were moving towards a style which has affinities with the French method.[76] The technique involved the stylisation of the essential features of a landscape into planes of flat colour, eschewing traditional representational devices to suggest distance and perspective and evoking the atmosphere of place by a patterning of colour-tones. John felt of Innes that his 'growing accentuation and delight in pattern compensated to some extent for the weak draughtsmanship'.[77] The method was consciously to promote the painterly qualities of the canvas as a lyrical, personal statement about landscape. John was to employ the technique largely for the backgrounds to his figure-studies of nudes or gypsies, though on occasion even the figures were evoked in bold flat masses of colour, the direction of the brushstrokes suggesting the modelling of the physical form.[78] Innes' deployment of the technique intimates at once his strange personality struggling with the tuberculosis that was to claim his life in 1914 and knowing by turns elation and cynical despair. It is the rhythms established by his brushwork that capture his prevailing moods: calmly undulating, vigorously assertive or jagged and nervous.[79] At his finest as in *The Waterfall* of 1910,[80] swirling, tumbling forms (there is not a single vertical on the canvas) can generate a dark, mysterious mood at once timeless and monumental yet full of potency, energy and tension, suggestive not of a transient, restless activity but of a life of endurance and perennial growth, the perpetuity behind seasonal change. Writing an appreciation of Gregory's paintings, Yeats found himself calling to mind Wordsworth's 'Leech Gatherer', feeling that his canvases 'share certain moods with great lyric poetry';[81] Innes could attain the profound elegiac note too: clear-eyed, dispassionate, rapt with intensity.

Lyricism, however, is the only serious point of contact between Innes and Gregory, for there is little that is playful or histrionic about Gregory's work. Vibrant colour is but sparingly used, reserved chiefly for imaginary landscapes where an Arcadian ease and serenity prevail or for still-life themes, such as *Roses*.[82] His preferred subjects (Coole Lake and the demesne; the shores of Galway Bay and the bleak villages near Mount Vernon, his summer home and Lady Gregory's gift on his marriage to Margaret Graham-Parry; and the wild reaches of the Burren) are a sparer, less dramatic landscape than Innes' chosen sites in Wales and the Pyrenees, harsh and angular, without majestic grandeurs and less prone to sudden changes of light. His palette is confined chiefly to a range of blues, gold, browns and grey-washed purples; as the *Illustrated London News* commented of his 1914 show:

Mr. Robert Gregory's Ireland is green after a fashion, but the chief note of his work at the Chenil Gallery is one of storm-coloured hills, dun earth and purple rocks.[83]

Such barren, impoverished vistas imposed an austere decorum: to render smooth or curvaceous the strange humped hills or oddly poised and tumbled rocks strewn across the Gort or Burren landscape where stunted trees intensify rather than relieve the mood of 'extravagant loneliness',[84] would be to succumb to sentimentality. Human forms where they occur are small in scale and usually in postures indicative of resignation; they and the mathematically precise shapes of the clusters of cottages serve by contrast to emphasize the contorted land-masses. Unlike Innes, Gregory is not moved to distort what his eye reveals into a rhetoric of despair or of protest. As with the figures in his landscapes his response is one of awareness and acceptance. Gregory's sense of rhythm is appropriately different from Innes's too: the irregularity, the 'broken' quality in the landscape is its distinctive feature and one that resists the kind of patterning with shapes that Innes exploits (though stretches of water feature in many of Gregory's paintings, reflected and inverted images rarely afford the major focus of interest that they do for Innes).[85] Rather Gregory angles his view so that, within the confines of the frame, the irregularities make their impact as such but are disposed about the canvas in pleasing asymmetrical arrangements (a distinctly Celtic quality of design); further relationships within a canvas are established less by shape than by colour parallels and contrasts bringing to the seemingly representational decorative qualities akin to abstraction. Again the familiar is made strange as rhythms which in nature incline to the chaotic are brought by art into a tentative order. There is at the heart of these works a sense of the primordial ('primitive' is an epithet that recurs throughout the press criticism of Gregory's two exhibitions); but the agelessness, the permanence of natural forms and forces does not suggest passivity, rather a gathering of intensity awaiting release. As the *Illustrated London News* observed, 'Though Mr. Gregory's Ireland is distressful, it has poetry':[86] the landscape for him is imbued with intimations of the tragic.

At times the melancholy finds release in an exaltation in natural movement, as in *Belharbour*,[87] where a cloud-rack races before the wind casting weird shadows over the bogland. Occasionally the asymmetries fail to find a point of balance, as in the visionary subject *Orpheus*,[88] where, despite the self-consciously decorative handling, the eye is attracted this way and that by the multiplicity of detail in a restless, nervy motion quite at odds with the stillness Orpheus by repute brought to animals, birds and trees with his music; the manner distracts from the matter to an irritating degree. More typical of his strengths as a painter are works like *The Natural Bridge*,[89] where the shelves of rock in Coole Park spread down beneath the trees to dam the river into a dark pool before it descends beneath the outcrop. Though summer light permeates the tree trunks, the dominant atmosphere is ominous rather than refreshing, as if one has chanced upon a place of immemorial gloom, a situation both remote and, because of its wealth of association, sinister. The stillness is alive with mystery. It is a subtle study in shades of blue deepening to tones of slate. It was Gregory's achievement to make the subject of his art what has been a major preoccupation of Irish literature — the celebration of places as rich repositories of associations, personal, historical, religious, mythical. His finished paintings demand attention and occasion reverie; they are Gregory's most private creative works, asking us to share a melancholy but by no means morbid sensibility in the contemplation of the bleak realities of Irish life and landscape — a chastening experience that nonetheless offers as a reward the appreciation of a new beauty in fortitude. This is very much the burden of Yeats's praise of Gregory as artist:

> We dreamed that a great painter had been born
> To cold Clare rock and Galway rock and thorn,
> To that stern colour and that delicate line
> That are our secret discipline
> Wherein the gazing heart doubles her might.[90]

In January 1915 Yeats wrote to Lady Gregory on seeing what was to be Robert's last publicly exhibited painting, *The Island*,[91] at the New English Art Club: 'I thought it very beautiful. It was the only thing there that I cared for. The picture is hung very well, given the central place of a wall.'[92] Its presence in the show and its position marked the completion of a rite of passage and an arrival for Gregory, an honour to Irish culture (noticeably, nothing else that was on display as 'New' or 'English' excited Yeats's approval) and the fulfilment of Lady Gregory's ambitions for her son. Within weeks of the exhibition Robert was to enlist with the 4th Connaught Rangers, transferring in January 1916 to the Royal Flying Corps. His melancholy disposition met its match in the challenge and danger of flying; the fearlessness he demonstrated frequently in his hunting and boxing pursuits now was at a premium. As Shaw observed to Lady Gregory after meeting her son at this time:

To a man with his power of standing up to danger — which must mean enjoying it — war must have intensified his life as nothing else could; he got a grip of it that he could not through art or love.[93]

The acceptance, the fortitude that the art intimates found new, exhilarating expression — 'A lonely impulse of delight' in the daily 'tumult in the clouds'.[94] Perfection of the art gave place as a priority to perfection of the life and the formerly disparate impulses defining Gregory's character found a mode of expression that spoke for the whole man:

> I balanced all, brought all to mind,
> The years to come seemed waste of breath,
> A waste of breath the years behind
> In balance with this life, this death.[95]

Unity of being was his and that in acting out of duty in a public cause. The rewards too were public: the Military Cross for displaying 'the highest courage and skill' and the Légion d'Honneur for 'many acts of conspicuous bravery'. On 23 January 1918, Gregory died in action on the North Italian front, shot down in error by an Italian pilot. Yeats was left to mourn a private and a cultural loss:

Robert Gregory painted the Burren hills and thereby found what promised to grow into a great style, but he had hardly found it before he was killed.[96]

The *Illustrated London News* concluded its short but pithy review of Gregory's 1914 exhibition by remarking that there was a degree of extravagance in the loneliness of his landscapes 'that would fit them admirably for stage-scenes to a less humorous "Playboy" '.[97] The comment is clearly intended in its context to be commendatory; the sense is not that Gregory's work partakes of the stagey. Several of Robert's designs for Abbey productions were included in his two shows and it argues considerable sensitivity in the reviewer of the *Illustrated London News* that he could perceive a serious relationship between the two aspects of Gregory's art: the intensely realised sense of place in the landscapes could hardly have been achieved with such immediacy and without reliance on rhetorical or symbolist devices had it not been for his successful endeavours in theatre design and for a very specialised kind of repertory. A good setting is more than a convenient background: it should be felt to have significance on its first impact and that significance should be felt to be increasingly right as the action progresses. From the first Gregory appears to have possessed aptitude in this respect; it was his good fortune to work either directly or at one remove from Yeats, Sturge Moore, Edward Gordon Craig and Charles Ricketts, who taught him in different ways how to realise his designs effectively in practice, encouraging him from diverse standpoints to make a virtue of artistic economy and to experiment with stylisation in the interests of a subtler and more resonant poetic suggestiveness. It was equally fortunate that working for the Irish National Theatre Society and the Abbey he had to learn to make a virtue of economic restraint. The poetry of his later landscapes was very much the product of Gregory's apprenticeship in the theatre.

Collaboration was the key to many of the successes of the Irish theatre movement in its initial stages; the décor for Yeats's *The Hour Glass* (14 March 1903) was the first instance of collaboration in the field of design with Sturge Moore working at Yeats's invitation to transform colour sketches by Gregory into an easily erected and stored, practicable scenic unit. A single performance in the Molesworth Hall necessitated something cheap and efficient; the play itself asks for an austere interior beyond which the audience must imagine richer, sunnier possible modes of living to be called to the eye of the mind by the Fool's words and the Angel's. Moore's solution was to adapt an idea of Gordon Craig's that was in itself an imaginative redeployment of the box set,[98] but with its three walls made of taut or hanging fabric, in this instance 'raw undyed' canvas (the tone under stage light was according to Yeats olive green) with a reddled floor cloth. 'As long as the costumes are dark and rich', Moore concluded, 'they will harmonise.'[99] Purple was the chosen colour, character-distinctions being effected by highlights of brown and green (' "The Angel" and "The Fool" alone being clad in tints with a little warmth in them').[100] The setting was dominated by the Wise Man's desk, tall and narrow, its proportions echoed in the two doorways (simple cutouts without actual doors) at stage right to the Wife's kitchen and at the rear to the outside world, this last surmounted by a plain square window through which a bell was visible as in Gregory's sketch. Moore preserved the extreme simplicities of Gregory's conception and the effect of imprisoning angularity; if anything, he intensified the harshness by substituting a tall cramped desk for Gregory's table[101] and by making more severe the dimensions of the doorway, which was to act as a frame in the production, not for the students as in the sketch but — developing Gregory's suggestion there — for the Angel poised at an intersection of Time with time.[102]

Yeats's play shared the bill with Lady Gregory's first independent venture for the Theatre Society, *Twenty-Five*; and between the plays Yeats lectured on 'The Reform of the Theatre'. Judging by the *Samhain* resumé of his address, he advocated four points of change: that the theatre become 'a place of intellectual excitement'; that words regain their 'sovereignty' on the stage; that acting be simplified 'especially in poetic drama'; and finally that 'the form and colour of scenery and costume' be simplified too. This last point was elaborated to be virtually a defence of the method adopted in *The Hour Glass*: there should be a background of 'a single colour, so that the persons in the play wherever they stand, may harmonise with it, and preoccupy our attention . . . as if it were the background of a portrait. . . . There must be nothing unnecessary, nothing that will distract the attention from speech and movement.' Whereas the Gregory/Moore scheme achieved a unity of design and with it a decided professionalism, the setting of *Twenty-Five* was fussy, ill-considered and amateurish. The lesson was plain. What cannot unfortunately be resolved from the few records that survive is the degree to which Yeats prescribed a scheme for *The Hour Glass* which Gregory and Sturge Moore then implemented or the degree to which their artistry inspired him to theorise. The important factor, whoever initiated it, however, was the decision to make aesthetic criteria the dominant motivating impulse behind the design rather than representational, naturalistic or superficially educational objectives.[103] To appreciate the originality of Yeats's reforms and Gregory's practice as a designer one need but compare the décor for *The Hour Glass* with the setting of a scholar's study for Irving's 1885 production of *Faust* with its vast reading-desk, heaps of ancient manuscripts, globes, retorts, shelves of books, cases of skulls, a skeleton and dried alligator carcase — 'the whole breathing the very spirit of musty Gothicism'.[104] Yeats wished to elicit from his audience a concentrated aural and intellectual response; Irving from his one that was predominantly emotional and visual; his ambition was to create 'a thoroughly authentic and atmospheric period set'.[105] In Yeats's play it is language that creates an awareness of time and place and the opposition of different modes of speech (the supernatural with the human characters, the Fool's visionary with the Wise Man's cerebral discourse) that generates atmosphere and tension. Nothing must distract attention from verbal nuance.

The criteria that made for success with *The Hour Glass* were closely followed by Gregory in two further settings for Yeats, *On*

Baile's Strand (April 1906) and *The Shadowy Waters* (December 1906): 'A background that does not insist on itself' and 'two predominant colours in remote fanciful plays. One colour predominant in actors, one in backcloth.'[106] Unfortunately scant visual evidence remains as a record of the productions. Photographs of the 'unauthorised' 1904 production of *The Shadowy Waters* (which Gregory had no hand in) indicate that the setting was merely an adaptation of Moore's design for *The Hour Glass*: a box-structure of draped canvas with, to suggest place, a heap of rope and ship's tackle down stage right, against which Forgael could recline in the opening sequence and across the full width of the stage at the rear a ground row suggesting an upward-curving gunwale or bulwark.[107] The design though adequate lacks poetic feeling; there is little of the 'remote' or 'fanciful' about it. All that Yeats retained in his 1906 production was the colour scheme of dark blues and greens. It would seem that Yeats consulted Sturge Moore initially but disliked his proffered design for *The Shadowy Waters* because its colour range would prove intrusive (black, white and brown with highlights in red) while its arrangement of sail and bulwark would, Yeats thought, prove impractical.[108] Yeats posited a semi-circular disposition for the backcloth in the manner of a cyclorama with a bulwark traversing the stage diagonally and a low-hung sail positioned downstage right but filling most of the stage as it curved round and away over the bulwark, thus creating a decidedly enclosed and intimate playing space for Forgael and Dectora's discovery of passion and relegating the querulous, drunken sailors to menacing presences, heard more than seen, in the dim recesses of the deck.[109] As Sturge Moore in the summer of 1906 was getting increasingly involved with Ricketts in promoting an English Literary Theatre Society, it doubtless fell to Robert to realise Yeats's ideas. Certainly Gregory is referred to by Yeats as the sole originator of the designs in every subsequent edition of the play, testifying to his pleasure in the result, but his description of the setting with 'decorated boat and sail', the green of the sail and the costumes against the blue of the deck and darker blue sky offset by touches of glimmering copper and gold,[110] conjures up most forcefully his own earlier recommendations to Sturge Moore:

The play is dreamy and dim and the colours should be the same — (say) a blue-green sail against an indigo blue backcloth and the mast and bulwark indigo blue. The persons in blue and green with some copper ornaments.[111]

If the production was truly dream-like in effect and avoided the fustian qualities of the 1904 version, the responsibility was largely Gregory's in involving himself in a new branch of theatre art — stage lighting.[112] Yeats began early in preparations for staging *The Shadowy Waters* to be concerned about the Abbey's lighting resources. On 5 October he wrote asking Synge to check with Henderson to ensure there was a good stock of amber lamps for the new season and continued:

I for my own purposes require a large number of blue and green lamps. During the playing of the harp the light upon the stage is green. During the rest of the play there will have to be blue ground rows. We have I think but we cannot be satisfied with suppositions, blue and green glasses for the limelight. If all these lamps are not in when I go up I wont be able to get the lighting of Shadowy Waters in order and the whole effect depends on the lighting. Robert Gregory is coming up to work at that and the scenery though a little later than me.[113]

He concluded by asking for absolute confirmation that the costumes, properties and backcloth were ready or at least in hand, since 'it will be necessary to have all these things before we begin work on the lighting'. Doubtless wanting to know what scope there was for innovation, his last question was 'as a matter of curiosity, whether Fay finds that he can work the limes from the bridge all right'. What this reveals is the surprisingly early date by which this design scheme was completed and put in preparation, that is some four or five months before the opening; and further, Yeats and Gregory's determination to rehearse the technical aspects of this production virtually from the start of that season to get them right by the most exacting of standards. Subtle control over graduating coloured light was a cumbersome business at this date requiring painstaking skill; moreover blue and green were notoriously difficult colours to manage, needing careful matching with the dyes of costumes and settings, if the results were not to be garish in the extreme.[114] Time to experiment and if necessary rework features of the design was essential if the performance were truly to appeal as a dream-vision. If Yeats's prescriptions for the reform of the theatre were to carry conviction, his own practice could in no way afford to be slapdash. In Gregory he appears to have found a like dedication that set perfection of the work beyond either personal inconvenience or prestige. A similarly sensitive collaboration between poet and artist had occurred in mounting the revised *On Baile's Strand* earlier that same year.

When first produced at the Abbey's inauguration (27 December 1904) it had also been staged much after the pattern set by *The Hour Glass*; Joseph Holloway records:

The novel staging proved most effective, the figures of the players stood well out in relief against the amber coloured draperies of which the boxed-in set was composed.[115]

It is not clear to what extent Gregory was involved at this stage or to what extent the Fays and Yeats were privately adapting the proven Moore/Gregory formula. The rich colouring was achieved by projecting amber floods against hangings of undyed jute to achieve an effect like cloth of gold, which would have offset Miss Horniman's costumes (predominantly red with grey for trimmings) with a sumptuous clarity.

Yeats's 1906 revision of the play was to give far greater weight to the arrival of the mysterious young man whom Cuchulain befriends then, despite his private intuitions, fights and kills at Conchubar's bidding, only to discover that his headstrong opponent was his own son. In revising the setting of the play Gregory chose to shift the visual focus in a way that is reflected in Yeats's different stage directions for the two versions. In 1904 the audience's attention was drawn to 'two great chairs on either side of the hall, each raised a little from the ground, and on the back of the one chair is carved and painted a woman with a fish's tail, and on the back of the other a hound', which established the opposition of Conchubar and Cuchulain as the principal theme of the play. Only after listing properties that indicate this is the great feasting chamber, a 'great ale vat' and so forth, does Yeats mention 'a large door at the back through which one can see the sea'.[116] The 1906 text gives the situation of the play at Dundealgan, then gives as the dominant image 'A big door at the back, and through the door misty light as of sea mist'; only one chair now is prominent among the many that circle the stage and the vat is replaced by a table with flagons and drinking horns.[117] Now it is the sense of an enclosed space with trappings indicative of material well-being and a mysterious world beyond that impresses itself on the audience, preparing them for the drives which determine so many of Cuchulain's responses in the action — his restlessness within the confines of the hall and his longing for the uncertainty and daring of a world without domestic allegiances and responsibilities where his heroism can renew itself. Gregory's design indeed made the doorway a commanding image: the two panels were vast, nine feet in height, of studded gold and hung with six large round shields. Moreover he added to the strangeness and threat of the young man's arrival by a simple but effective change in the lighting. While the doors were closed during the oath-taking ceremony, the grey-blue light used to evoke the mist during the scene with the beggars was replaced so that, in Willie Fay's words, 'when the doors were opened to Aoife's son, he stood silhouetted against a background of topaz blue giving an effect of sea and sky with an atmosphere that could never be obtained by paint'.[118] The sensitive staging of this episode must have given considerable dynamism to the playing of the second half of the tragedy, which is fundamentally concerned with exploring why Cuchulain behaves here so impulsively. The continuing presence of the topaz light framed by the great doors throughout the remainder of the action would also serve as an emblematic reminder of the youth, his high spirits and fearlessness, during the Blind Man's cruel taunting of Cuchulain with the knowledge that he has slain his own son; it would too provide a valuable focus resonant with significance towards or within which the actor taking the Fool's role could play out the long account of Cuchulain's madness and fight with the waves. It is a formidable episode, taxing on a performer's resources in being made up of short, flat, repeated sentences full of tragic import that the Fool in his innocence does not comprehend until the final moment ('the waves have mastered him'); the tone is one of child-like exhilaration in the fight beyond which the audience must sense a more terrible reality. By steadily endowing the lighting effect here with symbolic references, the staging would go a long way towards helping the actor avoid the hazard of bathos and unwelcome laughter so as to sustain the complex mood Yeats has devised for his dénouement. Perhaps it is no coincidence that the most graphic account of the 1906 staging of On Baile's Strand is Willie Fay's — the first interpreter of the Fool.

The device of a curtained box-setting that formed the basic principle of design for these three Yeats productions had been created in large measure to avoid what the poet considered the bane of contemporary staging — bad scene painting — bad because, however artfully or ingeniously executed, 'the moment the stage is filled the painted forms of the background are broken up and lost'.[119] All three plays required interior or at least enclosed settings where a precise environment could be readily evoked by a careful choice of colours and a central visual emblem — the scholar's desk and hourglass, a vast sail, the great doors of Dundealgan feasting chamber. Open-air situations would obviously pose problems which the curtained box could not meet. Yeats in his lecture, 'The Reform of the Theatre', had recommended finding a different mode of stylisation: 'Even when one has to represent trees or hills they should be treated in most cases decoratively, they should be little more than an unobtrusive pattern'.[120] Synge's *The Well of the Saints* (staged 4 February 1905) was the first Abbey play to extend the discussion into practice but the Colman Smith/Edith Craig designs though adequate were no more than that; and Yeats soon began to press Gregory into devising replacements.[121] That Yeats turned to Robert is indicative of his whole-hearted approval of Gregory's designs for his mother's tragedy *Kincora* staged a month after Synge's play. For a long time it remained Yeats's ideal for presenting open-air scenes, being decorative in the manner of Japanese art but wholly Irish in conception, colour-range and detail. It occasioned too a surprisingly fulsome outburst from Joseph Holloway:

The truth of the old saying 'A thing of beauty is a joy forever' struck me forcibly on seeing a full dress rehearsal of *Kincora* at the Abbey Theatre tonight. The costumes and scenery harmonised like an exquisite piece of music. I heard Lady Gregory say with motherly pride that it was her son's part in the production that pleased her most, and I don't wonder at it.[122]

Lady Gregory's pride remained undiminished by time; many years later she could recall the staging in considerable detail for Sean O'Casey's appreciation.

Kincora was a major undertaking for Gregory: not only were three quite distinct scenes to be set and changed rapidly but also it was his 'first experience of having to enlarge a finished design to many times the size of the original'[123] for he chose to execute the work personally. Bearing in mind the successful formula for *The Hour Glass* and Yeats's insistence on the decorative and suggestive in preference to the realistic or spectacular, Gregory devised a scheme of painted curtains rather than employ a definite box set for King Brian's hall at Kincora or backcloth with wing pieces for the woods at Clontarf. For the prologue, 'front-scene', where Aoibhell of the Sidhe tempts Brian to 'give up the sweetheart you have chosen, that hard sweetheart, Ireland' and go with her 'into the hidden houses of the hills', where she will give him love and eternal youth,[124] Gregory created 'a pattern of tree stems interlaced and of leaves edged with gold';[125] the foliage and contorted trunks were overwashed with grey and blue to suggest a dark, silent world in the depths of the forest; the forms were indistinct, 'suggesting without picturing a wood'[126] but were given a three-dimensional effect by the folds in the hangings catching the light and making further vertical patterns of brightness and shadow. The Great Hall, setting of the first two acts and the initial scene of the third, was suggested by a brilliant green curtain that was given some visual interest by a repeat pattern stencilled over its expanse in duller shades; this was caught up in places by shields embossed with gold designs to reveal set-piece doors with heavy mouldings. For the final scene at the battle of Clontarf where Brian is assassinated while at prayer, 'a great orange curtain filled the background' representing the King's tent.[127] All the settings toned with the costumes to advantage — the kings were similarly attired in 'red with a grey cloak and sword and a minn or ancient Irish coronet on the head. No glaring embroidery or glittering jewellry. Chief amongst the female personages is Queen Gormleith; and she wears a very bright orange dress ornamented with black and gold. The costume of the Danish warriors, who appear at the end of the play, is to be black with yellow fringes. Attendants at the palace are clad in green and brown or grey green.'[128] Class and national divisions were simply but efficiently caught, while the dressing of the three kings, Brian, Malachi and Maelmora, alike would encourage the actor playing Brian (Frank Fay) to establish his preeminence, his right to be High King, by force of temperament and authority, the qualities that win him Gormleith's love. Yeats, ever one to delight in symbolic effects achieved through design, pointed out to Joseph Holloway how the dressing of Gormleith in orange made her the dominant stage presence throughout Acts One and Two while the fluctuating of her desire between Malachi and Brian is shaping Ireland's destiny, but 'how the background of the last scene [that is the orange of the tent] blotted out her importance at the same time as the dramatist ended her career of power'.[129] Lady Gregory herself was impressed by how the vibrant orange became symbolic of Brian's greatness of spirit that won him immortality through fame, and how the colour threw into sharp relief the keening figures of Maire, Brennain and Derrick, his devoted servants, as they stood against it at the close 'in green, in red, in grey'.[130]

   At the time that Gregory embarked on the designs for *Kincora* (early November 1904), Yeats met him at Ricketts's studio; Yeats reported to Lady Gregory that Ricketts 'offered to do scenery for

a play . . . . He is full of fine ideas. If Robert wants advice about
Kincora he will give it him.'[131] What is particularly of interest in
Ricketts's concern to advise and be involved is that he had not yet
engaged in any theatre work himself, though theatre-going was a
regular activity.[132] Tantalizingly Ricketts's diaries record no
details of any discussions about scenery with Robert, his mother or
Yeats, only barbed comments on Irish politics if they chanced to be
mentioned, which makes it impossible to verify what influence *if
any* he had on Robert's solutions to the problems posed by
mounting *Kincora* at the Abbey. Equally impossible to verify is the
degree to which Gregory may have influenced Ricketts. One can
but point to remarkable parallels. Effects with curtains and
hangings are a notable feature of Ricketts's work at all stages of his
career; indeed he and his disciples Wilkinson and Rutherston
developed and refined the technique to the extent that Fuerst and
Hume in their monumental study *Twentieth-Century Stage
Decoration* (1928) designate the curtain-effect particularly English.
While Gregory only once imitated Ricketts's early method of
suspending groups of curtains against a clear cyclorama or sky-
cloth as in his first *Salomé* design of 1906, Ricketts came
increasingly to employ techniques initiated in *The Hour Glass* and
Kincora. The Death of Tintagiles (December 1912, for Granville
Barker at the St. James's Theatre) used a box set of tightly pleated
curtains with a metallic sheen lit from the stage floor to suggest
great height; these were caught back to reveal different doorways
— a narrow slit in a brick wall and, later, a huge, coffin-nail-
studded structure — to suggest the various locations within the
palace that Maeterlinck specifies.[133] For Shaw's *Saint Joan* (March
1924, at the New Theatre) Ricketts centred each scene on a
symbolically representative structure and created atmosphere by
surrounding it with appropriate curtaining or tapestries:[134] one
example — the setting for Warwick's tent was particularly
reminiscent of King Brian's at Clontarf as realised by Gregory, in
being suggested by a patterned curtain in deep folds, running stage
right to stage left with one fold flung back to reveal a descending
flight of steps. The principle behind these designs was in accord
with a philosophy of stage setting that Ricketts had outlined in 1913:

My personal bias is all towards imaginative emphasis in the preliminary
choice of scenic conditions. If 'a part is often better than the whole', it is
certainly so in scenery: a staircase alone may suggest more of the majesty
of a building than an entire palace.[135]

Gordon Bottomley describing the production of *Saint Joan* concluded: Ricketts 'invented a new kind of presentational stage . . . when he found he could mount *Saint Joan* more appropriately and conveniently by suggestion than by actualisation'.[136] But Ricketts merely refined for the commercial stage a theory and practice of theatre design in operation at the Abbey two decades previously. *The Times* obituary for Ricketts claimed 'he was in all probability the first to use pictorial curtains on the stage, as well as the first in the use of intensive colour or restricted range of colour, as, for instance, the all-red scene in *Attila* and the blue and green set in *Salomé*'.[137] Gregory had amply prepared the ground for such innovations. It was in the wake of Gregory's success with *Kincora* that Albert Rutherston tried to persuade him to take charge of design for the Mermaid Repertory or Repertoire Theatre, a task he had refused himself.[138] When in 1912–13 Rutherston under Ricketts's influence joined Norman Wilkinson as designer for Granville Barker's productions at the Savoy and the St. James's Theatres, he achieved his most conspicuous success with a woodland setting for the prologue of Shaw's *Androcles and the Lion* (1913): after the fashion of Gregory's presentation of the forest of Clontarf, he painted as a front-scene an airy woodland landscape on a billowing pleated curtain that was hung in broad folds. The method was lighter in execution than Gregory's (the effect being aimed at was, appropriately for Shaw, more fantastic and akin to caricature); but the principle was the same.[139] With all such designs, the audience's perception of pattern in the setting concentrates the eye on the movement and stance of the actors. Albert Rutherston ends his exposition of the value of curtained scenery in his 1915 lecture, 'Decoration in the Art of the Theatre' by claiming that 'The Barker Theatre is in England the only one which has the courage of experiment, and — may I be allowed to say it — thoughtful experiment'.[140] But 'thoughtful experiment' had characterised Yeats and Gregory's approach to stage design from 1903.[141] It was not in Robert Gregory's nature to be a theorist — words, as his letters reveal, he handled efficiently but not with eloquence — but the quality of his designs show that he subscribed to Ricketts and Rutherston's principles wholeheartedly, his practice anticipating their work and formulations by some years. Ricketts observed once ruefully that 'the production of our poetic drama usually fails in the sense of "concentration", in taste and in imagination';[142] Gregory's work at the Abbey is a notable exception.

Gregory's versatility is ably demonstrated by his next collaboration with his mother in staging her tragi-comedy *The White Cockade* (December 1905); it was his first attempt at a 'period' play where the date was precise and not some remote saga world of prehistory. The challenge posed by the play in production is the sustaining of the comic tone while allowing darker moods and episodes of pathos to make their mark. The great temptation with a comedy in eighteenth-century attire would be to overdress it, seeking to provoke laughter by exaggeration, pushing the style of the play towards caricature and farce. A surviving costume design — that for the Old Lady Dereen — shows Gregory's refusal to adopt the easy way: he has achieved a sense of period through the line of the light blue bodice at the neck and of the over-skirt or polonaise as it is swathed about the hips, while decoration is kept to a minimum — lace at the sleeve-ends, mauve ribbon bows on the corsage, a simply patterned petticoat of fawn spotted with brick red, and a mauve-blue cloak lined with brown.[143] Lady Dereen is a complex figure: she trusts blindly in the Stuart cause and refuses to recognise the cowardly, effete James as her king; she could appear merely ridiculous but Lady Gregory makes her an object of pity. She is a study not of self-deception which would be the obvious comic approach but a more subtle exploration of kinds of betrayal which endows her with a quiet dignity. Maire Nic Shiubhlaigh had great success in the role (Holloway thought she 'suggested Cathleen ni Houlihan at almost every turn' and found her lament for her lost king 'one of the most thrilling moments of the play')[144] and considerable support for her interpretation must have been afforded her by the grace and restraint of Gregory's costume design.

Scant details have survived concerning the setting of *The White Cockade*: Holloway notes unhelpfully that 'quite a series of beautiful historical pictures were exhibited to your gaze during its progress' and that Gregory's 'harmonious colouring' had 'charm'.[145] Of more value is his information about the atmospheric lighting effects that were experimented with:

Witness the mysterious sense of limitless expanse created by the dark blue backcloth with the pale limelight thrown on it from the front in Act III [the pier at Duncannon harbour by night], and the formation of the speck of yellow introduced into the colouring from the lamp's flickering ray as it twinkles suspended from a beacon post.[146]

After a couple of performances the staging at the end of Act II was
changed when the Williamite soldiers burst into the Kellehers' inn
in pursuit of the king who is hiding there:

The candles were extinguished and the stage became pitch dark; on the
candles being relighted only their feeble rays illuminated the scene, the
footlights not being turned on. The effect thus produced reminded one of
a Dutch interior by some old master, and the figures silhouetted against
the flickering tiny flames had a weird, creepy effect.[147]

It was such dramatic and poetic effects which helped to sustain the
play's tragi-comic tone. Holloway's untypical excitement at the
production and his pleasure for Lady Gregory ('she pardonably
waxed enthusiastic over her boy's artistic achievement')[148] offer
convincing support for a judgement of A. E. Malone, who
reviewing the first two decades or so of the Abbey's work noted
one major deficiency — that, 'except for occasional designs and
scenes by Robert Gregory, the stage effects at the Abbey Theatre
were never very impressive or striking, even if they were always
adequate'.[149]

For both Lady Gregory's The Image (November 1909) and
Douglas Hyde's The Nativity (January 1911), Gregory faced the
problem of creating a stylised open-air setting that would require
practicable units (cottages, the stable) not reducible to the kind of
patterned curtain effect achieved in Kincora. Painted backcloth and
wing pieces were inevitable. What is interesting here is how he
achieved pattern and variety. The backcloth for The Image is
essentially made up of horizontal bars of colour, a streaked and
pale-washed sky, a low-lying grey-green promontory, the sea and
the stone wall from which the characters view the bay where the
whales whose oil is to bring such wealth to the community have
been sighted. Shades of grey predominate, but the sea, catching the
sunshine, is a brighter tone (at the actors' head-height offsetting
their features with a fine clarity) that is designed to lead the eye into
the whitewashed cottage (stage left) of the Coppingers which is
balanced to the right by the dark silhouette in the shade of an
identically shaped cottage for Peggy Mahon.[150] This creates a
suitably dramatic environment, remote and secret, for so strange
a character, older than anyone can recall and with her eyes set
constantly on a heavenly reunion with her lost lover. It is a
sensitive design: in the night-time scene (Act II) when the strongest
source of light is the 'candle and firelight shining from the open

half-door of Coppinger's house',[151] the band of bright colour
representing the sea on the backcloth would catch enough of the
moonlight effects to glimmer and so add depth and form to the
scene (necessary with night scenes and silhouette-effects which can
make scenery look obviously two-dimensional). Staging the
episodes involving Peggy largely in shadow would greatly have
helped the actress, Maire O'Neill, then a mere twenty-two, to
project a convincing impersonation of a woman four times her own
age; having found an appropriate posture, she could then
concentrate on her vocal resources to characterise Peggy.

The design for *The Nativity* is simple and traditional:[152] the
stable, where the Holy Family will be disclosed, holds the centre of
the stage and the eye is led to it firmly by the line of hills and fields
on the backcloth and the sweep of the low stone wall and the
stylised thorn trees, two stage right and two left, achieved with cut-
out ground-rows. The sky pales in hue as it descends to the line of
the hills, again giving prominence to the stable. Calm, subdued in
tone and effect, it nonetheless creates a sense of expectation as all
things prepare the divine event. This was the tone struck from the
first by an ingenious lighting-effect; the stable was built of wattle
and 'through the chinks the flickering light from within strays
mysteriously into the darkness that precedes the dawn'.[153] Once
again the design is achieved with solid bands of colour; but, despite
the flatness of the technique, the setting has rhythm and a keen
feeling for dramatic possibilities. The simple and the homely is at
the point of transcendence.

Undoubtedly the triumph of Gregory's career as a stage designer
came with his work on the Deirdre plays of Yeats and Synge. Late
in life Yeats still was haunted (his own word) by the passionate,
solitary portrayal of his Deirdre by Mrs Patrick Campbell in 1908;
earlier in gratitude he had dedicated the play to her and to 'Robert
Gregory who designed the beautiful scene she played it in'.[154]
After several performances at the Abbey in the week of 9
November, Mrs Pat performed the play later that month as part of
a double-bill with the Hofmannsthal/Sophocles *Electra* at the New
Theatre, London, 'borrowing' Sara Allgood to play the first
Musician and Chrysothemis but otherwise casting the production
from her own company.[155] Fortunately several production
photographs exist to give a clear idea of Gregory's setting and
costumes as realised in the London performances.[156] A substantial
box set exactly evokes Yeats's directions for 'a rough house of
timber' through the doors and windows of which are to be seen

suggestions of a thickly wooded landscape; at the rear of the stage three steps lead up to an inner room full of hunting gear, animal skins and weapons, which is separated off from the main acting area by heavy, thickly pleated curtains. Ornament is restricted to a panel of material with a design of overlapping circles down the side borders of the curtains; at intervals about the walls are brackets with unlighted torches as Yeats specifies; there is stage right beside one doorway a brazier of logs for the musicians and to the left a low table with a chess game and simple curved stools. Gregory has created a stark and ominous playing space; it is well capable, since the entrances and windows are simply gaps in the structure without doors or hangings, of revealing as Yeats intended the arrival, departure or lurking presence of characters and of achieving a particular visual effect Yeats sought for — a poignant loneliness as the fated lovers try to calm their rising fears by playing chess while the daylight slowly fades in the woods without, reaching a point where their voices seem to come from a depth of shadow before the musicians light the torches by turn at the brazier. When light returns, the woodland landscape, Deirdre's proper element, is lost to sight, emphasizing the lovers' growing perception of being caught in a trap that has been most artfully sprung.

Though more detailed than Gregory's interior settings usually are, everything is subordinate to the need to create a precise mood of imminent disaster which motivates the heroine to explore a range of lyric feeling from despair at the thought of death to resolution for it as the only way of preserving her integrity. Even the properties dimly visible behind the curtains in the inner chamber have emblematic connotations of cruelty and sport that augment the sense of danger: it is a place of death where Naisi is dragged entangled like a boar in a net to be gutted at the whim of Conchubar's malice and where Deirdre will choose to go, proud and absolute, to find peace and revenge in suicide. From the opening of the play the chamber waits, a focus of attention, an embodiment of fate and inevitability whither the lovers *must* come for all the pathos of their struggles to resist. Gregory's design subtly complements the tragic inexorability of the play's structure. The contrast of the gloomy interior (its confines accentuated by the stylised painting of the logs from which it is supposedly built) and the woodland beyond clearly helped convey the mood Yeats wanted so effectively that later, when he envisaged staging the play with an arrangement of Craig's screens which might have necessitated abandoning windows and doors, he still wished to convey the sense of a woodland by projecting 'shadows of leaves seen on the wall beside the door under a shifting light' during the Musicians' opening exchange.[157] The original scheme had proved its worth and was not easily to be sacrificed.[158]

Synge sees Deirdre's tragedy, as did Yeats, as in part the taming and humiliating of a great spirit; he too conveys this theme by visual means. The three settings he envisages (each evoking meticulously a precise sense of place and time of year) subtly complement the play's tragic structure and underline the pathos of Deirdre's situation in her two impulsive choices — her opening the door of Lavarcham's house to Naisi and later her insisting on returning from the freedom of Alban, whither the lovers have fled, to Conchubar's fortress at Emain — that mark the passing of her springtime of independence and her summertide of passion and that bring her to a winter of loneliness and desolation. Two of Gregory's settings for *Deirdre of the Sorrows* have survived showing his sensitivity to the play's imagery of seasonal change as emblematic of Deirdre's psyche: the designs in watercolour for Acts II and III. Synge specifies for Act II that the time is 'early morning in the beginning of winter';[159] Gregory responded to the prevailing mood of the scene with a sombre setting washed with a cold, clear-grey light. The dark waters of a great bay that curves to a peninsula marking the horizon reflect a dull, lowering sky. In the foreground mounds of smooth grey rock break the surface of a grassy cliff-top on which Deirdre's rude tent is constructed (stage-left) of tree-branches and brown hangings. The stage-picture is framed by two narrow wing-pieces in the form of tree-trunks, one silvery-grey and bare, the other of dark brown bark and close black foliage suggestive of a yew. The few touches of colour — the pale green sward, the brown curtains, the cramped blackened furze-bushes accentuating the line of the rocky outcrop — serve only to stress the dominant tone of grey in the expanses of sea and sky. The atmosphere the setting conveys is bleak, still, expectant; it is a world to which the lovers in the fullness of their ecstasy might bring a vitality but 'seven years so sweet and shining' have passed and now 'the gods would be hard set to give us seven days the like of them'.[160] Gregory's setting seems to embody all the melancholy future Deirdre dreads will come into being, if she and Naisi once grow weary of their love. Fear of that possibility goads her to return to Emain preferring certain death to a lifetime of grey indifference.

Before discussing Gregory's design for Act III, something must be said of its provenance. Yeats had in his possession a design showing a despairing figure stooping in the opening of a vast tent through which can be seen a desolate winter landscape beneath a night sky. The tent is suggested by curtains of grey-brown patterned with circles in brick red and with borders in dark brown and red at top and base; above hangs a ragged black canopy. These curtains are suspended in the fashion of the box-shape devised for *The Hour Glass* but they are torn and pulled back to reveal a thicket of bare trees starkly silhouetted against the sky, the trunks white in the moonlight in contrast with what is nearer to view — a blackened mound of earth. The design has generally been described as an idealised setting for Yeats's *Deirdre*: 'idealised' because it does not accord with most of Yeats's stage-directions.[161] Gregory was not a designer who took great liberties with a dramatist's prescriptions for a setting. Though the design certainly does not match Yeats's directions, it matches Synge's perfectly. Yeats asks for a wooden cabin and that was what Gregory provided; Synge asks for a 'Tent below Emain', and that, to judge by the critic of the *Daily Express*, is what the Abbey audience saw: 'the third act sees the arrival of Deirdre and Naisi in a bare brown tent . . . parting the curtains, a newly-made grave is discerned'.[162] Both dramatists require few properties — Yeats specifies the brazier, chessboard and curtained recess;[163] Synge calls for tables on which an old woman arranges food and fruits and asks that the hangings be practicable (Deirdre remarks that though Conchubar has 'riches in store for us it's a shabby, ragged place he's put us waiting', then pulling at a curtain in distaste and despair she discovers 'new earth on the ground and a trench dug').[164] The design shows two tables on left and right of the parted curtains, bearing urns and a flagon and a bowl of fruit. In the catalogue of paintings exhibited by Gregory in June 1912 at the Baillie Gallery, item 8 is entitled 'Scene for Deirdre of the Sorrows, Act III . . . . . . 15 gns'. The critic of *The Morning Post* (5 June 1912) considered that 'Of the stage scenes, that for "Deirdre of the Sorrows" (8) is the most impressive'. He continued by describing the exhibit in detail:

The long, straight lines of the curtain, and the tree trunks, pale in the troubled starlight, emphasise the anguish of the crouching figure.[165]

It is not clear whether Yeats bought the design from the exhibition or whether Gregory subsequently gave it to him. The evidence shows beyond a doubt that the design was for Synge's play, not for Yeats's *Deirdre*.

Ricketts's influence on this setting is unmistakable (especially of the *Salomé* design of 1906 and some features of his work on *Attila* (1907) for Oscar Asche and *King Lear* (1909) for Herbert Trench). But inspiration has transcended influence: the colour-scheme of grey-washed browns is peculiarly Gregory's own, as are the gaunt stylised trees of the backcloth. What impresses is the ease with which the securely curtained box, the hall-mark of Gregory's design schemes, here opens up as the action progresses to reveal more and yet more of the bleak landscape without, transforming Conchubar's trap, as its nature becomes ever clearer to the lovers, into a place of desolation that enfolds them all, the High King included. How powerful the effect would be in performance within this setting of Synge's direction, 'a red glow is seen behind the grave',[166] at the point of climax when Naisi lies buried and Fergus in revolt has set Emain on fire. The palid hue of the backcloth would reflect the light strongly and the browns and reds of the curtains would begin to glow as if Conchubar's whole world were aflame with destruction. While ironically as that chill, forbidding scene begins to burn, Deirdre knows only that 'it is a cold place I must go to be with you, Naisi'.[167] At Deirdre's suicide, 'the red glow fades, leaving the stage very dark'[168] and the play ends with voices only: Lavarcham keens the lovers and Conchubar, reduced by frantic despair to senility, moans querulously for help and pity. The great curtains, pulled apart by the characters in their anguish, appear now in dark, tattered and looming silhouette, a fitting emblem for a world in ruins destroyed by unassuageable passions. In this way a tragic conflagration leaving in its wake only 'a hard and naked earth'[169] has been suggested without recourse to any spectacular effects but through the simplest devices of stylisation, so that attention never wavers from its focus on the characters in their suffering:

Because of me there will be weasels and wildcats crying on a lonely wall where there were queens and armies and red gold, the way there will be a story told of a ruined city and a raving king and a woman will be young for ever.[170]

The secret of Gregory's success lay in his choosing to offer support for the powerfully visual quality of Synge's writing and not to compete with it. Given this noble setting for high tragedy it is regrettable that circumstances prevented Gregory from staging Sophocles' *Antigone* with Sara Allgood as he had planned in 1906 and that by the time the Abbey turned to Greek drama in the 1920s Gregory was dead.

The production of *Deirdre of the Sorrows* (13 January 1910) brought Gregory's association with the Abbey virtually to an end — but not quite: the parting was to be more in sorrow than in triumph. The principal reason for his abandoning theatre business would appear to be a desire to dedicate himself wholeheartedly to easel painting at least temporarily in preparation for his exhibitions. A further reason would seem to be Yeats's growing involvement with Edward Gordon Craig and his enthusiasm for Craig's system of scenic decoration involving the use of screens. On 5 January 1910, anticipating a meeting with Craig, Yeats informed Lady Gregory from Woburn Buildings: 'I am inclined to get his advice on all our scenic difficulties — perhaps to come to Dublin for the purpose. It would be a fine new start for us and put new force in much that we do'. He took care to add: 'It would not prevent Robert designing but would give us all the mechanism — a mountain to put our mountain on.'[171] Wary of Lady Gregory's often sceptical responses to his enthusiasms, Yeats was being markedly tactful.

Within a year the Abbey had a set of screens to Craig's specifications and on 12 January 1911 Yeats's *The Hour Glass* and Lady Gregory's *The Deliverer* were staged employing the new system. There was general acclaim for Yeats's morality as 'entirely beautiful and convincing'[172] in its new guise; but Lady Gregory's bitter satire was an infelicitous choice by which to test the new scenic arrangements. Its mood is not poetic and elevated but bleak and sarcastic in its attack on Irish vacillation and apathy. The Israelites are seen stoning to death Moses, their would-be deliverer, out of envy of his fearlessness and dread of the challenge of escaping Egypt to create a new life. The deployment of Kiltartan dialect in the dialogue would have forced analogies home on the Dublin audience; Yeats himself quite openly referred to it as Lady Gregory's 'Parnell' play.[173] *The Deliverer* was bound to provoke discomfort, indeed it aimed at doing so. While the Abbey as 'a laboratory for dramatic experiment'[174] was right to explore disinterestedly where Craig's system would work and where not, it was a gross error of judgement on Yeats's part to select Lady Gregory's play when the screens received their first public showing. Ill-feeling provoked by the play was bound to be directed in some measure at the mode of presentation. The critic of *The Times* found the setting impressive — 'several square pillars with a plain background ranging obliquely across the stage . . . the costuming is bright and looks well against the plain surroundings';[175] and the *Freeman's Journal* thought the 'vastness' of it all 'with its temple pillars and amber lighting' resplendent but deemed it quite out of keeping with the play, for the pithy political realism of the action was not in accord with the evocative spaciousness of the scenery.[176] Joseph Holloway considered Craig's innovation an 'affected failure' and found obvious relish in recording Sara Allgood's view of Lady Gregory's play as 'Tripe!'[177] Yeats as was his custom addressed the audience from the stage after the performance and doubtless seeking to defend his own enthusiasm for Craig, blamed the failure of *The Deliverer* on the costumes. Holloway describes these as 'unsightly and ungainly . . . The ladies wore a sort of short hobble skirt that reached a little below the knees and brought to mind to Mr. Hughes *The Playboy*'s description of "the twelve eastern maidens in their shifts" '.[178] It was generally believed that they were the work of Gordon Craig: those for *The Hour Glass* had indeed been 'carried out from sketches supplied by Craig';[179] those for *The Deliverer* were, however, the work of Robert Gregory. In a difficult moment, Yeats had forgotten his scruples.

Early the previous November Robert had written apologetically to his mother, busy rehearsing *The Deliverer* in Dublin:

My dear Mama — I'm very sorry I lost your letter in which you talked of Moses costumes. I got it just as I was going hunting, glanced through it, and gave it to M[argaret, his wife] to read, saying I'd read it again when I came back; M put it away carefully, but it can't be found. Will you write about it again. I'm sorry to give you the trouble.[180]

Lady Gregory must have replied promptly for by 8 November Robert had finished her commission and despatched it to Dublin with the following covering letter:

I have sent off tonight sketches for Moses. (I just remember I have written 'Joseph' instead of 'Moses' on his costume). You had better send them to Miss Block I think, with measurements. I don't see Miss A[llgood] in these garments. I think they are best fitted to the leaner members. Miss O'N[eill] would look well in them.

(Sara Allgood and her sister Maire O'Neill played Malachi's Wife and Dan's Wife respectively). Two days later, presumably in response to a criticism by his mother or the actor (J. M. Kerrigan), Gregory wrote promising 'another Moses design — the rest can be used for anyone for whom they are suitable'.

It was unfortunate that Yeats focussed his criticism on the costume designs. The screens were not to prove the inestimable benefit to the Abbey he had supposed; their use was infrequent and rarely successful other than with *The Hour Glass*. Interestingly the critic of the *Freeman's Journal* in attempting to explain his own dissatisfaction with Craig's experiments drew attention to a number of factors that limited their operation and effect:

One did not get, however, the sense of space which was intended by the artist. Possibly this is the fault of the construction of the theatre, the proscenium being so close to the auditorium, but it seemed to be in some measure due to the arrangement of the background. . . and why was there so much amber and so little white light?[181]

Had Craig personally supervised the installation of his screens and directed the first plays to use them, these limitations might have been overcome and the worth of the invention proven. It was a misjudgement by Yeats to lay the blame in but one quarter. Was it perhaps to redeem a difficult situation that in March 1913 he wrote informing Lady Gregory of Craig's excitement on seeing some of Robert's designs and of his own decision to include some of Robert's theatre work in a 'refurbished' collected edition by Bullen of his writings? He explained: 'The books will be rearranged, all the *Samhains* and theatre essays in general making up one volume, and it is into this volume I would like to get Robert's work.'[182] To Bullen he argued the case for including 'two of Gregory's designs' on interesting historical grounds which attest to Yeats's sense of the value and innovation of Robert's methods and achievement:

Coming at this moment when people have in their memories the Reinhardt productions, the scenery and costumes of the Russian Ballet, the Barker productions of Shakespeare — all examples of the new decorative method — it would probably get considerable attention.[183]

He is in part referring to his own theories of stage design but also to Gregory's practice. It is proud company he keeps, but fitting: here is Gregory's proper place along with Ricketts and with Craig. O'Casey, ever alert to Irish bombast and pretension, had no irony in mind, when, after talking with Lady Gregory about her son and seeing examples of his work at Coole, he observed:

When Robert Gregory fell on the hilly soil of Italy, Ireland may have lost an Irish, and more colourful, Gordon Craig.[184]

This is a fine epitaph; and yet, in arguing that Gregory's achievement in the art of stage design deserves to be viewed in an international context, it is imperative to stress that his best work was for plays that called richly on his Irish sensibility, when he could make 'visible through his art the beauty of what had been looked upon but as barrenness'.[185] This was a quality that his art as painter and designer shared with his mother's art as dramatist and one which she took pleasure in observing. Perhaps the finest testimony of the way the strengths of Gregory's artistry reflected the inner strengths of the man which were in their turn the reflection of a parental and national inheritance was expressed by Sir Arthur Clay. On 23 January 1905 Sir Arthur wrote to Lady Gregory about her son who was then staying as a guest at Hyde Park Gate during his Slade years; a chance occurrence had allowed the older man, himself a painter of some repute, to see the younger with a sudden clarity of insight:

My dear Lady Gregory,

I must write a note to tell you how (agreeably) startled I was by a picture of a weaver's house which Robert has shown me.

I had not before seen anything he had done and had not the slightest idea that he was so far and so successfully advanced.

Prophecy is dangerous but I shall be as much disappointed as surprised (which is putting it strongly) if he does not do great things.

My only crticism is that the picture is almost *too* good for his age — it does not give the impression of being the work of a young man — the excellence of the values — the lighting — the sobriety & breadth of treatment and the reticence — suggest a long experience in the painter! The only explanation is that he has lived all his life in an atmosphere friendly to the development of the higher artistic nature — and that the 'feeling' by which he is led to right selection of method is hereditary — I have no doubt that this is the true explanation — the same qualities of thought and taste are shown in his conversation which is far in advance of his years. . .

Here, exactly delineated, is the friend of Ricketts and Augustus John, the Gregory celebrated in Yeats's elegies, the painter of the Burren wastes, and the Abbey's first designer: self-effacing, subtly poetic, Irish.

NOTES

A NOTE ON REFERENCES TO THE COOLE EDITION

In this volume all references to Lady Gregory's works in the Coole Edition are referred to by their title and number in the edition: e.g. *Gods and Fighting Men*, C.E.2. Bibliographical details are given below. The Edition is published in Great Britain by Colin Smythe Ltd., and except for *Seventy Years*, by Oxford University Press Inc., New York, in North America.

1   *Visions and Beliefs in the West of Ireland*, with a foreword by Elizabeth Coxhead (1970).
2   *Cuchulain of Muirthemne*, with a foreword by Daniel Murphy (1970).
3   *Gods and Fighting Men*, with a foreword by Daniel Murphy (1970).
4   *Our Irish Theatre*, with a foreword by Roger McHugh (1972).
5   *Collected Plays I, The Comedies* (1971).
6   *Collected Plays II, The Tragedies and Tragic-Comedies* (1971).
7   *Collected Plays III, Wonder and the Supernatural Plays* (1971).
8   *Collected Plays IV, Translations, Adaptations and Collaborations* (1971).
    The Collected Plays were edited, with forewords to each volume, by Ann Saddlemyer.
9   *The Kiltartan Books* (containing the *Poetry, History* and *Wonder Books*), with a foreword by Padraic Colum (1972).
10 *Sir Hugh Lane, His Life and Legacy*, with a foreword by James White (1973).
11 *Poets and Dreamers*, with a foreword by T. R. Henn (1974).
12 *A Book of Saints and Wonders*, with a foreword by Edward Malins (1972).
13 *Seventy Years 1852–1922*, edited with a foreword by Colin Smythe (1974). Published in the U.S.A. by Macmillan Publishing Co. Inc., New York, in 1976.
14 *The Journals, part I: Books 1–29*, edited and with a foreword by Daniel Murphy (1978).
15 *The Journals part II: Books 30–44*, edited by Daniel Murphy, and with an Afterword by Colin Smythe (1987).
16 *The Lectures*, with a foreword by A. Norman Jeffares.
17 and 18   *The Shorter Writings*, edited and with a foreword by Mary FitzGerald.
19 *The Autobiography of Sir William Gregory*, transcribed by Lady Gregory, edited by Colin Smythe. With a foreword by Edward McCourt (1987).
20 Mr. *Gregory's Letter-Box 1813–85*, with a foreword by Jon Stallworthy (1981).
21 will contain a General Index to the Edition, a Bibliography of Lady Gregory's writings, and a list of the books in Coole Library.

General Editors of the Coole Edition: T. R. Henn and Colin Smythe

INTRODUCTION
Ann Saddlemyer and Colin Smythe

1 'Where Wild Swans Nest', *Inishfallen, Fare Thee Well* (Macmillan, London, 1949), p. 150, *Autobiographies II* (Macmillan, London, 1981), p. 121.
2 Quoted by A. Norman Jeffares, *W. B. Yeats: Man and Poet* (Routledge & Kegan Paul, London, 1949), p. 106.
3 Elizabeth Coxhead, *Lady Gregory, A Literary Portrait* (Macmillan, London; Harcourt Brace & World, New York, 1961; 2nd edition Secker & Warburg, London, 1966); Michelle Dalmasso, *Lady Gregory et la Renaissance Irlandaise* (Université de Provence, Aix-en-Provence, 1982); Micheál MacLiammóir, 'Yeats, Lady Gregory, Denis Johnston' (*The Bell*, VI, 1). Other relevant works include Ann Saddlemyer, *In Defence of Lady Gregory, Playwright* (Dolmen Press, Dublin, 1966); Anne Dedio, *Das Dramatische Werk von Lady Gregory* (Francke Verlag, Berne, 1967); Hazard Adams, *Lady Gregory* (Bucknell University Press, Lewisburg, 1973); Colin Smythe, *A Guide to Coole Park, Home of Lady Gregory* (Colin Smythe, Gerrards Cross, 1973, revised and enlarged, 1983); Edward A. Kopper Jr., *Lady Isabella Persse Gregory* (Twayne Publishers, Boston 1967); E. H. Mickhail, editor, *Lady Gregory, Interviews and Recollections* (Macmillan, London; Barnes & Noble, New York, 1977); and Mary Lou Kohfeldt, *Lady Gregory, The Woman Behind the Irish Renaissance* (Atheneum, New York; Andre Deutsch, London, 1985). See also E. H. Mikhail, *Lady Gregory: An Annotated Bibliography of Criticism* (Whitston, Troy, N.Y., 1982).
4 Lady Gregory, *Coole* (Dolmen Press, Dublin, 1971), p. 47.
5 *Ibid.*, p. 41.

'PERFECTION OF THE LIFE': LADY GREGORY'S AUTOBIOGRAPHICAL WRITINGS
Mary FitzGerald

1 *The Poems of W. B. Yeats: A New Edition*, ed. Richard J. Finneran (Macmillan, New York, 1983), p. 246. These lines were originally part of 'Coole and Ballylee' and were thus apparently written with Lady Gregory in mind. Cf. Finneran, *Editing Yeats's Poems* (Macmillan Press, London and Basingstoke; St. Martin's Press, New York, 1983), p. 34.
2 *Seventy Years*, C.E.13, p. 197.
3 *Our Irish Theatre*, C.E.4, p. 57.
4 Memoirs, Holograph version, in the Henry W. and Albert A. Berg Collection of the New York Public Library, Astor, Lenox and Tilden Foundations.
5 *Seventy Years*, p. 152.
6 Diaries, Berg Collection.
7 See note 2 above.
8 *The Autobiography of Sir William Gregory* (John Murray, London, 1894); *Mr. Gregory's Letter-Box, 1813–1835* (Smith Elder, London, 1898), *Our Irish Theatre: A Chapter of Autobiography* (A. G. Putnam's Sons, New York, 1913 and London, 1914); *Hugh Lane's Life and Achievement* (John Murray,

London, 1921; E. P. Dutton, New York, 1922); *Coole* (Cuala Press, Dublin, 1931).
9 *Lady Gregory's Journals, Part 1*, C.E.14. Volume 2 of the *Journals* is forthcoming, and there are plans to publish the diaries, which predate the journals.
10 Journals, March 1925. Berg Collection.
11 Letters to John Quinn, Manuscript Room, New York Public Library, Astor, Lenox and Tilden Foundations; and Elizabeth Longford, *Pilgrimage of Passion: The Life of Wilfrid Scawen Blunt* (Weidenfeld & Nicolson, London, 1979; Knopf, New York, 1980).
12 Journals, March 1925, Berg Collection.
13 See note 9 above.

THE CLOUD OF WITNESSES
Mary Lou Kohfeldt Stevenson

1 *Seventy Years*, C.E.13, p. 1.
2 *Ibid.*, p. 3.
3 Genealogical information about the Persses throughout this article is from their entry in *Burke's Irish Family Records* (Burke's Peerage, London, 1976).
4 Folklore Archives, University College, Dublin. Collected by Sean O'Flannagain, 15 February 1938, in Ard Rathain, Dun Cillin, Co. Galway, from Maidhei Connors, farmer, eighty years old, MS.455.
5 Sir William Gregory, *Autobiography*, ed. Lady Gregory 2nd. edition (John Murray, London, 1894), p. 41.
6 *Seventy Years*, p. 5.
7 Gregory Holograph Memoirs, Vol. 10. Henry W. and Albert A. Berg Collection, New York Public Library, Aston, Lenox & Tilden Foundations.
8 Holograph Diaries, Vol. 12, 11 April 1896. Berg Collection.
9 Charles Kickham, *Knocknagow* (James Duffy, Dublin 1879), Chapter 32.
10 Gregory, Holograph Diary, Vol. 12 11 April 1896. Berg Collection.
11 Gregory, Holograph Memoirs, Vol. 9. Berg.
12 *Ibid.*, Vol. 1.
13 Folklore Archives, University College, Dublin, MS.455.
14 *Seventy Years*, p. 5.
15 *Ibid.*, pp. 22–23.
16 Gregory, Holograph Memoirs, Vol. 10, Berg.
17 *The Kiltartan Books*, C.E. 9, p. 19.
18 *Sir Hugh Lane: His Life and Legacy*, C.E.10, p. 27.
19 *Ibid.*, p. 28.
20 Gregory, Holograph Diaries, Vol. 10, p. 63, Berg.
21 Gregory, Holograph Memoirs, Vol. 2, Berg.
22 *The Kiltartan Books*, p. 17.
23 *Ibid.*
24 *Ibid.*
25 *The Spirit of the Nation*, ed. Charles Gavan Duffy (James Duffy, Dublin, 1845), p. 6.
26 *Seventy Years*, p. 14.
27 Gregory, Holograph Memoirs, Vol. 2, Berg.

28 *Seventy Years*, p. 13.
29 Gregory, Holograph Memoirs, Vol. 3, Berg.
30 *Ibid.*
31 *Our Irish Theatre*, C.E.4, p. 44.
32 Malcolm Brown, *The Politics of Irish Literature* (University of Washington Press, Seattle, 1972), p. 194.
33 *Seventy Years*, p. 1.
34 *Ibid.*, p. 17.
35 Gregory, Holograph Memoirs, Vol. 9, Berg.
36 *Seventy Years*, p. 10.
37 Gregory, Holograph Memoirs, Vol. 2, Berg.
38 *Seventy Years*, p. 10.
39 *Ibid.*, p. 11.
40 *Ibid.*, p. 12.
41 *Ibid.*, p. 11.
42 Gregory, Holograph Memoirs, Vol. 2, Berg.
43 *Ibid.*
44 *Seventy Years*, p. 14.
45 Gregory, Holograph Memoirs, Vol. 10, Berg.
46 *Seventy Years*, pp. 14–15.
47 George Moore, *Vale. Hail and Farewell*, (Appleton, New York, 1920), p. 184.
48 Gregory, Holograph Diaries, Vol. 12, 20 May 1896, Berg.
49 Gregory, Holograph Memoirs, Vol. 10, Berg.
50 *Seventy Years*, p. 453.
51 *Ibid.*, p. 4.
52 *Ibid.*, pp. 15–16.
53 Gregory, Holograph Memoirs, Vol. 10, Berg.
54 *Seventy Years*, p. 16.
55 W. B. Yeats, *Memoirs*, ed. Denis Donoghue (Macmillan, London and New York, 1972), p. 190.
56 Gregory, Holograph Memoirs, Vol. 10, Berg.
57 *Ibid.*, Vol. 8.
58 *Ibid.*, Vol. 10.
59 *Ibid.*
60 *Ibid.*
61 *Seventy Years*, p. 18.
62 Gregory, Holograph Memoirs, Vol. 10., Berg.
63 *Ibid.*
64 *Ibid.*
65 *Seventy Years*, p. 20.
66 Gregory, Holograph Memoirs, Vol. 10, Berg.
67 *Ibid.*
68 Lady Gregory, Letter to Lennox Robinson. Robinson Papers, Manuscript Room, Morris Library, Southern Illinois University, Carbondale, III. No. 74, 3 July 1926.
69 George Eliot, *Middlemarch*, London 1872, Ch. 3.

THE MARRIAGE
Brian Jenkins

1 Anne Fremantle, *Three-Cornered Heart* (New York, 1971), pp. 97–8.
2 *Ibid.*
3 William Gregory (WHG) to Bess Gregory, 17 August 1873, Gregory Papers, Robert W. Woodruff Library, Emory University (copyright © 1985 Anne de Winton and Catharine Kennedy). All manuscript citations are to the Gregory Papers unless otherwise identified.
4 *Tuam Herald*, 9 June 1877.
5 Sir Henry Layard to WHG, 12 September 1877, Layard Papers, British Museum (BM) Add. Ms. 38949.
6 WHG to Layard, 27 September 1877; F. Standish to WHG, 20 March 1878.
7 WHG to Layard, 7 August 1879.
8 WHG to Bess Gregory, 29 October 1873.
9 WHG to Augusta Persse, 21 March 1879.
10 *Seventy Years*, C.E.13. p. 26 n. 2.
11 WHG to Augusta Persse, 28 January 1880.
12 WHG to Augusta Persse, 1 February 1880.
13 James O'Hara to WHG, 14 February 1880.
14 C. Redington to WHG, 15 February 1880.
15 WHG to Layard, 15 February 1880.
16 WHG to Augusta Persse, 16 February 1880; *ibid.*, 1 February.
17 WHG to Layard, 17 May 1883; *ibid.*, 9 March 1880.
18 Diary of Lady Layard, 7 May 1880, Layard Papers, BM Add. MS. 46157.
19 WHG to Layard, 9 May 1889.
20 WHG to Augusta Gregory (AG), 13 February 1881.
21 WHG to Layard, 6 January 1883.
22 WHG to Layard, 26 October 1880.
23 WHG to Layard, 25 November 1882.
24 WHG to Layard, 27 June 1883.
25 WHG to AG, 11 June 1886.
26 WHG to AG, 4 January 1884.
27 WHG to AG, 22 September 1883.
28 WHG to AG, 12 January 1884; *ibid.*, 5 June 1890.
29 Sir Mountstewart Elphinestone Grant Duff, *Notes from a Diary − 1881–86*, 2 vols. (John Murray, London, 1899), vol. 2, pp. 175–178.
30 WHG to AG, 3 October 1883.
31 WHG to AG, 13 January 1884.
32 WHG to AG, 8 April 1884.
33 Rev. William Dodge to WHG, 11 June 1884.
34 AG to Comte de Basterot, 17 March 1892.

LADY GREGORY AND WILFRID SCAWEN BLUNT
Elizabeth Longford

1 *Seventy Years*, C.E.13, p. 436.
2 Blunt Papers, Fitzwilliam Museum, Cambridge MS 454/1975 1 April 1920.

3 Elizabeth Longford, *A Pilgrimage of Passion: The Life of Wilfrid Scawen Blunt* (Weidenfield & Nicolson, London, 1979), p. ix.
4 Edith Finch, *Wilfrid Scawen Blunt* (Jonathan Cape, London, 1938) p. 41, and also quoted in *Pilgrimage of Passion*, p. 132.
5 Blunt Papers, MS 44/1975, p. 53.
6 Lady Gregory's diary 1880–1882, Robert W. Woodruff Library, Emory University.
7 *Ibid.*
8 *Seventy Years*, C.E.13, p. 33.
9 *The Secret History of the English Occupation of Egypt*, (Fisher Unwin, London, 1907. Republished Gregg, Hampshire, 1969) p. 197.
10 Lady Gregory, diary.
11 *Ibid.*
12 *Ibid.*
13 *Ibid.*
14 Diary of Lady Anne Blunt, British Library, Add. Ms. 53917.
15 *Seventy Years*, p. 47.
16 Blunt Papers, *Alms to Oblivion* MS. 324/1975 p. 53. (Repeated in MS. 44, pp. 205–7).
17 *Ibid.*
18 *Ibid.*, p. 55
19 *Ibid.*, p. 56–9. Quoted in *Pilgrimage of Passion*, p. 91.
20 Lady Gregory's diary.
21 *Ibid.*
22 *Seventy Years*, p. 46.
23 *Seventy Years*, p. 51. 'The Trial of Arabi Pasha' by Blunt appeared in *The Times*, 27 November 1882, p. 8c.
24 Blunt Papers, MS. 44, pp. 207 and 209–15.
25 *Ibid.*, MS. 32, 9 May 1892.
26 *Seventy Years*, p. 54.
27 *Pilgrimage of Passion*, p. 268.
28 *Seventy Years*, p. 203; and *Pilgrimage of Passion*, p. 426.
29 Blunt Papers, MS. 32.
30 *Ibid.*, MS. 343/1975, 29 November 1894, (Repeated in MS. 3/1975).
31 Sonnet 6.
32 Anne Gregory, *Me & Nu; Childhood at Coole* (Colin Smythe, Gerrards Cross, 1970), p. 61.
33 Blunt Papers, MS. 7/1975, 8 January 1905 and MS. 15/1975, 15 May 1915.
34 *Ibid.*, MS. 36 and MS. 374; also *Pilgrimage of Passion*, p. 349.
35 *Me & Nu* p. 29.
36 Blunt Papers, MS. 375, 19 October 1903.
37 *Ibid.*, MS. 417/1976, 6 and 11 January 1914 MS 14/1975, 6–19 January 1914.
38 *Seventy Years* pp. 478–80.
39 Blunt Papers, MS. 434/1975, 25 November 1916. MS. 16/1975, same date.
40 *Ibid.*, MS. 10, 12 February 1910.
41 *Ibid.*, MS. 13, 28–29 December 1913.
42 *Ibid.*, MS. 14/1975
43 *Ibid.*, MS. 8/1975, 9 August 1906. Letters, 1 August 1906, D. Carleton to Blunt, *Pilgrimage of Passion*, p. 368.
44 Blunt Papers, MS. 3, 29 November 1894.
45 Preface to *My Diaries* (Knopf, New York 1921), p. xiv.

46   Letter in possession of Lady Mary Lyon.
47   Sonnet 7.
48   Sonnet 12.

COMMENTARY TO 'A WOMAN'S SONNETS'
James Pethica

1   George Moore, *Ave* (Heinemann, London, 1911) p. 275, *Vale* (Heinemann, London, 1914) p. 173.
2   Blunt's diary, quoted in Elizabeth Longford, *A Pilgrimage of Passion*, (Weidenfeld & Nicolson, London, 1979) p. 193.
3   No manuscript copy of the poem seems to have survived, but the text as published in the Kelmscott volume (pp. 71–72) presumably includes alterations by Blunt, for he had written in 1888 when first asking to use the poem: 'Of course if you are ever likely to publish a volume of your own I wd not do it, and I have altered a few lines & added a couple of verses. But it wd be pleasant to me to have this little pearl in my oyster' (Letter of 27 August 1888, MS. 65b1272 Berg Collection).
4   Berg Collection 65b1291. Lady Gregory omitted this passage when using the letter in her memoirs (*Seventy Years*, C.E.13, pp. 260–61). 'From words by A. G.' remained in the margin by the poem.
5   Undated letter (7 October 1891), Berg Collection 65b3456/v.
6   Sotheby auction catalogue p. 13 for 20–21 March 1972.
7   Undated letter (14 October 1891), Berg Collection 65b3457, i.
8   MS. 31–1975, Fitzwilliam Museum, Cambridge.
9   She had written to Blunt disarmingly on 17 May 1883: 'I hope all yr political talk did not distract yr mind from yr poems wh ought to engross you just now — I wrote a sonnet once, & a song — a prologue — & several translations — & am nearly as good as a rhyming dictionary' Undated letter, Berg 65b3440, ii.
10   Diary entry for 29 December 1913, Fitzwilliam MS. 416–1975, p. 66.
11   One of her letters to Blunt in summer 1891 for example presumably refers to a poem sent to him: 'I am glad you liked the lines — If you put the idea they express into better words (as you are sure to do) please let me see them. They are yours, I did not keep a copy' Berg 3456/i.
12   Blunt's diary, quoted by Longford, p. 194. His diary also gives some account of the ending of the affair: 'It ended by a mutual pact made between us in the summer of 1883 at the moment of my leaving for India that this [passionate] part of our friendship should be replaced by one of a saner and less intimate kind' Fitzwilliam MS. 44–1975 p. 207.
13   The title of Lady Gregory's play *A Losing Game* echoes this line accidentally. A letter dated 25 November 1902 from John Quinn to Lady Gregory shows that this title was chosen by the editor of *The Gael*, which published the play in America in December 1902. The original title, *Twenty-Five*, referred to a card game which was thought unlikely to be widely known in America (Quinn papers, MS. division NYPL).
14   Longford, p. 287.
15   This ambivalence is paralleled by emendations made in Blunt's diary. His fair copy reads: 'we found comfort in each other's arms. . . She wrote them for me as a farewell to our passion and put them in my hand the morning that

we parted after a last night spent together in the room over the bow window at Crabbet.' (Longford p. 191, p. 194). An earlier draft (Fitzwilliam Museum MS. 44–1975) shows 'arms' as an addition above a deleted 'affection'. Similarly, 'put them in my hand. . . Crabbet' one of few confirmations of the physicality of the affair, is also a later addition.

16 W. B. Yeats, *A Vision* (Macmillan, London, 1937) p. 171.

17 E. Coxhead, *Lady Gregory: A Literary Portrait*, (Macmillan, London, 1961) pp. 39–40.

18 *The Sketch*, 25 March 1896 (p. 376), but the story was written in 1894.

19 *Ibid*.

20 *Passim*, Vols. 11 and 12 holograph diary, Berg Collection. The main plot of 'Dies Irae' seems to have been based on an actual marital break-up (Lady Gregory noted in her diary that the story was 'founded on the Marcus Lynchs') but its ending is clearly fictional.

21 Holograph Memoirs v. 13 (Berg Collection), entry dated 22 May 1918. Published in *Lady Gregory's Journals 1916–30* ed. Lennox Robinson (Putnam, London, 1946) p. 33.

22 *Grania, Tragedies & Tragic-Comedies*, C.E. 6, p. 21.

23 Berg Collection, holograph notebook 64b8034, though this change might be accounted for by variants in the Grania legend on which the play is based.

24 Lady Gregory refers several times to Blunt's 'extraordinary good looks' (*Seventy Years*, p. 35), in their correspondence and elsewhere. His charisma was notorious — Margot Asquith, for example, considered him 'one of the four best-looking men' she had ever seen (*The Autobiography of Margot Asquith* (Thornton Butterworth, London, 1920), p. 185).

25 *Grania*, p. 20.

26 Coxhead, pp. 146–47. Later critics have followed Coxhead in remarking on the autobiographical element in *Grania*, but without attempting to clarify it. See M. Dalmasso, *Lady Gregory et la Renaissance Irlandaise* (Publications Université de Provence, 1982), p. 323. Kopper in *Lady Gregory* (Twayne, Boston, 1976), p. 99, suggested that in *Grania* Lady Gregory "attempts to cope with the natural repressions caused by her widowhood".

27 Notes to *Spreading the News*, *Comedies*, C.E.5, p. 253.

28 See W. B. Yeats, *Memoirs*, ed. D. Donoghue (Macmillan, London, 1972), pp. 256–57.

29 *Grania*, p. 37.

'DEAR JOHN QUINN'
Daniel J. Murphy

1　J. B. Yeats to John Quinn, 14 May 1920. This and the subsequent letters are from the Manuscript Division of the New York Public Library.
2　John Quinn, 'Lady Gregory and the Abbey Theatre', in *Outlook*, 16 December 1911, pp. 917–18; *Our Irish Theatre*, C.E. 4, p. 248.
3　Quinn, p. 918; *Our Irish Theatre*, p. 251.
4　*Poets and Dreamers*, C.E. 11, p. 137; *Our Irish Theatre*, C.E. 4, p. 251.
5　Quinn, p. 917; *Our Irish Theatre*, p. 250.
6　Quinn, p. 918; *Our Irish Theatre*, p. 250.
7　Quinn, pp. 918, 917; *Our Irish Theatre*, pp. 252, 249.
8　J. B. Yeats, *Letters to his son W. B. Yeats and others 1869–1922*, ed. Joseph Hone (Faber & Faber, London, 1944; E. P. Dutton, New York, 1946), p. 73.
9　Irish Literary Society of New York, *Constitution and Officers* (New York, 1903), p. 5.
10　*The Letters of W. B. Yeats*, ed. Allan Wade (Rupert Hart-Davis, London, 1954; Macmillan, New York, 1955), p. 403. The Society produced *The Pot of Broth, Cathleen ni Houlihan* and *The Land of Heart's Desire* at the Carnegie Lyceum, June 1903 (*The Theatre Magazine*, III, July 1903, pp. 158–59).
11　2 August 1907.
12　2 August 1907.
13　Lady Gregory to Quinn, 3 January 1909.
14　Walter Patch, *Queer Thing, Painting* (New York, 1938), p. 207.
15　*Our Irish Theatre*, C.E. 4, p. 105.
16　*Ibid.*, p. 111.
17　*Ibid.*
18　*Ibid.*, p. 119.
19　B. L. Reid, *The Man from New York, John Quinn and His Friends* (Oxford, New York, 1968), p. 114.
20　The following letters from Lady Gregory to John Quinn are in the Manuscript Division of the New York Public Library, Astor, Lenox and Tilden Foundations, by whose permission, and the permission of Anne de Winton and Catherine Kennedy, they are published here.
21　William M. Murphy, in *Prodigal Father* (Cornell University Press, Ithaca, 1978) states that recently retreived letters seem to confirm that they continued the affair in 1913. I have been unable to find such letters.
22　*Journals*, C.E. 14, p. 569.

THE PATTERN OF THREE THREADS:
THE HYDE GREGORY FRIENDSHIP
Gareth W. Dunleavy

1　*Seventy Years*, C.E. 13, pp. 382, 391.
2　*Ibid.* p. 317.
3　*Ibid.* p. 306.
4　*Ibid.* p. 319.

5 I should like to thank the administration of the Research Libraries of the New York Public Library [NYPL] for permission to quote from the Hyde letters in the John Quinn Papers in Special Collections and the Lady Gregory Papers in the Henry W. and Albert A. Berg Collection, New York Public Library, Astor, Lenox and Tilden Foundations. I am indebted especially to Dr. Lola Szladits, Curator of the Berg Collection, for assistance in locating significant items. I am grateful also to the Trustees of the National Library of Ireland [NLI] for permission to publish extracts from the Douglas Hyde papers, and to Alf MacLochlainn, until recently Director of the National Library of Ireland, and now University Librarian at University College, Galway, for his continuing help with and encouragement of my research on Douglas Hyde. Among private collectors, Aidan Heavey has generously made his Hyde letters available to me for examination. Support for my research, of which this essay is one result, has been supplied in part by grants from the American Philosophical Society, the Graduate School of the University of Wisconsin-Milwaukee, and the Guggenheim Foundation.

6 Hyde to Gregory, 19 August 1897. NYPL. For the benefit of readers, spelling and punctuation have been normalized in this and other letters quoted here.

7 Gregory to Hyde, 23 October 1897. NLI MS 17,291. For transcriptions of passages from this and other letters of Lady Gregory to Hyde in the National Library, I am indebted to Colin Smythe.

8 Hyde to Gregory, 23 October 1897. Private papers, Aidan Heavey.

9 Hyde to Gregory, 26 October 1897. NYPL.

10 NLI MSS G1050, G1051.

11 Hyde to Gregory, 6 January 1898. NYPL.

12 Hyde to Gregory, 26 January 1898. NYPL.

13 Hyde to Gregory, 21 February 1898. NYPL.

14 Hyde to Gregory, 27 May 1898. NYPL.

15 Hyde to Gregory, 13 January 1899, translated by Professor Maureen Murphy of Hofstra University. NYPL.

16 Hyde to Gregory, 1 February 1899, 20 February 1899. NYPL.

17 NLI MS 10,874, translated by Professor Janet Egleson Dunleavy of The University of Wisconsin-Milwaukee. The viewpoint of the anti-Literary Theatre element in the Gaelic League was expressed by P. H. Pearse in a letter to editor MacNeill of 13 May, 1899: 'The Irish Literary Theatre is in my opinion more dangerous, because glaringly anti-national, than Trinity College. If we once admit the Irish literature in English idea, then the language movement is a mistake. . . . Let us strangle it at its birth.' By 1905 Pearse himself was speaking well of Lady Gregory's plays, but others still held to the ideas he previously had expressed. See *The Letters of P. H. Pearse*, ed. Séamas Ó Buachalla (Colin Smythe, Gerrards Cross, 1980), p. 9.

18 Hyde to Gregory, 15 May 1900. NYPL.

19 Hyde to Gregory, 5 June 1900. NYPL.

20 Hyde to Gregory, [n.d.] September 1900. NYPL.

21 Hyde to Gregory, 31 December 1900. NYPL.

22 Hyde to Gregory, 7 January 1901 [postmark]. NYPL. D. P. Moran, a journalist who in 1900 launched his own nationalist newspaper, the *Leader*, called for an 'Irish-Ireland', particularly an Irish-speaking Ireland.

23 Gregory to Hyde, 1 March 1901. NLI MS 17,291.

24 *Seventy Years*, C.E. 13, p. 321.

25 *Ibid.*, p. 391.

26 *Ibid.*, p. 394.
27 Hyde to Gregory, 13 March 1901. NYPL.
28 Gregory to Hyde, 11 May 1901. NLI MS 17,291.
29 *Letters to W. B. Yeats*, ed. Richard J. Finneran, G. M. Harper, and W. M. Murphy (Macmillan, London; Barnes & Noble, New York, 1977) I, 89.
30 *Seventy Years*, p. 400.
31 *Ibid.*, p. 402.
32 Gregory to Hyde, 11 May 1901. NLI MS 17,291. Two of Hyde's one-act plays *An Pósadh (The Marriage)* and *An Cleamhnas (The Matchmaking)* benefited from revisions and alterations suggested by Lady Gregory: "Yeats came to dine, and we went through the Match Making and I enclose the proposed alterations for your consideration — and shall be anxious to hear what you think." Gregory to Hyde (date indecipherable), probably written 1903–04. For her translations of these and other Hyde plays, see *Poets and Dreamers*, C.E. 11. See also *Selected Plays of Douglas Hyde*, eds. Gareth W. and Janet Egleson Dunleavy, forthcoming from Colin Smythe Ltd. and Catholic University of America Press.
33 Hyde to Gregory, 14 March 1902, 5 May 1902. NYPL.
34 Hyde to Gregory, 14 March 1902. NYPL.
35 Hyde to Gregory, 9 November 1903. NYPL.
36 Hyde to Gregory, 29 November 1905. NYPL.
37 Hyde to Gregory, 2 January 1906. NYPL.
38 Hyde may have alluded to Lady Gregory's and Yeats's theatre in his 'literary' lectures given at several American colleges at this time, but he appears to have avoided mention of their work in the giant fund-raising rallies across the country. His letter to Lady Gregory asserts that he unfailingly promoted their work in every speech.
39 Hyde to Gregory, 12 April 1908. NYPL.
40 Hyde to Gregory, 8 October 1908. NYPL.
41 Gregory to Hyde, 11 October 1908. NLI MS 17,291.
42 Hyde to Gregory, 14 July 1910. NYPL.
43 Quoted in *Lady Gregory—Interviews and Recollections*, ed. E. H. Mikhail (Macmillan, London, Barnes & Noble, New York, 1977), p. 5.
44 B. L. Reid, *The Man From New York John Quinn and His Friends* (Oxford, New York, 1968), p. 119. Hyde's cable disclaiming any connection between the League and the Abbey Theatre had been sent in response to a communication from the League's delegate in New York, Father Michael O'Flanagan: '(John) Devoy told me a few days ago that he would do nothing for the Gaelic League until you gave [sic] official denial to Lady Gregory's claim that the plays of the Abbey Theatre were inspired by the Gaelic League.' O'Flanagan continued that unless Hyde sent a cable disassociating the League from the Abbey 'I am convinced the Gaelic League must begin all over again in America and look for new friends in a most unpromising field.' O'Flanagan to Hyde, 2 December 1911. NLI Ms. 25,070.
45 Gregory to Hyde, 7 December 1911. NLI MS 17,291.
46 *Ibid.*
47 Hyde to Gregory, 18 December 1911. NYPL.
48 Hyde to Gregory, 11 May 1912. NYPL. In a letter, undated but probably written in May, 1912, Lady Gregory sought to reassure Hyde: 'Yes indeed, you would not willingly have done anything to hurt us, and I have always said you did what you believed best for the interest of the League. . .'.

49 Hyde to Gregory, 21 December 1915. NLI MS 22, 957.
50 Hyde to Gregory, 9 October 1916. NYPL. Writing to Hyde in 1918, Lady Gregory reminded him of what they had achieved: '. . . but you and I anyhow didn't put off the rebuilding until Home Rule! Your League encompasses the end of the earth — and our theatre is anyhow marking time till we can hand it over to a National Movement.' Gregory to Hyde. 20 July 1918.
51 *Journals*, C.E. 14, p. 524.
52 Hyde to Quinn, 1 January 1911. John Quinn Papers, NYPL.
53 *Seventy Years*, p. 306.

LADY GREGORY AND THE GAELIC LEAGUE
Maureen Murphy

1 Lady Gregory, Introduction to 'The Kiltartan Poetry Books', *The Kiltartan Books* C.E. 9, p. 19. See also Lady Gregory, Interview with *The Evening Post* (N.Y.), December 6, 1911 in *Our Irish Theatre*, C.E. 4, p. 156.
2 *The Kiltartan Books*, p. 19.
3 Douglas Hyde, 'The Necessity for De-Anglicising Ireland', in Vivian Mercier and David H. Greene, eds., *1000 Years of Irish Prose* (Universal Library, New York, 1961), p. 79.
4 See Breandan S. MacAodha, 'Was This a Social Revolution?' in Seán O'Tuama, ed., *The Gaelic League Idea* (Mercier, Cork, 1972), pp. 10–30 and the unpublished paper 'Peasants and Emigrants: Some Considerations of the Gaelic League as a Social Movement' (1973) by the late Martin J. Waters.
5 Elizabeth Coxhead suggests Robert Gregory's request to learn Irish was made in 1894, *Lady Gregory: A Literary Portrait* (Macmillan, London; Harcourt, Brace and World, New York, 1961), p. 39; however, Lady Gregory records the date as 1897 in *Seventy Years* C.E. 13, p. 318.
6 Pádraig O'Fearáil, *The Story of Conradh na Gaeilge* (Conradh na Gaeilge, Baile Átha Cliath [Dublin] 1975), p. 7. When Father O'Growney died 18 October 1899, Eoin Mac Neill wrote Parts IV and V of this series that provided the foundation for most League learners. Brian O'Cuiv, 'Mac Neill and the Irish Languages', in F. X. Martin and F. J. Byrne, eds., *The Scholar Revolutionary: Eoin Mac Neill, 1867–1945 and the Making of the New Ireland* (Irish University Press, Shannon, 1973), p. 7.
7 *The Kiltartan Books*, p. 19. See also *Our Irish Theatre*, p. 142.
8 Lady Gregory's dates are a little vague. Her references in her diaries and in *Seventy Years* (p. 332) suggest she studied with Miss Borthwick in Spring, 1897, but it was no doubt Spring, 1898.
9 'I first saw J. M. Synge in the North Island of Aran. I was staying there gathering folk-lore, talking to the people, and felt quite angry when I passed another outsider walking here and there, talking also to the people. I was jealous of not being alone on the island among the fishers and seaweed gatherers. I did not speak to the stranger, nor was he inclined to speak to me; he also looked on me as an intruder, I only heard his name.' *Our Irish Theatre*, p. 73. 'Synge's first visit in 1898 lasted from May 10th to June 25th, with two weeks spent on the main island and four on the middle island.' David H. Greene and Edward M. Stephens, *J. M. Synge 1871–1909* (The Macmillan Company, New York, 1959), p. 76. Lady Gregory recorded in her diary that Synge arrived at Coole on June 28. Lady Gregory first visited Aran in October

1893. See Mary Lou Kohfeldt, *Lady Gregory, the Woman behind the Irish Renaissance* (Atheneum, New York; Deutsch, London, 1985), p. 94.

10 'I had almost forgotten, by the by, that I have begun Irish and am getting on fairly well with it,' W. B. Yeats to Lily Yeats, July 11, 1898. Allan Wade, ed., *The Letters of W. B. Yeats* (Rupert Hart-Davis, London, 1954), p. 302. Yeats was a willing though unsuccessful student of Irish. See his letter to *The Gael* published in December, 1899. 'I have taken up Gaelic again, and though I shall never have entire mastery of it, I hope to be able to get some feeling of the language . . .' Wade, p. 328.

11 *Seventy Years*, p. 319.

12 *Ibid.*, p. 320.

13 *Ibid.*, p. 310.

14 *Ibid.*, p. 382.

15 Vere R. T. Gregory, *The House of Gregory* (Browne and Nolan, Dublin, 1943), p. 89.

16 *Seventy Years*, p. 343.

17 *Ibid.*, p. 363.

18 *Ibid.*, p. 382.

19 *Ibid.*, p. 393.

20 *Our Irish Theatre*, p. 147.

21 Lady Gregory is probably responsible for 'Public Meeting at Kiltartan', 29 Iúl [July] 1899, pp. 314–315; "Lecture in Gort", 12 Lughnasa [August] 1899, pp. 342–343, and, indirectly, for 'Dr. Hyde in Gort', 19 Lughnasa [August], 1899, p. 365.

22 *Seventy Years*, p. 360.

23 *An Claidheamh Soluis* (5 Deireadh Fómhair [October], 1901), p. 471. Padraic Pearse's only appearance before the Irish bar in 1905 involved defending another man brought to court for the same offence. Pearse lost. Séamus O'Buachalla, *Padraig Mac Piarais agus Eire lena Linn* (Mercier, Cork, 1979), p. 18.

24 A. C. Edwards, ed., 'The Lady Gregory Letters to Sean O'Casey', *Modern Drama*, 8, 1 (May, 1965), p. 99.

25 Lady Gregory, 'Ireland, Real and Ideal', *The Nineteenth Century* (November, 1898), p. 780.

26 Quoted in Dominic Daly, 'Notes on Douglas Hyde's Plays', *Poets and Dreamers* C.E. 11, pp. 225–226.

27 *Seventy Years*, p. 394.

28 Cú Uladh, 'Árd-Smuainte ar Eirinn', *An Claidheamh Soluis* (23 March 1901), p. 19.

29 Wade, p. 532.

30 Tomás O'Concheanainn, 'Anonn agus Anall', *An Claidheamh Soluis* (16 Seacht-mhí, 1899), pp. 419–421.

31 Lady Gregory, Unpublished Diary, Henry W. and Albert A. Berg Collection, New York Public Library, Astor, Lenox and Tilden Foundations. Redington was Christopher Redington, the first Commissioner of Education in Ireland. See: 'I set to work to learn Irish. I had wished to do so long before, but was discouraged, first by the advice of a Chief Commissioner of Irish Education who had told me it would be a waste of time to learn a language which had 'no literature,' and again by the shyness of the people about teaching a language they had felt was looked down on.' *Our Irish Theatre*, pp. 141–142.

32 *Poets and Dreamers*, C.E. 11, p. 136.

33 See the text of the play in Robert Hogan and James Kilroy, *The Irish Literary Theatre 1899–1901* (Dolmen, Dublin, 1975), pp. 137–144.
34 *Our Irish Theatre*, p. 54.
35 *Ibid.*, p. 35.
36 Hogan and Kilroy, p. 135. Hugh Hunt, *The Abbey. Ireland's National Theatre 1904–1979* (Columbia University Press, New York; Gill & Macmillan, Dublin, 1979), p. 17. While Lady Gregory maintained that *Casadh an tSúgáin* was 'the first play ever given in Irish in a Dublin theatre . . .' (*Seventy Years*, p. 381), George Moore's essay 'The Irish Literary Theatre' in *Samhain*, 1901 acknowledges that Hyde's play was not the first play in Irish.

'I thought till the other day that it would be the first play produced in Dublin but now I hear that an organization called Inghean [sic] na h-Eireann has produced at the Antient Concert Rooms (it was in this room *The Countess Cathleen* and *The Heather Field* were performed), a play in Irish. In a way it would have pleased our vanity to have been the first in Dublin with an Irish play, but this would have been a base vanity and unworthy of a Gaelic Leaguer'.

37 W. G. Fay and Catherine Carswell. *The Fays of the Abbey Theatre* (Rich and Cowan, London, 1935), pp. 113–114. Robert Hogan and James Kilroy consider the claims of both George Moore and William Fay that they directed *Casadh an tSúgáin* and conclude it is impossible to decide who did what (p. 95). Hogan and Kilroy do not, however, mention Fay's experience directing the Dinneen play. Dominic Daly attributed the direction of *Casadh an tSúgáin* to Fay, *The Young Douglas Hyde* (Irish University Press, Shannon, 1974), p. 135.
38 *Our Irish Theatre*, pp. 54–55, Wade, pp. 384, 391.
39 *Our Irish Theatre*, p. 57.
40 See Daly, pp. 216–217, note 39 and *Poets and Dreamers*, C.E. 11, pp. 224–226.
41 *Poets and Dreamers*, pp. 69–70. Lady Gregory, *The Rising of the Moon, Comedies*, C.E. 5, p. 301.
42 *Seventy Years*, p. 410.
43 *Comedies*, C.E. 5, p. 60.
44 *Ibid. Comedies* p. 67.
45 *Tragedies and Tragic-Comedies*, C.E. 6, p. 241.
46 An Craoibhin Aobhinn, *Mo Thurus go hAmerice* (Oifig Diolta Foillseacháin Rialtais, Baile Átha Cliath, 1937), p. 3.
47 A *feis* programme with sketches by Jack Yeats is in the Quinn Papers, Berg Collection, New York Public Library. The programme is reproduced in B. L. Reid, *The Man from New York* (Oxford University Press, New York, 1968), p. 9.
48 John Quinn, 'Lady Gregory and the Abbey Theatre', *The Outlook* (December 16, 1911), p. 917; *Our Irish Theatre*, p. 249.
49 Ruth Dudley Edwards, *Patrick Pearse, The Triumph of Failure* (Victor Gollancz, London, 1977), p. 30.
50 P. H. Pearse, 'The "Irish" Literary Theatre', *An Claidheamh Soluis* (20 Bealtaine 1899), 157. Pearse later changed his opinion of Yeats. In February 1903, when Pearse was canvassing for support for his bid to edit *An Claidheamh Soluis*, he proposed 'leading writers in English like Lady Gregory, W. B. Yeats and W. P. Ryan should contribute literary articles'. Edwards, p.

62. While editor of *An Claidheamh Soluis* he wrote, 'We may not all agree with his theories on art and literature, but we can not forget that he has spent his life in an endeavor to free our ideas from the trammels of foreign thought, or that it was through his writings many of us made our first acquaintance with our early traditions and literature. He has never ceased to work for Ireland' (28 Samhain, 1908). Pearse was also grateful to Yeats for his support when he invited Pearse to bring his St. Enda's production of *An Rí* to the Abbey Theatre on May 17, 1913.

51 'Public Meeting at Kiltartan', *An Claidheamh Soluis* (29 Iúl, 1899), 314–315.

52 *An Claidheamh Soluis* (5 Lughnasa, 1899), 329.

53 Ó Fearáil, p. 5.

54 Lady Gregory, trans., 'The Last Class', *An Claidheamh Soluis — Duillanchán an Oireachtas* (1901), p. 1.

55 *Our Irish Theatre*, p. 167.

56 W. B. Yeats, *Beltaine* (February, 1900), p. 4.

57 Wade, pp. 350–351.

58 See the discussion in Declan Kiberd, *Synge and the Irish Language* (Macmillan, London; Rowman and Littlefield, Totowa, 1979), pp. 236–237, 238.

59 *Seventy Years*, p. 414.

60 C. A. 'Taisbeántas Pictéar', *An Claidheamh Soluis* (2 Samhain, 1901), 531.

61 *Seventy Years*, p. 418.

62 *Seventy Years*, p. 548.

63 Daniel Murphy, ed., 'Letters from Lady Gregory: Her Friendship with T. J. Kiernan, Part II', *Bulletin of the New York Public Library*, 72 (January, 1968), pp. 51–52.

64 Lady Gregory, Unpublished Diary, Henry W. and Albert A. Berg Collection. The New York Public Library. Astor, Lenox and Tilden Foundations.

65 *Lady Gregory's Journals I*, C.E. 14, p. 328.

66 *Seventy Years*, p. 306.

67 *Seventy Years*, p. 321.

68 W. B. Yeats, *Dramatis Personae* (Macmillan, New York, 1936), p. 14, *Autobiographies*, (Macmillan, London, 1955), p. 395.

LADY GREGORY AND SEAN O'CASEY: AN UNLIKELY FRIENDSHIP REVISITED
Ronald Ayling

1 Lady Gregory and O'Casey continued to exchange letters occasionally after the quarrel, but the relationship was never to be the same again; the later letters are quire different from earlier ones, as can be seen in the examples quoted in the present article. Mostly, O'Casey's letters after the break with the Abbey appear to be 'duty' letters, written to acknowledge Christmas greetings from Lady Gregory. An important exception is the letter of 25 October 1931, printed in full in the present article.

2 David Krause, 'Sean O'Casey,' *Recent Research on Anglo-Irish Writers*, ed. Richard J. Finneran (Modern Language Association of America, New York

1983), p. 230. In this instance he is reviewing Ronald Ayling's essay on 'Sean O'Casey and the Abbey Theatre, Dublin' in *Sean O'Casey: Centenary Essays*, ed. David Krause and Robert G. Lowery, (Colin Smythe, Gerrards Cross, 1983), pp. 13–40.

3 *Recent Research on Anglo-Irish Writers*, p. 231.

4 In *Sean O'Casey: Centenary Essays*, pp. 67–99. This essay should be read in tandem with another by FitzGerald, 'How the Abbey Said No: Readers' Reports and the Rejection of *The Silver Tassie*', a piece whose provenance extends well beyond the Theatre's controversial handling of this play in 1928; it is printed in *O'Casey Annual No. 1*, ed. Robert G. Lowery (Macmillan, London 1982), pp. 73–87.

5 *Lady Gregory: A Literary Portrait* (2nd revised edition, Secker & Warburg, London 1966); there is additional material on O'Casey in this edition.

6 *Modern Drama*, VIII: 1 (May 1965), p. 95. Even Elizabeth Coxhead has helped to bolster this myth, claiming that, of all at the Abbey theatre, Lady Gregory 'was the first to discern' the playwright's literary gifts even in 'the fumbling of his early efforts' (*Lady Gregory: A Literary Portrait*, p. 183).

7 'Editor's Notes', *O'Casey Annual No. 1*, p. xi.

8 Quoted by Lennox Robinson in a letter to O'Casey dated 5 November 1921; see *The Letters of Sean O'Casey, Vol. 1*, ed. David Krause (Macmillan, New York,1975), p. 96.

9 St. John Ervine, *The Theatre in My Time* (Rich & Cowan, London, 1933), p. 156.

10 *Oak Leaves and Lavender* (Macmillan, London, 1946) is not one of O'Casey's better plays but, in the form of a salute to the heroic efforts of the common people in the Battle of Britain, it offers a conscious refutation of W. B. Yeats's pessimism in the present age and in modern democracy in such plays as *Purgatory* and *The Words Upon the Window-Pane*. O'Casey uses a chorus of eighteenth-century figures (themselves uttering sentiments similar to those of Yeats) to point the change: the fate of the civilised world no longer rests upon the swords and pens of aristocrats but, in 1940–41, upon the efforts of the common folk in Britain and Russia. The aristocratic lady of the manor house, upon losing her airman son in battle, can yet look to a future that she knows has no place for her and can declare (in direct contradiction to the attitude realised in *Purgatory*): 'The house must change; but it must not die.' One can somehow hear the voice of the old woman who wrote: 'But the days of landed property have passed. It is better so. Yet I wish some one of our blood would after my death care enough for what has been a home for so long, to keep it open.' (*Lady Gregory's Journals* ed. Lennox Robinson (Putnam, London, 1946), p. 340).

11 I cannot think of any Irish writer or critic who has written more copiously or with such unstinting appreciation of Lady Gregory and her work as did Sean O'Casey. Indeed, the obverse is the more usual case: a good number of Irish writers and critics (several with considerable artistic or financial indebtedness to her) have been cruelly critical of her: examples would include Oliver St. John Gogarty, Denis Johnston and (most notably and certainly with less justification) James Joyce.

12 In his essay, 'The Lady of Coole' published in *The 1943 Saturday Book* (Hutchinson, London, 1942) O'Casey added 'A charwoman, right enough, but one with a star on her forehead'.

13 See 'A Protestant Bridget' (1946) and 'A Sprig of Rosemary among the Laurel'

(1962) in *Blasts and Benedictions* (Macmillan, London, 1967), pp. 205–215. The two chapters in *Inishfallen, Fare Thee Well* (Macmillan, London & New York, 1949) are entitled 'Blessed Bridget O'Coole' and 'Where Wild Swans Nest'.

14 *Sean O'Casey: Centenary Essays*, p. 94.

15 *Ibid.*, p. 94.

16 Roger McHugh, 'Sean O'Casey and Lady Gregory,' *James Joyce Quarterly*, VIII: 1 (Fall 1970), p. 121.

17 This quotation is taken direct from the manuscript of 'I Come to Coole', among the O'Casey papers in the Berg Collection of the New York Public Library.

18 This episode is also taken from the ms. of 'The Lady of Coole'.

19 Letter, once in the possession of Mr Colin Smythe to whom I am grateful for assistance (and much patience) in the preparation of this article, now belonging to Robert W. Woodruff Library, Emory University.

20 I am indebted to Miss Hannah D. French, formerly reference librarian at Wellesley College in Massachusetts, for details of this holograph letter now in that college's library.

21 Letter now in the possession of the Robert W. Woodruff Library.

22 Something should be said about this collection of twenty-three letters by Lady Gregory. In some cases Edwards seems to have based his text on a typewritten transcription made by O'Casey; the dangers in such reliance were pointed out by the playwright himself. In one instance, copying out a letter, he paused to add a comment: 'Standard Hotel, Dublin. 2nd April, 1930 (Note: L. Gregory's writing is so atrocious that it is hard work making the words out, and giving them their meaning. I have replied to a number of them without knowing what had been said by her; and a number of others I destroyed because they were indecipherable to me; and I had to save my eyes from the strain of trying to decode them. S.O.'C.)' The difficulties can be seen from this very letter alone which, in O'Casey's version (printed by Edwards and by David Krause in the first volume of O'Casey's letters) reads: 'I must write — because my mind is so full of *The Plough and The Stars*, that I saw last evening — a wonderful play — always next morning — even without B. Fitzgerald — though of course no one can fill his place. I cannot help hoping that you will *give and forgive* — give another great play — and give us a new opportunity. Anyhow whether you do or not, I feel I must thank you for this — and for *Juno* — but I put *The Plough* first in my own mind. And the audience last night was full of enthusiasm . . ' This is an important letter in the context of their relationship but it appears garbled: 'always next morning'? a comparison with the original text reveals that the almost unreadable phrase, referring to *The Plough and the Stars*, is almost certainly meant to be 'always and ever moving'. It is likely that the other texts printed by Edwards and Krause are equally suspect in places.

23 Letter now in the possession of the Robert W. Woodruff Library, Emory University.

'FRIENDSHIP IS THE ONLY HOUSE I HAVE':
LADY GREGORY AND W. B. YEATS
John Kelly

1   'The Sunset of Fantasy', *Dublin Magazine*, XIII (January 1938), p. 6.
2   Diary, c. June 1894 (Berg Collection).
3   *Variorum Poems of W. B. Yeats (V.P.)*, ed. Allt and Alspach, p. 489.
4   *Memoirs*, p. 102.
5   Mary Lou Kohfeldt, *Lady Gregory, The Woman Behind the Irish Renaissance* (New York, 1985; London, 1986), p. 118.
6   *V.P.*, p. 602.
7   *V.P.*, p. 489.
8   T. J. Kiernan, 'Lady Gregory and W. B. Yeats'. *Southerly*, 4 (1953), p. 241.
9   Diary, 6 March 1893.
10 *Seventy Years 1852–1922* C.E.13, p. 109.
11 Diary, 5 November 1894.
12 Diary, March and August 1896; she wrote to Blunt (3 January 1898) that their deaths gave her a 'sense of my foundations having slipped away'.
13 *Ibid.*, January 1894.
14 *Ibid.*, 21 December 1894.
15 *Ibid.*, March 1895.
16 *Ibid.*, 8 April 1895.
17 *Ibid.*, 13 February 1896.
18 W. B. Yeats, *Autobiographies* (Macmillan, London, 1955), pp. 33–4.
19 This extended to the English middle classes also; in an unpublished letter to his wife of 17 November 1931 WBY reports that the 'earlier middle class part' of Trollope's *Can You Forgive Her* annoyed Lady Gregory. She said: '"I dislike those English middle-classes. I think very little of them" . . . Lady Gregory always thinks people unworthy of attention unless they have an inherited code which makes fussy thinking unnecessary.'
20 Diary, 30 January 1894.
21 Unpublished letter from Lady Gregory to Wilfrid Blunt, 5 May 1885.
22 Diary, 30 July 1886.
23 *Ibid.*, 1 January 1901, see also entry for 10 May 1900.
24 See for example Diary 28 June 1898, and *Seventy Years* 28, 81, 380–1, 384, 400.
25 *Bleak House* (Oxford, 1966), p. 108.
26 'An Emigrant's Notebook'.
27 *Ibid.*
28 *Ibid.*
29 *Argosy*, (June 1891), p. 474.
30 *Collected Letters of W. B. Yeats*, ed. J. S. Kelly (Oxford, 1986), p. 399.
31 *Ideals in Ireland*, ed. Lady Gregory, (London, 1901), p. 91.
32 *The Letters of W. B. Yeats*, ed. Allan Wade (London, 1954), p. 286.
33 *Ibid.*
34 *Collected Letters of W. B. Yeats*, p. 263, note 2.
35 Anne Gregory,*Me and Nu* (Gerrards Cross, 1970), p. 31.

36 See for example George Moore, *Hail and Farewell*, ed. Richard Allen Cave (Gerrards Cross, 1976), pp. 203–7.
37 W. B. Yeats *Memoirs*, transcribed and edited by Denis Donoghue (London, 1972), pp. 160–1.
38 William Murphy, *Prodigal Father* (Ithaca and London, 1978), pp. 86, 217.
39 *Ibid.*, 215.
40 *Ibid.*, 115.
41 Unpublished letter to Lady Gregory, 4 January 1900.
42 Unpublished letter to Olivia Shakespear, 20 May 1900.
43 See *Autobiographies*, p. 31.
44 Unpublished letter to Lady Gregory, 3 August 1904.
45 Unpublished letter from Ellen O'Leary to W. B. Yeats, 23 April [1887].
46 This was Anna Elizabeth, Comtesse de Bremont, a widow, novelist and ex-singer.
47 *Seventy Years*, pp. 1, 17.
48 Diary, 30 November 1897.
49 *V.P.* pp. 478–9.
50 Jon Stallworthy, *Between the Lines* (Oxford, 1963), p. 185.
51 Diary, 30 November 1898.
52 *Ibid.*
53 *Ibid.*
54 *Ibid.*, 14 February 1898.
55 *Ibid.*
56 Unpublished letter to Lady Gregory, 10 December 1897.
57 Unpublished letter to Lady Gregory, 2 June 1900.
58 Unpublished letter to Lady Gregory, 15 December 1898.
59 *Memoirs*, pp. 125–6.
60 Unpublished letter to Lady Gregory, 21 December 1898.
61 Diary, 30 November 1897.
62 *Ibid.*
63 *Ibid.*, 21 March 1897.
64 *Ibid.*, November 1899.
65 *ibid.*, 16 December 1898.
66 Reported in an unpublished letter from WBY to Lady Gregory, 9 February 1908.
67 Diary, 4 November 1900.
68 *Ibid.*, 23 January 1900.
69 Letter of 24 June 1901, quoted in *Seventy Years*, p. 373.
70 *The Spectator*, 20 April 1895, p. 20.
71 Diary, 10 October 1895, 9 February 1897, 16 March 1897.
72 *Ibid.*, 30 November 1897.
73 *Ibid.*
74 *Autobiographies*, pp. 399–400.
75 Unpublished letter to Katharine Tynan, 28 July 1904.
76 Inscription quoted in *Gazette of the Grolier Club*, N.S. No. 2, October 1966, p. 12.
77 W. B. Yeats, *Explorations* (Macmillan, London, 1962), p. 3.
78 *Ibid.*, p. 7.
79 *Ibid.*, p. 28.
80 Diary.
81 *Autobiographies*, p. 455.
82 Diary, 30 November 1894.

83 *Ibid.*, 'My reflections', 1900.
84 *My First Play: Colman and Guaire* (London, 1930).
85 *Hail and Farewell*, pp. 243–55.
86 Diary, 13 October 1900.
87 *Collected Plays II*, C.E.6, p. 27.
88 *Ibid.*
89 'Manifesto of the Literary Theatre', quoted in Lady Gregory's *Our Irish Theatre*, C.E.4, p. 20.
90 Unpublished letter, Lady Gregory to WBY, November 1902.
91 *Collected Plays III*, C.E.7, p. 207.
92 *Our Irish Theatre*, p. 52.
93 See Maurice Browne, *Too Late to Lament*, 117, and E. H. Mikhail, *Lady Gregory, Interviews and Recollections* (London, 1977).
94 'Manifesto of the Irish Literary Theatre', quoted in *Our Irish Theatre*, p. 20.
95 Unpublished letter from Lady Gregory to WBY, 20 May 1902.
96 Wade, p. 352.
97 Unpublished letter to Lady Gregory, 26 February 1904.
98 *Autobiographies*, p. 317.
99 *Ibid.*, p. 355.
100 *Memoirs*, p. 163.
101 *V.P.*, pp. 217–19.
102 *Ibid.*, p. 218.
103 *The Oxford Book of Modern Verse*, ed. W. B. Yeats, (Oxford, 1936), p. xi.
104 *V.P.*, p. 198.
105 In June 1902 a sect of British-Israelites tried to dig up the Hill of Tara in an attempt to find the Ark of the Covenant. Yeats, George Moore and Douglas Hyde wrote in protest to *The Times* on 24 June 1902.
106 Unpublished letter to Lady Gregory, c. 14 September 1899.
107 Wade, p. 403.
108 *V.P.*, p. 264.
109 *Memoirs*, p. 226.
110 *Ibid.*
111 *Autobiographies*, p. 491.
112 *V.P.*, p. 264.
113 *Ibid.*, p. 265.
114 *Ibid.*
115 *Ibid.*, p. 435.
116 A. N. Jeffares, 'The New Faces', *RES* XXIII (October 1947), p. 92.
117 Unpublished letters to Lady Gregory, 7 and 12 December 1912.
118 Unpublished letter to Lady Gregory, 8 January 1913.
119 *Memoirs*, p. 230.
120 Unpublished letter to Lady Gregory, 18 May 1905.
121 *Memoirs*, pp. 154–5.
122 *Ibid.*, p. 257.
123 *Ibid.*, p. 256.
124 *Ibid.*, p. 257.
125 *Ibid.*, p. 258.
126 *Ibid.*, pp. 257–8.
127 *Autobiographies*, p. 463.
128 *V.P.*, p. 418.
129 See *Memoirs*, 269–70 and *Hail and Farewell passim*.

130 Unpublished letter to Lady Gregory [January 1914].
131 The document is in the Berg Collection and is quoted in part in *Prodigal Father*, 404–5. Another example of her flattering Quinn occurs in an unpublished letter of 12 July 1914 thanking him for a photograph of himself and WBY: 'It is especially good of you. I said to Hugh Lane, "John Quinn is the beauty of these two", and he said "Yes, and the intellectual one!"'
132 Unpublished letter to Lady Gregory, 22 September 1917.
133 Unpublished letter from Mrs Tucker to Lady Gregory, October 1917.
134 Unpublished letter WBY to George Yeats, 4 October 1917.
135 Unpublished letter from Mrs Tucker to Lady Gregory, 9 October 1917.
136 Unpublished letter, George Yeats to Lady Gregory, 10 October 1917.
137 Unpublished letter, WBY to Lady Gregory, 13 October 1917.
138 Wade, p. 634.
139 *Seventy Years*, pp. 553–4.
140 See above, p. 228.
141 Unpublished letter from Lady Gregory to WBY, 2 February 1918.
142 Unpublished letter from Lady Gregory to WBY, 5 February 1918.
143 Unpublished letter from Lady Gregory to WBY, 10 February 1918.
144 Wade, p. 646.
145 Unpublished letter, WBY to Iseult Gonne, 9 February 1918.
146 'Major Robert Gregory'. *The Observer*, 17 February 1918, reprinted in *Uncollected Prose* II, 429–31.
147 Unpublished letter from Lady Gregory to WBY, 25 February 1918.
148 Unpublished letter to Iseult Gonne, 9 February 1918.
149 Wade, p. 646.
150 Wade, p. 648.
151 Unpublished letters, Lady Gregory to WBY, 13 and 18 February 1918.
152 *V.P.*, p. 340.
153 Unpublished letter, Lady Gregory to WBY, 25 February 1918.
154 *V.P.*, pp. 340–1.
155 *Ibid.*, p. 341.
156 Unpublished letter, WBY to George Yeats, May 1918.
157 *V.P.*, p. 325.
158 *Ibid.*, p. 326.
159 *Ibid.*, p. 327.
160 Unpublished letter Lady Gregory to WBY, 25 February 1917.
161 *V.P.*, p. 327.
162 Unpublished letter to an unidentified correspondent, c. March 1923.
163 *V.P.*, p. 328.
164 *Ibid.*
165 See, for example, Robert Graves quoted in *The Listener*, 15 July 1971, p. 75.
166 *V.P.*, p. 791.
167 *Journals I*, p. 351.
168 Unpublished letter. MacColl to Lady Gregory, 7 January 1917.
169 Unpublished letter to Lady Gregory, 18 December 1916.
169a Unpublished letter, George Yeats to Dorothy Pound, 22 August [1931].
170 See *Journals, pt. II*, C.E. 15, pp. 633–38
171 *V.P.*, p. 489.
172 'You have been to me a well of peace and happiness.' See above, p. 201.
173 *V.P.*, p. 491. My italics.
174 *Ibid.* My italics.

175   *Ibid.*, p. 490.
176   *Ibid.*, pp. 491–2.
177   *Autobiographies*, p. 116.
178   *V.P.*, p. 402.
179   *Ibid.*, pp. 605–7.
180   Wade, p. 796.
181   Unpublished letter to John Quinn, 30 September [1921].
182   Unpublished letter to Lady Gregory, [13 October 1908].
183   Wade, p. 855.

A LANGUAGE FOR HEALING
Robert Welch

1   *Visions and Beliefs in the West of Ireland*, C.E.I, p. 135
2   *Ibid.*, p. 149.
3   *Hail and Farewell* (Colin Smythe, Gerrards Cross, 1976), p. 223.
4   *Uncollected Prose by W. B. Yeats*, vol. 1 edited by John P. Frayne (Macmillan, London, 1970), p. 295.
5   *The Kiltartan Books*, C.E.9, p. 19.
6   W. B. Yeats, *Mythologies* (Macmillan, London, 1959), p. 25
7   Songs Ascribed to Raftery: *Abhráin atá Leagtha ar an Reachtúire*, edited by Douglas Hyde (Irish University Press reprint, Shannon, 1973), pp. 330–2.
8   W. B. Yeats, *Collected Poems* (Macmillan, London, 1950), p. 276.
     We were the last romantics — chose for theme
     Traditional sanctity and loveliness;
     Whatever's written in what poet's name
     The book of the people. . .
9   *Seventy Years*, C.E. 13, p. 410.
10   *Poets and Dreamers*, C.E.11, p. 15.
11   *Songs Ascribed to Raftery*, p. 98.
12   *Poets and Dreamers*, p. 29.
13   *Ibid.*, p. 40.
14   *Ibid.*, p. 36.
15   *Ibid.*, p. 159.
16   *The Kiltartan Books*, C.E.9, p. 20.
17   *Seventy Years*, p. 392.
18   *Ibid.*, p. 394.
19   *Cuchulain of Muirthemne*, C.E.2, p.5.
20   *Our Irish Theatre*, C.E.4, pp. 142–43.
21   *Seventy Years*, p. 413.
22   *Bricriu's Feast*, edited by George Henderson (Irish Texts Society London, 1899) p. 126.
23   *Cuchulain of Muirthemne*, p. 75.
24   *Ibid.*, p. 68.
25   *Bricriu's Feast*, p. 72.
26   *Collected Poems*, p. 182.
27   *Ibid.*, p. 225.
28   Martin Heidegger, *On the Way to Language* (Harper & Row, New York and San Francisco, 1971), p. 47. It is a pleasure to acknowledge that the thinking on language in this essay owes a great deal to Heidegger's insights in this and in others of his works.

FOUR FRENCH COMEDIES: LADY GREGORY'S
TRANSLATIONS OF MOLIÈRE
Mary FitzGerald

1   An early version of this paper was delivered at the annual meeting of the Irish
    Studies Section of the South Atlantic Modern Language Association, October
    1983. On 19 May 1923, Shaw showed Lady Gregory something he had written
    for the *Times Literary Supplement* which she quoted in her journal: 'Some
    writers have a natural gift of writing dialogue and need no training, and the
    first that come to mind in a literary sense are Molière, Goldsmith, Chesterton
    and Lady Gregory.' *Lady Gregory's Journals*, Vol. 1, Books 1–29, 10 October
    1916 – 24 February 1925, ed. Daniel J. Murphy, C.E.14, p. 455.
2   *Our Irish Theatre, A Chapter of Autobiography*, C.E.4 pp. 34–35; *Seventy
    Years*, C.E.13, p. 315.
3   *Our Irish Theatre*, p. 60.
4   *Our Irish Theatre*, p. 198.
5   *The Boston Evening Transcript*, 7 October 1911, quoted in *Our Irish Theatre*,
    p. 168.
6   *Seventy Years, Being the Autobiography of Lady Gregory*, C.E.13, p. 420.
7   *Theatre Business: The Correspondence of the First Abbey Theatre Directors:
    William Butler Yeats, Lady Gregory and J. M.Synge*, ed. Ann Saddlemyer
    (Colin Smythe, Gerrards Cross; Penn State Press, University Park, PA, 1982),
    p. 75.
8   *Theatre Business*, p. 131.
9   *The Translations and Adaptations of Lady Gregory and Her Collaborations
    with Douglas Hyde and W. B. Yeats*, ed. Ann Saddlemyer C.E.8, p. 367.
10 Robert Hogan and James Kilroy, *The Abbey Theatre: The Years of Synge,
    1905–09, The Modern Irish Drama*, 3 (Dolmen Press, Dublin; Humanities
    Press, Atlantic Highlands, NJ., 1978), p. 65.
11 *Translations and Adaptations*, pp. 45–46.
12 *Theatre Business*, p. 217.
13 See *The Comedies of Lady Gregory*, ed. Ann Saddlemyer, C.E.5, pp.
    299–304, for an allegorical parody of the play, and for Lady Gregory's
    comments (p. 260) that indicate she may have thought of it in allegorical
    terms.
14 Lady Gregory's unpublished Diary, 1910, the Henry W. and Albert A. Berg
    Collection of the New York Public Library, Astor, Lenox and Tilden
    Foundations.
15 *The Freeman's Journal*, 6 April 1908, quoted by Hogan and Kilroy, p. 220.
16 *Translations and Adaptations*, p. 79.
17 *Translations and Adaptations*, p. 91.
18 Hogan and Kilroy, pp. 274–75.
19 Unpublished letter of Lennox Robinson, 8 July [1924]. Berg Collection.
20 *Guregorii Fujin Gikyoku Zenshu*, Kondo Kotaro honyaku (Shinchosha,
    Tokyo, 1924).
21 *Lady Gregory's Journals*, vol. I, p. 595.
22 *Lady Gregory's Journals*, vol. I, p. 598.
23 *Lady Gregory's Journals*, vol I, pp. 606–13.
24 *Lady Gregory's Journals*, vol. I, p. 607.
25 *Translations and Adaptations*, p. 191.

IN RETROSPECT: LADY GREGORY'S PLAYS FIFTY YEARS LATER
Lorna D. Young

1 The date of composition is shown in parentheses after the first reference to a play.
2 W. B. Yeats, *Autobiographies* (Macmillan, London, 1961) p. 457.
3 *The Wonder and Supernatural Plays*, C.E.7, p. 400.
4 *The Comedies*, C.E.5, p. 24.
5 Molière is more inclined to conduct this type of dialogue between two persons only as in the case of the "galley scene" in *Les Fourbéries de Scapin*, where he has old Geronte alternate his speeches between a pertinent response to Scapin on the one hand, and on the other the much quoted rhetorical question: "What the devil was he doing in that galley?"
6 *The Comedies*, pp. 155–57.
7 Her translations of the work of the Rev. Peter O'Leary and D'Annunzio will appear in the *Shorter Writings*.
8 Frank O'Connor, *The Backward Look: A Survey of Irish Literature* (Macmillan, London, 1967) pp. 84, 191–2.
9 *The Travelling Man* is one of the very few of her plays set in a cottage kitchen, though Lady Gregory is regularly maligned as the originator of the Abbey's kitchen drama.
10 *The Wonder and Supernatural Plays*, p. 342.
11 *Ibid.*, p. 400.
12 *Ibid.*, p. 364.
13 *Ibid.*, p. 266.
14 *Ibid.*, p. 300.
15 *Ibid.*, p. 206.
16 Over the years I have seen *The Rising of the Moon* performed several times in Ireland, in both English and Irish; the audience finds it hilarious from start to finish.
17 Three different views of this relationship are shown in *The Travelling Man, Dave* and *The Jester*.

THE GLORY OF THE WORLD AND THE PEASANT MIRROR
Ann Saddlemyer

1 *Lady Gregory's Journals 1916–1930*, ed. Lennox Robinson (Macmillan, New York, 1947), p. 318. The title page of *A Vision* is dated 1925, but the book was not distributed until 15 January 1926.
2 All quotations from *A Vision* are taken from the Macmillan, London, 1962 edition, pp. 169–72.
3 A phrase frequently employed by Lady Gregory; cf. *Our Irish Theatre*, C.E. 4, p. 33.
4 'Per Amica Silentia Lunae', *Mythologies* (Macmillan, London, 1959), p. 326.

5 'Dramatis Personae', *Autobiographies* (Macmillan, London, 1955), pp. 456–57; see also p. 395.

6 *Lady Gregory's Journals vol. I, Books 1–29*, C.E.14, p. 619.

7 *Journals*, ed. Murphy, p. 444; ed. Robinson, p. 334.

8 'The Trembling of the Veil', *Autobiographies*, p. 380.

9 Notes to *The Full Moon*, in *Wonder and the Supernatural Plays*, C.E. 7, p. 374. All references to Lady Gregory's plays are to this edition.

10 *Ibid.*

11 Introductory notes to 'The Fool of the Forth', *Visions and Beliefs in the West of Ireland*, C.E.1 p. 250; cf. notes to *The Full Moon*, pp. 374–75.

12 'Ireland in Letters', *The Book Monthly*, April 1904, p. 471.

13 'West Irish Ballads', *Poets and Dreamers*, C.E.11, p. 51.

14 cf. notes to *The Wrens, The Comedies*, C.E.5, pp. 265–66; dedications to *Poets and Dreamers* and *The Kiltartan History Book*, and her review of P. W. Joyce's *A Social History of Ancient Ireland, The Academy and Literature*, 31 October 1903, p. 464. ' "The voice of the people" my dictionary!' she wrote to T. J. Kiernan, disclaiming reference books, 27 June 1930, 'Letters from Lady Gregory: Her Friendship with T. J. Kiernan', ed. Daniel J. Murphy, *Bulletin of the New York Public Library*, vol. 72, no. 1 (January 1968), p. 54.

15 cf. J. M. Synge, *Prose*, ed. Alan Price (Oxford University Press, 1966; Colin Smythe, Gerrards Cross,1982), p. 351.

16 21 June 1902. Writing to Bernard Shaw of Robert's death, she comforted herself, 'I am glad to know the last thing he looked at was the Italian sky and not bursting shells or the faces of enemies', 'The Lady Gregory Letters to G. B.Shaw', ed. Daniel J. Murphy, *Modern Drama*, vol X, no. 4 (February, 1968), p. 344.

17 *Journals*, Vol. 1, C.E. 14, p. 465.

18 Her report in *The Speaker* of the establishment of the Kiltartan branch of the Gaelic League, 12 August 1899.

19 17 May 1903.

20 'The Felons of our Land', *Cornhill Magazine*, May 1900, p. 622.

21 *Journals*, C.E.14, p. 616. She wrote to John Quinn of Blake and Swedenborg on 22 February 1916, 'They all bring one back to the simplicity of "I saw a new heaven and a new earth". I suppose that is what we are always hoping for.' (letter in the Foster-Murphy collection, courtesy of Professor William Murphy).

22 'Modern Art in Dublin', *The Spectator*, 25 January 1908, on the opening of Hugh Lane's gallery. In her biography of Lane, she quotes this as having been written for *Claidheamh Soluis*. Writing to John Quinn on 30 June 1912 about Lane's efforts to build a modern gallery in Dublin to house his pictures, 'I believe he will have to do it himself in the end. One generally has to carry out one's schemes either with one's own money or time or both'. (Foster-Murphy collection).

23 Editor's Note, *Ideals in Ireland* (At the Unicorn, London, 1901), pp. 9–10. The quotation, used by Yeats as title for his novel *The Speckled Bird*, is from Jeremiah 12:9.

24 Paul Ruttledge in *Where There is Nothing* at the climax of his sermon, 'We must destroy the World . . .', Act IV. A speech in Act I of this play is one Yeats would later attribute to Synge, 'I only know that I want to upset everything. Have you not noticed that it is a complaint many of us have in this country? and whether it comes from love or hate I don't know, they are so mixed together here.'

25 To T. J. Kiernan, *Bulletin of the New York Public Library*, vol. 71, no. 10, (December 1967), pp. 642, 649.
26 'Modern Art in Dublin', *The Spectator*, 25 January 1908.
27 To T. J. Kiernan, 9 April 1928, p. 21.
28 To Bernard Shaw, 13 November 1923, pp. 344–345.
29 *Journals*, C.E. 14, p. 353 after reading of Montaigne's 'fenc[ing] with poverty', 'I have had that thought, that the muscles of the mind may be strengthened by the battle'.
30 *Collected Plays I*, C.E.5, pp. 253 and 259.
31 Notes to *Damer's Gold, Collected Plays I*, p. 262.
32 Notes to *The Bogie Men, Collected Plays I*, p. 260.
33 'Lady Gregory's Strenuous Effort to Found National Theatres and Quell Mobs Dissatisfied with Plays', a clipping dated April 1913 from her American cutting book, unidentified.
34 Cf. her note to *Spreading the News, The Comedies*, p. 253.
35 *The Tragedies and Tragic Comedies*, C.E.6, pp. 164–65.
36 Letter to George Roberts, 24 February 1904, Houghton Library, Harvard University. She wrote in her Journal (ed. Robinson, pp.97–98) of Pearse's speech as used in *The Plough and the Stars*, 'One feels those who heard it were forced to obey its call, not to be afraid to fight even in the face of defeat. One honours and understands their emotion'. And, on the question of the Republicans and the oath, 'one should no more be angry with Government or Republicans than with different sections of one's own mind, tilting to good or bad on one or the other side, in many questions besides this' (C.E.14, p. 496).
37 *Wonder and the Supernatural Plays*, C.E.7, p. 167.
38 *Ibid.*, p.182.
39 *The Tragedies and Tragic Comedies*, p. 277.
40 'At 9, Merrion Row', *The Leader*, 9 November 1901.
41 *Wonder and the Supernatural Plays*, pp. 395, 398.
42 'The Felons of our Land', p. 634.
43 *Journals*, Vol. 1, C.E.14,p. 590.
44 29 January 1925, p. 621.
45 The entire poem, untitled, is quoted in her notes, C.E.7, p. 400; *Dave* is dedicated to AE.
46 Notes to *The Dragon, Wonder and the Supernatural Plays*, p. 392.
47 *Journals*, ed. Robinson, p. 103; cf. pp. 323–24 for Robinson's advice with *Dave*.
48 'Ireland: Real and Ideal', *Nineteenth Century*, November 1898, p. 769.
49 *Memoirs*, ed. Denis Donoghue (Macmillan, London, 1972), p. 168. Yeats's note to *The Unicorn from the Stars, Translations and Adaptations*, C.E.8, pp. 362–63, doubtless also owes much to Lady Gregory: 'The strange characters, her handiwork, on whom he [Paul Ruttledge] sheds his light, delight me. She has enabled me to carry out an old thought for which my own knowledge is insufficient, and to commingle the ancient phantasies of poetry with the rough, vivid, ever-contemporaneous tumult of the roadside; to share in the creation of a form that otherwise I could but dream of, though I do that always, an art that murmured, though with worn and failing voice, of the day when Quixote and Sancho Panza, long estranged, may once again go out gaily into the bleak air.'
50 Note to *Sancho's Master, Translations and Adaptations*, pp. 360–61.
51 Bernard Shaw to Lady Gregory, 26 June 1928; of the *Three Last Plays*, Shaw preferred *Dave*.

52   Notes to *Sancho's Master, Translations and Adaptations*, p. 361.
53   *Journals*, ed. Robinson, p. 324.
54   'The Whirligig of Time and the Irish Language', *The Leader*, 6 December 1902, p. 235.

LADY GREGORY'S CONTRIBUTIONS TO PERIODICALS: A CHECKLIST
Colin Smythe

1   The other works in which Lady Gregory had a major hand — *The King's Threshold, On Baile's Strand, Deirdre*, and the acting edition of *The Shadowy Waters* were not published in periodicals, and for that reason only are not included in this list.
2   An article 'Lady Augusta Gregory thanks friends in America for help given workers in Ireland' appeared in a Chicago paper on March 15 1905; an article or letter on Sir Henry Layard's Will was published in *The Observer* c. 1926.
3   The Abbey Theatre scrapbooks, compiled by Lady Gregory, were mislaid by Lennox Robinson on Cork Station on the return of the Abbey Theatre Company from one of their U.S. tours. Some of them were recovered by Mrs. Yeats, many years later, on a barrow bookstall, and returned to the Abbey's safekeeping. They are now in the Natonal Library of Ireland, available to students on microfilm. Lady Gregory's personal scrapbooks are now in the Robert W. Woodruff Library, Emory University.
4   Allan Wade, *A Bibliography of the Writings of W. B. Yeats*, 3rd edition revised and edited by Russell K. Alspach, (Rupert Hart-Davis, London, 1968). I am presently working on the 4th edition for Oxford University Press, who have taken over the Soho Bibliographies series from Hart-Davis.

ROBERT GREGORY: ARTIST AND STAGE DESIGNER
Richard Allen Cave

1   The letters quoted in this essay are reproduced by courtesy of the Robert W. Woodruff Library, Emory University; Anne de Winton and Catherine Kennedy. All letters reproduced in this essay are © Anne de Winton and Catherine Kennedy, 1982.
2   *The Journals*. part 1. C.E. 14, p. 459.
3   *Seventy Years*, C.E. 13, p. 559.
4   Though not the finest of Yeats's elegies for Robert Gregory, "Shepherd and Goatherd" with its pastoral mode and domestic idiom observes an appropriate decorum and reflects a social fact:

>   He that was best in every country sport
>   And every country craft, and of us all
>   Most courteous to slow age and hasty youth,
>   Is dead.

5 *Sir Hugh Lane: His Life and Legacy*, C.E. 10, p. 66.
6 *Ibid.* p. 155.
7 The letter is undated but enclosed in an envelope bearing the postmark 11 March 1900.
8 *Seventy Years*, p. 282. Before Elstree and Harrow, Robert Gregory had been educated at Park Hill. The headmaster there wrote of him in later years that "he had, as a boy, an affectionate nature and a penetrating mind, and seemed to me to be one of the ablest boys I ever had under me" (*Seventy Years.* p. 557).
9 *Ibid.*, p. 281.
10 The letter is undated and the postmark is indecipherable but is likely, given the subject matter, to have been written during Gregory's first session at Oxford.
11 *Seventy Years*, pp. 393–94.
12 The letter is undated but postmarked 14 March 1903. On 6 November 1902 Gregory had remarked in a letter to his mother: "I have been getting through a good lot of work — chiefly philosophy; but I seem to get a more confused idea the more I read".
13 The letter is undated but postmarked 14 May 1903.
14 *Theatre Business*. Selected and edited by Ann Saddlemyer (Colin Smythe, Gerrards Cross, Penn State University Press, University Park, 1982), p. 143. Nothing came of this scheme but those features of the actress that would have made her an ideal Antigone — her youth, simplicity, the fierce determination in the set of the chin and the elegant carriage of the head — are beautifully caught in Gregory's portrait-drawing of Miss Allgood which was reproduced in the 1908 volume of *Samhain*. This sketch has been reproduced on p. 32 of *Robert Gregory 1881–1918: A Centenary Tribute*, ed. Colin Smythe (Colin Smythe, Gerrards Cross, 1982).
15 These details are recorded in an obituary notice for Gregory in the *Illustrated Sporting and Dramatic News* of 23 February 1918: 'A good shot, a fine boxer, an excellent slow-break bowler, and a fearless horseman and point-to-point rider'.
16 Undated but bears a forwarding stamp from Gort dated 2 February 1901.
17 The forwarding stamp from London is dated 9 February 1903.
18 The forwarding stamp is dated 23 February 1903.
19 Yeats must have been on the point of leaving London with Lady Gregory for Dublin for a performance of the Irish National Theatre Society at the Molesworth Hall (the programme combined his morality, *The Hour Glass*, with her first comedy, *Twenty Five*) so his being released from the engagement was doubtless welcome.
20 Undated but the postmark reads 7 May 1903.
21 The postmark reads 14 May 1903. This passage is characteristic of Gregory's rapid epistolary style; there is every suggestion that his letters were not read through after composition and corrected. The main sentence here appears to require the insertion of a negative to make grammatical sense, though the drift of his ideas is clear enough.
22 D. J. Gordon and Ian Fletcher: 'Persons and Places: III In Memory of Major Robert Gregory', *Images of a Poet*, ed. D. J. Gordon, (Manchester University Press, Manchester, 1961), p. 32.
23 *Theatre Business*, pp. 44–5.
24 One of Gregory's sketches for *The Hour Glass* is reproduced as Plate One in

Yeats and the Theatre, eds. Robert O'Driscoll and Lorna Reynolds, (Macmillan of Canada, Toronto, 1975).

25 *Joseph Holloway's Abbey Theatre*, eds. Robert Hogan and M. J. O'Neill, (Southern Illinois University Press, Carbondale, 1967), p. 22.

26 Augustus John, *Chiaroscuro* (Jonathan Cape, London, 1952), pp. 41–2.

27 Lennox Robinson, *Curtain Up*, (Michael Joseph, London, 1942), p. 25. Robinson stayed in Yeats's quarters after being despatched to London by the poet to learn the theatrical trade by acting as Shaw's amanuensis and observing his method of directing plays.

28 The letters of the Slade years are the most informative about Robert's development as an artist and they are therefore transcribed here virtually in full. The remaining letters in the collection fall into two categories: a group sent while he was on active service in the Great War; and a considerable number sent from Coole to his mother during the years 1908–15 while she was away in Dublin, England or America with the Abbey company giving her news of the estate and the family and information about business transactions. In transcribing the letters, the present writer has observed wherever possible the layout and style of punctuation of the originals. Capital letters have been given to words initiating sentences, which Gregory in his haste does not always give himself. His preference for dashes rather than full stops in many letters has been retained. Omission marks (i.e. as follows: ". . .") indicate the omission of short references to members of the family, Lady Gregory's circle or the servants at Coole, to his various dogs, his gunsmith and his cricketing companions. It is not often that Gregory dates letters; where dates are given in square brackets, these are surmised from the postmarks on the envelopes or the forwarding stamps from Gort (designated 'p.mk.' before the date). Where words are printed in square brackets preceded by a question mark, this indicates that the original is not clearly legible and a reading has been hazarded by the present writer. Where it is impossible even to surmise a reading — a rare occurrence — this is indicated by square brackets enclosing a question mark.

29 The Irish National Theatre Society would have been rehearsing Yeats's *The King's Threshold* and Synge's *In The Shadow of the Glen* for performance on 8th October in the Molesworth Hall when Robert passed through Dublin.

30 Sir Arthur Temple Felix Clay (1842–1928), the fourth Baronet, a barrister at the Inner Temple and a landscape and portrait painter of some distinction, was the brother of Sir William Gregory's first wife Elizabeth. Lady Gregory fostered a close relationship with her predecessor's family even after Sir William's death; Sir Arthur and his wife Margaret (née Barcley) lived at 19 Hyde Park Gate; their son, George Felix Neville, was Robert's senior by ten years.

31 A former college friend of Gregory, see above p. 350.

32 Arthur Clifton's Carfax Gallery in Bury Street housed exhibitions at this time for a range of Gregory's friends and associates — Will Rothenstein, Augustus and Gwen John, Nettleship, Tonks and Wilfrid Blunt's son-in-law, Neville Lytton. The Blake exhibition of forty-one works (largely Biblical scenes with the Job series predominating) was an unusual departure for Clifton, but its success justified a follow-up exhibition of sixty-three illustrations by Calvert the next April.

33 It was eventually situated in an outhouse by the laundry.

34 Henry Arthur Jones's *Joseph Entangled* had opened for a successful run at the

Haymarket Theatre on 19 January 1904 with Cyril Maude and Herbert Waring in the leading roles. The plot concerns a bachelor and a married lady who unwittingly and quite innocently spend a night alone in a house each believes empty. The servants, their acquaintance and the lady's husband put the worst construction on the facts when they are discovered; the lady's passionate refusal to elope with the bachelor and make the best of a nasty situation is overheard by her husband who at last accepts her plea of innocence. The play has some potential as a Sheridan-like exposure of the cruelty that accompanies man's hunger for scandal but Gregory is right to criticise the basic premise of its construction as forced, while Jones patently enjoys the titillative aspects of what he sets out to condemn.

35 Pinero's *Letty* had been enjoying a good run at the Duke of York's Theatre where it opened on 8 October 1903; it follows the career of a working-class girl who toys with the idea of becoming mistress to an aristocrat and a transient success in 'fast' society but chooses the lasting securities of a marriage to a caring and industrious if humbler man of her own background. All indeed 'turns upon Letty's character', but her major decisions are all taken off-stage between the acts so that there is a cloying weight of retrospect and reminiscence.

36 *The Letters of W. B. Yeats*, edited by Allan Wade, (Rupert Hart-Davis, London, 1954, Macmillan, New York, 1955), p. 432.

37 Elinor Mary Monsell of Curragh Chase, Adare, Co. Limerick had entered the Slade in 1896 but continued to befriend students there with an Irish connection; she visited Coole regularly (several of her sketches of equestrian subjects grace Robert's album) and she designed both 'Maeve and the Wolfhound', which Yeats and Lady Gregory subsequently used as the Abbey Theatre emblem, and the Dun Emer pressmark of 'Lady Emer and the tree'.

38 Sydney Cockerell was soon to visit Wilfrid Scawen and Lady Anne Blunt at Sheykh Obeyd, their residence near Cairo.

39 British sympathies were strongly pro-Japanese in the Russo-Japanese War for the occupation of Manchuria and Korea which broke out this month.

40 Frank Curzon's production of Robert Marshall's *The Duke of Killicrankie* had just opened at the Criterion; despite Gregory's astute criticism of its improbabilities (the Duke kidnaps the heroine and keeps her locked in his remote castle to gain the chance of proving the strength of his love for her), the play was a popular success and ran till August.

41 British Library Ms. No. 58116. The entry is for 20 March.

42 *Ibid.*

43 On 26th June, Shannon records; 'Went in the evening to see Yeats play at Court with Lady Gregory's party also dined with her at a little restaurant close by the theatre. The play was very interesting [this was *Where There Is Nothing*, directed by Granville Barker] but not quite a complete success as far as acting was concerned. Thomas Hardy was also in our box but he did not stagger one with his intelligence'. On 4 November he notes: 'Yates [sic] & American friend Gregory & friend came in evening & Pissarro', while on 12 November he records: 'Dined with Lady Gregory with R[icketts] to meet Yeats & young Gregory'. All quotations are from British Library Ms. No. 58116.

44 British Library Ms. No. 58117.

45 British Library Ms. No. 58103. The entry is for 23 January 1905.

46 *The Letters of W. B. Yeats*. p. 442.

47   *Theatre Business*. p. 66. This was dated 15 November; a week later, on 24 November, Yeats wrote asking Lady Gregory whether Robert 'could find time to look up some prints and to make me a wing of this sort in the next three or four days' (*The Letters of W. B. Yeats*, p. 445). Amongst Yeats's effects now in Anne Yeats's possession is a design by Gregory for some tree wings; they show clusters of pine trees to stage left and right, the elongated trunks overlapping in shades of reddish brown while high aloft the foliage is suggested by simple masses of grey-blue and blue-green flat colour; a backcloth that sketchily depicts a further group of trees of a similar design and a mountainside together with two figures (a woman in a flowing robe and an armed man) complete the design. It is the most Japanese in inspiration of Gregory's surviving theatre settings. It is not clear whether it was ever used for a particular play or whether, as seems more likely, this is Robert's response to Yeats's request for 'the sort of tree one finds in Japanese prints'.

48   *Samhain*. November 1905. p. 3.

49   Undated but Shaw's *John Bull's Other Island*, which Barker and Vedrenne revived throughout the month at the Royal Court opened on 7 February.

50   In the event Gregory did cross over to Dublin to supervise the preparation and painting of the sets, see p.

51   Hilary Pyle in her biography, *Jack B. Yeats* (Routledge & Kegan Paul, London, 1970) does not include the exhibition at Baillie's Gallery in her checklist of the artist's public shows.

52   Eric Browell Hoare and George Kennedy from Cookham, Berkshire, entered the Slade as Gregory's contemporaries in 1903 but Hoare left after one session.

53   Hugh Lane with the assistance of Dermot O'Brien had in the New Year mounted an exhibition of the Staats Forbes collection at the Royal Hibernian Academy. Lady Gregory comments: 'in accordance with the testator's wish it was to be given for a lower price than in the open market, should it be purchased to find a place in some public gallery [and] Hugh saw the opportunity for Dublin' (*Sir Hugh Lane: His Life and Legacy*, C.E. 10, p. 58). The paintings, chiefly nineteenth-century works, were amplified by a wealth of French Impressionist canvases on loan from Durand Ruel (Lady Gregory dates Lane's enthusiasm for the style from this year); many were purchased by gift or subscription to form the nucleus of a Gallery of Modern Art for Dublin, including a landscape 'An October Morning' by Stott of Oldham, given by the Gregorys in memory of the Comte de Basterot of Duras. Lane was often in two minds about which of the exhibited works to purchase for a permanent collection: O'Brien remarks that he was constantly as treasurer having to explain to people 'why when they had given their money for one picture yesterday, their name would appear today upon another' (*Ibid*. p. 62). This doubtless explains his appeal for Robert Gregory's help.

54   British Library Ms. No. 58117.

55   *Ibid*.

56   British Library Ms. No. 58103. The entry is for 28 April 1905.

57   The National Theatre Society now firmly established at the Abbey were investigating the possibility of a week's season of their current repertoire in London; in the event the visit did not occur until the last week in November preceded by performances in Oxford and Cambridge.

58   Albert Daniel Rothenstein (better known by his adopted name of Rutherston) was William Rothenstein's precocious younger brother who had entered the Slade with Wyndham Lewis and Augustus John in 1899 at sixteen. Though he

resisted this particular invitation to design for the theatre, he was to work for two years (1912–13) with Granville Barker, most notably on *Androcles and the Lion*, and on a number of ballet projects for Anna Pavlova.

59 Charles Wallington Furse, a former Slade scholar and member of the New English Art Club, had died on 17 October 1904.

60 Charles Archer's translation of Ibsen's *Lady Inger* was mounted by the Incorporated Stage Society in a production by Herbert Jarman at the Scala Theatre on 28 January 1906 with a cast that included Edythe Olive as Lady Inger, Henry Ainley as Nils Lykke, Charles Doran and Harcourt Williams.

61 William Rothenstein, *Men and Memories: Recollections 1872–1900* (Faber & Faber, London, 1931), p. 333.

62 *The Letters of W. B. Yeats*. p. 504. Yeats observed to Florence Farr at this time that 'Robert watches him [John] with visible admiration and discipleship' (*Letters*, p. 492).

63 *Hyacinth Halvey*, which opened at the Abbey on 19 February, was to establish Lady Gregory's talent as a writer of farce: Joseph Holloway for one found it 'if anything funnier than *Spreading the News*' (*Joseph Holloway's Abbey Theatre*), p. 70.

64 British Library Ms. No. 58117.

65 British Library Ms. No. 58118.

66 *Ibid.*

67 John Fothergill, *James Dickson Innes* (Faber & Faber, London), 1946, p. 6.

68 Augustus John's gift of his gypsy lexicon was the fulfilment of a promise made to Lady Gregory in May 1904 after receiving a presentation copy of her *Poets and Dreamers* which astonished him for its rendering of tinker speech, beside which the language of English tinkers appeared to him impoverished and derivative: 'Your book proves how much original feeling there is in the Irish peasant'. He volunteered to send Lady Gregory 'the hundred words or so I know of English Shelta' but recommended her also to consult John Sampson, Librarian at Liverpool University, as the true 'custodian' of Irish gipsy dialects. (See Michael Holroyd, *Augustus John: A Biography*. Vol. I. (Wm. Heinemann, London 1974, p. 163).

69 Agnew's exhibition — 'Some Examples of Independent Art Today: English, Scottish, Irish' — ran throughout February and March 1906 at the Bond Street gallery and included works by Steer, Tonks, Sickert, Will Rothenstein, Fry, Conder and James Pryde.

70 Ricketts's canvas, one of his most successful, was *The Betrayal of Christ* (1904), a composition of considerable intensity and dramatic gesture; it was further exhibited at the International Exhibition in Rome (1911) and posthumously at the Royal Academy (1933).

71 Shannon's exhibits were his Titian-inspired *Tibullus in the House of Delia* (1900–1905), an exploration of the power of colours to pulsate and shimmer against a prevailing dark background, and a landscape, *The Millpond*. Compared with Ricketts's painting, Shannon's do lack psychological power; painterly execution seems the total *raison d'être*.

72 *The Variorum Edition of the Plays of W. B. Yeats*, ed. R. K. Alspach. (Macmillan, London and New York, 1966), p. 526.

73 It is said that the Italianate Renaissance idiom was the wish of Lady Gregory but Titian and Bellini were declared influences on Shannon's work at this date; indeed the modelling of the head against the dark wall, the highlighting of the chin-structure and the finely proportioned nose against the near-black tones

of the canvas on which it is to be supposed that Gregory is working is arguably Shannon's finest assumption of the grand manner. The portrait is reproduced on page 14 of the *Centenary Tribute* and on page 49 of *Images of a Poet.*

74 Augustus John 'Fragment of an Autobiography'. *Horizon.* Vol. XI. No. 64. April 1945. p. 255.

75 See *Images of a Poet.* p. 32.

76 Interestingly Innes in the Spring of 1908 painted in Collioure and Bozouls, a terrain visited some three or four years earlier by both Matisse and Derain. See *Augustus John: A Biography.* Vol. I, p. 375.

77 'Fragment of an Autobiography', p. 255.

78 See for example the oil painting, *Dorelia and the children at Martiques,* now in the possession of the Fitzwilliam Museum, Cambridge.

79 Innes could be naive and whimsical, yet in a darker vein, he could exaggerate and contort the angularities of a Welsh or Pyrenean landscape to evoke a doomed or diabolic world. See plates 16 and 17 and plates 8, 16 and 34 in Fothergill's *James Dickson Innes* for examples of these contrasting moods.

80 Reproduced as plate 15 in Fothergill and as plate 32 in *Images of a Poet,* p. 119. The painting is in the possession of the Tate Gallery, London.

81 W. B. Yeats, 'A Note of Appreciation', *The Observer.* 17 February 1918. It is reprinted in *Robert Gregory — A Centenary Tribute,* p. 15.

82 See for example *An Imaginary Landscape with Riders* reproduced in *Robert Gregory — A Centenary Tribute* on page 37. The original is alive with vibrant colour: the foreground rocks and trees are a light grey through which can be seen naked figures riding white or buff horses and disporting themselves across a meadow scattered with flowers. In the distance beyond a further line of grey trees a lake gleams at the foot of purple and pink hills and is edged with a golden strand and bushes. *Roses* is reproduced in *The Centenary Tribute* on page 37.

83 *Illustrated London News,* 6 June 1914, p. 970.

84 *Ibid.*

85 An exception is perhaps *Coole Lake* reproduced as plate 29 in *Images of a Poet* on page 116. Examples of Innes's patterning with reflections of land masses in water or of clouds echoing or inverting the line of mountains or the layout of fields and hedgerows can be found in his 1910–11 studies of Bala Lake (plates 18, 19 and 20 in Fothergill).

86 *Illustrated London News,* 6 June 1914, p. 970.

87 Reproduced in the *Centenary Tribute* on page 39.

88 See plate 30 in *Images of a Poet* on page 117.

89 See the *Centenary Tribute,* page 38.

90 W. B. Yeats, *The Collected Poems* (Macmillan, London, 1950), pp. 150–1.

91 This was the last full-scale canvas exhibited; a *Sketch for a Decoration* was shown at the New English Art Club's spring exhibition in 1915.

92 *Seventy Years,* p. 491.

93 *Ibid.,* p. 558.

94 W. B. Yeats, 'An Irish Airman Foresees His Death', *The Collected Poems,* p. 152.

95 *Ibid.*

96 Yeats's footnote of 1924 to his essay, 'Ireland and the Arts' (1901) reprinted in *Ideas of Good and Evil* and subsequently in *Essays and Introductions* (Macmillan, London, 1961), p. 209.

97 *Illustrated London News.* 6 June 1914, p. 970.

98 Craig's *The Masque of Love* of 1901 was set in a box of grey canvas flooded with pools of different coloured lights.
99 *W. B. Yeats and T. Sturge Moore: Their Correspondence, 1901–1937* ed. Ursula Bridge (Routledge & Kegan Paul, & Oxford, New York, 1953), pp. 4–5. The letter from Moore to Yeats together with a reproduction of his sketch for the setting of *The Hour Glass* is also reproduced in Liam Miller, *The Noble Drama of W. B. Yeats* (Dublin, 1977), pp. 80–81.
100 *Joseph Holloway's Abbey Theatre*, pp. 21–2.
101 In performance it appears from a surviving photograph showing the Fay brothers as the Wise Man and the Fool that a trestle table akin in proportions to that in Gregory's sketch was used rather than a desk. Instead a chair with a high, narrow, open back was used to achieve the effect Moore was aiming for. This photograph is reproduced amongst the plates in *Theatre Business* and as plate 5 in James W. Flannery, *W. B. Yeats and the Idea of a Theatre* (Macmillan of Canada, Toronto; Yale University Press, New Haven, 1976).
102 This was to be an image that resonated in Yeats's imagination finding further dramatic life most notably in the conclusion to *The King of the Great Clock Tower*.
103 These were the criteria adhered to by most designers and directors during the Victorian and Edwardian period; settings were required to look authentic, much historical research frequently going into the quest for accuracy of representation on the grounds of the immense educational value for the audience of the result.
104 Michael R. Booth, *Victorian Spectacular Theatre 1850–1910*, (Routledge & Kegan Paul, Boston, London, Henley 1981), p. 103. I am indebted to Professor Booth for this account of Irving's *Faust*.
105 *Ibid.*, p. 103.
106 *W. B. Yeats and T. Sturge Moore: Their Correspondence, 1901–1937*, pp. 5–6.
107 See plates 8 and 17 in *W. B. Yeats and the Idea of a Theatre*.
108 *W. B. Yeats and T. Sturge Moore: Their Correspondence, 1901–1937*, pp. 5–7. The letter is reprinted in *The Noble Drama of W. B. Yeats*, pp. 95–7.
109 *Ibid.*, pp. 6–7. Yeats's letter included rough sketches of how he thought the setting for *The Shadowy Waters* should be arranged. The drawings are also reproduced in *The Noble Drama of W. B. Yeats*, p. 96.
110 *The Variorum Edition of the Plays of W. B. Yeats*, p. 341.
111 *W. B. Yeats and T Sturge Moore: Their Correspondence, 1901–1937*, p. 7.
112 Craig (inspired by his first-hand knowledge of Irving's brilliant, imaginative deployment of gas lighting at the Lyceum, by his masterly handling of darkness and his sense of the sculptural possibilities of subtly angled light) had from his first production of *Dido and Aeneas* impressed Yeats by the range of poetic effects he had achieved simply by virtue of light subtly modulated and coloured in unconventional positioning. More recently Ricketts had insisted on lighting his staging of Wilde's *Salomé* (10 June 1906) at the King's Hall, Covent Garden. Moonlight preoccupies Wilde's characters, becoming a crucial, even obsessive, strand in the pattern of imagery and Ricketts saw it as essential that the stage-picture should in no way mar the impact of the verbal artistry. His setting — a vast terrace, dominated by an austere distant column and hung about with dense pale green curtains in the manner of a colonnade to create areas of coolness and privacy — would offer considerable possibilities for ethereal and sinister effects if imaginatively lit. The design is now in the collection of the Victoria and Albert Museum, London. There is

no record of Gregory seeing this production (Yeats certainly did), but he was
still in London during that June.

113   *Theatre Business*, p. 156.
114   As late as 1926, Harold Ridge, one of England's foremost lighting designers,
      was warning of the difficulty of getting good, clear effects with green and
      especially blue light in his *Stage Lighting for Little Theatres* (Heffer,
      Cambridge, 1926).
115   *Joseph Holloway's Abbey Theatre*, p. 50.
116   *The Variorum Edition of the Plays of W. B. Yeats*, p. 456.
117   Ibid. p. 459.
118   W. G. Fay: 'The Poet and the Actor', *Scattering Branches: Tributes to the
      Memory of W. B. Yeats* ed. S. Gwynne (Macmillan, London, 1940), p. 134.
119   *Samhain*. September, 1903, p. 10.
120   *Ibid.*, p. 10.
121   In the event Gregory did not complete a commission to re-stage the play for
      perfomances in 1908. After his marriage the previous September he had gone
      to study in Paris; he finished a sketch for the blackcloth during a visit to Coole
      in the spring of 1908 and took his ideas for sally wings back with him to Paris
      to work on them in more detail. Appeals from Synge and Lady Gregory met
      with silence and in desperation Yeats approached Charles Ricketts who hastily
      devised sets and costumes with Yeats advising virtually at his elbow since
      Ricketts had never been to Ireland. Lady Gregory tried to save face for Robert
      by herself copying designs for wings from an illustration of Beardsley's — his
      'Perseus with the Gorgon's head'. These show a dense thicket of slender tree
      trunks across which stylised willow and thorn saplings curve as if arching
      against the wind. Synge, generally the appeaser in crises at the Abbey,
      consoled Robert with the hope that 'the blackcloth at least may come in handy
      for my Deirdre which is to be ready in autumn' (*Theatre Business* p. 276).
122   *Joseph Holloway's Abbey Theatre*, p. 54.
123   W. G. Fay and C. Carswell, *The Fays of the Abbey Theatre*. (Rich and
      Cowan, London, 1935), p. 170.
124   *Kincora* in *Tragedies and Tragic-Comedies*, C.E.6, p. 316.
125   *Our Irish Theatre*, C.E.4, p. 65.
126   An article giving preliminary details about the staging of *Kincora* from *The
      Freeman's Journal* of 25 March. It is quoted in Robert Hogan and James
      Kilroy, *The Abbey Theatre: The Years of Synge, 1905–1909*, (Dolmen Press,
      Dublin, 1978), p. 23.
127   *Our Irish Theatre*, p. 65.
128   *The Abbey Theatre: The Years of Synge, 1905–1909*, p. 23.
129   *Ibid.*, p. 26.
130   *Our Irish Theatre*, p. 65.
131   *The Letters of W. B. Yeats*. p. 422. The following 12 November, Ricketts and
      Shannon dined with Lady Gregory who was then visiting London and
      Ricketts's Diary enigmatically notes. 'In evening to Lady Gregory to discuss
      scenery etc.' (British Library MS. No. 58102). From then until the following
      February was a period when Shannon was working intermittently on
      Gregory's portrait so occasions for discussions on the settings for *Kincora*
      certainly presented themselves. Ricketts was unsparing in his encouragement
      of younger artists.
132   Ricketts's first designs were for Binyon's *Paris and Oenone*, Sturge Moore's
      Aphrodite against Artemis and Wilde's *Salome* in March, April and June 1906.

133 Photographs of the setting can be seen in the Theatre Collection at the Victoria and Albert Museum, London.

134 The designs are reproduced in G. B. Shaw, *Saint Joan* (with illustrations by Ricketts, Constable, London, 1924.) Photographs of the production are reproduced in Joseph Darracott, *The World of Charles Ricketts* (Eyre Methuen, London, 1980), pp. 172–3.

135 Charles Ricketts, 'The Art of Stage Decoration', *Pages on Art* (Constable, London, 1913), p. 246.

136 Gordon Bottomley, 'Charles Ricketts, R. A.', *Theatre Arts Monthly*, May 1932, p. 379.

137 *The Times*, 9 October 1931, p. 7.

138 See above, p. 367.

139 The design is reproduced in Albert Rutherston, *Sixteen Designs for the Theatre* (Humphrey Milford, London, 1928); and with the text of his lecture 'Decoration in the Theatre' in *The Monthly Chapbook* (Number Two, Vol. I. August 1919).

140 'Decoration in the Theatre', p. 19.

141 To read Ricketts's essay of 1913, 'The Art of Stage Decoration', is to encounter again Yeats's baldly stated criteria of 1903 being applied to a review of stage-practice over the intervening decade. The ideas, often even the terms, coalesce; Ricketts argues that the designer's ambition should be for a new simplicity that is not naiveté but a concentration of effects; that such a simplification once found opens up an infinite variety of possibilities and that it will be found ideally only in one set of circumstances — 'as the action grows in intensity so should the imagination of the artist be at its intensest' (p. 247).

142 'The Art of Stage Decoration', p. 230.

143 The design is reproduced on page 32 of *Robert Gregory: A Centenary Tribute*.

144 *Joseph Holloway's Abbey Theatre*. p. 63.

145 *Ibid.*, p. 64

146 *Ibid.*, p. 64.

147 *Ibid.*, p. 64.

148 *Ibid.*, p. 65.

149 A. E. Malone, *The Irish Drama* (Constable, London, Scriber's, New York, 1929; reprinted Benjamin Blom, New York & London, 1965), p. 298.

150 The design is reproduced on page 34 of *Robert Gregory: A Centenary Tribute*. It was exhibited as Item 20 of Gregory's 1912 show at the Baillie Gallery.

151 *The Image* in *Collected Plays II*, C.E.6, p. 147.

152 The design is reproduced on page 34 of *Robert Gregory: A Centenary Tribute*; it too was exhibited at the Baillie Gallery in 1912, as Item 3.

153 *The Irish Times*, 6 January 1911, p. 4.

154 *The Variorum Edition of the Plays of W. B. Yeats*, p. 344.

155 Naisi was played by Claude King and Conchubar by Arthur Homes-Gore. In *Electra*, Florence Farr appeared as Clytemnestra, Arthur Holmes-Gore as Aegisthus and Vernon Steel as Orestes.

156 *The Sketch* and *The Tatler* for 9 December 1908 carried photographs of the production. Flannery reproduces one as plate 12 in *W. B. Yeats and the Idea of a Theatre*.

157 *The Noble Drama of W. B. Yeats*, p. 174, quoting from *Plays for an Irish Theatre*, 1911, p. 215.

158 Plate 14 in *W. B. Yeats and the Idea of a Theatre* is entitled by James Flannery as 'Scene from Yeats's *Deirdre* (1906). *Source*: Senator Yeats'. The situation

could be Deirdre mourning the dead Naisi watched over by Conchubar and an attendant Musician. But the presence of a sword near the dead man's hand when Yeats specifies that Naisi is entangled in a net and disarmed before being slain leaves room for doubt whether this is an illustration of the climax of Yeats's tragedy. There is, also, no curtain or hanging behind which the deaths might be effected; a curtained inner stage is fundamental to his conception of the drama. There is no record of Mrs. Campbell asking for a new setting from Gregory for her appearances in Dublin or for her London season. The photographs of Mrs. Campbell's performances show a setting that, were it the original Abbey staging, was simple and would be readily transportable; her season at the New Theatre was limited to a few matinées and economies would be essential. The ascription of the photograph to the 1906 production of *Deirdre* is troubling because it is quite unlike the style of Gregory's theatre work at any period; the construction is crude (wooden framed flats backed by canvas) and amateurish while the painting is distractingly fussy with a multiplicity of patterns and devices; the costumes lack grace of line being heavily ornamented and worn with sashes and cowled cloaks. Moreover this setting does not accord with reviewers' accounts of what they saw; that is a 'guesthouse in the woods' or 'poor hut, destitute of comfort'. There is too no suggestion of the forest that all-importantly surrounds the hut. Several reviewers summarising the action imply or confirm the presence of a curtain at the rear of the stage for the death-scenes. The mode of construction of the set with flats and its cramped dimensions much resembles those in photographs of early performances of Yeats's *Cathleen ni Houlihan* by the National Theatre Society while the costumes call to mind those devised for the first production of AE's *Deirdre* in George Coffey's garden, being similar in design and execution. AE's *Deirdre* was performed by the society in 1902 and the play was revived by the 'Theatre of Ireland Company' at the Abbey in 1907; this could be a record of that production. There is no conclusive proof but the evidence suggests that the photograph reproduced by Flannery has been mistitled; that the setting and costumes to be seen in photographs of Mrs. Campbell's London season are substantially those used at the Abbey in 1906 and 1908 in Yeats's play; and that these alone are the work of Robert Gregory.

159 J. M. Synge, *Plays Book 2*, ed. Ann Saddlemyer (Colin Smythe, Gerrards Cross, 1982), p. 217. The direction continues: "A wood, outside the tent of DEIRDRE and NAISI". A further design survives but only as a photograph, which may be a preliminary attempt at this scene. Lady Gregory had her copies of the catalogues for Gregory's two exhibitions bound together with photographs of several of the paintings on show. The volume commemorating the Chenil Gallery exhibition includes a photograph which Lady Gregory has entitled in her own hand 'Woodscene for Deirdre'; a painting of that title was item 12 in her catalogue. This depicts a backcloth representing a vigorous wooded landscape, alive with movement created by great upward-sweeping arcs formed by myriad intersecting branches. The manner is reminiscent of Van Gogh in the swirling, stabbing brushstrokes that evoke the mass of leaves and the stylised forms of rock and undergrowth. The whole expresses joy in vitality. Clearly the design could not be for Yeats's play which asks for an interior setting. Only Act II of Synge's tragedy has a direction mentioning a wood, though there is talk of a wild woodland outside the house of Deirdre's nurse, Lavarcham, where Act I is set. It is possible that this is a backcloth to be viewed by the audience through the door and windows of that interior

setting; but it seems too detailed for such a purpose. More likely, it was intended as a setting for Act II, that was rejected in favour of the cliff-top design which is more responsive to the sense of place conjured forth by the dialogue. The feeling of openness and freedom would contrast more effectively with the trapped, claustrophobic interior setting envisaged for Act III. The woodland design is reproduced on page 33 of *Robert Gregory: A Centenary Tribute*.

160 Synge, *Plays Book 2*, p. 233.

161 See for example plate 13 in *W. B. Yeats and the Idea of a Theatre*, while as plate VI in *The Noble Drama of W. B. Yeats*, it is titled 'Scene Design for *Deirdre*, 1906'. This same description is given to the design in *Robert Gregory: A Centenary Tribute* on page 33.

162 *The Daily Express* (Dublin), 14 January 1910, p. 5.

163 'In the centre, a part of the house is curtained off; the curtains are drawn. There are unlighted torches in brackets on the walls. There is at one side a small table with a chess-board and chessmen upon it. At the other side of the room there is a brazier with a fire.' (*The Variorum Edition of the Plays of W. B. Yeats*, p. 345.)

164 Synge, *Plays Book 2*, p. 249.

165 *The Morning Post* (London), 5 June 1912, p. 5.

166 Synge, *Plays Book 2*, p. 265.

167 *Ibid.*, p. 269.

168 *Ibid.*, p. 269.

169 *Ibid.*, p. 269.

170 *Ibid.*, p. 267.

171 *The Letters of W. B. Yeats*, pp. 545–6.

172 *The Freeman's Journal*, 13 January 1911, p. 10.

173 See for example his comment on *The Deliverer* to his father, J. B. Yeats, on 24 November 1910: "I shall get all my plays into the Craig scene and a new one of Lady Gregory's which is a symbolical play ostensibly about Moses really about Parnell". (*The Letters of W. B. Yeats*, p. 555.)

174 *The Freeman's Journal*, 13 January 1911, p. 10.

175 *The Irish Times*, 13 January 1911, p. 8.

176 *The Freeman's Journal*, 13 January 1911, p. 10.

177 *Joseph Holloway's Abbey Theatre*, p. 148.

178 *Ibid.*, p. 148.

179 *Ibid.*, p. 148.

180 The letter from Coole Park is simply dated 'Sunday'; the postmark is for Oranmore, but only the month — 'Nov' — is legible. The postmark of the next letter quoted is clearly readable as 'Oranmore Nov 8'; the contents of this letter obviously date it as later than the undated missive quoted here.

181 *The Freeman's Journal*, 13 January 1911, p. 10.

182 *The Letters of W. B. Yeats*, p. 578.

183 *Ibid.*, p. 579.

184 Sean O'Casey, 'Where Wild Swans Nest', *Inishfallen, Fare Thee Well* (Macmillan, London, 1949), p. 153.

185 *The Journals*, Part 1, C.E. 14, p. 283.

NOTES ON CONTRIBUTORS

RONALD AYLING, Professor of English at the University of Alberta, Canada, is literary advisor to the Estate of Sean O'Casey. He has published extensively on O'Casey and also on Shaw, Yeats, Synge, Lady Gregory, Wole Soyinka, Olive Schreiner and contemporary South African literature.

RICHARD ALLEN CAVE, Reader in Drama at Royal Holloway and Bedford New College in the University of London, has published *A Study of the Novels of George Moore* and editions of Moore's *Hail and Farewell!* and *The Lake*; *Terence Gray and the Festival Theatre Cambridge*; *The Dublin Gate Theatre: 1928–1978* (with Richard Pine); and a range of essays on modern theatre and on Anglo-Irish drama.

GARETH W. DUNLEAVY is Professor of English and Comparative Literature at the University of Wisconsin-Milwaukee. A recent Guggenheim and Camargo Fellow, he is presently completing (with Janet Egleson Dunleavy) a biography of Douglas Hyde. He is the author of *Colum's Other Island* (1960) and *Douglas Hyde* (1974).

GABRIEL FALLON (1898–1980) was a spare-time actor with the Abbey Theatre company from 1920 to 1928, and acted in first productions of the early plays of Sean O'Casey. He was a Director of the Theatre from 1959 until his death. His *Sean O'Casey; The Man I Knew* was published in 1965. His history of the Abbey Theatre, from which the extracts in this volume are taken, remains unpublished.

WILLIAM G. FAY (1872–1947), with his brother Frank J. Fay founded W. G. Fay's Irish National Dramatic Society while at the same time making his living as an electrician. The only member of the original Abbey Theatre company with experience on the professional stage, he was principal actor, stage manager/director of the company until resigning in 1909 over a disagreement with the Directors concerning the management of the Irish National Theatre Society Limited. He continued to perform, mainly in London and in films, until his death.

MARY FITZGERALD, Professor of English at the University of New Orleans, specialises in contemporary Irish poetry and the Abbey Theatre, and is Reviews Editor of *Yeats: An Annual of Critical and Textual Studies*. She is also the editor of Lady Gregory's *Shorter Writings*, two forthcoming volumes in the Coole Edition.

ANNE GREGORY is the elder of Lady Gregory's grand-daughters. Her recollections of her grandmother are told in her *Me & Nu; Childhood at Coole*.

The Rt. Rev. THOMAS ARNOLD HARVEY (1878–1966) was Robert Gregory's tutor at Coole for his Oxford entrance. He was Professor of pastoral Theology at Trinity College, Dublin 1929–34, Dean of St. Patrick's 1933–35, and Bishop of Cashel and Waterford, 1935–58. He officiated at Robert's marriage to Lily Margaret Graham Parry in 1907 and at Lady Gregory's funeral in 1932.

BRIAN JENKINS, a Fellow of the Royal Historical Society, has long been interested in Anglo-Irish as well as Anglo-American relations. He has published *Fenians and Anglo-American Relations during Reconstruction* (1969), two volumes on *Britain and the War for the Union* (1974 and 1980). His biography *Sir William Gregory of Coole* appeared in 1986, and he has just completed a study of William Gregory (Sir William's grandfather) and the Government of Ireland between 1812 and 1830.

JOHN S. KELLY, Senior English Fellow at St. John's College, Oxford, is Editor of *The Collected Letters of W. B. Yeats*, the first volume of which, covering the years to 1895, has just been published by Oxford University Press.

DAN H. LAURENCE, literary and dramatic advisor to the Shaw Estate, is editor of Shaw's collected letters, plays and prefaces, and music criticism. His comprehensive *Bernard Shaw: A Bibliography* was published in 1983.

ELIZABETH LONGFORD (THE COUNTESS OF LONGFORD), C.B.E., has written biographies of Wilfrid Scawen Blunt, the First Duke of Wellington, Lord Byron, Queen Victoria, and Queen Elizabeth II.

BRINSLEY MACNAMARA (1890–1963), pen name of John Weldon, best known as a novelist for *The Valley of the Squinting Windows*, had nine plays produced at the Abbey Theatre between 1919 and 1945. Briefly a member of the Abbey's Board of Directors in 1935, he resigned in protest over Sean O'Casey's *The Silver Tassie*, and was later the drama critic for *The Irish Times*.

ANDREW E. MALONE (1888–1939), pen name of Laurence Patrick Byrne, journalist, author and drama critic, published in 1929 *The Irish Drama*, one of the first book-length serious critical studies of the Abbey Theatre and its companion movements.

GEORGE MOORE (1852–1933) gained a solid reputation as novelist and essayist before he turned his attention to the theatre and back to Ireland, where he collaborated with his cousin Edward Martyn and with Yeats, and was intimately involved with the Irish Literary Theatre. His trilogy *Hail and Farewell!* provides an idiosyncratic and highly entertaining picture of the Irish Literary Revival from its beginnings to 1911 when he returned to London.

DANIEL J. MURPHY, of the City University of New York, is the co-author of six books on various aspects of English grammar and style. He is editor of *Lady Gregory's Journals,* volumes 14 and 15 of the Coole Edition.

MAUREEN MURPHY is Dean of Students at Hofstra University, Vice-President of the American Committee for Irish Studies, Historiographer of the American Irish Historical Society, and Bibliographer of the International Association for the Study of Anglo-Irish Literature. She has written on Irish history, literature, folklore and the Irish language, and her current project is a book on the Irish Servant Girl in America.

MAIRE Nic SHIUBHLAIGH (d. 1938) was the stage name of Mary Walker, later Mrs. Eamon Price. She and her brother Frank had been members of W. G. Fay's Irish National Dramatic Society; later two sisters also joined the company. Her reminiscences, written with her nephew Edward Kenny, *The Splendid Years,* document the early years of the dramatic movement.

SEAN O'CASEY (1880–1964), playwright, essayist, polemicist, and autobiographer, contributed three plays to the Abbey Theatre (*The Shadow of a Gunman, Juno and the Paycock, The Plough and the Stars*) before the rejection of *The Silver Tassie* severed his close connection with the Theatre and its Directors. After Lady Gregory's death he reached a rapprochement with Yeats.

JAMES PETHICA is a Junior Research Fellow at Wolfson College, Oxford, and is currently editing Lady Gregory's diaries for the years 1892 to 1902.

ANN SADDLEMYER, Professor of English and Drama at the University of Toronto and past Chairman of the International Association for the Study of Anglo-Irish Literature, has published extensively on Irish drama, as well as editing Synge's and Lady Gregory's Collected Plays. Her most recent books are *Theatre Business, The Correspondence of the First Abbey Theatre Directors* and *The Collected Letters of John Millington Synge.* She is also co-Editor of *Theatre History in Canada.*

[GEORGE] BERNARD SHAW (1856–1950), one of the most outstanding and certainly the most prolific dramatist in the twentieth century, left his native Ireland in 1876 and after devoting his considerable energies to novels, music and art criticism, and Fabian politics, received his first professional production as a playwright alongside W. B. Yeats in 1894. His relationship with the Irish dramatic movement began with the rejection by the Abbey of *John Bull's Other Island* because it was too large and too difficult for its resources, and continued primarily through his close friendship with Lady Gregory.

COLIN SMYTHE, publisher and bibliographer, is General Editor of the Coole Edition of Lady Gregory's works, co-General Editor of the Collected Works of G. W. Russell (AE), editor of *Robert Gregory 1881–1918*, Lady Gregory's *Coole*, and her autobiography *Seventy Years 1852–1922* and author of *A Guide to Coole Park, Home of Lady Gregory*. He is presently working on the 4th edition of Alan Wade's *A Bibliography of the Writings of W. B. Yeats* and a bibliography of Lady Gregory's works.

MARY LOU KOHFELDT STEVENSON's biography *Lady Gregory, The Woman Behind the Irish Renaissance* was published in 1985. She received her doctorate from the University of North Carolina at Chapel Hill, where she taught English Literature.

SIGNE TOKSVIG (1891–c. 1975), novelist and biographer, married Irish novelist and historian Francis Hackett in the U.S.A. When her first novel, *Eve's Doctor* had the dubious honour of sharing the fate of her husband's novel in being banned by the Irish Censorship Board, the couple settled in her native Denmark. A visit to the United States in 1939 was prolonged when Germany occupied her homeland. Her last publication was *Emmanuel Swedenborg, Scientist and Mystic*.

ROBERT WELCH is Professor of English and Head of the Department of English, Media and Theatre Studies at the University of Ulster. He is author of *Irish Poetry from Moore to Yeats*; editor of *The Way Back*, and his *History of Verse Translation from the Irish: 1789–1897* will be published in 1987. He is at work on a *Companion to Irish Literature*.

ANNE YEATS, one of Ireland's leading artists, began her career in the Abbey Theatre, where she designed, among other plays, the first production of her father's *Purgatory*. She has held many one-artist shows both in Ireland and North America and, after her mother's death in 1968, took responsibility, with her brother Michael B. Yeats, for the Cuala Press.

W. B. YEATS (1865–1939), poet, playwright, essayist and critic, founder of the Abbey Theatre, member of the Irish Free State Senate, and winner of the 1923 Nobel Prize for literature, is one of the outstanding literary figures of the twentieth century. With Lady Gregory, whom he first met in 1894, he established the Irish Literary Theatre and together they worked, in words of Lady Gregory often quoted by Yeats, 'to restore to Ireland its native dignity'.

LORNA D. YOUNG, Professor of English at Carleton University, has specialised in Anglo-Irish and American literature. Her thesis on Lady Gregory's plays for Trinity College, Dublin, was the first full study of Lady Gregory's work.

INDEX

the Poor', 148, 151, 154, 327;
The Rising of the Moon, 4, 5,
6, 40–1, 42, 44, 154, 155, 160,
274, 283, 295, 303 304, 313,
314, 332, 335; *The
Rogueries of Scapin* (Molière),
5, 43, 279, 284–5, 296; *Sancho's
Master* (after Cervantes), 11,
315, 319–21; *Selected Plays*, x,
12; *Seven Short Plays*, 6, 9, 10,
332–3, 335, 336, 338; *Seventy
Years*, x, 12, 48, 51–3, 86, 234,
267, 347, 349, 350; *Shanwalla*,
8, 10, 299; *The Shoelace*, 11,
313; *A Short Catechism on the
Financial Claims of Ireland*, 2;
*Sir Hugh Lane's Life and
Achievement*, 10, 48, 53; *Sir
Hugh Lane: His Life and
Legacy*, 341, 342, 343; *Sir
William Gregory, K.C.M.G.,
An Autobiography*, 2, 48, 49,
52, 186, 347; 'A Sorrowful
Lament for Ireland', 328;
Spreading the News, 4, 5, 6,
10, 11, 36, 38, 121, 213, 275,
282, 292, 293–4, 304, 332, 335,
336, 339, 364; *The Story
Brought by Brigit*, 10, 42, 213,
292, 299, 300, 305, 315–7, 344;
Teja (Sudermann), 283–4;
'Three Kiltartan Folk Tales',
340; *Three Last Plays*, 280;
Three Wonder Plays, 10;
'Through Portugal', 83, 323;
The Tinker and the Fairy
(Hyde), 154; for translations of
other authors' works, *see* under
English titles here, and below;
for translations of Lady
Gregory's work, *see* Linati,
Carlo; Ó Siochghradha,
Padraig; *The Travelling Man*,
4, 6, 41, 42, 299–300, 303, 305,
313, 315, 335; *Twenty-Five (A
Losing Game)*, 3, 313, 330–1,
381; *The Twisting of the Rope*
(Hyde), 3, 137, 296, 329; *The
Unicorn from the Stars* (with
W. B. Yeats) 5, 6, 283, 312,
313, 317; *Visions and Beliefs in
the West of Ireland*, 9, 12, 206,
325, 329; 'A Week in Ireland',
'A Second Week in Ireland',
etc., 10, 245, 246, 342–3; *The
White Cockade*, 4, 7, 42, 43,
44, 154, 155, 160, 214, 215,
281, 298, 299, 304, 313, 314,
335, 336, 337, 390–1; 'A
Woman's Sonnets', 2, 91, 93,
96, 97, 98–122; *The Workhouse
Ward*, 5, 6, 40, 154, 274, 275,
283, 292, 304, 313, 336, 338; *The
Would-be Gentleman* (Molière),
10, 43, 277, 280, 287–90, 296;
The Wrens, 8, 10, 215, 313
see also under W. B. Yeats,
Plays for an Irish Theatre
translations: d'Annunzio, 296;
Daudet, 158–9, 328; Goldoni,
40, 43, 44, 296; Hyde, 3, 40,
137, 147, 150, 154, 265, 296,
329, 330, 331, 333, 337, 344;
Maeterlinck, 5; Molière, 4, 40,
43, 44, 276–90, 295, 296;
O'Leary, 296; Pearse, 161;
Raftery, 147, 150, 155, 267,
268, 330, 331; Sudermann, 40,
296
Gregory, Margaret (*née* Graham-
Parry), later Mrs Guy Gough
(daughter-in-law), 148, 195,
234, 235, 238, 374, 375, 398;
illustrations for *Kiltartan
Wonder Book*, 7; ambushed,
246–7, 287; second marriage, 11
Gregory, Major Richard
(grandson), 6, 51, 93, 237,
347
GREGORY, MAJOR (WILLIAM)
ROBERT (son), ix, 29, 49, 50,
83, 96, 184, 187, 194, 227, 238,

347–400; birth, 76, 79, 347;
childhood, 84, 347; schooling,
349; at Coole, 15, 17, 134;
travels in Italy, 349, 350; at
Oxford University, 3, 348–53;
and Irish language, 145, 203;
art studies, 4, 353–73, 375;
interest in Greek tragedy, 350;
marriage, 5, 375, 376; war
service, 8, 234–4, 378; honours,
379; death, 9, 132, 228, 234–5,
287, 379, 400; tributes, 347,
400; portrait (by Shannon),
360–1, 362, 366, 378, 370, 372,
374
career as painter and stage
designer: sketches and
paintings, 376; 'Belharbour',
377; 'Death of the Firstborn',
371, 372; 'The Island', 378; 'The
Natural Bridge', 377–8;
'Orpheus', 377; illustrations in
the *Kiltartan History Book*, 6
designs for sets and costumes
for the Abbey Theatre, 364,
374, 379, 389; in collaboration
with AG, 390; in collaboration
with Sturge Moore, 380–1; *On
Baile's Strand* (Yeats), 272–3,
382, 383–5; *Deirdre* (Yeats),
392–4, 395; *Deirdre of the
Sorrows* (Synge), 394–7; *The
Deliverer* (Gregory), 398–9; *The
Hour Glass* (Yeats), 354, 380–1,
382, 386; *The Image* (Gregory),
391–2; *Kincora* (Gregory),
363–5, 366–7, 386–8, 389, 391;
The Nativity (Hyde), 391, 392;
The White Cockade (Gregory),
390–1
designs for Dun Emer Press: *A
Book of Saints and Wonders*
(Gregory), 369; *Stories of Red
Hanrahan* (Yeats), 369
letters to mother, 347, 349,
350–73 *passim*, 398; AG and,

120, 149, 185, 186, 189, 190,
255
Yeats on, 235–6, 239, 349, 350,
376, 379; his attitude to, 228,
229, 235, 237, 348; poems in
memory of, 239–49
Gregory, Vere, 146
Gregory, Sir William Henry
(husband), 1, 13, 39, 49, 66,
67–8, 69, 70–84, 85, 90, 92, 95,
120, 225, 349; career, 70–1;
first marriage, 71; marriage to
AG, 1, 75–84; in Egypt, 85–9;
letters to *The Times* from
Egypt, 88; death, 2, 93, 184,
347;
Griffith, Arthur, 218
Guest, Lady Charlotte, 207
Gyles, Althea, 202

Hans Anderson German Theatre
Company, 368
Hardy, Thomas, 238
Harmsworth, Baron, later 1st the
Viscount Northcliffe, 361
Harrow School: RG at, 2, 349
Hart, Henry, 66–7
Harvey, Rt. Rev. Thomas Arnold,
11, 12; 'Memories of Coole',
15–17, 442
Harvey, Sir Paul, 194–5
Heidegger, Martin: 'A Dialogue
on the Language', 272
Hélène of Orleans, Princesse, 85
Henderson, George: translation of
Cuchulain stories, 269, 270, 271
Henderson, W. A., 383
Henley, W.E., 256, 257
Herald Tribune (New York), 340
Hoare, Mr., 365
Holloway, Joseph, 354, 384, 386,
387, 390, 391, 398
Horniman, Annie Elizabeth
Frederika, 15, 26, 44, 50–1, 52,
217, 281, 384
Houghton, 1st Baron, 88